EVERYTHING EVERYWHERE...

rick kirkman
jerry scott

Collection

NO. 41

Andrews McMeel
PUBLISHING®

EVERYTHING EVERYWHERE...

Other *Baby Blues®* Books from Andrews McMeel Publishing

Guess Who Didn't Take a Nap?
I Thought Labor Ended When the Baby Was Born
We Are Experiencing Parental Difficulties . . . Please Stand By
Night of the Living Dad
I Saw Elvis in My Ultrasound
One More and We're Outnumbered!
Check, Please . . .
Threats, Bribes & Videotape
If I'm a Stay-at-Home Mom, Why Am I Always in the Car?
Lift and Separate
I Shouldn't Have to Scream More Than Once!
Motherhood Is Not for Wimps
Baby Blues®: Unplugged
Dad to the Bone
Never a Dry Moment
Two Plus One Is Enough
Playdate: Category 5
Our Server Is Down
Something Chocolate This Way Comes
Briefcase Full of Baby Blues®
Night Shift
The Day Phonics Kicked In
My Space
The Natural Disorder of Things
We Were Here First
Ambushed! In the Family Room
Cut!
Eat, Cry, Poop
Scribbles at an Exhibition
Bedlam
Wetter, Louder, Stickier
No Yelling!
Gross!
Binge Parenting
Adult Time
Surviving the Great Indoors
Stink Eye
Multitasking
NOT GUILTY-ish

Treasuries

The Super-Absorbent Biodegradable Family-Size Baby Blues®
Baby Blues®: Ten Years and Still in Diapers
Butt-Naked Baby Blues®
Wall-to-Wall Baby Blues®
Driving Under the Influence of Children
Framed!
X-Treme Parenting
BBXX: Baby Blues: Decades 1 and 2
BB3X: Baby Blues: The Third Decade

Gift Books

It's a Boy
It's a Girl

To Aunt Elaine, joy and kindness personified.

—R.K.

For Kim

—J.S.

FIRST ICE-CUBE-DOWN-THE-SHIRT OF 2023!
SHRIEK!

FIRST WEDGIE OF 2023!
YAWP!
FIRST NOOGIE OF 2023!
DOINK! DOINK! DOINK!
OW!
FIRST ICE-CUBE-DOWN-THE-SHIRT OF 2023!
SHRIEK!
©2023, BABY BLUES BROS LLC DIST. BY ANDREWS MCMEEL SYNDICATION
FIRST WET WILLIE OF 2023!
STOP!!!
FIRST ARREST AND CONVICTION OF 2023?
ACTUALLY, THIS IS NUMBER THREE. I GOT UP EARLY.
KIRKMAN & SCOTT 1-1

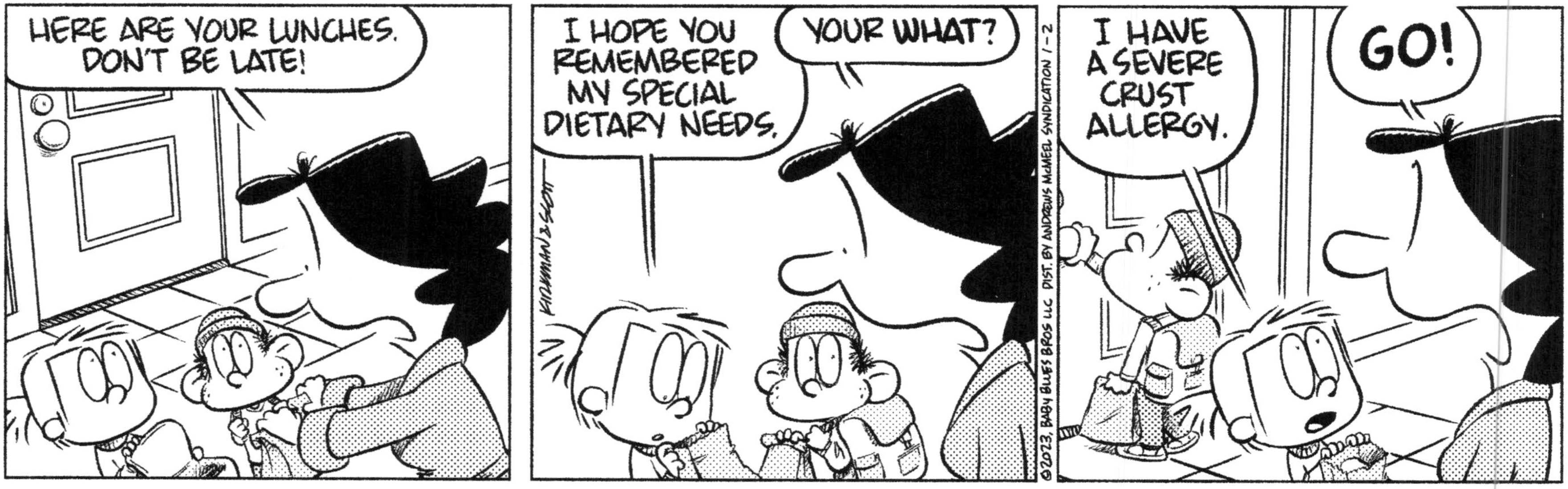
HERE ARE YOUR LUNCHES. DON'T BE LATE!
I HOPE YOU REMEMBERED MY SPECIAL DIETARY NEEDS.
YOUR WHAT?
I HAVE A SEVERE CRUST ALLERGY.
GO!
KIRKMAN & SCOTT
©2023, BABY BLUES BROS LLC DIST. BY ANDREWS McMEEL SYNDICATION 1-2

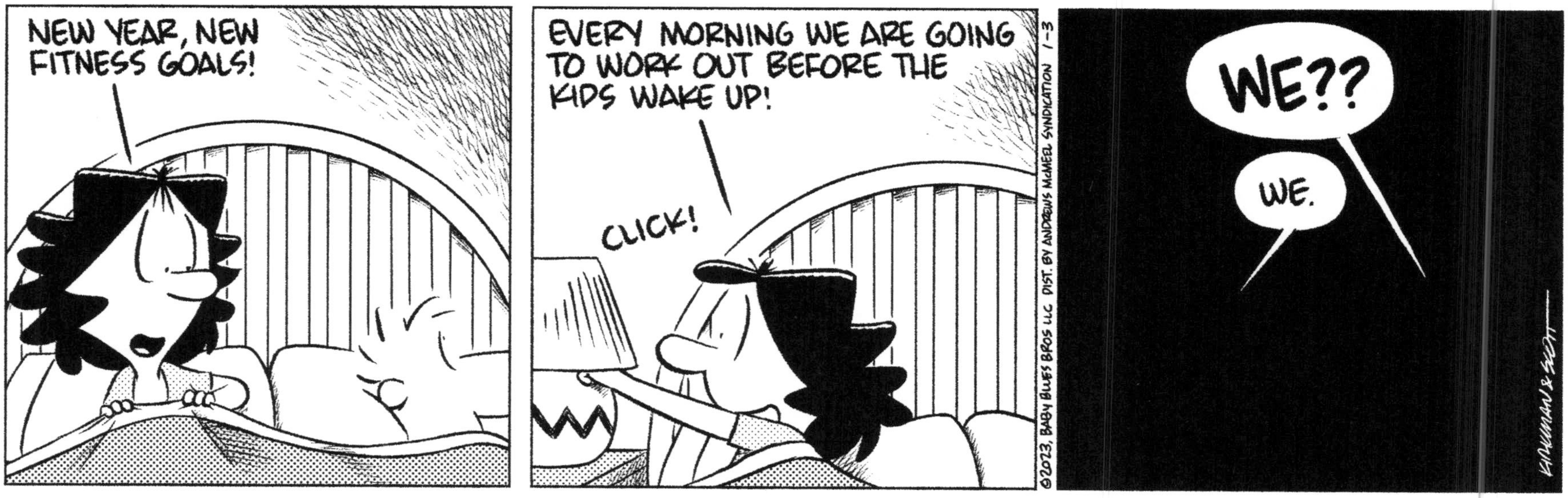
NEW YEAR, NEW FITNESS GOALS!
EVERY MORNING WE ARE GOING TO WORK OUT BEFORE THE KIDS WAKE UP!
CLICK!
WE??
WE.
KIRKMAN & SCOTT
©2023, BABY BLUES BROS LLC DIST. BY ANDREWS McMEEL SYNDICATION 1-3

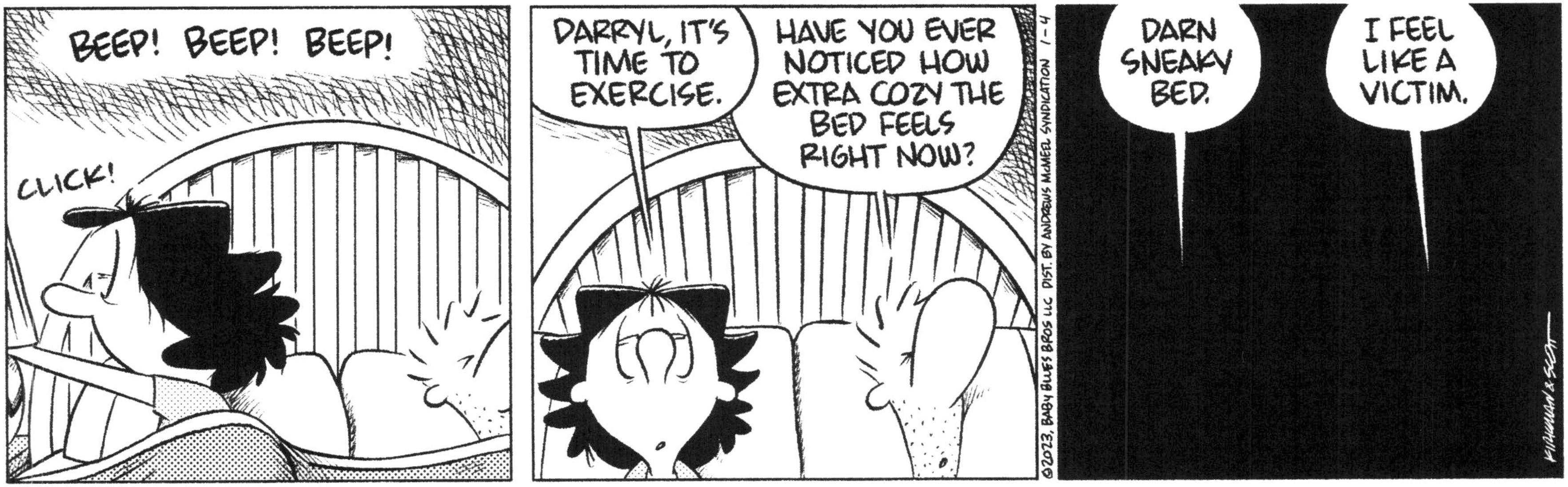
BEEP! BEEP! BEEP!
CLICK!
DARRYL, IT'S TIME TO EXERCISE.
HAVE YOU EVER NOTICED HOW EXTRA COZY THE BED FEELS RIGHT NOW?
©2023, BABY BLUES BROS LLC DIST. BY ANDREWS McMEEL SYNDICATION 1-4
DARN SNEAKY BED.
I FEEL LIKE A VICTIM.
KIRKMAN & SCOTT

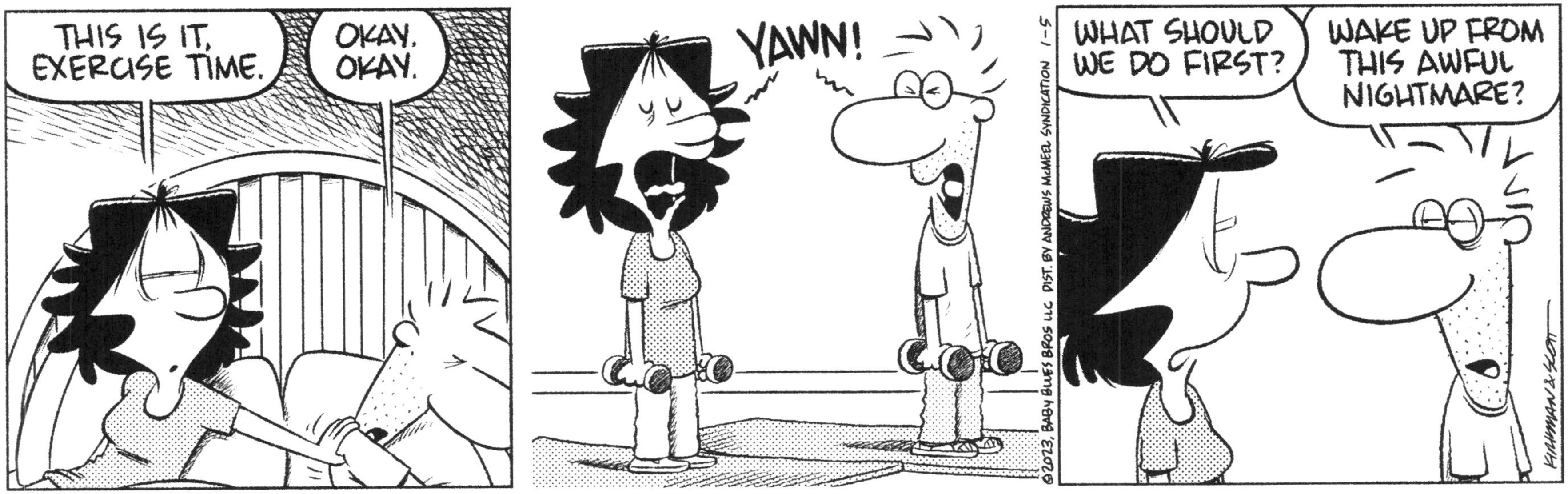
THIS IS IT, EXERCISE TIME.
OKAY. OKAY.
YAWN!
©2023, BABY BLUES BROS LLC DIST. BY ANDREWS McMEEL SYNDICATION 1-5
WHAT SHOULD WE DO FIRST?
WAKE UP FROM THIS AWFUL NIGHTMARE?
KIRKMAN & SCOTT

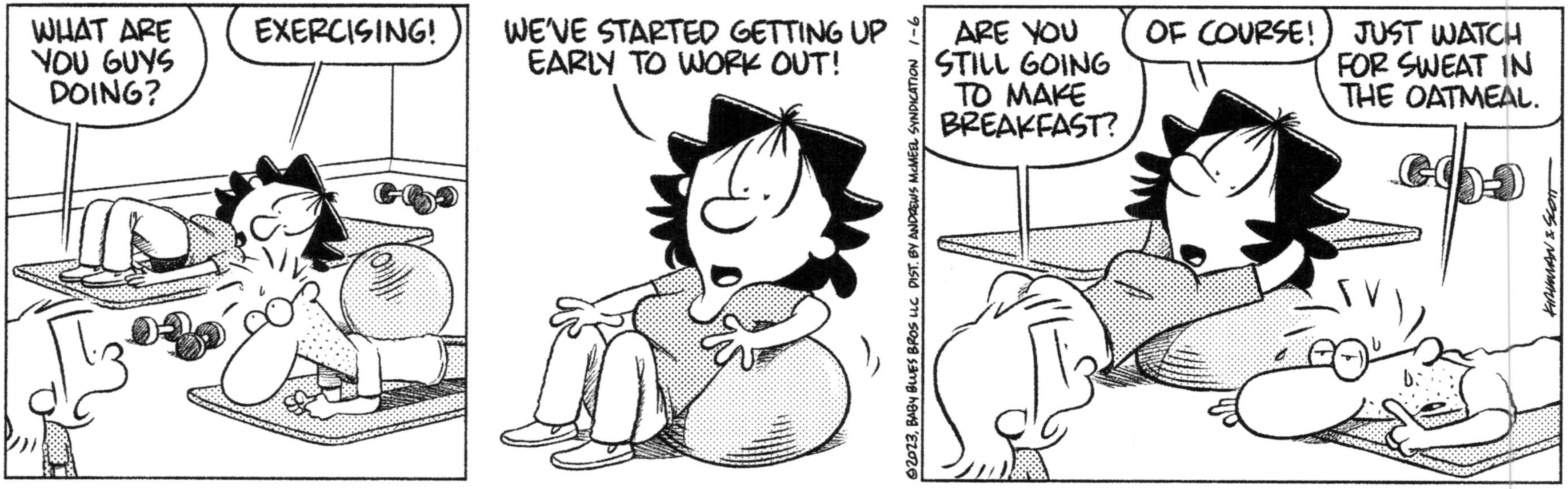
WHAT ARE YOU GUYS DOING?
EXERCISING!
WE'VE STARTED GETTING UP EARLY TO WORK OUT!
1-6
©2023, BABY BLUES BROS LLC DIST. BY ANDREWS MCMEEL SYNDICATION
ARE YOU STILL GOING TO MAKE BREAKFAST?
OF COURSE!
JUST WATCH FOR SWEAT IN THE OATMEAL.
KIRKMAN & SCOTT

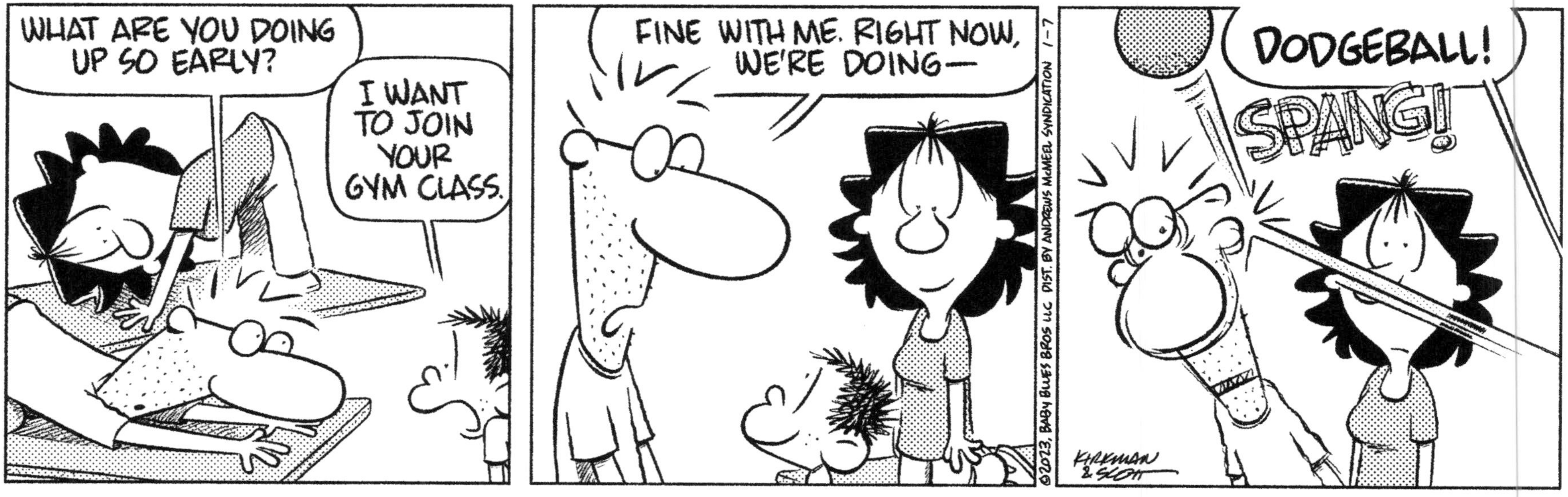
WHAT ARE YOU DOING UP SO EARLY?
I WANT TO JOIN YOUR GYM CLASS.
FINE WITH ME. RIGHT NOW, WE'RE DOING—
1-7
©2023, BABY BLUES BROS LLC DIST. BY ANDREWS MCMEEL SYNDICATION
DODGEBALL!
SPANG!
KIRKMAN & SCOTT

SHE'S GONNA
FLIP WHEN
SHE SEES THIS!

OH, WOW! A HEART-SHAPED ROCK!
MOM LOVES THESE THINGS!
SHE'S GONNA FLIP WHEN SHE SEES THIS!
SHE'LL PROBABLY TAKE US TO DISNEYLAND, OR MAKE US GIANT ICE-CREAM SUNDAES JUST TO THANK US.
1-8
ANOTHER HEART-SHAPED ROCK. CUTE!
©2023, BABY BLUES BROS LLC DIST. BY ANDREWS MCMEEL SYNDICATION
KIRKMAN & SCOTT
NEVER PUT TOO MUCH FAITH IN A ROCK.

I'M HOME!
HI, SWEETIE.
NICE HAIRCUT!
THANK YOU!
I'M SO LUCKY TO HAVE A HUSBAND WHO NOTICES THE LITTLE THINGS.
©2023, BABY BLUES BROS LLC DIST. BY ANDREWS MCMEEL SYNDICATION
I CAN ALWAYS COUNT ON YOU TO BE THE SAME SWEET, SENSITIVE MAN I MARRIED ALL THOSE YEARS AGO.

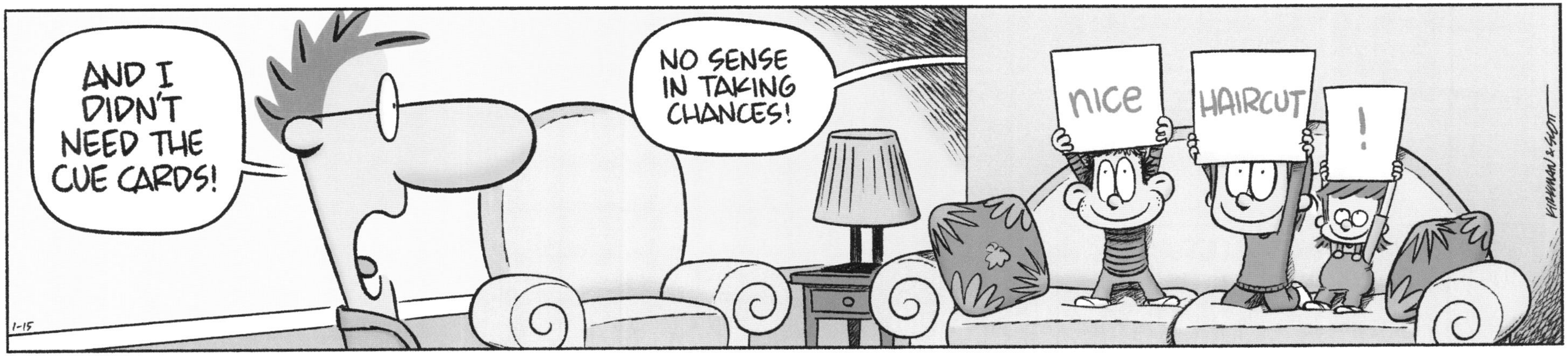
AND I DIDN'T NEED THE CUE CARDS!
NO SENSE IN TAKING CHANCES!
nice
HAIRCUT
!
1-15
KIRKMAN & SCOTT

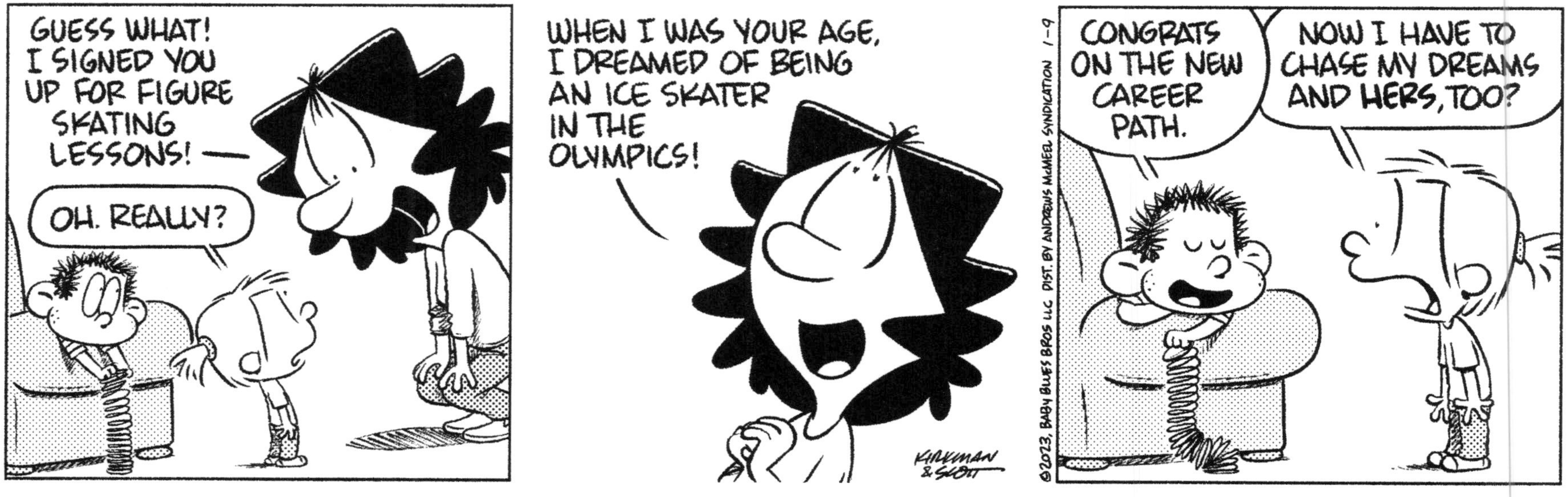
GUESS WHAT! I SIGNED YOU UP FOR FIGURE SKATING LESSONS!
OH. REALLY?
WHEN I WAS YOUR AGE, I DREAMED OF BEING AN ICE SKATER IN THE OLYMPICS!
KIRKMAN & SCOTT
©2023, BABY BLUES BROS LLC DIST. BY ANDREWS MCMEEL SYNDICATION 1-9
CONGRATS ON THE NEW CAREER PATH.
NOW I HAVE TO CHASE MY DREAMS AND HERS, TOO?

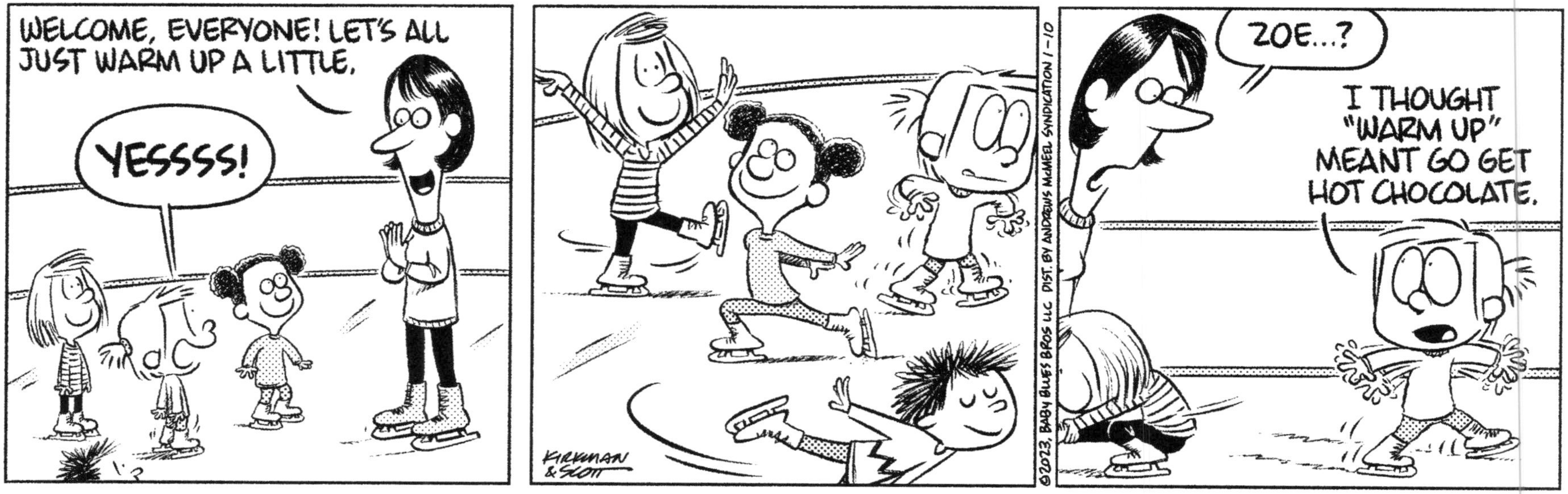
WELCOME, EVERYONE! LET'S ALL JUST WARM UP A LITTLE.
YESSSS!
KIRKMAN & SCOTT
©2023, BABY BLUES BROS LLC DIST. BY ANDREWS MCMEEL SYNDICATION 1-10
ZOE...?
I THOUGHT "WARM UP" MEANT GO GET HOT CHOCOLATE.

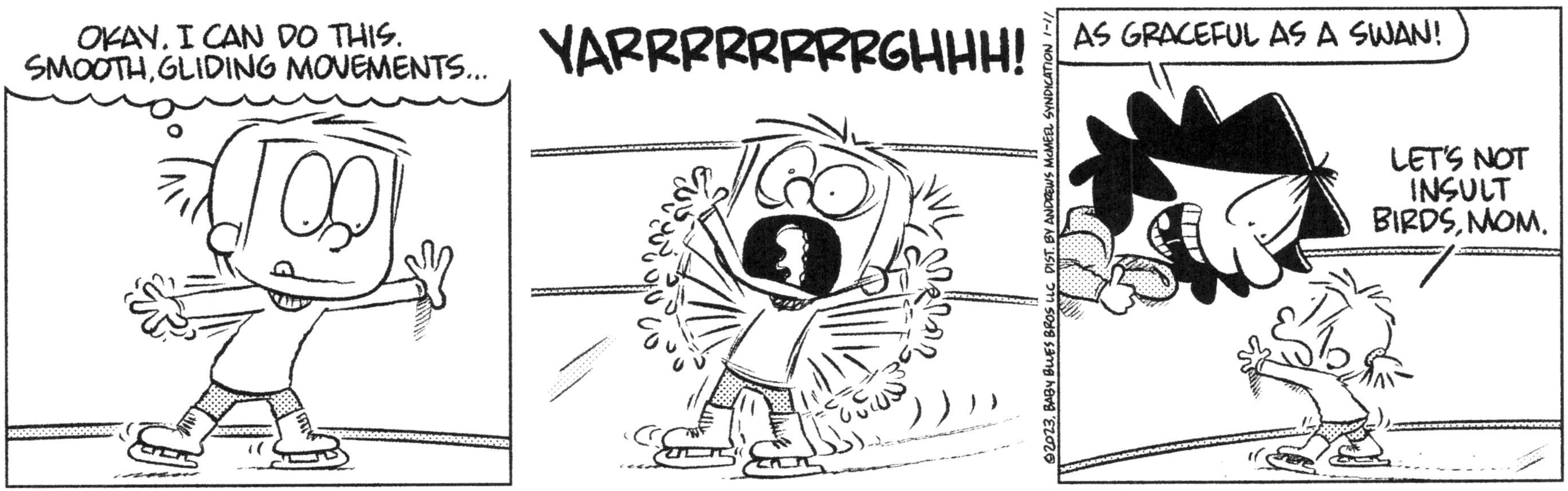
OKAY. I CAN DO THIS. SMOOTH, GLIDING MOVEMENTS...
YARRRRRRRRGHHH!
1-11
©2023, BABY BLUES BROS LLC DIST. BY ANDREWS McMEEL SYNDICATION
AS GRACEFUL AS A SWAN!
LET'S NOT INSULT BIRDS, MOM.

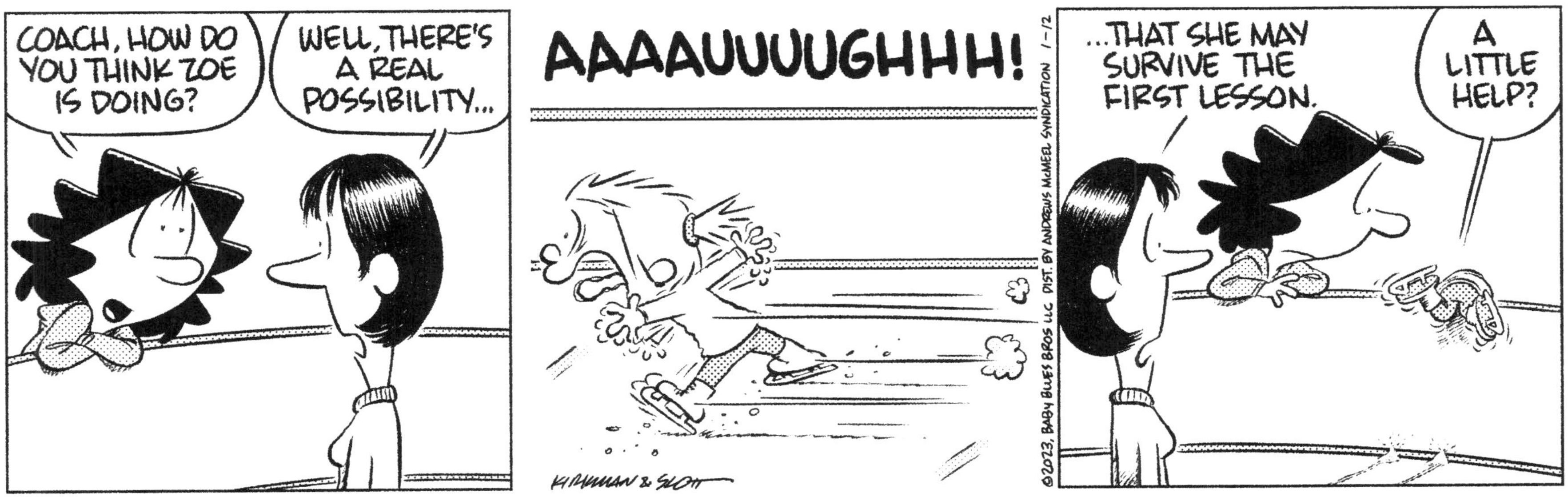
COACH, HOW DO YOU THINK ZOE IS DOING?
WELL, THERE'S A REAL POSSIBILITY...
AAAAUUUUGHHH!
KIRKMAN & SCOTT
1-12
©2023, BABY BLUES BROS LLC DIST. BY ANDREWS McMEEL SYNDICATION
...THAT SHE MAY SURVIVE THE FIRST LESSON.
A LITTLE HELP?

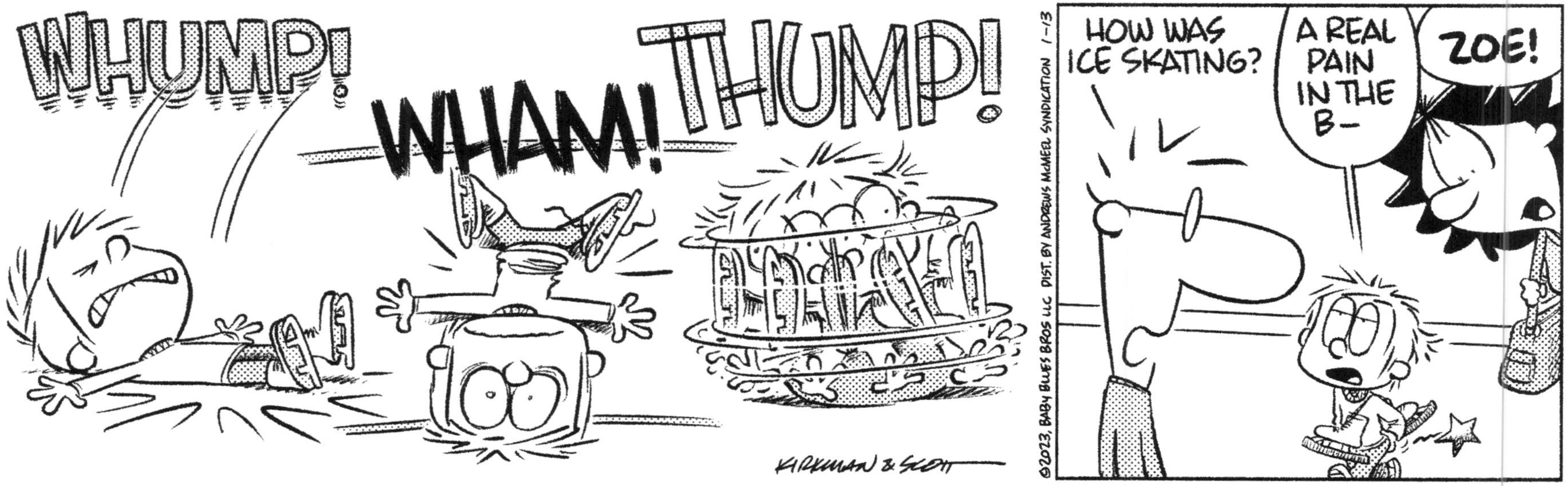
WHUMP!
WHAM!
THUMP!
KIRKMAN & SCOTT
©2023, BABY BLUES BROS LLC DIST. BY ANDREWS McMEEL SYNDICATION 1-13
HOW WAS ICE SKATING?
A REAL PAIN IN THE B—
ZOE!

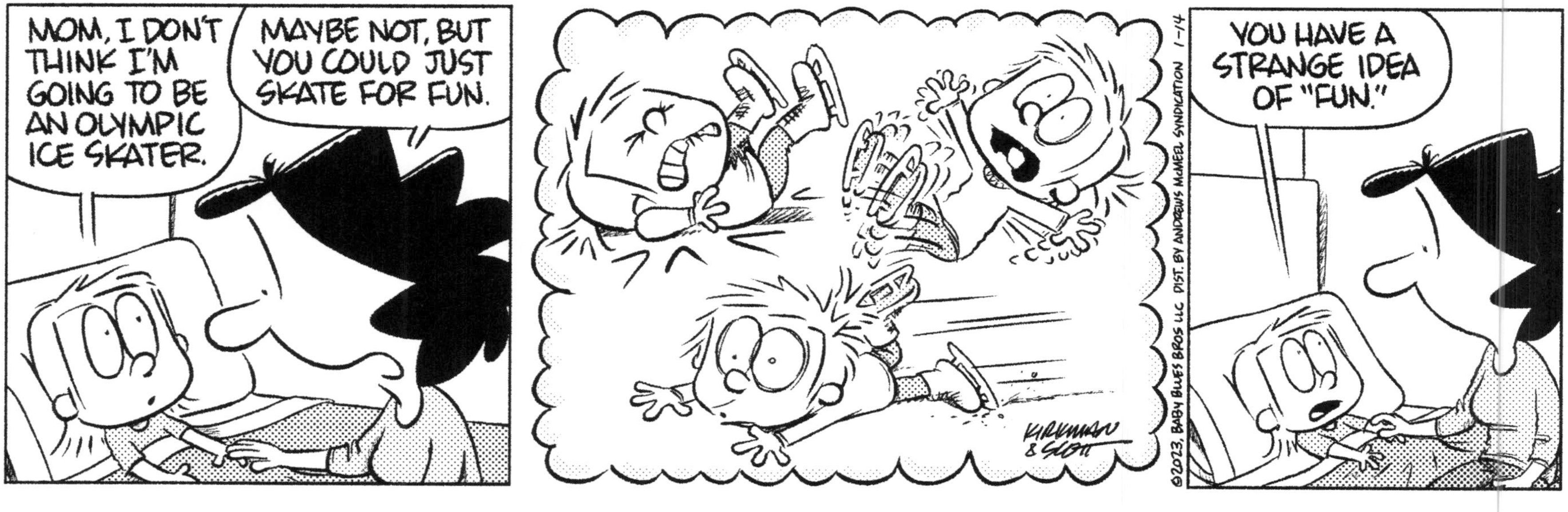
MOM, I DON'T THINK I'M GOING TO BE AN OLYMPIC ICE SKATER.
MAYBE NOT, BUT YOU COULD JUST SKATE FOR FUN.
KIRKMAN & SCOTT
©2023, BABY BLUES BROS LLC DIST. BY ANDREWS McMEEL SYNDICATION 1-14
YOU HAVE A STRANGE IDEA OF "FUN."

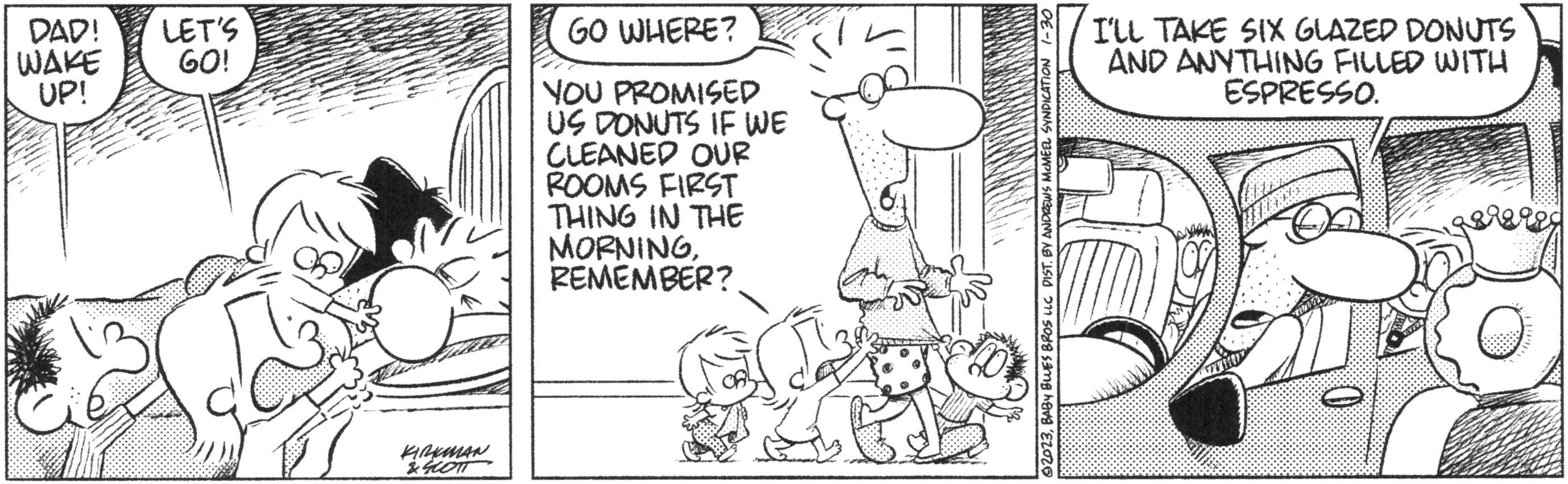
DAD! WAKE UP!
LET'S GO!
KIRKMAN & SCOTT
GO WHERE?
YOU PROMISED US DONUTS IF WE CLEANED OUR ROOMS FIRST THING IN THE MORNING, REMEMBER?
©2023, BABY BLUES BROS LLC DIST. BY ANDREWS McMEEL SYNDICATION 1-30
I'LL TAKE SIX GLAZED DONUTS AND ANYTHING FILLED WITH ESPRESSO.

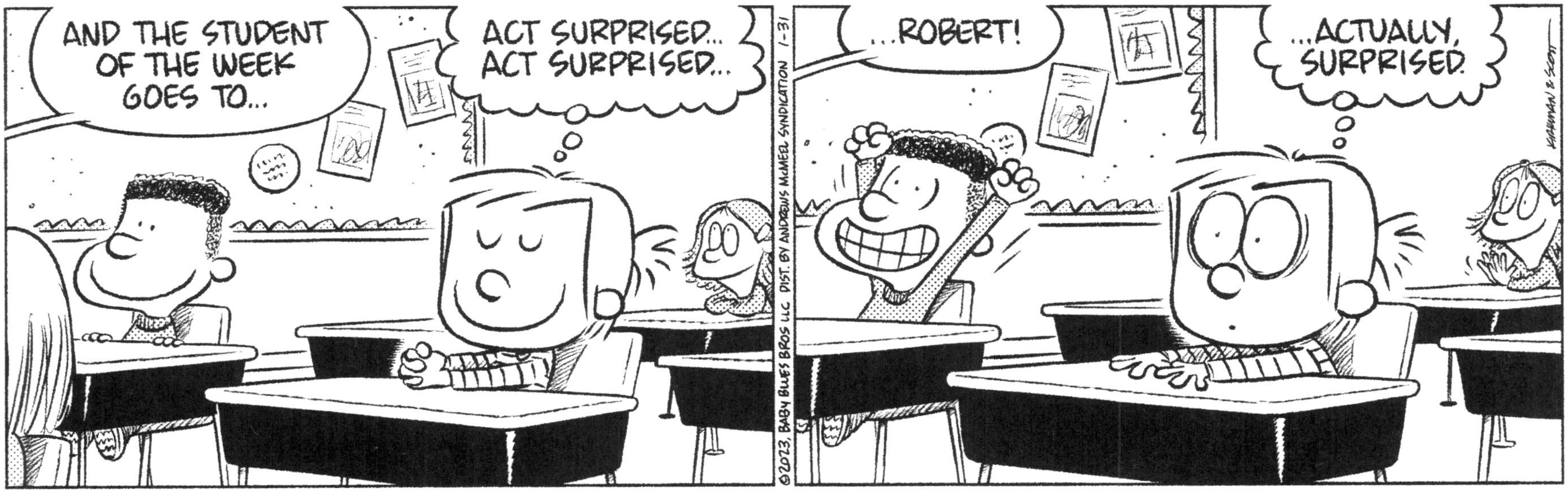
AND THE STUDENT OF THE WEEK GOES TO...
ACT SURPRISED... ACT SURPRISED...
©2023, BABY BLUES BROS LLC DIST. BY ANDREWS McMEEL SYNDICATION 1-31
...ROBERT!
...ACTUALLY, SURPRISED.
KIRKMAN & SCOTT

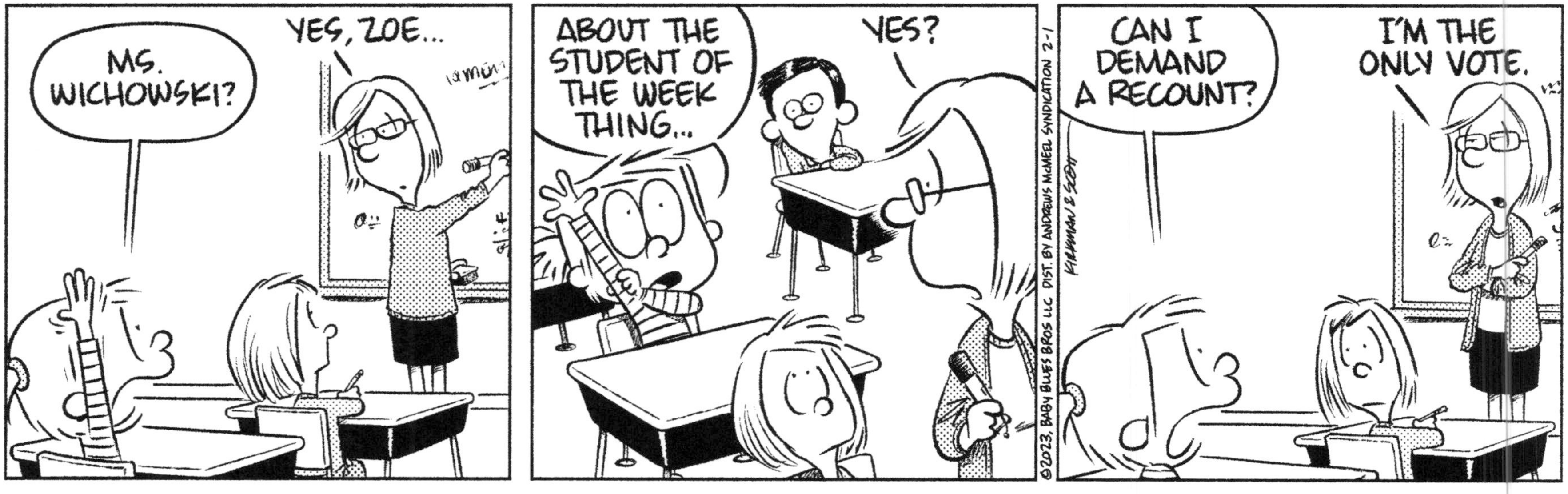
MS. WICHOWSKI?
YES, ZOE...
ABOUT THE STUDENT OF THE WEEK THING...
YES?
CAN I DEMAND A RECOUNT?
I'M THE ONLY VOTE.
©2023, BABY BLUES BROS LLC DIST. BY ANDREWS MCMEEL SYNDICATION 2-1
KIRKMAN & SCOTT

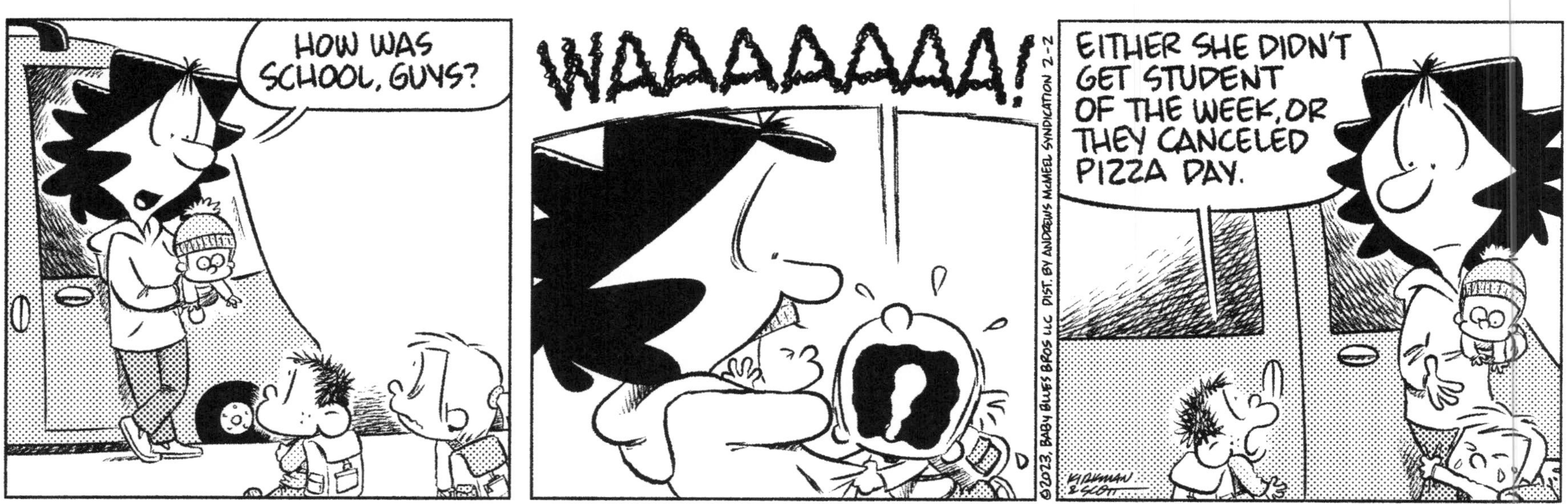
HOW WAS SCHOOL, GUYS?
WAAAAAAA!
EITHER SHE DIDN'T GET STUDENT OF THE WEEK, OR THEY CANCELED PIZZA DAY.
©2023, BABY BLUES BROS LLC DIST. BY ANDREWS MCMEEL SYNDICATION 2-2
KIRKMAN & SCOTT

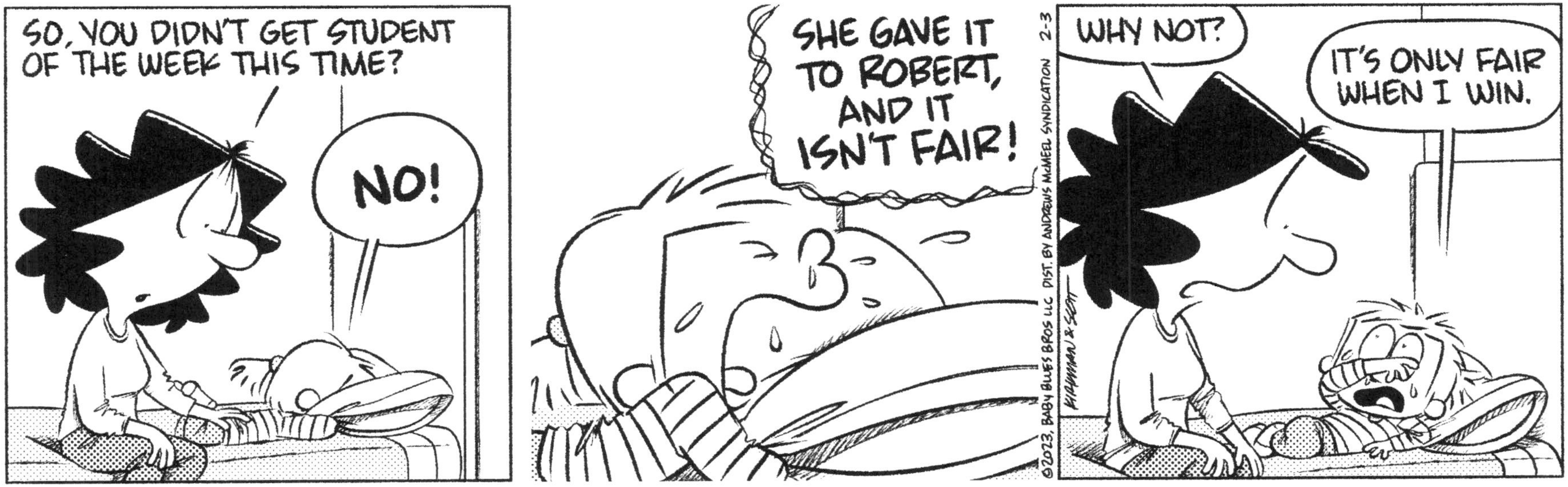

SO, YOU DIDN'T GET STUDENT OF THE WEEK THIS TIME?
NO!
SHE GAVE IT TO ROBERT, AND IT ISN'T FAIR!
©2023, BABY BLUES BROS LLC DIST. BY ANDREWS McMEEL SYNDICATION 2-3
KIRKMAN & SCOTT
WHY NOT?
IT'S ONLY FAIR WHEN I WIN.

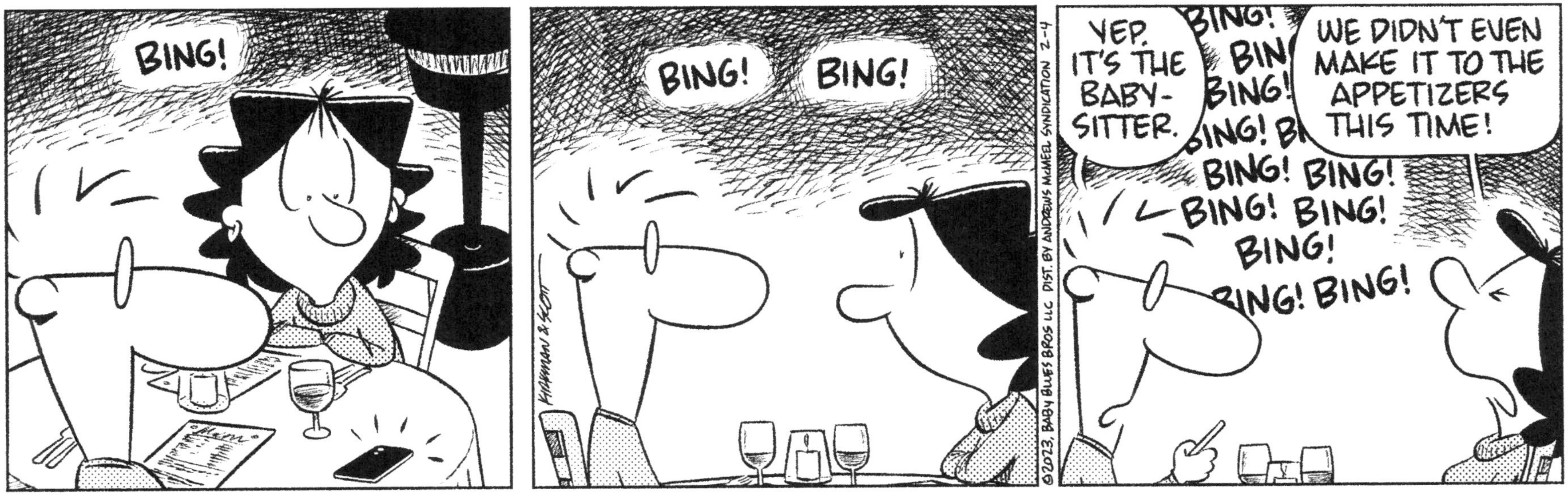

BING!
KIRKMAN & SCOTT
BING! BING!
©2023, BABY BLUES BROS LLC DIST. BY ANDREWS McMEEL SYNDICATION 2-4
YEP. IT'S THE BABY-SITTER.
BING! BING! BING! BING! BING! BING! BING!
WE DIDN'T EVEN MAKE IT TO THE APPETIZERS THIS TIME!

MOM! CHECK THIS OUT!

AH-CHOO!
BURP!
TOOT!
A SNEEZE, A BURP, AND A TOOT! I **SNURPOOTED**!
IN ANCIENT TIMES, THAT WOULD MAKE YOU THE KING.
©2023, BABY BLUES BROS LLC DIST. BY ANDREWS McMEEL SYNDICATION
REALLY?
OH, YEAH. PEOPLE WITH SPECIAL SKILLS WERE ALWAYS PUT IN CHARGE BACK THEN.
MOM! CHECK THIS OUT!
1-22
AH-CHOO! BURP! TOOT!
SO, ARE YOU IN CHARGE NOW?
NO. SHE GAVE ME TISSUES, AIR FRESHENER, AND PUT ME IN EXILE.
KIRKMAN & SCOTT

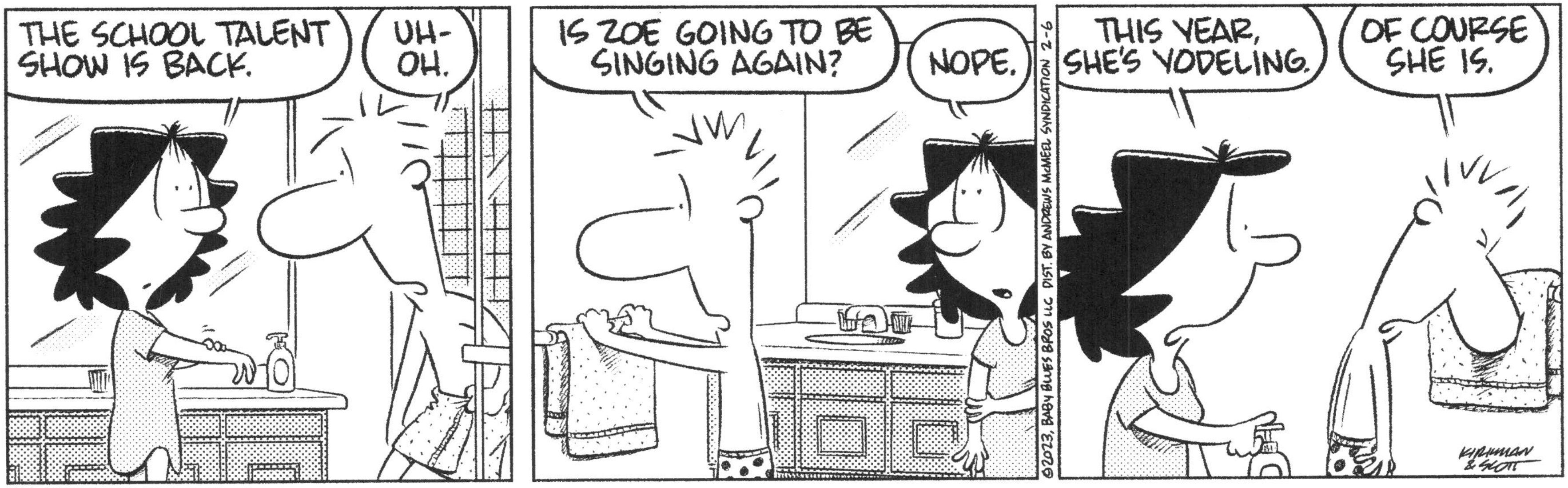
THE SCHOOL TALENT SHOW IS BACK.
UH-OH.
IS ZOE GOING TO BE SINGING AGAIN?
NOPE.
©2023, BABY BLUES BROS LLC DIST. BY ANDREWS McMEEL SYNDICATION 2-6
THIS YEAR, SHE'S YODELING.
OF COURSE SHE IS.
KIRKMAN & SCOTT

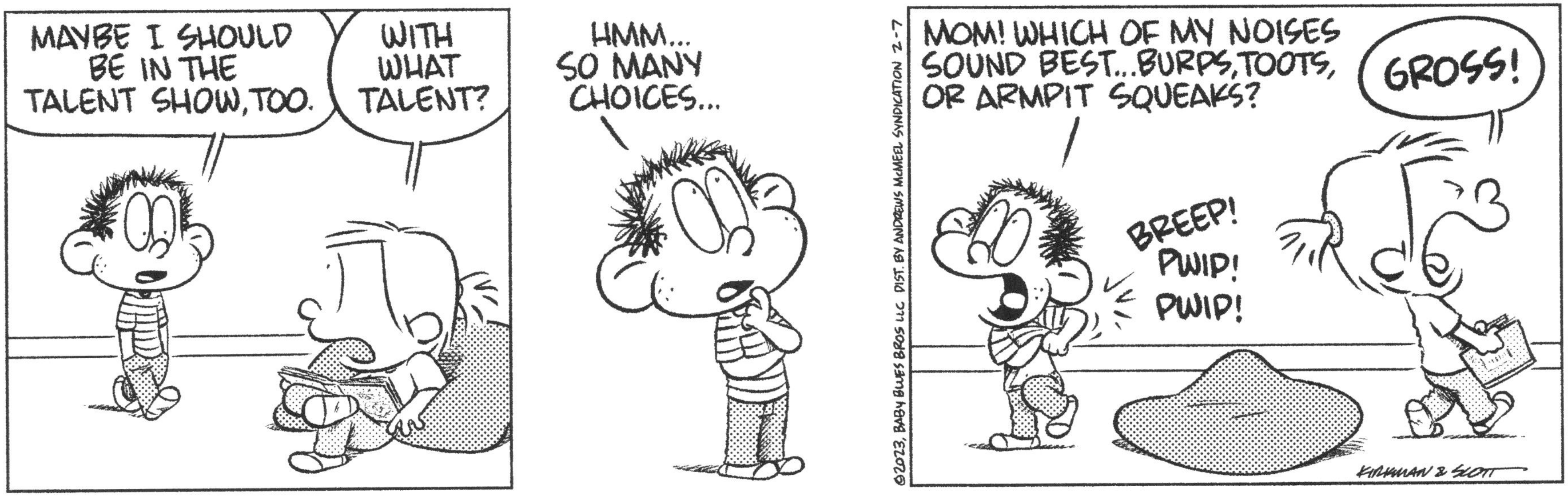
MAYBE I SHOULD BE IN THE TALENT SHOW, TOO.
WITH WHAT TALENT?
HMM... SO MANY CHOICES...
©2023, BABY BLUES BROS LLC DIST. BY ANDREWS McMEEL SYNDICATION 2-7
MOM! WHICH OF MY NOISES SOUND BEST...BURPS, TOOTS, OR ARMPIT SQUEAKS?
GROSS!
BREEP!
PWIP!
PWIP!
KIRKMAN & SCOTT

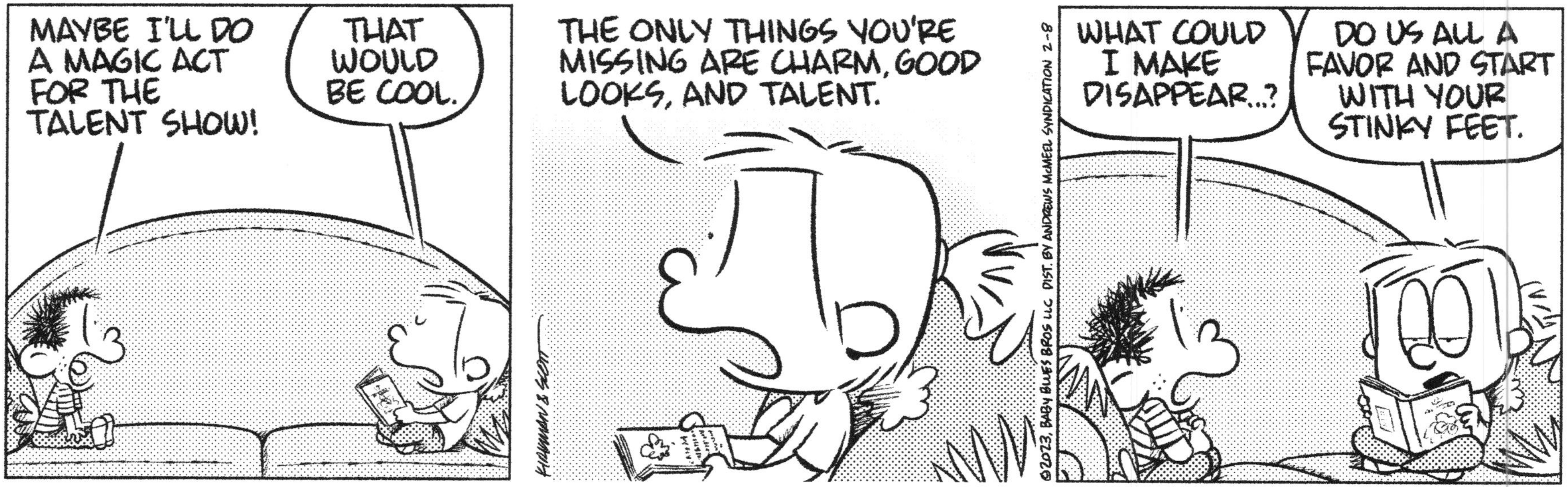
MAYBE I'LL DO A MAGIC ACT FOR THE TALENT SHOW!
THAT WOULD BE COOL.
THE ONLY THINGS YOU'RE MISSING ARE CHARM, GOOD LOOKS, AND TALENT.
KIRKMAN & SCOTT
©2023, BABY BLUES BROS LLC DIST. BY ANDREWS McMEEL SYNDICATION 2-8
WHAT COULD I MAKE DISAPPEAR...?
DO US ALL A FAVOR AND START WITH YOUR STINKY FEET.

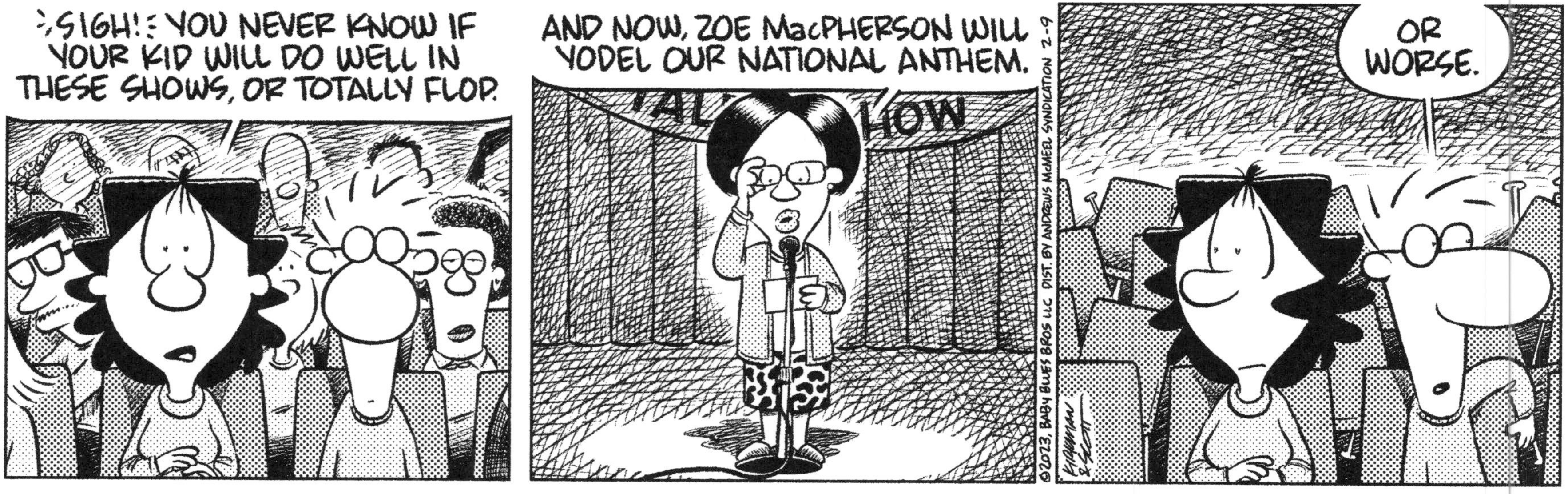
:SIGH!: YOU NEVER KNOW IF YOUR KID WILL DO WELL IN THESE SHOWS, OR TOTALLY FLOP.
AND NOW, ZOE MacPHERSON WILL YODEL OUR NATIONAL ANTHEM.
©2023, BABY BLUES BROS LLC DIST. BY ANDREWS McMEEL SYNDICATION 2-9
KIRKMAN & SCOTT
OR WORSE.

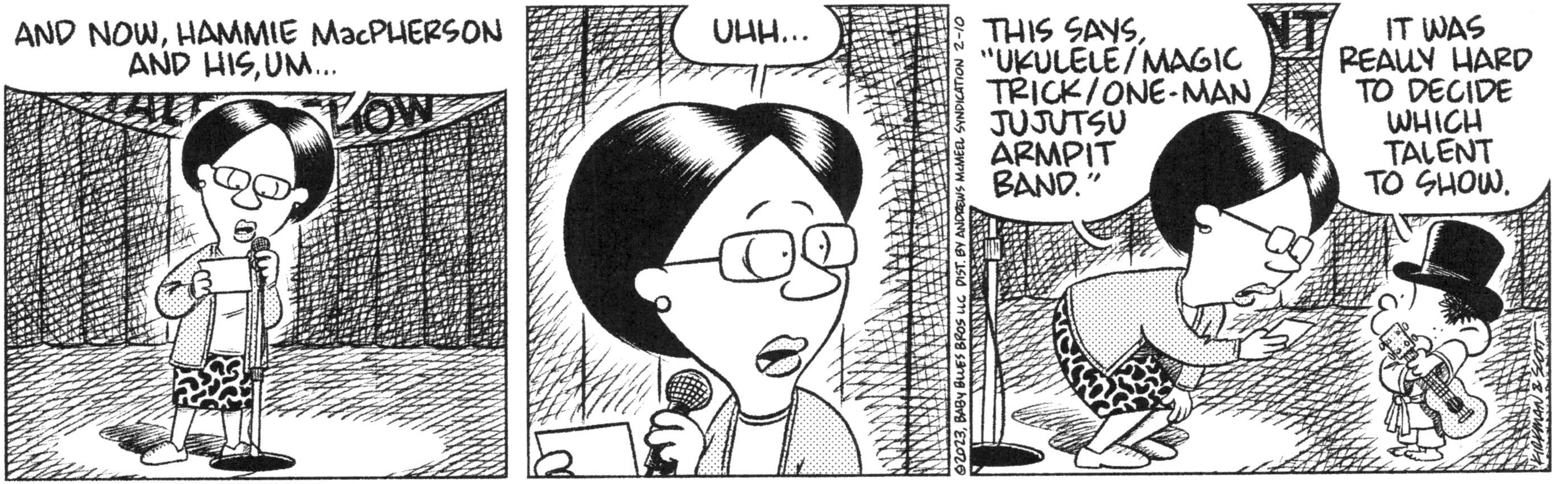
AND NOW, HAMMIE MacPHERSON AND HIS, UM...
UHH...
©2023, BABY BLUES BROS LLC DIST. BY ANDREWS McMEEL SYNDICATION 2-10
THIS SAYS, "UKULELE/MAGIC TRICK/ONE-MAN JUJUTSU ARMPIT BAND."
IT WAS REALLY HARD TO DECIDE WHICH TALENT TO SHOW.
KIRKMAN & SCOTT

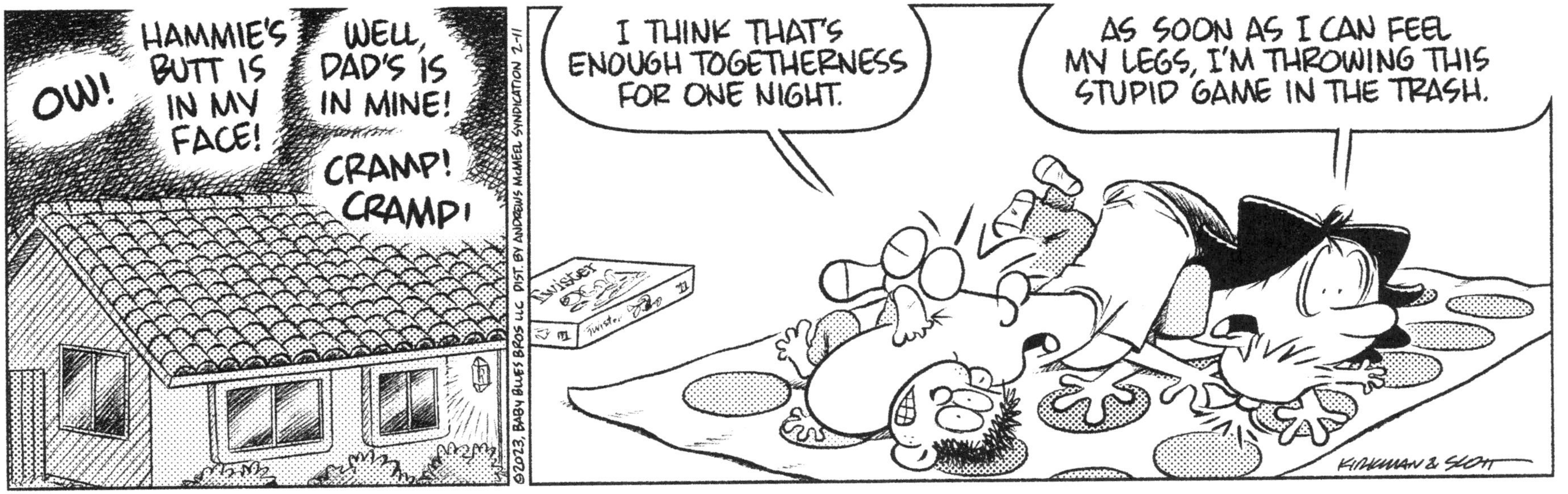
OW!
HAMMIE'S BUTT IS IN MY FACE!
WELL, DAD'S IS IN MINE!
CRAMP! CRAMP!
©2023, BABY BLUES BROS LLC DIST. BY ANDREWS McMEEL SYNDICATION 2-11
I THINK THAT'S ENOUGH TOGETHERNESS FOR ONE NIGHT.
AS SOON AS I CAN FEEL MY LEGS, I'M THROWING THIS STUPID GAME IN THE TRASH.
Twister
KIRKMAN & SCOTT

SNORT! SNUFFLE! GROWL!
WHAT ARE YOU SUPPOSED TO BE?

SNORT! SNUFFLE! GROWL!
WHAT ARE YOU SUPPOSED TO BE?
A WILD GRIZZLY BEAR, OBVIOUSLY.
SKRITCH! SKRITCH!
©2022, BABY BLUES BROS LLC DIST. BY ANDREWS McMEEL SYNDICATION
GRIZZLY BEARS EAT SALMON. YOU HATE SALMON.
OH. THAT'S RIGHT. WHAT SHOULD I DO?
JUST PRETEND TO BE SOMETHING THAT LIKES WHAT YOU LIKE.
SUCH AS?
1-29
KIRKMAN & SCOTT
SPYORK! SPYORK! I'M A MUTANT DUCK-BILLED PLATYPUS WITH A VICIOUS SWEET-TOOTH!
LET ME GUESS. ZOE SUGGESTED THIS.
JUST HAND OVER THE COCOA PUFFS, AND NOBODY GETS HURT.

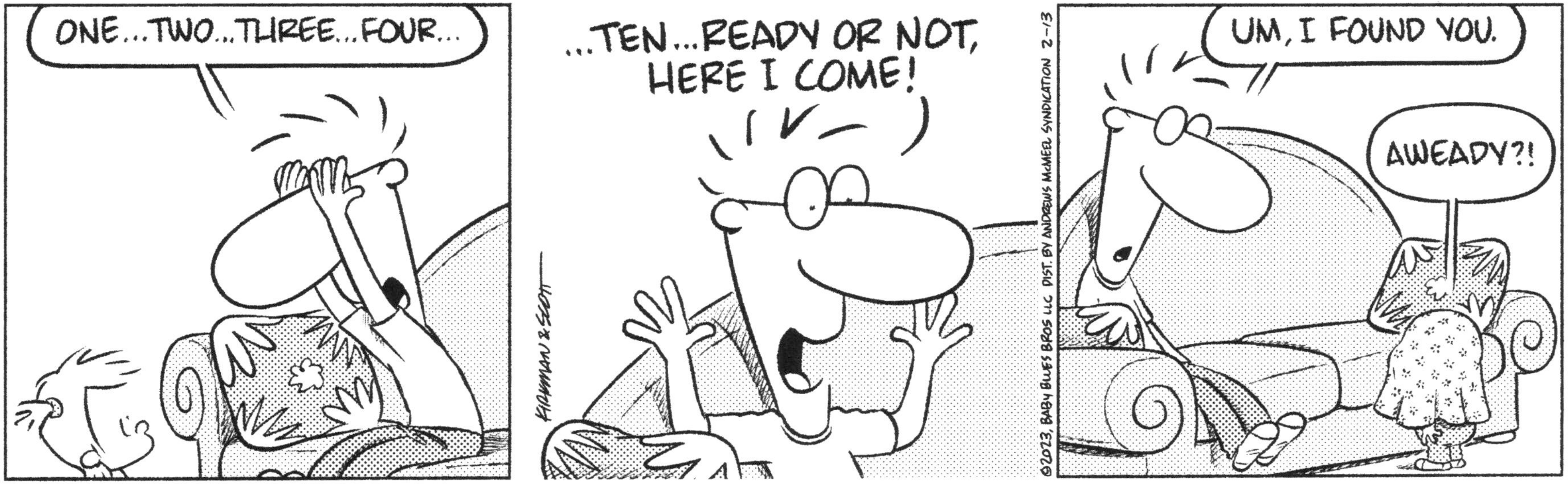
ONE...TWO...THREE...FOUR...
KIRKMAN & SCOTT
...TEN...READY OR NOT, HERE I COME!
©2023, BABY BLUES BROS LLC DIST. BY ANDREWS McMEEL SYNDICATION 2-13
UM, I FOUND YOU.
AWEADY?!

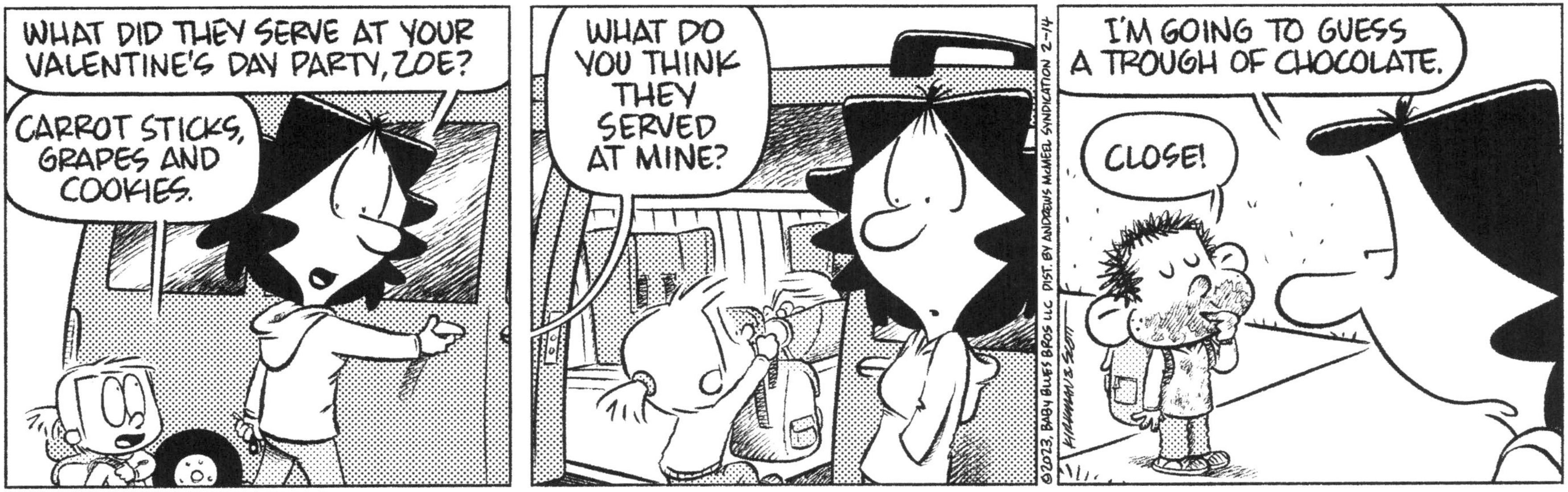
WHAT DID THEY SERVE AT YOUR VALENTINE'S DAY PARTY, ZOE?
CARROT STICKS, GRAPES AND COOKIES.
WHAT DO YOU THINK THEY SERVED AT MINE?
©2023, BABY BLUES BROS LLC DIST. BY ANDREWS McMEEL SYNDICATION 2-14
KIRKMAN & SCOTT
I'M GOING TO GUESS A TROUGH OF CHOCOLATE.
CLOSE!

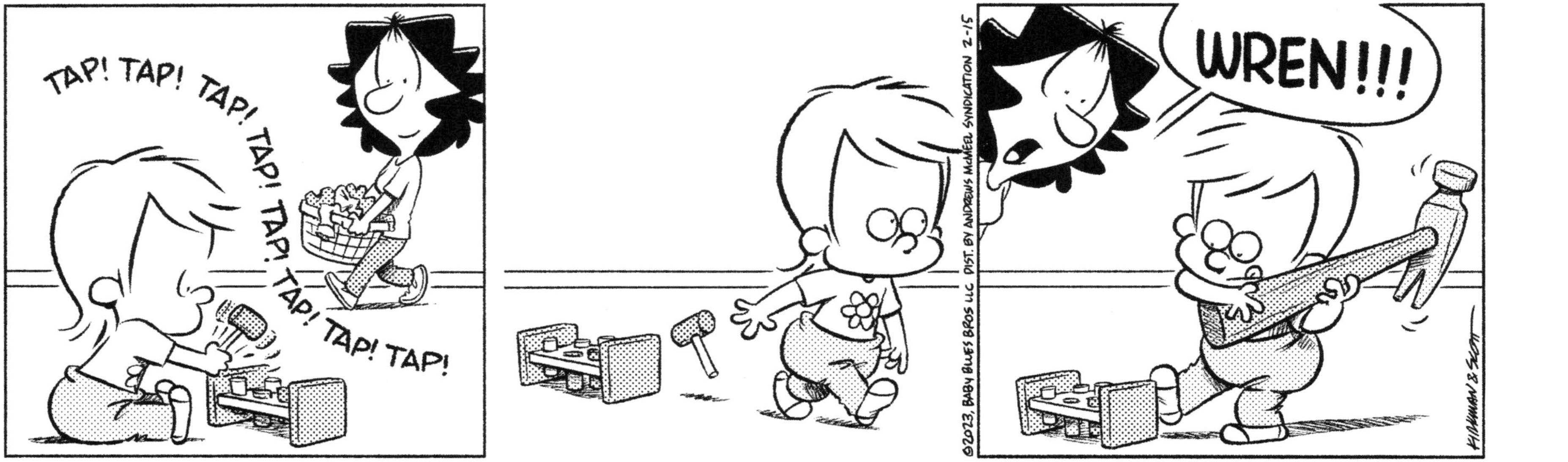
TAP! TAP! TAP! TAP! TAP! TAP! TAP! TAP! TAP!
©2023, BABY BLUES BROS LLC DIST. BY ANDREWS McMEEL SYNDICATION 2-15
WREN!!!
KIRKMAN & SCOTT

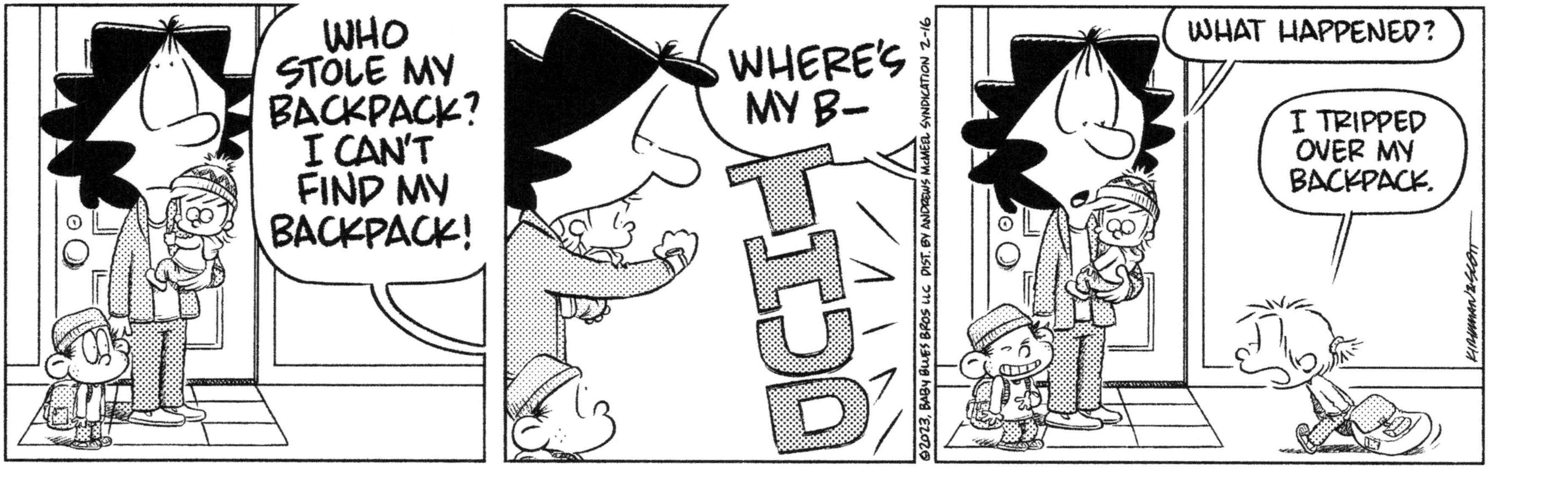
WHO STOLE MY BACKPACK? I CAN'T FIND MY BACKPACK!
WHERE'S MY B—
THUD
©2023, BABY BLUES BROS LLC DIST. BY ANDREWS McMEEL SYNDICATION 2-16
WHAT HAPPENED?
I TRIPPED OVER MY BACKPACK.
KIRKMAN & SCOTT

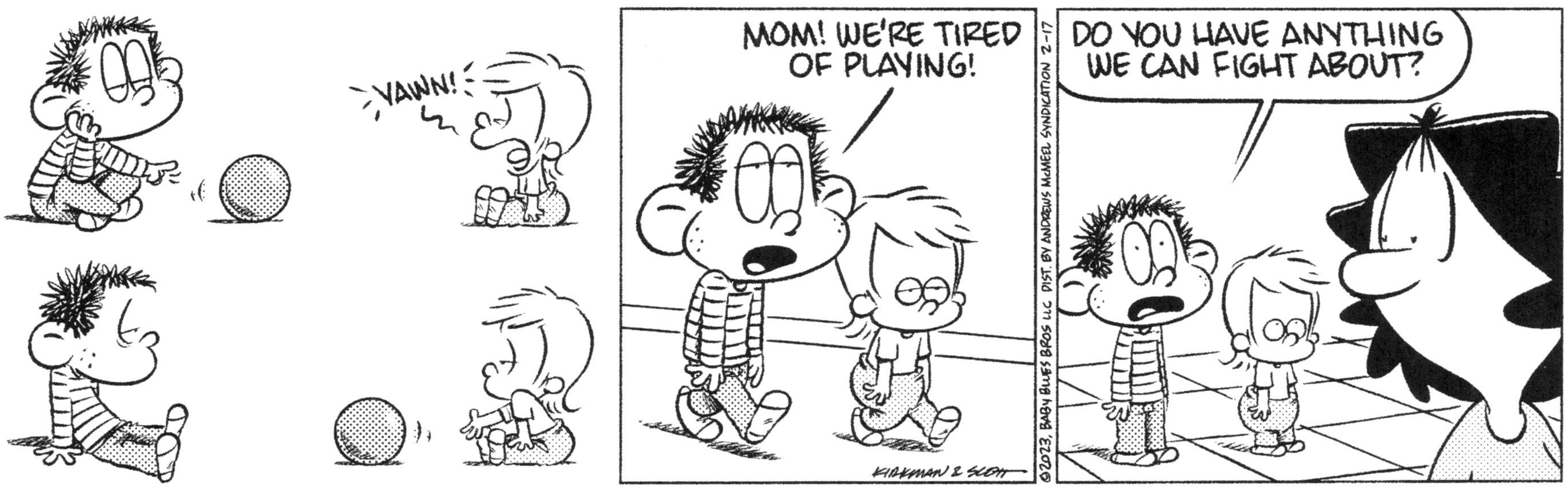
YAWN!
MOM! WE'RE TIRED OF PLAYING!
DO YOU HAVE ANYTHING WE CAN FIGHT ABOUT?
KIRKMAN & SCOTT
©2023, BABY BLUES BROS LLC DIST. BY ANDREWS McMEEL SYNDICATION 2-17

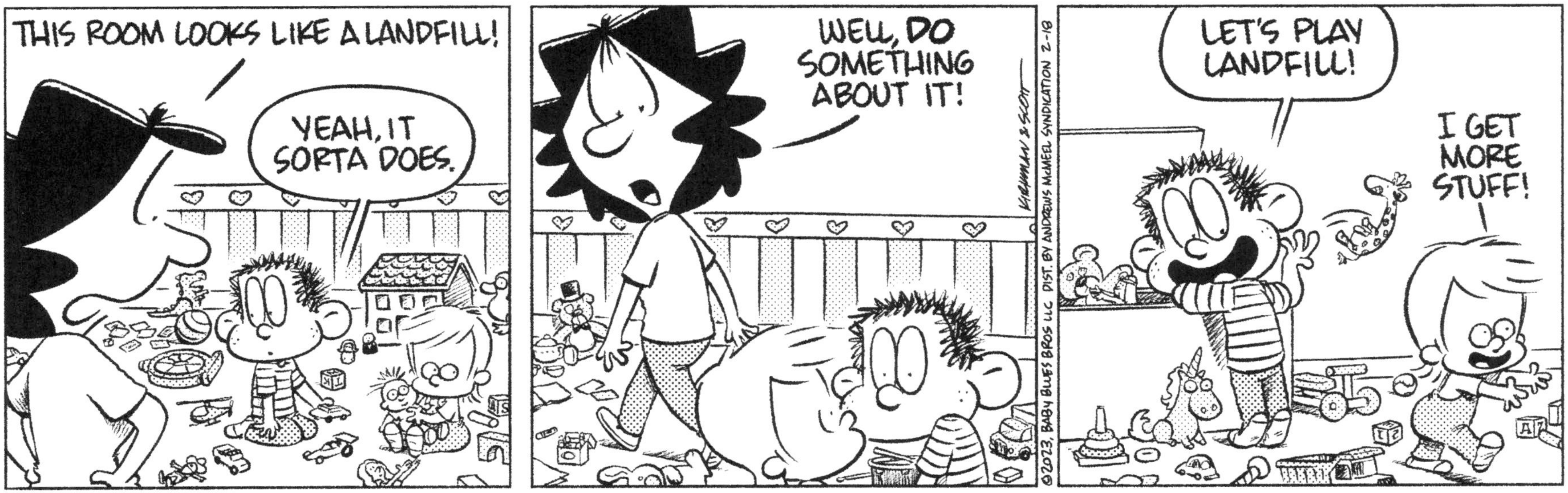
THIS ROOM LOOKS LIKE A LANDFILL!
YEAH, IT SORTA DOES.
WELL, DO SOMETHING ABOUT IT!
KIRKMAN & SCOTT
©2023, BABY BLUES BROS LLC DIST. BY ANDREWS McMEEL SYNDICATION 2-18
LET'S PLAY LANDFILL!
I GET MORE STUFF!

DAD! COME PLAY WITH US!

DAD! COME PLAY WITH US!
WHAT ARE WE PLAYING?
WE'RE NOT SURE YET.
©2013, BABY BLUES BROS LLC DIST. BY ANDREWS MCMEEL SYNDICATION
SHAKE! SHAKE! SHAKE! SHAKE! SHAKE! SHAKE!
SINCE NONE OF OUR GAMES HAVE ALL THE PIECES, WE'RE PUTTING EVERYTHING TOGETHER AND MAKING UP A NEW ONE.
DID I HEAR YOU PLAYING A BOARD GAME WITH THE KIDS?
YOU'RE LOOKING AT THE NEW MONOPO-CLUE-YAHTZEE-UNO-SORRY-CANDY-TRAP CHAMPION.
KIRKMAN & SCOTT 2-5

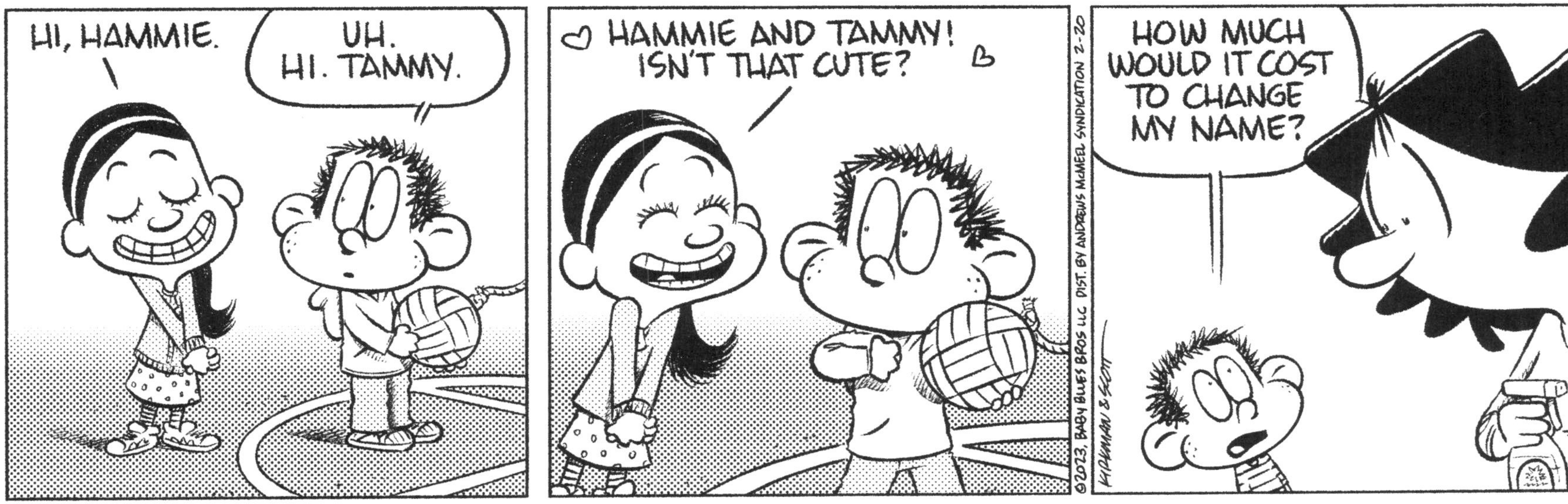
HI, HAMMIE.
UH. HI. TAMMY.
HAMMIE AND TAMMY! ISN'T THAT CUTE?
©2023, BABY BLUES BROS LLC DIST. BY ANDREWS McMEEL SYNDICATION 2-20
KIRKMAN & SCOTT
HOW MUCH WOULD IT COST TO CHANGE MY NAME?

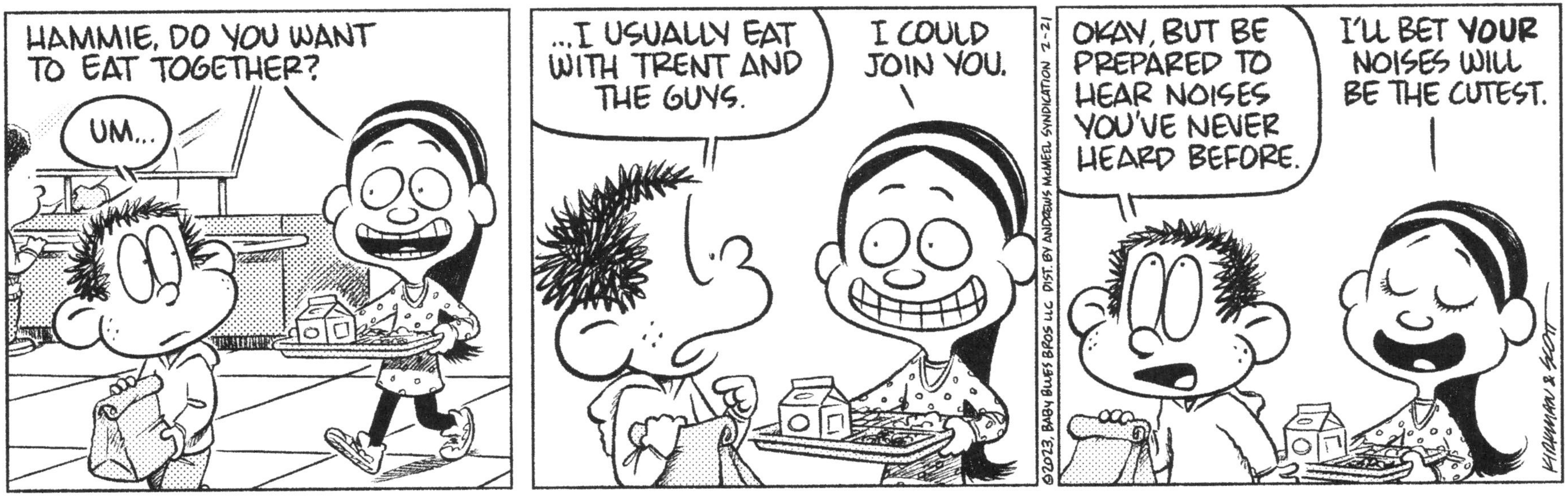
HAMMIE, DO YOU WANT TO EAT TOGETHER?
UM...
...I USUALLY EAT WITH TRENT AND THE GUYS.
I COULD JOIN YOU.
©2023, BABY BLUES BROS LLC DIST. BY ANDREWS McMEEL SYNDICATION 2-21
OKAY, BUT BE PREPARED TO HEAR NOISES YOU'VE NEVER HEARD BEFORE.
I'LL BET **YOUR** NOISES WILL BE THE CUTEST.
KIRKMAN & SCOTT

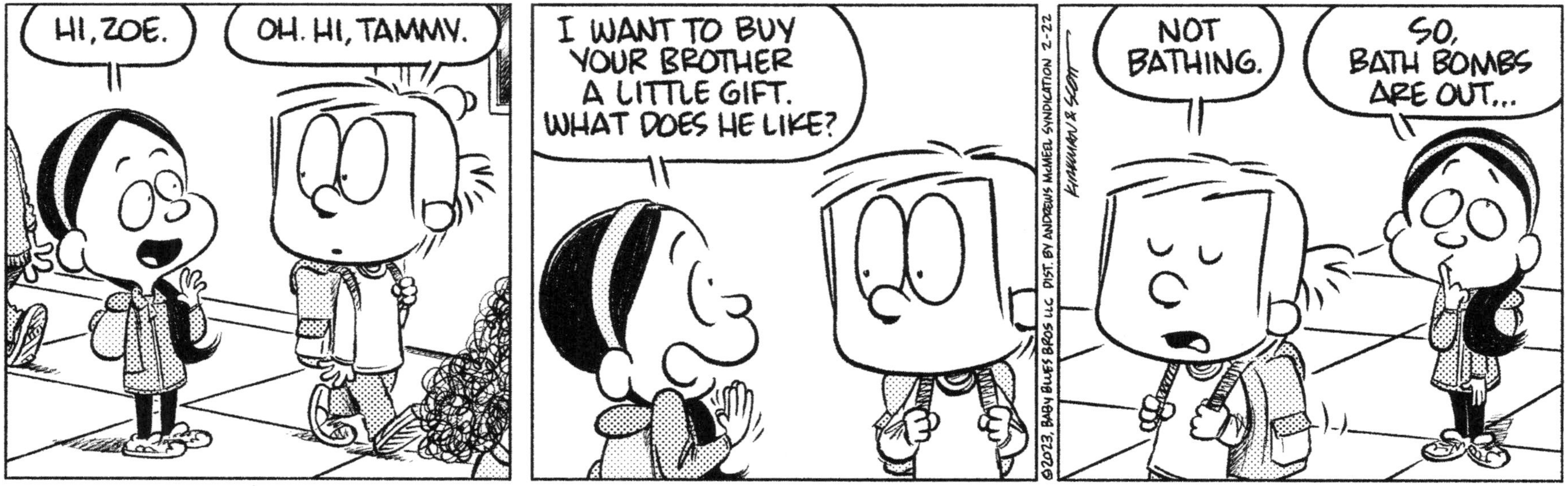
HI, ZOE.
OH. HI, TAMMY.
I WANT TO BUY YOUR BROTHER A LITTLE GIFT. WHAT DOES HE LIKE?
NOT BATHING.
SO, BATH BOMBS ARE OUT...
©2023, BABY BLUES BROS LLC. DIST. BY ANDREWS McMEEL SYNDICATION 2-22
KIRKMAN & SCOTT

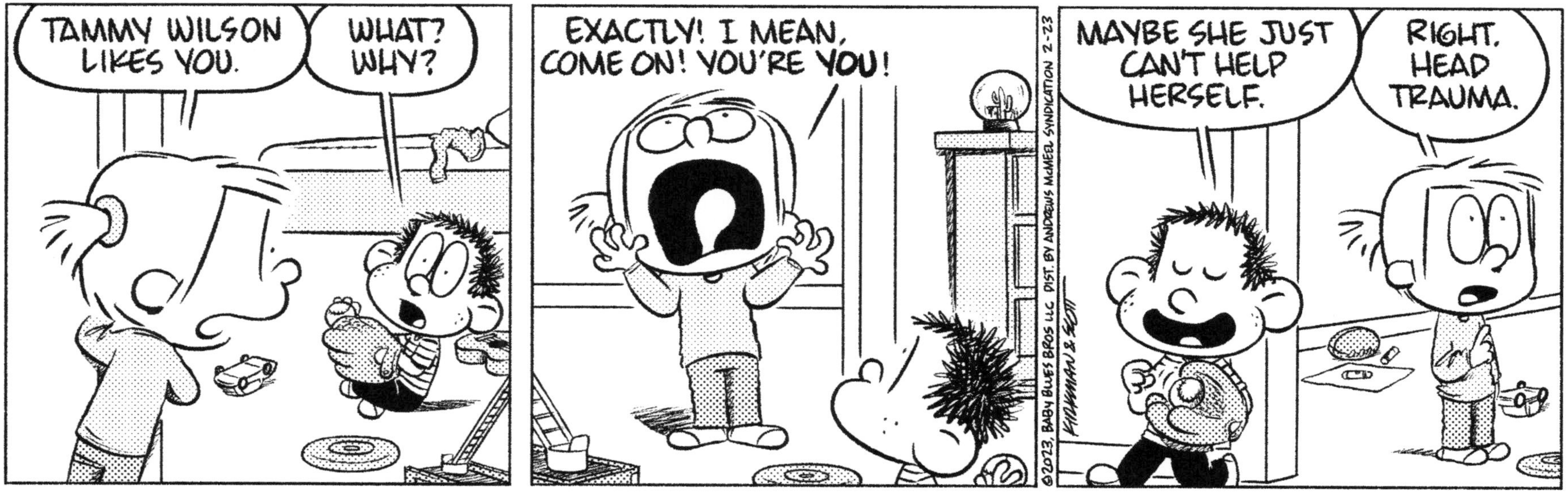
TAMMY WILSON LIKES YOU.
WHAT? WHY?
EXACTLY! I MEAN, COME ON! YOU'RE **YOU**!
MAYBE SHE JUST CAN'T HELP HERSELF.
RIGHT. HEAD TRAUMA.
©2023, BABY BLUES BROS LLC. DIST. BY ANDREWS McMEEL SYNDICATION 2-23
KIRKMAN & SCOTT

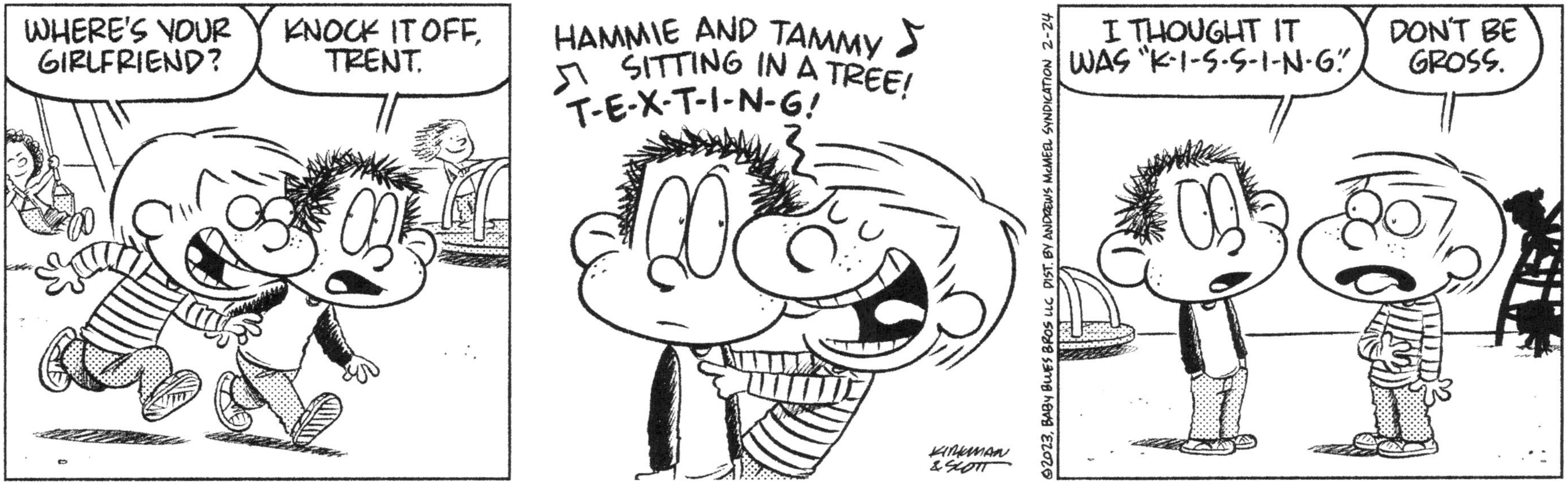
WHERE'S YOUR GIRLFRIEND?
KNOCK IT OFF, TRENT.
HAMMIE AND TAMMY SITTING IN A TREE! T-E-X-T-I-N-G!
KIRKMAN & SCOTT
©2023, BABY BLUES BROS LLC DIST. BY ANDREWS McMEEL SYNDICATION 2-24
I THOUGHT IT WAS "K-I-S-S-I-N-G."
DON'T BE GROSS.

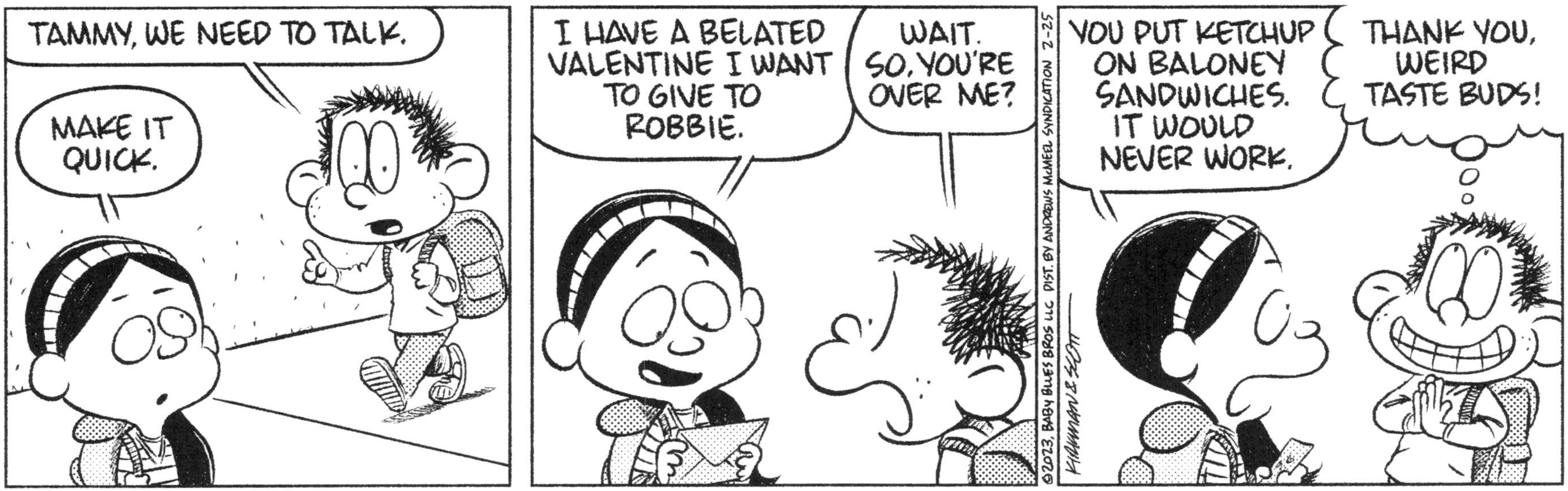
TAMMY, WE NEED TO TALK.
MAKE IT QUICK.
I HAVE A BELATED VALENTINE I WANT TO GIVE TO ROBBIE.
WAIT. SO, YOU'RE OVER ME?
©2023, BABY BLUES BROS LLC DIST. BY ANDREWS McMEEL SYNDICATION 2-25
KIRKMAN & SCOTT
YOU PUT KETCHUP ON BALONEY SANDWICHES. IT WOULD NEVER WORK.
THANK YOU, WEIRD TASTE BUDS!

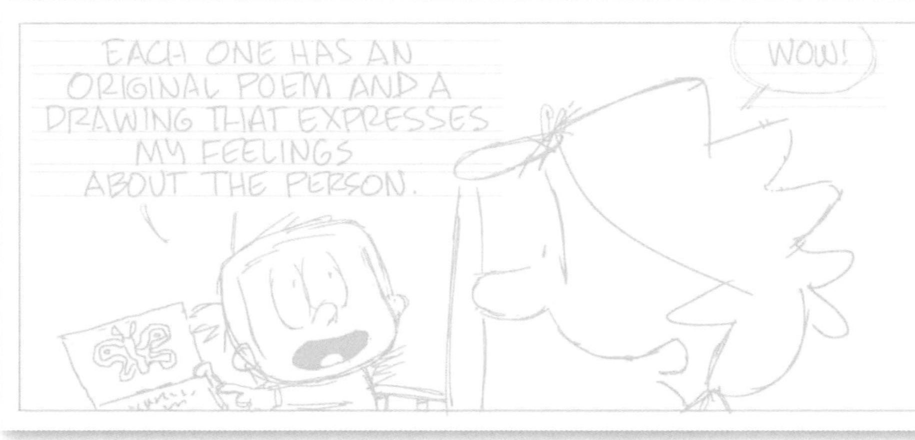
EACH ONE HAS AN ORIGINAL POEM AND A DRAWING THAT EXPRESSES MY FEELINGS ABOUT THE PERSON.
WOW!

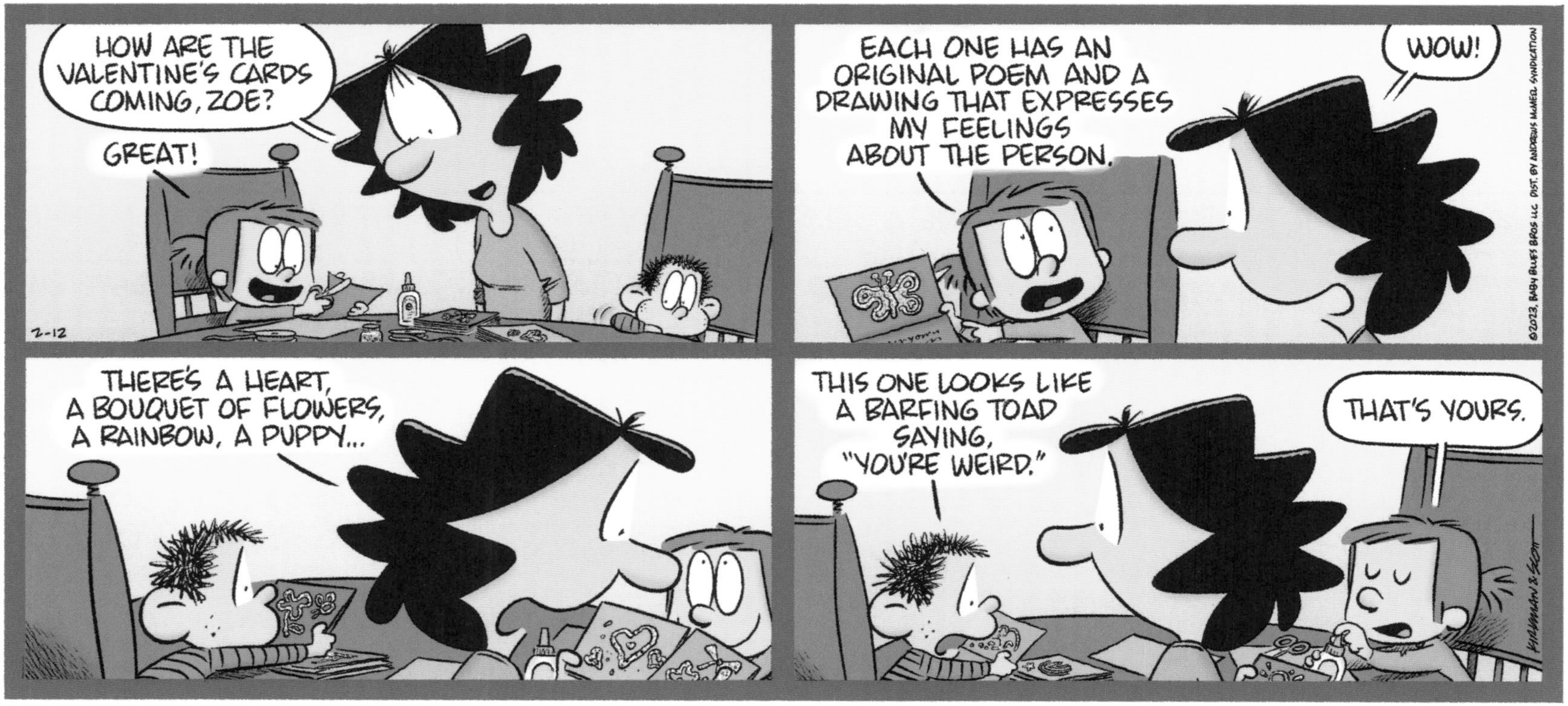
HOW ARE THE VALENTINE'S CARDS COMING, ZOE?
GREAT!
2-12
EACH ONE HAS AN ORIGINAL POEM AND A DRAWING THAT EXPRESSES MY FEELINGS ABOUT THE PERSON.
WOW!
©2023, BABY BLUES BROS LLC DIST. BY ANDREWS MCMEEL SYNDICATION
THERE'S A HEART, A BOUQUET OF FLOWERS, A RAINBOW, A PUPPY...
THIS ONE LOOKS LIKE A BARFING TOAD SAYING, "YOU'RE WEIRD."
THAT'S YOURS.
KIRKMAN & SCOTT

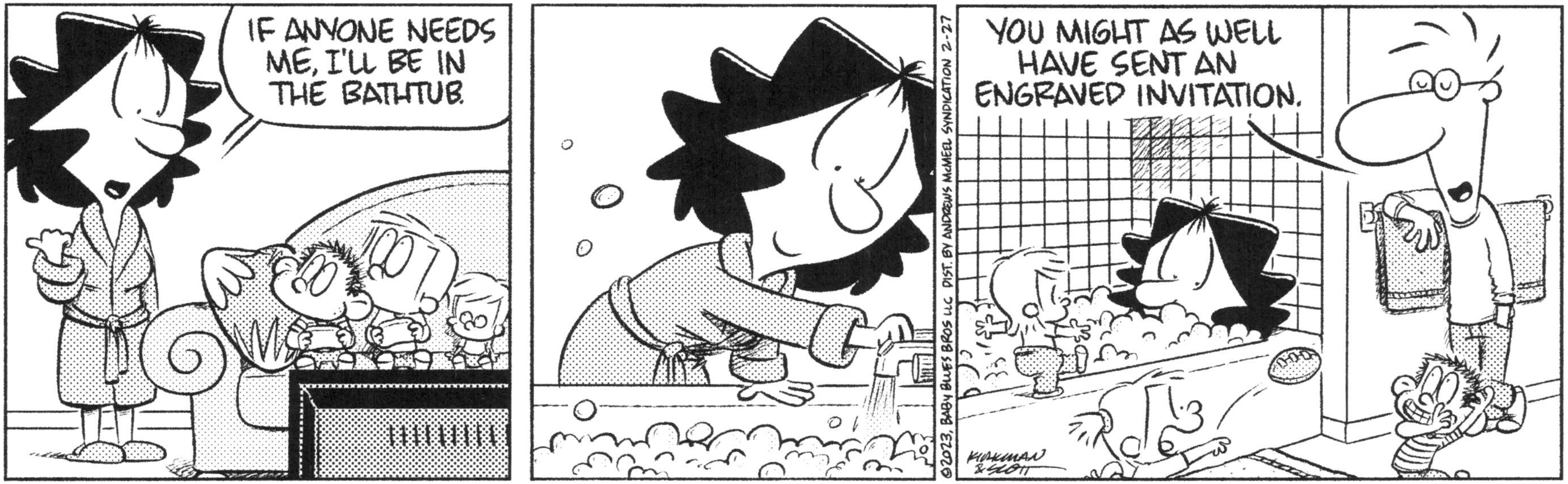
IF ANYONE NEEDS ME, I'LL BE IN THE BATHTUB.
©2023, BABY BLUES BROS LLC DIST. BY ANDREWS MCMEEL SYNDICATION 2-27
YOU MIGHT AS WELL HAVE SENT AN ENGRAVED INVITATION.
KIRKMAN & SCOTT

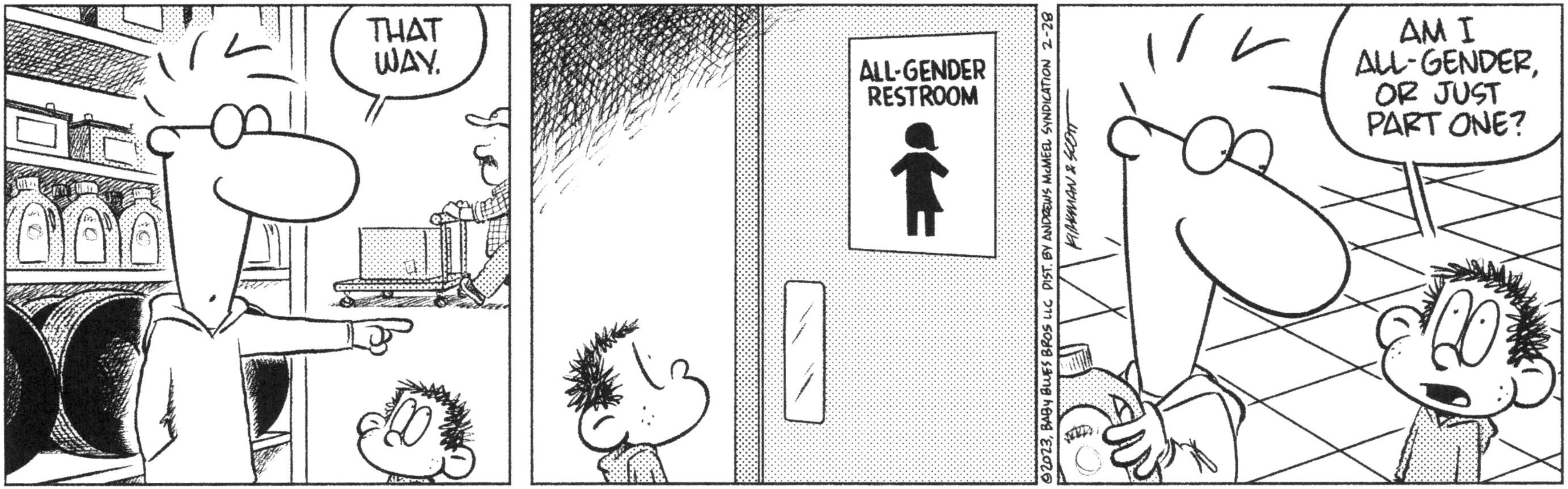
THAT WAY.
ALL-GENDER RESTROOM
©2023, BABY BLUES BROS LLC DIST. BY ANDREWS MCMEEL SYNDICATION 2-28
KIRKMAN & SCOTT
AM I ALL-GENDER, OR JUST PART ONE?

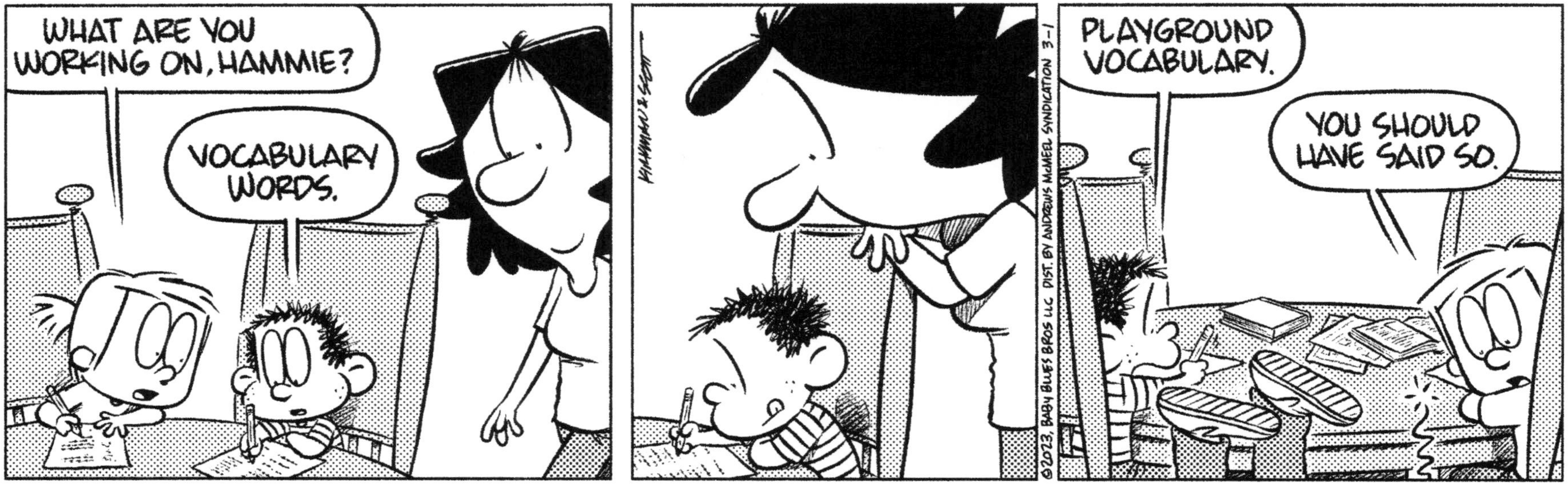
WHAT ARE YOU WORKING ON, HAMMIE?
VOCABULARY WORDS.
PLAYGROUND VOCABULARY.
YOU SHOULD HAVE SAID SO.
KIRKMAN & SCOTT
©2023, BABY BLUES BROS LLC DIST. BY ANDREWS McMEEL SYNDICATION 3-1

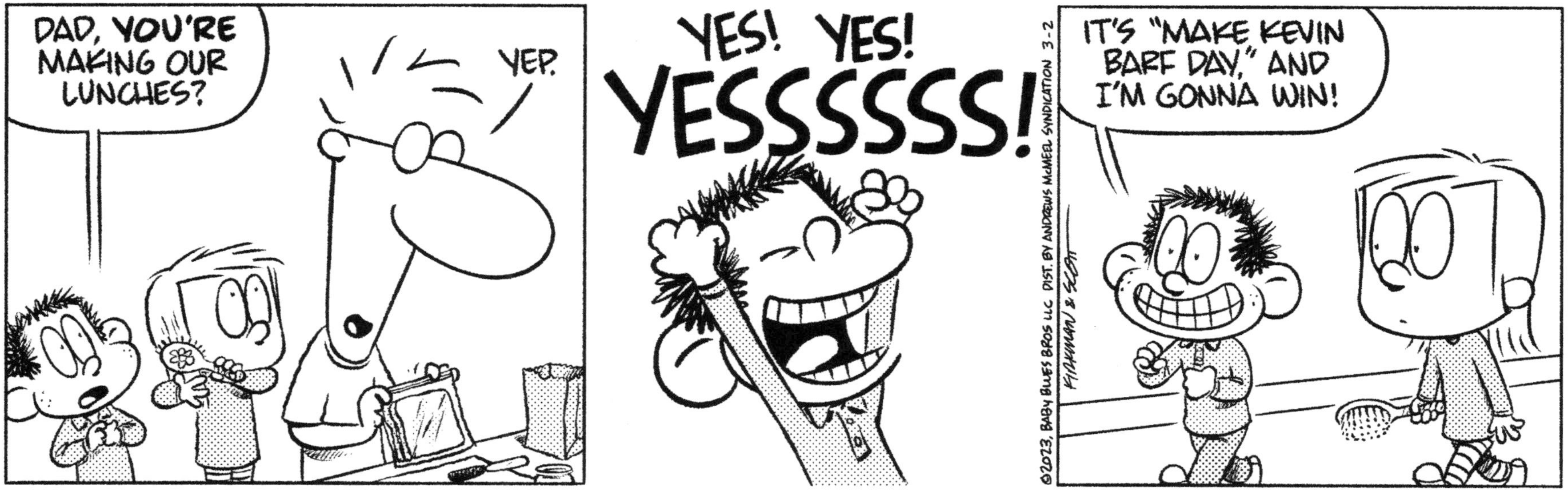
DAD, YOU'RE MAKING OUR LUNCHES?
YEP.
YES! YES! YESSSSSS!
IT'S "MAKE KEVIN BARF DAY," AND I'M GONNA WIN!
KIRKMAN & SCOTT
©2023, BABY BLUES BROS LLC DIST. BY ANDREWS McMEEL SYNDICATION 3-2

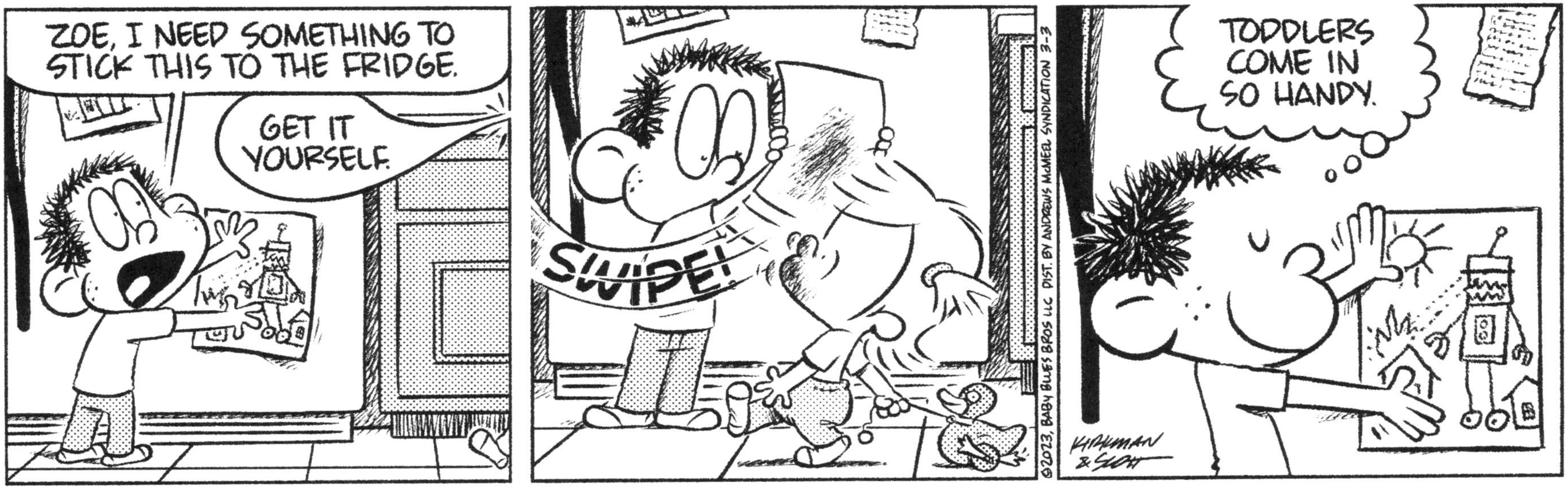
ZOE, I NEED SOMETHING TO STICK THIS TO THE FRIDGE.
GET IT YOURSELF.
SWIPE!
©2023, BABY BLUES BROS LLC DIST. BY ANDREWS MCMEEL SYNDICATION 3-3
TODDLERS COME IN SO HANDY.
KIRKMAN & SCOTT

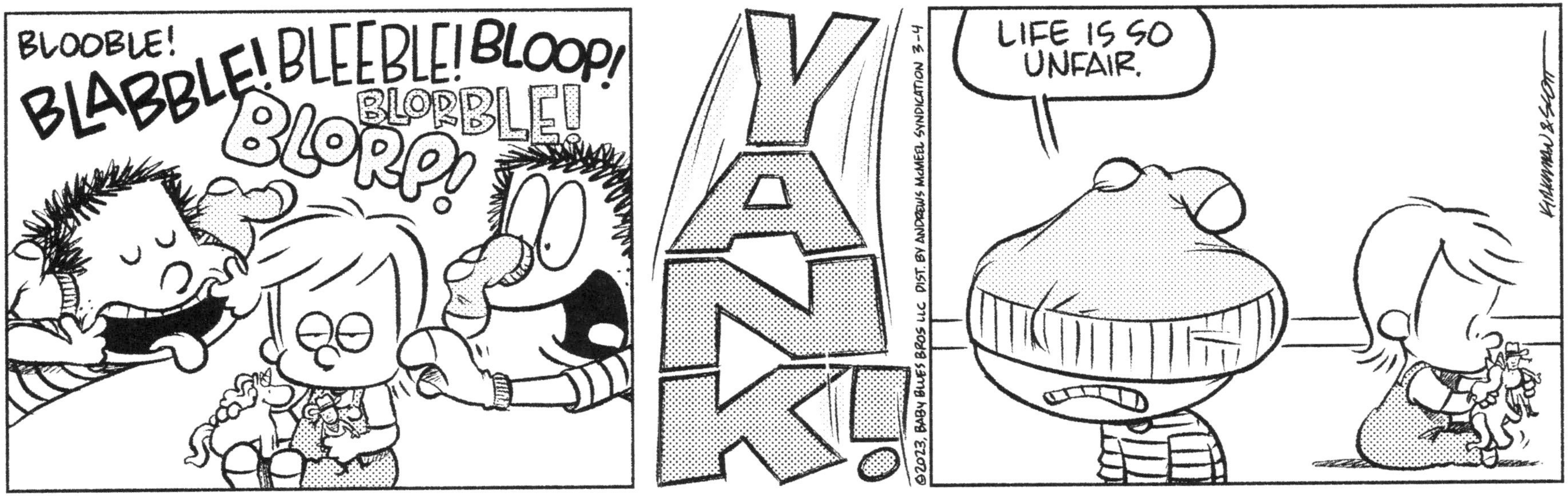
BLOOBLE!
BLABBLE!
BLEEBLE!
BLOOP!
BLORBBLE!
BLORP!
YANK!
©2023, BABY BLUES BROS LLC DIST. BY ANDREWS MCMEEL SYNDICATION 3-4
LIFE IS SO UNFAIR.
KIRKMAN & SCOTT

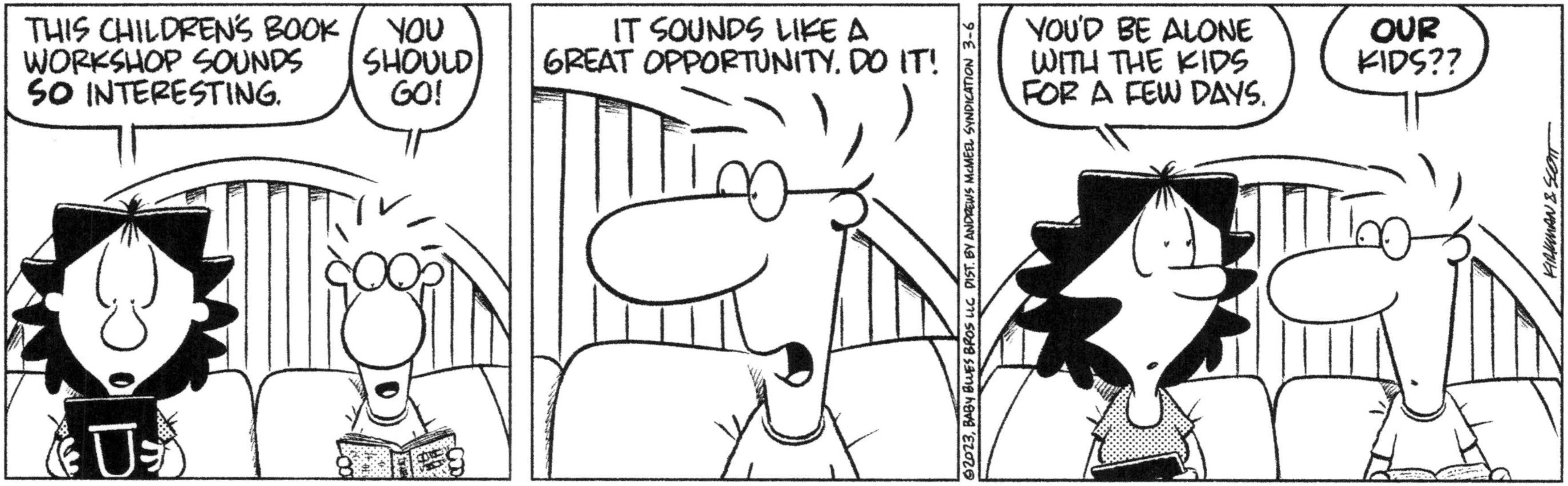
THIS CHILDREN'S BOOK WORKSHOP SOUNDS **SO** INTERESTING.
YOU SHOULD GO!
IT SOUNDS LIKE A GREAT OPPORTUNITY. DO IT!
©2023, BABY BLUES BROS LLC DIST. BY ANDREWS McMEEL SYNDICATION 3-6
YOU'D BE ALONE WITH THE KIDS FOR A FEW DAYS.
OUR KIDS??
KIRKMAN & SCOTT

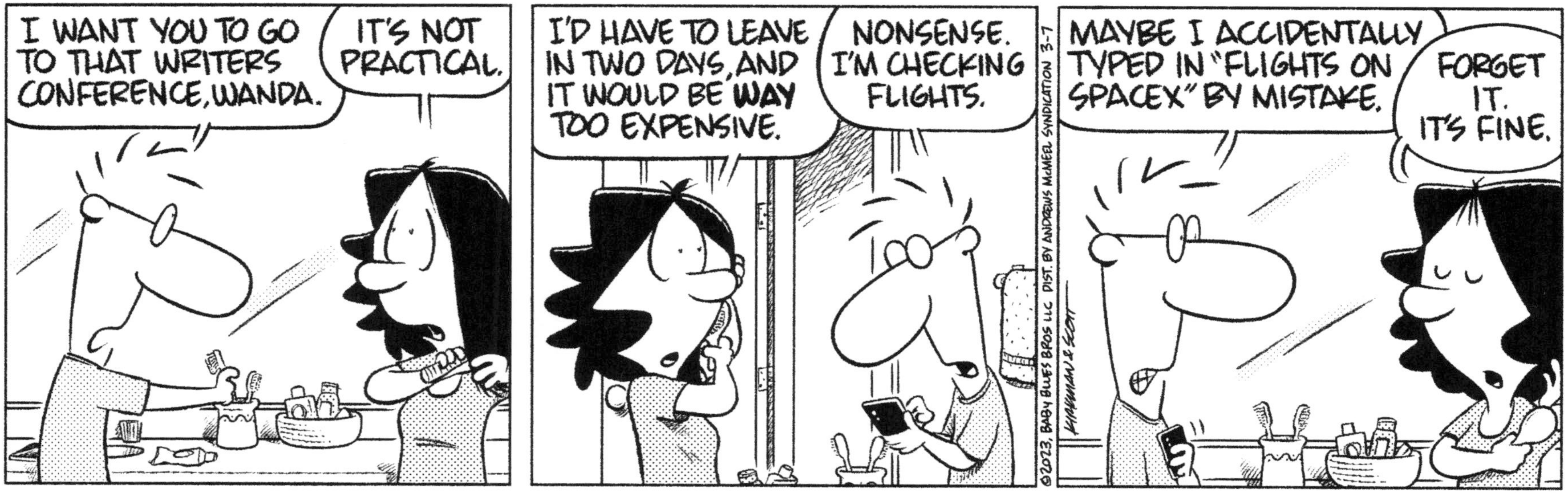
I WANT YOU TO GO TO THAT WRITERS CONFERENCE, WANDA.
IT'S NOT PRACTICAL.
I'D HAVE TO LEAVE IN TWO DAYS, AND IT WOULD BE **WAY** TOO EXPENSIVE.
NONSENSE. I'M CHECKING FLIGHTS.
©2023, BABY BLUES BROS LLC DIST. BY ANDREWS McMEEL SYNDICATION 3-7
KIRKMAN & SCOTT
MAYBE I ACCIDENTALLY TYPED IN "FLIGHTS ON SPACEX" BY MISTAKE.
FORGET IT. IT'S FINE.

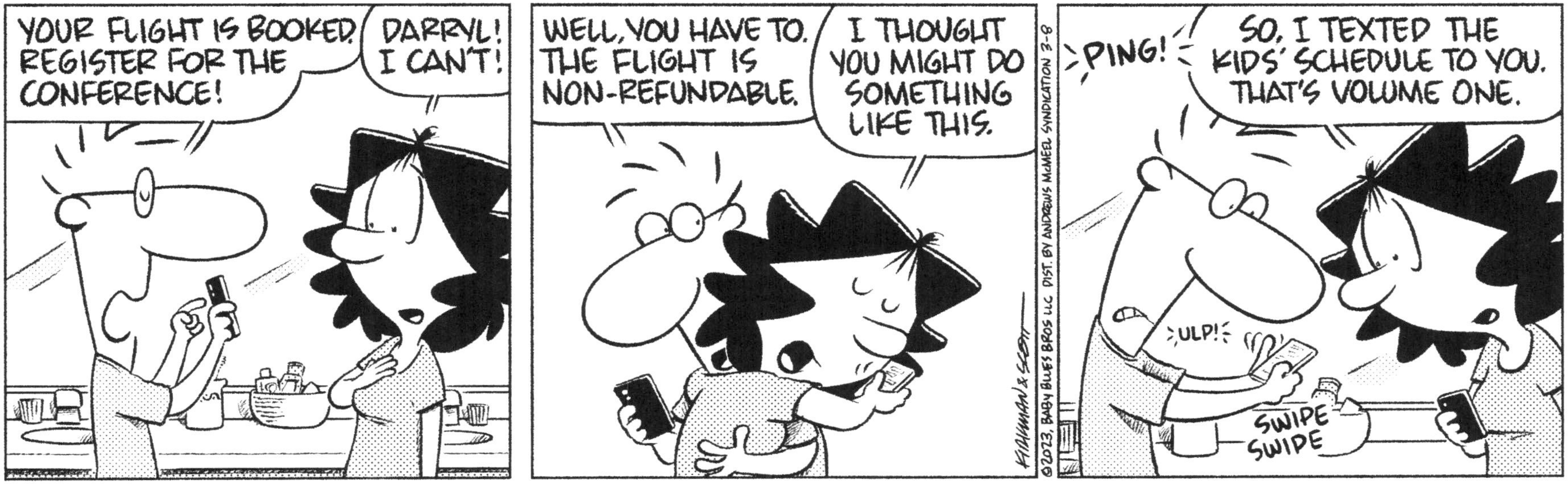
YOUR FLIGHT IS BOOKED. REGISTER FOR THE CONFERENCE!
DARRYL! I CAN'T!
WELL, YOU HAVE TO. THE FLIGHT IS NON-REFUNDABLE.
I THOUGHT YOU MIGHT DO SOMETHING LIKE THIS.
KIRKMAN & SCOTT
©2023, BABY BLUES BROS LLC DIST. BY ANDREWS McMEEL SYNDICATION 3-8
PING!
SO, I TEXTED THE KIDS' SCHEDULE TO YOU. THAT'S VOLUME ONE.
ULP!
SWIPE SWIPE

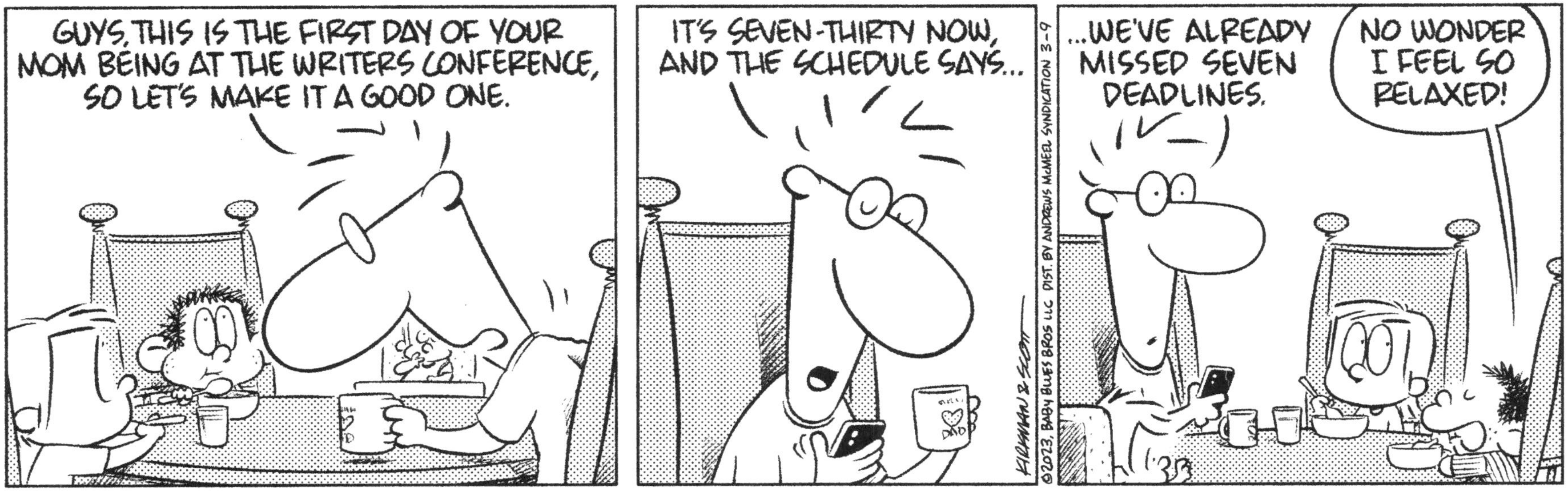
GUYS, THIS IS THE FIRST DAY OF YOUR MOM BEING AT THE WRITERS CONFERENCE, SO LET'S MAKE IT A GOOD ONE.
IT'S SEVEN-THIRTY NOW, AND THE SCHEDULE SAYS...
KIRKMAN & SCOTT
©2023, BABY BLUES BROS LLC DIST. BY ANDREWS McMEEL SYNDICATION 3-9
DAD
...WE'VE ALREADY MISSED SEVEN DEADLINES.
NO WONDER I FEEL SO RELAXED!

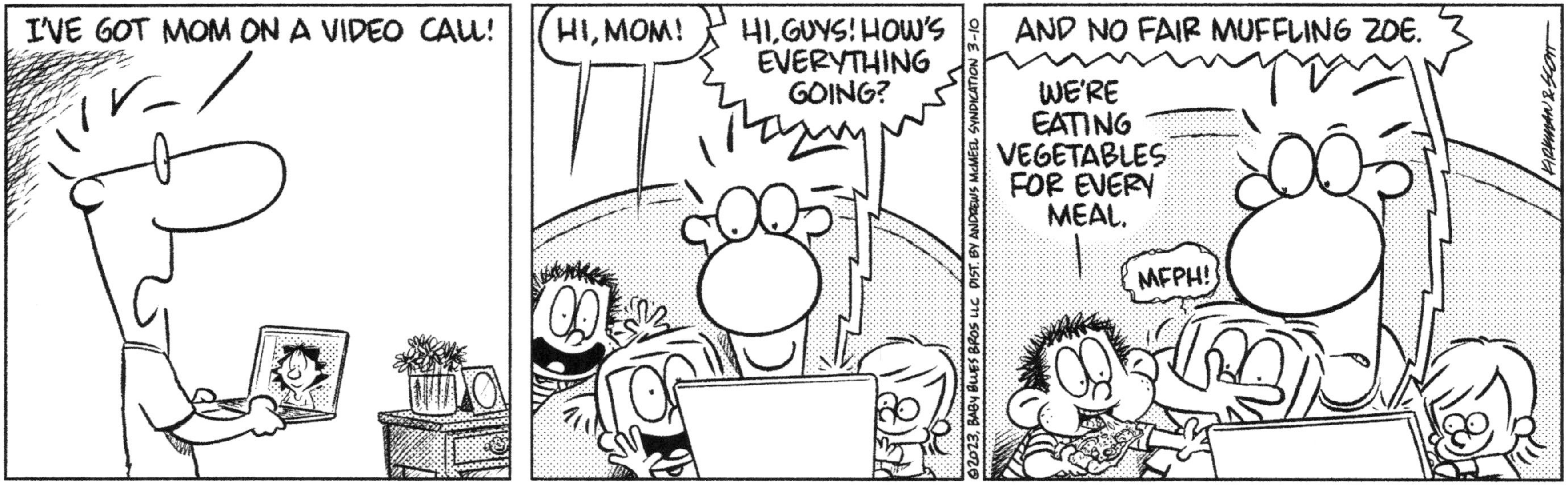
I'VE GOT MOM ON A VIDEO CALL!
HI, MOM!
HI, GUYS! HOW'S EVERYTHING GOING?
©2023, BABY BLUES BROS LLC DIST. BY ANDREWS McMEEL SYNDICATION 3-10
AND NO FAIR MUFFLING ZOE.
WE'RE EATING VEGETABLES FOR EVERY MEAL.
MFPH!
KIRKMAN & SCOTT

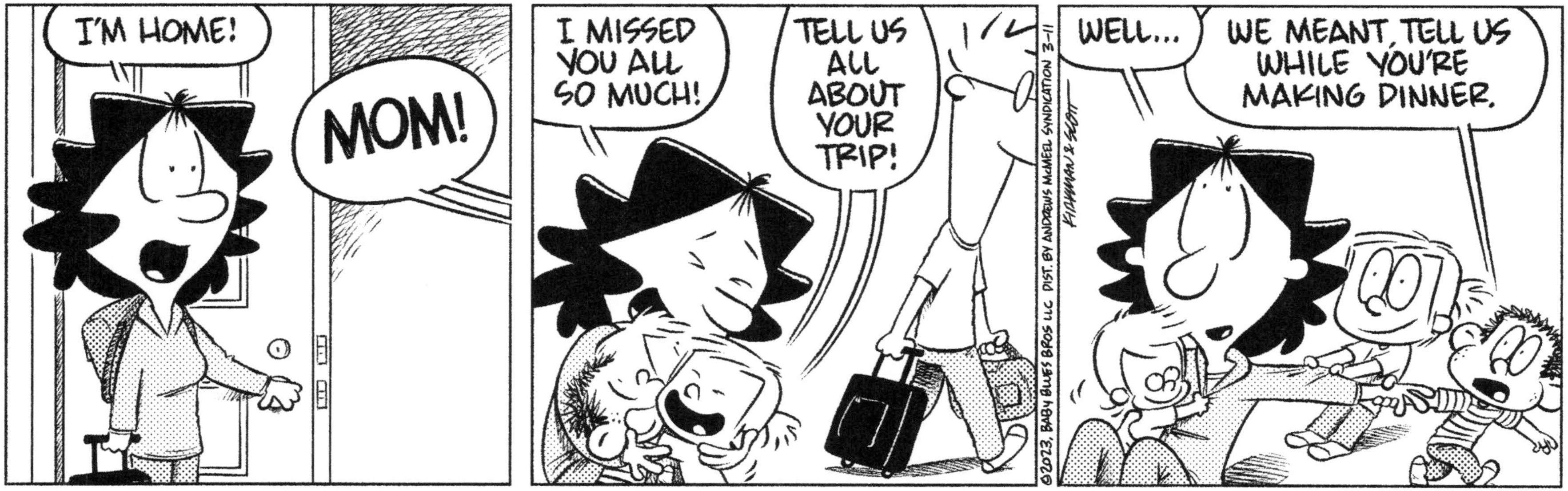
I'M HOME!
MOM!
I MISSED YOU ALL SO MUCH!
TELL US ALL ABOUT YOUR TRIP!
©2023, BABY BLUES BROS LLC DIST. BY ANDREWS McMEEL SYNDICATION 3-11
KIRKMAN & SCOTT
WELL...
WE MEANT, TELL US WHILE YOU'RE MAKING DINNER.

WHAT DID I JUST SAY??

WHAT DID I JUST SAY??
WHAT DID I JUST SAY.
WHAT?
©2023, BABY BLUES BROS LLC DIST. BY ANDREWS MCMEEL SYNDICATION
YOU ASKED WHAT YOU JUST SAID, AND I SAID, "WHAT DID I JUST SAY," BECAUSE THAT'S WHAT YOU JUST SAID.
NO! I MEAN, BEFORE THAT!
WELL, IF YOU WANT ME TO TELL YOU WHAT YOU SAID BEFORE WHAT YOU JUST SAID, YOU SHOULD'VE SAID, "WHAT DID I SAY BEFORE WHAT DID I JUST SAY," NOT JUST "WHAT DID I JUST SAY." IT'S CONFUSING.
3-5
KIRKMAN & SCOTT
MOM DOESN'T WANT YOU PLAYING WIFFLE BALL IN THE LIVING ROOM.
WHY DIDN'T SHE JUST SAY SO?

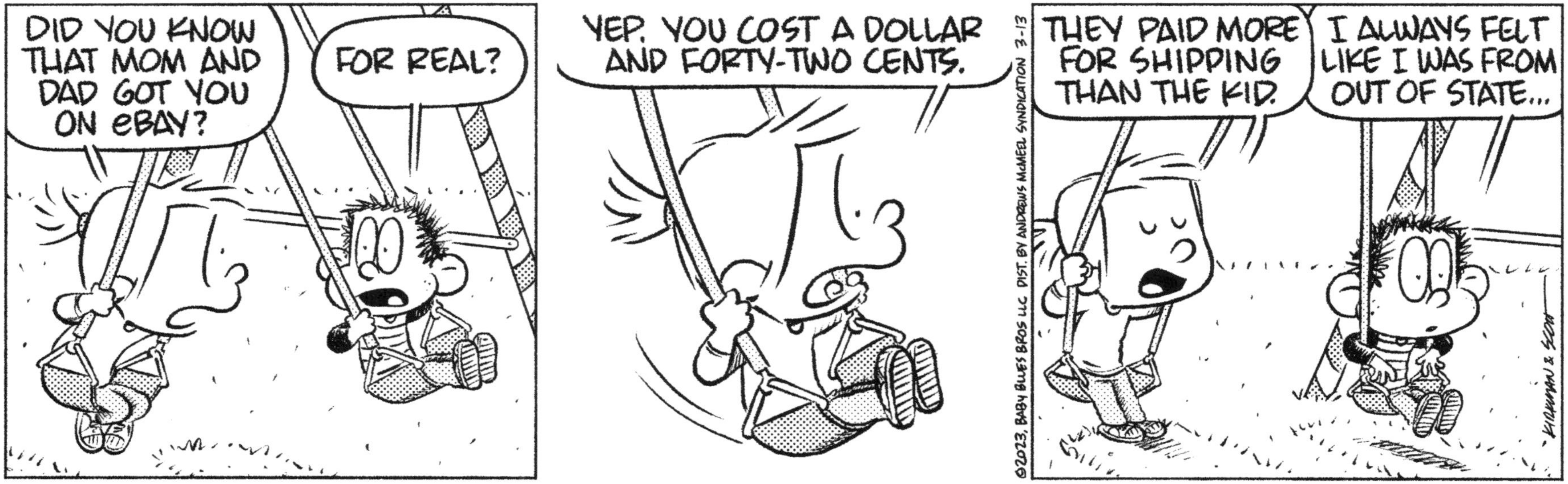
DID YOU KNOW THAT MOM AND DAD GOT YOU ON eBAY?
FOR REAL?
YEP. YOU COST A DOLLAR AND FORTY-TWO CENTS.
©2023, BABY BLUES BROS LLC DIST. BY ANDREWS McMEEL SYNDICATION 3-13
THEY PAID MORE FOR SHIPPING THAN THE KID.
I ALWAYS FELT LIKE I WAS FROM OUT OF STATE...
KIRKMAN & SCOTT

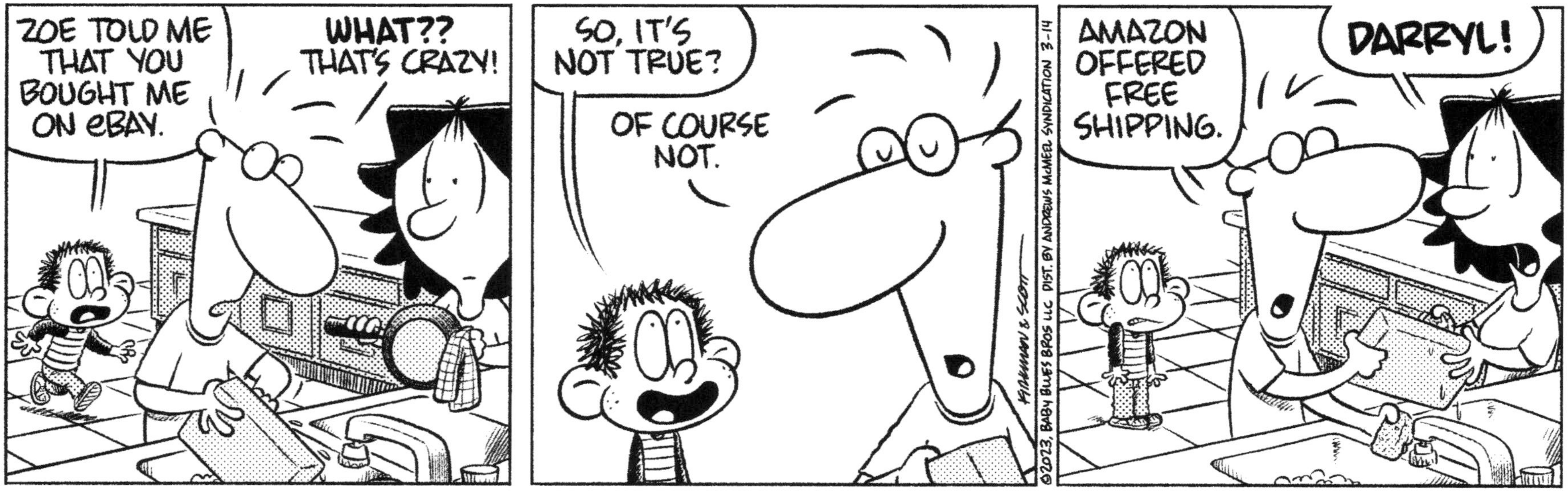
ZOE TOLD ME THAT YOU BOUGHT ME ON eBAY.
WHAT?? THAT'S CRAZY!
KIRKMAN & SCOTT
SO, IT'S NOT TRUE?
OF COURSE NOT.
©2023, BABY BLUES BROS LLC DIST. BY ANDREWS McMEEL SYNDICATION 3-14
AMAZON OFFERED FREE SHIPPING.
DARRYL!

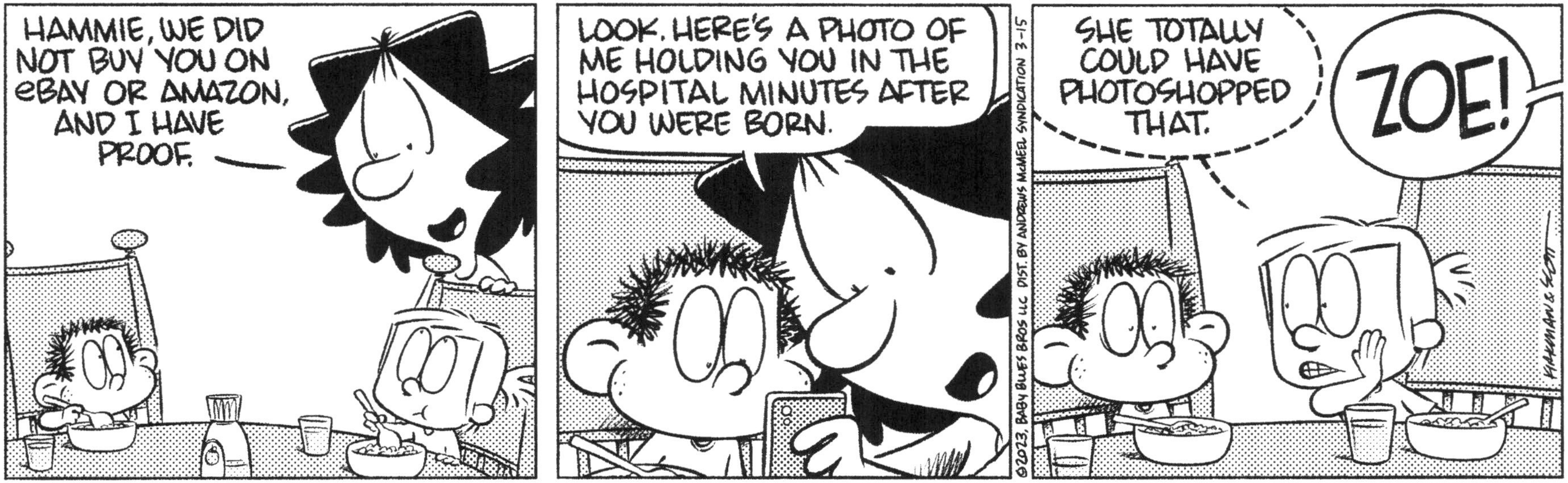
HAMMIE, WE DID NOT BUY YOU ON eBAY OR AMAZON, AND I HAVE PROOF.
LOOK. HERE'S A PHOTO OF ME HOLDING YOU IN THE HOSPITAL MINUTES AFTER YOU WERE BORN.
©2023, BABY BLUES BROS LLC DIST. BY ANDREWS MCMEEL SYNDICATION 3-15
SHE TOTALLY COULD HAVE PHOTOSHOPPED THAT.
ZOE!
KIRKMAN & SCOTT

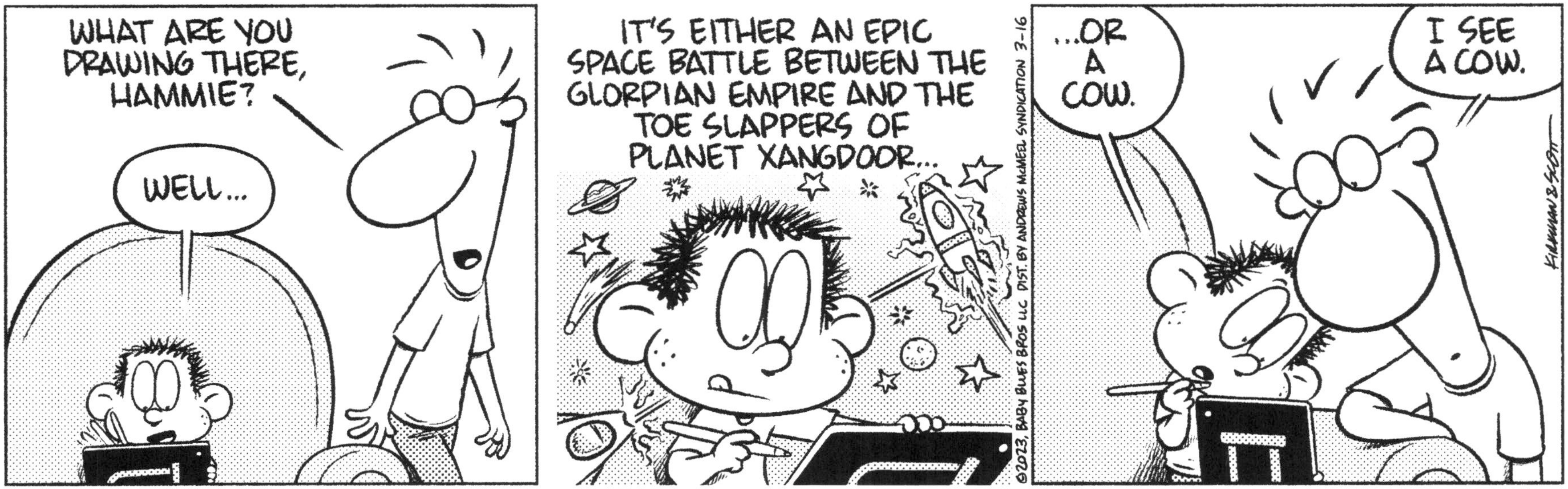
WHAT ARE YOU DRAWING THERE, HAMMIE?
WELL...
IT'S EITHER AN EPIC SPACE BATTLE BETWEEN THE GLORPIAN EMPIRE AND THE TOE SLAPPERS OF PLANET XANGDOOR...
©2023, BABY BLUES BROS LLC DIST. BY ANDREWS MCMEEL SYNDICATION 3-16
...OR A COW.
I SEE A COW.
KIRKMAN & SCOTT

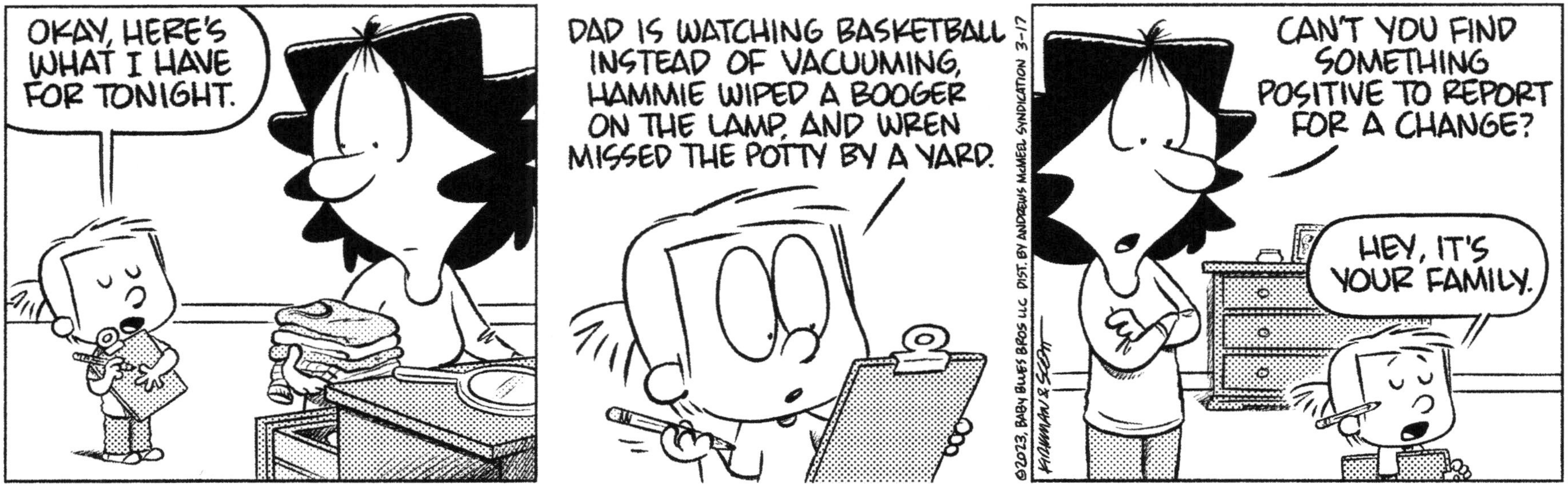
OKAY, HERE'S WHAT I HAVE FOR TONIGHT.
DAD IS WATCHING BASKETBALL INSTEAD OF VACUUMING, HAMMIE WIPED A BOOGER ON THE LAMP, AND WREN MISSED THE POTTY BY A YARD.
©2023, BABY BLUES BROS LLC DIST. BY ANDREWS McMEEL SYNDICATION 3-17
KIRKMAN & SCOTT
CAN'T YOU FIND SOMETHING POSITIVE TO REPORT FOR A CHANGE?
HEY, IT'S YOUR FAMILY.

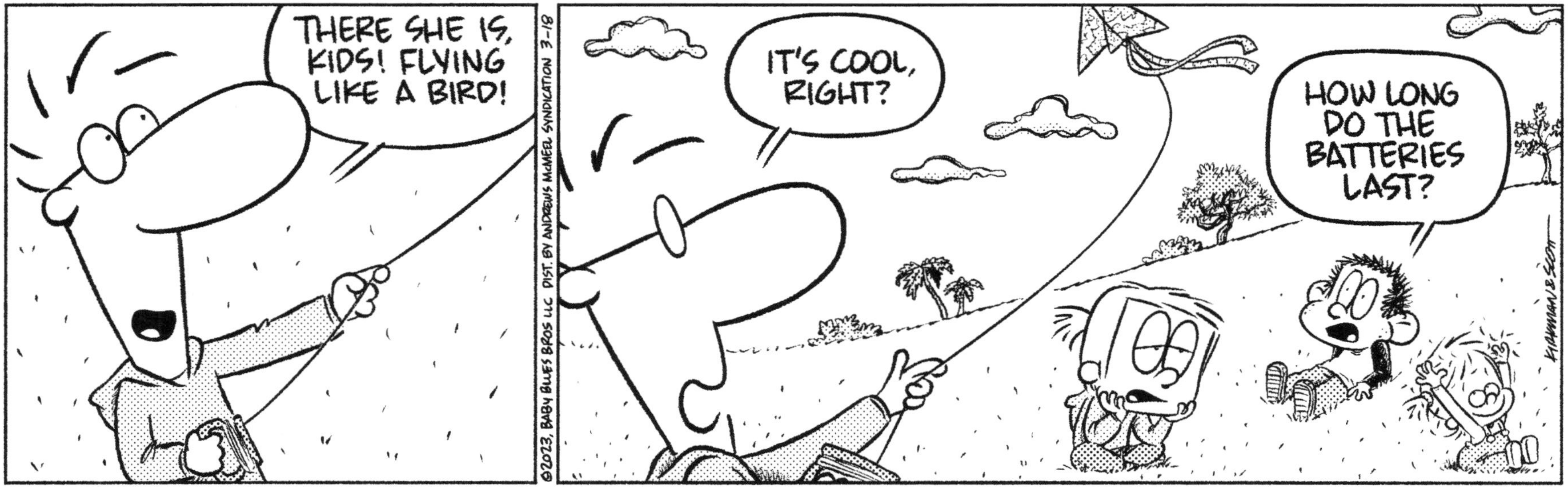
THERE SHE IS, KIDS! FLYING LIKE A BIRD!
©2023, BABY BLUES BROS LLC DIST. BY ANDREWS McMEEL SYNDICATION 3-18
IT'S COOL, RIGHT?
HOW LONG DO THE BATTERIES LAST?
KIRKMAN & SCOTT

IS THERE A PROBLEM WITH THAT?
PARENTING RULE #619-B...

WE GOT THE LAUNDRY ALL CLEANED AND FOLDED.
THE KITCHEN IS SPOTLESS, THE KIDS ARE ASLEEP...
©2023, BABY BLUES BROS LLC DIST. BY ANDREWS McMEEL SYNDICATION
...AND THE WHOLE HOUSE SEEMS TO BE UNDER CONTROL!
IS THERE A PROBLEM WITH THAT?
PARENTING RULE #619-B...
3-26
..."IF EVERYTHING IS GOING WELL, YOU'RE NOT PAYING ATTENTION."

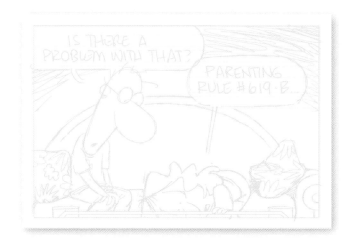

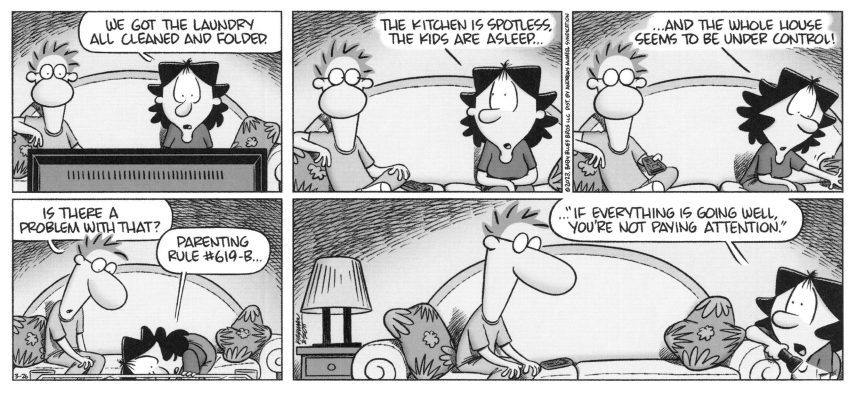

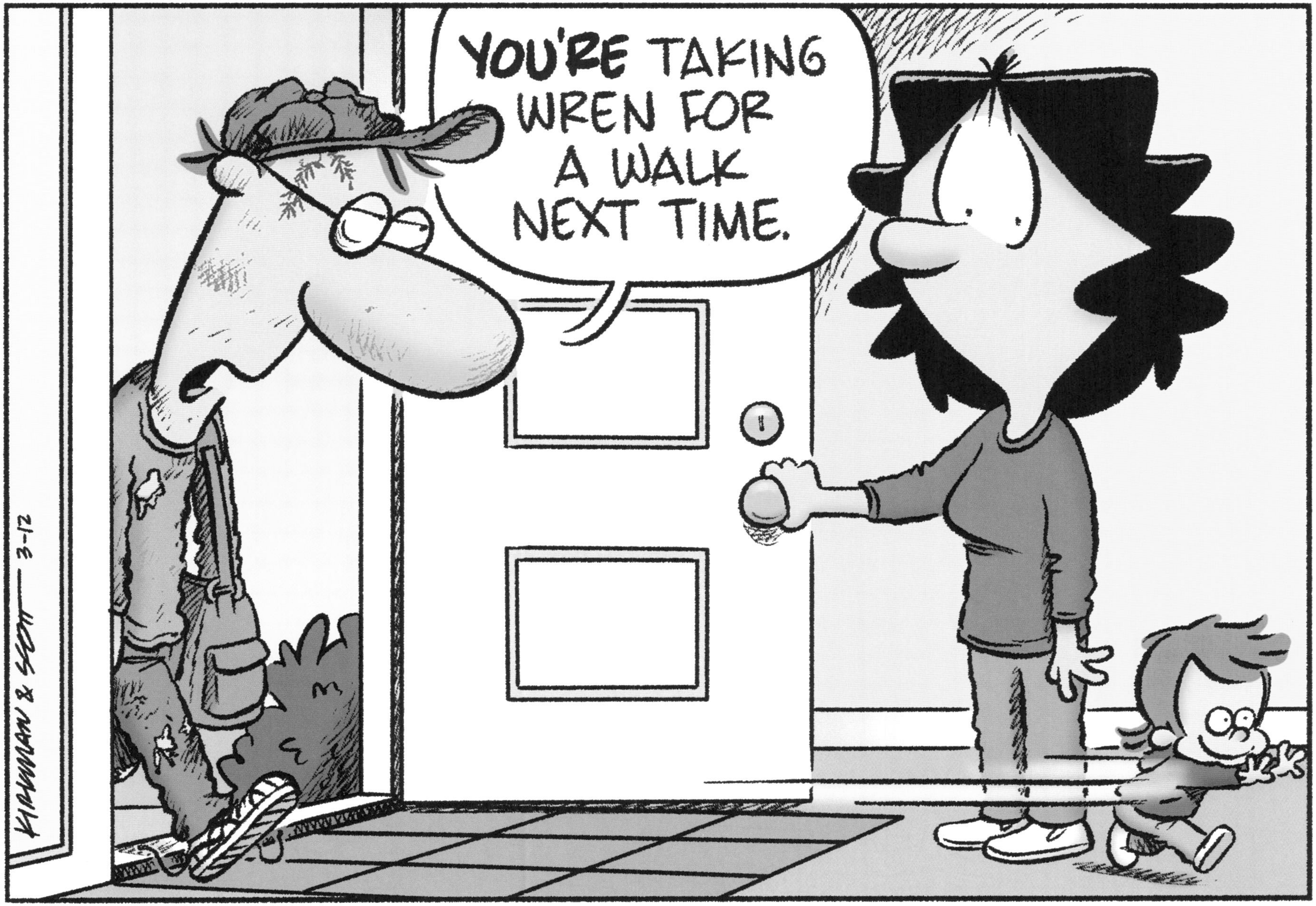
YOU'RE TAKING WREN FOR A WALK NEXT TIME.
KIRKMAN & SCOTT 3-12

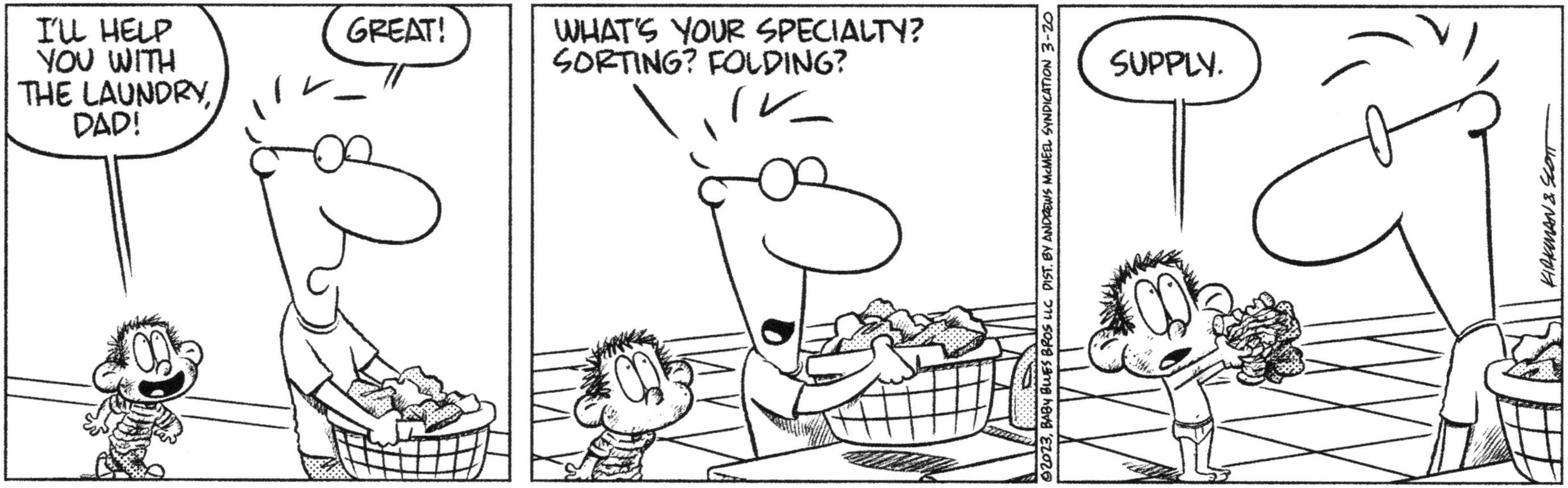
I'LL HELP YOU WITH THE LAUNDRY, DAD!
GREAT!
WHAT'S YOUR SPECIALTY? SORTING? FOLDING?
SUPPLY.
©2023, BABY BLUES BROS LLC DIST. BY ANDREWS McMEEL SYNDICATION 3-20
KIRKMAN & SCOTT

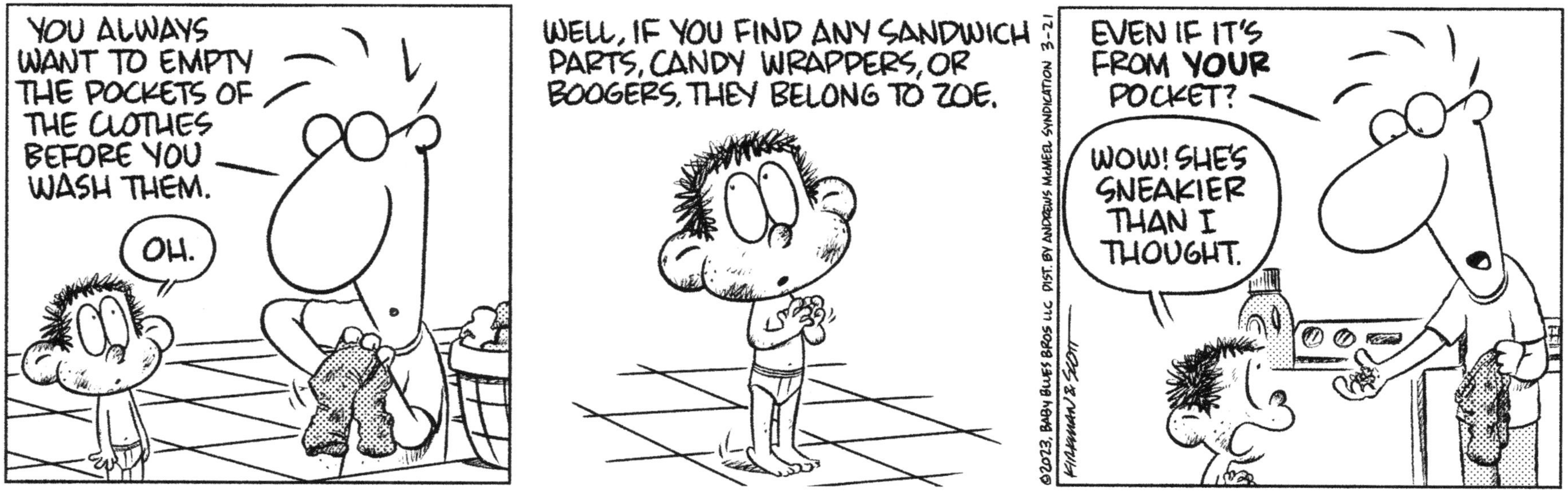
YOU ALWAYS WANT TO EMPTY THE POCKETS OF THE CLOTHES BEFORE YOU WASH THEM.
OH.
WELL, IF YOU FIND ANY SANDWICH PARTS, CANDY WRAPPERS, OR BOOGERS, THEY BELONG TO ZOE.
EVEN IF IT'S FROM **YOUR** POCKET?
WOW! SHE'S SNEAKIER THAN I THOUGHT.
©2023, BABY BLUES BROS LLC DIST. BY ANDREWS McMEEL SYNDICATION 3-21
KIRKMAN & SCOTT

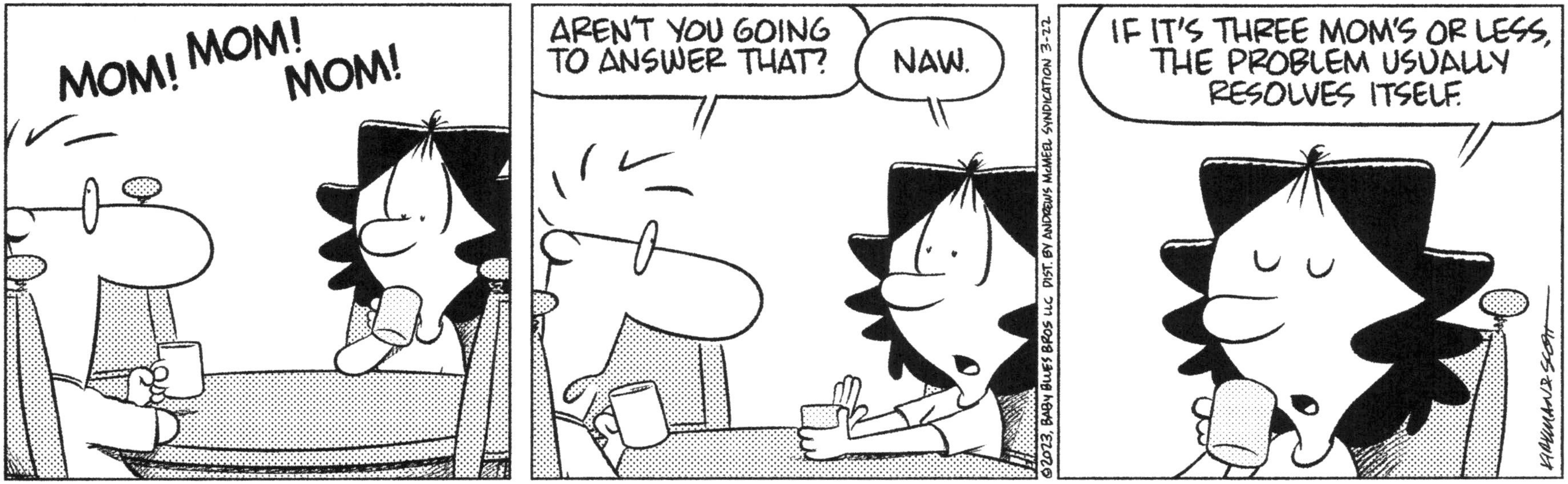
MOM! MOM! MOM!
AREN'T YOU GOING TO ANSWER THAT?
NAW.
©2023, BABY BLUES BROS LLC DIST. BY ANDREWS McMEEL SYNDICATION 3-22
IF IT'S THREE MOM'S OR LESS, THE PROBLEM USUALLY RESOLVES ITSELF.
KIRKMAN & SCOTT

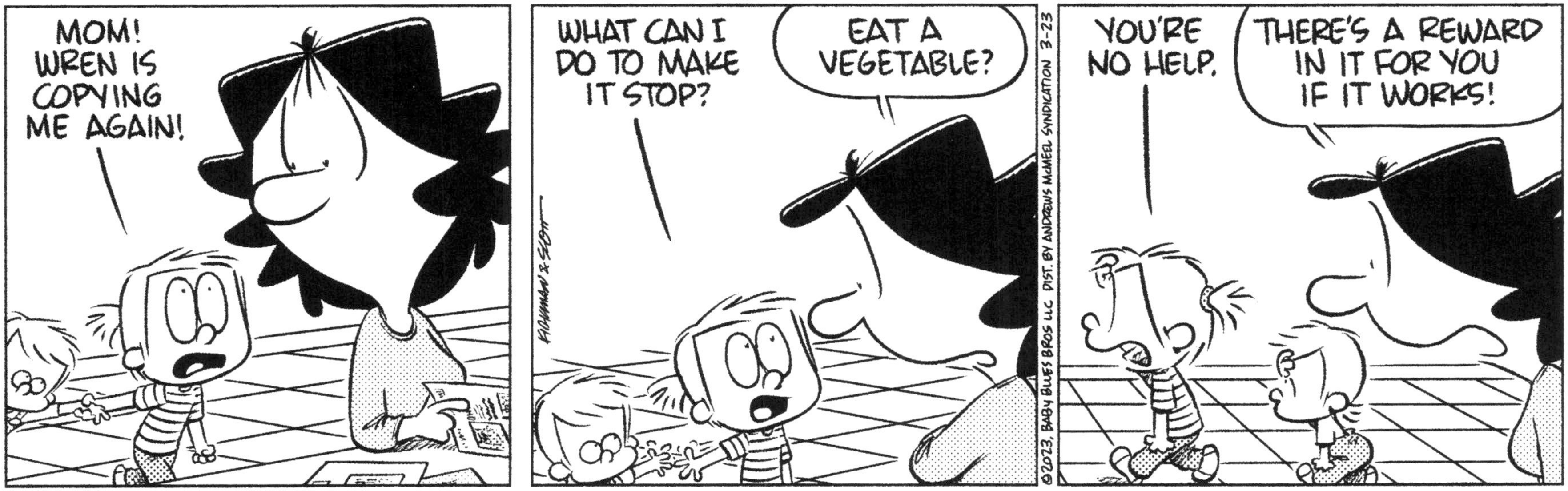
MOM! WREN IS COPYING ME AGAIN!
KIRKMAN & SCOTT
WHAT CAN I DO TO MAKE IT STOP?
EAT A VEGETABLE?
©2023, BABY BLUES BROS LLC DIST. BY ANDREWS McMEEL SYNDICATION 3-23
YOU'RE NO HELP.
THERE'S A REWARD IN IT FOR YOU IF IT WORKS!

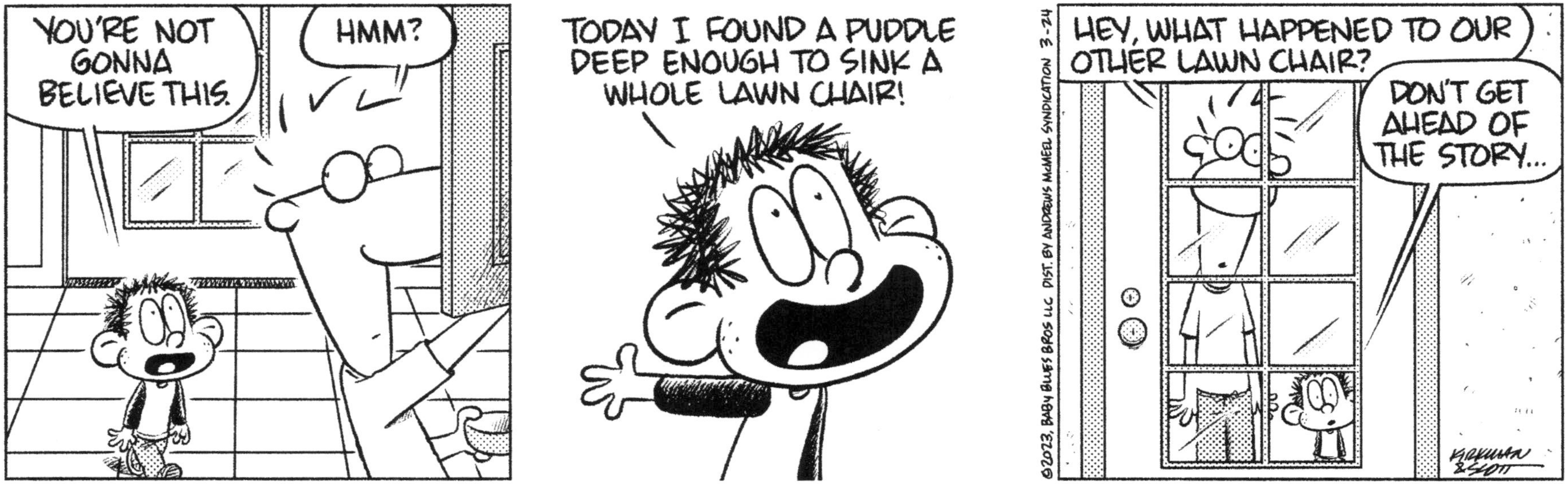
YOU'RE NOT GONNA BELIEVE THIS.
HMM?
TODAY I FOUND A PUDDLE DEEP ENOUGH TO SINK A WHOLE LAWN CHAIR!
©2023, BABY BLUES BROS LLC DIST. BY ANDREWS McMEEL SYNDICATION 3-24
HEY, WHAT HAPPENED TO OUR OTHER LAWN CHAIR?
DON'T GET AHEAD OF THE STORY...
KIRKMAN & SCOTT

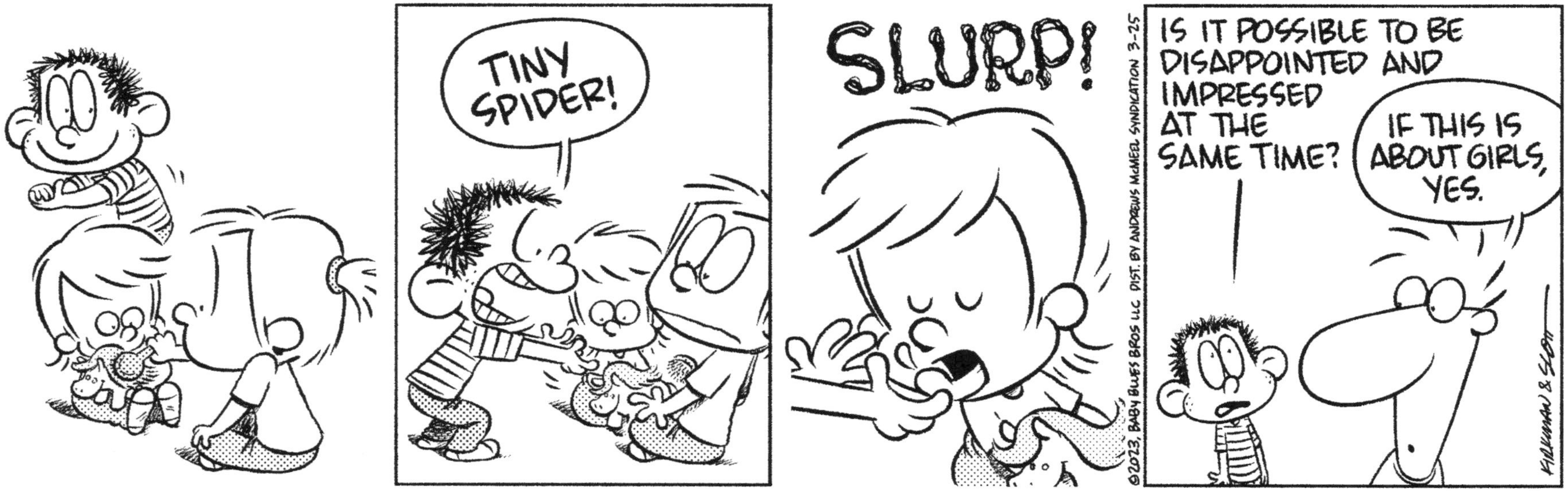
TINY SPIDER!
SLURP!
©2023, BABY BLUES BROS LLC DIST. BY ANDREWS McMEEL SYNDICATION 3-25
IS IT POSSIBLE TO BE DISAPPOINTED AND IMPRESSED AT THE SAME TIME?
IF THIS IS ABOUT GIRLS, YES.
KIRKMAN & SCOTT

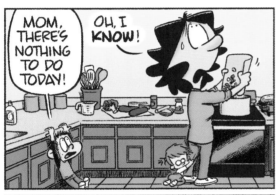

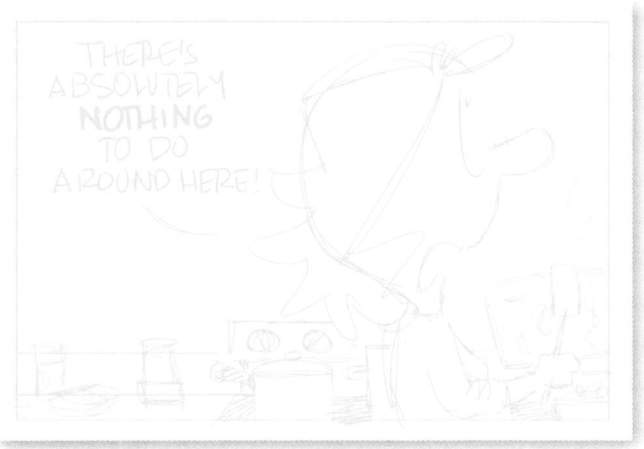

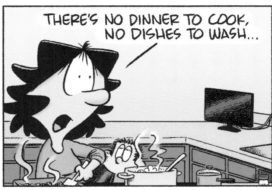

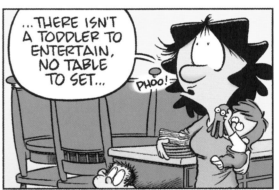

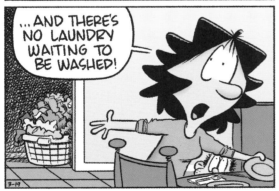

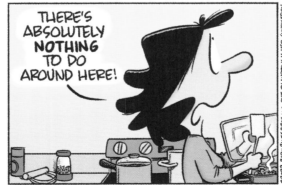

THERE'S ABSOLUTELY NOTHING TO DO AROUND HERE!

MOM, THERE'S NOTHING TO DO TODAY!
OH, I KNOW!
THERE'S NO DINNER TO COOK, NO DISHES TO WASH...
...THERE ISN'T A TODDLER TO ENTERTAIN, NO TABLE TO SET...
PHOO!
...AND THERE'S NO LAUNDRY WAITING TO BE WASHED!
3-19
THERE'S ABSOLUTELY NOTHING TO DO AROUND HERE!
©2013, BABY BLUES BROS LLC. DIST. BY ANDREWS McMEEL SYNDICATION
EVEN MOM AGREES.

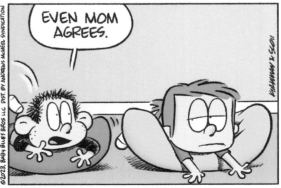

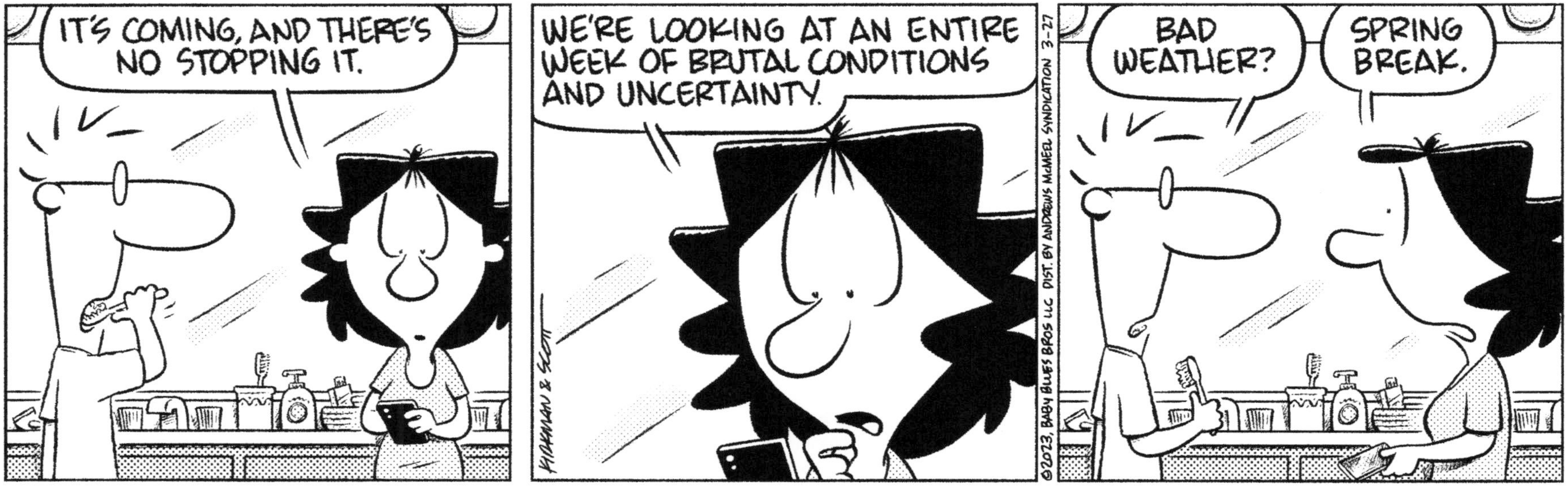
IT'S COMING, AND THERE'S NO STOPPING IT.
WE'RE LOOKING AT AN ENTIRE WEEK OF BRUTAL CONDITIONS AND UNCERTAINTY.
KIRKMAN & SCOTT
©2023, BABY BLUES BROS LLC DIST. BY ANDREWS MCMEEL SYNDICATION 3-27
BAD WEATHER?
SPRING BREAK.

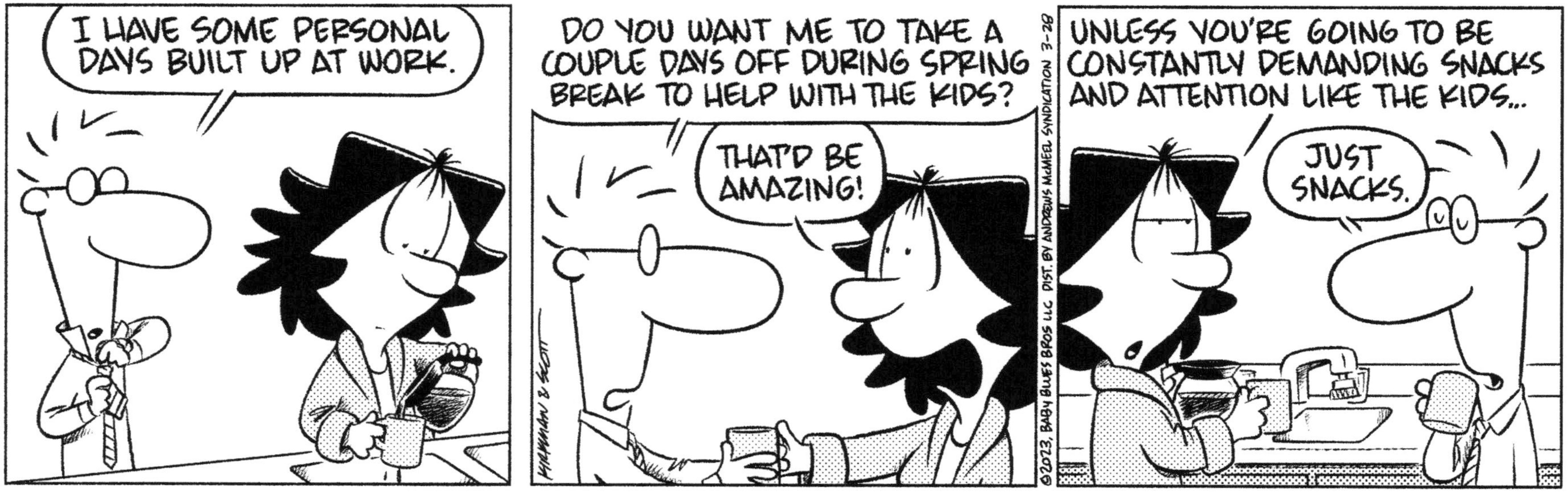
I HAVE SOME PERSONAL DAYS BUILT UP AT WORK.
DO YOU WANT ME TO TAKE A COUPLE DAYS OFF DURING SPRING BREAK TO HELP WITH THE KIDS?
THAT'D BE AMAZING!
KIRKMAN & SCOTT
©2023, BABY BLUES BROS LLC DIST. BY ANDREWS MCMEEL SYNDICATION 3-28
UNLESS YOU'RE GOING TO BE CONSTANTLY DEMANDING SNACKS AND ATTENTION LIKE THE KIDS...
JUST SNACKS.

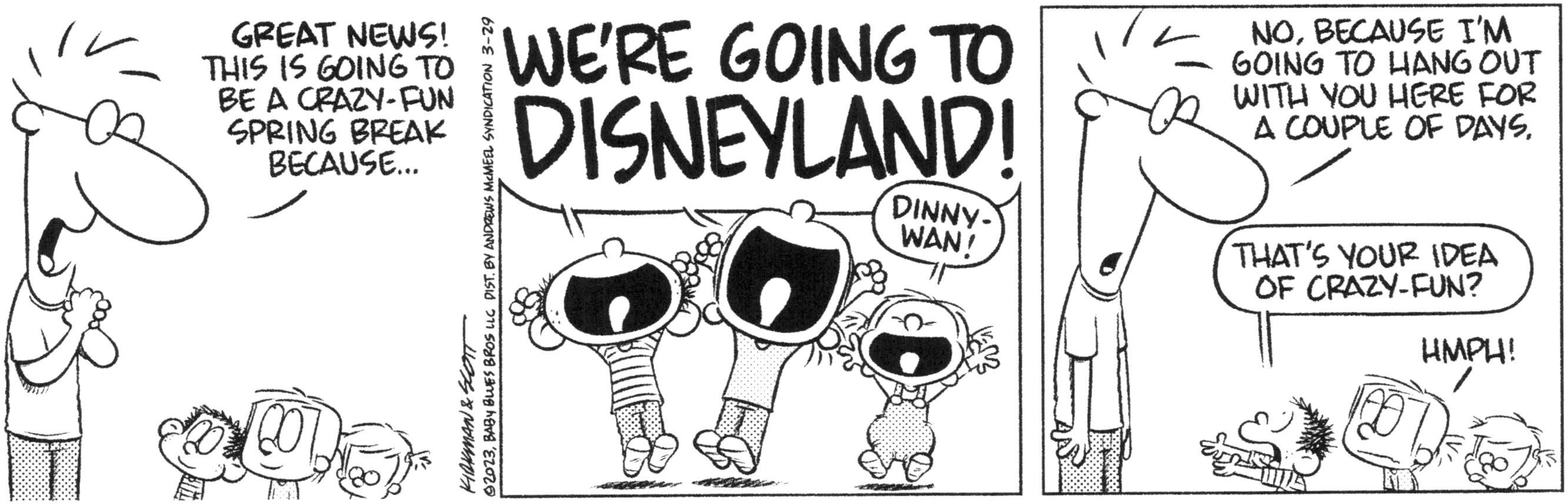
GREAT NEWS! THIS IS GOING TO BE A CRAZY-FUN SPRING BREAK BECAUSE...
KIRKMAN & SCOTT
©2023, BABY BLUES BROS LLC DIST. BY ANDREWS MCMEEL SYNDICATION 3-29
WE'RE GOING TO DISNEYLAND!
DINNY-WAN!
NO, BECAUSE I'M GOING TO HANG OUT WITH YOU HERE FOR A COUPLE OF DAYS.
THAT'S YOUR IDEA OF CRAZY-FUN?
HMPH!

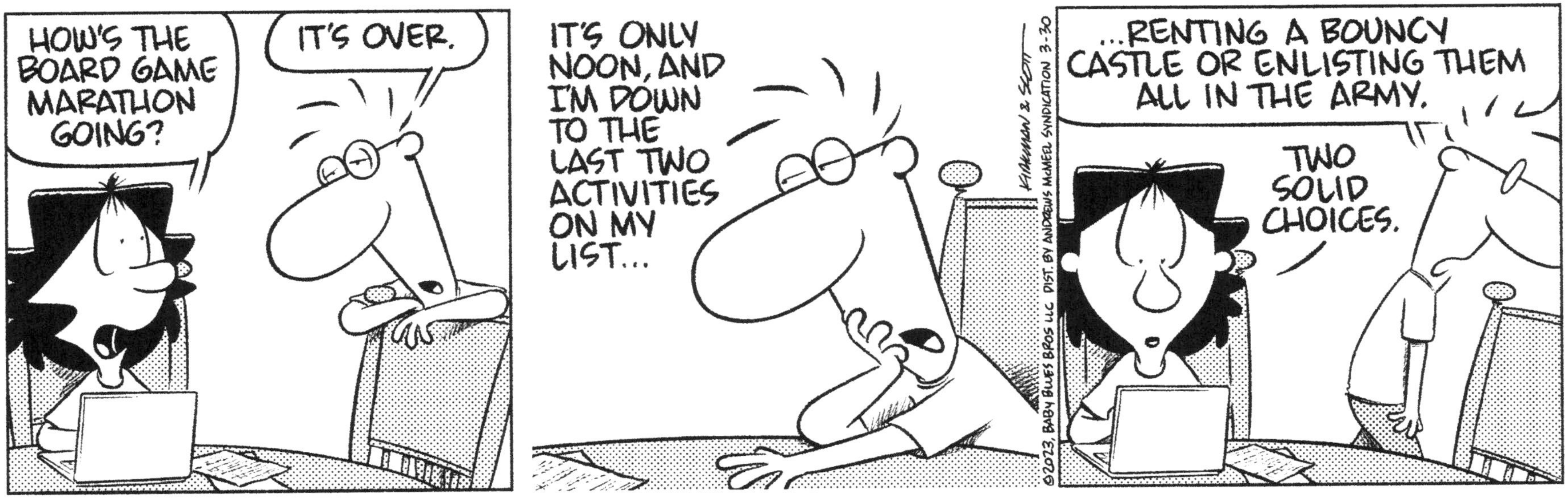
HOW'S THE BOARD GAME MARATHON GOING?
IT'S OVER.
IT'S ONLY NOON, AND I'M DOWN TO THE LAST TWO ACTIVITIES ON MY LIST...
KIRKMAN & SCOTT
©2023, BABY BLUES BROS LLC DIST. BY ANDREWS MCMEEL SYNDICATION 3-30
...RENTING A BOUNCY CASTLE OR ENLISTING THEM ALL IN THE ARMY.
TWO SOLID CHOICES.

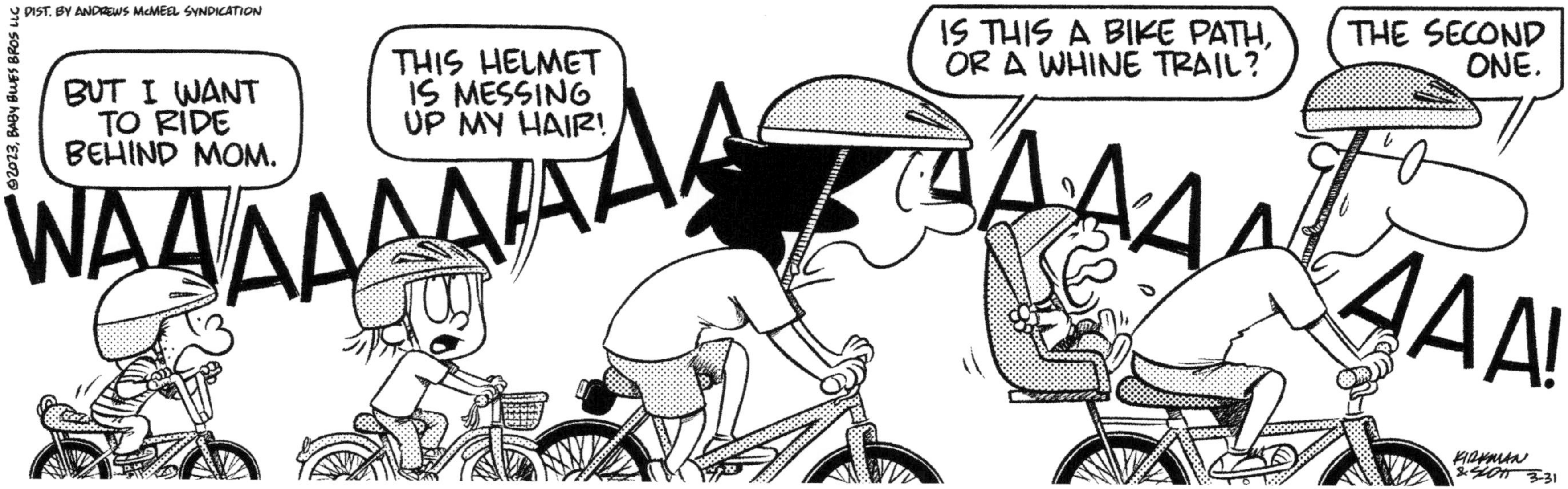
©2023, BABY BLUES BROS LLC DIST. BY ANDREWS McMEEL SYNDICATION
BUT I WANT TO RIDE BEHIND MOM.
THIS HELMET IS MESSING UP MY HAIR!
WAAAAAAAAAAAAAAAAAA!
IS THIS A BIKE PATH, OR A WHINE TRAIL?
THE SECOND ONE.
KIRKMAN & SCOTT 3-31

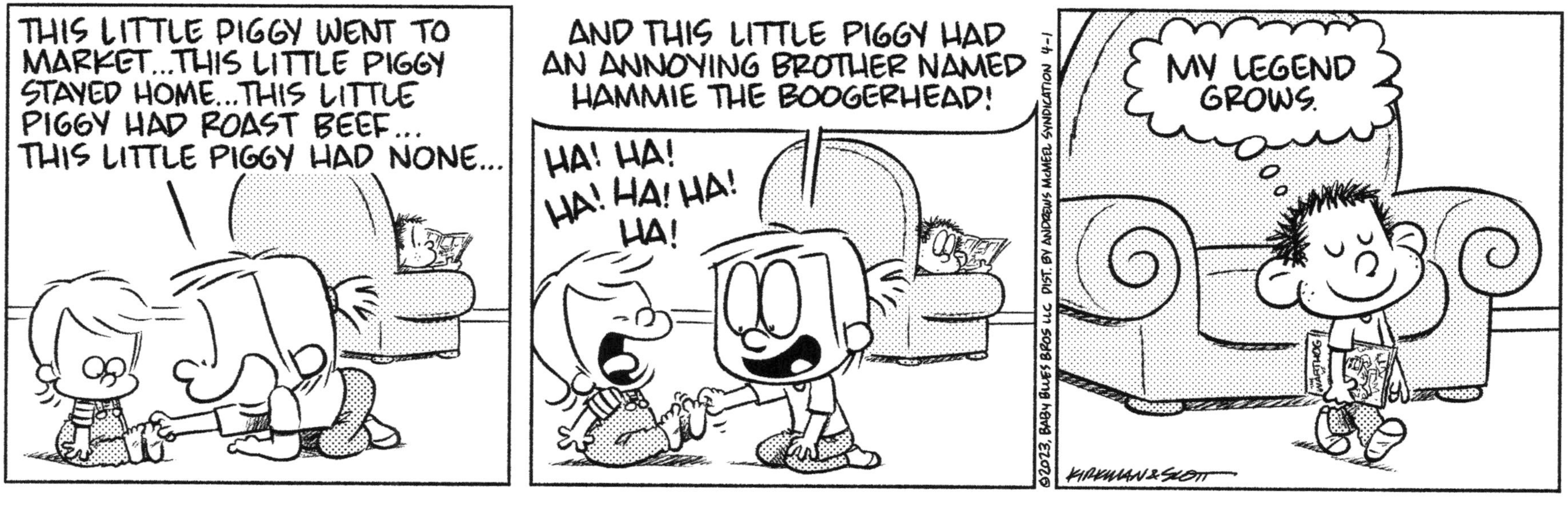
THIS LITTLE PIGGY WENT TO MARKET...THIS LITTLE PIGGY STAYED HOME...THIS LITTLE PIGGY HAD ROAST BEEF... THIS LITTLE PIGGY HAD NONE...
AND THIS LITTLE PIGGY HAD AN ANNOYING BROTHER NAMED HAMMIE THE BOOGERHEAD!
HA! HA! HA! HA! HA! HA!
©2023, BABY BLUES BROS LLC DIST. BY ANDREWS McMEEL SYNDICATION 4-1
MY LEGEND GROWS.
KIRKMAN & SCOTT

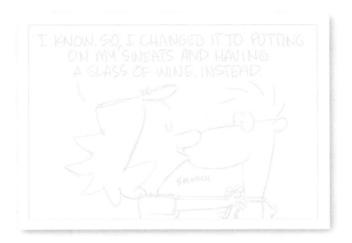

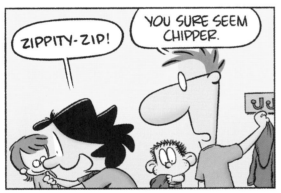

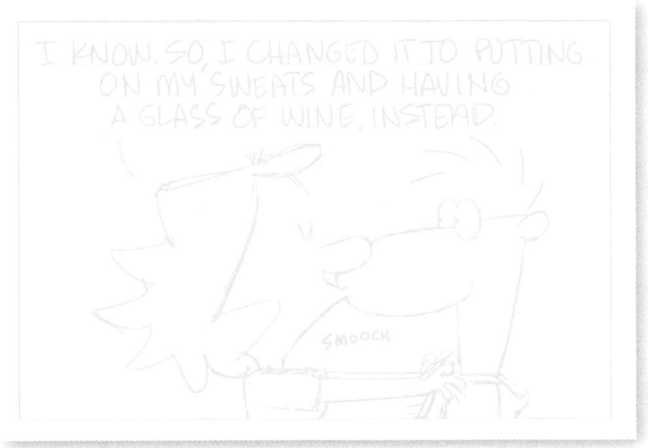

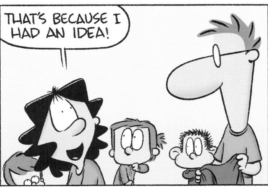

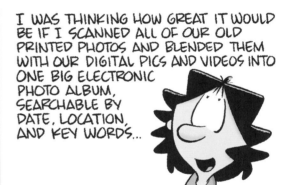

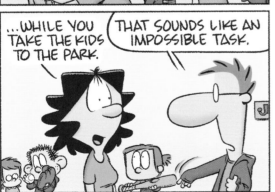

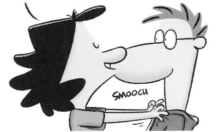

I KNOW. SO, I CHANGED IT TO PUTTING ON MY SWEATS AND HAVING A GLASS OF WINE, INSTEAD.
SMOOCH

ZIPPITY-ZIP!
YOU SURE SEEM CHIPPER.
THAT'S BECAUSE I HAD AN IDEA!
I WAS THINKING HOW GREAT IT WOULD BE IF I SCANNED ALL OF OUR OLD PRINTED PHOTOS AND BLENDED THEM WITH OUR DIGITAL PICS AND VIDEOS INTO ONE BIG ELECTRONIC PHOTO ALBUM, SEARCHABLE BY DATE, LOCATION, AND KEY WORDS...
...WHILE YOU TAKE THE KIDS TO THE PARK.
THAT SOUNDS LIKE AN IMPOSSIBLE TASK.
I KNOW. SO, I CHANGED IT TO PUTTING ON MY SWEATS AND HAVING A GLASS OF WINE, INSTEAD.
SMOOCH
4-2
©2013, BABY BLUES BROS LLC DIST. BY ANDREWS MCMEEL SYNDICATION
IF YOU NEED ME, I'LL BE HERE, MEETING MY GOALS!
KIRKMAN & SCOTT

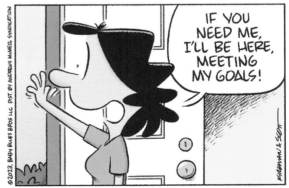

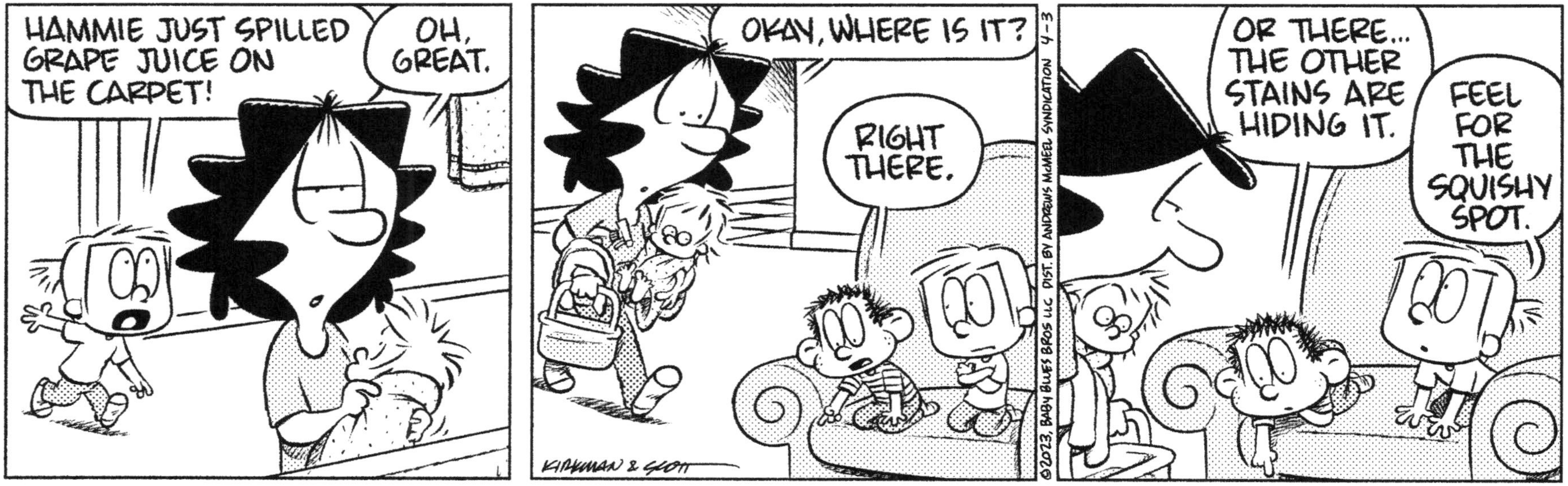
HAMMIE JUST SPILLED GRAPE JUICE ON THE CARPET!
OH, GREAT.
OKAY, WHERE IS IT?
RIGHT THERE.
KIRKMAN & SCOTT
©2023, BABY BLUES BROS LLC DIST. BY ANDREWS McMEEL SYNDICATION 4-3
OR THERE... THE OTHER STAINS ARE HIDING IT.
FEEL FOR THE SQUISHY SPOT.

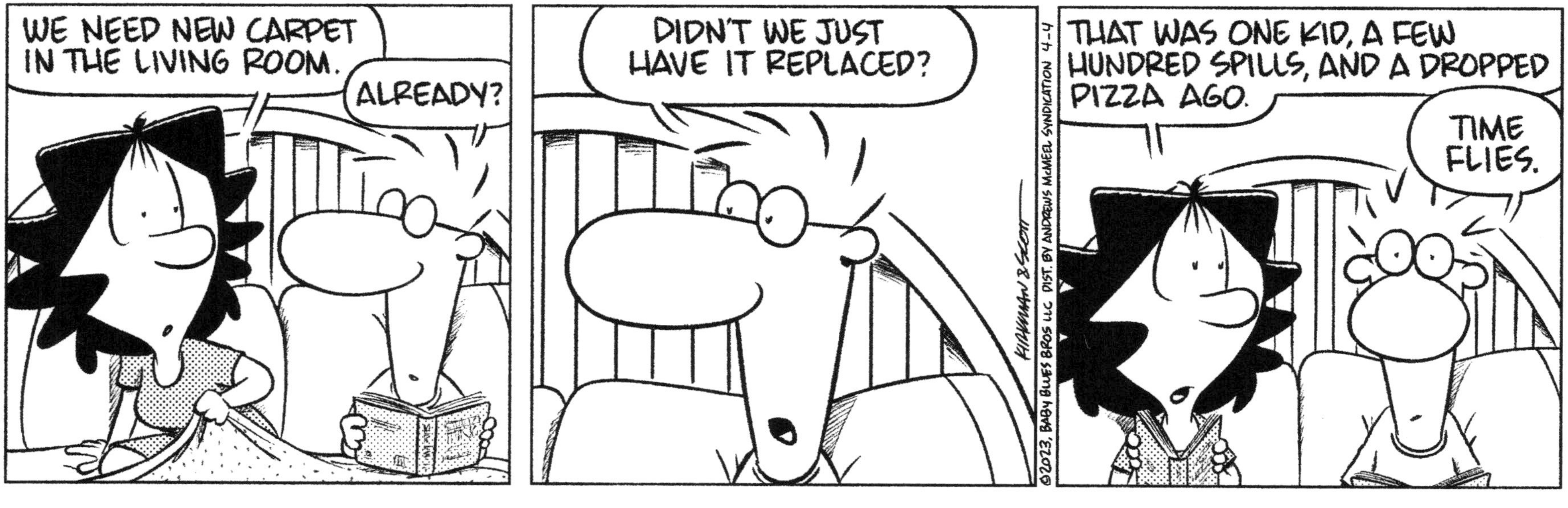
WE NEED NEW CARPET IN THE LIVING ROOM.
ALREADY?
DIDN'T WE JUST HAVE IT REPLACED?
KIRKMAN & SCOTT
©2023, BABY BLUES BROS LLC DIST. BY ANDREWS McMEEL SYNDICATION 4-4
THAT WAS ONE KID, A FEW HUNDRED SPILLS, AND A DROPPED PIZZA AGO.
TIME FLIES.

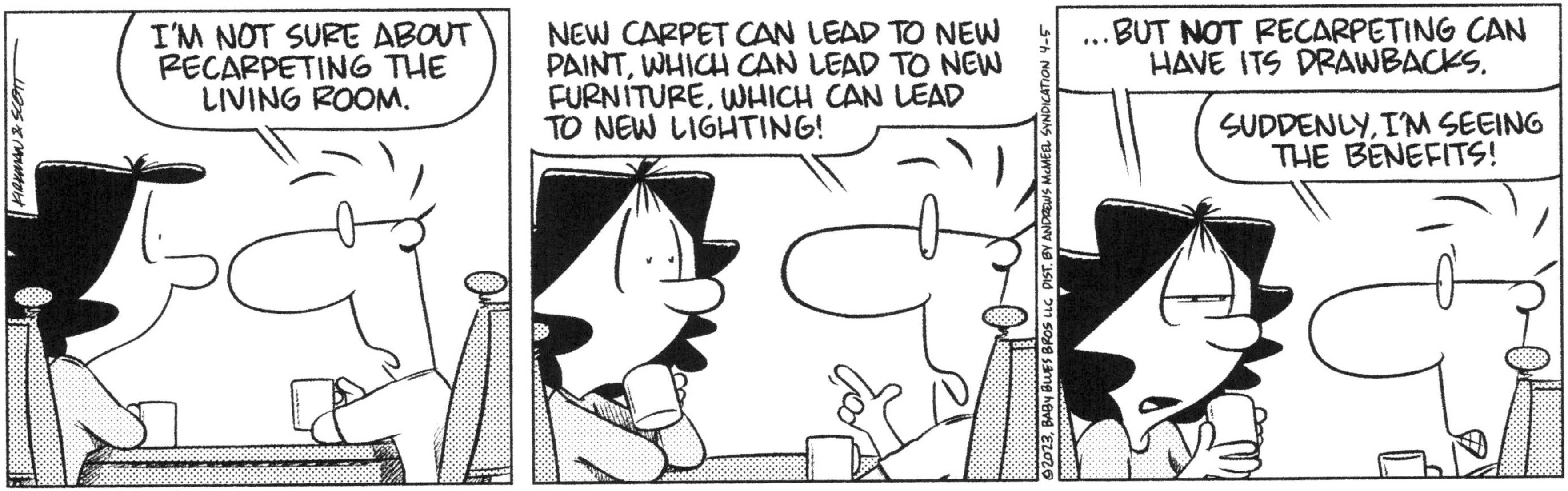
I'M NOT SURE ABOUT RECARPETING THE LIVING ROOM.
NEW CARPET CAN LEAD TO NEW PAINT, WHICH CAN LEAD TO NEW FURNITURE, WHICH CAN LEAD TO NEW LIGHTING!
...BUT NOT RECARPETING CAN HAVE ITS DRAWBACKS.
SUDDENLY, I'M SEEING THE BENEFITS!
KIRKMAN & SCOTT
©2023, BABY BLUES BROS LLC DIST. BY ANDREWS MCMEEL SYNDICATION 4-5

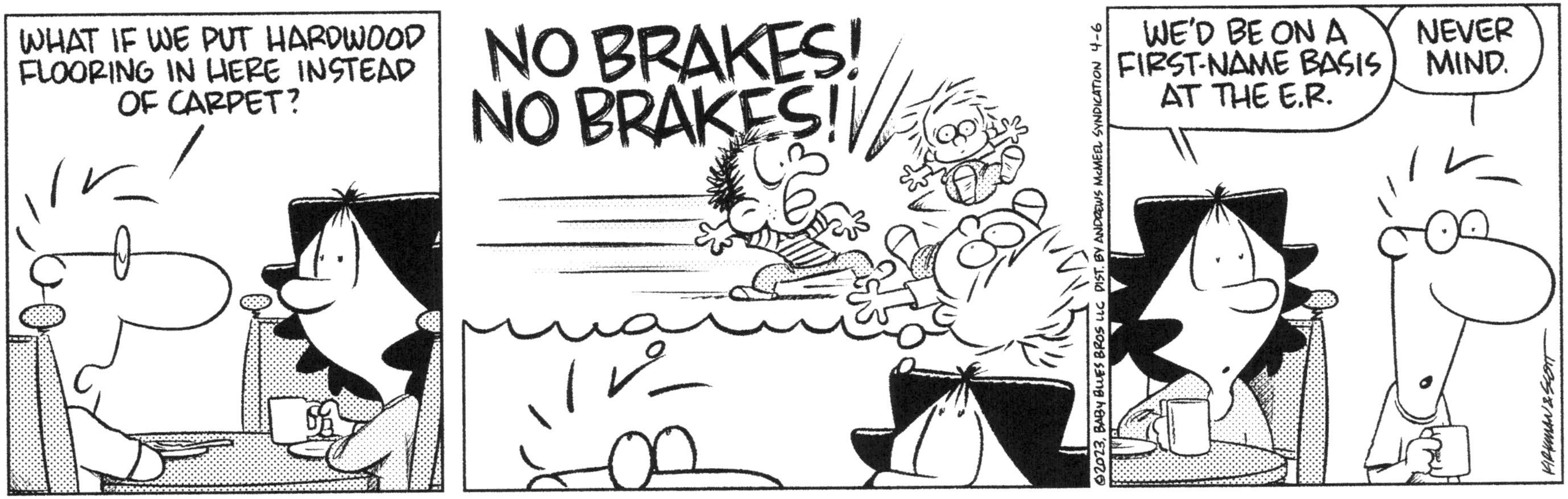
WHAT IF WE PUT HARDWOOD FLOORING IN HERE INSTEAD OF CARPET?
NO BRAKES! NO BRAKES!
WE'D BE ON A FIRST-NAME BASIS AT THE E.R.
NEVER MIND.
KIRKMAN & SCOTT
©2023, BABY BLUES BROS LLC DIST. BY ANDREWS MCMEEL SYNDICATION 4-6

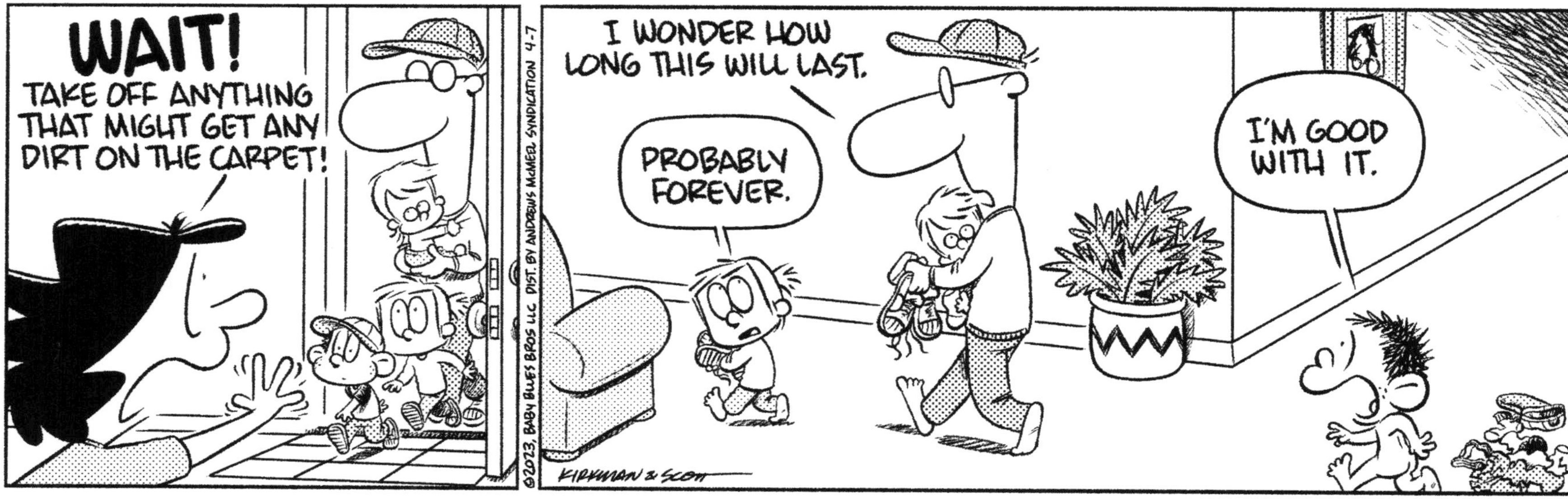
WAIT!
TAKE OFF ANYTHING THAT MIGHT GET ANY DIRT ON THE CARPET!
©2023, BABY BLUES BROS LLC DIST. BY ANDREWS McMEEL SYNDICATION 4-7
I WONDER HOW LONG THIS WILL LAST.
PROBABLY FOREVER.
I'M GOOD WITH IT.
KIRKMAN & SCOTT

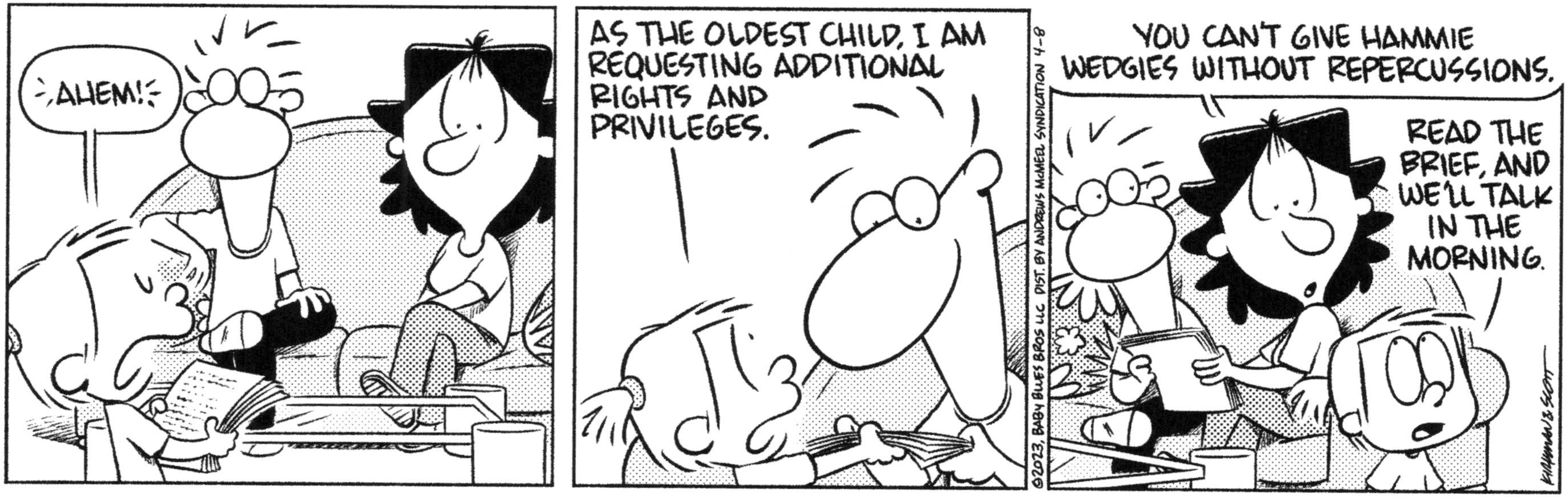
AHEM!
AS THE OLDEST CHILD, I AM REQUESTING ADDITIONAL RIGHTS AND PRIVILEGES.
©2023, BABY BLUES BROS LLC DIST. BY ANDREWS McMEEL SYNDICATION 4-8
YOU CAN'T GIVE HAMMIE WEDGIES WITHOUT REPERCUSSIONS.
READ THE BRIEF, AND WE'LL TALK IN THE MORNING.
KIRKMAN & SCOTT

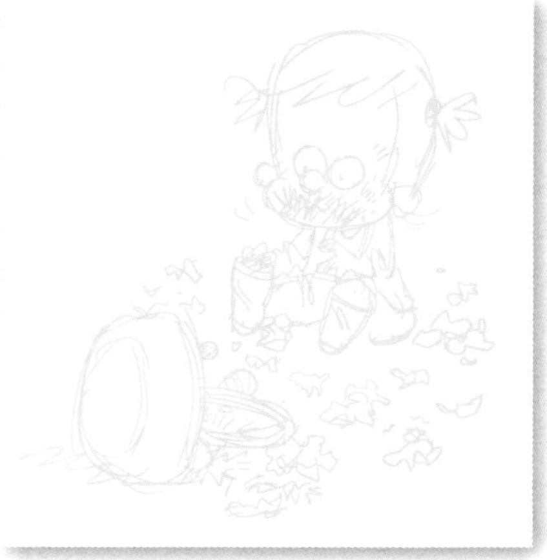

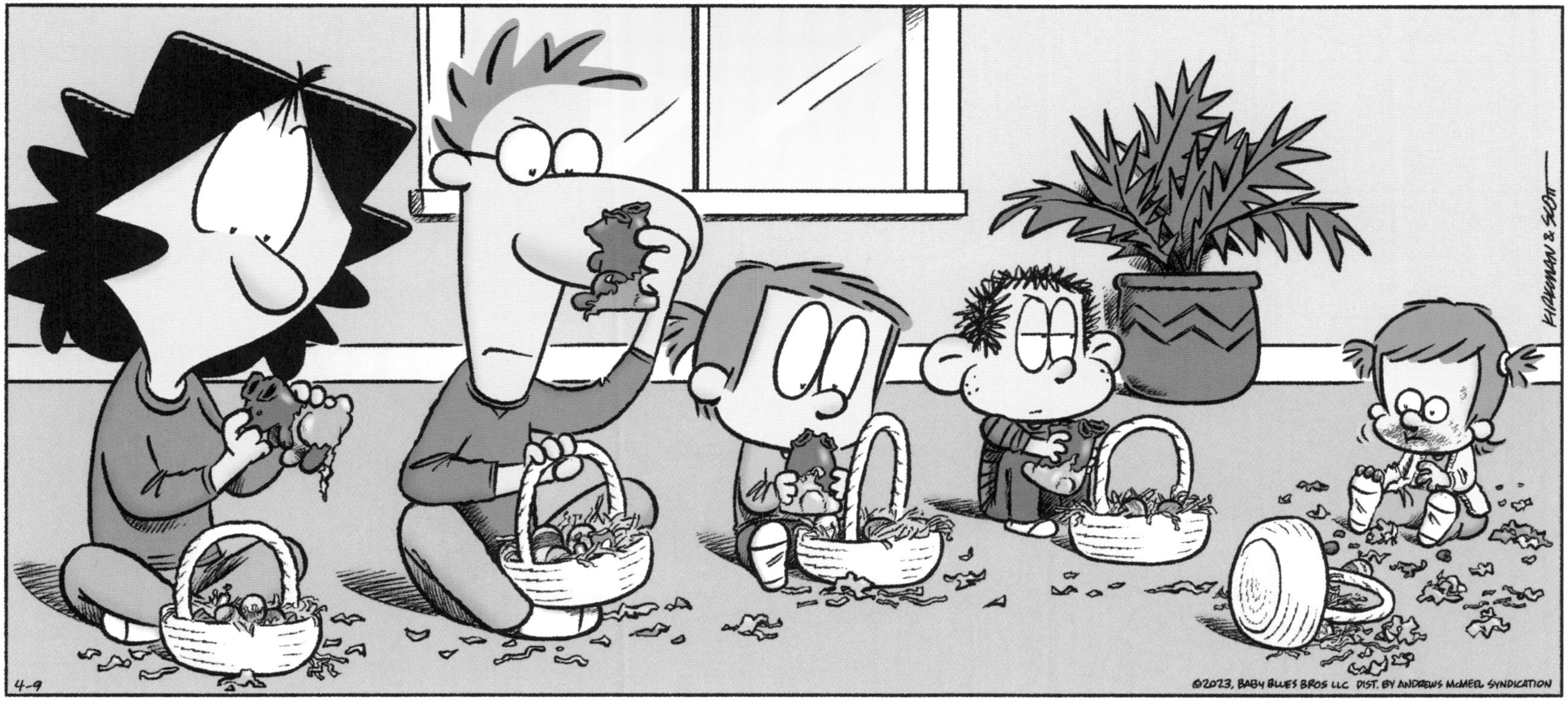
KIRKMAN & SCOTT
4-9
©2023, BABY BLUES BROS LLC DIST. BY ANDREWS McMEEL SYNDICATION

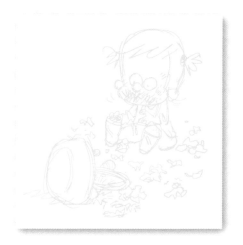

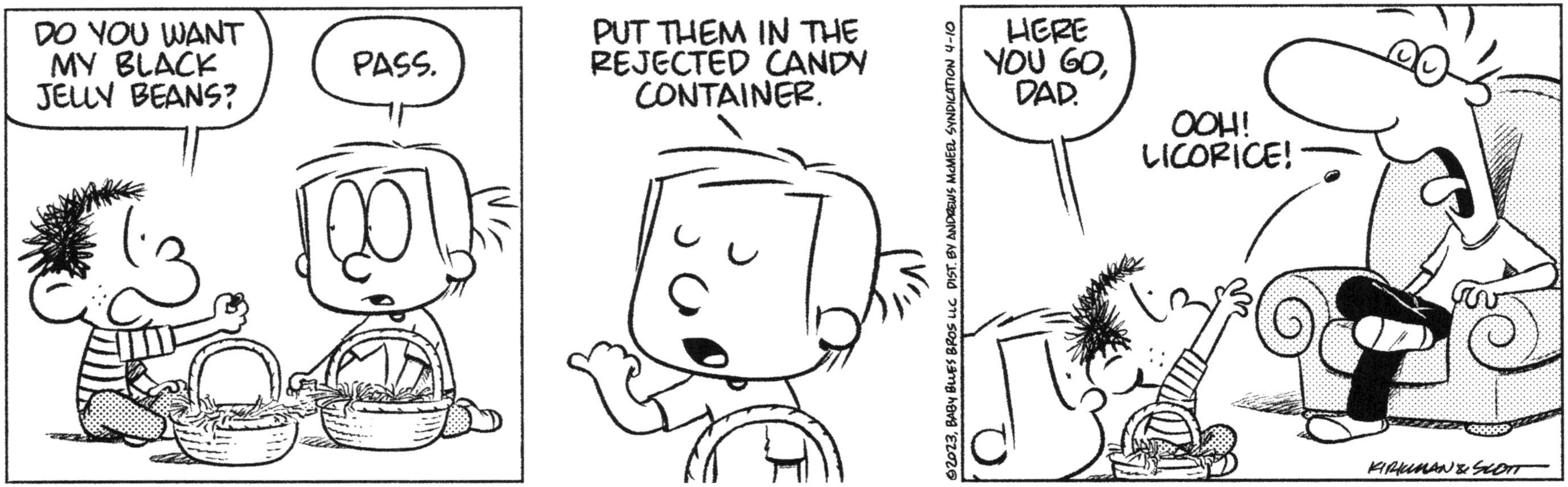
DO YOU WANT MY BLACK JELLY BEANS?
PASS.
PUT THEM IN THE REJECTED CANDY CONTAINER.
©2023, BABY BLUES BROS LLC DIST. BY ANDREWS McMEEL SYNDICATION 4-10
HERE YOU GO, DAD.
OOH! LICORICE!
KIRKMAN & SCOTT

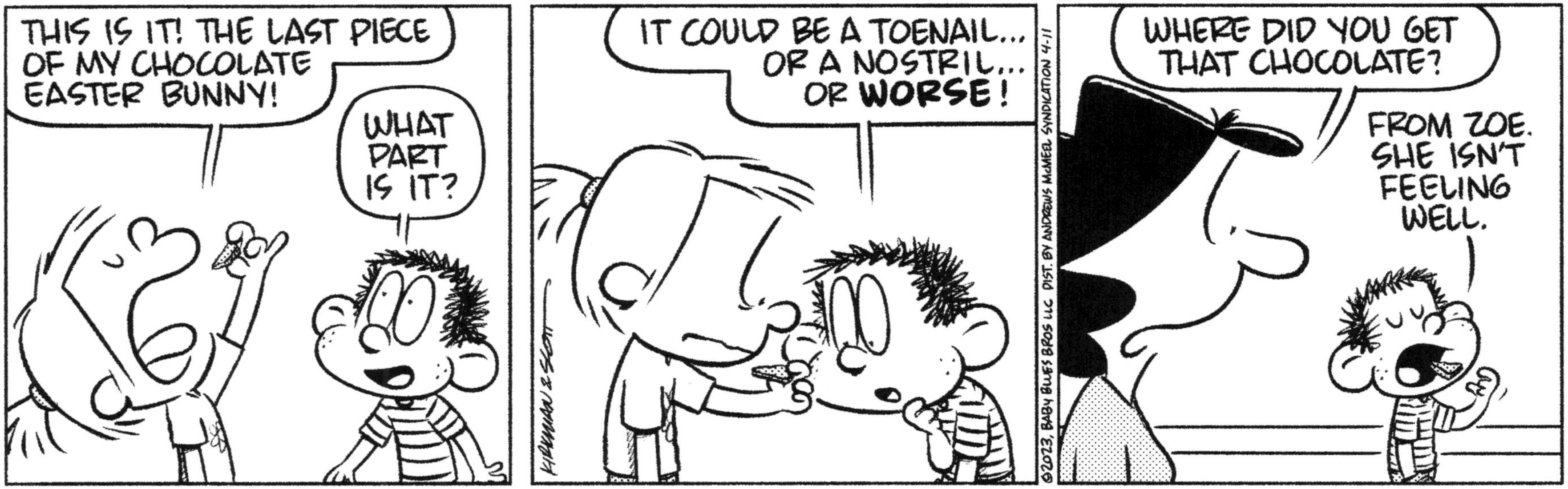
THIS IS IT! THE LAST PIECE OF MY CHOCOLATE EASTER BUNNY!
WHAT PART IS IT?
KIRKMAN & SCOTT
IT COULD BE A TOENAIL... OR A NOSTRIL... OR **WORSE**!
©2023, BABY BLUES BROS LLC DIST. BY ANDREWS McMEEL SYNDICATION 4-11
WHERE DID YOU GET THAT CHOCOLATE?
FROM ZOE. SHE ISN'T FEELING WELL.

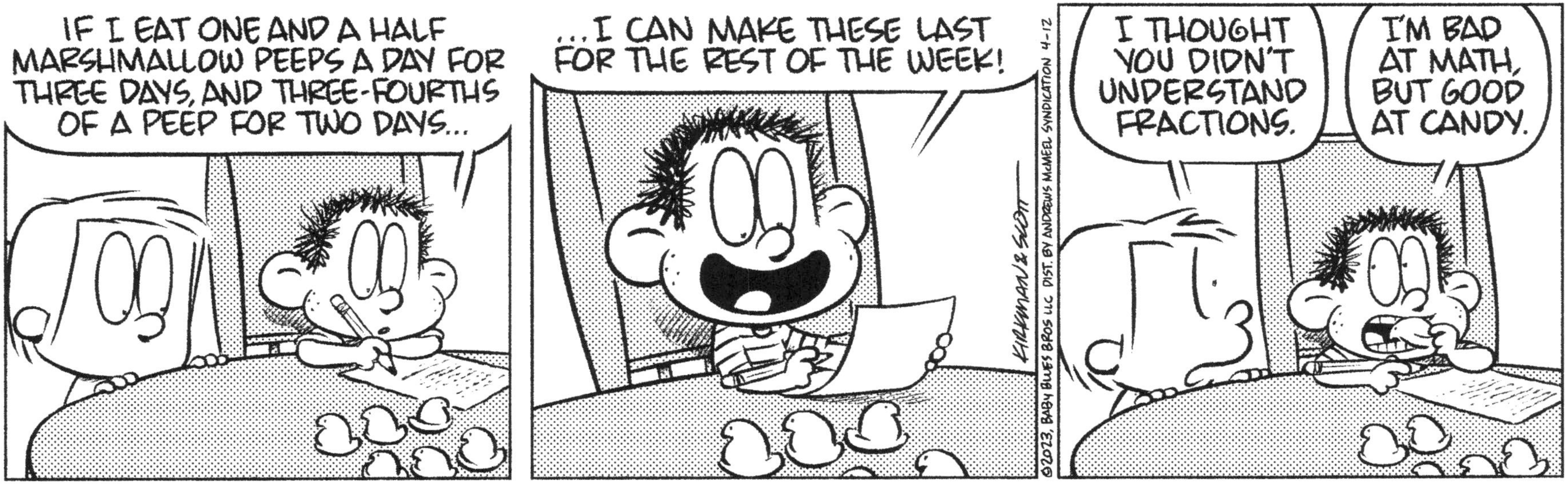
IF I EAT ONE AND A HALF MARSHMALLOW PEEPS A DAY FOR THREE DAYS, AND THREE-FOURTHS OF A PEEP FOR TWO DAYS...
...I CAN MAKE THESE LAST FOR THE REST OF THE WEEK!
KIRKMAN & SCOTT
©2023, BABY BLUES BROS LLC DIST. BY ANDREWS McMEEL SYNDICATION 4-12
I THOUGHT YOU DIDN'T UNDERSTAND FRACTIONS.
I'M BAD AT MATH, BUT GOOD AT CANDY.

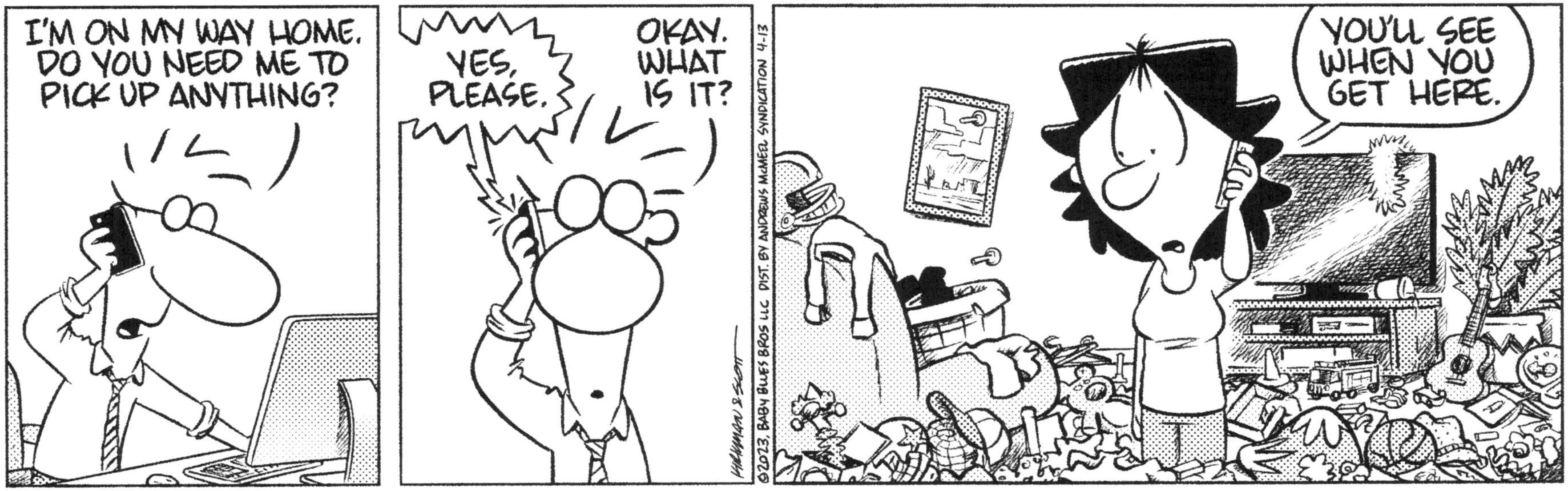
I'M ON MY WAY HOME. DO YOU NEED ME TO PICK UP ANYTHING?
YES, PLEASE.
OKAY. WHAT IS IT?
KIRKMAN & SCOTT
©2023, BABY BLUES BROS LLC DIST. BY ANDREWS McMEEL SYNDICATION 4-13
YOU'LL SEE WHEN YOU GET HERE.

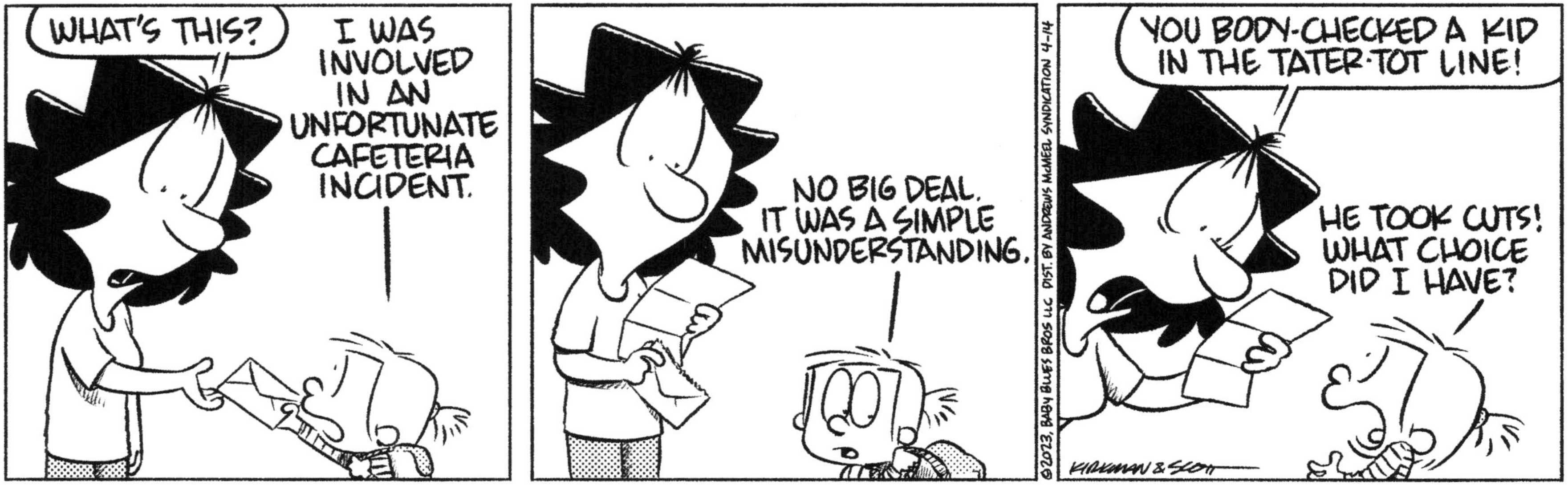
WHAT'S THIS?
I WAS INVOLVED IN AN UNFORTUNATE CAFETERIA INCIDENT.
NO BIG DEAL. IT WAS A SIMPLE MISUNDERSTANDING.
©2023, BABY BLUES BROS LLC DIST. BY ANDREWS McMEEL SYNDICATION 4-14
YOU BODY-CHECKED A KID IN THE TATER-TOT LINE!
HE TOOK CUTS! WHAT CHOICE DID I HAVE?
KIRKMAN & SCOTT

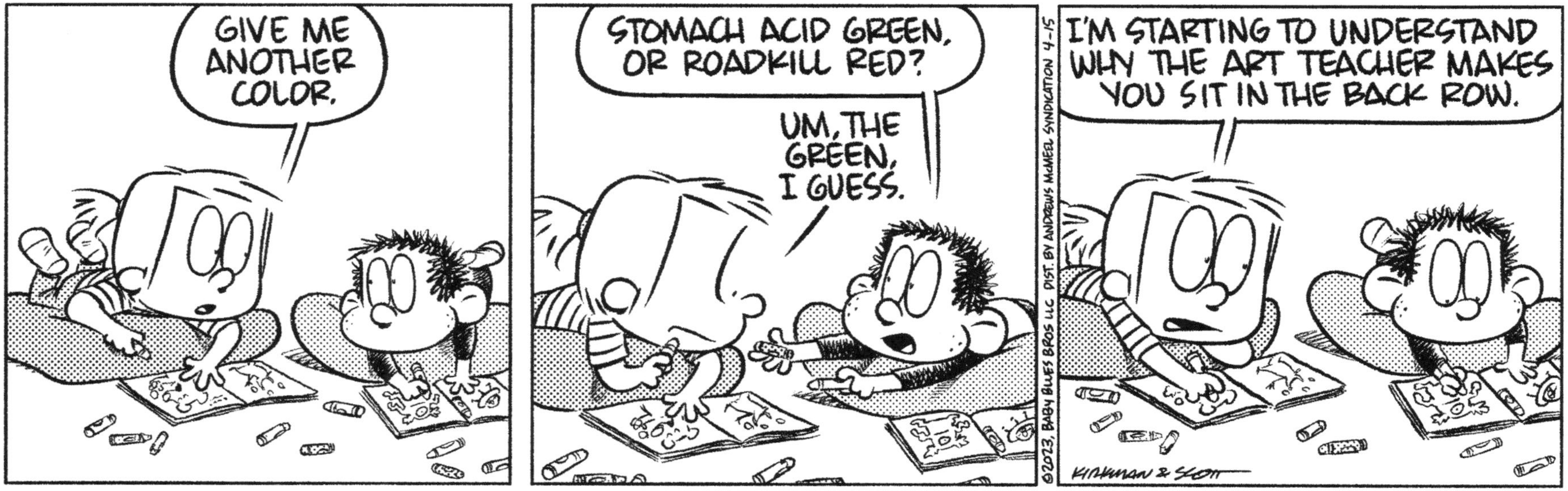
GIVE ME ANOTHER COLOR.
STOMACH ACID GREEN, OR ROADKILL RED?
UM, THE GREEN, I GUESS.
©2023, BABY BLUES BROS LLC DIST. BY ANDREWS McMEEL SYNDICATION 4-15
I'M STARTING TO UNDERSTAND WHY THE ART TEACHER MAKES YOU SIT IN THE BACK ROW.
KIRKMAN & SCOTT

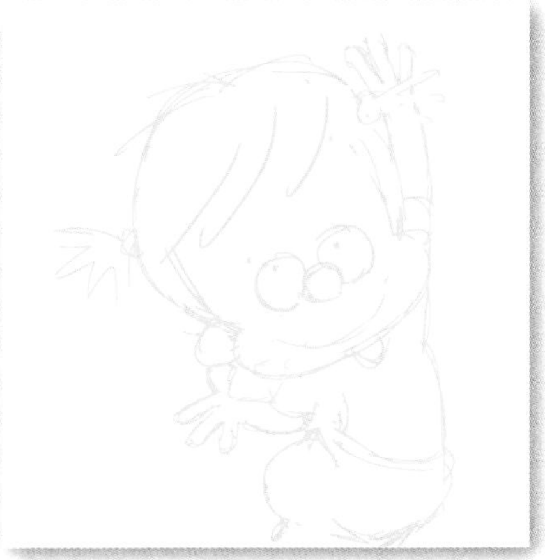

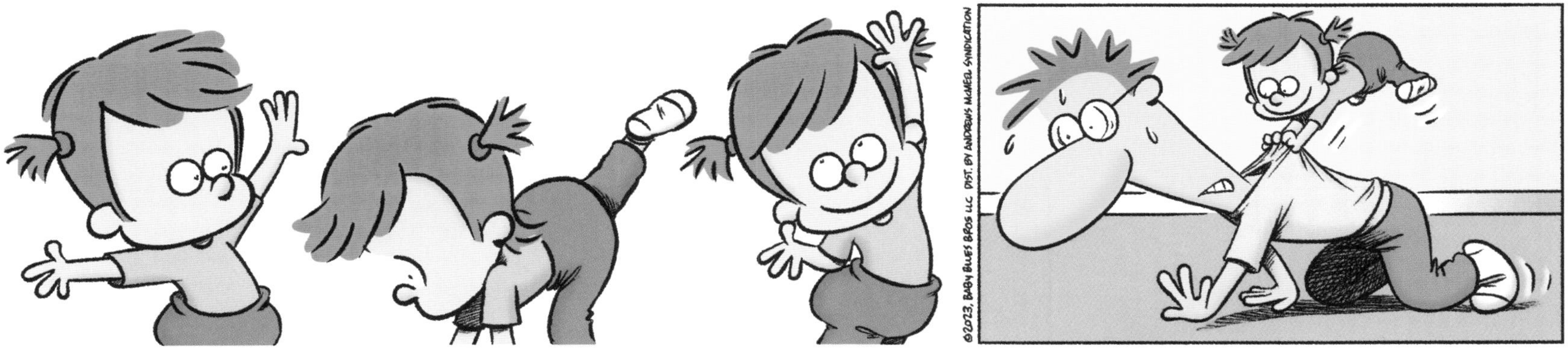
©2023, BABY BLUES BROS LLC DIST. BY ANDREWS MCMEEL SYNDICATION

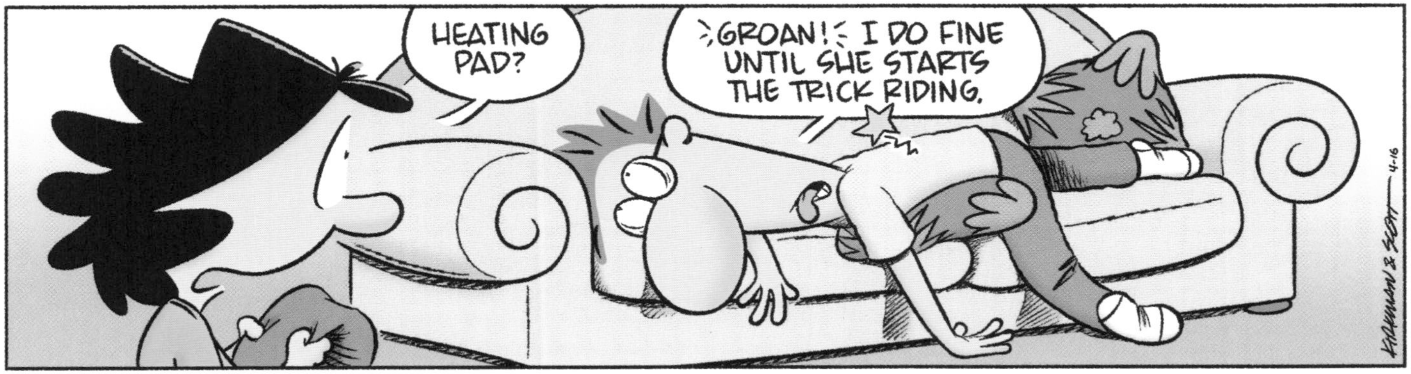
HEATING PAD?
GROAN! I DO FINE UNTIL SHE STARTS THE TRICK RIDING.
KIRKMAN & SCOTT
4-16

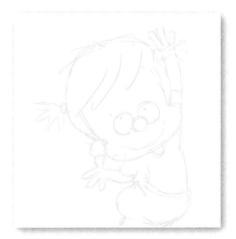

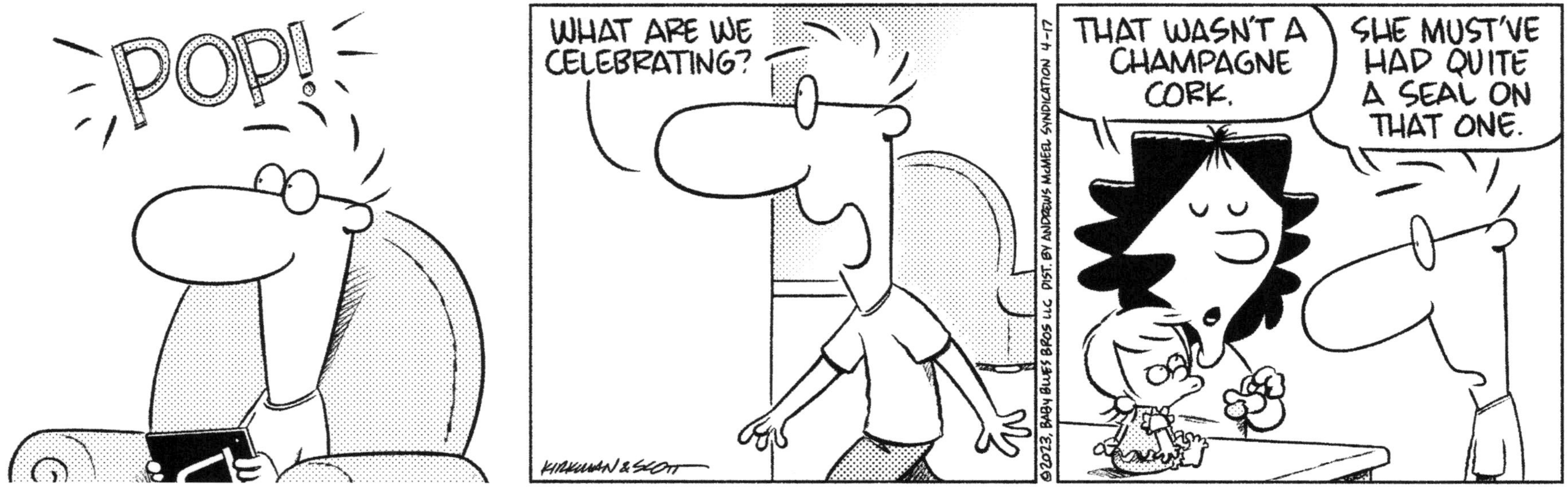
POP!
WHAT ARE WE CELEBRATING?
KIRKMAN & SCOTT
©2023, BABY BLUES BROS LLC DIST. BY ANDREWS MCMEEL SYNDICATION 4-17
THAT WASN'T A CHAMPAGNE CORK.
SHE MUST'VE HAD QUITE A SEAL ON THAT ONE.

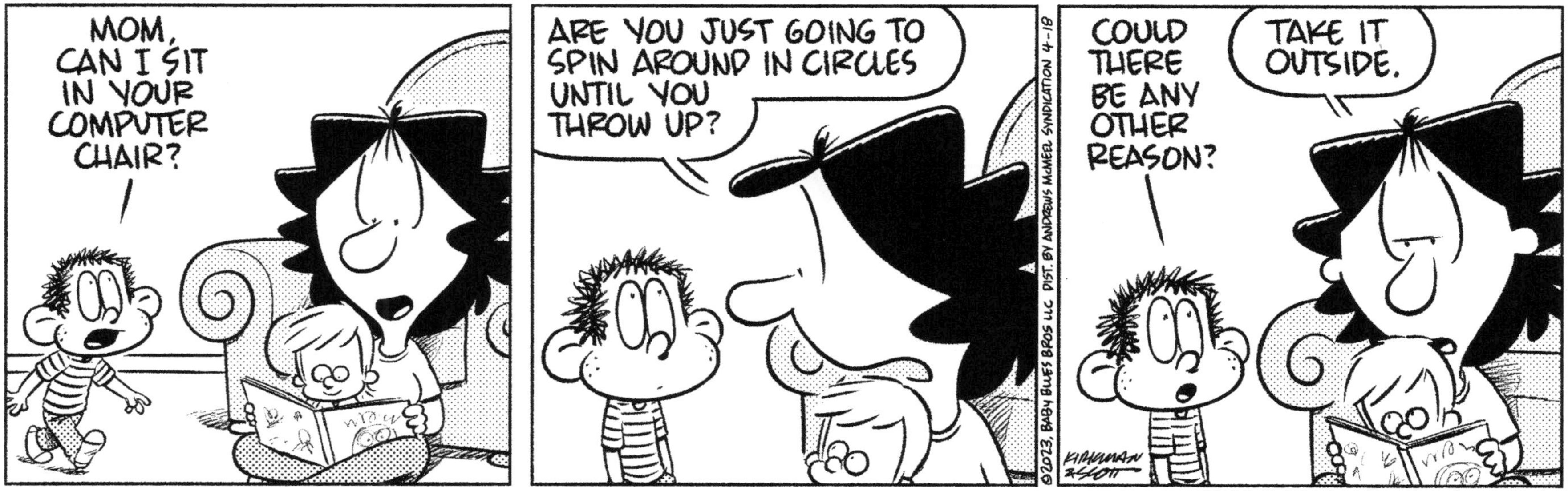
MOM, CAN I SIT IN YOUR COMPUTER CHAIR?
ARE YOU JUST GOING TO SPIN AROUND IN CIRCLES UNTIL YOU THROW UP?
©2023, BABY BLUES BROS LLC DIST. BY ANDREWS MCMEEL SYNDICATION 4-18
COULD THERE BE ANY OTHER REASON?
TAKE IT OUTSIDE.
KIRKMAN & SCOTT

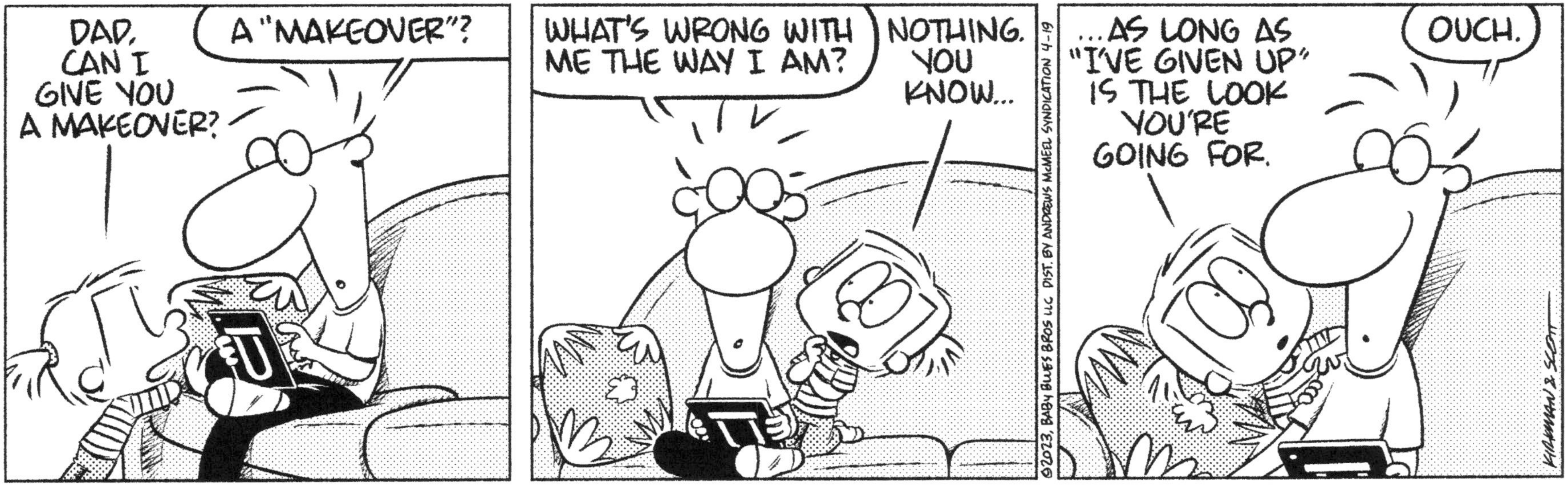
DAD, CAN I GIVE YOU A MAKEOVER?
A "MAKEOVER"?
WHAT'S WRONG WITH ME THE WAY I AM?
NOTHING. YOU KNOW...
©2023, BABY BLUES BROS LLC DIST. BY ANDREWS McMEEL SYNDICATION 4-19
...AS LONG AS "I'VE GIVEN UP" IS THE LOOK YOU'RE GOING FOR.
OUCH.
KIRKMAN & SCOTT

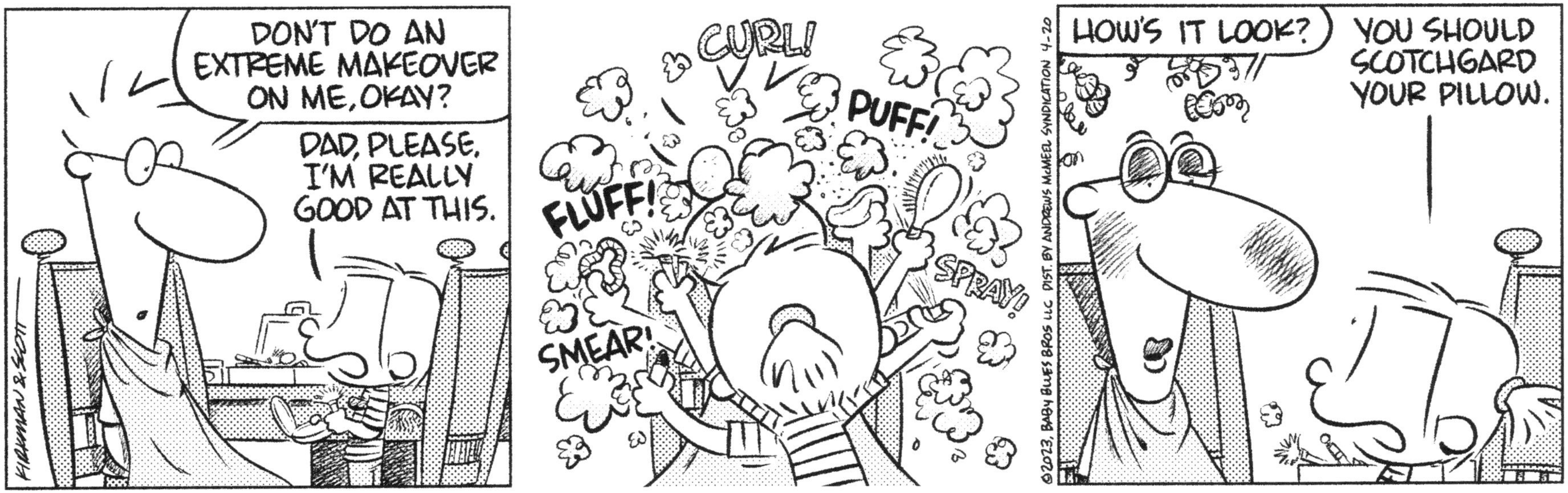
DON'T DO AN EXTREME MAKEOVER ON ME, OKAY?
DAD, PLEASE, I'M REALLY GOOD AT THIS.
KIRKMAN & SCOTT
CURL!
PUFF!
FLUFF!
SPRAY!
SMEAR!
©2023, BABY BLUES BROS LLC DIST. BY ANDREWS McMEEL SYNDICATION 4-20
HOW'S IT LOOK?
YOU SHOULD SCOTCHGARD YOUR PILLOW.

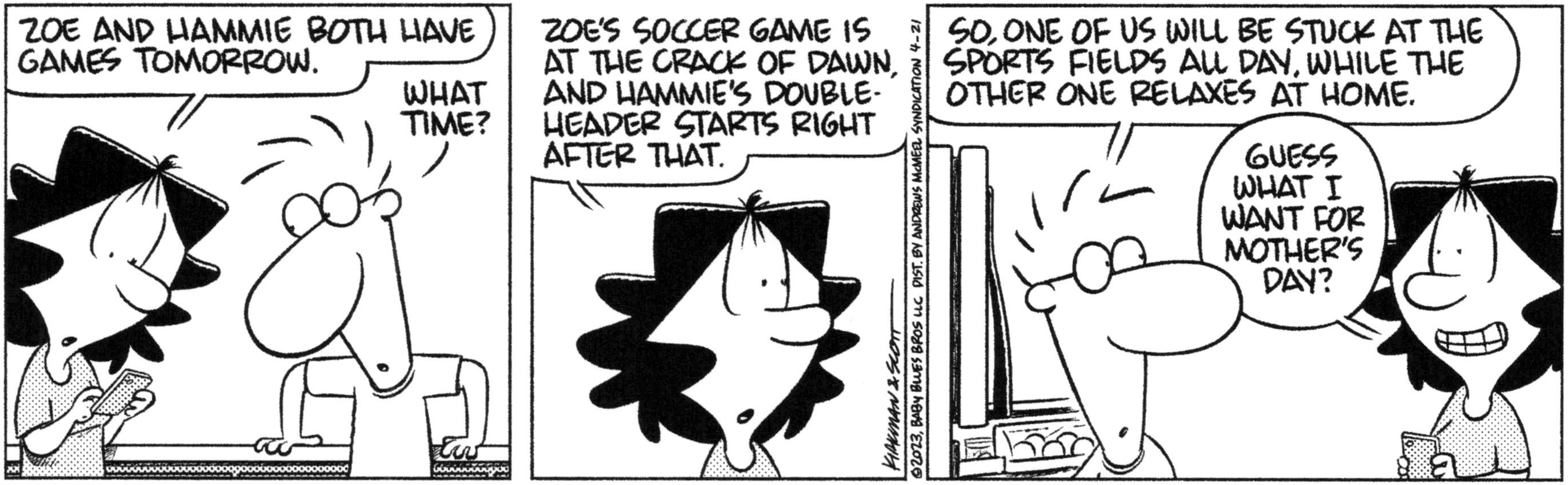
ZOE AND HAMMIE BOTH HAVE GAMES TOMORROW.
WHAT TIME?
ZOE'S SOCCER GAME IS AT THE CRACK OF DAWN, AND HAMMIE'S DOUBLE-HEADER STARTS RIGHT AFTER THAT.
KIRKMAN & SCOTT
©2023, BABY BLUES BROS LLC DIST. BY ANDREWS McMEEL SYNDICATION 4-21
SO, ONE OF US WILL BE STUCK AT THE SPORTS FIELDS ALL DAY, WHILE THE OTHER ONE RELAXES AT HOME.
GUESS WHAT I WANT FOR MOTHER'S DAY?

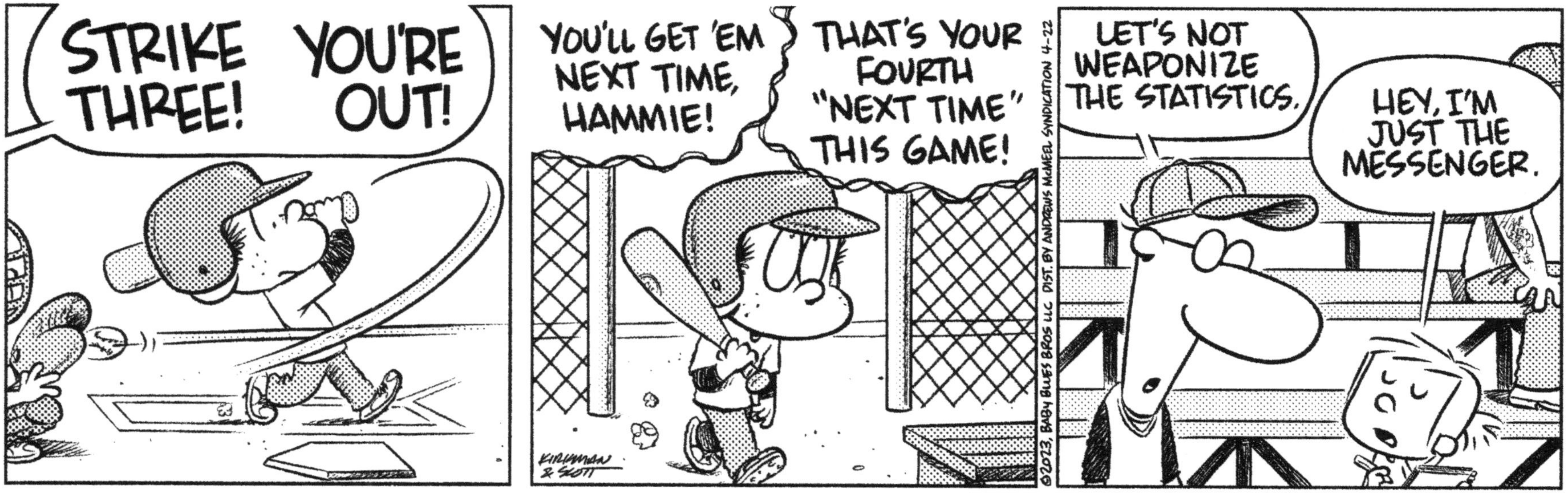
STRIKE THREE! YOU'RE OUT!
YOU'LL GET 'EM NEXT TIME, HAMMIE!
THAT'S YOUR FOURTH "NEXT TIME" THIS GAME!
KIRKMAN & SCOTT
©2023, BABY BLUES BROS LLC DIST. BY ANDREWS McMEEL SYNDICATION 4-22
LET'S NOT WEAPONIZE THE STATISTICS.
HEY, I'M JUST THE MESSENGER.

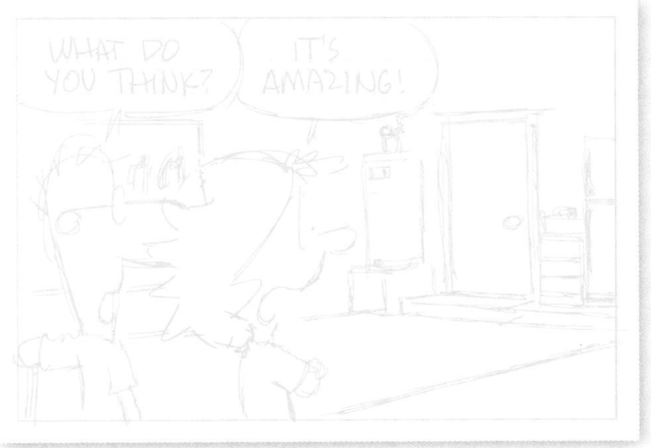
WHAT DO YOU THINK?
IT'S AMAZING!

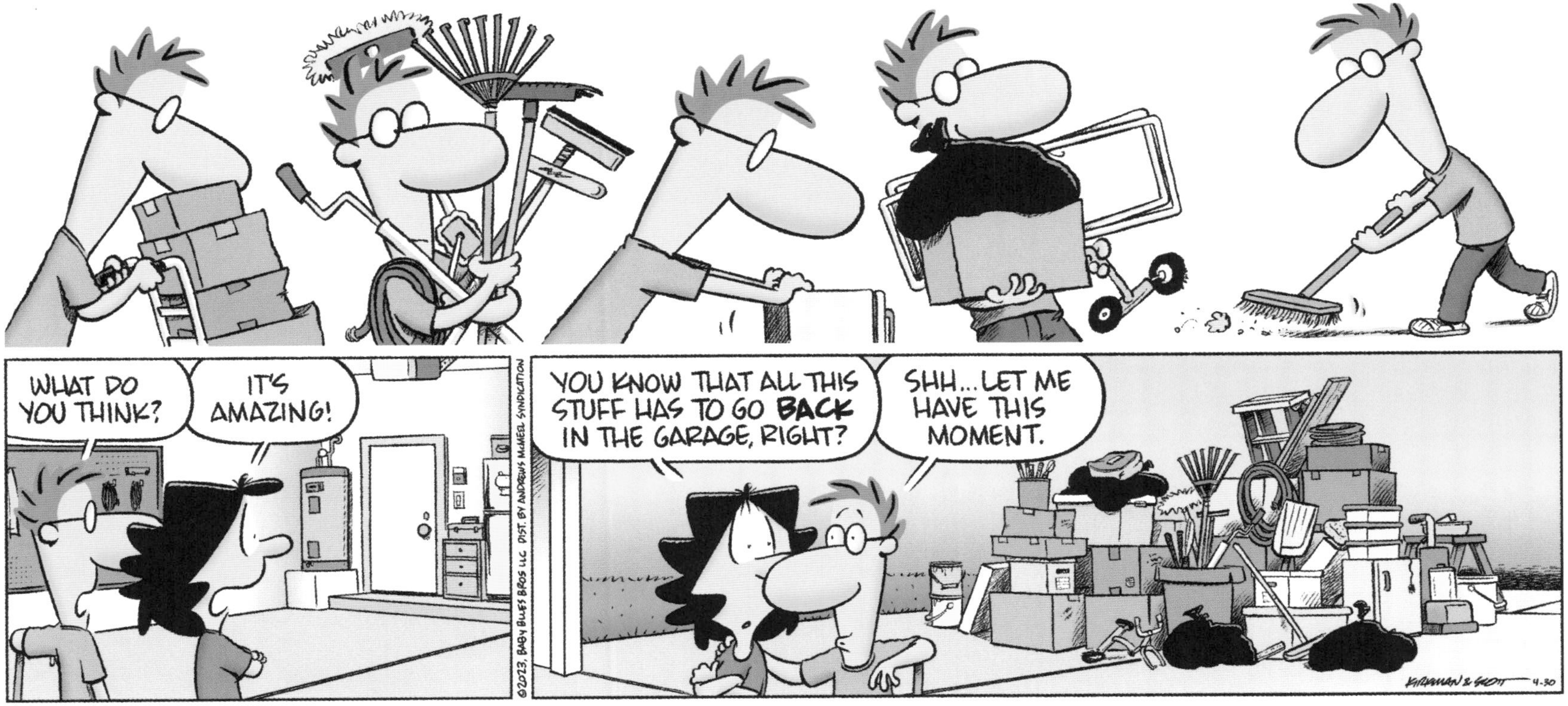
WHAT DO YOU THINK?
IT'S AMAZING!
©2023, BABY BLUES BROS LLC DIST. BY ANDREWS McMEEL SYNDICATION
YOU KNOW THAT ALL THIS STUFF HAS TO GO **BACK** IN THE GARAGE, RIGHT?
SHH... LET ME HAVE THIS MOMENT.
KIRKMAN & SCOTT 4.30

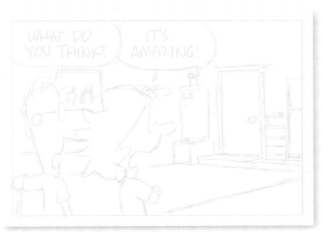

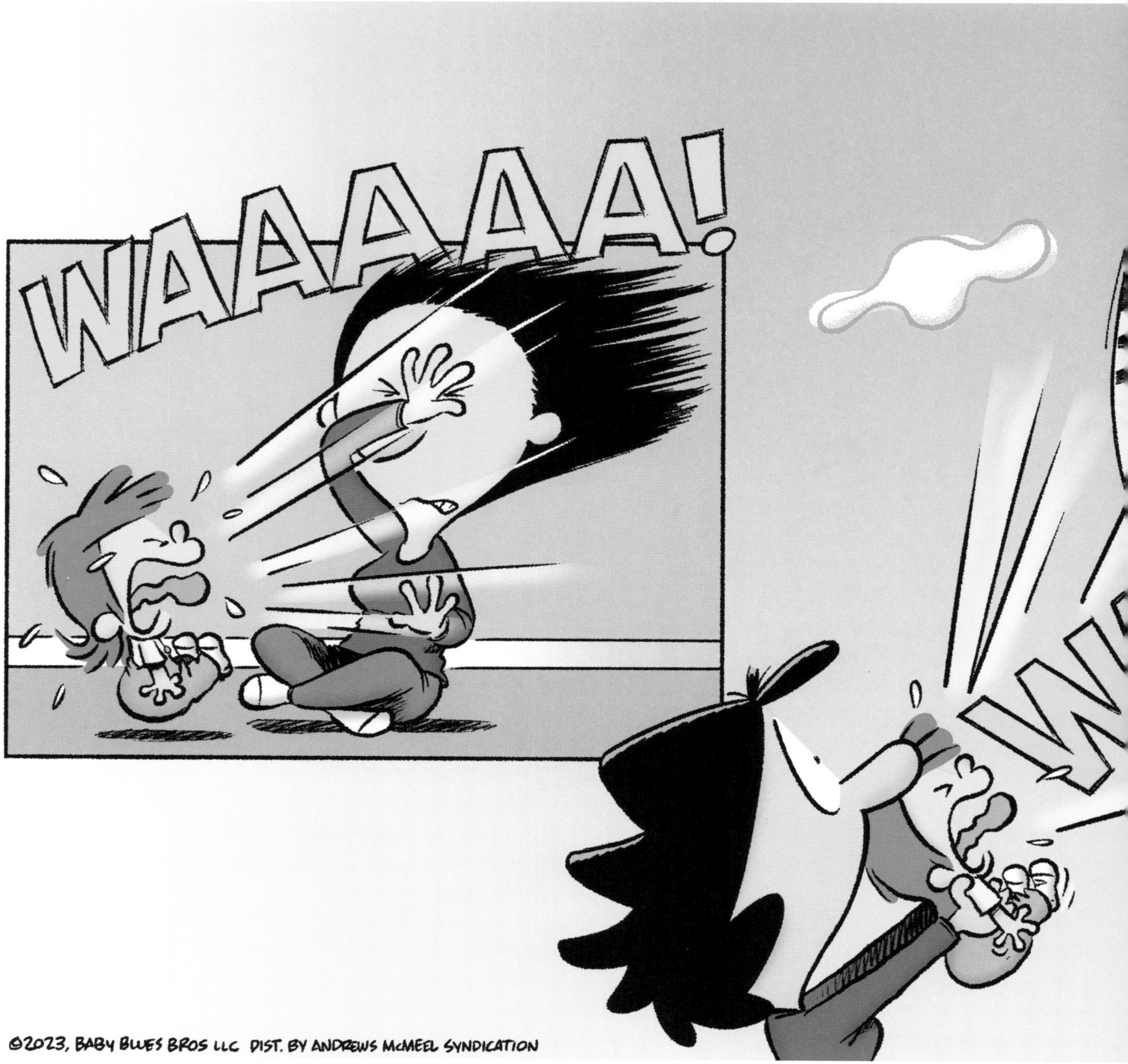
WAAAAAA!
©2023, BABY BLUES BROS LLC DIST. BY ANDREWS McMEEL SYNDICATION

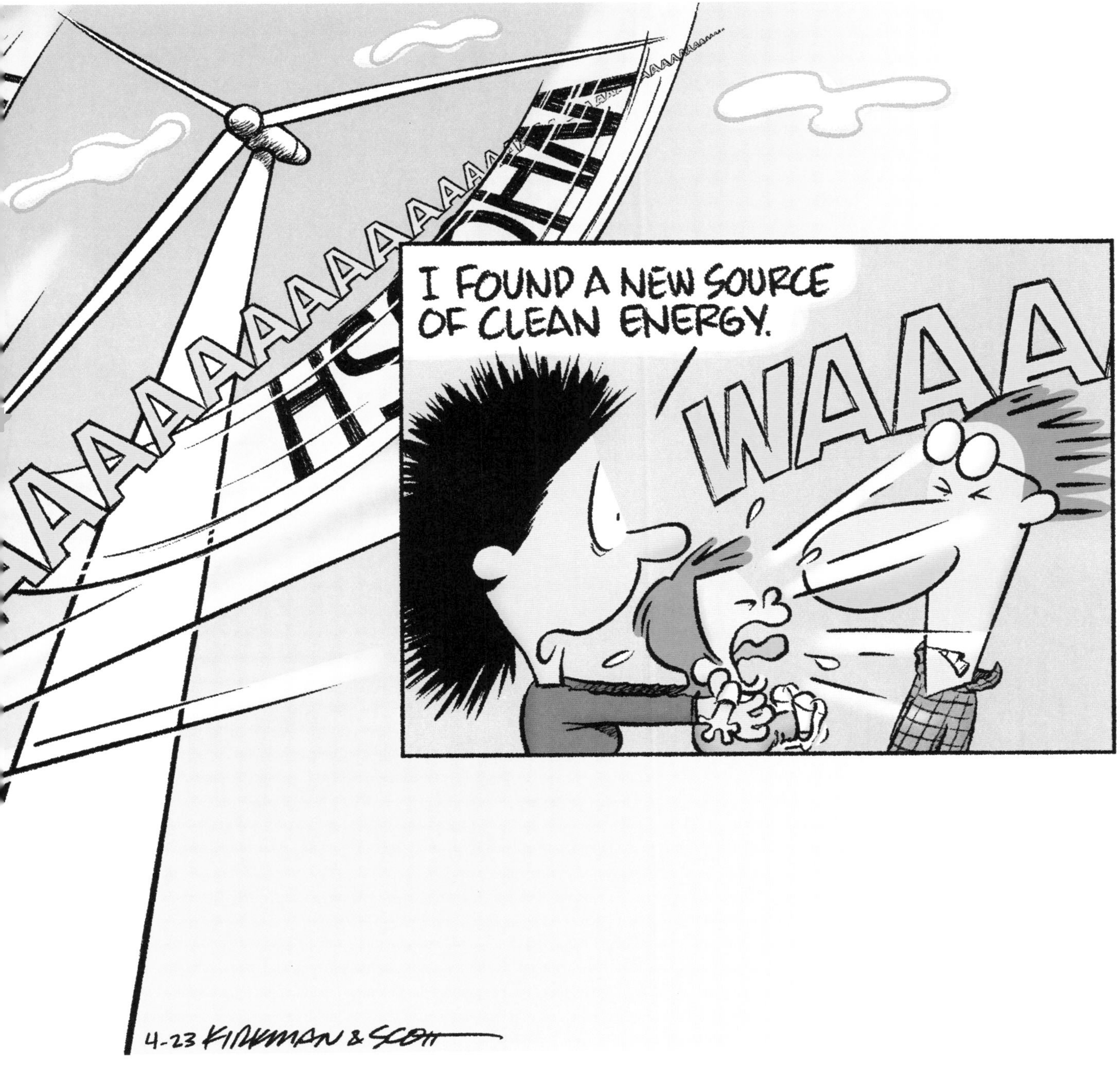
I FOUND A NEW SOURCE OF CLEAN ENERGY.
WAAA
4-23 KIRKMAN & SCOTT

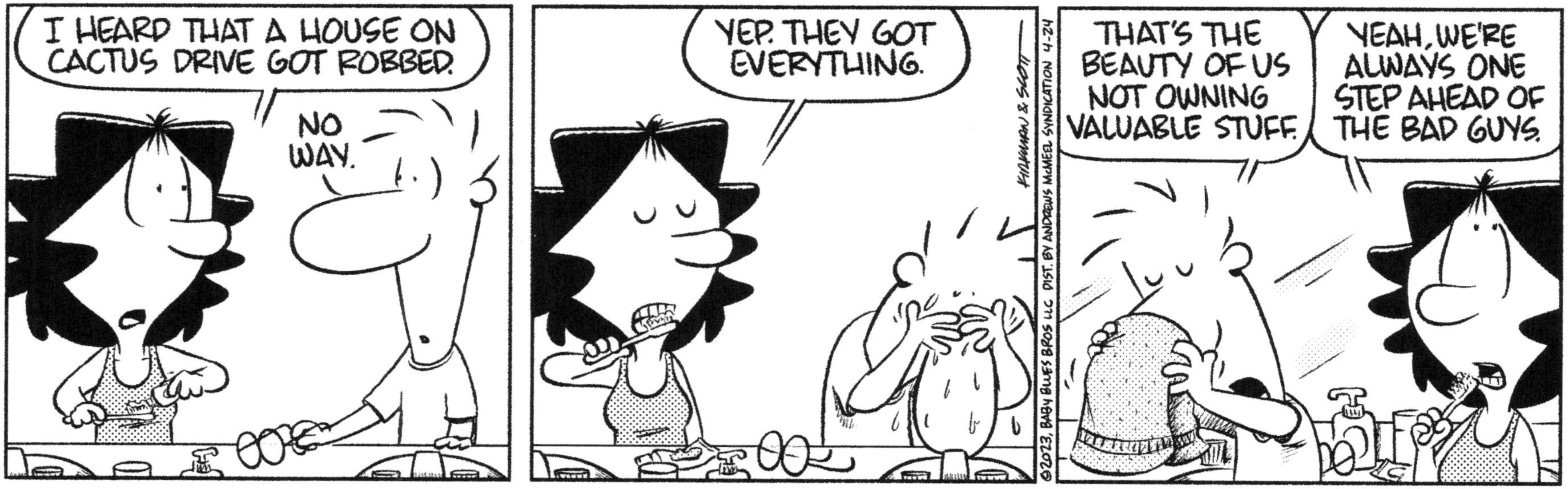
I HEARD THAT A HOUSE ON CACTUS DRIVE GOT ROBBED.
NO WAY.
YEP. THEY GOT EVERYTHING.
KIRKMAN & SCOTT 4-24
©2023, BABY BLUES BROS LLC DIST. BY ANDREWS MCMEEL SYNDICATION
THAT'S THE BEAUTY OF US NOT OWNING VALUABLE STUFF.
YEAH, WE'RE ALWAYS ONE STEP AHEAD OF THE BAD GUYS.

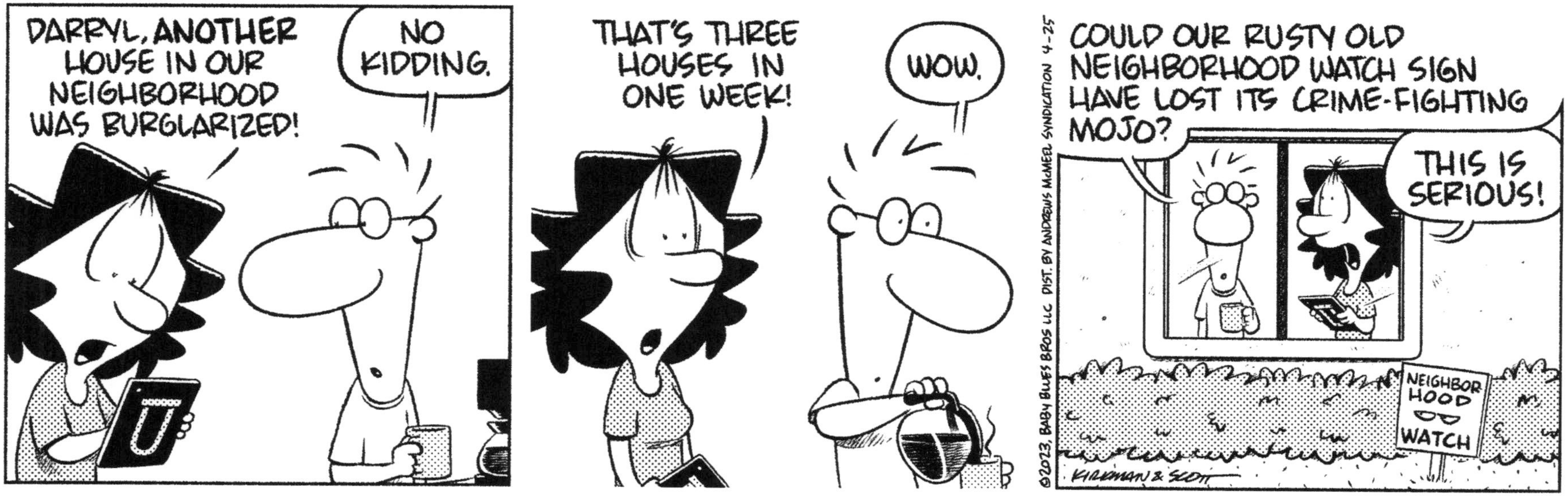
DARRYL, ANOTHER HOUSE IN OUR NEIGHBORHOOD WAS BURGLARIZED!
NO KIDDING.
THAT'S THREE HOUSES IN ONE WEEK!
WOW.
©2023, BABY BLUES BROS LLC DIST. BY ANDREWS MCMEEL SYNDICATION 4-25
COULD OUR RUSTY OLD NEIGHBORHOOD WATCH SIGN HAVE LOST ITS CRIME-FIGHTING MOJO?
THIS IS SERIOUS!
NEIGHBOR HOOD WATCH
KIRKMAN & SCOTT

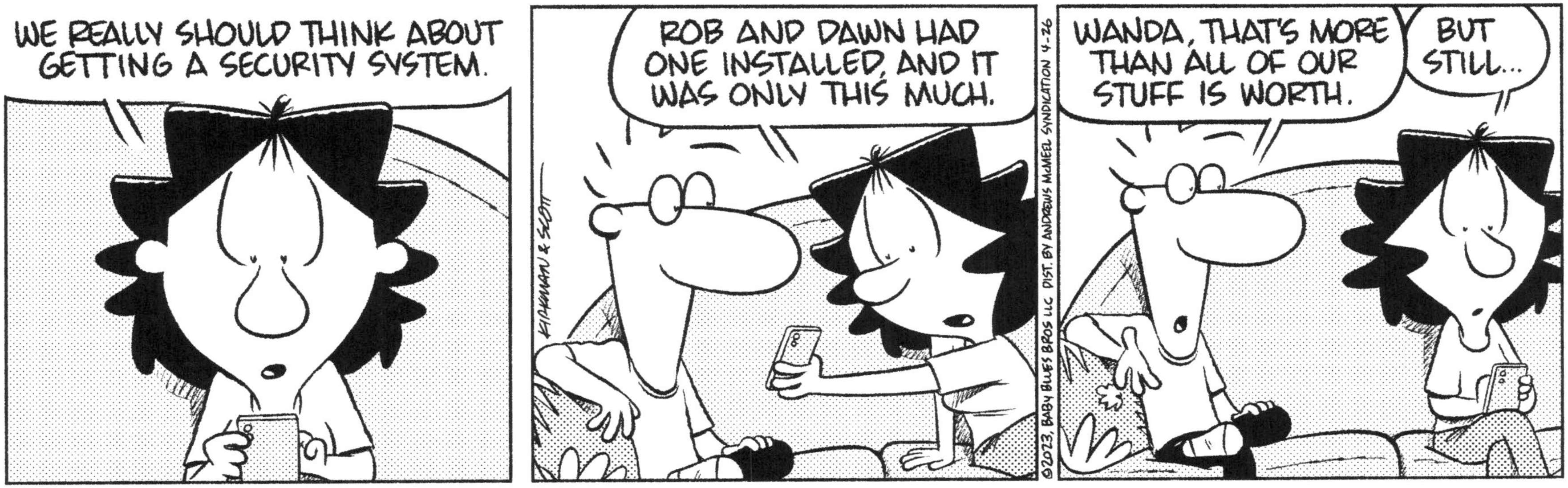
WE REALLY SHOULD THINK ABOUT GETTING A SECURITY SYSTEM.
ROB AND DAWN HAD ONE INSTALLED, AND IT WAS ONLY THIS MUCH.
KIRKMAN & SCOTT
©2023, BABY BLUES BROS LLC DIST. BY ANDREWS McMEEL SYNDICATION 4-26
WANDA, THAT'S MORE THAN ALL OF OUR STUFF IS WORTH.
BUT STILL...

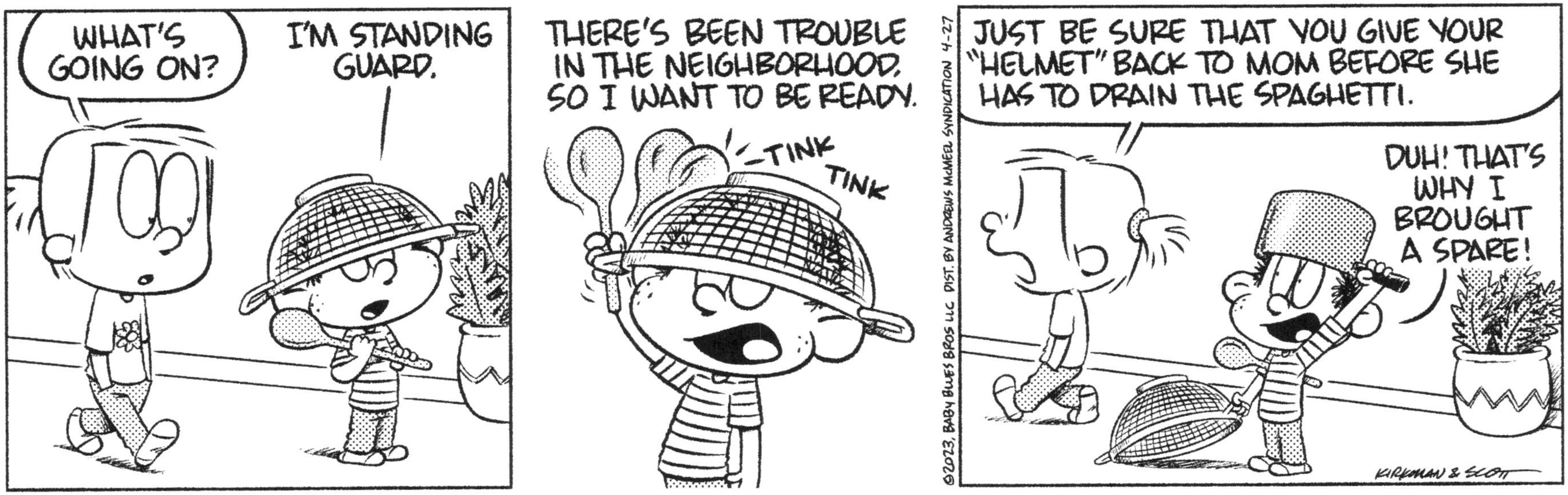
WHAT'S GOING ON?
I'M STANDING GUARD.
THERE'S BEEN TROUBLE IN THE NEIGHBORHOOD, SO I WANT TO BE READY.
TINK
TINK
©2023, BABY BLUES BROS LLC DIST. BY ANDREWS McMEEL SYNDICATION 4-27
JUST BE SURE THAT YOU GIVE YOUR "HELMET" BACK TO MOM BEFORE SHE HAS TO DRAIN THE SPAGHETTI.
DUH! THAT'S WHY I BROUGHT A SPARE!
KIRKMAN & SCOTT

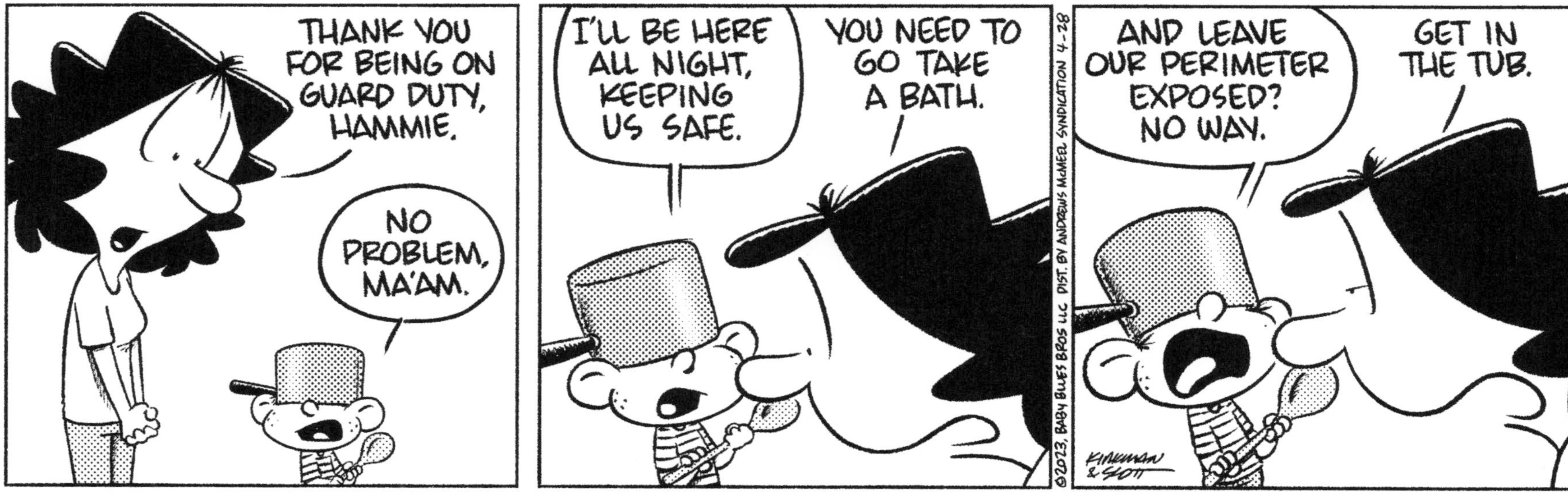
THANK YOU FOR BEING ON GUARD DUTY, HAMMIE.
NO PROBLEM, MA'AM.
I'LL BE HERE ALL NIGHT, KEEPING US SAFE.
YOU NEED TO GO TAKE A BATH.
©2023, BABY BLUES BROS LLC DIST. BY ANDREWS McMEEL SYNDICATION 4-28
AND LEAVE OUR PERIMETER EXPOSED? NO WAY.
GET IN THE TUB.
KIRKMAN & SCOTT

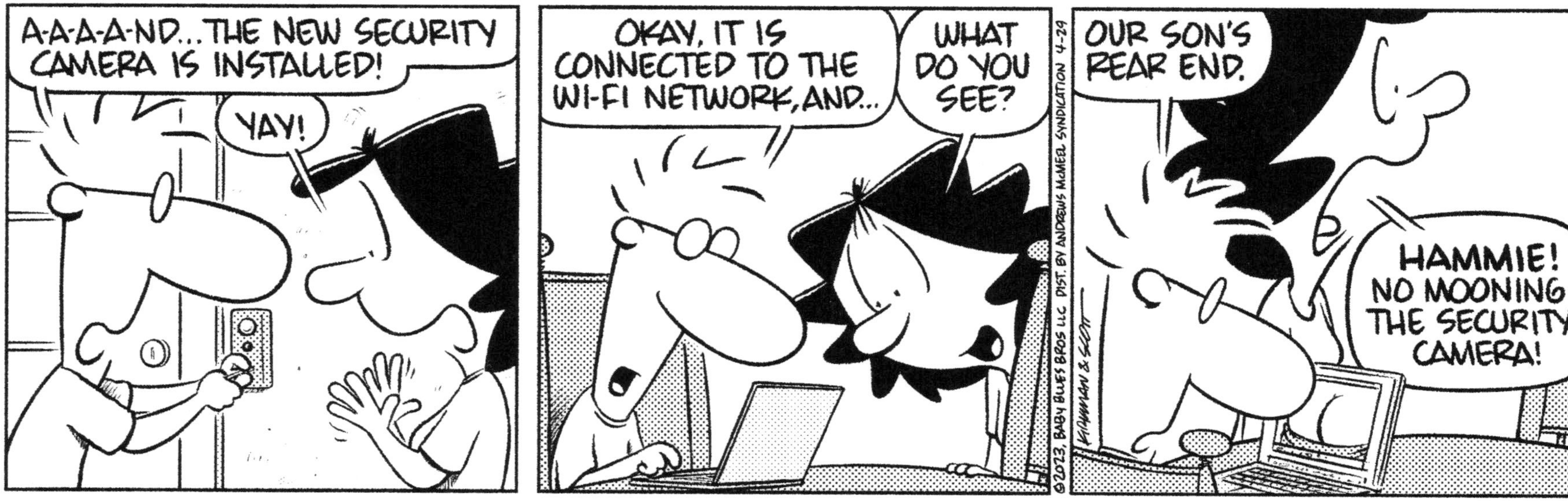
A-A-A-A-ND...THE NEW SECURITY CAMERA IS INSTALLED!
YAY!
OKAY, IT IS CONNECTED TO THE WI-FI NETWORK, AND...
WHAT DO YOU SEE?
©2023, BABY BLUES BROS LLC DIST. BY ANDREWS McMEEL SYNDICATION 4-29
KIRKMAN & SCOTT
OUR SON'S REAR END.
HAMMIE! NO MOONING THE SECURITY CAMERA!

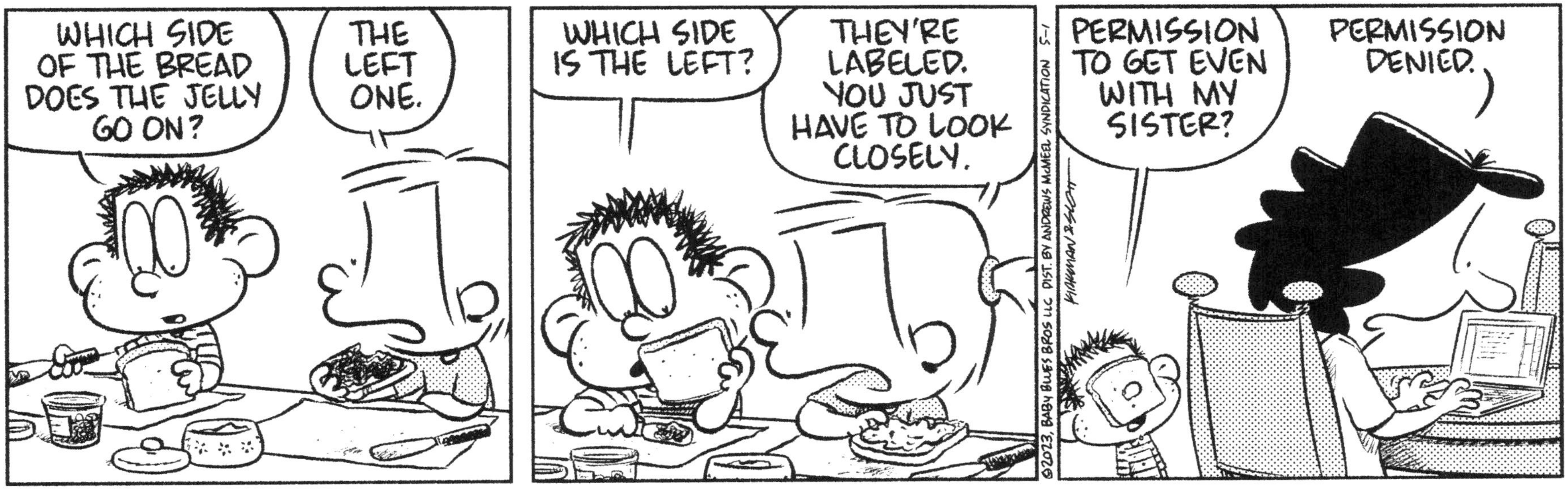
WHICH SIDE OF THE BREAD DOES THE JELLY GO ON?
THE LEFT ONE.
WHICH SIDE IS THE LEFT?
THEY'RE LABELED. YOU JUST HAVE TO LOOK CLOSELY.
©2023, BABY BLUES BROS LLC DIST. BY ANDREWS McMEEL SYNDICATION 5-1
KIRKMAN & SCOTT
PERMISSION TO GET EVEN WITH MY SISTER?
PERMISSION DENIED.

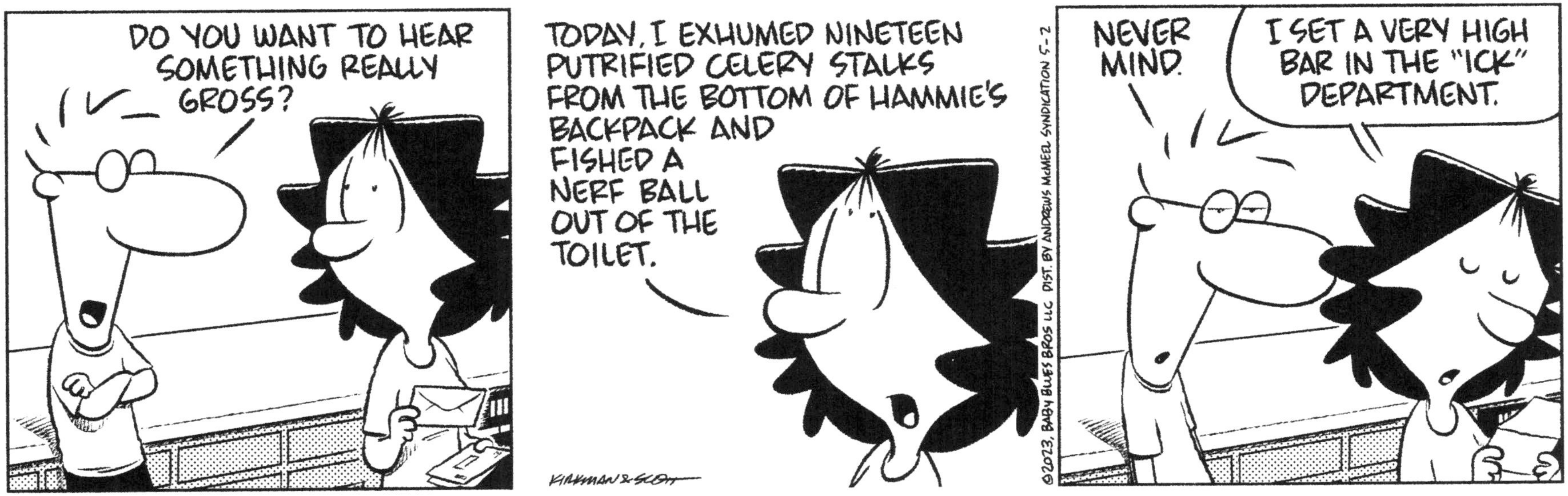
DO YOU WANT TO HEAR SOMETHING REALLY GROSS?
TODAY, I EXHUMED NINETEEN PUTRIFIED CELERY STALKS FROM THE BOTTOM OF HAMMIE'S BACKPACK AND FISHED A NERF BALL OUT OF THE TOILET.
KIRKMAN & SCOTT
©2023, BABY BLUES BROS LLC DIST. BY ANDREWS McMEEL SYNDICATION 5-2
NEVER MIND.
I SET A VERY HIGH BAR IN THE "ICK" DEPARTMENT.

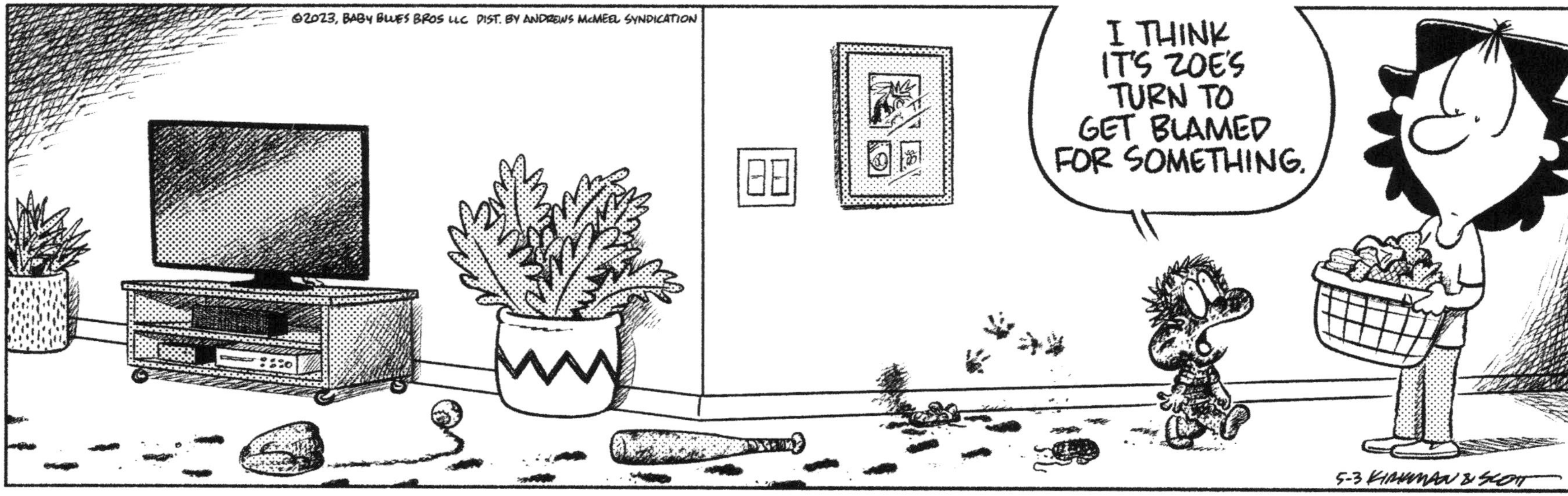
©2023, BABY BLUES BROS LLC DIST. BY ANDREWS McMEEL SYNDICATION
I THINK IT'S ZOE'S TURN TO GET BLAMED FOR SOMETHING.
5-3 KIRKMAN & SCOTT

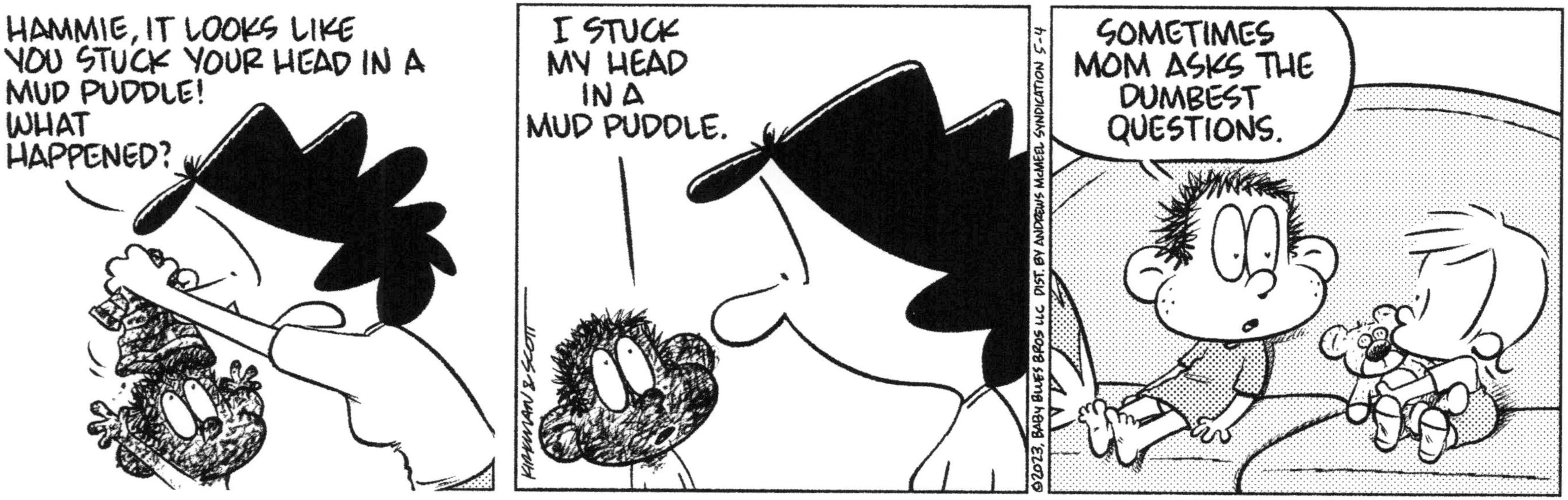
HAMMIE, IT LOOKS LIKE YOU STUCK YOUR HEAD IN A MUD PUDDLE! WHAT HAPPENED?
I STUCK MY HEAD IN A MUD PUDDLE.
KIRKMAN & SCOTT
©2023, BABY BLUES BROS LLC DIST. BY ANDREWS McMEEL SYNDICATION 5-4
SOMETIMES MOM ASKS THE DUMBEST QUESTIONS.

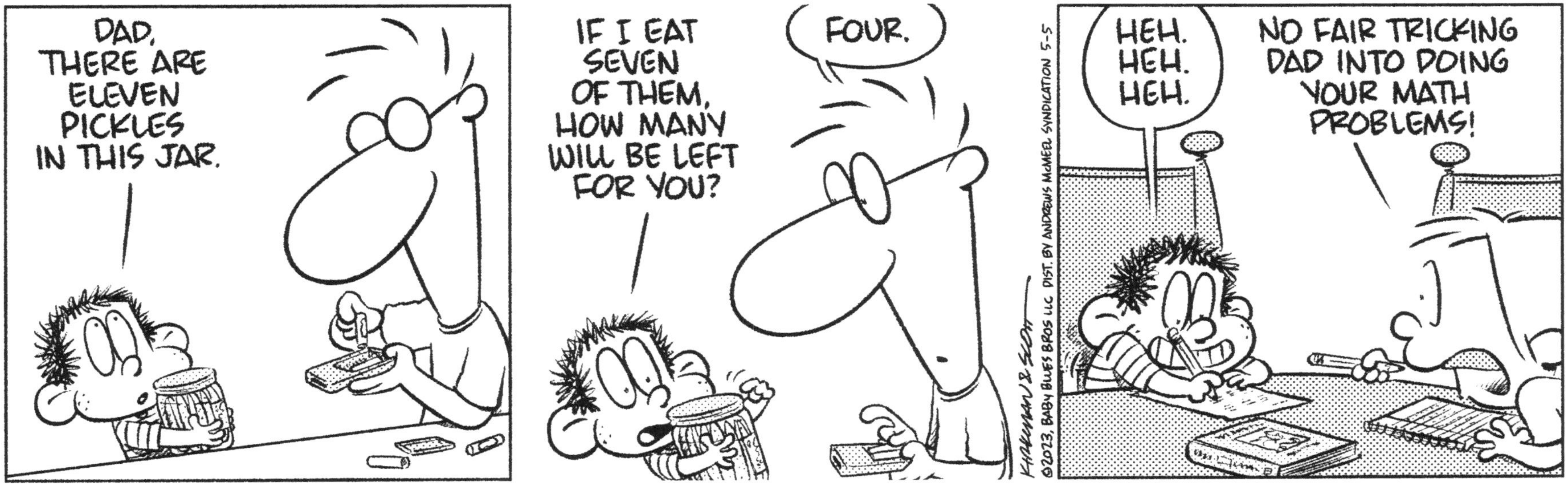
DAD, THERE ARE ELEVEN PICKLES IN THIS JAR.
IF I EAT SEVEN OF THEM, HOW MANY WILL BE LEFT FOR YOU?
FOUR.
KIRKMAN & SCOTT
©2023, BABY BLUES BROS LLC DIST. BY ANDREWS McMEEL SYNDICATION 5-5
HEH. HEH. HEH.
NO FAIR TRICKING DAD INTO DOING YOUR MATH PROBLEMS!

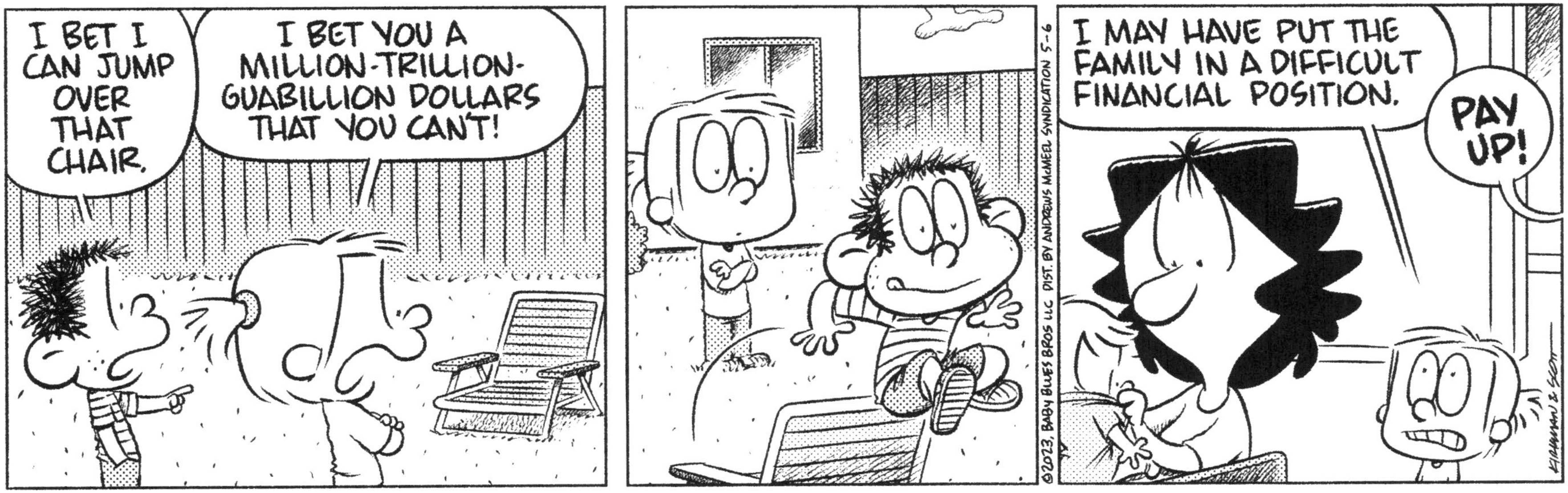
I BET I CAN JUMP OVER THAT CHAIR.
I BET YOU A MILLION-TRILLION-GUABILLION DOLLARS THAT YOU CAN'T!
©2023, BABY BLUES BROS LLC DIST. BY ANDREWS McMEEL SYNDICATION 5-6
I MAY HAVE PUT THE FAMILY IN A DIFFICULT FINANCIAL POSITION.
PAY UP!
KIRKMAN & SCOTT

IT COULD BE TAX DEDUCTIBLE IF USED FOR THERAPEUTIC PORPOISES.

DAD! I KNOW WHAT WE SHOULD GET FOR MOM FOR MOTHER'S DAY!
YEAH? WHAT?
5-7
ONE OF THOSE!
UH, BUDDY, THAT'S AN EIGHT-THOUSAND-DOLLAR JACUZZI.
WE CAN'T AFFORD IT.
BUT SHE WOULD REALLY LOVE IT!
I'M SURE SHE WOULD, BUT IT'S TOO EXPENSIVE.
MAYBE NOT, THOUGH.
IT COULD BE TAX DEDUCTIBLE IF USED FOR THERAPEUTIC PORPOISES.
©2013, BABY BLUES BROS LLC DIST. BY ANDREWS McMEEL SYNDICATION
KIRKMAN & SCOTT
PURPOSES... NOT PORPOISES.
YEAH. THAT.
NICE TRY, WANDA.

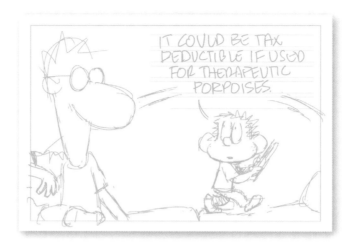

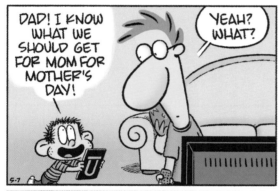

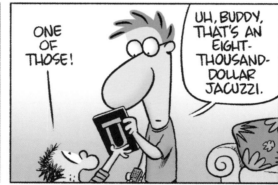

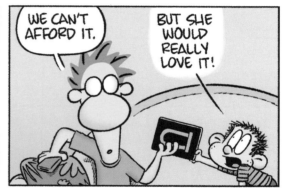

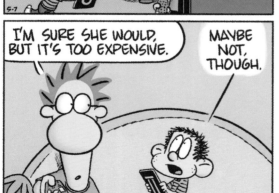

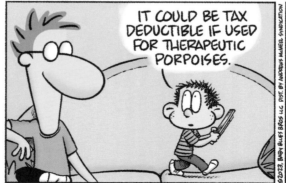

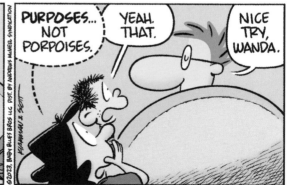

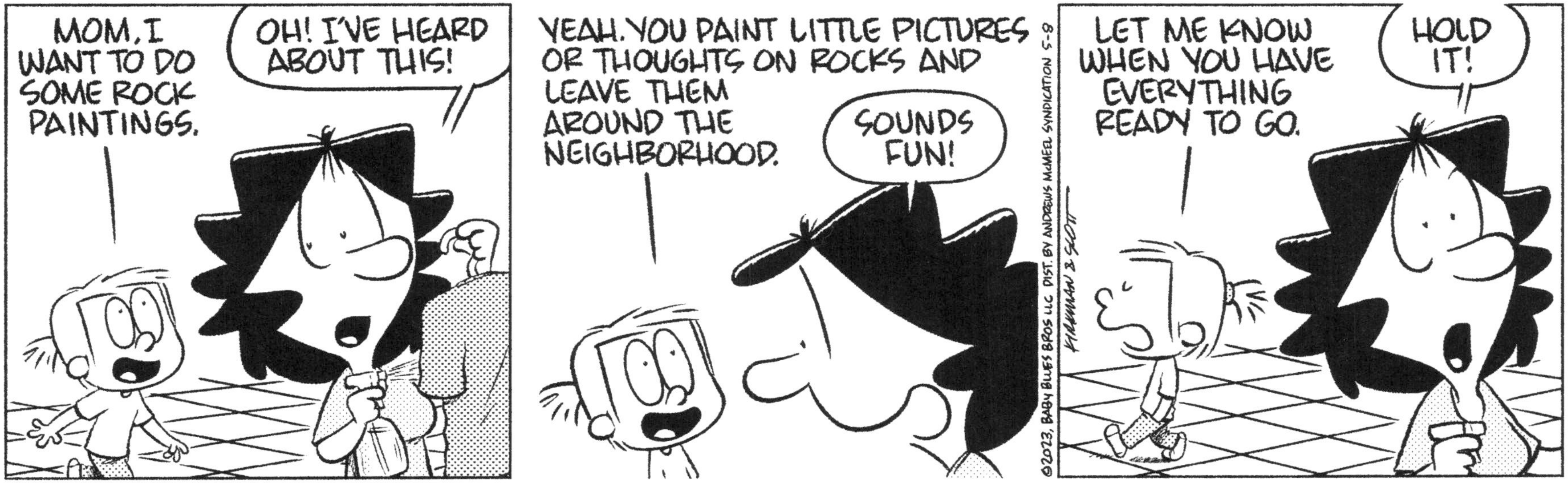
MOM, I WANT TO DO SOME ROCK PAINTINGS.
OH! I'VE HEARD ABOUT THIS!
YEAH. YOU PAINT LITTLE PICTURES OR THOUGHTS ON ROCKS AND LEAVE THEM AROUND THE NEIGHBORHOOD.
SOUNDS FUN!
LET ME KNOW WHEN YOU HAVE EVERYTHING READY TO GO.
HOLD IT!
©2023, BABY BLUES BROS LLC DIST. BY ANDREWS McMEEL SYNDICATION 5-8
KIRKMAN & SCOTT

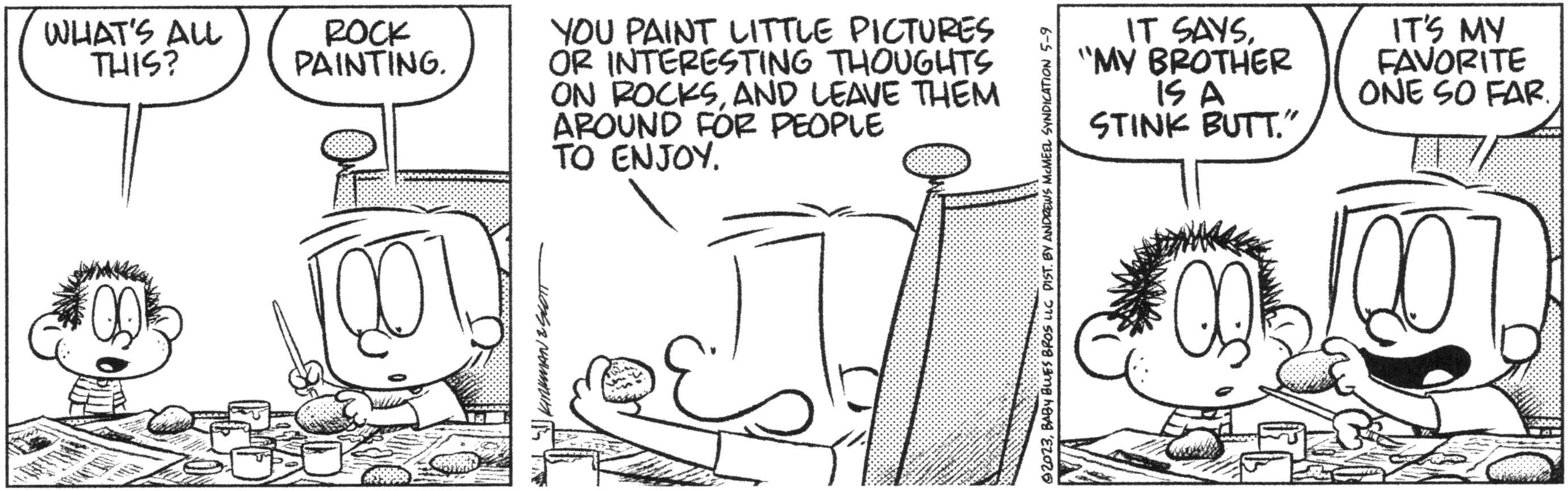
WHAT'S ALL THIS?
ROCK PAINTING.
YOU PAINT LITTLE PICTURES OR INTERESTING THOUGHTS ON ROCKS, AND LEAVE THEM AROUND FOR PEOPLE TO ENJOY.
IT SAYS, "MY BROTHER IS A STINK BUTT."
IT'S MY FAVORITE ONE SO FAR.
©2023, BABY BLUES BROS LLC DIST. BY ANDREWS McMEEL SYNDICATION 5-9
KIRKMAN & SCOTT

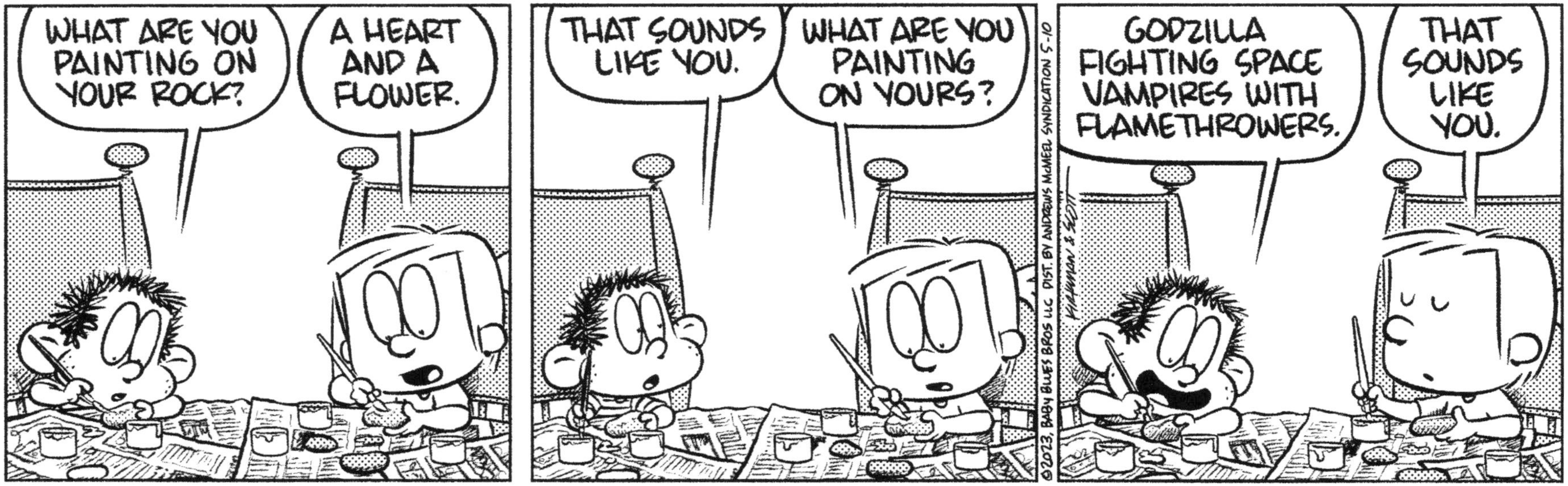
WHAT ARE YOU PAINTING ON YOUR ROCK?
A HEART AND A FLOWER.
THAT SOUNDS LIKE YOU.
WHAT ARE YOU PAINTING ON YOURS?
©2023, BABY BLUES BROS LLC DIST. BY ANDREWS McMEEL SYNDICATION 5-10
KIRKMAN & SCOTT
GODZILLA FIGHTING SPACE VAMPIRES WITH FLAMETHROWERS.
THAT SOUNDS LIKE YOU.

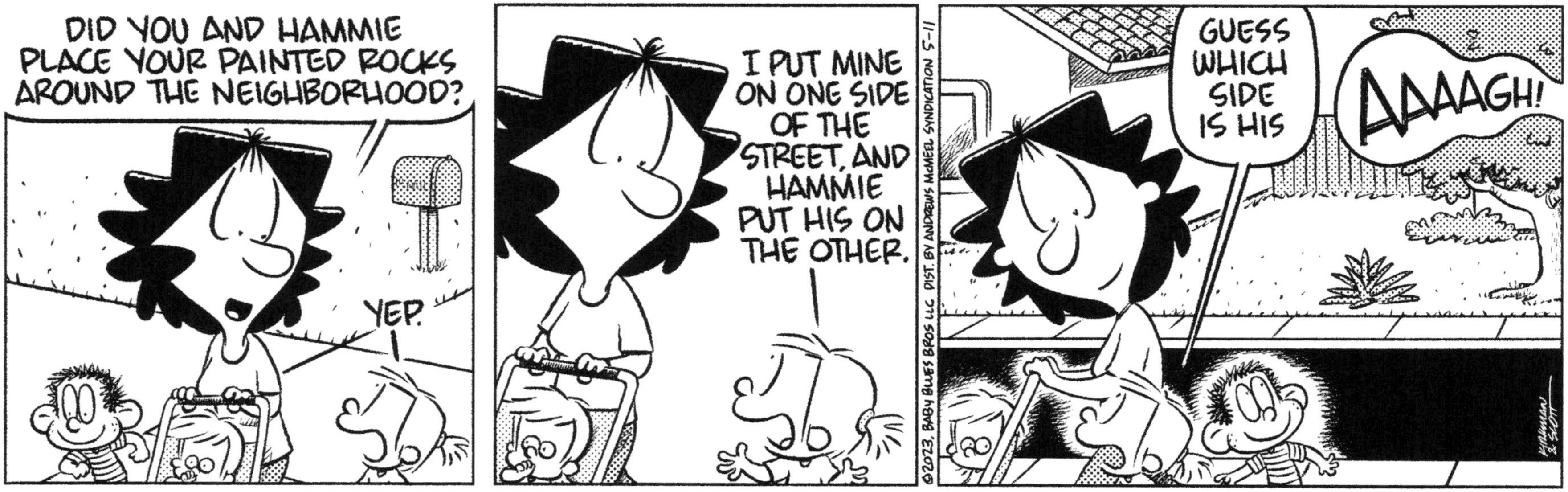
DID YOU AND HAMMIE PLACE YOUR PAINTED ROCKS AROUND THE NEIGHBORHOOD?
YEP.
I PUT MINE ON ONE SIDE OF THE STREET, AND HAMMIE PUT HIS ON THE OTHER.
©2023, BABY BLUES BROS LLC DIST. BY ANDREWS McMEEL SYNDICATION 5-11
GUESS WHICH SIDE IS HIS
AAAAGH!
KIRKMAN & SCOTT

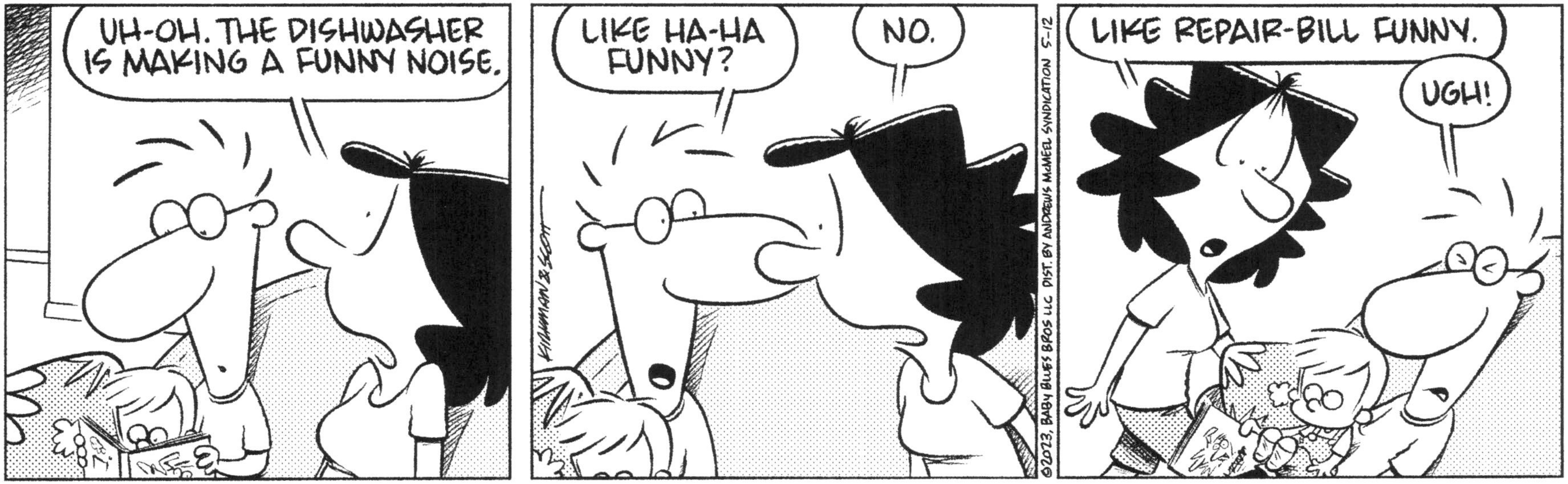
UH-OH. THE DISHWASHER IS MAKING A FUNNY NOISE.
LIKE HA-HA FUNNY?
NO.
LIKE REPAIR-BILL FUNNY.
UGH!
KIRKMAN & SCOTT
©2023, BABY BLUES BROS LLC DIST. BY ANDREWS McMEEL SYNDICATION 5-12

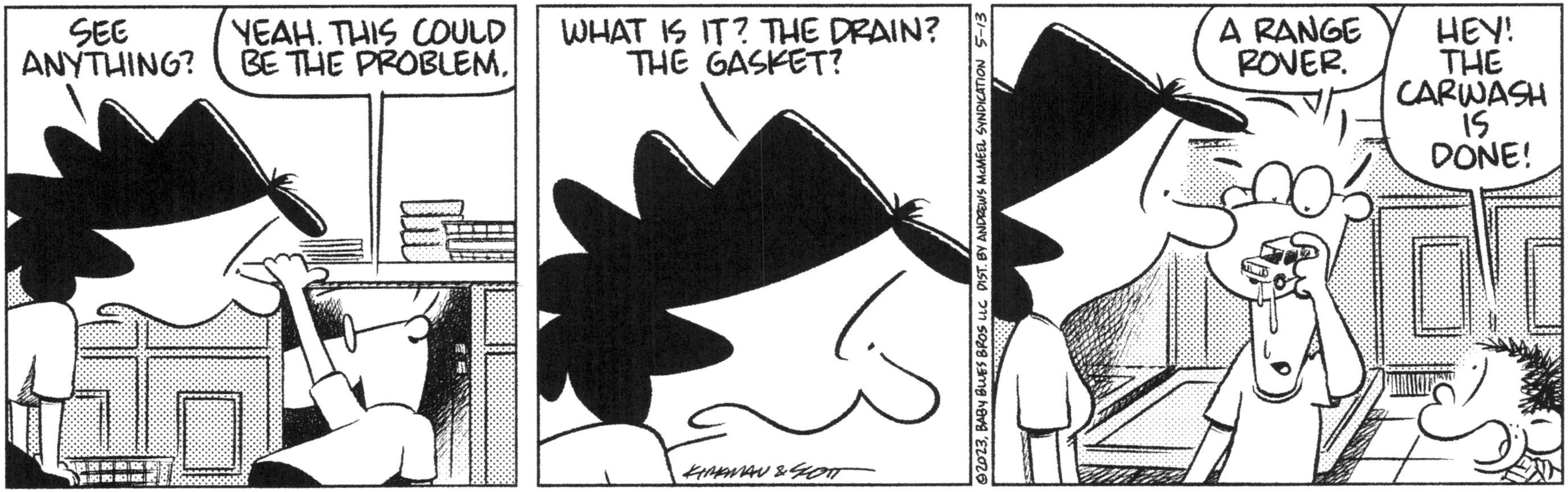
SEE ANYTHING?
YEAH. THIS COULD BE THE PROBLEM.
WHAT IS IT? THE DRAIN? THE GASKET?
A RANGE ROVER.
HEY! THE CARWASH IS DONE!
KIRKMAN & SCOTT
©2023, BABY BLUES BROS LLC DIST. BY ANDREWS McMEEL SYNDICATION 5-13

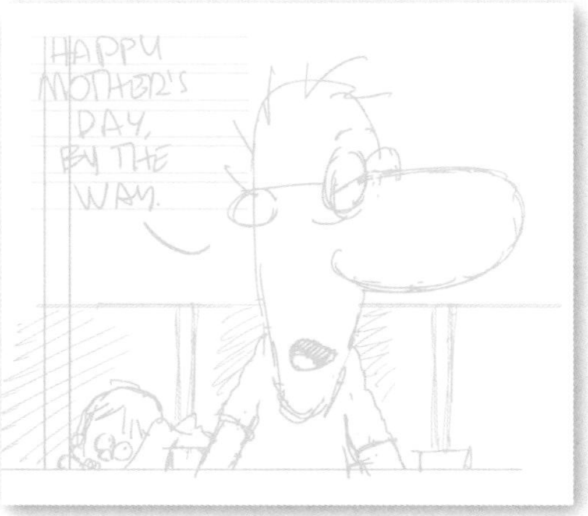
HAPPY MOTHER'S DAY, BY THE WAY.

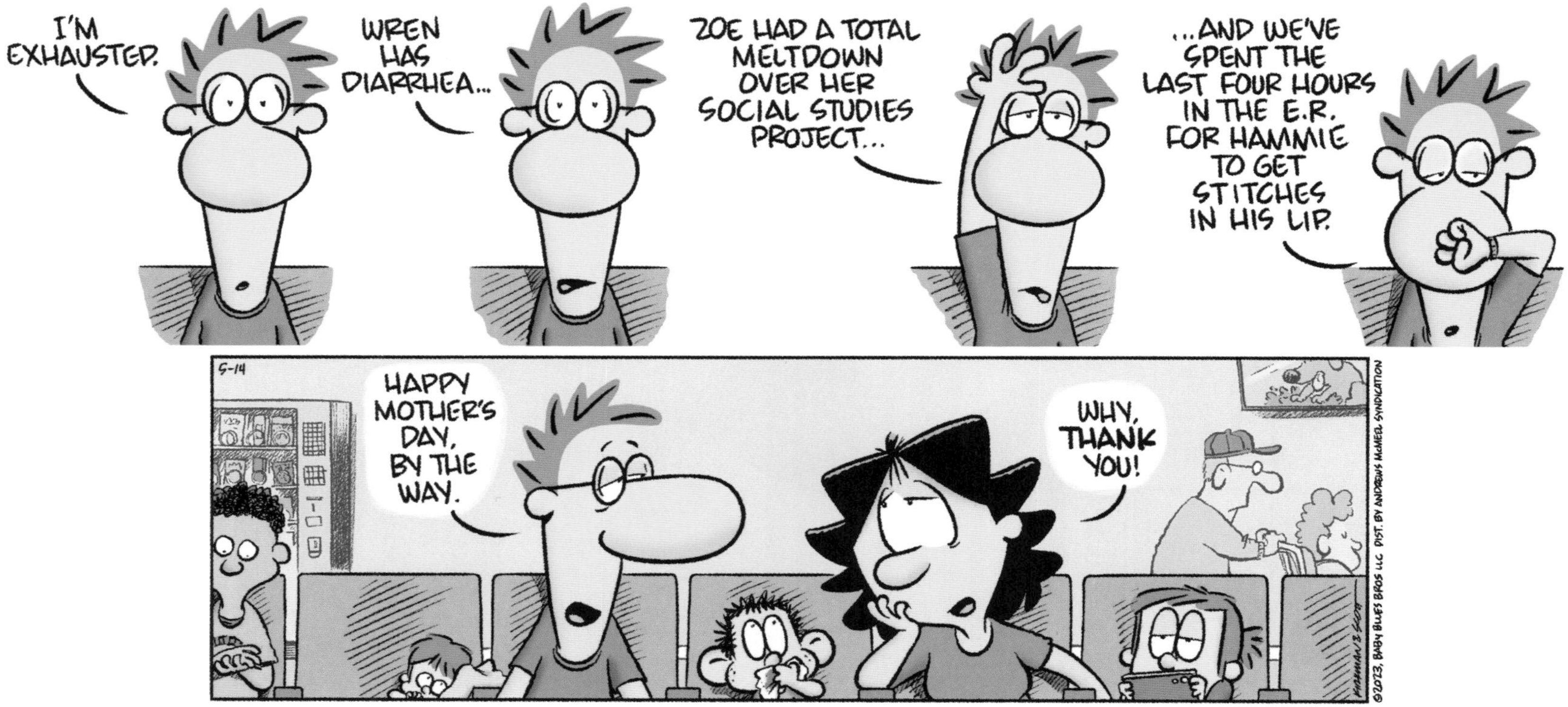
I'M EXHAUSTED.
WREN HAS DIARRHEA...
ZOE HAD A TOTAL MELTDOWN OVER HER SOCIAL STUDIES PROJECT...
...AND WE'VE SPENT THE LAST FOUR HOURS IN THE E.R. FOR HAMMIE TO GET STITCHES IN HIS LIP.
5-14
HAPPY MOTHER'S DAY, BY THE WAY.
WHY, THANK YOU!
©2013, BABY BLUES BROS LLC DIST. BY ANDREWS McMEEL SYNDICATION

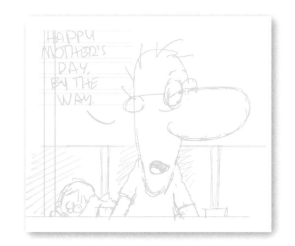

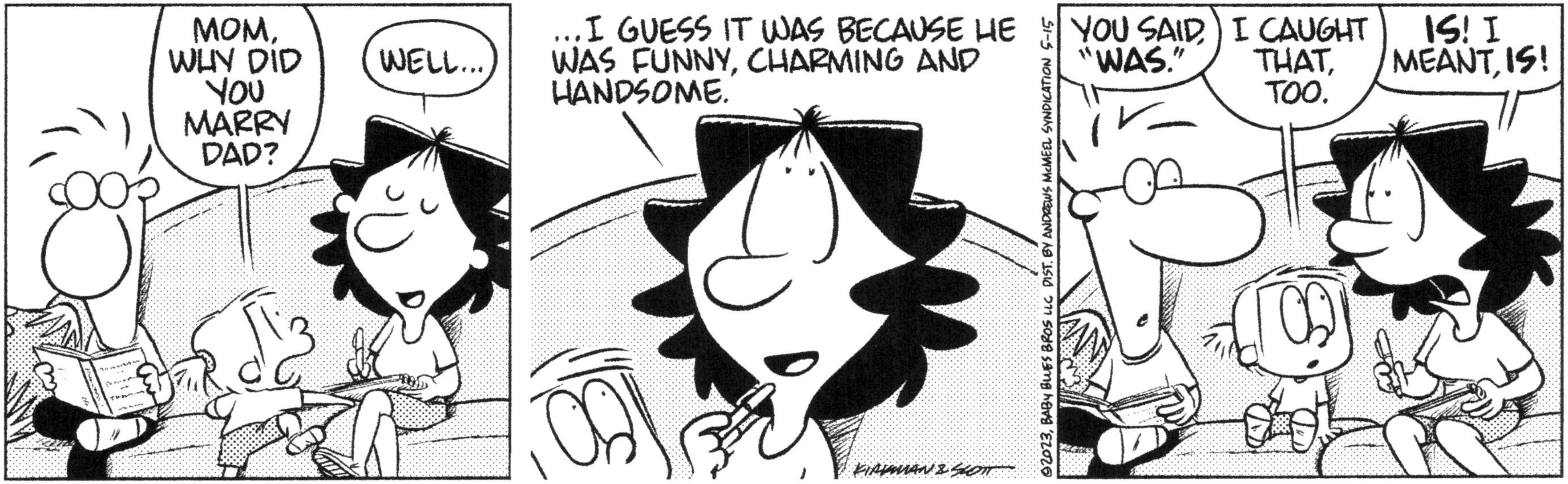
MOM, WHY DID YOU MARRY DAD?
WELL...
...I GUESS IT WAS BECAUSE HE WAS FUNNY, CHARMING AND HANDSOME.
KIRKMAN & SCOTT
©2023, BABY BLUES BROS LLC DIST. BY ANDREWS McMEEL SYNDICATION 5-15
YOU SAID, "WAS."
I CAUGHT THAT, TOO.
IS! I MEANT, IS!

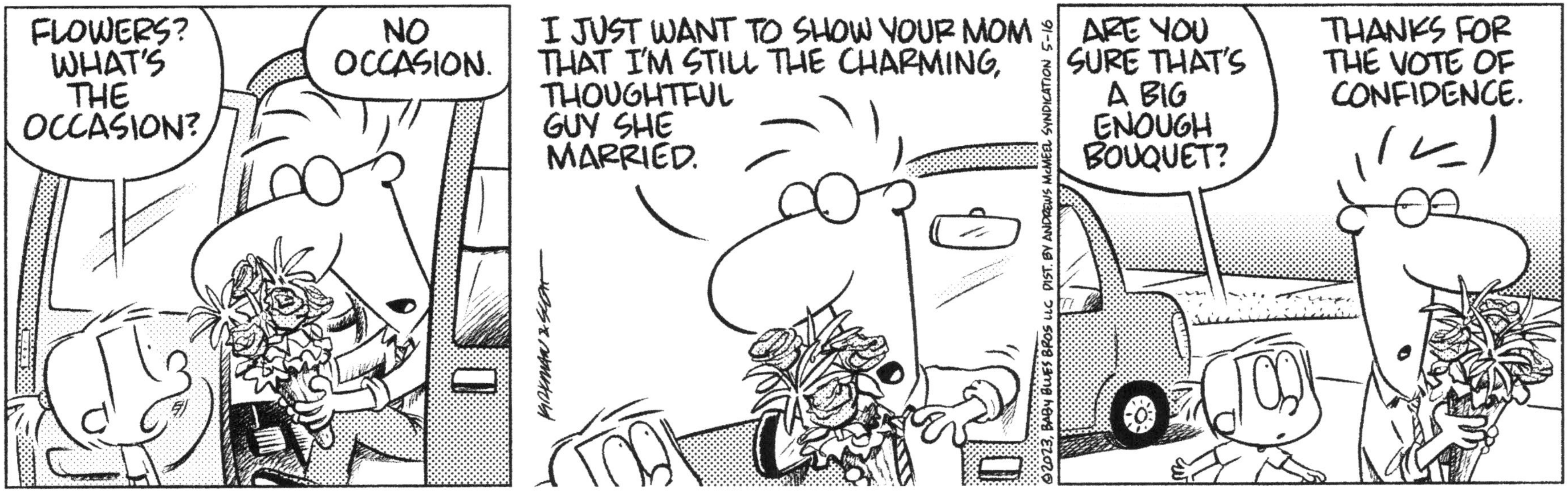
FLOWERS? WHAT'S THE OCCASION?
NO OCCASION.
KIRKMAN & SCOTT
I JUST WANT TO SHOW YOUR MOM THAT I'M STILL THE CHARMING, THOUGHTFUL GUY SHE MARRIED.
©2023, BABY BLUES BROS LLC DIST. BY ANDREWS McMEEL SYNDICATION 5-16
ARE YOU SURE THAT'S A BIG ENOUGH BOUQUET?
THANKS FOR THE VOTE OF CONFIDENCE.

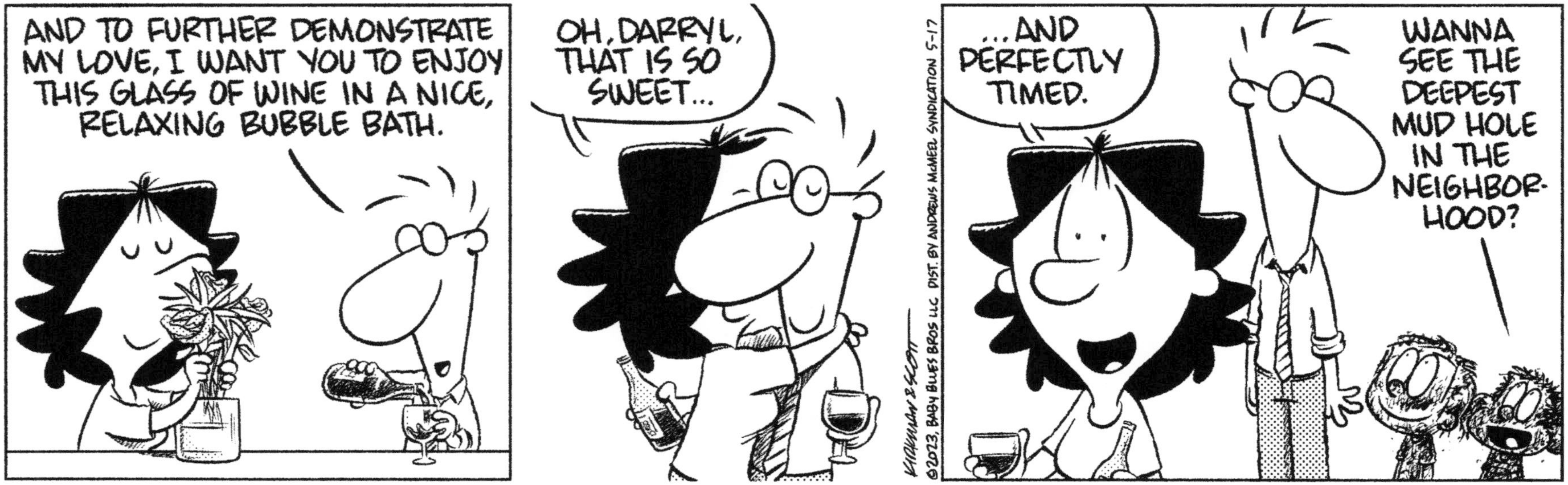
AND TO FURTHER DEMONSTRATE MY LOVE, I WANT YOU TO ENJOY THIS GLASS OF WINE IN A NICE, RELAXING BUBBLE BATH.
OH, DARRYL, THAT IS SO SWEET...
...AND PERFECTLY TIMED.
WANNA SEE THE DEEPEST MUD HOLE IN THE NEIGHBOR-HOOD?
©2023, BABY BLUES BROS LLC DIST. BY ANDREWS MCMEEL SYNDICATION 5-17

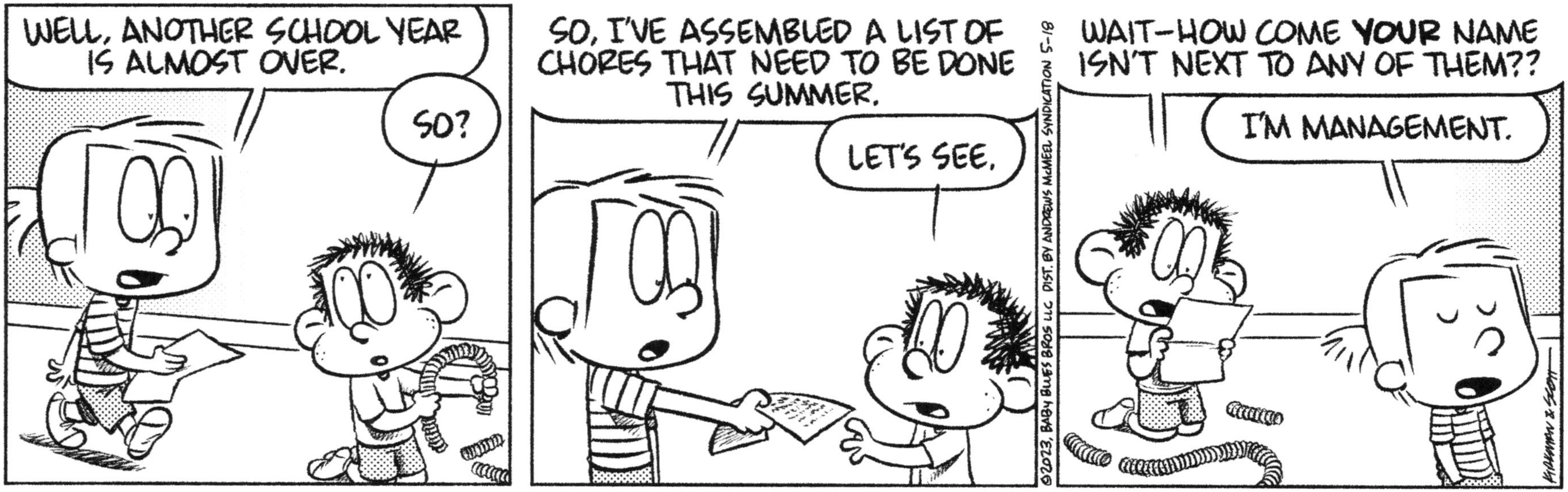
WELL, ANOTHER SCHOOL YEAR IS ALMOST OVER.
SO?
SO, I'VE ASSEMBLED A LIST OF CHORES THAT NEED TO BE DONE THIS SUMMER.
LET'S SEE.
WAIT–HOW COME **YOUR** NAME ISN'T NEXT TO ANY OF THEM??
I'M MANAGEMENT.
©2023, BABY BLUES BROS LLC DIST. BY ANDREWS MCMEEL SYNDICATION 5-18

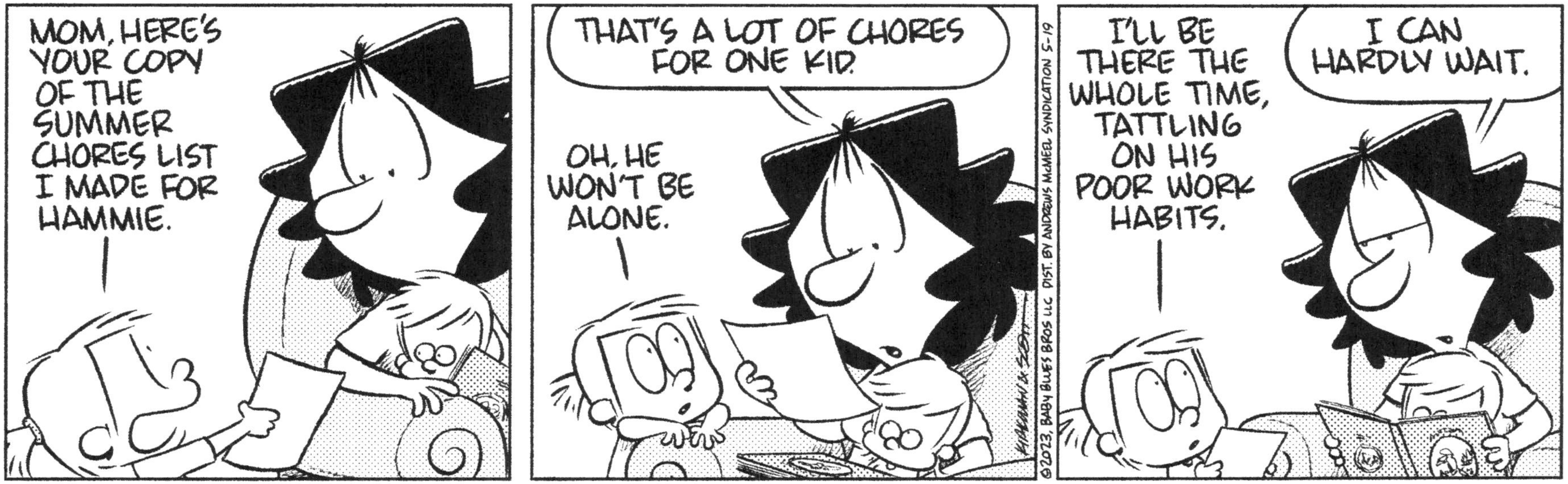
MOM, HERE'S YOUR COPY OF THE SUMMER CHORES LIST I MADE FOR HAMMIE.
THAT'S A LOT OF CHORES FOR ONE KID.
OH, HE WON'T BE ALONE.
KIRKMAN & SCOTT
©2023, BABY BLUES BROS LLC DIST. BY ANDREWS McMEEL SYNDICATION 5-19
I'LL BE THERE THE WHOLE TIME, TATTLING ON HIS POOR WORK HABITS.
I CAN HARDLY WAIT.

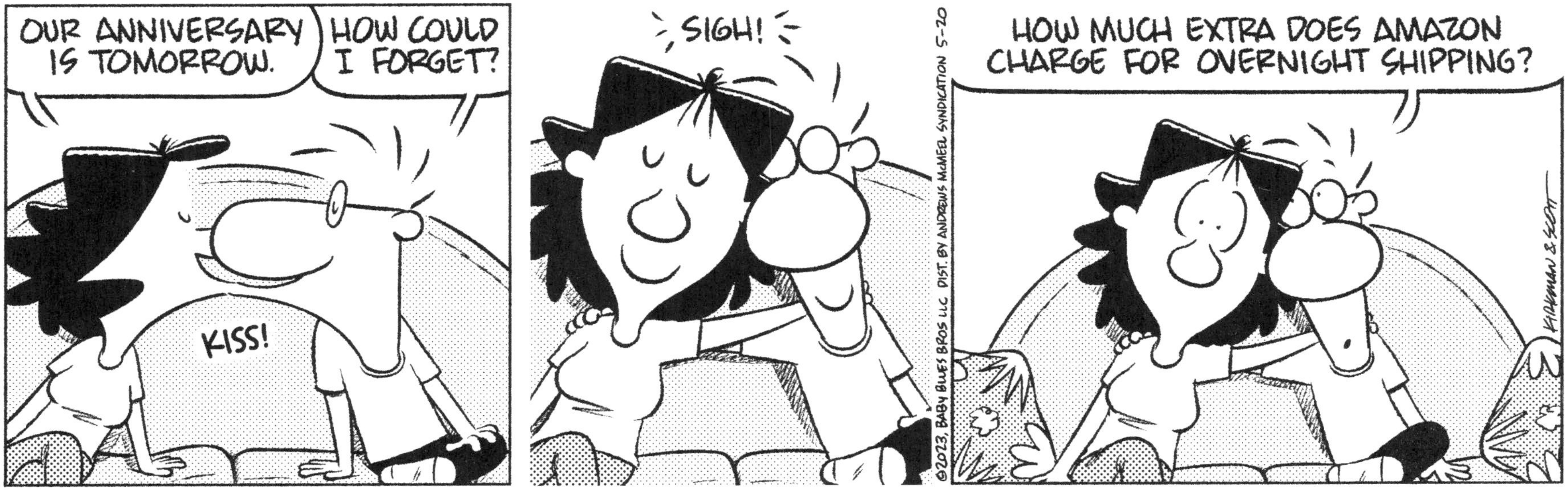
OUR ANNIVERSARY IS TOMORROW.
HOW COULD I FORGET?
KISS!
SIGH!
©2023, BABY BLUES BROS LLC DIST. BY ANDREWS McMEEL SYNDICATION 5-20
HOW MUCH EXTRA DOES AMAZON CHARGE FOR OVERNIGHT SHIPPING?
KIRKMAN & SCOTT

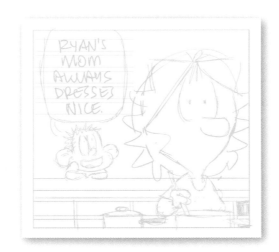

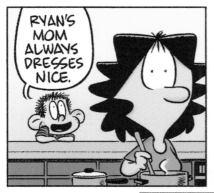

RYAN'S MOM ALWAYS DRESSES NICE.

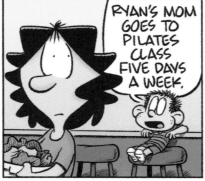

RYAN'S MOM ALWAYS DRESSES NICE.
RYAN'S MOM GOES TO PILATES CLASS FIVE DAYS A WEEK.
BAP! BAP! BAP!
RYAN'S MOM USED TO SING IN A BAND.
RYAN'S MOM-
CAN WE CHANGE THE SUBJECT?
LET'S NOT TALK ABOUT SOMEONE ELSE'S PERFECT LIFE WHILE I'M JUGGLING DINNER FOR FIVE PEOPLE, DOING LAUNDRY, AND ENTERTAINING A TODDLER!
OKAY.
5-21 KIRKMAN & SCOTT
©2013, BABY BLUES BROS LLC. DIST. BY ANDREWS MCMEEL SYNDICATION
RYAN'S MOM IS SURE RIGHT ABOUT STRESS CAUSING WRINKLES.
GAH!

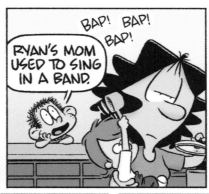

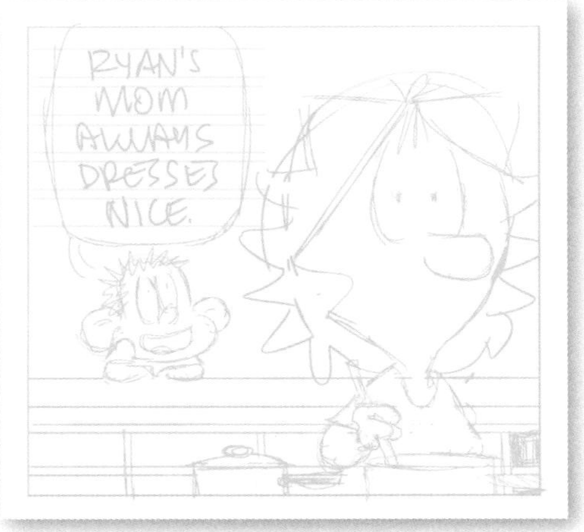

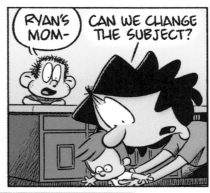

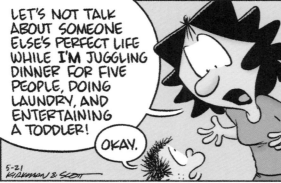

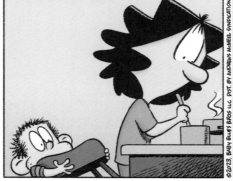

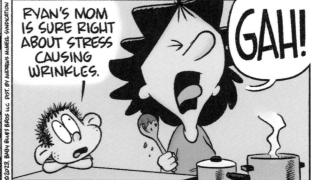

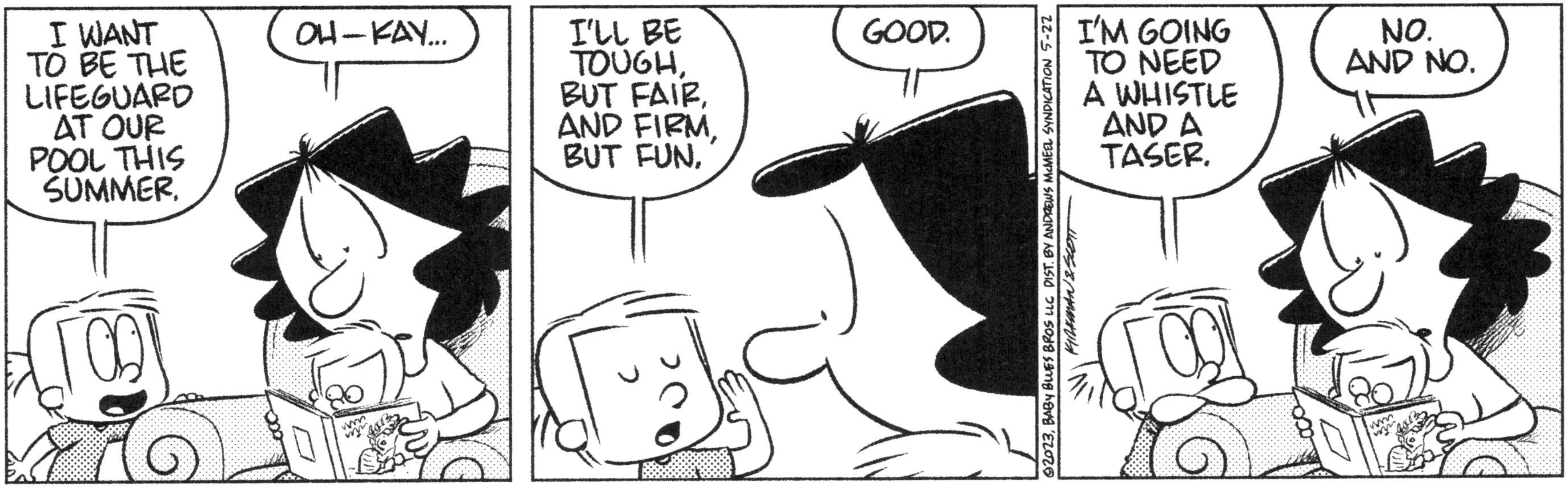
I WANT TO BE THE LIFEGUARD AT OUR POOL THIS SUMMER.
OH-KAY...
I'LL BE TOUGH, BUT FAIR, AND FIRM, BUT FUN.
GOOD.
©2023, BABY BLUES BROS LLC DIST. BY ANDREWS McMEEL SYNDICATION 5-22
KIRKMAN & SCOTT
I'M GOING TO NEED A WHISTLE AND A TASER.
NO. AND NO.

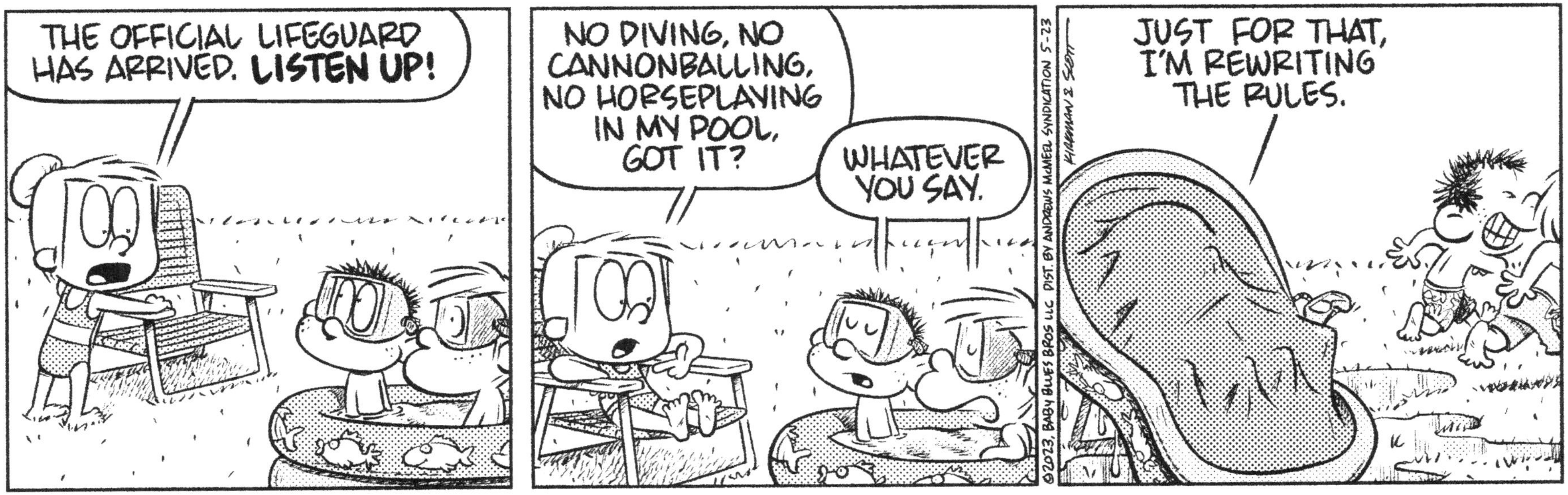
THE OFFICIAL LIFEGUARD HAS ARRIVED. **LISTEN UP!**
NO DIVING, NO CANNONBALLING, NO HORSEPLAYING IN MY POOL, GOT IT?
WHATEVER YOU SAY.
©2023, BABY BLUES BROS LLC DIST. BY ANDREWS McMEEL SYNDICATION 5-23
KIRKMAN & SCOTT
JUST FOR THAT, I'M REWRITING THE RULES.

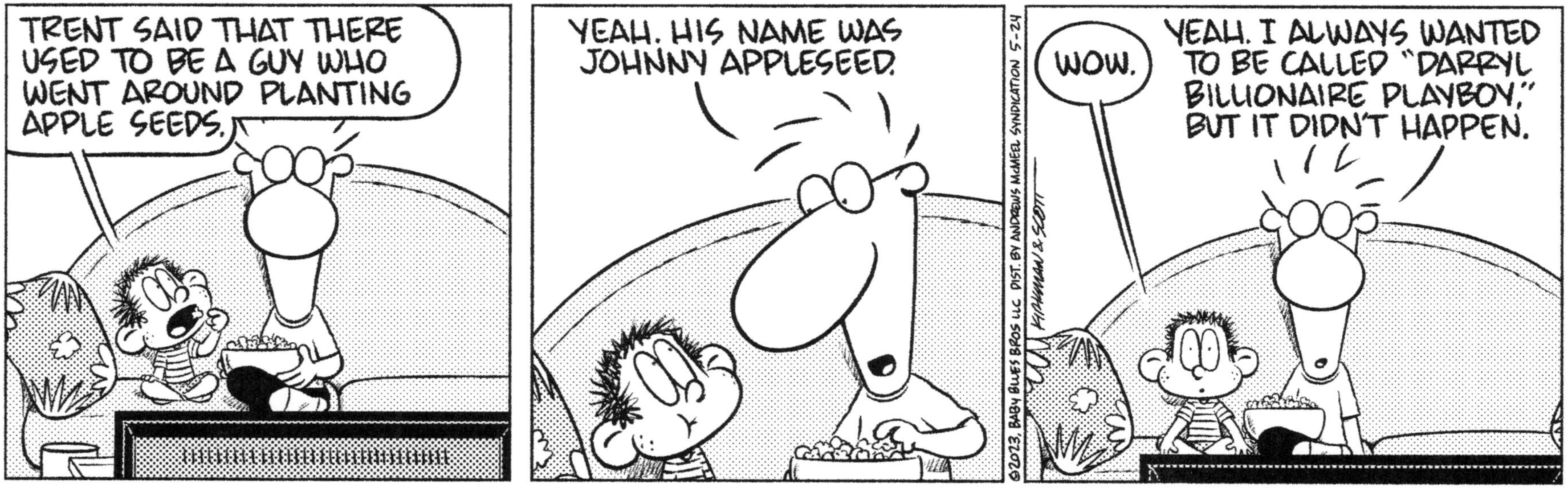
TRENT SAID THAT THERE USED TO BE A GUY WHO WENT AROUND PLANTING APPLE SEEDS.
YEAH. HIS NAME WAS JOHNNY APPLESEED.
©2023, BABY BLUES BROS LLC DIST. BY ANDREWS McMEEL SYNDICATION 5-24
KIRKMAN & SCOTT
WOW.
YEAH. I ALWAYS WANTED TO BE CALLED "DARRYL BILLIONAIRE PLAYBOY," BUT IT DIDN'T HAPPEN.

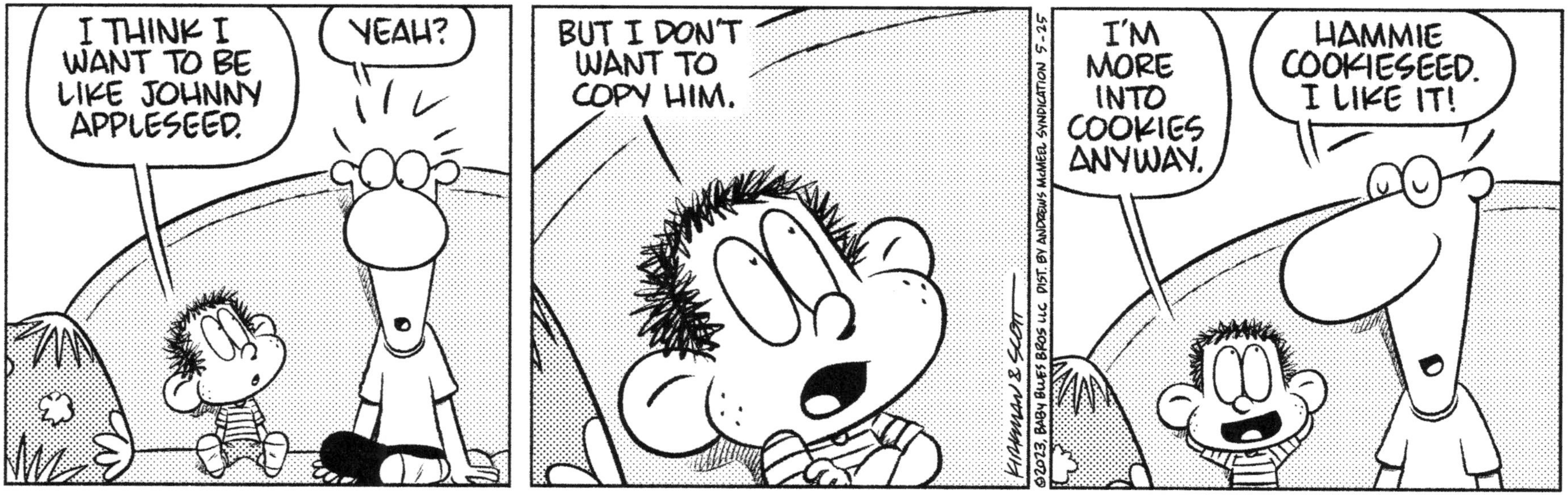
I THINK I WANT TO BE LIKE JOHNNY APPLESEED.
YEAH?
BUT I DON'T WANT TO COPY HIM.
KIRKMAN & SCOTT
©2023, BABY BLUES BROS LLC DIST. BY ANDREWS McMEEL SYNDICATION 5-25
I'M MORE INTO COOKIES ANYWAY.
HAMMIE COOKIESEED. I LIKE IT!

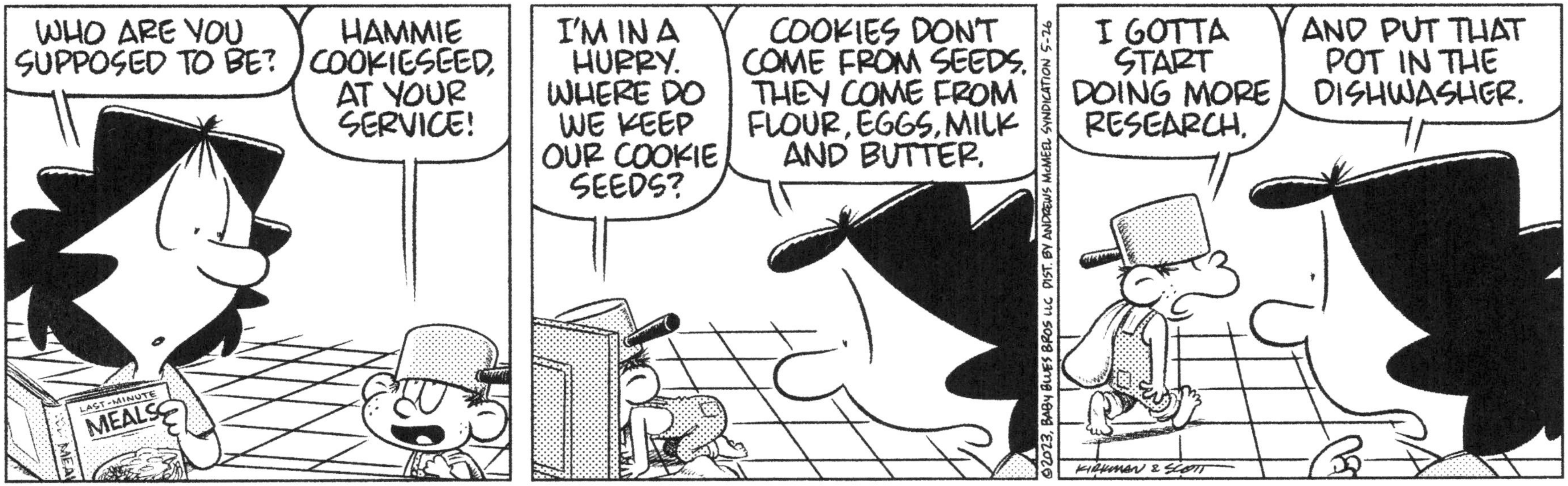
WHO ARE YOU SUPPOSED TO BE?
HAMMIE COOKIESEED, AT YOUR SERVICE!
LAST-MINUTE MEALS
I'M IN A HURRY. WHERE DO WE KEEP OUR COOKIE SEEDS?
COOKIES DON'T COME FROM SEEDS. THEY COME FROM FLOUR, EGGS, MILK AND BUTTER.
©2023, BABY BLUES BROS LLC DIST. BY ANDREWS MCMEEL SYNDICATION 5-26
I GOTTA START DOING MORE RESEARCH.
AND PUT THAT POT IN THE DISHWASHER.
KIRKMAN & SCOTT

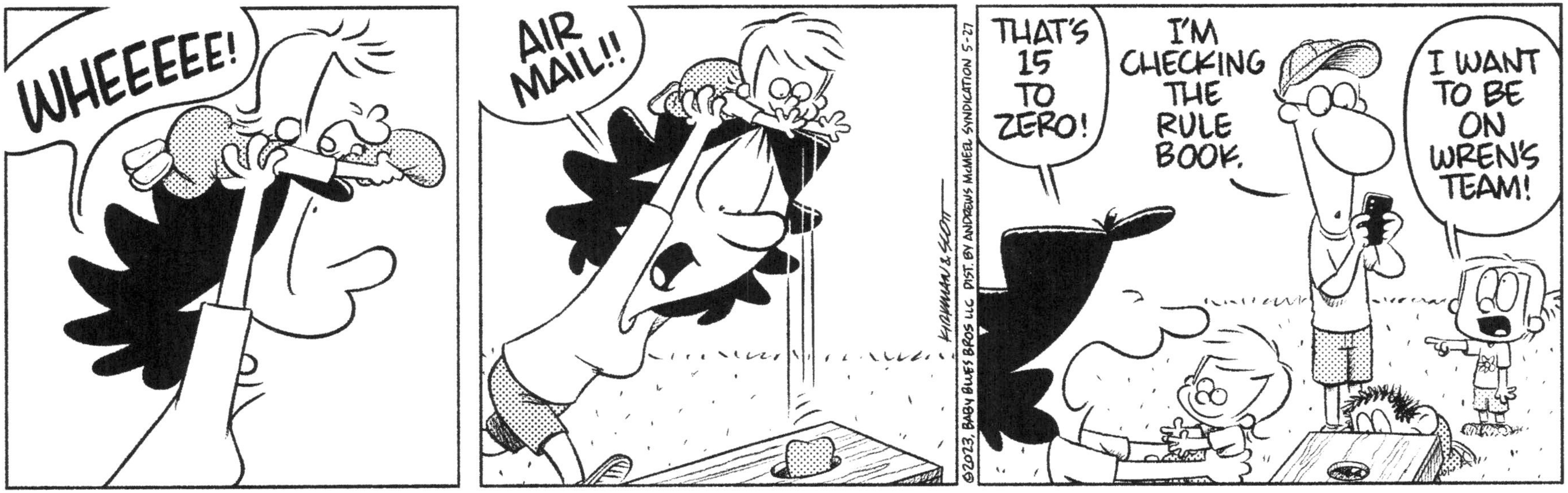
WHEEEEEE!
AIR MAIL!!
KIRKMAN & SCOTT
©2023, BABY BLUES BROS LLC DIST. BY ANDREWS MCMEEL SYNDICATION 5-27
THAT'S 15 TO ZERO!
I'M CHECKING THE RULE BOOK.
I WANT TO BE ON WREN'S TEAM!

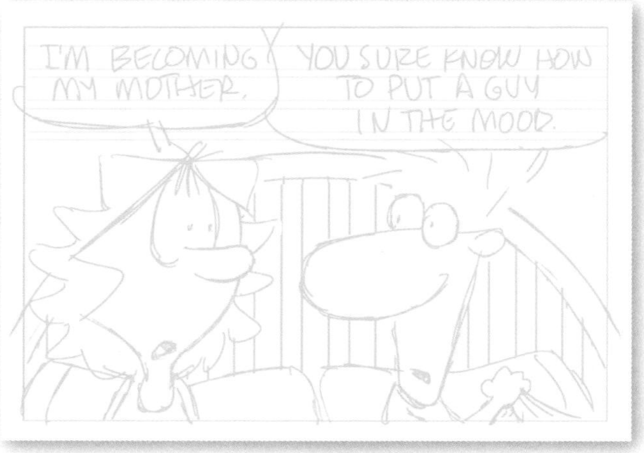
I'M BECOMING MY MOTHER.
YOU SURE KNOW HOW TO PUT A GUY IN THE MOOD.

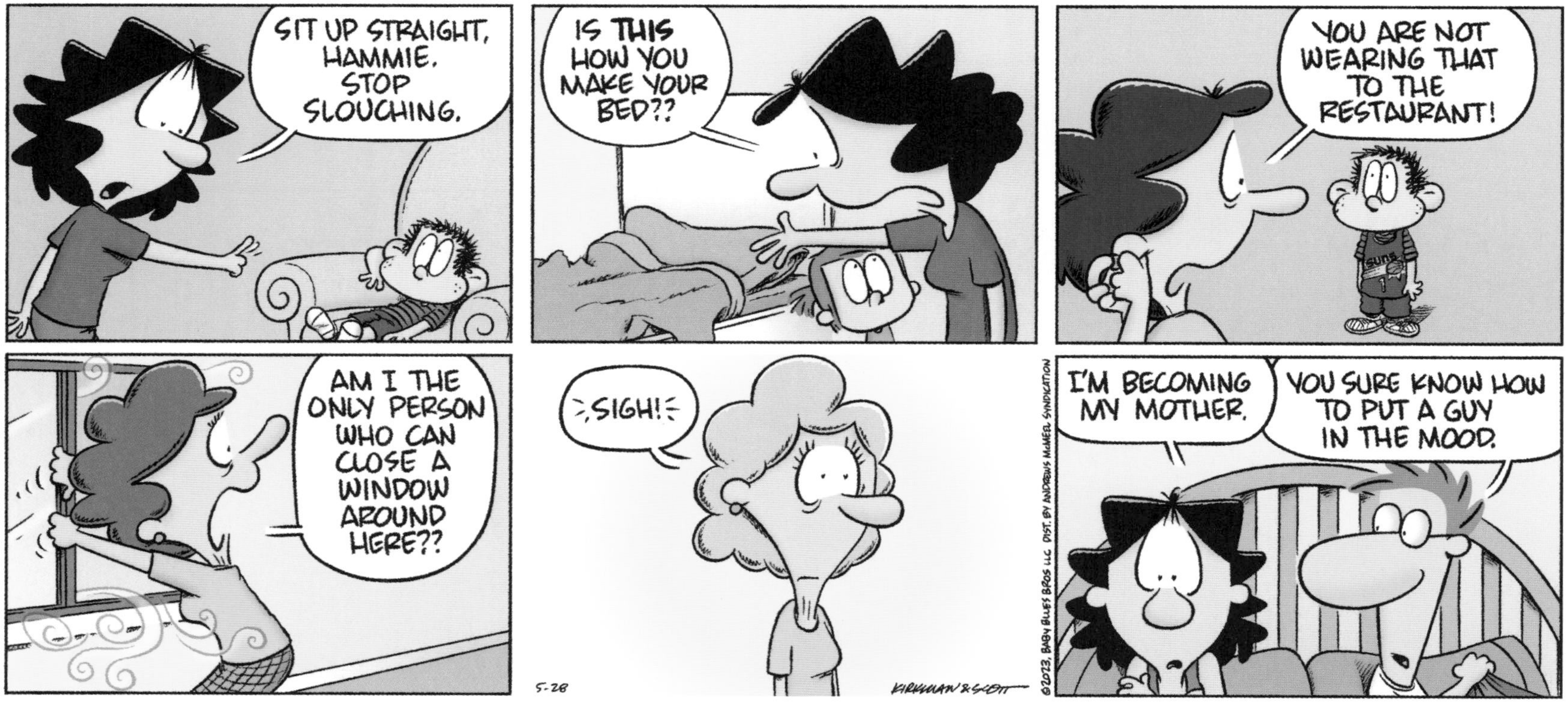
SIT UP STRAIGHT, HAMMIE. STOP SLOUCHING.
IS **THIS** HOW YOU MAKE YOUR BED??
YOU ARE NOT WEARING THAT TO THE RESTAURANT!
SUNS
AM I THE ONLY PERSON WHO CAN CLOSE A WINDOW AROUND HERE??
SIGH!
5-28
KIRKMAN & SCOTT
©2013, BABY BLUES BROS LLC. DIST. BY ANDREWS McMEEL SYNDICATION
I'M BECOMING MY MOTHER.
YOU SURE KNOW HOW TO PUT A GUY IN THE MOOD.

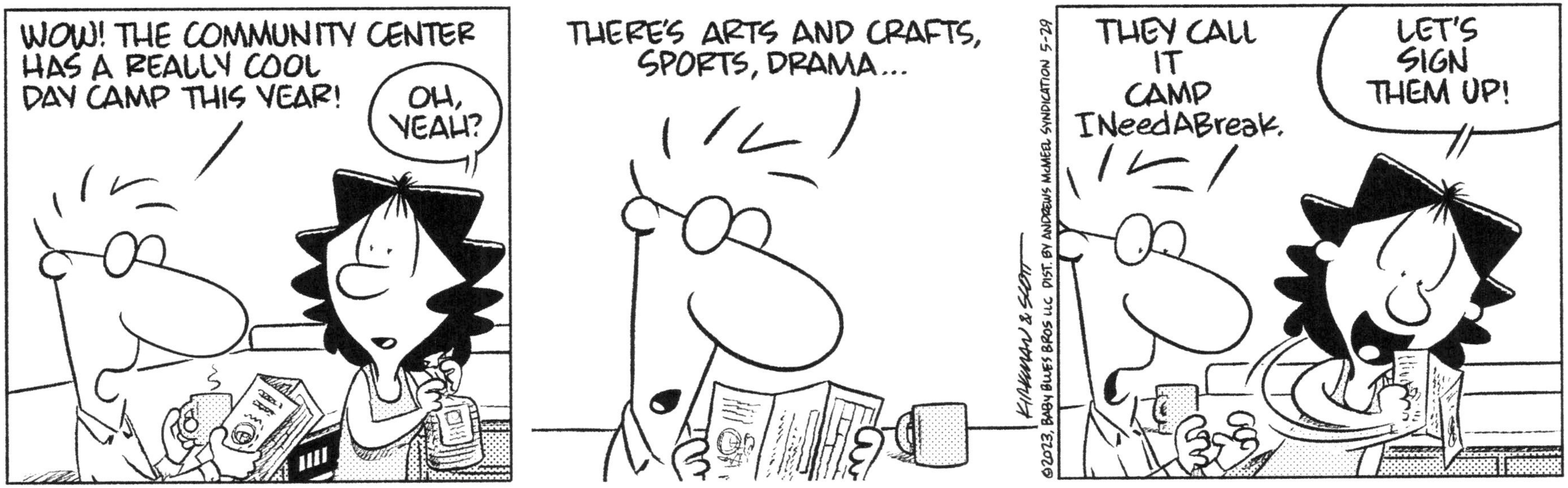
WOW! THE COMMUNITY CENTER HAS A REALLY COOL DAY CAMP THIS YEAR!
OH, YEAH?
THERE'S ARTS AND CRAFTS, SPORTS, DRAMA...
KIRKMAN & SCOTT
©2023, BABY BLUES BROS LLC DIST. BY ANDREWS MCMEEL SYNDICATION 5-29
THEY CALL IT CAMP INeedABreak.
LET'S SIGN THEM UP!

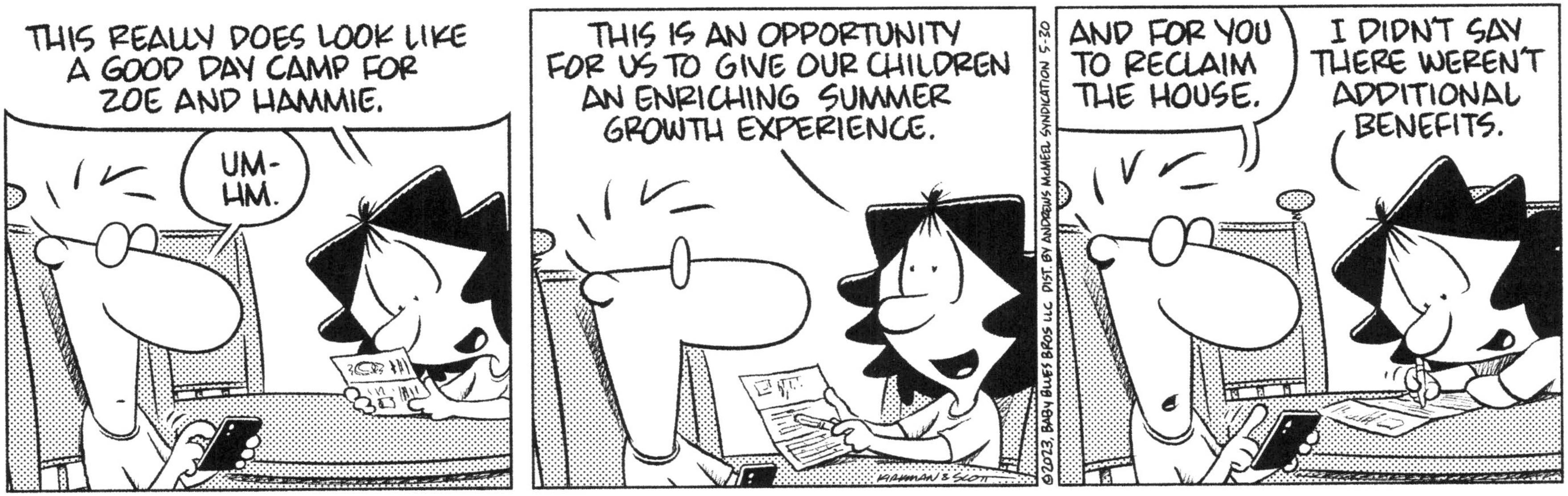
THIS REALLY DOES LOOK LIKE A GOOD DAY CAMP FOR ZOE AND HAMMIE.
UM-HM.
THIS IS AN OPPORTUNITY FOR US TO GIVE OUR CHILDREN AN ENRICHING SUMMER GROWTH EXPERIENCE.
KIRKMAN & SCOTT
©2023, BABY BLUES BROS LLC DIST. BY ANDREWS MCMEEL SYNDICATION 5-30
AND FOR YOU TO RECLAIM THE HOUSE.
I DIDN'T SAY THERE WEREN'T ADDITIONAL BENEFITS.

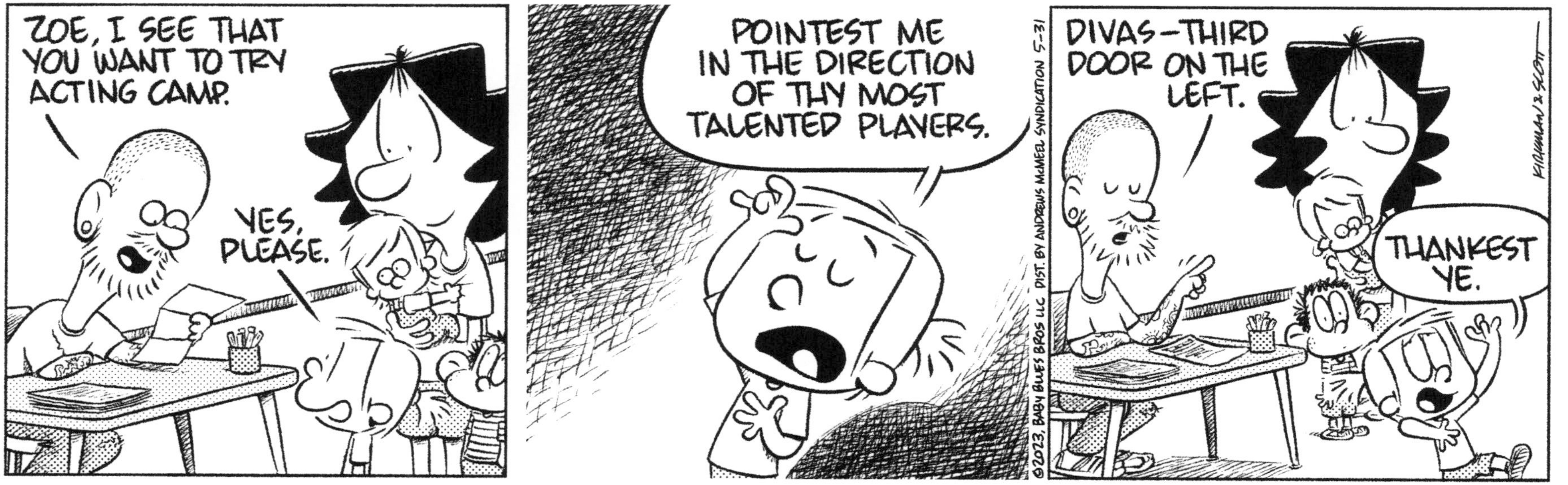
ZOE, I SEE THAT YOU WANT TO TRY ACTING CAMP.
YES, PLEASE.
POINTEST ME IN THE DIRECTION OF THY MOST TALENTED PLAYERS.
©2023, BABY BLUES BROS LLC DIST. BY ANDREWS McMEEL SYNDICATION 5-31
DIVAS—THIRD DOOR ON THE LEFT.
THANKEST YE.
KIRKMAN & SCOTT

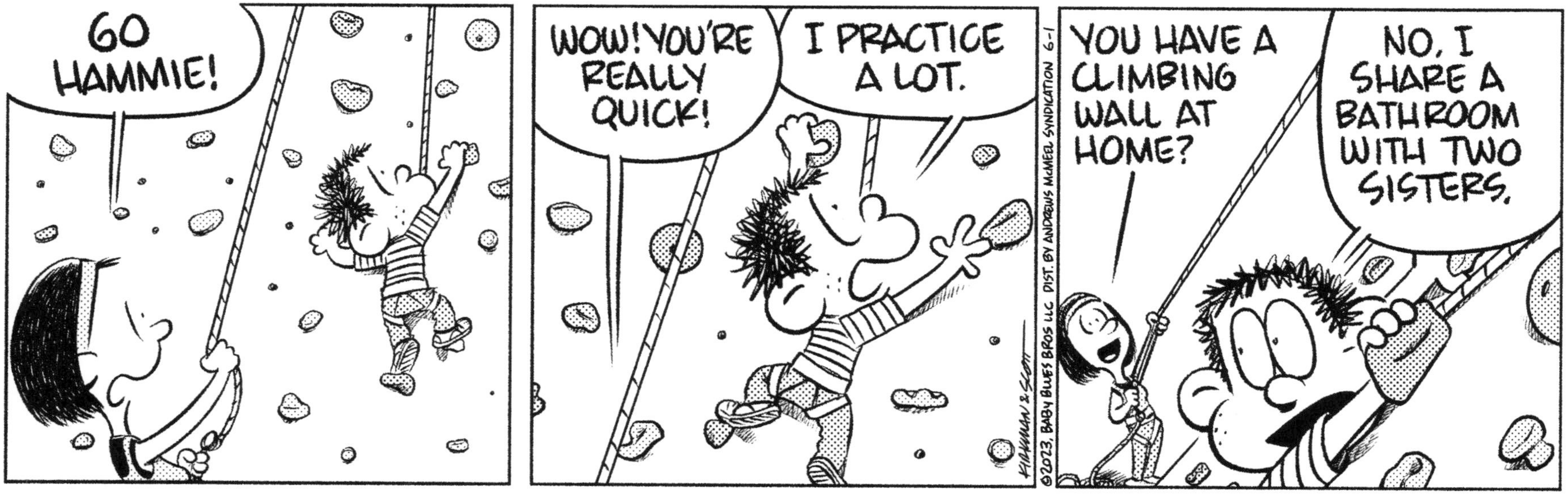
GO HAMMIE!
WOW! YOU'RE REALLY QUICK!
I PRACTICE A LOT.
KIRKMAN & SCOTT
©2023, BABY BLUES BROS LLC DIST. BY ANDREWS McMEEL SYNDICATION 6-1
YOU HAVE A CLIMBING WALL AT HOME?
NO, I SHARE A BATHROOM WITH TWO SISTERS.

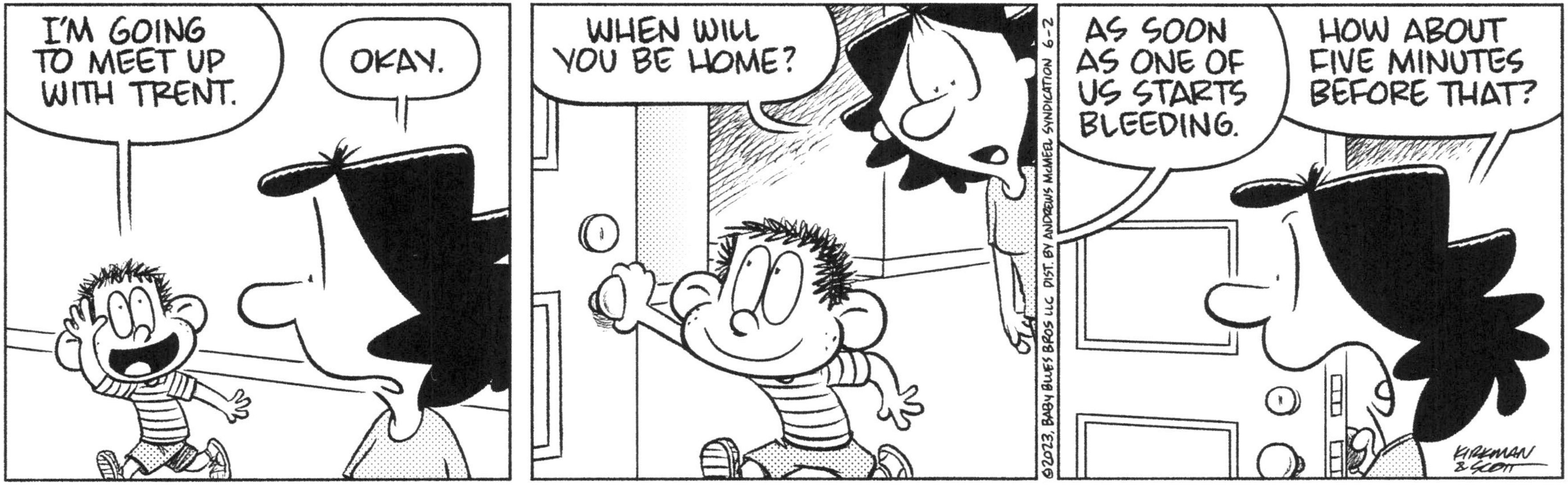
I'M GOING TO MEET UP WITH TRENT.
OKAY.
WHEN WILL YOU BE HOME?
©2023, BABY BLUES BROS LLC DIST. BY ANDREWS McMEEL SYNDICATION 6-2
AS SOON AS ONE OF US STARTS BLEEDING.
HOW ABOUT FIVE MINUTES BEFORE THAT?
KIRKMAN & SCOTT

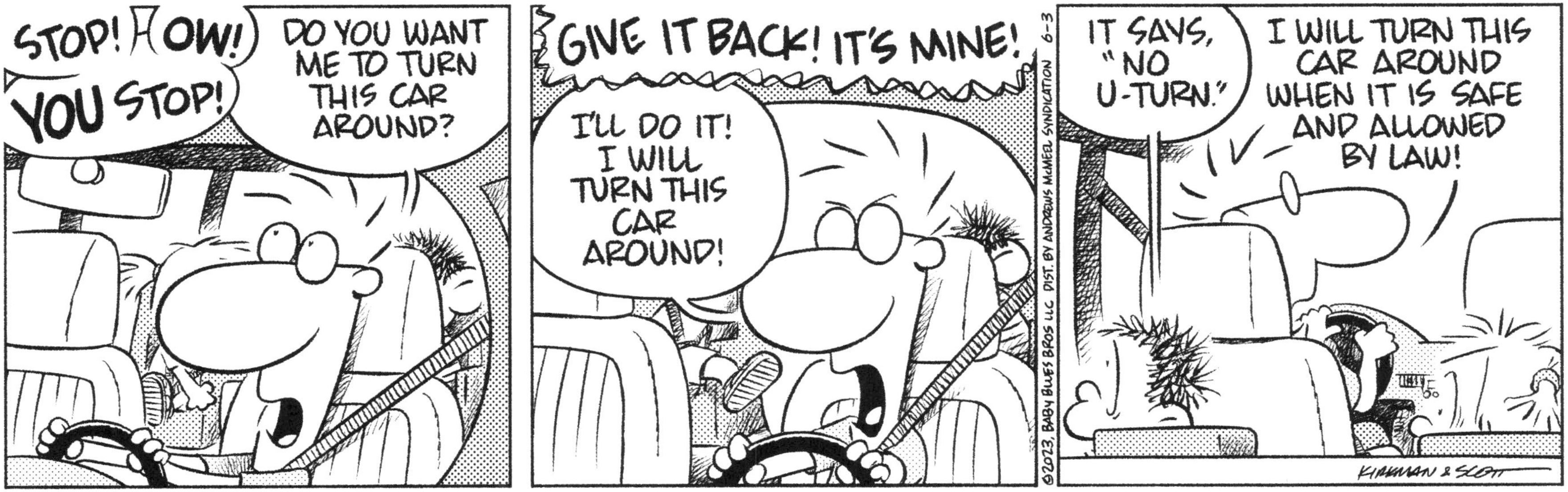
STOP! OW!
YOU STOP!
DO YOU WANT ME TO TURN THIS CAR AROUND?
GIVE IT BACK! IT'S MINE!
I'LL DO IT! I WILL TURN THIS CAR AROUND!
©2023, BABY BLUES BROS LLC DIST. BY ANDREWS McMEEL SYNDICATION 6-3
IT SAYS, "NO U-TURN."
I WILL TURN THIS CAR AROUND WHEN IT IS SAFE AND ALLOWED BY LAW!
KIRKMAN & SCOTT

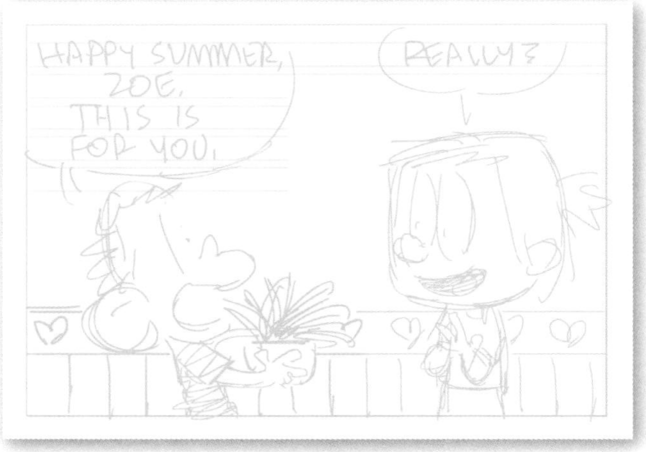
HAPPY SUMMER, ZOE. THIS IS FOR YOU.
REALLY?

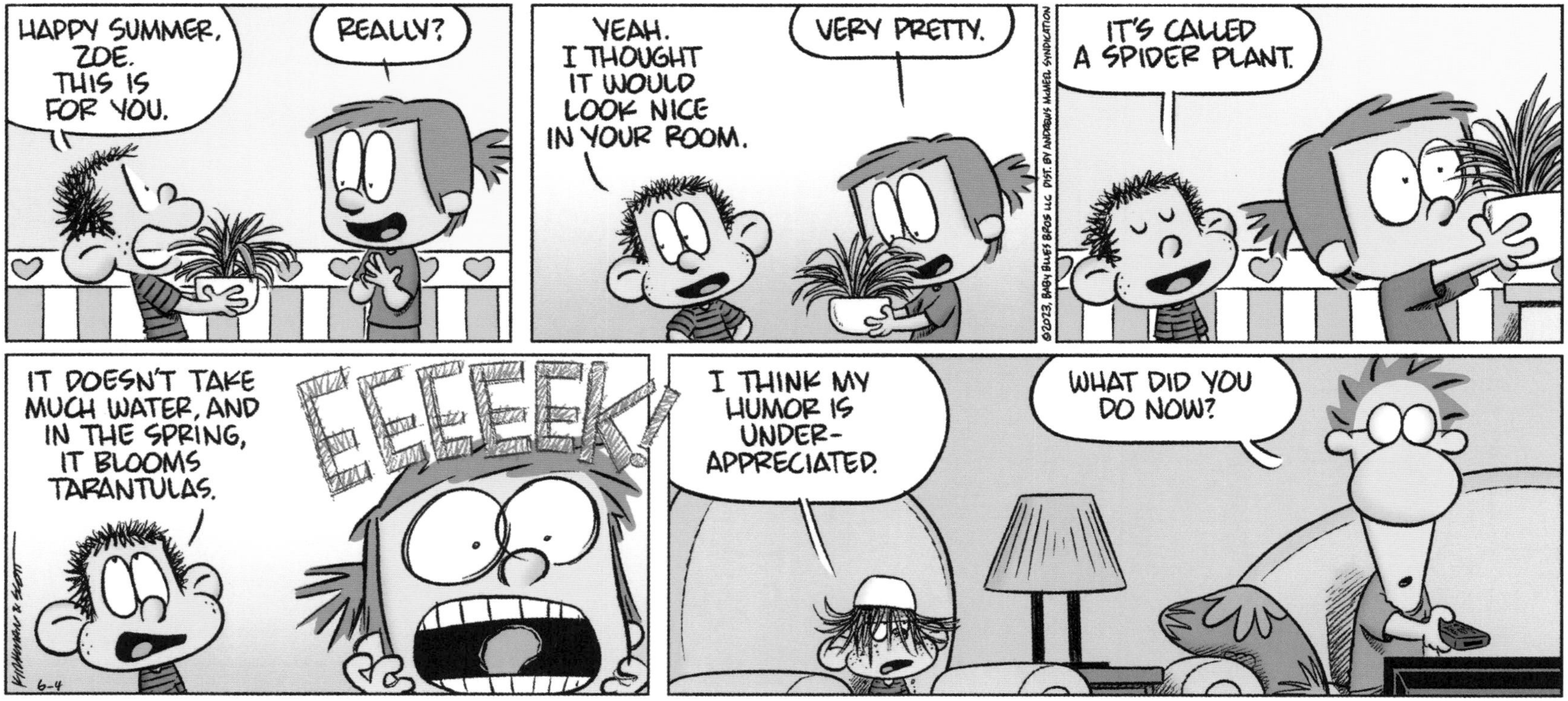
HAPPY SUMMER, ZOE. THIS IS FOR YOU.
REALLY?
YEAH. I THOUGHT IT WOULD LOOK NICE IN YOUR ROOM.
VERY PRETTY.
©2023, BABY BLUES BROS LLC DIST. BY ANDREWS McMEEL SYNDICATION
IT'S CALLED A SPIDER PLANT.
IT DOESN'T TAKE MUCH WATER, AND IN THE SPRING, IT BLOOMS TARANTULAS.
EEEEEK!
I THINK MY HUMOR IS UNDER-APPRECIATED.
WHAT DID YOU DO NOW?

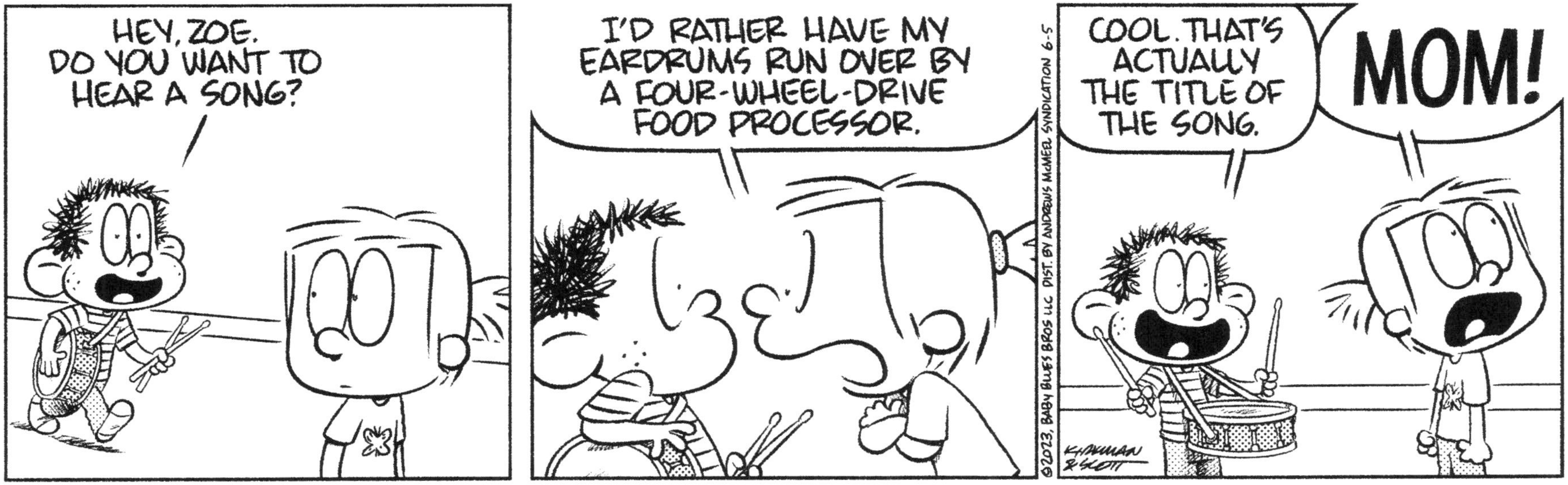
HEY, ZOE.
DO YOU WANT TO HEAR A SONG?
I'D RATHER HAVE MY EARDRUMS RUN OVER BY A FOUR-WHEEL-DRIVE FOOD PROCESSOR.
©2023, BABY BLUES BROS LLC DIST. BY ANDREWS MCMEEL SYNDICATION 6-5
COOL. THAT'S ACTUALLY THE TITLE OF THE SONG.
MOM!
KIRKMAN & SCOTT

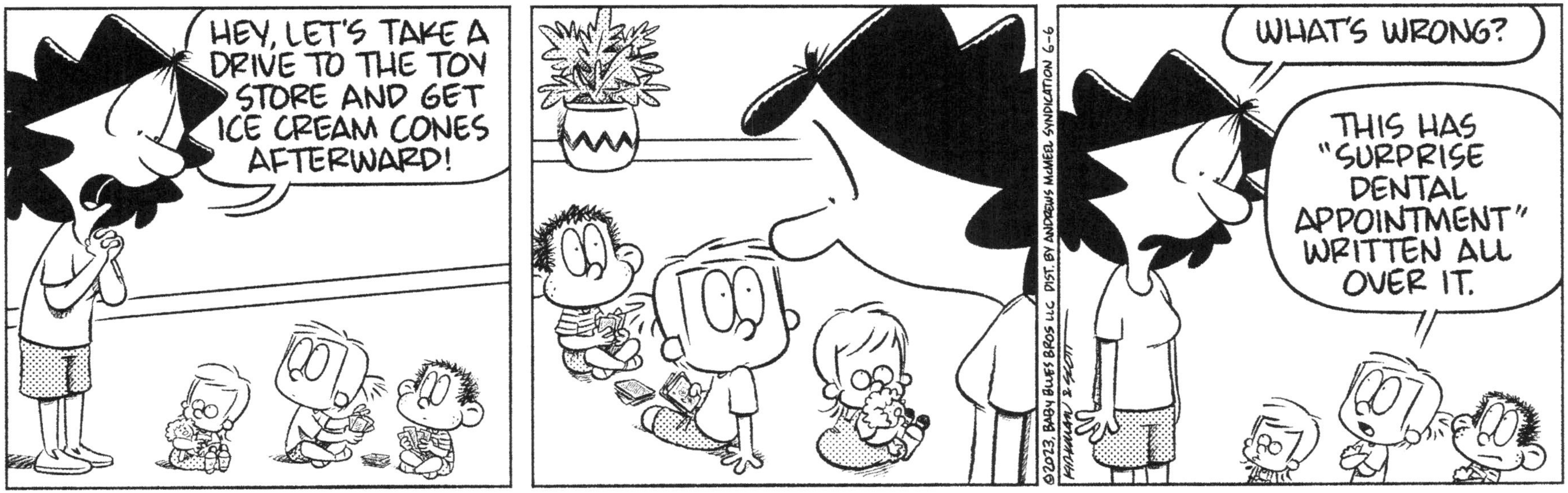
HEY, LET'S TAKE A DRIVE TO THE TOY STORE AND GET ICE CREAM CONES AFTERWARD!
©2023, BABY BLUES BROS LLC DIST. BY ANDREWS MCMEEL SYNDICATION 6-6
KIRKMAN & SCOTT
WHAT'S WRONG?
THIS HAS "SURPRISE DENTAL APPOINTMENT" WRITTEN ALL OVER IT.

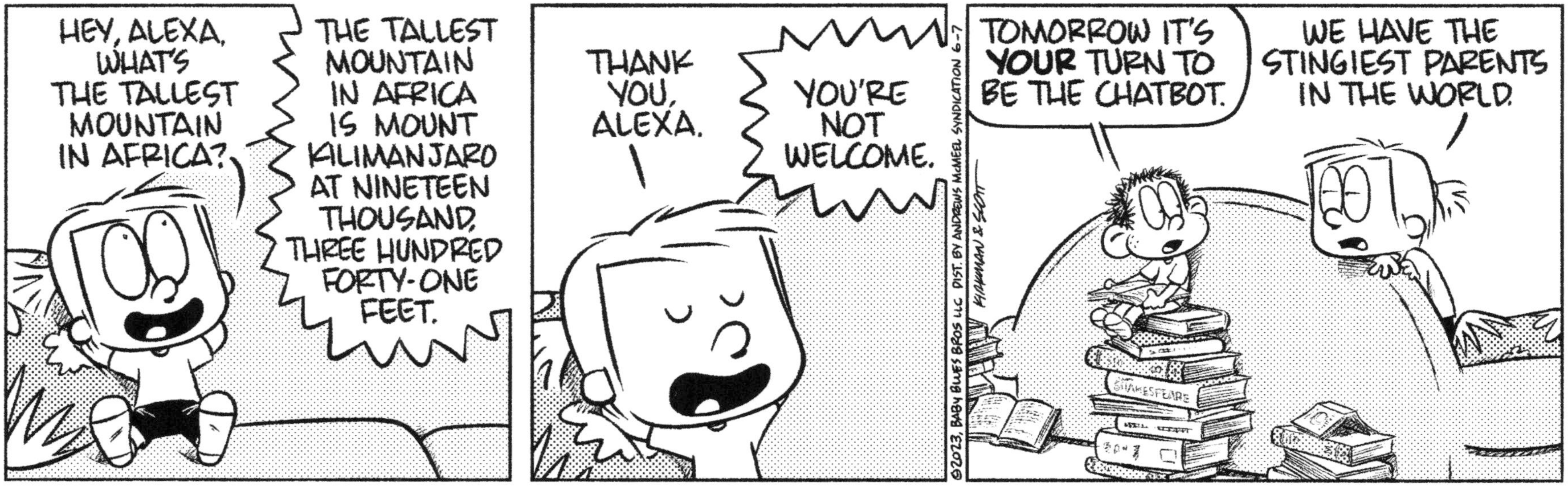
HEY, ALEXA. WHAT'S THE TALLEST MOUNTAIN IN AFRICA?
THE TALLEST MOUNTAIN IN AFRICA IS MOUNT KILIMANJARO AT NINETEEN THOUSAND, THREE HUNDRED FORTY-ONE FEET.
THANK YOU, ALEXA.
YOU'RE NOT WELCOME.
©2023, BABY BLUES BROS LLC DIST. BY ANDREWS McMEEL SYNDICATION 6-7
KIRKMAN & SCOTT
TOMORROW IT'S **YOUR** TURN TO BE THE CHATBOT.
WE HAVE THE STINGIEST PARENTS IN THE WORLD.
SHAKESPEARE

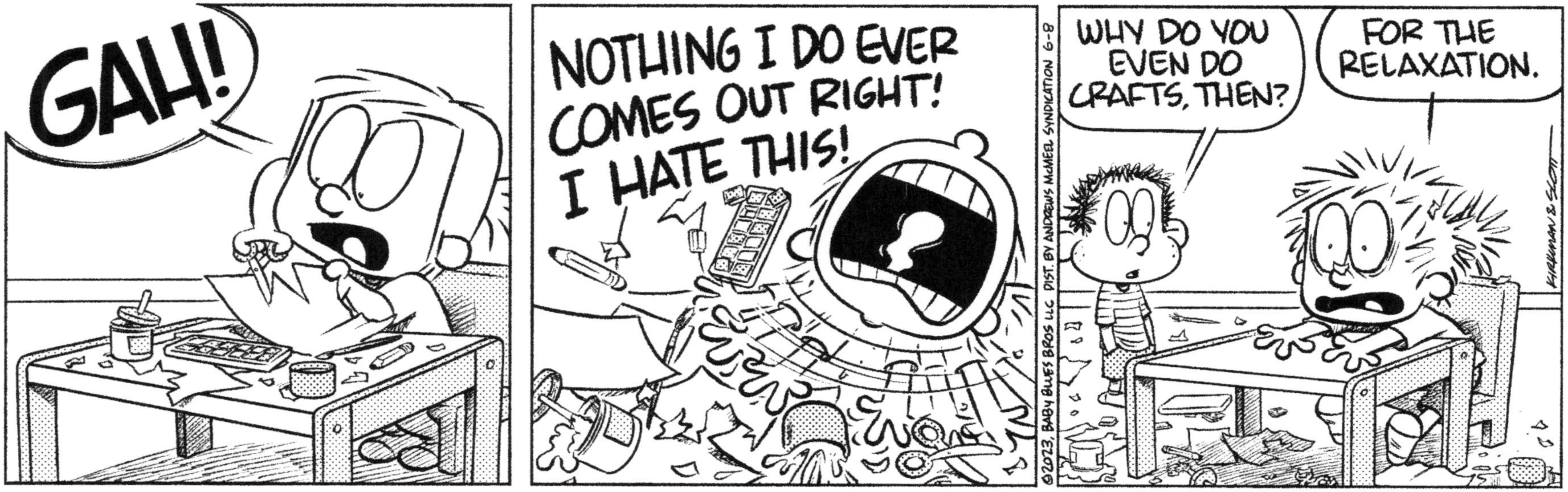
GAH!
NOTHING I DO EVER COMES OUT RIGHT! I HATE THIS!
©2023, BABY BLUES BROS LLC DIST. BY ANDREWS McMEEL SYNDICATION 6-8
WHY DO YOU EVEN DO CRAFTS, THEN?
FOR THE RELAXATION.
KIRKMAN & SCOTT

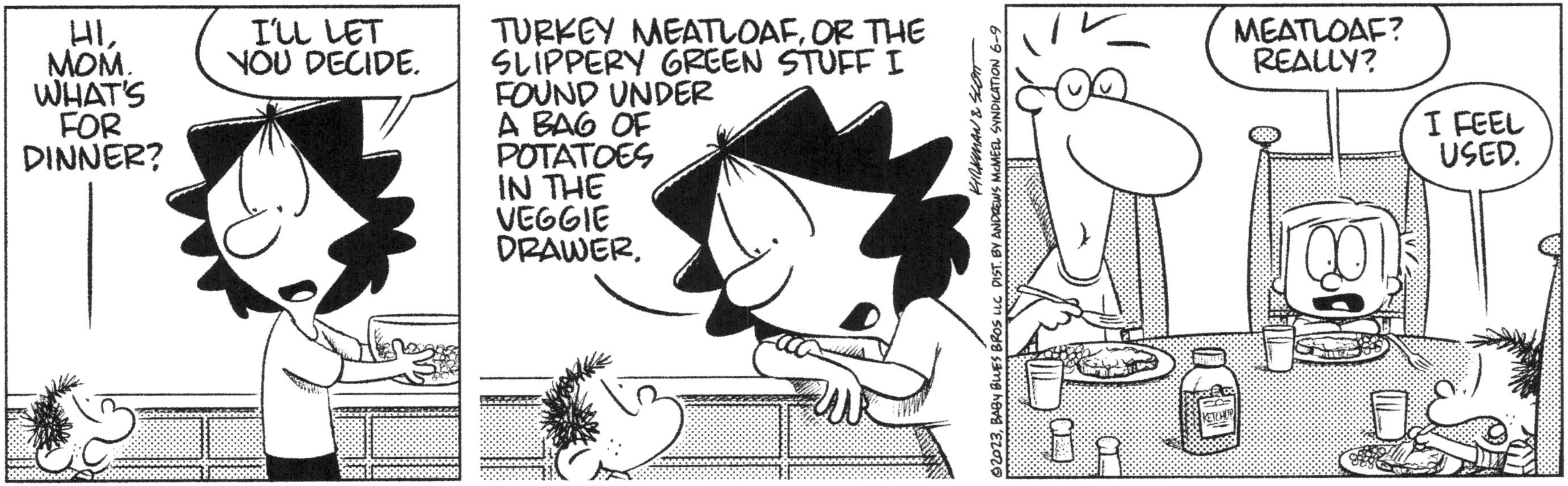
HI, MOM. WHAT'S FOR DINNER?
I'LL LET YOU DECIDE.
TURKEY MEATLOAF, OR THE SLIPPERY GREEN STUFF I FOUND UNDER A BAG OF POTATOES IN THE VEGGIE DRAWER.
KIRKMAN & SCOTT
©2023, BABY BLUES BROS LLC DIST. BY ANDREWS MCMEEL SYNDICATION 6-9
MEATLOAF? REALLY?
I FEEL USED.
KETCHUP

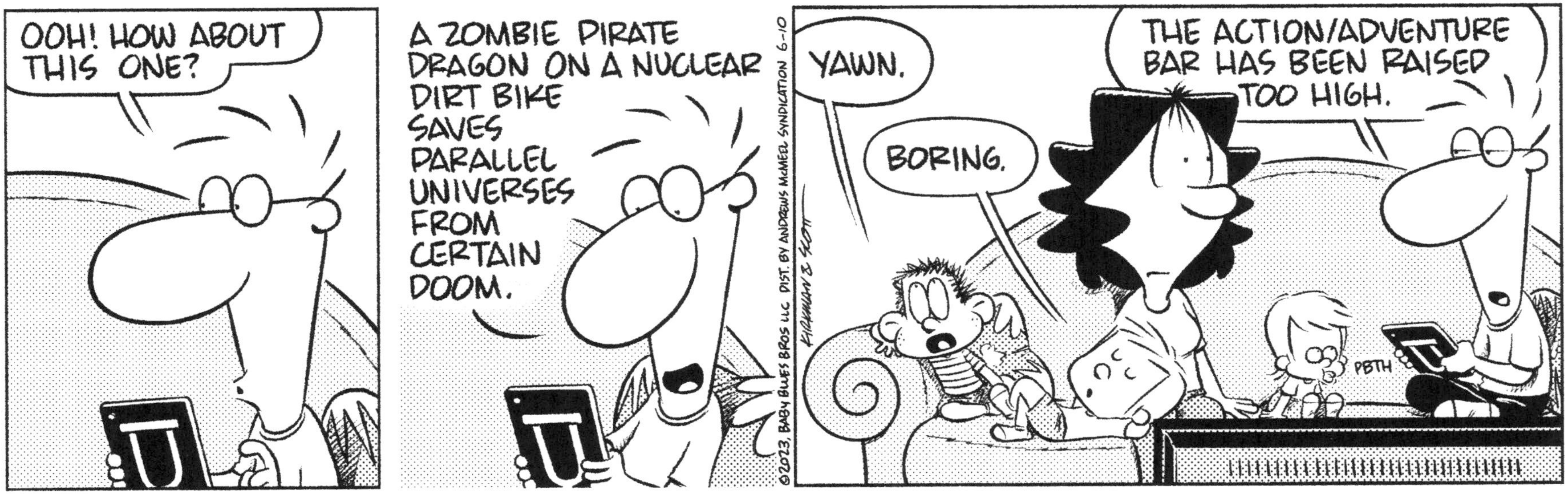
OOH! HOW ABOUT THIS ONE?
A ZOMBIE PIRATE DRAGON ON A NUCLEAR DIRT BIKE SAVES PARALLEL UNIVERSES FROM CERTAIN DOOM.
KIRKMAN & SCOTT
©2023, BABY BLUES BROS LLC DIST. BY ANDREWS MCMEEL SYNDICATION 6-10
YAWN.
BORING.
THE ACTION/ADVENTURE BAR HAS BEEN RAISED TOO HIGH.
PBTH

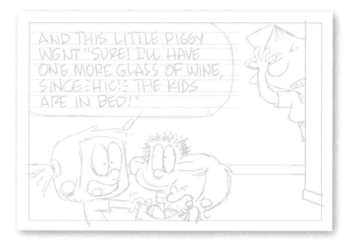

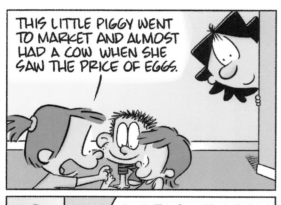

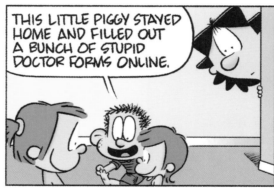

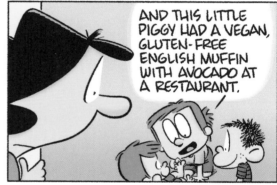

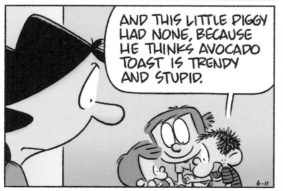

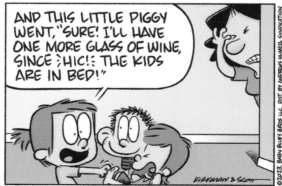

AND THIS LITTLE PIGGY WENT "SURE! I'LL HAVE ONE MORE GLASS OF WINE, SINCE ⋮HIC!⋮ THE KIDS ARE IN BED!"

THIS LITTLE PIGGY WENT TO MARKET AND ALMOST HAD A COW WHEN SHE SAW THE PRICE OF EGGS.
THIS LITTLE PIGGY STAYED HOME AND FILLED OUT A BUNCH OF STUPID DOCTOR FORMS ONLINE.
AND THIS LITTLE PIGGY HAD A VEGAN, GLUTEN-FREE ENGLISH MUFFIN WITH AVOCADO AT A RESTAURANT.
AND THIS LITTLE PIGGY HAD NONE, BECAUSE HE THINKS AVOCADO TOAST IS TRENDY AND STUPID.
6-11
AND THIS LITTLE PIGGY WENT, "SURE! I'LL HAVE ONE MORE GLASS OF WINE, SINCE ⋮HIC!⋮ THE KIDS ARE IN BED!"
KIRKMAN & SCOTT
©2023, BABY BLUES BROS LLC. DIST. BY ANDREWS MCMEEL SYNDICATION
REMEMBER WHEN I SAID THAT OUR CHILDREN NEVER PAY ATTENTION TO ANYTHING WE SAY?

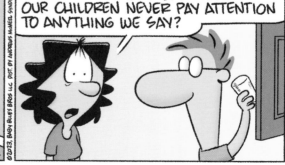

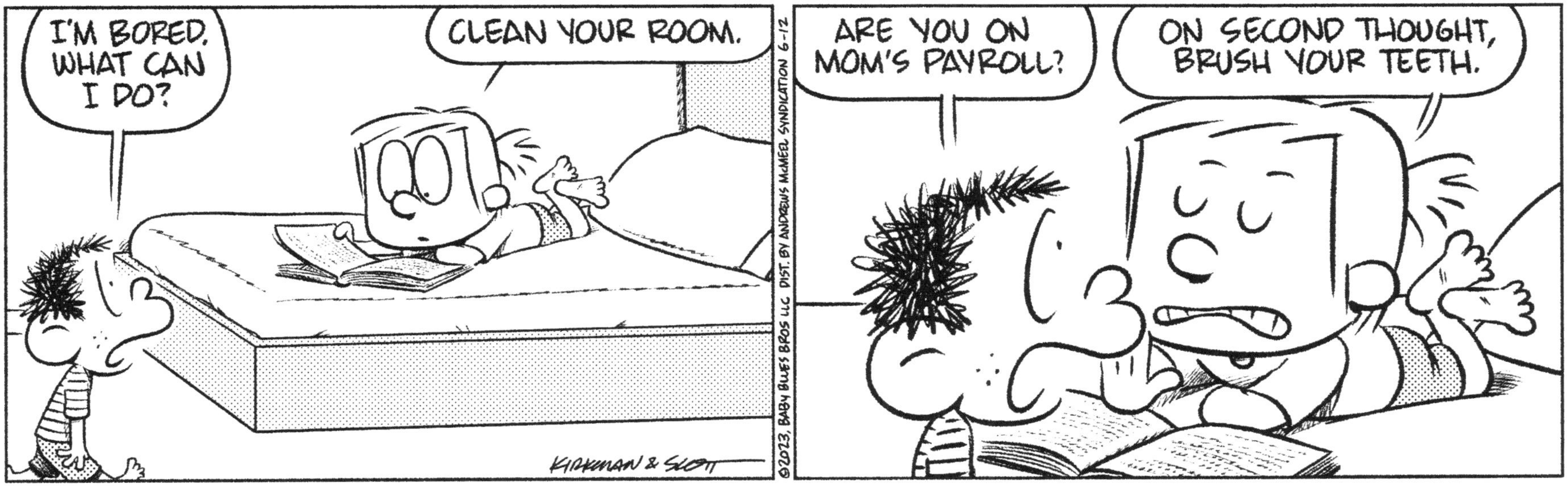
I'M BORED. WHAT CAN I DO?
CLEAN YOUR ROOM.
KIRKMAN & SCOTT
©2023, BABY BLUES BROS LLC DIST. BY ANDREWS McMEEL SYNDICATION 6-12
ARE YOU ON MOM'S PAYROLL?
ON SECOND THOUGHT, BRUSH YOUR TEETH.

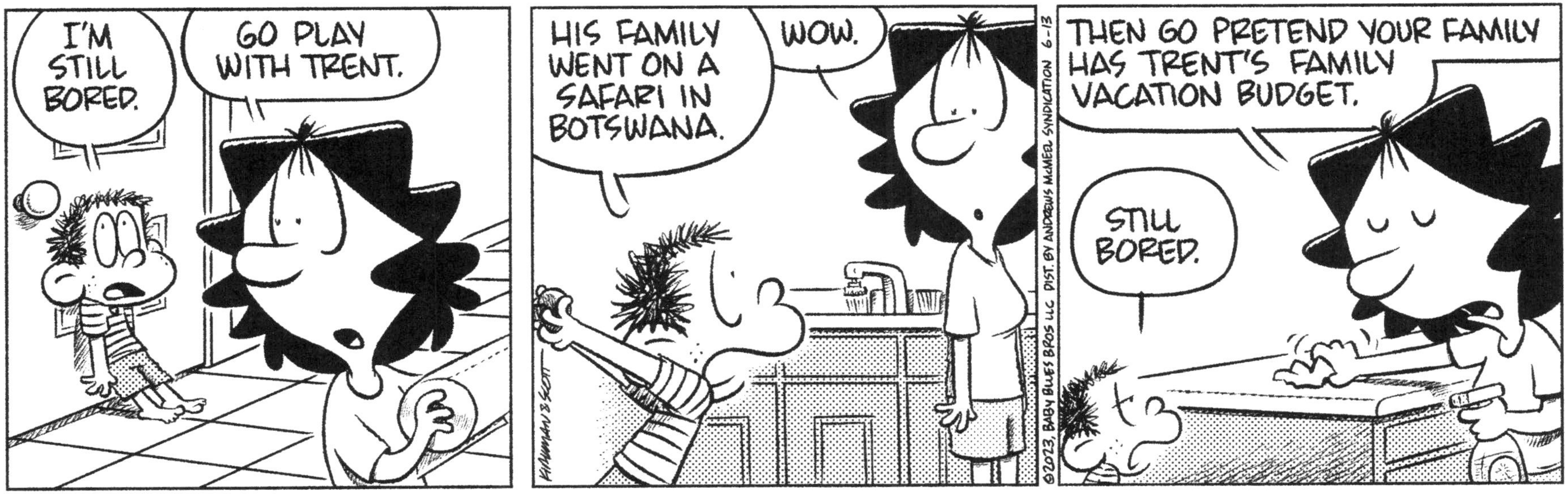
I'M STILL BORED.
GO PLAY WITH TRENT.
HIS FAMILY WENT ON A SAFARI IN BOTSWANA.
WOW.
KIRKMAN & SCOTT
©2023, BABY BLUES BROS LLC DIST. BY ANDREWS McMEEL SYNDICATION 6-13
THEN GO PRETEND YOUR FAMILY HAS TRENT'S FAMILY VACATION BUDGET.
STILL BORED.

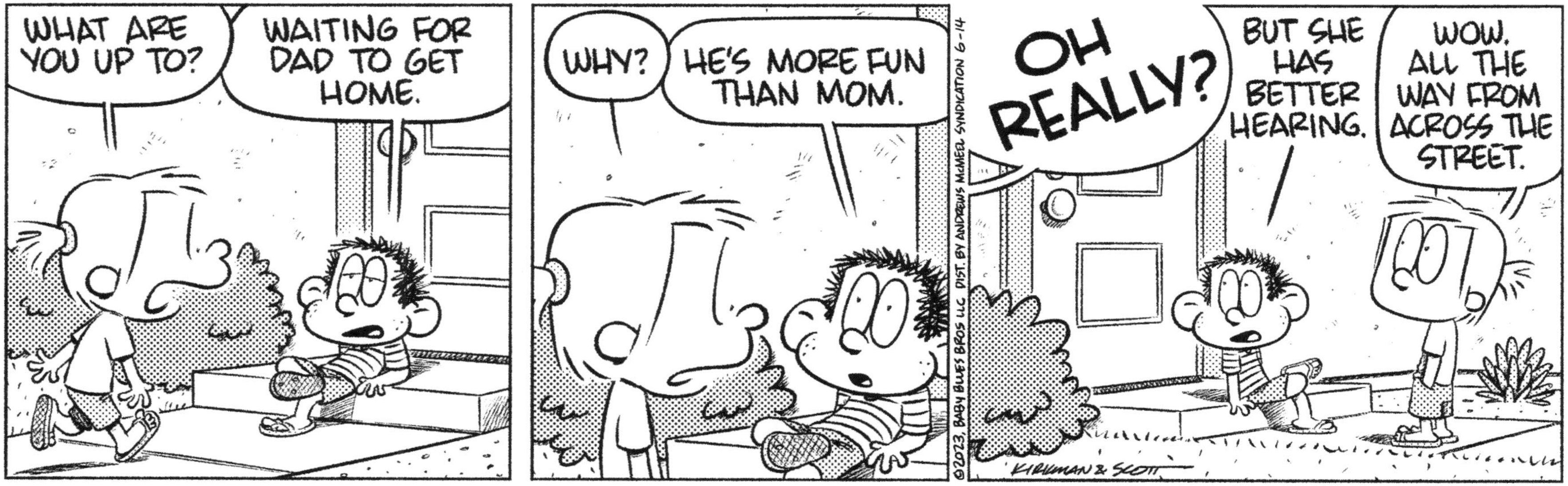
WHAT ARE YOU UP TO?
WAITING FOR DAD TO GET HOME.
WHY?
HE'S MORE FUN THAN MOM.
©2023, BABY BLUES BROS LLC DIST. BY ANDREWS McMEEL SYNDICATION 6-14
OH REALLY?
BUT SHE HAS BETTER HEARING.
WOW. ALL THE WAY FROM ACROSS THE STREET.
KIRKMAN & SCOTT

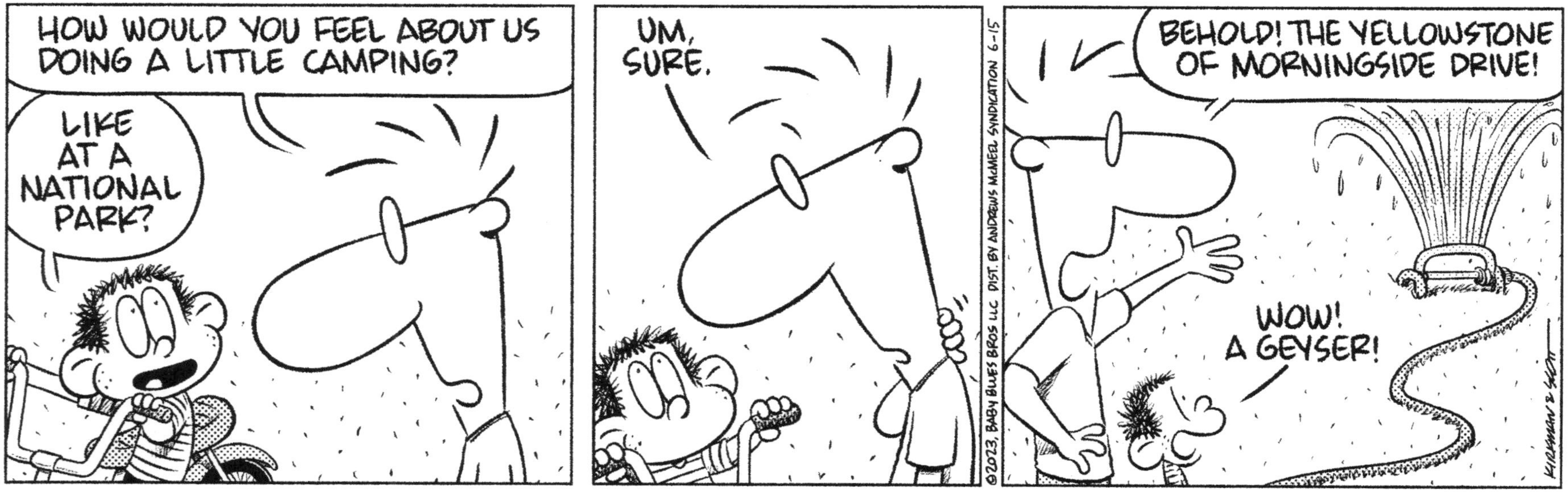
HOW WOULD YOU FEEL ABOUT US DOING A LITTLE CAMPING?
LIKE AT A NATIONAL PARK?
UM, SURE.
©2023, BABY BLUES BROS LLC DIST. BY ANDREWS McMEEL SYNDICATION 6-15
BEHOLD! THE YELLOWSTONE OF MORNINGSIDE DRIVE!
WOW! A GEYSER!
KIRKMAN & SCOTT

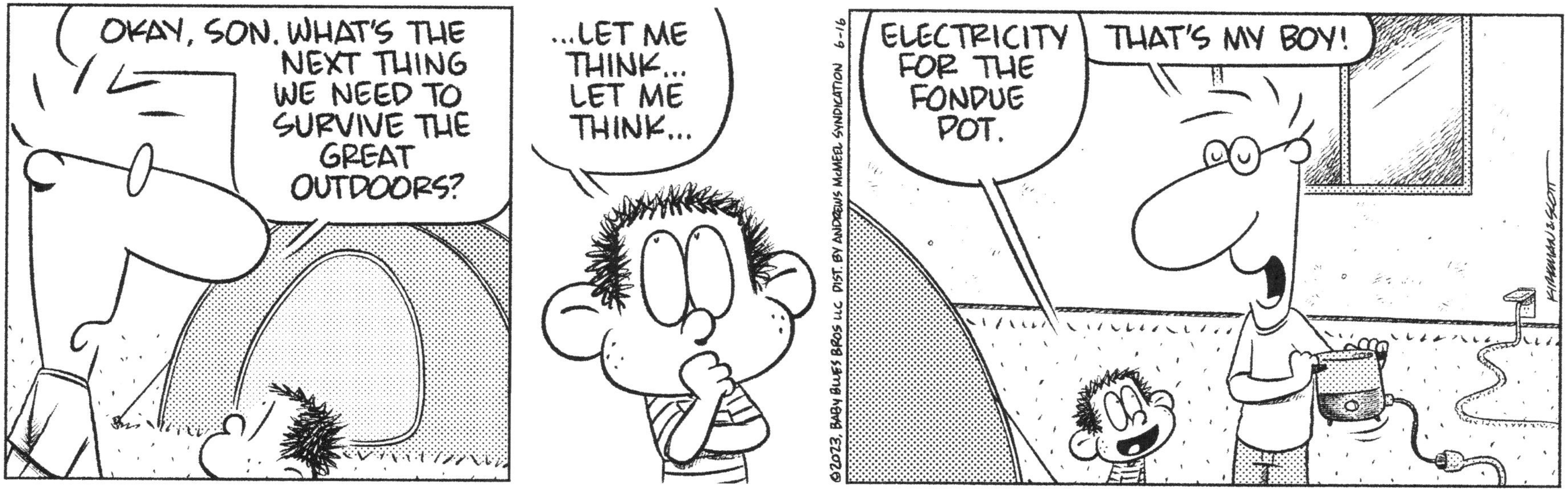
OKAY, SON. WHAT'S THE NEXT THING WE NEED TO SURVIVE THE GREAT OUTDOORS?
...LET ME THINK... LET ME THINK...
©2023, BABY BLUES BROS LLC DIST. BY ANDREWS McMEEL SYNDICATION 6-16
ELECTRICITY FOR THE FONDUE POT.
THAT'S MY BOY!
KIRKMAN & SCOTT

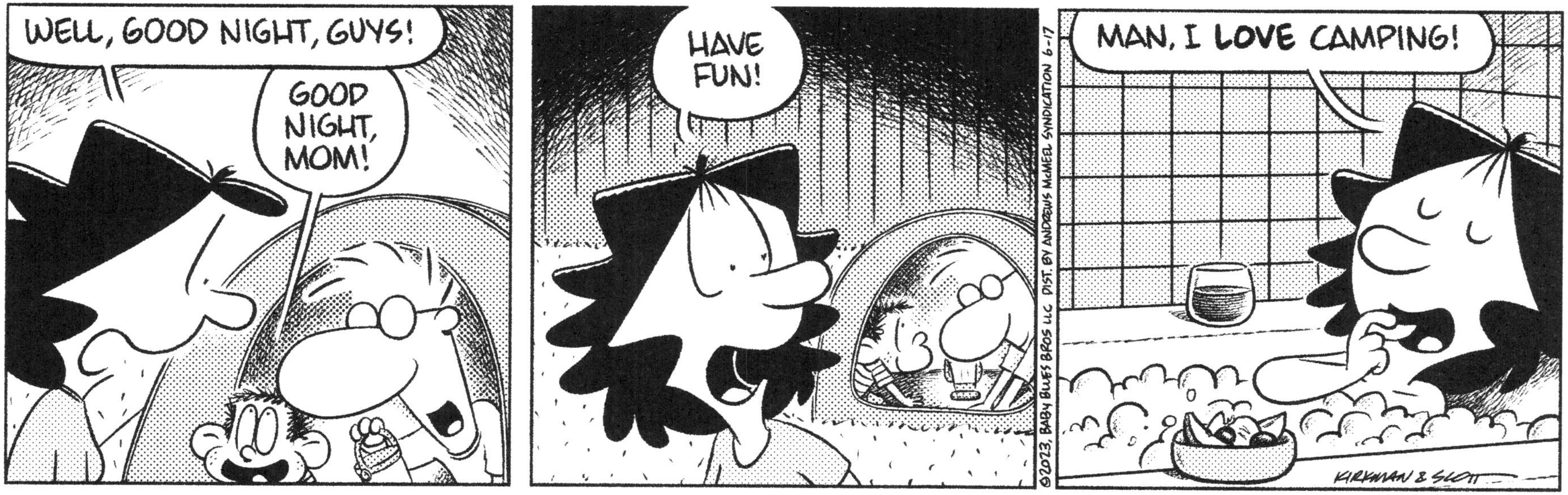
WELL, GOOD NIGHT, GUYS!
GOOD NIGHT, MOM!
HAVE FUN!
©2023, BABY BLUES BROS LLC DIST. BY ANDREWS McMEEL SYNDICATION 6-17
MAN, I **LOVE** CAMPING!
KIRKMAN & SCOTT

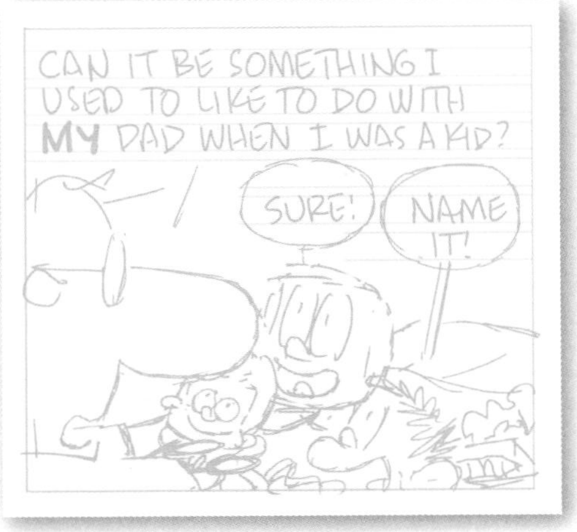
CAN IT BE SOMETHING I USED TO LIKE TO DO WITH **MY** DAD WHEN I WAS A KID?
SURE!
NAME IT!

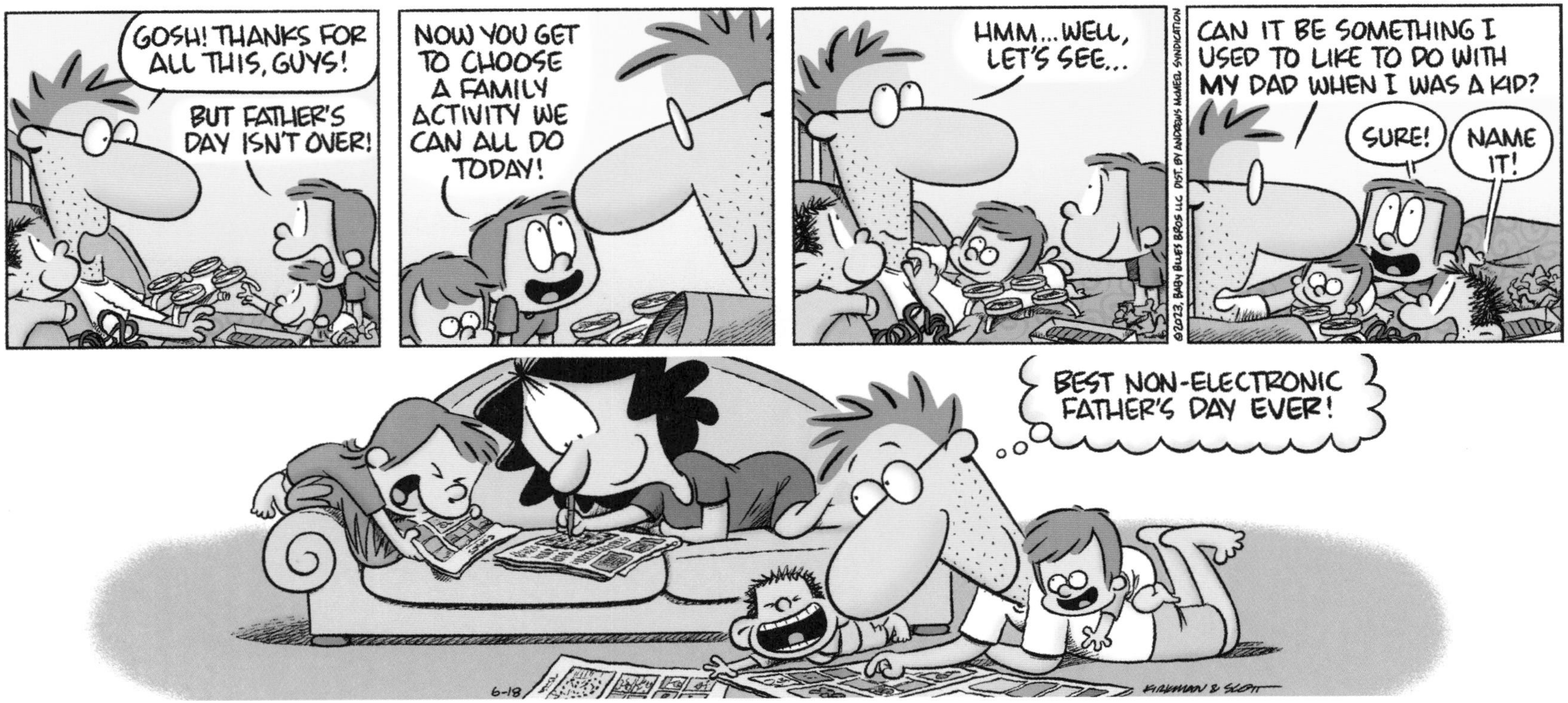
GOSH! THANKS FOR ALL THIS, GUYS!
BUT FATHER'S DAY ISN'T OVER!
NOW YOU GET TO CHOOSE A FAMILY ACTIVITY WE CAN ALL DO TODAY!
HMM... WELL, LET'S SEE...
©2013, BABY BLUES BROS LLC. DIST. BY ANDREWS McMEEL SYNDICATION
CAN IT BE SOMETHING I USED TO LIKE TO DO WITH **MY** DAD WHEN I WAS A KID?
SURE!
NAME IT!
BEST NON-ELECTRONIC FATHER'S DAY EVER!
6-18
KIRKMAN & SCOTT

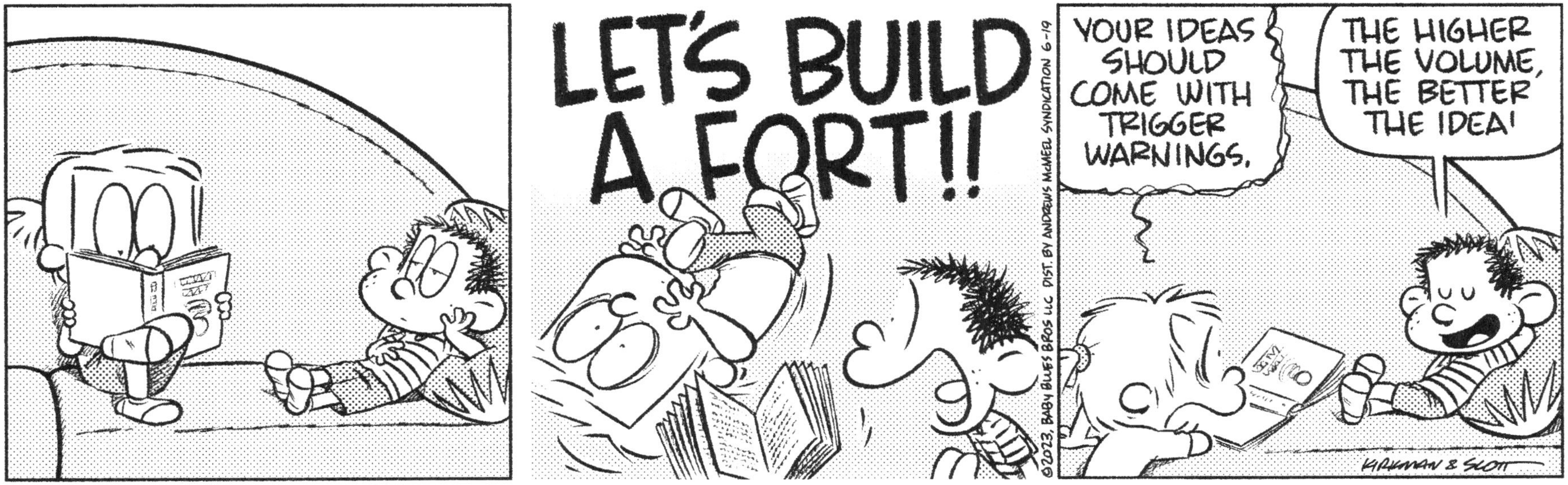
LET'S BUILD A FORT!!
©2023, BABY BLUES BROS LLC DIST. BY ANDREWS McMEEL SYNDICATION 6-19
YOUR IDEAS SHOULD COME WITH TRIGGER WARNINGS.
THE HIGHER THE VOLUME, THE BETTER THE IDEA!
KIRKMAN & SCOTT

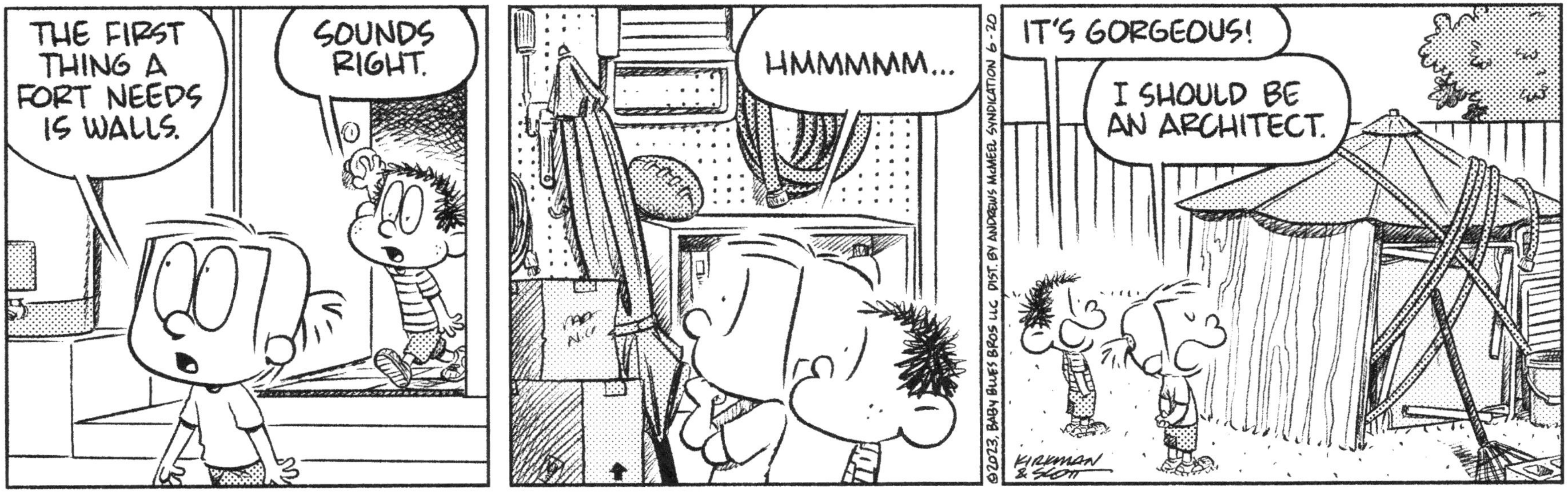
THE FIRST THING A FORT NEEDS IS WALLS.
SOUNDS RIGHT.
HMMMMM...
©2023, BABY BLUES BROS LLC DIST. BY ANDREWS McMEEL SYNDICATION 6-20
IT'S GORGEOUS!
I SHOULD BE AN ARCHITECT.
KIRKMAN & SCOTT

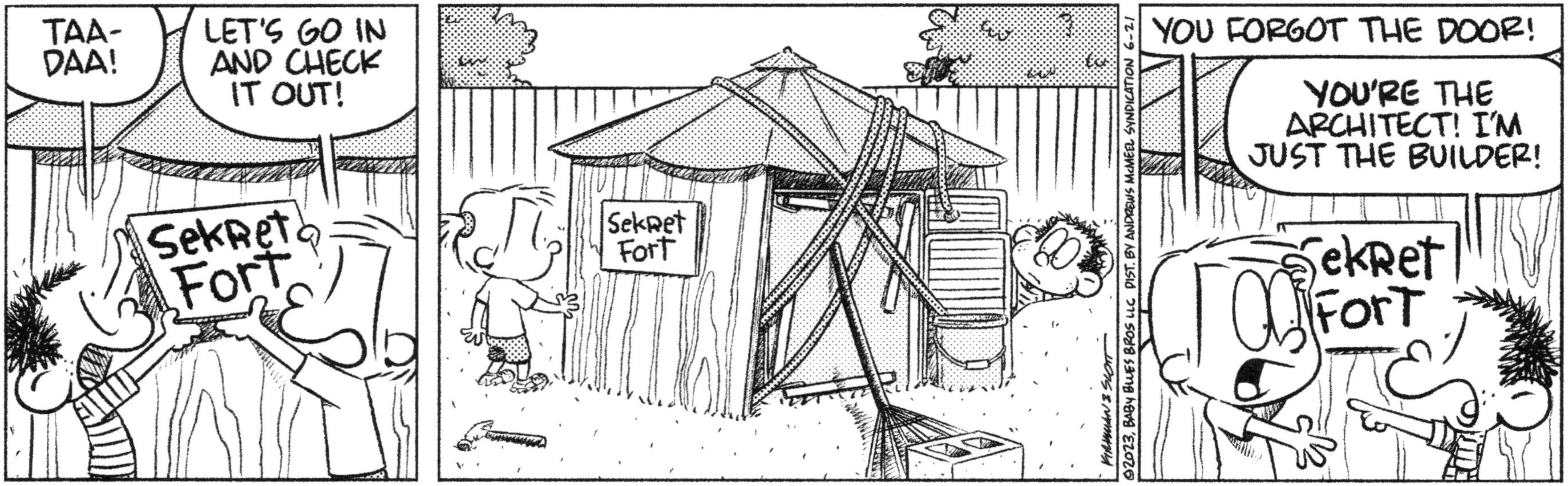
TAA-DAA!
LET'S GO IN AND CHECK IT OUT!
SekRet Fort
SekRet Fort
©2023, BABY BLUES BROS LLC DIST. BY ANDREWS McMEEL SYNDICATION 6-21
KIRKMAN & SCOTT
YOU FORGOT THE DOOR!
YOU'RE THE ARCHITECT! I'M JUST THE BUILDER!
SekRet FoRT

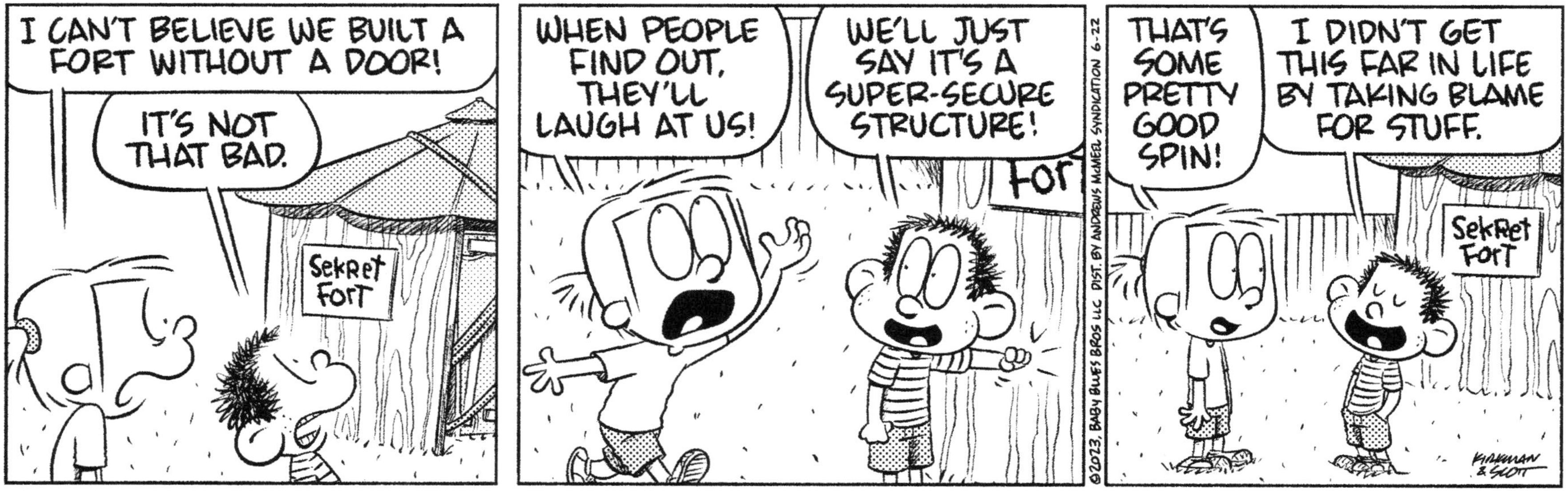
I CAN'T BELIEVE WE BUILT A FORT WITHOUT A DOOR!
IT'S NOT THAT BAD.
SekRet FoRT
WHEN PEOPLE FIND OUT, THEY'LL LAUGH AT US!
WE'LL JUST SAY IT'S A SUPER-SECURE STRUCTURE!
©2023, BABY BLUES BROS LLC DIST. BY ANDREWS McMEEL SYNDICATION 6-22
THAT'S SOME PRETTY GOOD SPIN!
I DIDN'T GET THIS FAR IN LIFE BY TAKING BLAME FOR STUFF.
SekRet FoRT
KIRKMAN & SCOTT

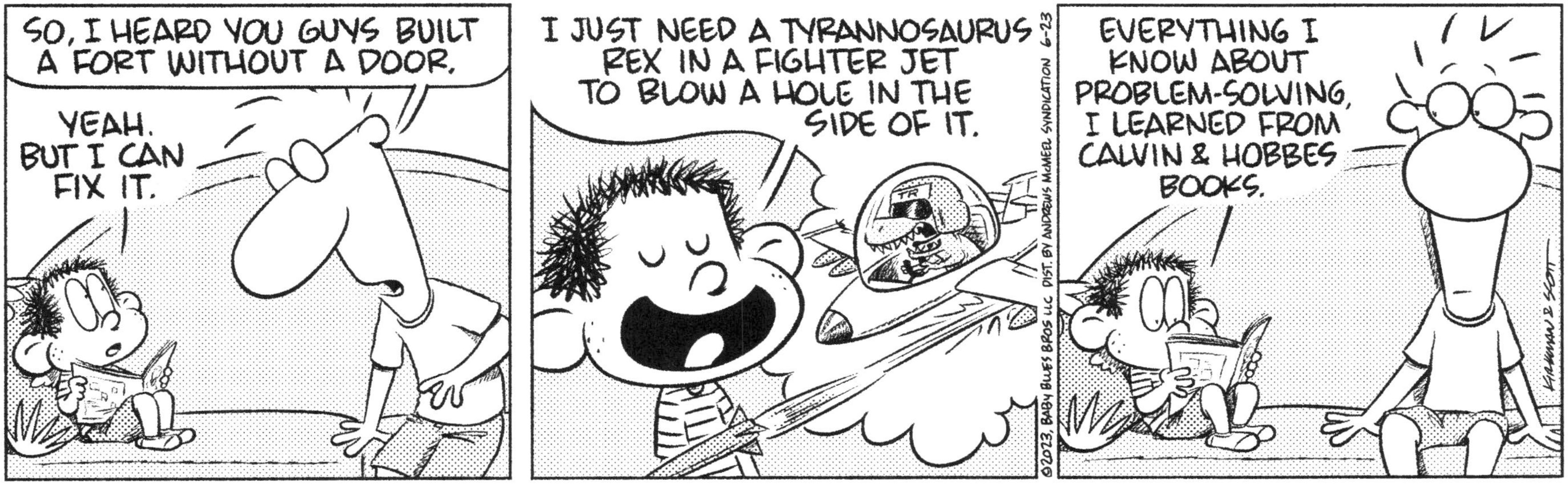
SO, I HEARD YOU GUYS BUILT A FORT WITHOUT A DOOR.
YEAH. BUT I CAN FIX IT.
I JUST NEED A TYRANNOSAURUS REX IN A FIGHTER JET TO BLOW A HOLE IN THE SIDE OF IT.
TR
©2023, BABY BLUES BROS LLC DIST. BY ANDREWS McMEEL SYNDICATION 6-23
EVERYTHING I KNOW ABOUT PROBLEM-SOLVING, I LEARNED FROM CALVIN & HOBBES BOOKS.
KIRKMAN & SCOTT

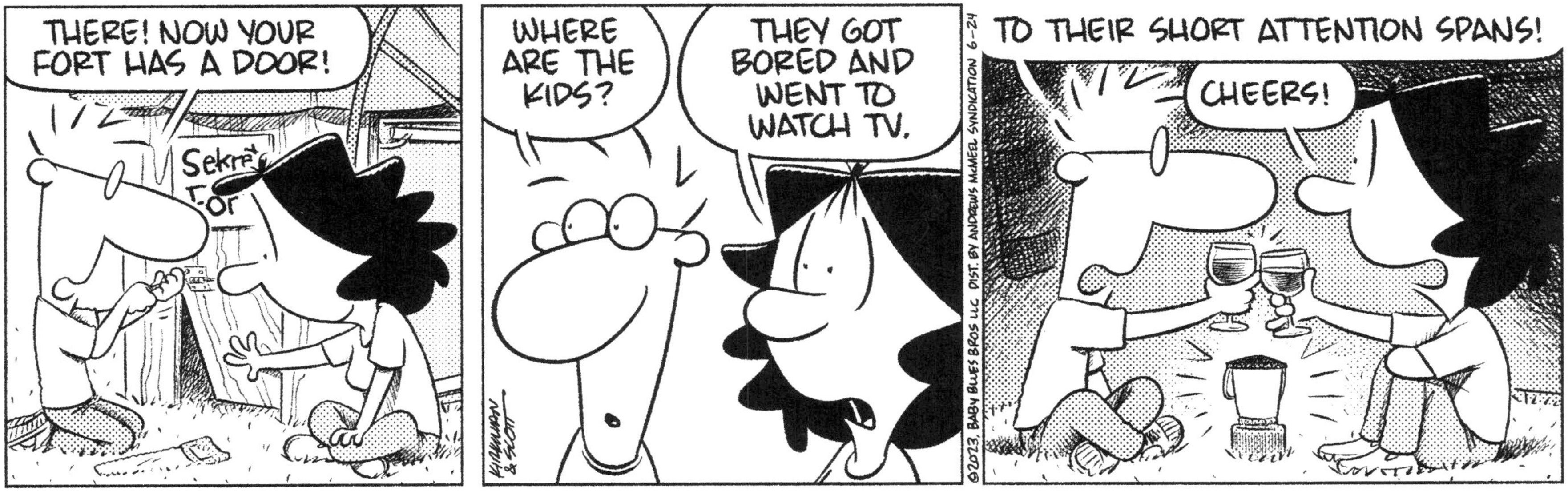
THERE! NOW YOUR FORT HAS A DOOR!
KIRKMAN & SCOTT
WHERE ARE THE KIDS?
THEY GOT BORED AND WENT TO WATCH TV.
©2023, BABY BLUES BROS LLC DIST. BY ANDREWS McMEEL SYNDICATION 6-24
TO THEIR SHORT ATTENTION SPANS!
CHEERS!

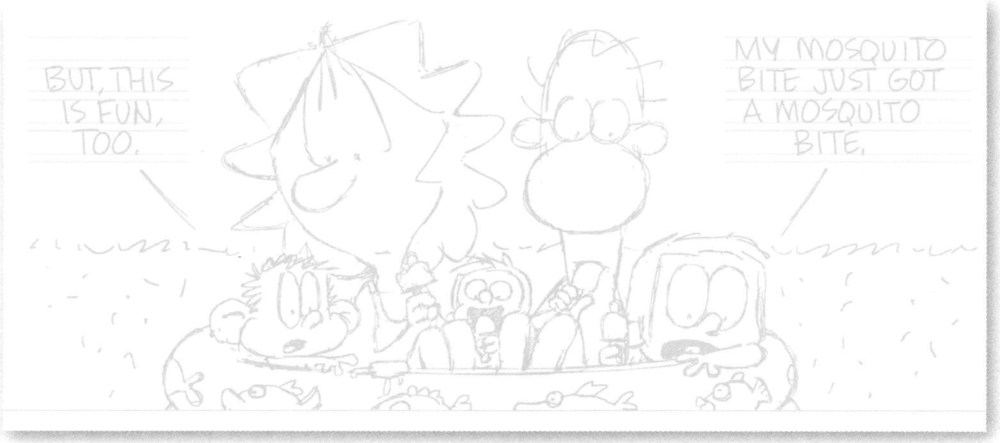
BUT, THIS IS FUN, TOO.
MY MOSQUITO BITE JUST GOT A MOSQUITO BITE.

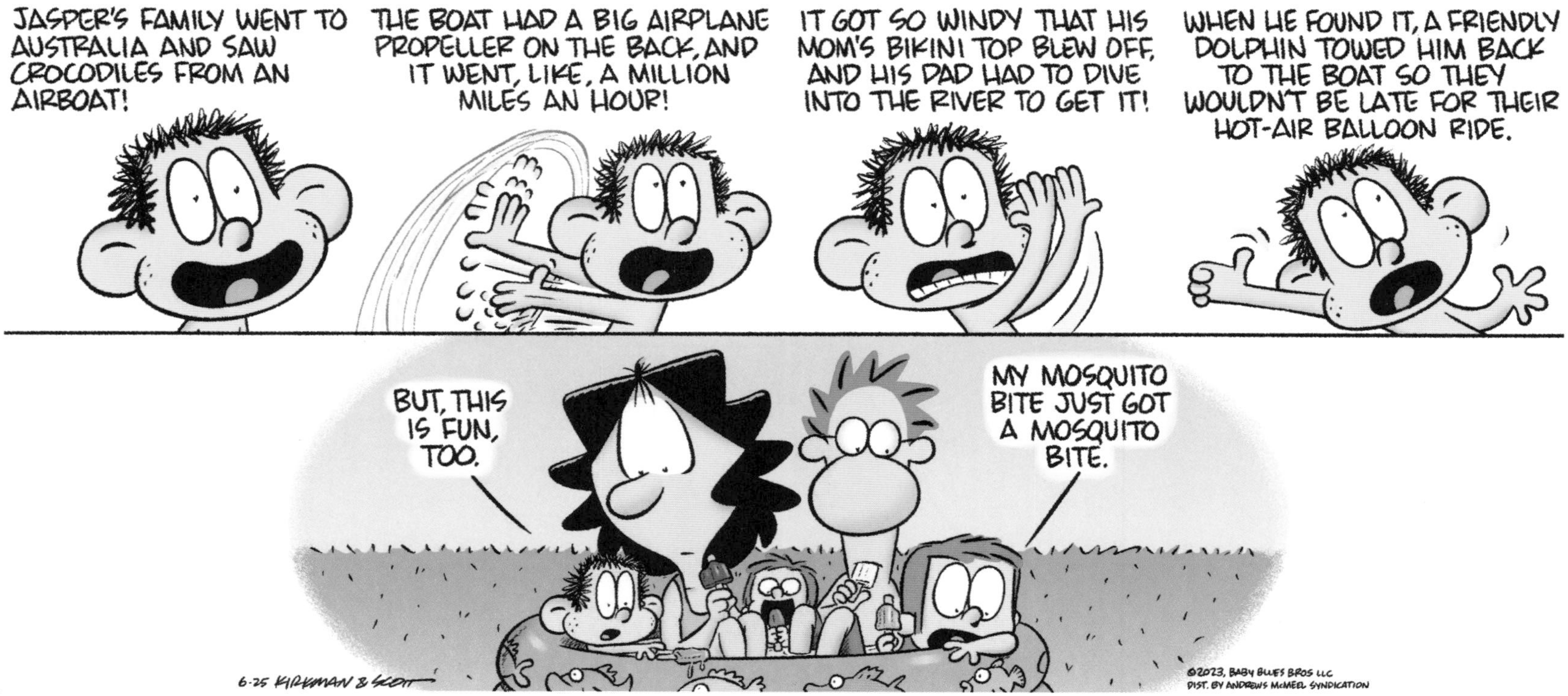
JASPER'S FAMILY WENT TO AUSTRALIA AND SAW CROCODILES FROM AN AIRBOAT!
THE BOAT HAD A BIG AIRPLANE PROPELLER ON THE BACK, AND IT WENT, LIKE, A MILLION MILES AN HOUR!
IT GOT SO WINDY THAT HIS MOM'S BIKINI TOP BLEW OFF, AND HIS DAD HAD TO DIVE INTO THE RIVER TO GET IT!
WHEN HE FOUND IT, A FRIENDLY DOLPHIN TOWED HIM BACK TO THE BOAT SO THEY WOULDN'T BE LATE FOR THEIR HOT-AIR BALLOON RIDE.
BUT, THIS IS FUN, TOO.
MY MOSQUITO BITE JUST GOT A MOSQUITO BITE.
6-25 KIRKMAN & SCOTT
©2023, BABY BLUES BROS LLC
DIST. BY ANDREWS McMEEL SYNDICATION

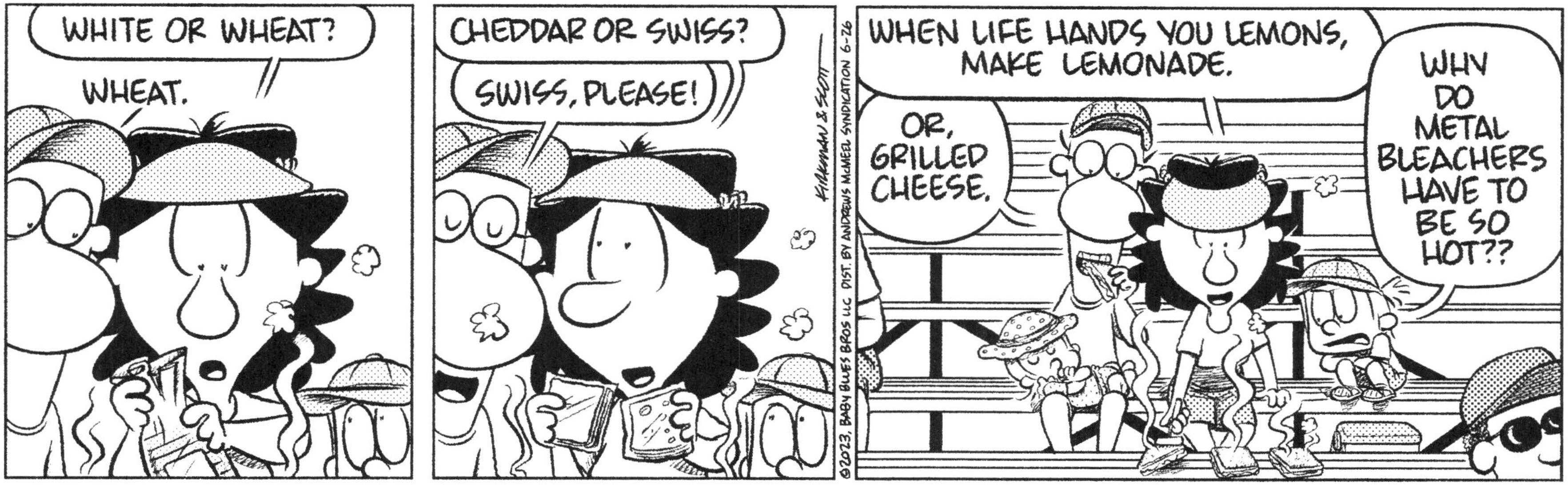
WHITE OR WHEAT?
WHEAT.
CHEDDAR OR SWISS?
SWISS, PLEASE!
KIRKMAN & SCOTT
©2023, BABY BLUES BROS LLC DIST. BY ANDREWS MCMEEL SYNDICATION 6-26
WHEN LIFE HANDS YOU LEMONS, MAKE LEMONADE.
OR, GRILLED CHEESE.
WHY DO METAL BLEACHERS HAVE TO BE SO HOT??

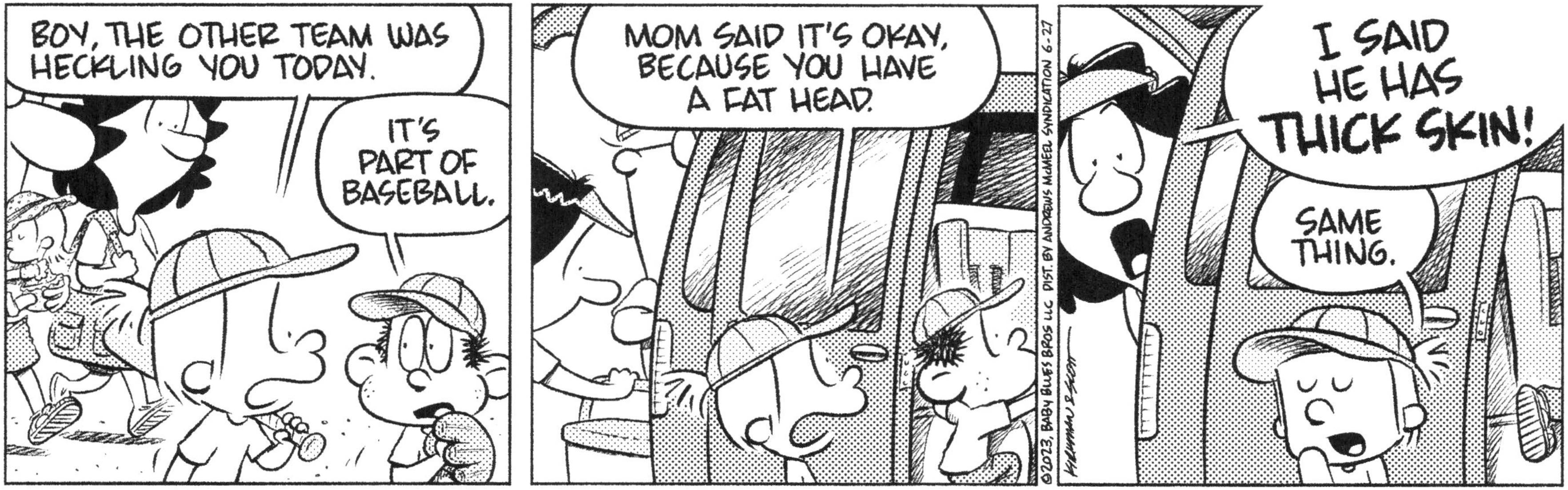
BOY, THE OTHER TEAM WAS HECKLING YOU TODAY.
IT'S PART OF BASEBALL.
MOM SAID IT'S OKAY, BECAUSE YOU HAVE A FAT HEAD.
©2023, BABY BLUES BROS LLC DIST. BY ANDREWS MCMEEL SYNDICATION 6-27
KIRKMAN & SCOTT
I SAID HE HAS THICK SKIN!
SAME THING.

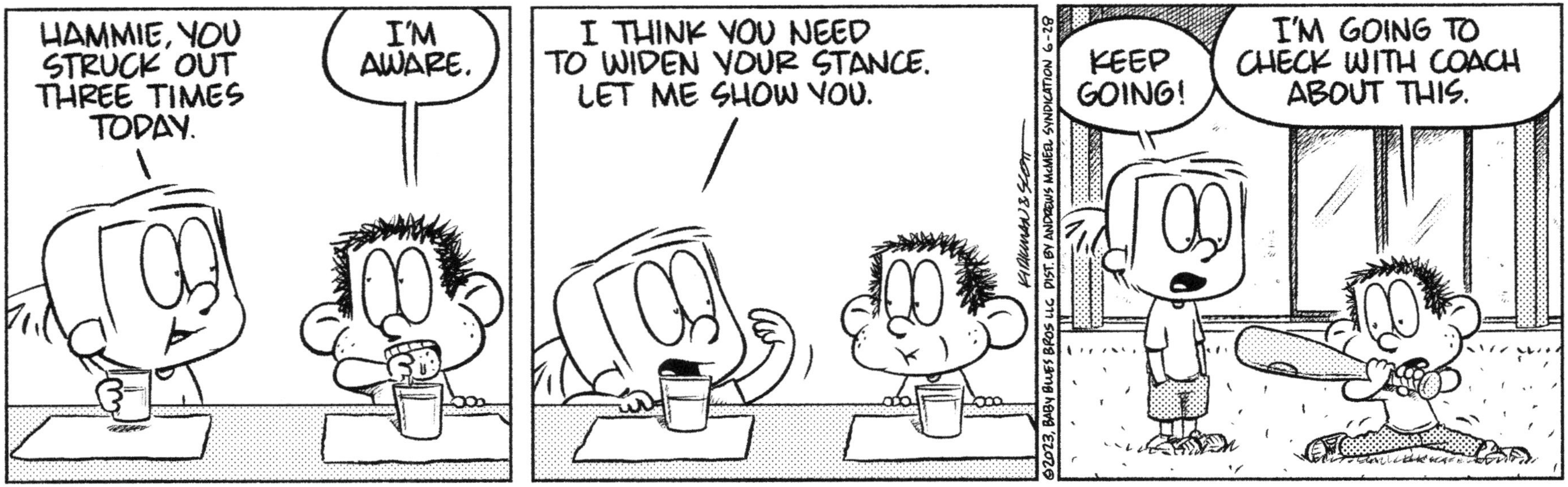
HAMMIE, YOU STRUCK OUT THREE TIMES TODAY.
I'M AWARE.
I THINK YOU NEED TO WIDEN YOUR STANCE. LET ME SHOW YOU.
KEEP GOING!
I'M GOING TO CHECK WITH COACH ABOUT THIS.
©2023, BABY BLUES BROS LLC DIST. BY ANDREWS MCMEEL SYNDICATION 6-28
KIRKMAN & SCOTT

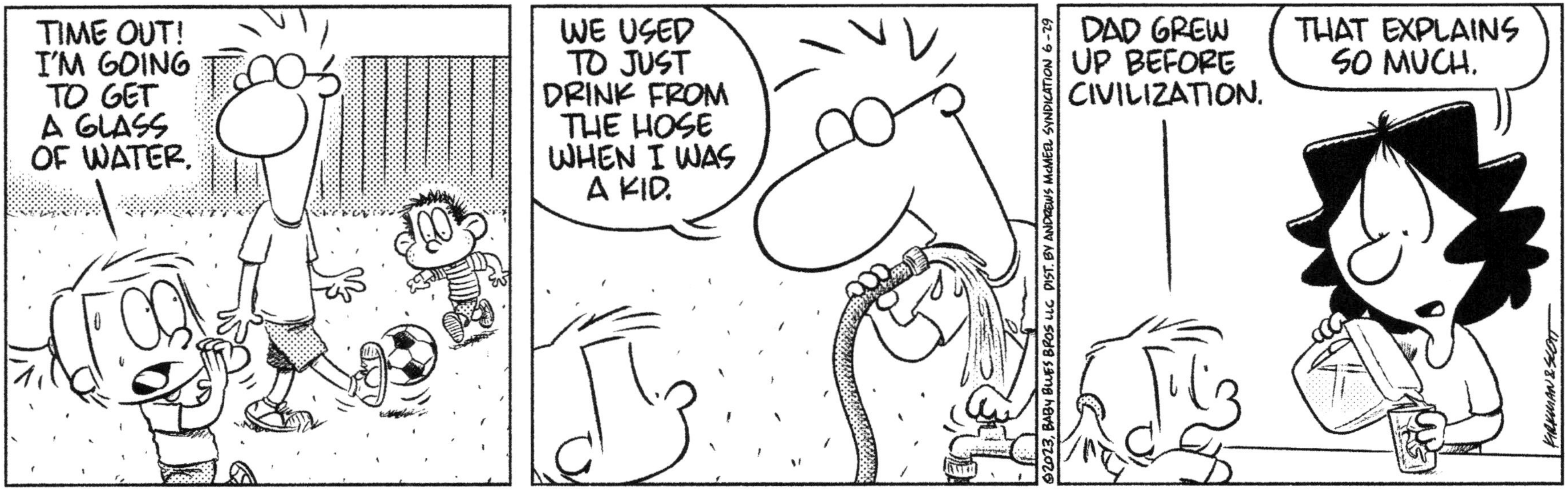
TIME OUT! I'M GOING TO GET A GLASS OF WATER.
WE USED TO JUST DRINK FROM THE HOSE WHEN I WAS A KID.
DAD GREW UP BEFORE CIVILIZATION.
THAT EXPLAINS SO MUCH.
©2023, BABY BLUES BROS LLC DIST. BY ANDREWS MCMEEL SYNDICATION 6-29
KIRKMAN & SCOTT

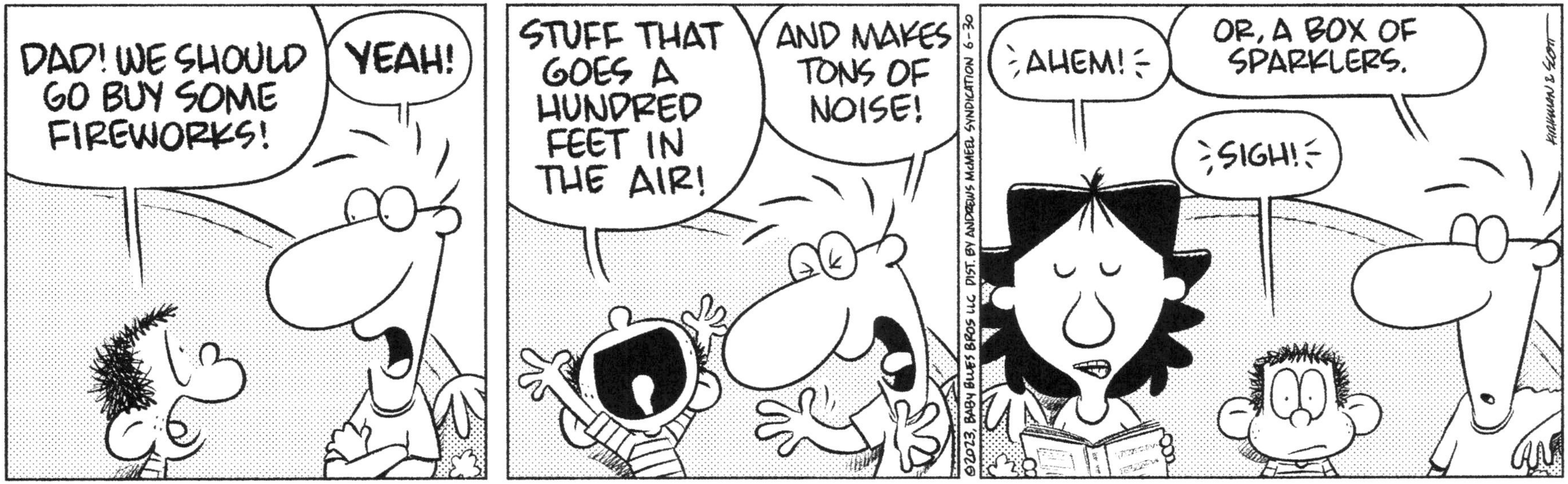
DAD! WE SHOULD GO BUY SOME FIREWORKS!
YEAH!
STUFF THAT GOES A HUNDRED FEET IN THE AIR!
AND MAKES TONS OF NOISE!
©2023, BABY BLUES BROS LLC DIST. BY ANDREWS MCMEEL SYNDICATION 6-30
AHEM!
OR, A BOX OF SPARKLERS.
SIGH!
KIRKMAN & SCOTT

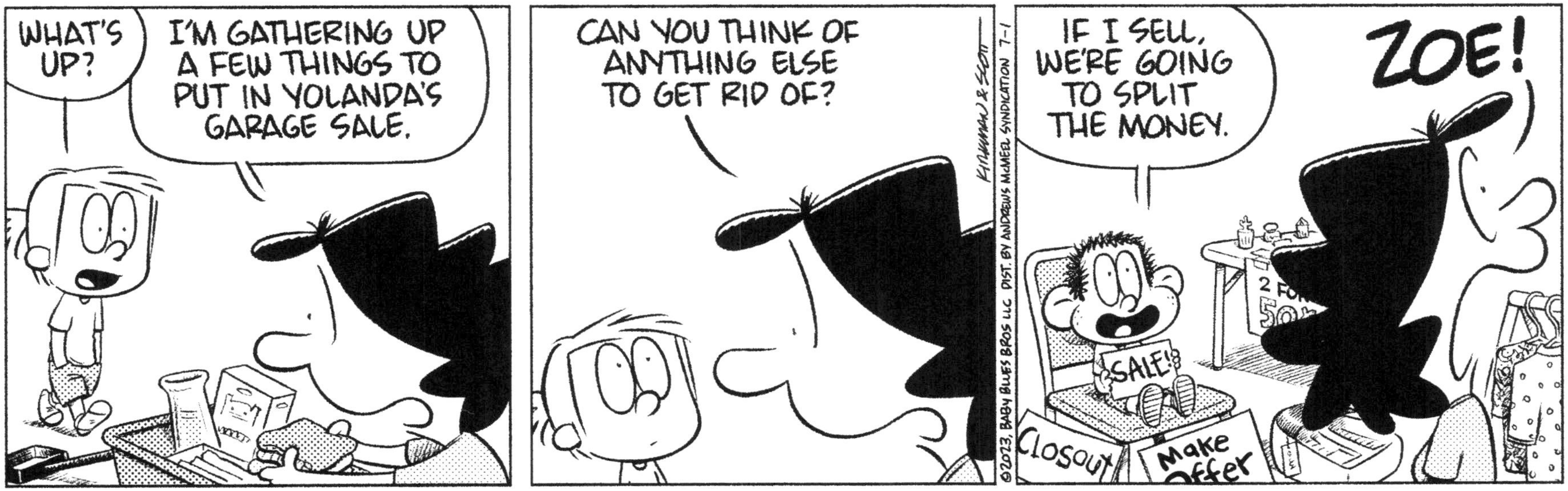
WHAT'S UP?
I'M GATHERING UP A FEW THINGS TO PUT IN YOLANDA'S GARAGE SALE.
CAN YOU THINK OF ANYTHING ELSE TO GET RID OF?
KIRKMAN & SCOTT
©2023, BABY BLUES BROS LLC DIST. BY ANDREWS MCMEEL SYNDICATION 7-1
IF I SELL, WE'RE GOING TO SPLIT THE MONEY.
ZOE!
SALE!
Closeout
Make Offer

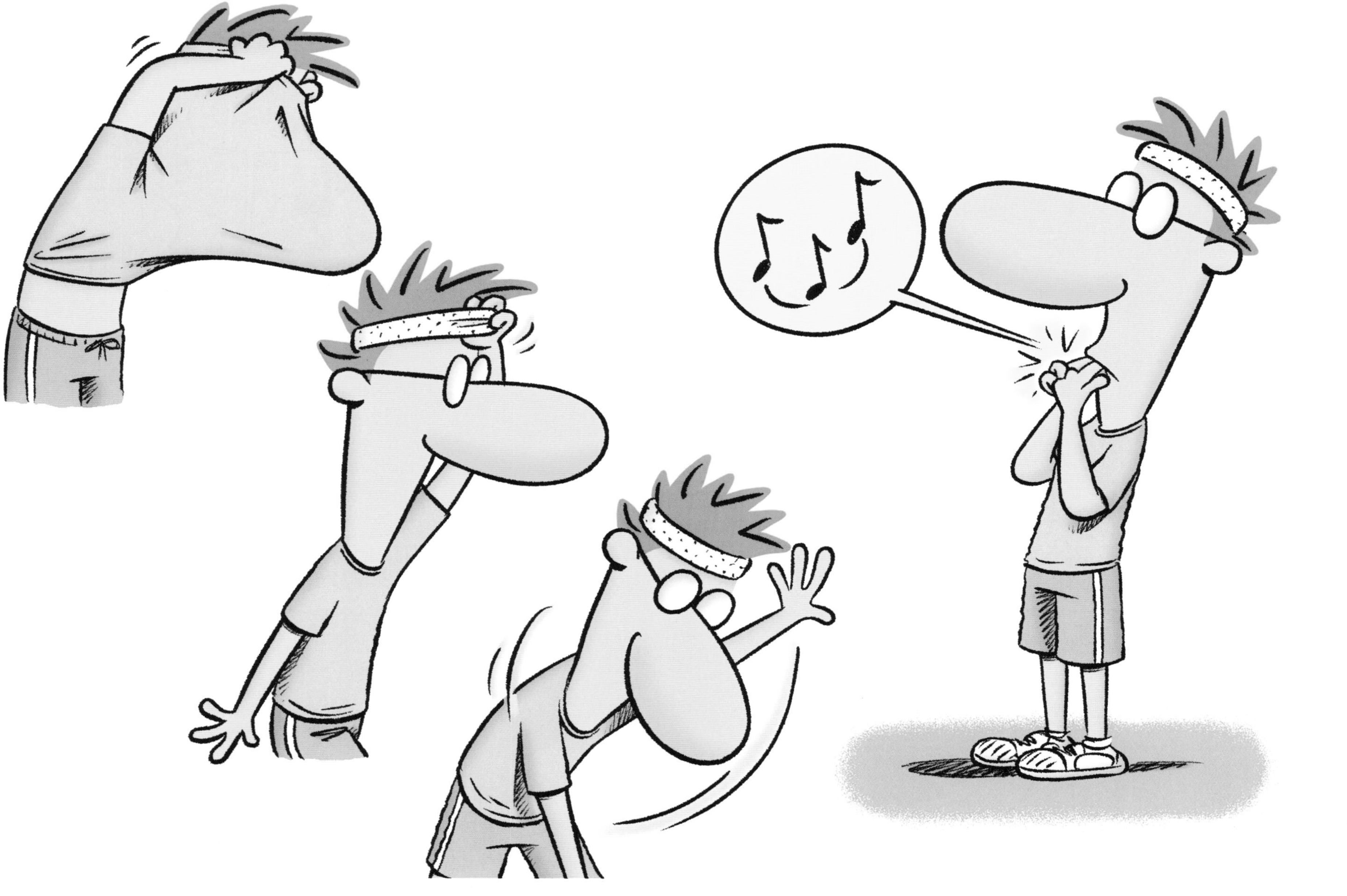

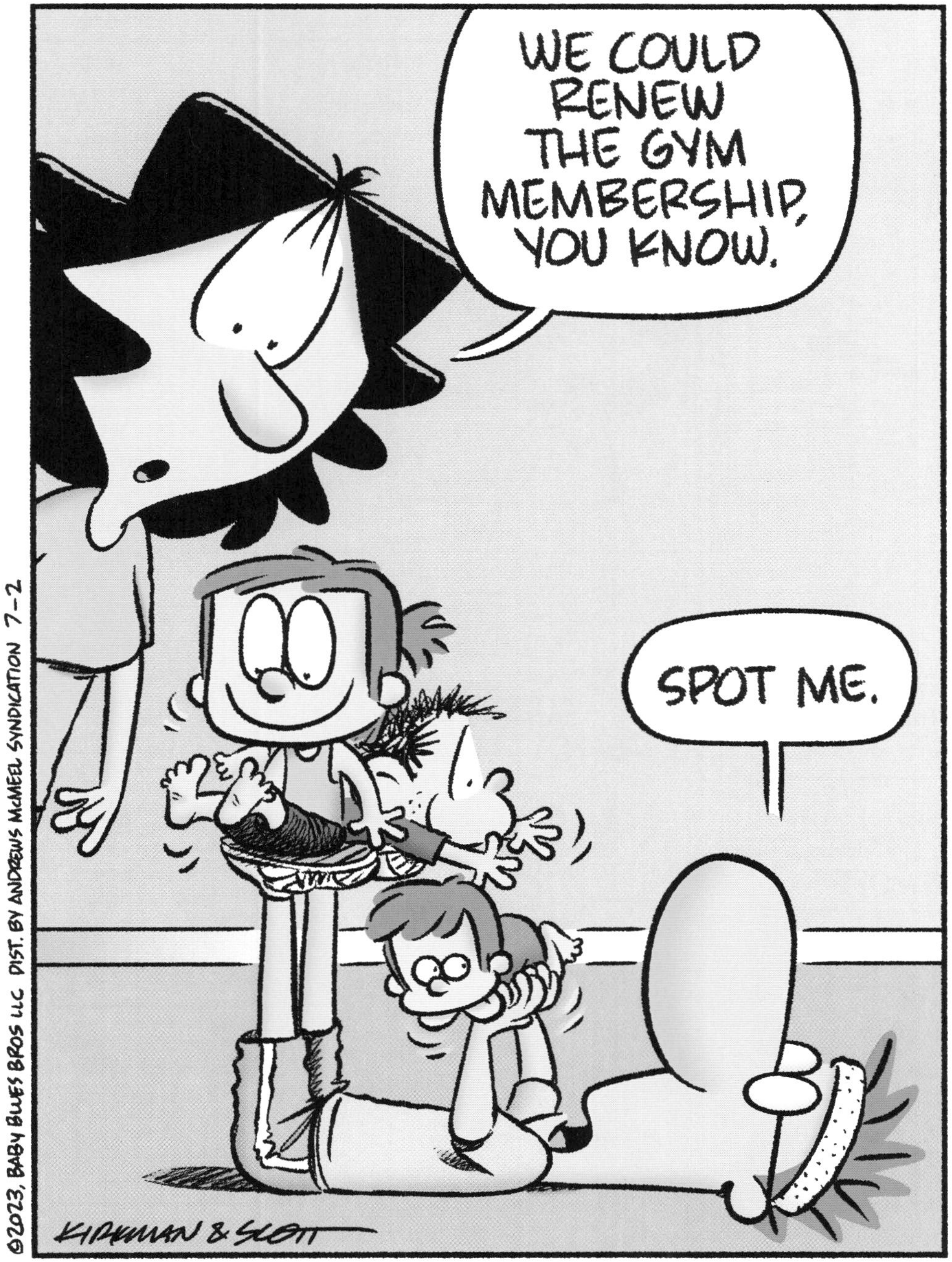
WE COULD RENEW THE GYM MEMBERSHIP, YOU KNOW.
SPOT ME.
KIRKMAN & SCOTT
©2023, BABY BLUES BROS LLC DIST. BY ANDREWS MCMEEL SYNDICATION 7-2

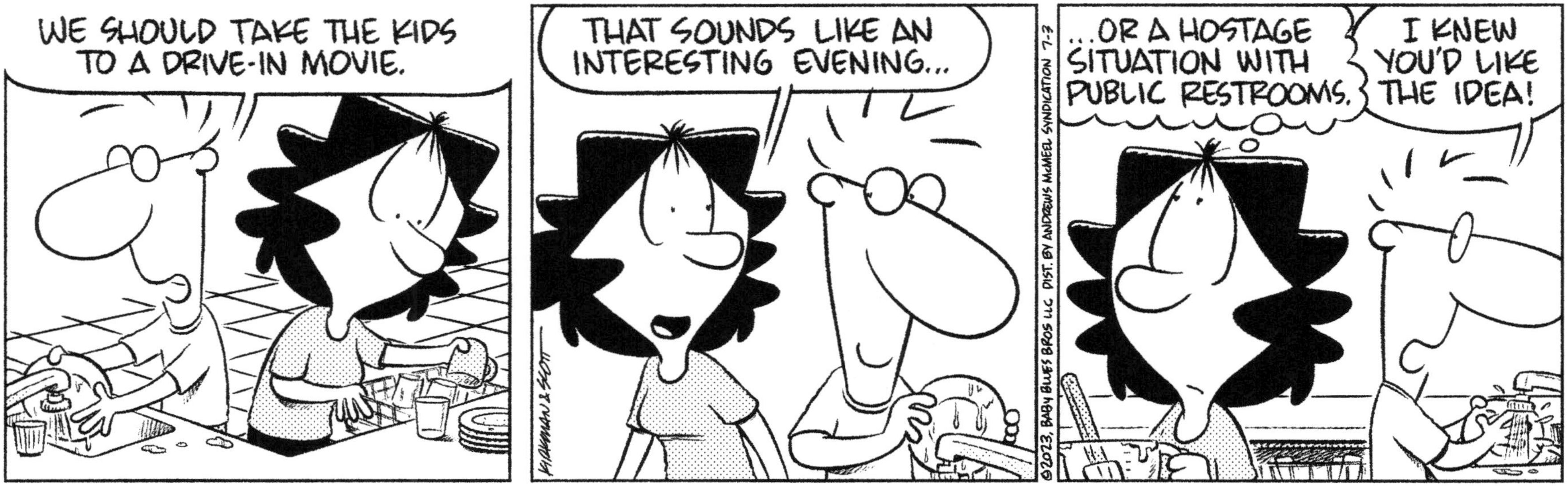
WE SHOULD TAKE THE KIDS TO A DRIVE-IN MOVIE.
KIRKMAN & SCOTT
THAT SOUNDS LIKE AN INTERESTING EVENING...
©2023, BABY BLUES BROS LLC DIST. BY ANDREWS MCMEEL SYNDICATION 7-3
...OR A HOSTAGE SITUATION WITH PUBLIC RESTROOMS.
I KNEW YOU'D LIKE THE IDEA!

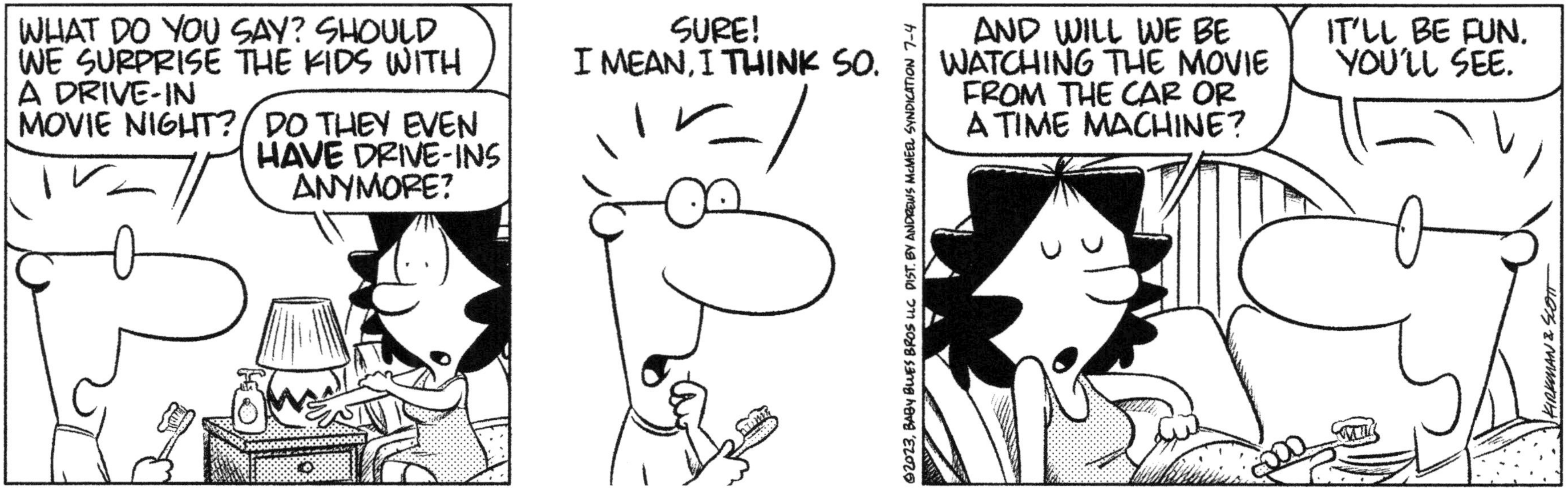
WHAT DO YOU SAY? SHOULD WE SURPRISE THE KIDS WITH A DRIVE-IN MOVIE NIGHT?
DO THEY EVEN **HAVE** DRIVE-INS ANYMORE?
SURE! I MEAN, I **THINK** SO.
©2023, BABY BLUES BROS LLC DIST. BY ANDREWS MCMEEL SYNDICATION 7-4
AND WILL WE BE WATCHING THE MOVIE FROM THE CAR OR A TIME MACHINE?
IT'LL BE FUN. YOU'LL SEE.
KIRKMAN & SCOTT

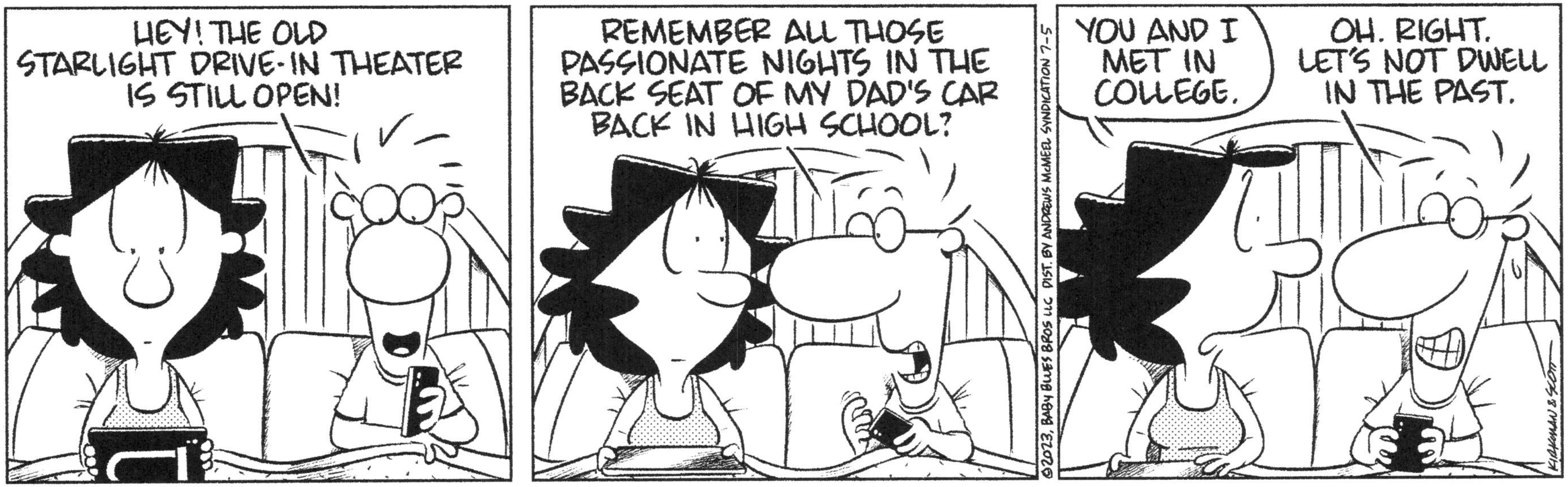
HEY! THE OLD STARLIGHT DRIVE-IN THEATER IS STILL OPEN!
REMEMBER ALL THOSE PASSIONATE NIGHTS IN THE BACK SEAT OF MY DAD'S CAR BACK IN HIGH SCHOOL?
©2023, BABY BLUES BROS LLC DIST. BY ANDREWS McMEEL SYNDICATION 7-5
YOU AND I MET IN COLLEGE.
OH. RIGHT. LET'S NOT DWELL IN THE PAST.
KIRKMAN & SCOTT

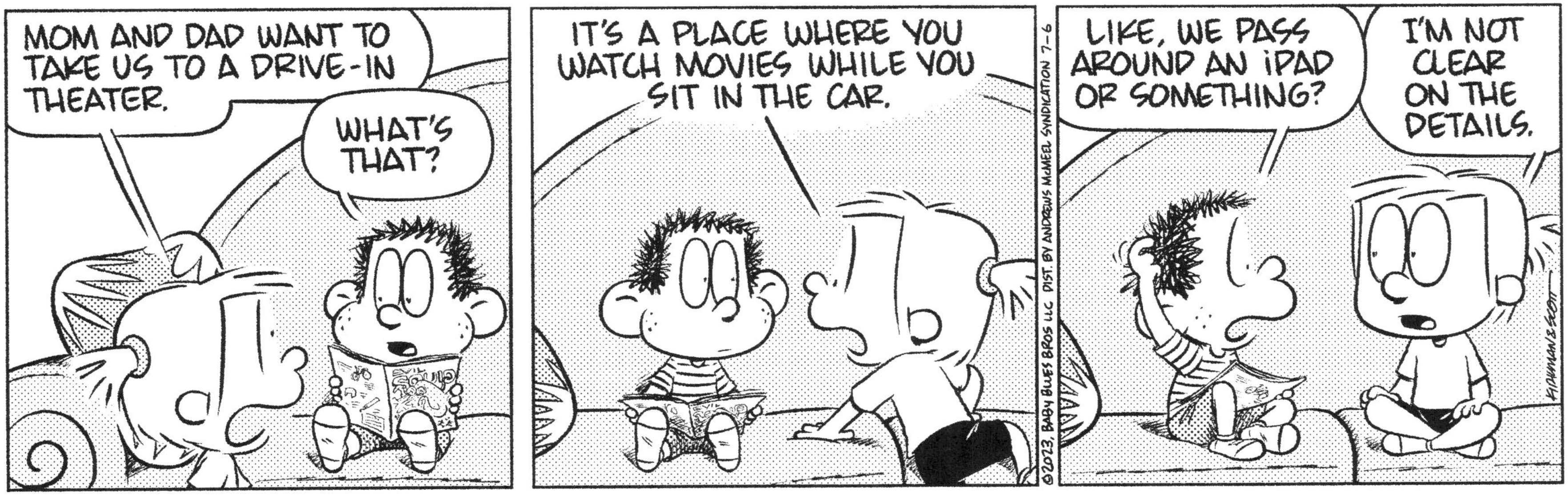
MOM AND DAD WANT TO TAKE US TO A DRIVE-IN THEATER.
WHAT'S THAT?
IT'S A PLACE WHERE YOU WATCH MOVIES WHILE YOU SIT IN THE CAR.
©2023, BABY BLUES BROS LLC DIST. BY ANDREWS McMEEL SYNDICATION 7-6
LIKE, WE PASS AROUND AN iPAD OR SOMETHING?
I'M NOT CLEAR ON THE DETAILS.
KIRKMAN & SCOTT

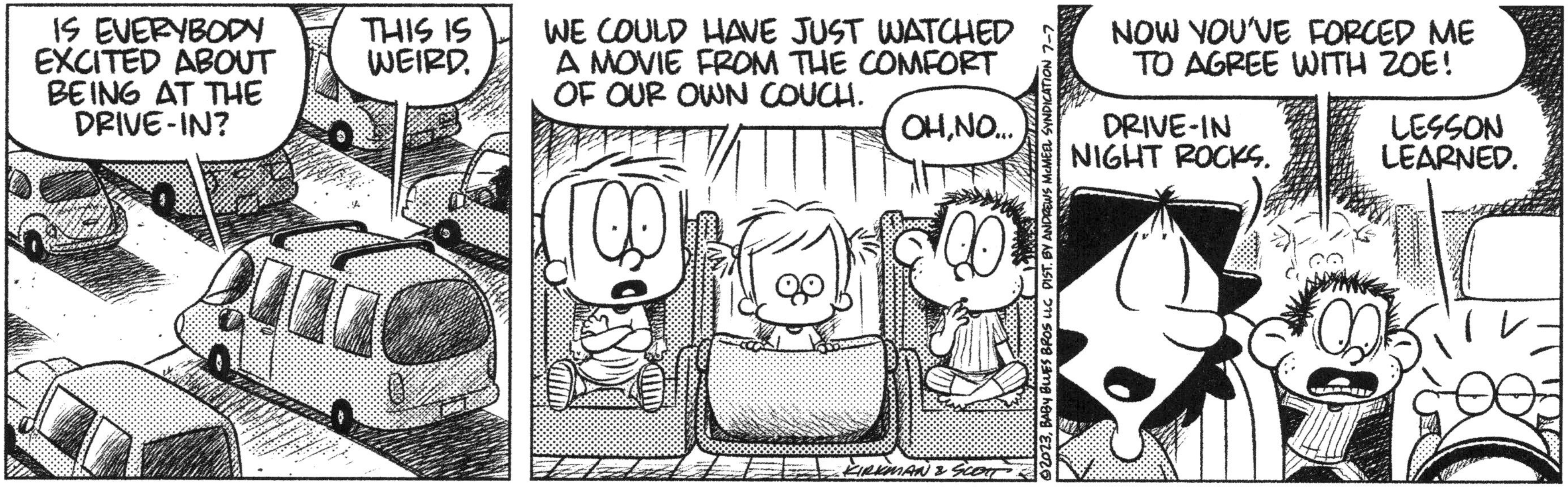
IS EVERYBODY EXCITED ABOUT BEING AT THE DRIVE-IN?
THIS IS WEIRD.
WE COULD HAVE JUST WATCHED A MOVIE FROM THE COMFORT OF OUR OWN COUCH.
OH, NO...
KIRKMAN & SCOTT
©2023, BABY BLUES BROS LLC DIST. BY ANDREWS MCMEEL SYNDICATION 7-7
NOW YOU'VE FORCED ME TO AGREE WITH ZOE!
DRIVE-IN NIGHT ROCKS.
LESSON LEARNED.

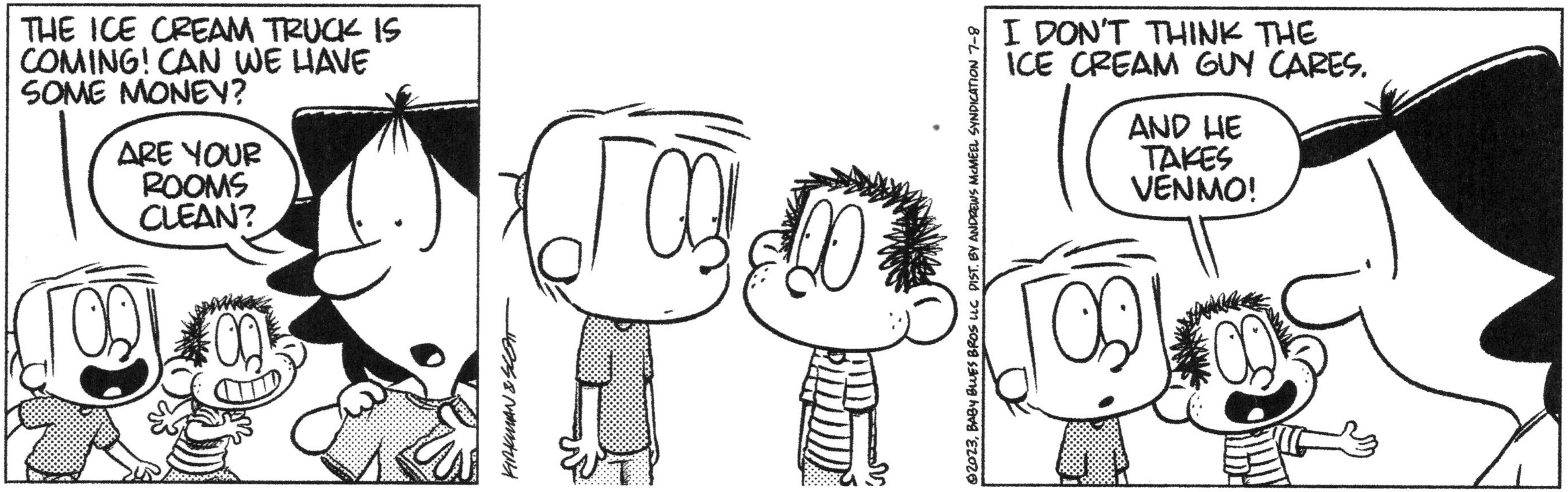
THE ICE CREAM TRUCK IS COMING! CAN WE HAVE SOME MONEY?
ARE YOUR ROOMS CLEAN?
KIRKMAN & SCOTT
©2023, BABY BLUES BROS LLC DIST. BY ANDREWS MCMEEL SYNDICATION 7-8
I DON'T THINK THE ICE CREAM GUY CARES.
AND HE TAKES VENMO!

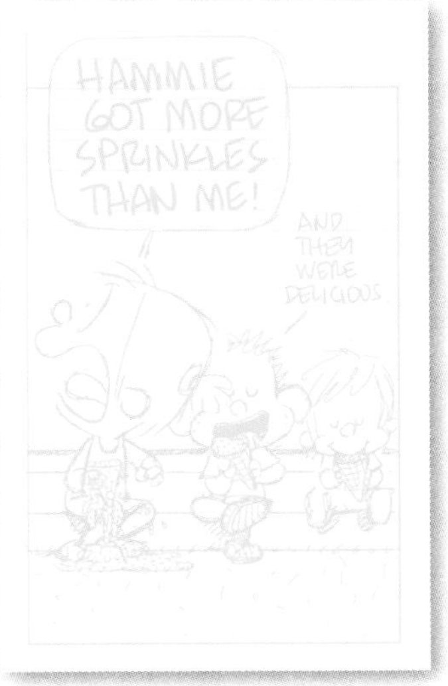
HAMMIE GOT MORE SPRINKLES THAN ME!
AND THEY WERE DELICIOUS

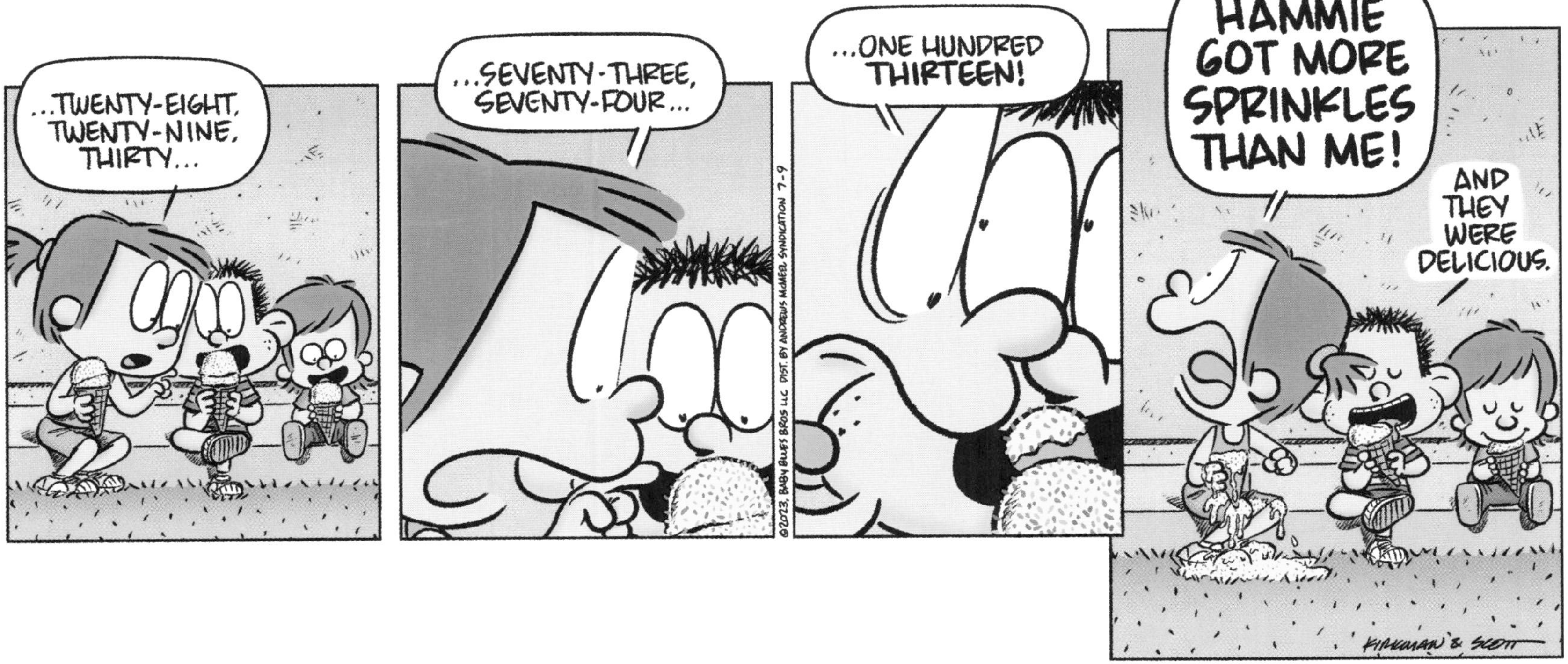
...TWENTY-EIGHT, TWENTY-NINE, THIRTY...
...SEVENTY-THREE, SEVENTY-FOUR...
©2013, BABY BLUES BROS LLC DIST. BY ANDREWS MCMEEL SYNDICATION 7-9
...ONE HUNDRED THIRTEEN!
HAMMIE GOT MORE SPRINKLES THAN ME!
AND THEY WERE DELICIOUS.
KIRKMAN & SCOTT

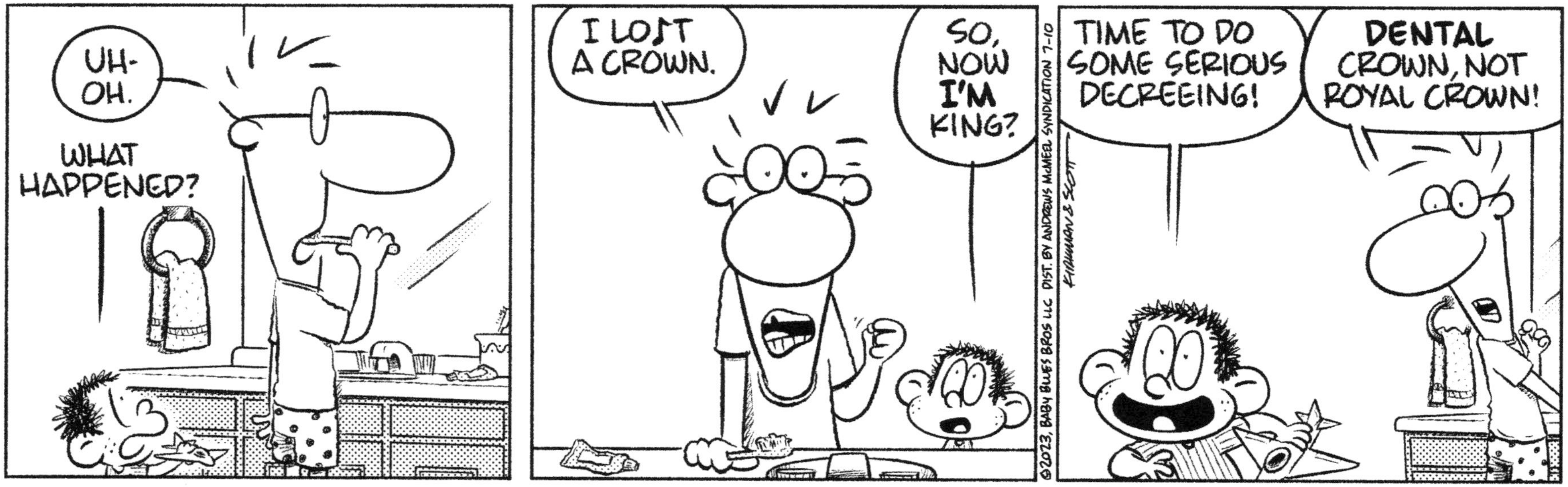
UH-OH.
WHAT HAPPENED?
I LOST A CROWN.
SO, NOW I'M KING?
©2023, BABY BLUES BROS LLC DIST. BY ANDREWS MCMEEL SYNDICATION 7-10
KIRKMAN & SCOTT
TIME TO DO SOME SERIOUS DECREEING!
DENTAL CROWN, NOT ROYAL CROWN!

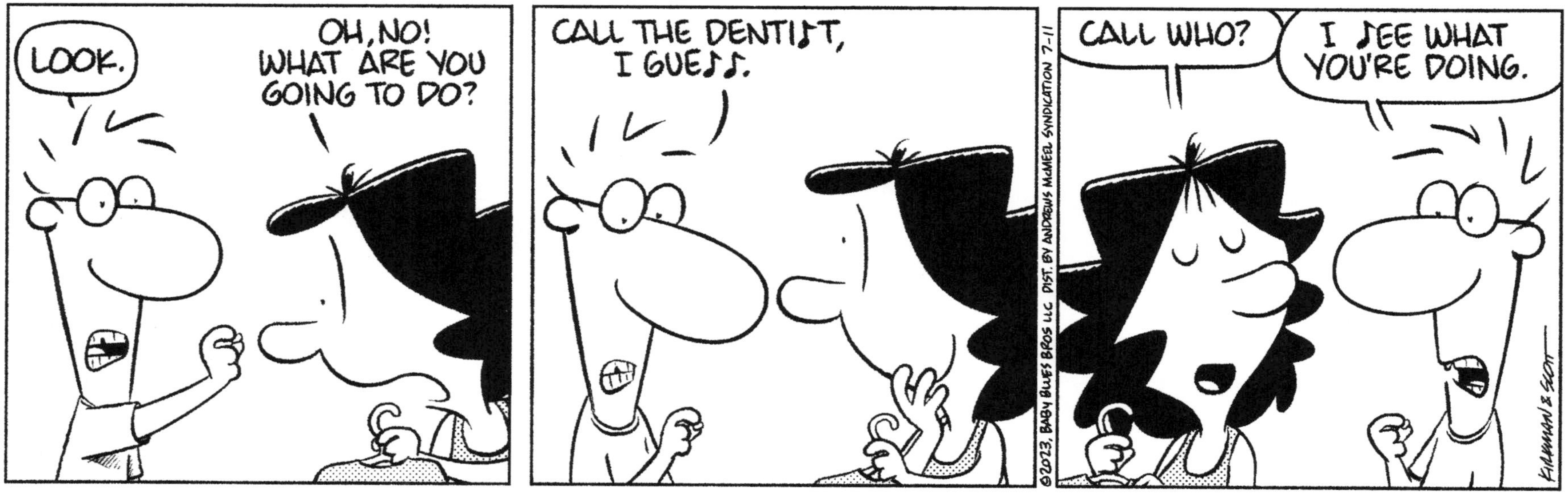
LOOK.
OH, NO! WHAT ARE YOU GOING TO DO?
CALL THE DENTIST, I GUESS.
©2023, BABY BLUES BROS LLC DIST. BY ANDREWS MCMEEL SYNDICATION 7-11
CALL WHO?
I SEE WHAT YOU'RE DOING.
KIRKMAN & SCOTT

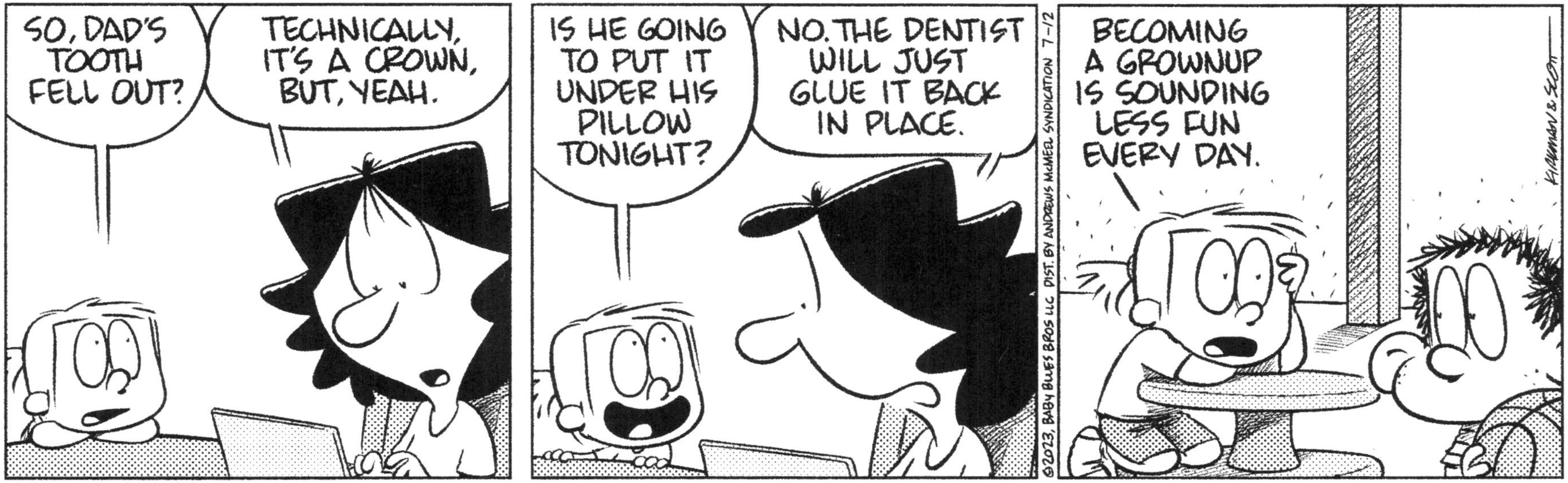
SO, DAD'S TOOTH FELL OUT?
TECHNICALLY, IT'S A CROWN, BUT, YEAH.
IS HE GOING TO PUT IT UNDER HIS PILLOW TONIGHT?
NO. THE DENTIST WILL JUST GLUE IT BACK IN PLACE.
©2023, BABY BLUES BROS LLC DIST. BY ANDREWS McMEEL SYNDICATION 7-12
BECOMING A GROWNUP IS SOUNDING LESS FUN EVERY DAY.
KIRKMAN & SCOTT

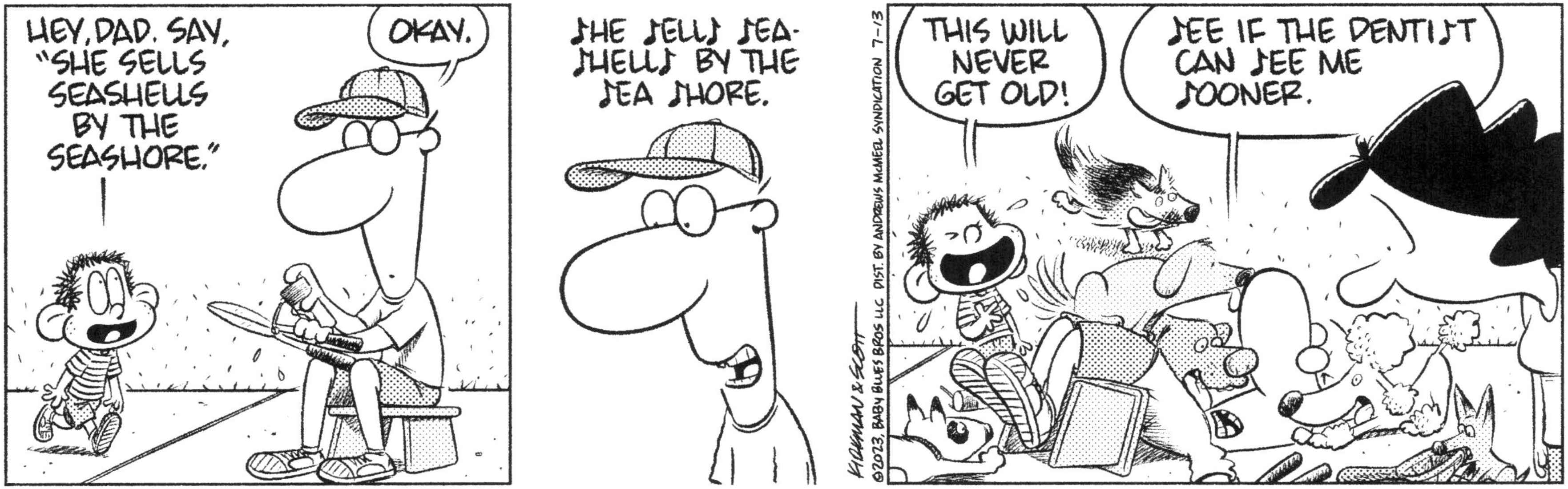
HEY, DAD. SAY, "SHE SELLS SEASHELLS BY THE SEASHORE."
OKAY.
♪HE ♪ELL♪ ♪EA-♪HELL♪ BY THE ♪EA ♪HORE.
KIRKMAN & SCOTT
©2023, BABY BLUES BROS LLC DIST. BY ANDREWS McMEEL SYNDICATION 7-13
THIS WILL NEVER GET OLD!
♪EE IF THE DENTI♪T CAN ♪EE ME ♪OONER.

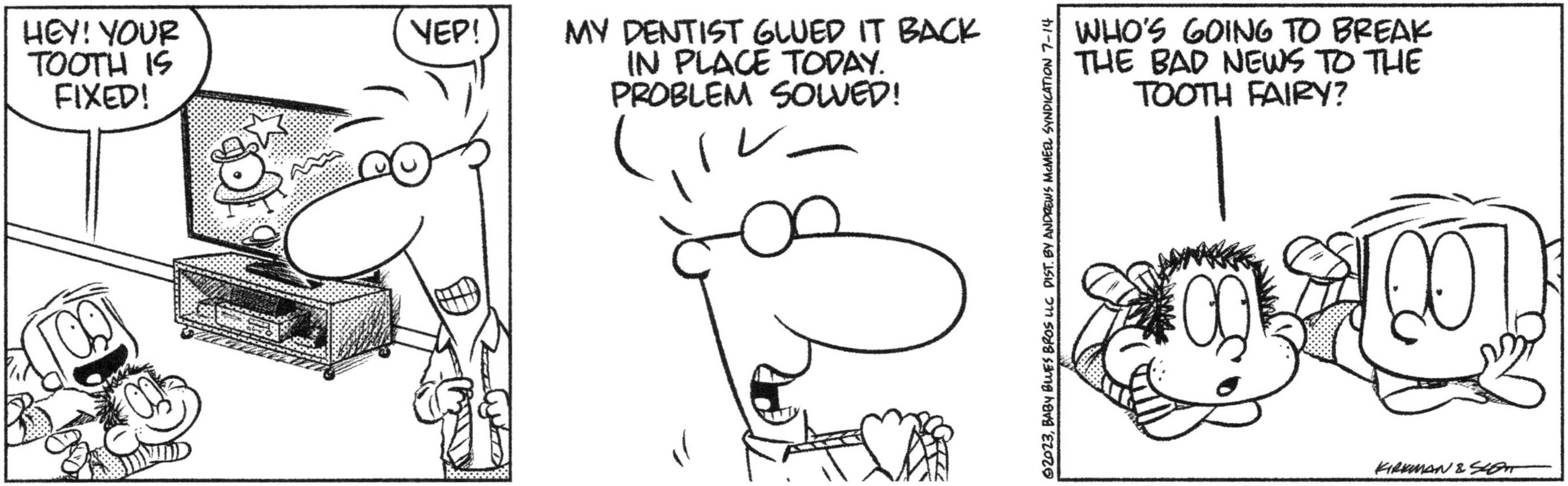
HEY! YOUR TOOTH IS FIXED!
YEP!
MY DENTIST GLUED IT BACK IN PLACE TODAY. PROBLEM SOLVED!
©2023, BABY BLUES BROS LLC DIST. BY ANDREWS MCMEEL SYNDICATION 7-14
WHO'S GOING TO BREAK THE BAD NEWS TO THE TOOTH FAIRY?
KIRKMAN & SCOTT

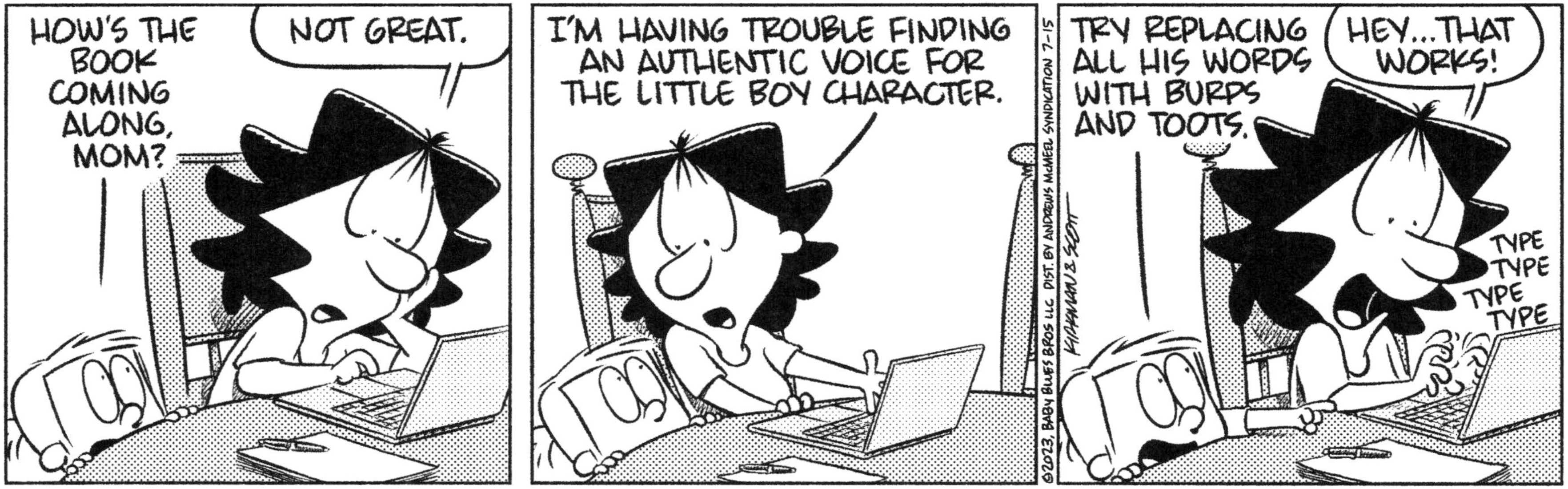
HOW'S THE BOOK COMING ALONG, MOM?
NOT GREAT.
I'M HAVING TROUBLE FINDING AN AUTHENTIC VOICE FOR THE LITTLE BOY CHARACTER.
©2023, BABY BLUES BROS LLC DIST. BY ANDREWS MCMEEL SYNDICATION 7-15
KIRKMAN & SCOTT
TRY REPLACING ALL HIS WORDS WITH BURPS AND TOOTS.
HEY...THAT WORKS!
TYPE TYPE TYPE TYPE

FLIP

FLIP FLIP
FLIP FLIP
©2023, BABY BLUES BROS LLC DIST. BY ANDREWS McMEEL SYNDICATION
FLIP
I WONDER WHO GOT THE DIRTBURGER.
THE WHAT?
KIRKMAN & SCOTT 7-23

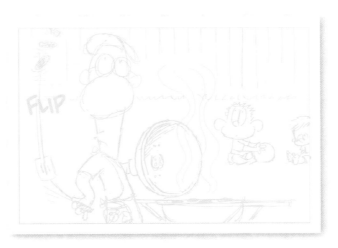

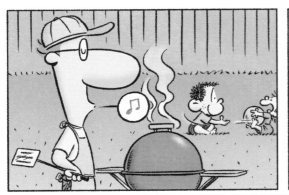

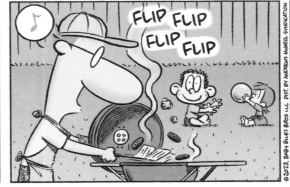

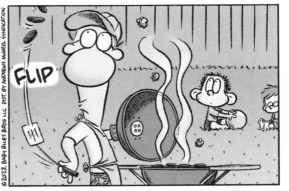

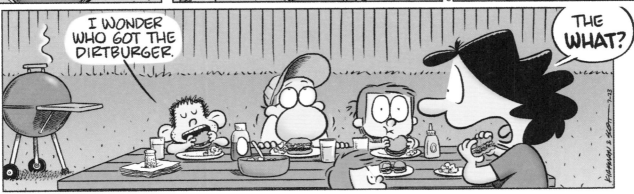

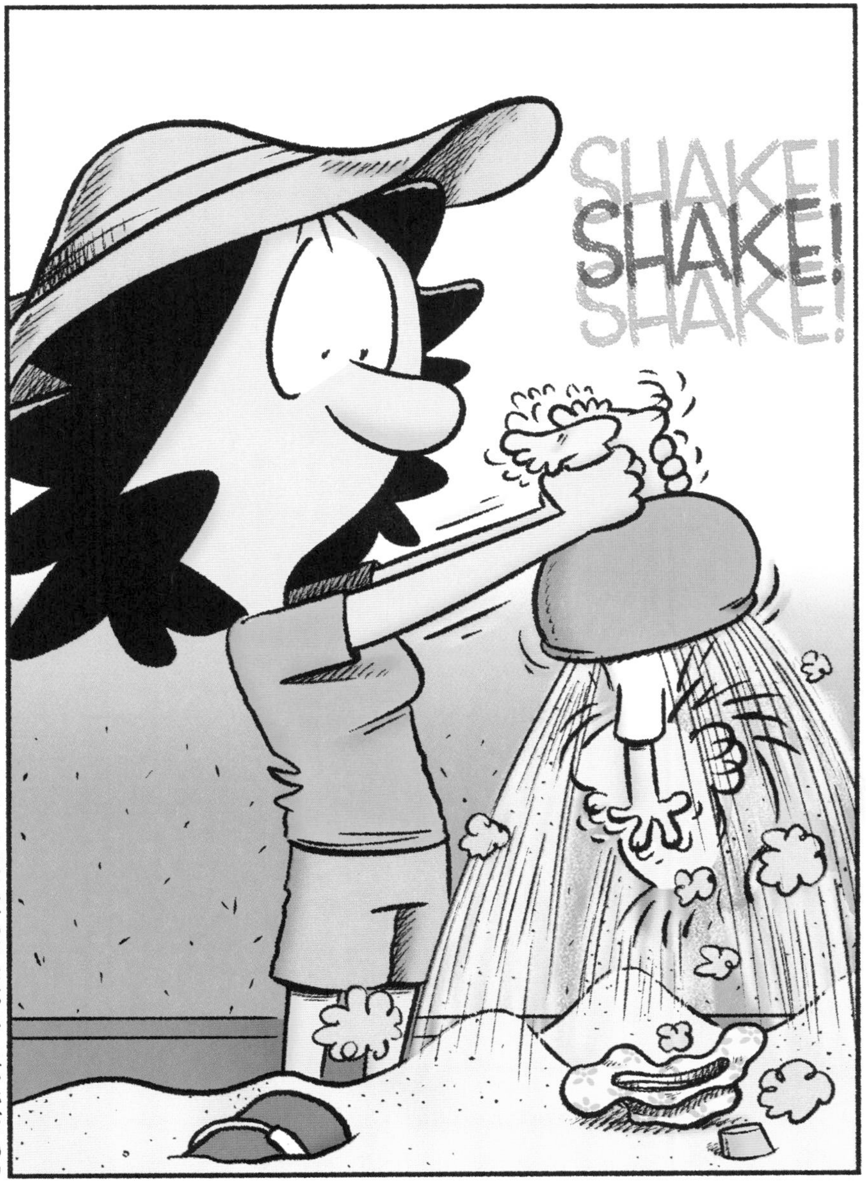
SHAKE!
SHAKE!
SHAKE!

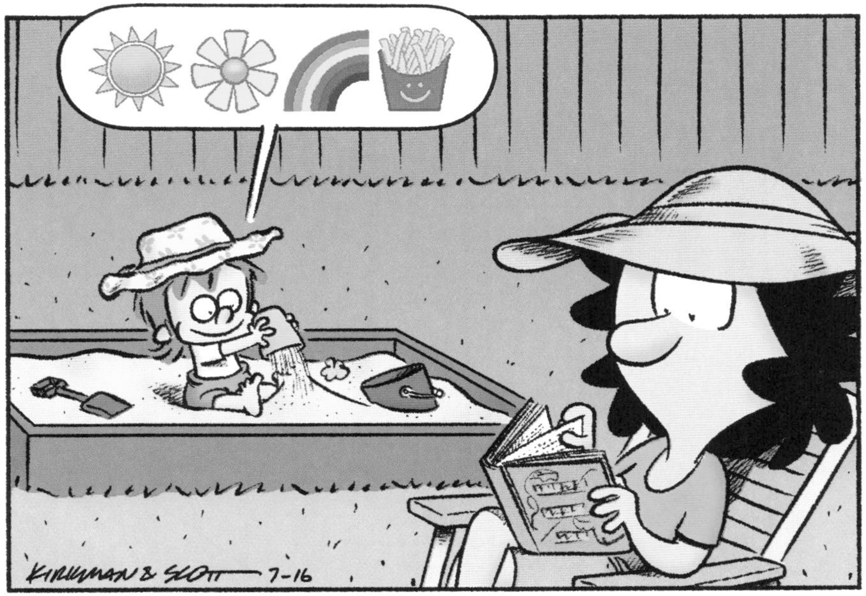
KIRKMAN & SCOTT 7-16

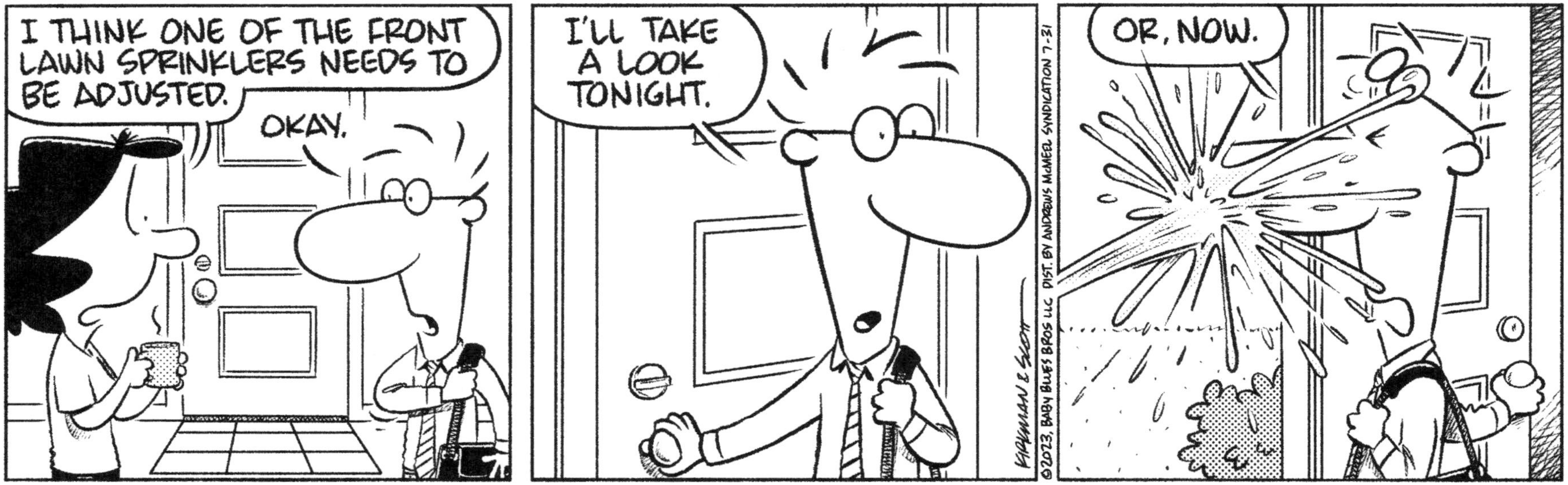
I THINK ONE OF THE FRONT LAWN SPRINKLERS NEEDS TO BE ADJUSTED.
OKAY.
I'LL TAKE A LOOK TONIGHT.
KIRKMAN & SCOTT
©2023, BABY BLUES BROS LLC DIST. BY ANDREWS MCMEEL SYNDICATION 7-31
OR, NOW.

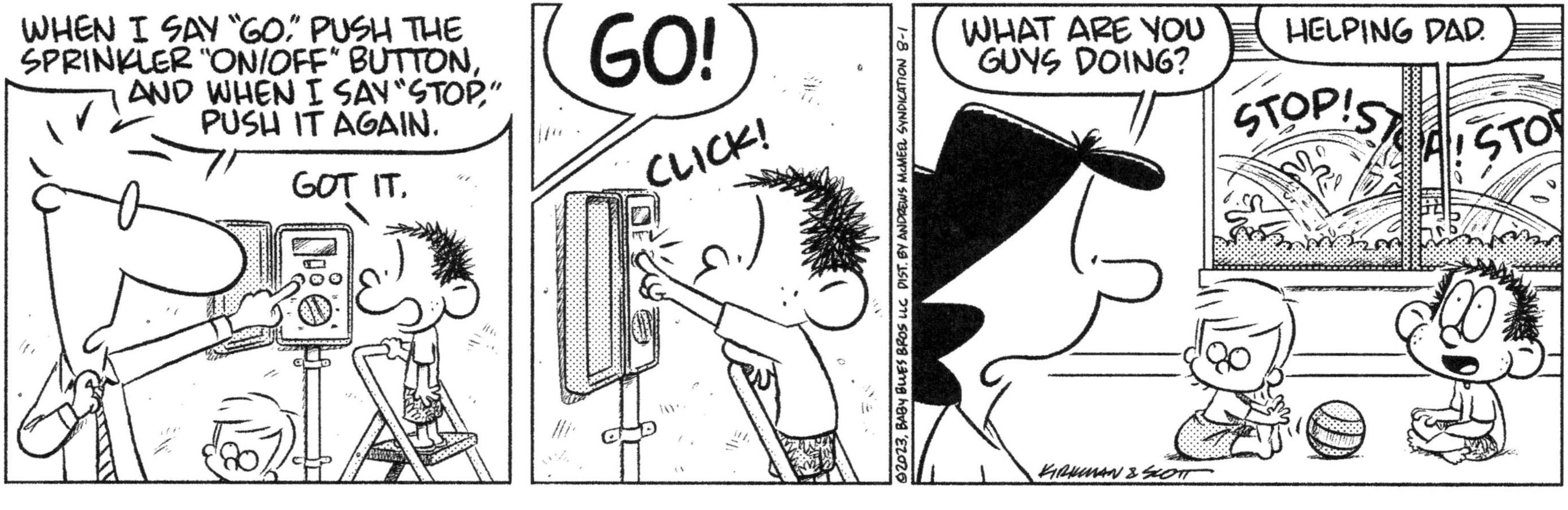
WHEN I SAY "GO," PUSH THE SPRINKLER "ON/OFF" BUTTON, AND WHEN I SAY "STOP," PUSH IT AGAIN.
GOT IT.
GO!
CLICK!
©2023, BABY BLUES BROS LLC DIST. BY ANDREWS MCMEEL SYNDICATION 8-1
WHAT ARE YOU GUYS DOING?
HELPING DAD.
STOP!
KIRKMAN & SCOTT

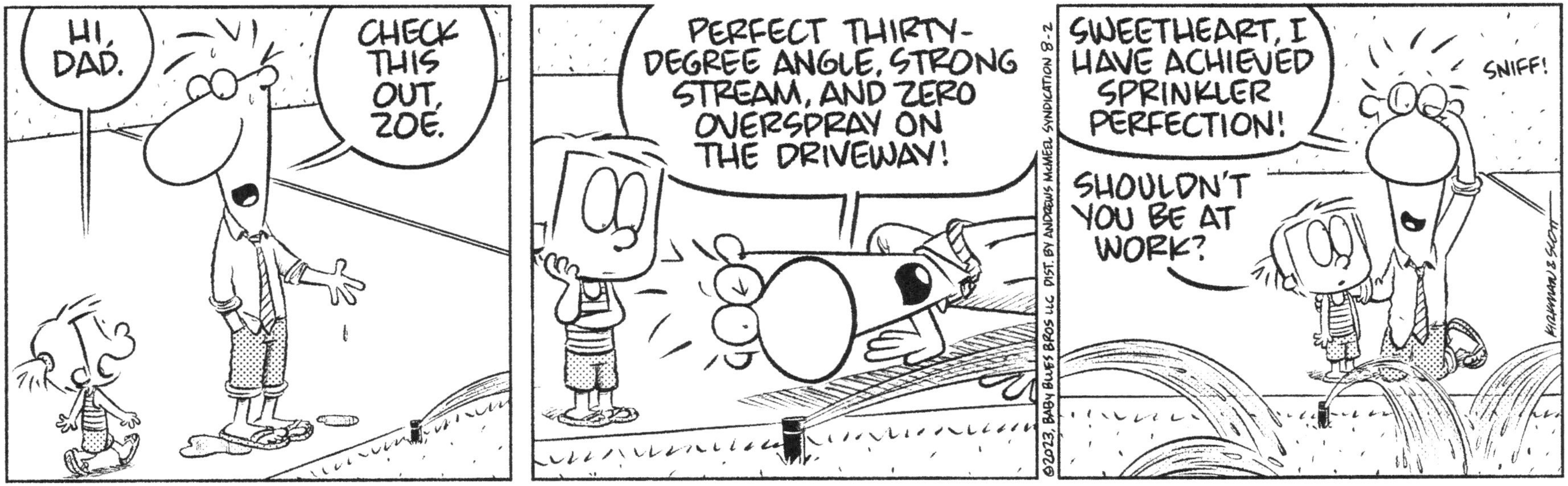
HI, DAD.
CHECK THIS OUT, ZOE.
PERFECT THIRTY-DEGREE ANGLE, STRONG STREAM, AND ZERO OVERSPRAY ON THE DRIVEWAY!
©2023, BABY BLUES BROS LLC DIST. BY ANDREWS McMEEL SYNDICATION 8-2
SWEETHEART, I HAVE ACHIEVED SPRINKLER PERFECTION!
SNIFF!
SHOULDN'T YOU BE AT WORK?
KIRKMAN & SCOTT

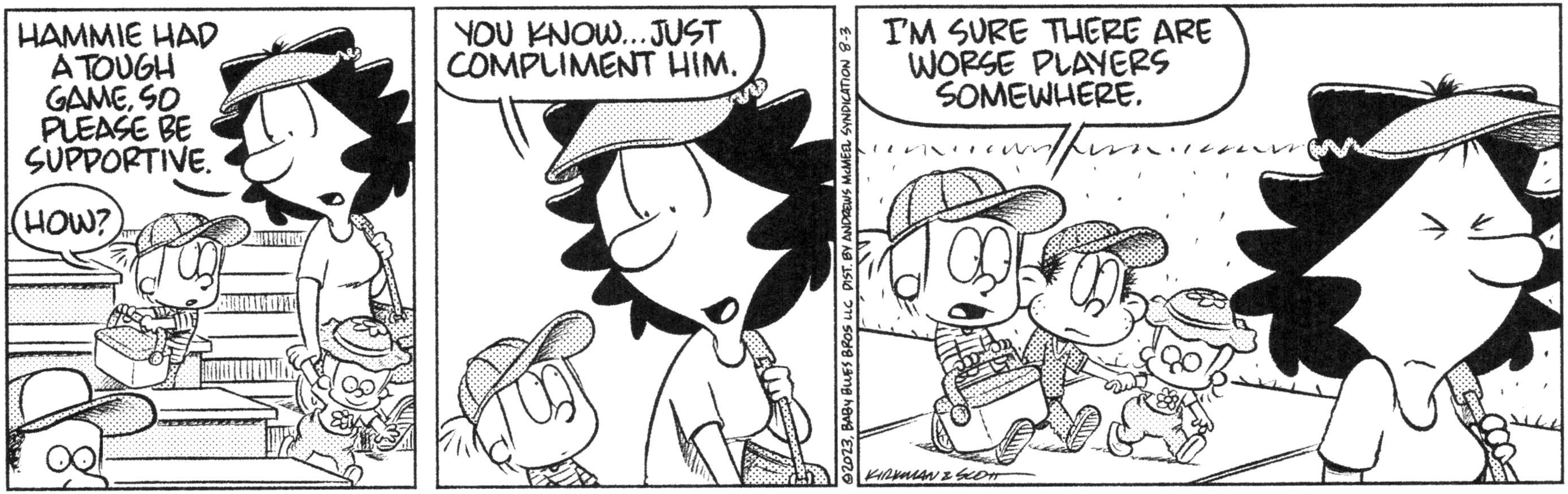
HAMMIE HAD A TOUGH GAME, SO PLEASE BE SUPPORTIVE.
HOW?
YOU KNOW... JUST COMPLIMENT HIM.
©2023, BABY BLUES BROS LLC DIST. BY ANDREWS McMEEL SYNDICATION 8-3
I'M SURE THERE ARE WORSE PLAYERS SOMEWHERE.
KIRKMAN & SCOTT

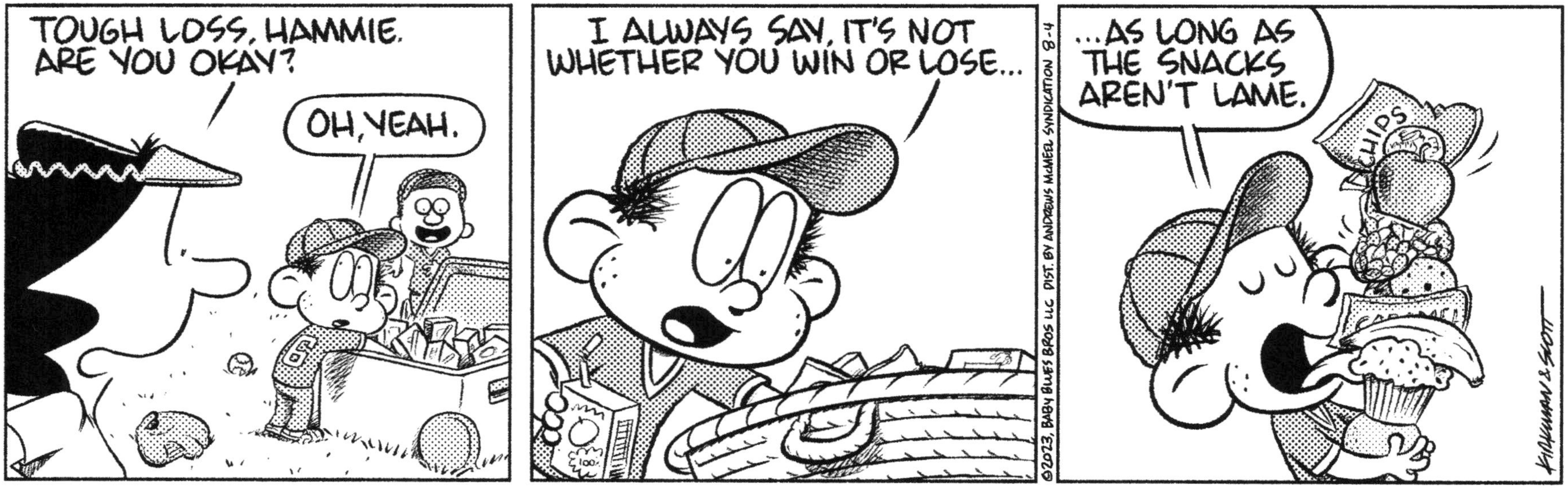
TOUGH LOSS, HAMMIE. ARE YOU OKAY?
OH, YEAH.
I ALWAYS SAY, IT'S NOT WHETHER YOU WIN OR LOSE...
...AS LONG AS THE SNACKS AREN'T LAME.
CHIPS
©2023, BABY BLUES BROS LLC DIST. BY ANDREWS McMEEL SYNDICATION 8-4
KIRKMAN & SCOTT

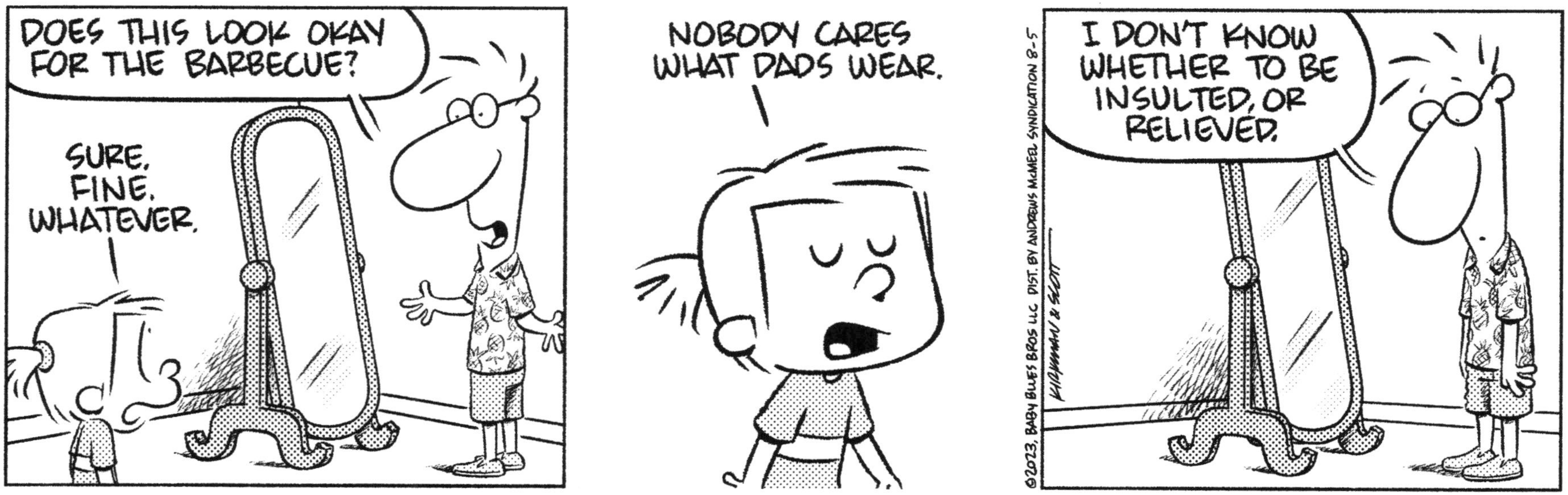
DOES THIS LOOK OKAY FOR THE BARBECUE?
SURE. FINE. WHATEVER.
NOBODY CARES WHAT DADS WEAR.
I DON'T KNOW WHETHER TO BE INSULTED, OR RELIEVED.
©2023, BABY BLUES BROS LLC DIST. BY ANDREWS McMEEL SYNDICATION 8-5
KIRKMAN & SCOTT

YOUR GRAPHIC NOVELS ARE GETTING A LITTLE TOO GRAPHIC.

Robot Sister
A Grafik NOVEL by Hammie M
I give you Robot SISTER 5.0!!
YO.
Yay!
CLap
CLap
CLap
RS-5, show us yor amaZE-ing SKILZ!
ZZT
CLIK!
poink
TWIST TWIST
Swish! Swish!
CLeen
SIENS HERO
Big PriZ
Yay!
Yay!
CLap
CLap
CLap!
YOUR GRAPHIC NOVELS ARE GETTING A LITTLE TOO GRAPHIC.
KIRKMAN & SCOTT
7/30
©2023, BABY BLUES BROS LLC DIST. BY ANDREWS McMEEL SYNDICATION

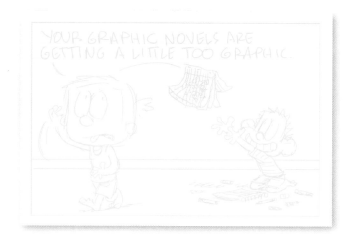

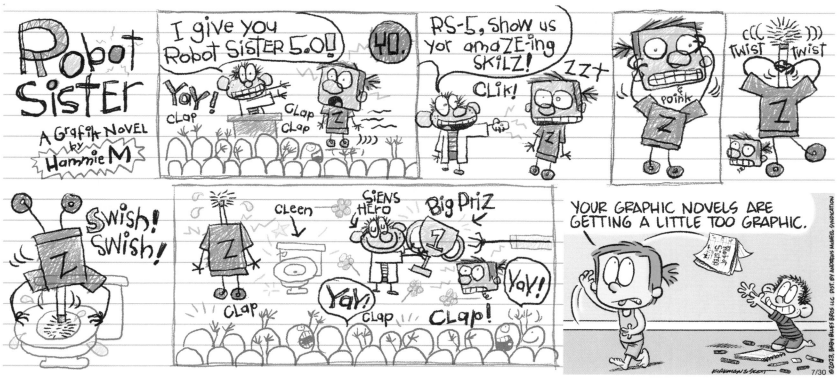

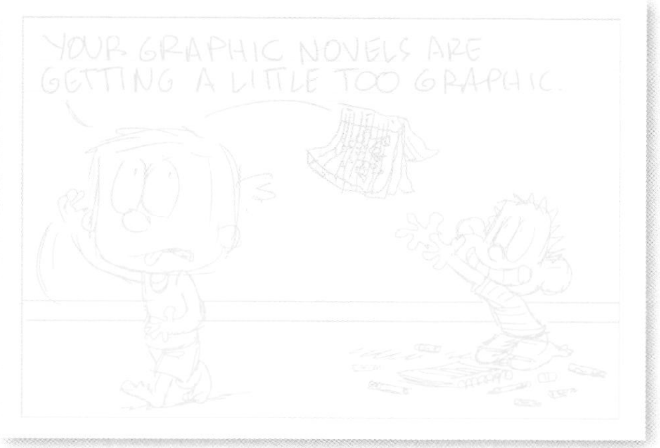

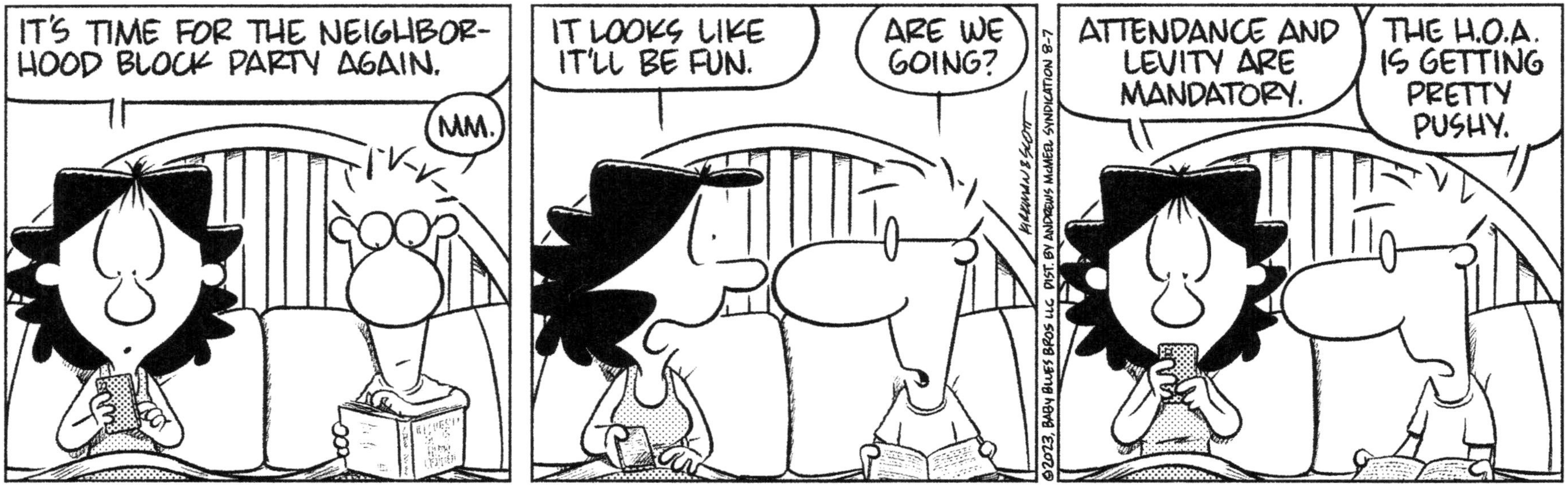
IT'S TIME FOR THE NEIGHBORHOOD BLOCK PARTY AGAIN.
MM.
IT LOOKS LIKE IT'LL BE FUN.
ARE WE GOING?
KIRKMAN & SCOTT
©2023, BABY BLUES BROS LLC DIST. BY ANDREWS McMEEL SYNDICATION 8-7
ATTENDANCE AND LEVITY ARE MANDATORY.
THE H.O.A. IS GETTING PRETTY PUSHY.

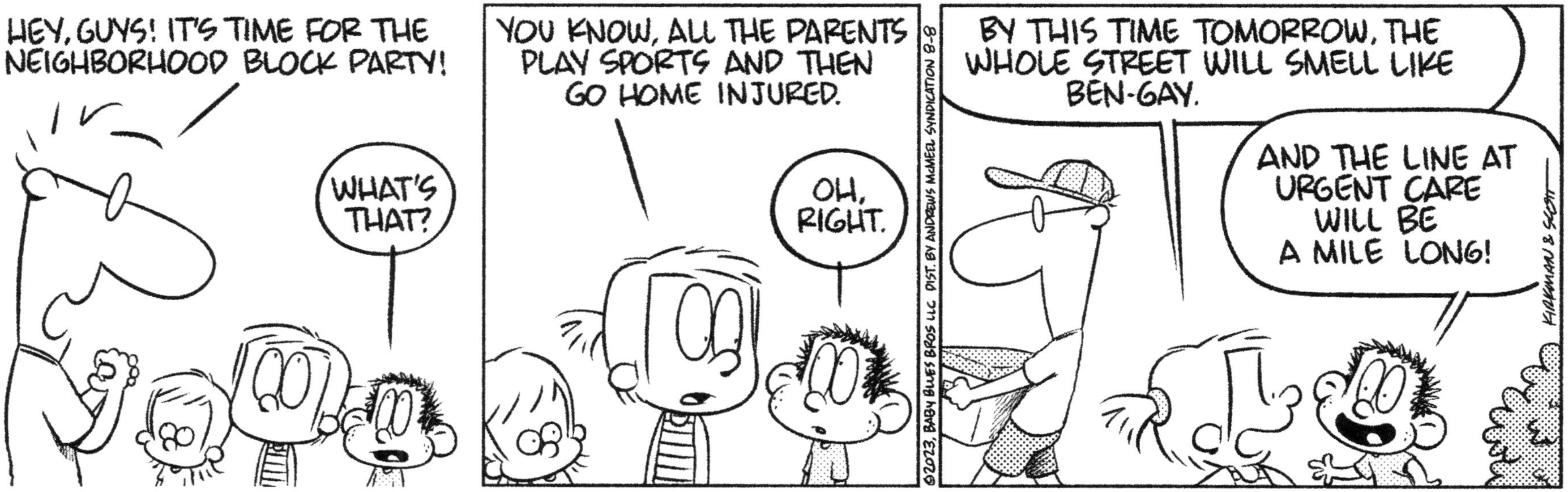
HEY, GUYS! IT'S TIME FOR THE NEIGHBORHOOD BLOCK PARTY!
WHAT'S THAT?
YOU KNOW, ALL THE PARENTS PLAY SPORTS AND THEN GO HOME INJURED.
OH, RIGHT.
©2023, BABY BLUES BROS LLC DIST. BY ANDREWS McMEEL SYNDICATION 8-8
BY THIS TIME TOMORROW, THE WHOLE STREET WILL SMELL LIKE BEN-GAY.
AND THE LINE AT URGENT CARE WILL BE A MILE LONG!
KIRKMAN & SCOTT

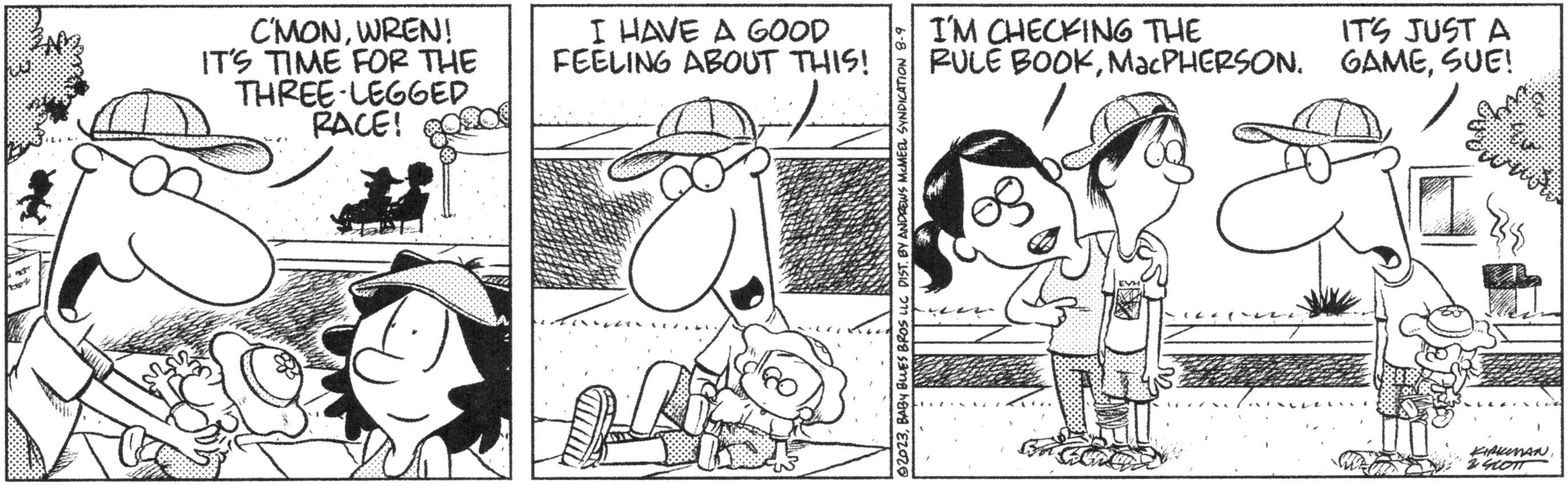
C'MON, WREN! IT'S TIME FOR THE THREE-LEGGED RACE!
I HAVE A GOOD FEELING ABOUT THIS!
©2023, BABY BLUES BROS LLC DIST. BY ANDREWS McMEEL SYNDICATION 8-9
I'M CHECKING THE RULE BOOK, MacPHERSON.
IT'S JUST A GAME, SUE!
KIRKMAN & SCOTT

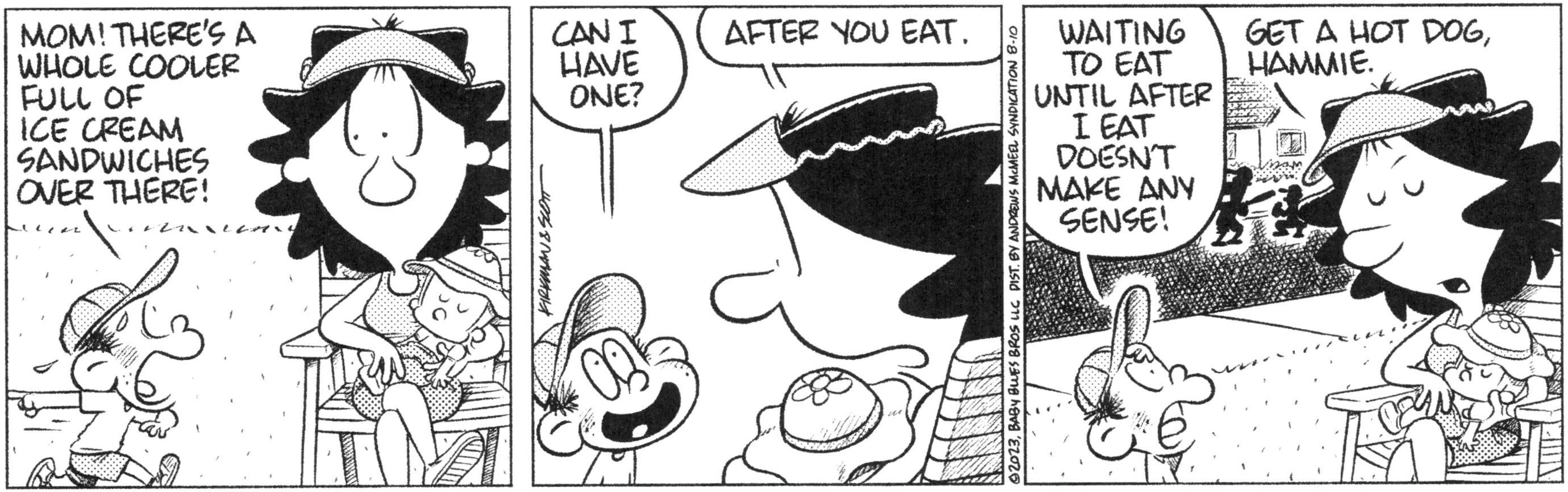
MOM! THERE'S A WHOLE COOLER FULL OF ICE CREAM SANDWICHES OVER THERE!
KIRKMAN & SCOTT
CAN I HAVE ONE?
AFTER YOU EAT.
©2023, BABY BLUES BROS LLC DIST. BY ANDREWS McMEEL SYNDICATION 8-10
WAITING TO EAT UNTIL AFTER I EAT DOESN'T MAKE ANY SENSE!
GET A HOT DOG, HAMMIE.

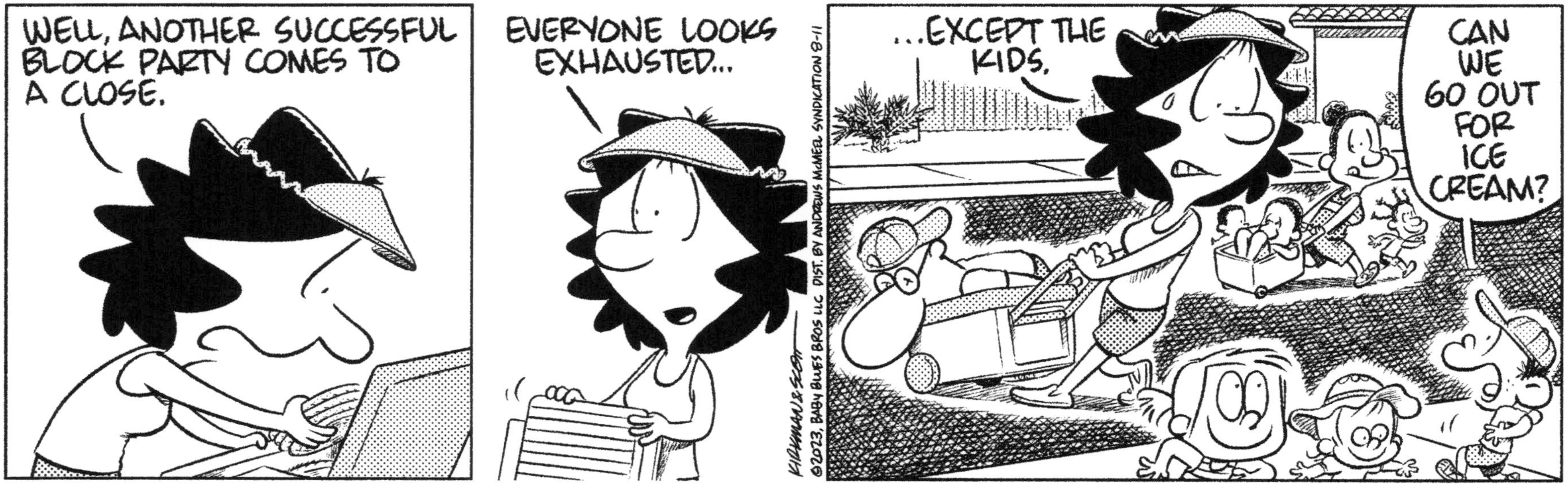
WELL, ANOTHER SUCCESSFUL BLOCK PARTY COMES TO A CLOSE.
EVERYONE LOOKS EXHAUSTED...
...EXCEPT THE KIDS.
CAN WE GO OUT FOR ICE CREAM?
KIRKMAN & SCOTT
©2023, BABY BLUES BROS LLC DIST. BY ANDREWS MCMEEL SYNDICATION 8-11

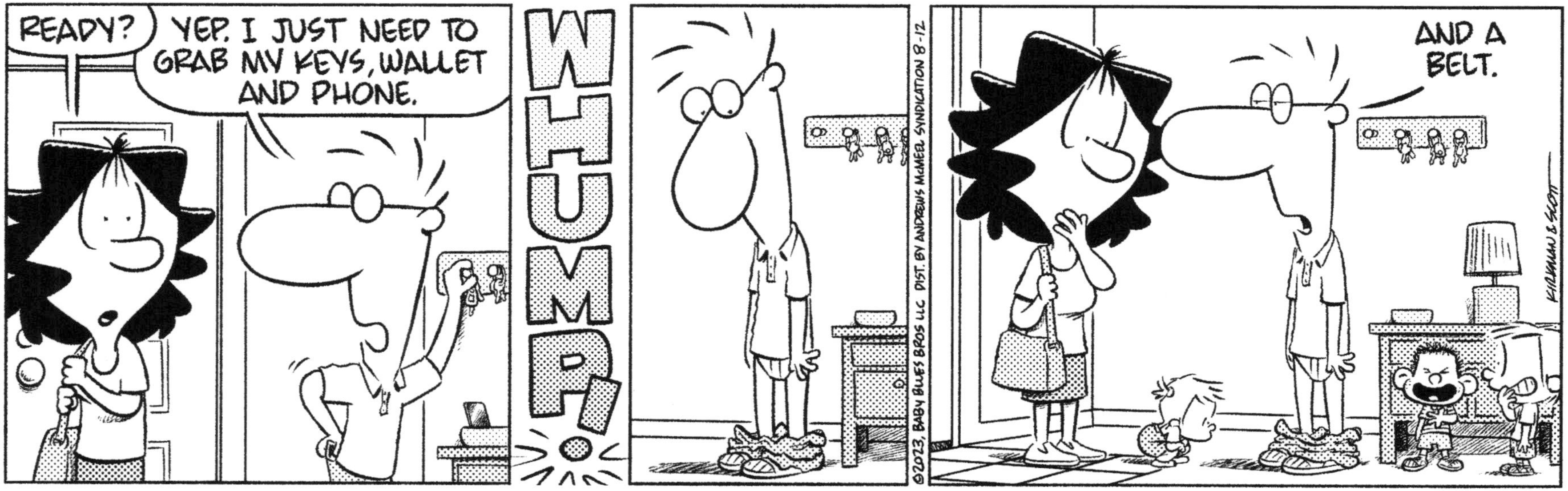
READY?
YEP. I JUST NEED TO GRAB MY KEYS, WALLET AND PHONE.
WHUMP!
AND A BELT.
©2023, BABY BLUES BROS LLC DIST. BY ANDREWS MCMEEL SYNDICATION 8-12
KIRKMAN & SCOTT

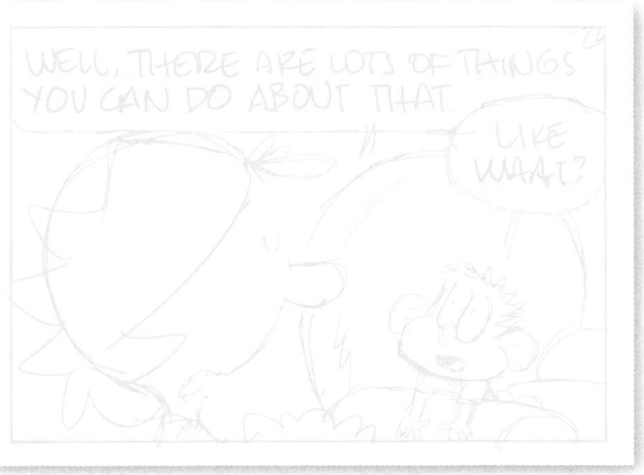
WELL, THERE ARE LOTS OF THINGS YOU CAN DO ABOUT THAT.
LIKE WHAT?

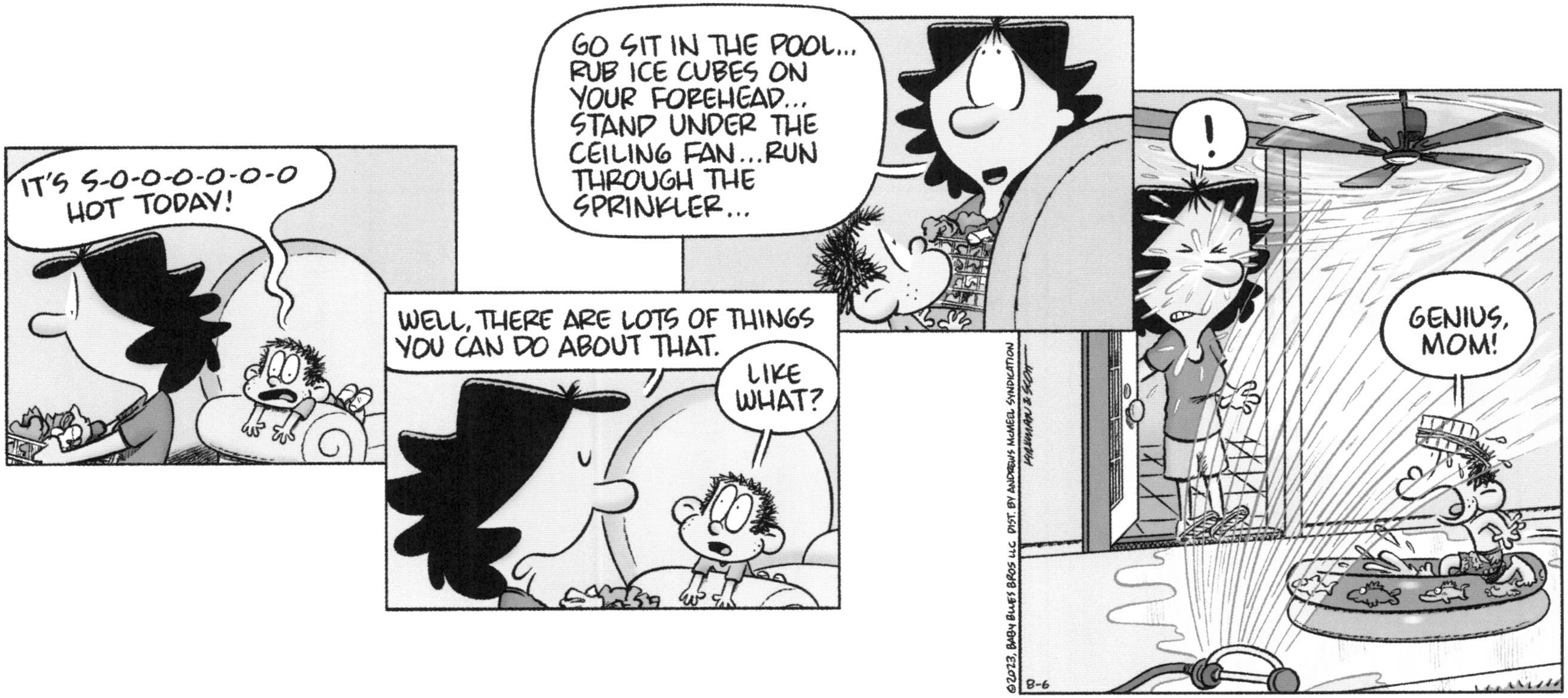
IT'S S-O-O-O-O-O-O-O HOT TODAY!
WELL, THERE ARE LOTS OF THINGS YOU CAN DO ABOUT THAT.
LIKE WHAT?
GO SIT IN THE POOL... RUB ICE CUBES ON YOUR FOREHEAD... STAND UNDER THE CEILING FAN...RUN THROUGH THE SPRINKLER...
!
GENIUS, MOM!
©2023, BABY BLUES BROS LLC DIST. BY ANDREWS MCMEEL SYNDICATION
KIRKMAN & SCOTT
8-6

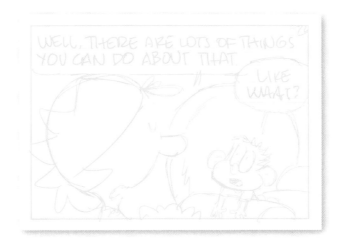

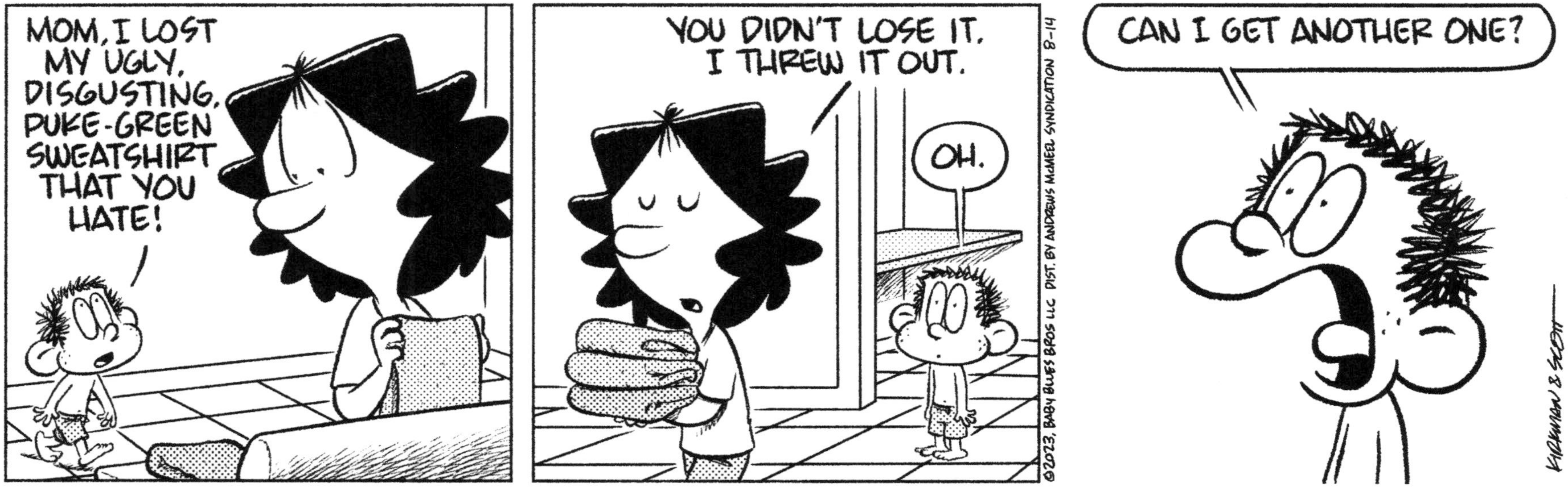
MOM, I LOST MY UGLY, DISGUSTING, PUKE-GREEN SWEATSHIRT THAT YOU HATE!
YOU DIDN'T LOSE IT. I THREW IT OUT.
OH.
CAN I GET ANOTHER ONE?
©2023, BABY BLUES BROS LLC DIST. BY ANDREWS McMEEL SYNDICATION 8-14
KIRKMAN & SCOTT

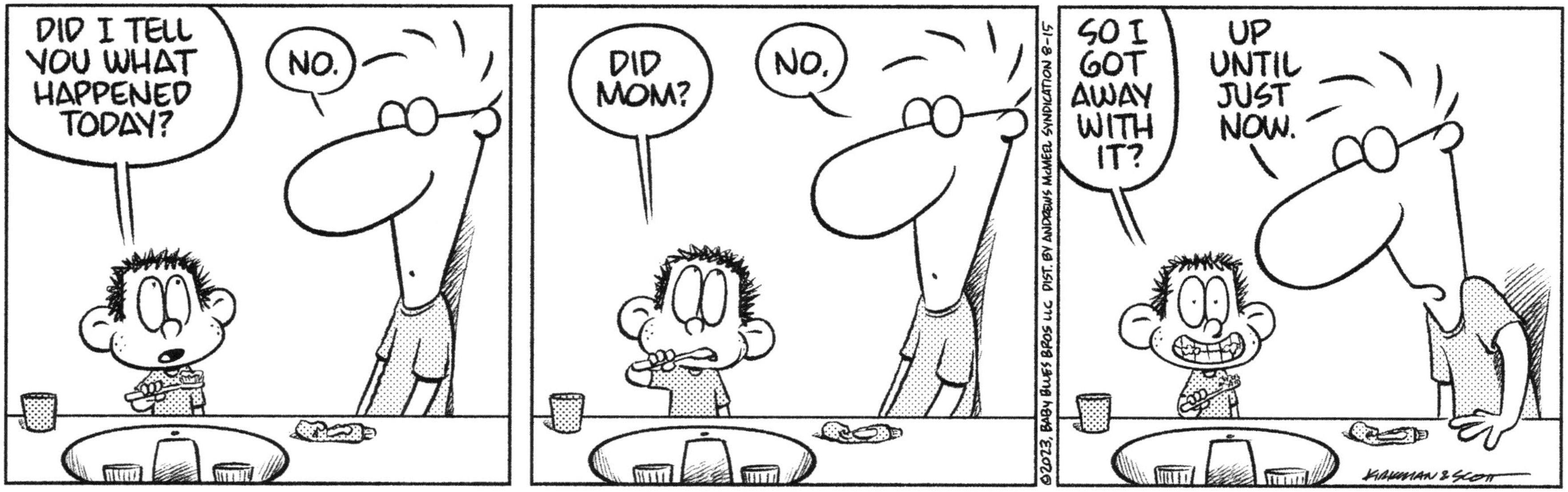
DID I TELL YOU WHAT HAPPENED TODAY?
NO.
DID MOM?
NO.
SO I GOT AWAY WITH IT?
UP UNTIL JUST NOW.
©2023, BABY BLUES BROS LLC DIST. BY ANDREWS McMEEL SYNDICATION 8-15
KIRKMAN & SCOTT

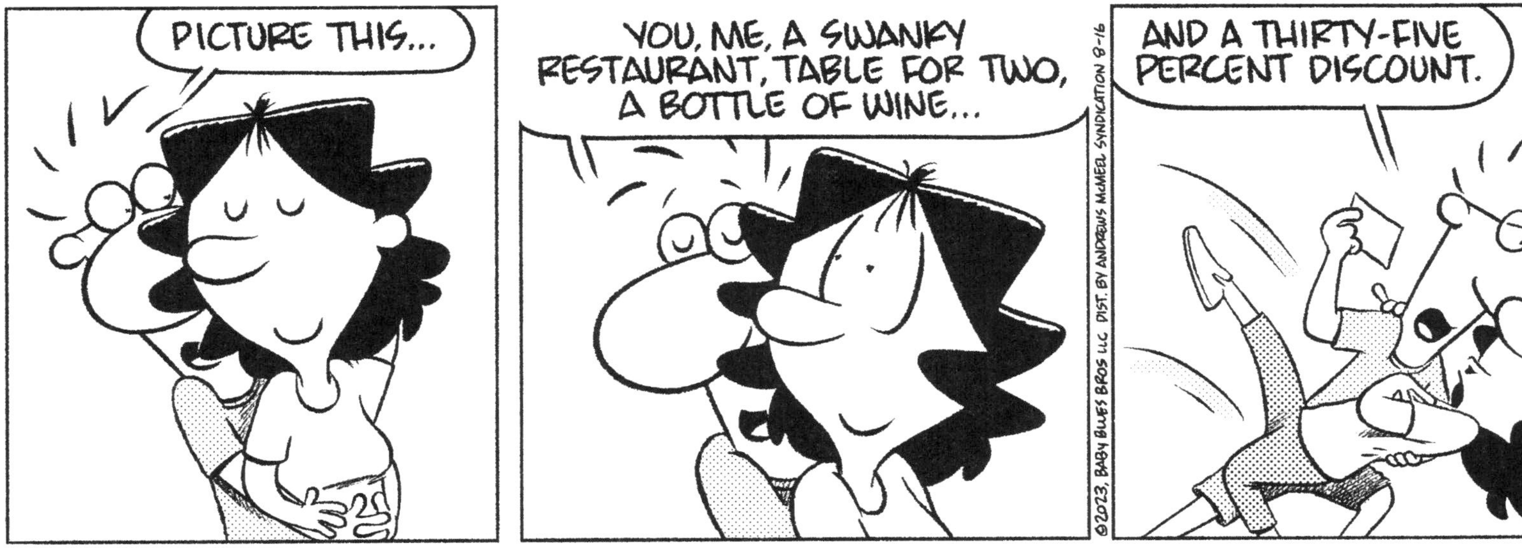
PICTURE THIS...
YOU, ME, A SWANKY RESTAURANT, TABLE FOR TWO, A BOTTLE OF WINE...
©2023, BABY BLUES BROS LLC DIST. BY ANDREWS McMEEL SYNDICATION 8-16
AND A THIRTY-FIVE PERCENT DISCOUNT.
COUPONS ARE MY LOVE LANGUAGE!
KIRKMAN & SCOTT

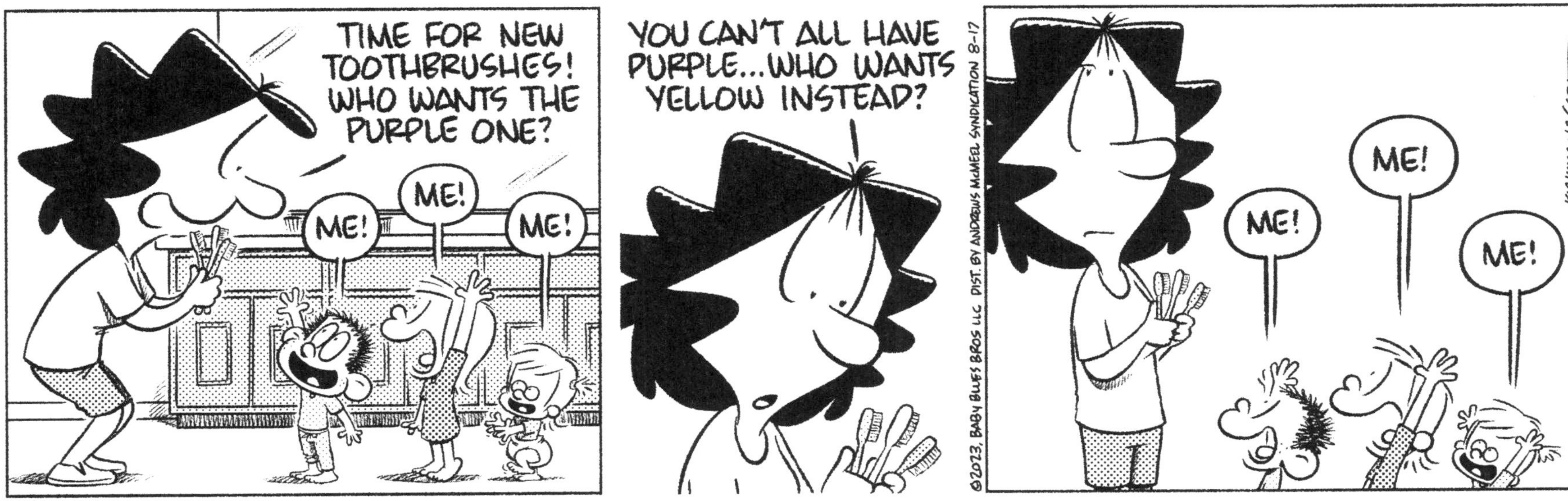
TIME FOR NEW TOOTHBRUSHES! WHO WANTS THE PURPLE ONE?
ME!
ME!
ME!
YOU CAN'T ALL HAVE PURPLE...WHO WANTS YELLOW INSTEAD?
©2023, BABY BLUES BROS LLC DIST. BY ANDREWS McMEEL SYNDICATION 8-17
KIRKMAN & SCOTT
ME!
ME!
ME!

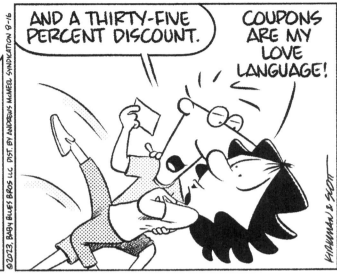

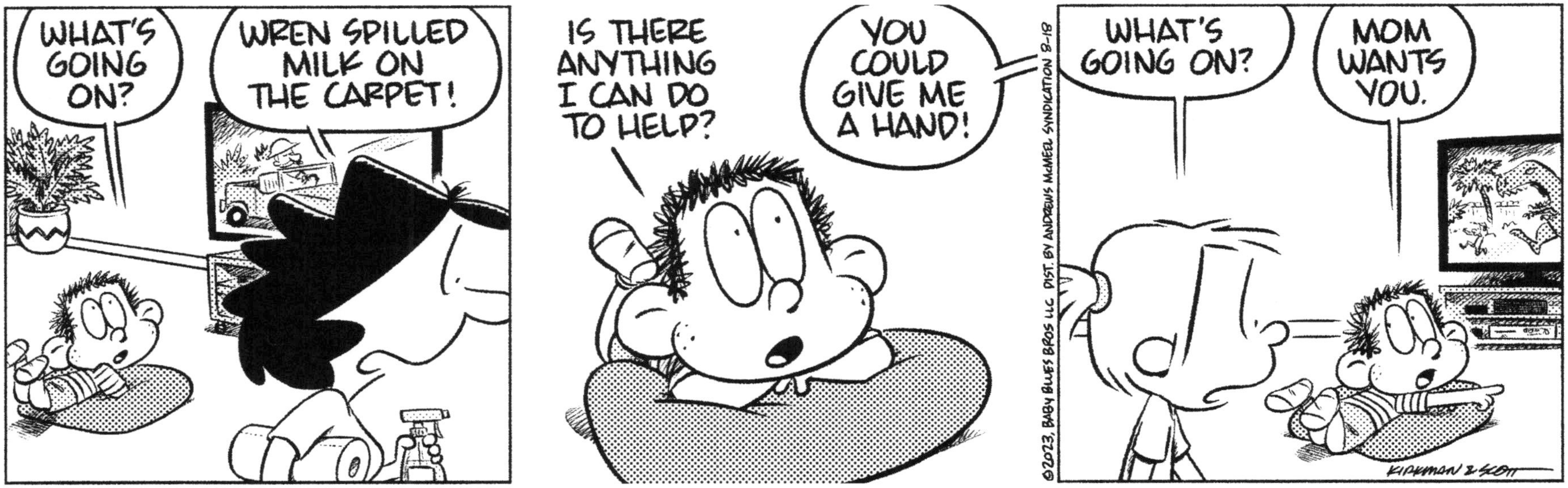
WHAT'S GOING ON?
WREN SPILLED MILK ON THE CARPET!
IS THERE ANYTHING I CAN DO TO HELP?
YOU COULD GIVE ME A HAND!
©2023, BABY BLUES BROS LLC DIST. BY ANDREWS McMEEL SYNDICATION 8-18
WHAT'S GOING ON?
MOM WANTS YOU.
KIRKMAN & SCOTT

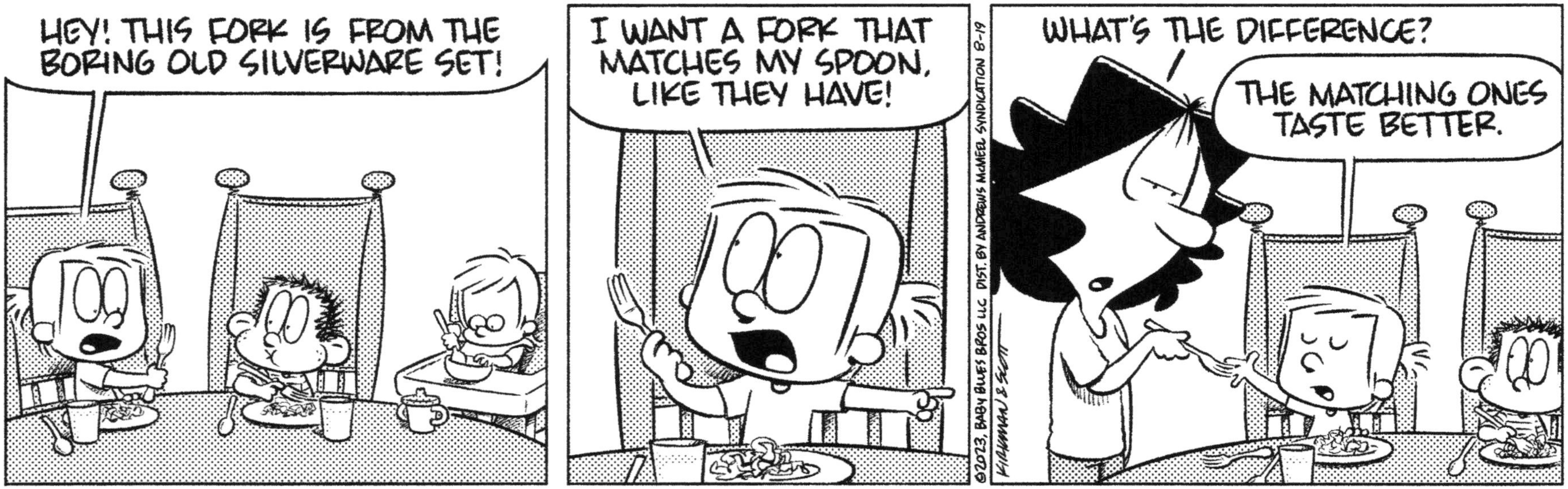
HEY! THIS FORK IS FROM THE BORING OLD SILVERWARE SET!
I WANT A FORK THAT MATCHES MY SPOON, LIKE THEY HAVE!
©2023, BABY BLUES BROS LLC DIST. BY ANDREWS McMEEL SYNDICATION 8-19
KIRKMAN & SCOTT
WHAT'S THE DIFFERENCE?
THE MATCHING ONES TASTE BETTER.

LET'S GO!
MEET YOU OUT BACK!

OOH! THERE'S A METEOR SHOWER TONIGHT!
REALLY?
THAT GIVES ME AN IDEA...
WE ZIP A COUPLE OF SLEEPING BAGS TOGETHER, GET A BOTTLE OF WINE, AND DO A LITTLE "METEOR-WATCHING" IN THE BACKYARD?
MMM... GIGGLE!
LET'S GO!
MEET YOU OUT BACK!
©2023, BABY BLUES BROS LLC DIST. BY ANDREWS McMEEL SYNDICATION
FIVE MINUTES LATER...
WHAT ARE WE MISSING?
SIGH!
KIRKMAN & SCOTT 8-13

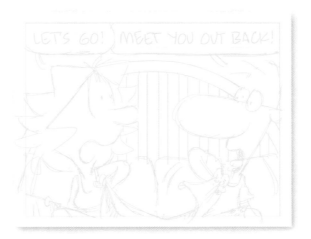

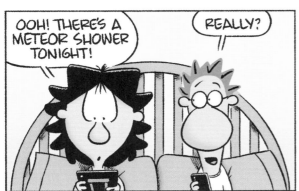

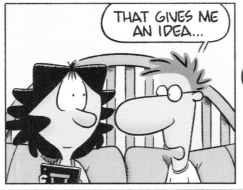

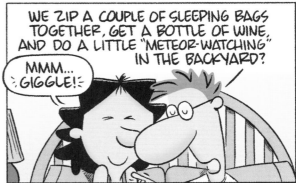

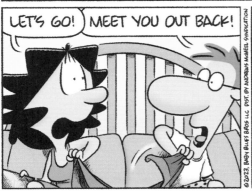

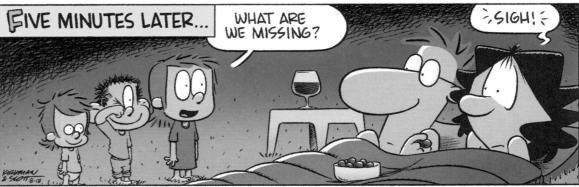

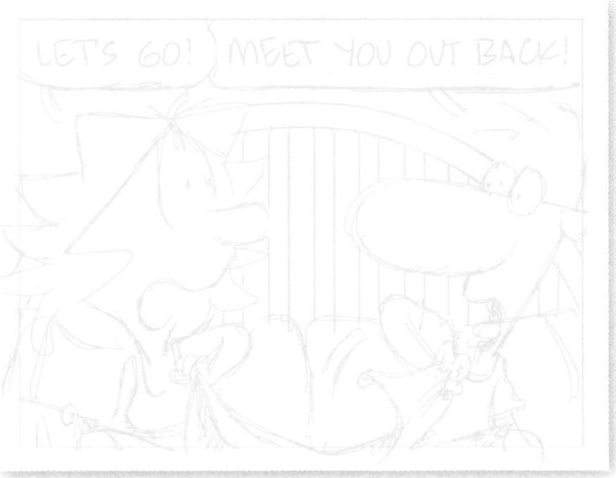

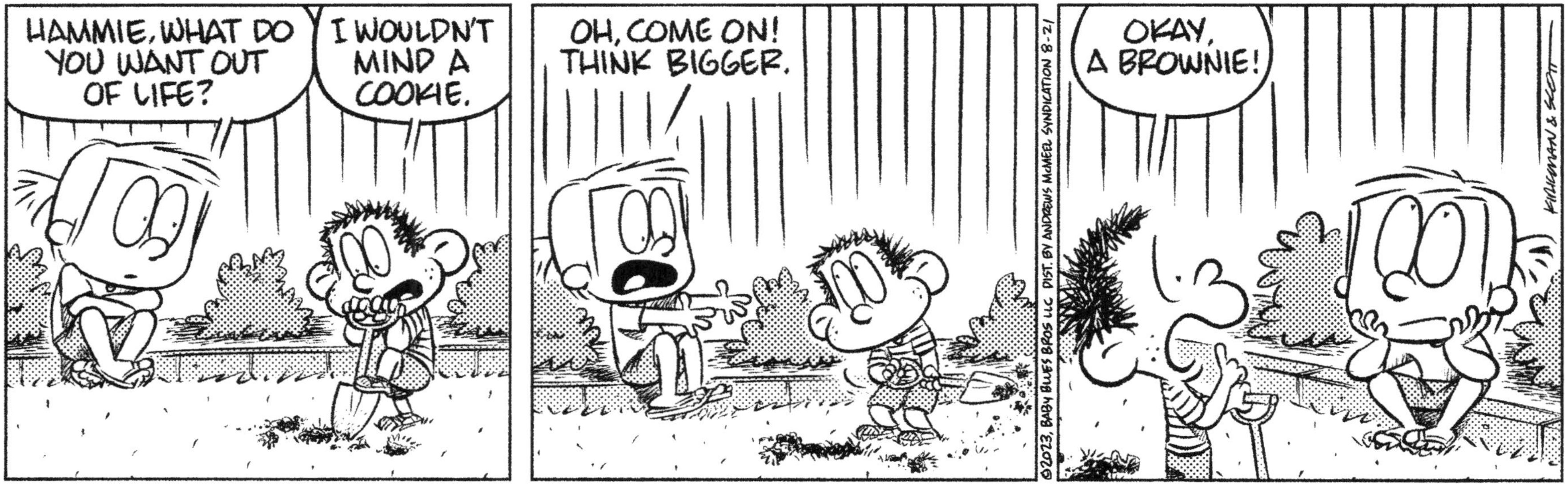
HAMMIE, WHAT DO YOU WANT OUT OF LIFE?
I WOULDN'T MIND A COOKIE.
OH, COME ON! THINK BIGGER.
OKAY, A BROWNIE!
©2023, BABY BLUES BROS LLC DIST. BY ANDREWS MCMEEL SYNDICATION 8-21
KIRKMAN & SCOTT

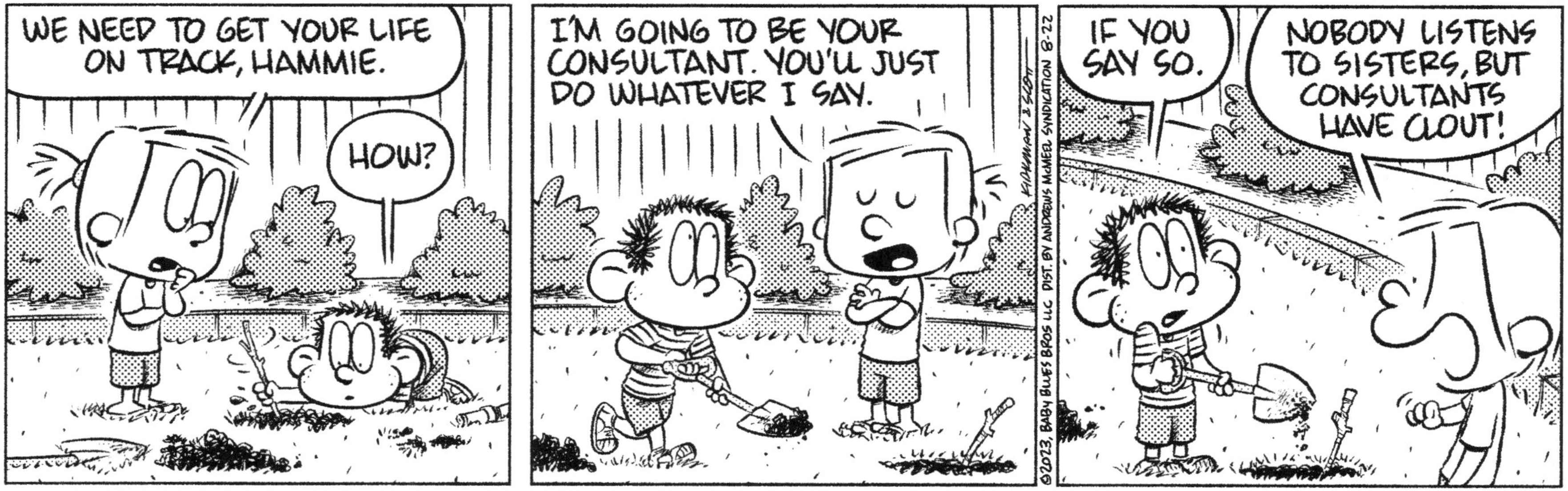
WE NEED TO GET YOUR LIFE ON TRACK, HAMMIE.
HOW?
I'M GOING TO BE YOUR CONSULTANT. YOU'LL JUST DO WHATEVER I SAY.
IF YOU SAY SO.
NOBODY LISTENS TO SISTERS, BUT CONSULTANTS HAVE CLOUT!
©2023, BABY BLUES BROS LLC DIST. BY ANDREWS MCMEEL SYNDICATION 8-22
KIRKMAN & SCOTT

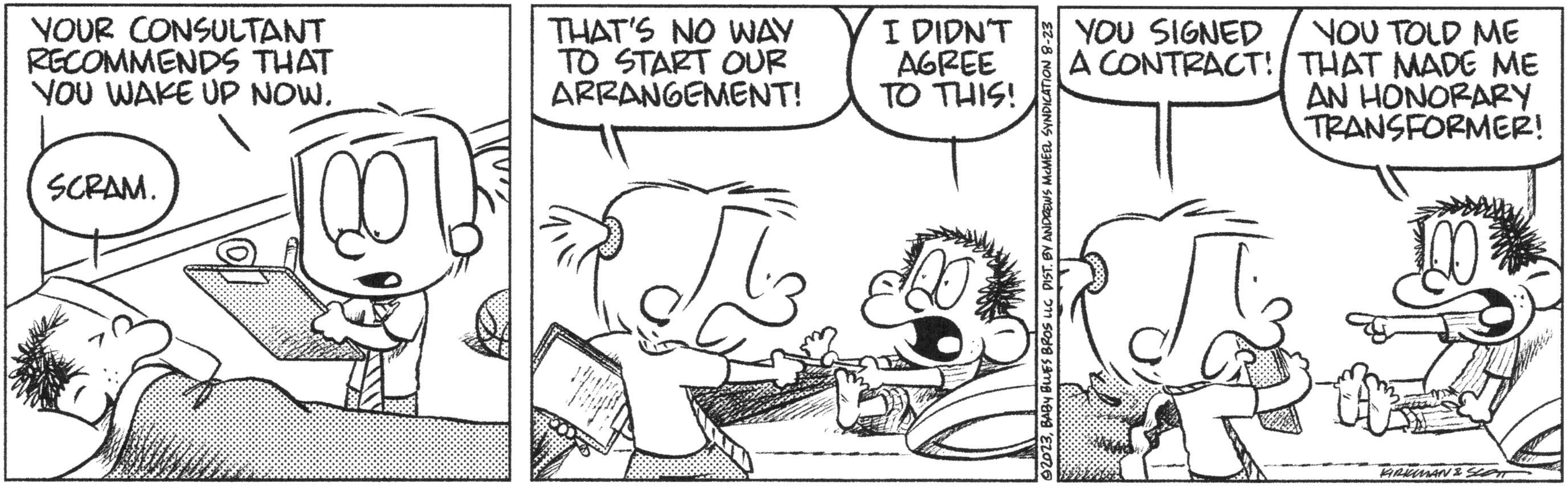
YOUR CONSULTANT RECOMMENDS THAT YOU WAKE UP NOW.
SCRAM.
THAT'S NO WAY TO START OUR ARRANGEMENT!
I DIDN'T AGREE TO THIS!
©2023, BABY BLUES BROS LLC DIST. BY ANDREWS McMEEL SYNDICATION 8-23
YOU SIGNED A CONTRACT!
YOU TOLD ME THAT MADE ME AN HONORARY TRANSFORMER!
KIRKMAN & SCOTT

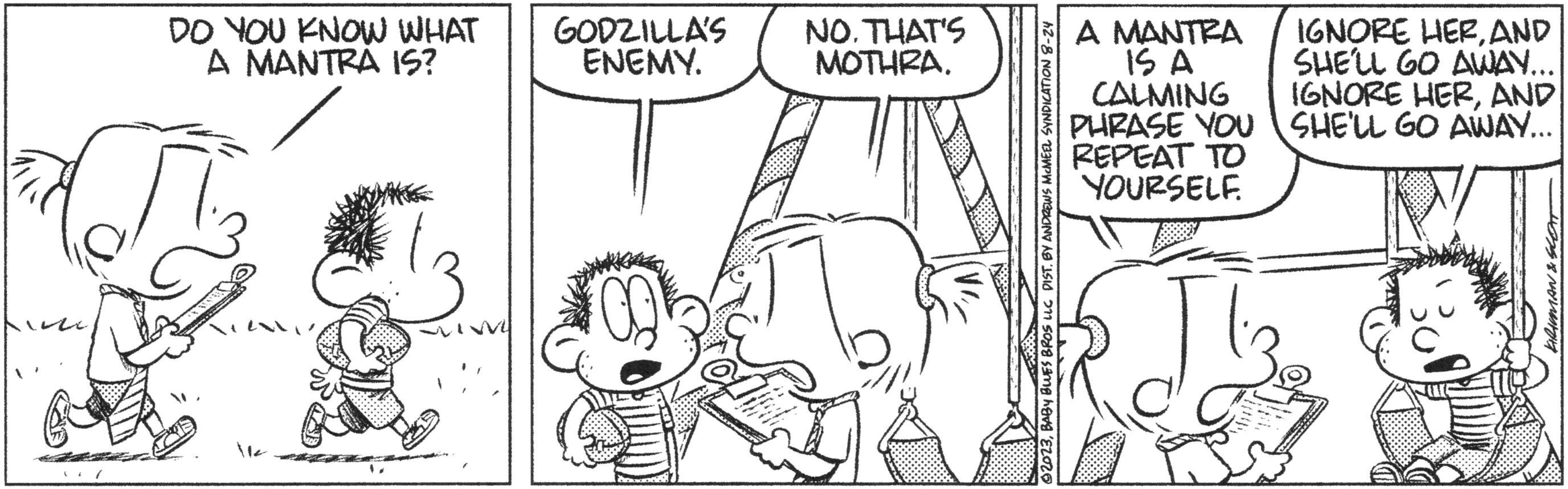
DO YOU KNOW WHAT A MANTRA IS?
GODZILLA'S ENEMY.
NO. THAT'S MOTHRA.
©2023, BABY BLUES BROS LLC DIST. BY ANDREWS McMEEL SYNDICATION 8-24
A MANTRA IS A CALMING PHRASE YOU REPEAT TO YOURSELF.
IGNORE HER, AND SHE'LL GO AWAY... IGNORE HER, AND SHE'LL GO AWAY...
KIRKMAN & SCOTT

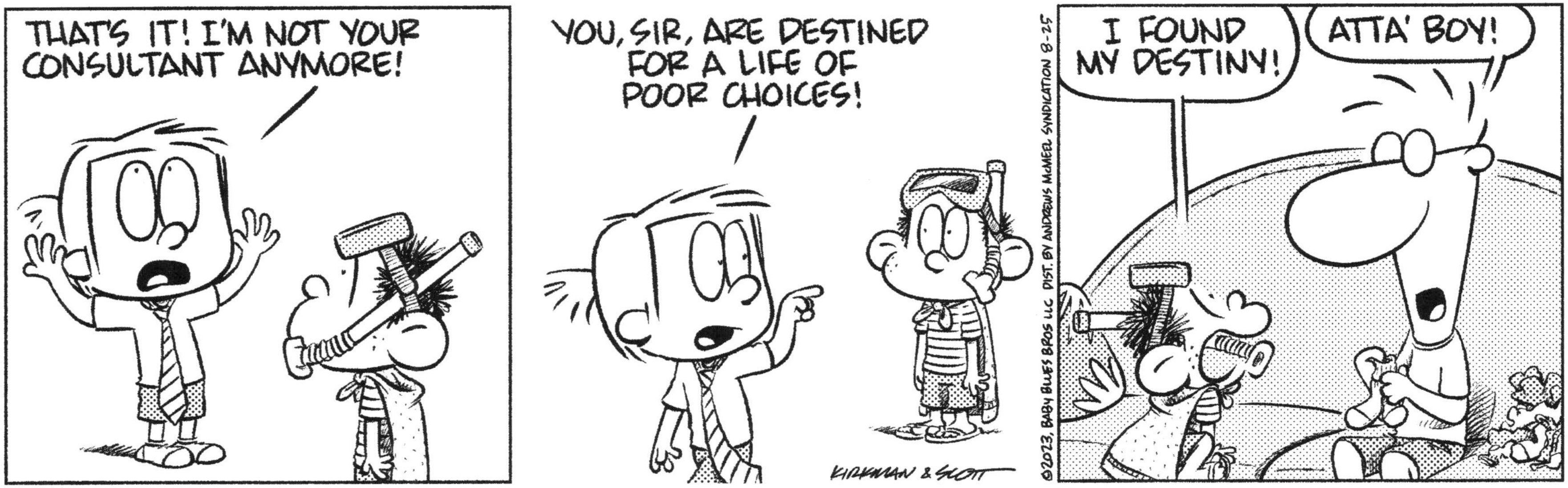
THAT'S IT! I'M NOT YOUR CONSULTANT ANYMORE!
YOU, SIR, ARE DESTINED FOR A LIFE OF POOR CHOICES!
KIRKMAN & SCOTT
©2023, BABY BLUES BROS LLC DIST. BY ANDREWS McMEEL SYNDICATION 8-25
I FOUND MY DESTINY!
ATTA' BOY!

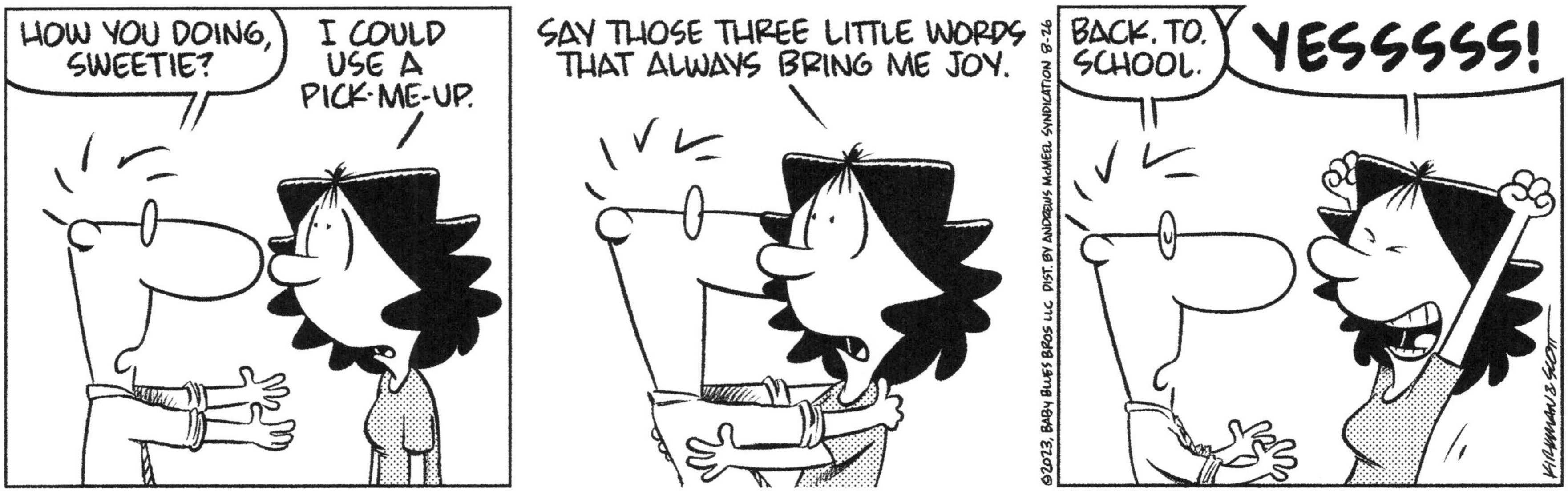
HOW YOU DOING, SWEETIE?
I COULD USE A PICK-ME-UP.
SAY THOSE THREE LITTLE WORDS THAT ALWAYS BRING ME JOY.
©2023, BABY BLUES BROS LLC DIST. BY ANDREWS McMEEL SYNDICATION 8-26
BACK. TO. SCHOOL.
YESSSSS!
KIRKMAN & SCOTT

THEY WOULD'VE TASTED BETTER MY WAY.

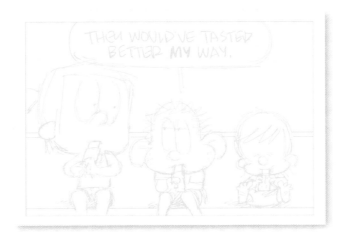

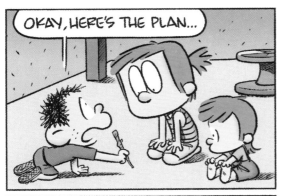

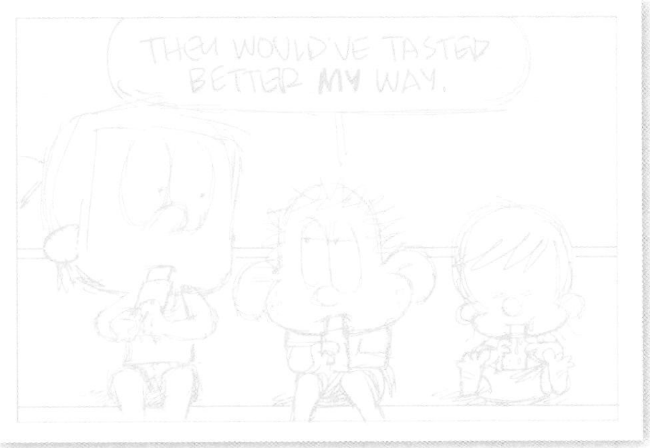

OKAY, HERE'S THE PLAN...
WREN WILL GO TO HER ROOM AND START CRYING, TO CREATE A DIVERSION.
WHEN MOM COMES TO SEE WHAT'S WRONG, YOU CLOSE THE DOOR BEHIND HER, AND THEN SIGNAL ME WITH THIS FLAG.
WHEN I SEE THE SIGNAL, I'LL PUSH THIS LAWN CHAIR OVER, CRAWL THROUGH THE KITCHEN WINDOW, TIPTOE TO THE FREEZER, AND...
9-3
MOM? CAN WE EACH HAVE AN ICE POP?
SURE.
©2023, BABY BLUES BROS LLC DIST. BY ANDREWS MCMEEL SYNDICATION
THEY WOULD'VE TASTED BETTER MY WAY.
KIRKMAN & SCOTT

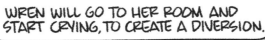

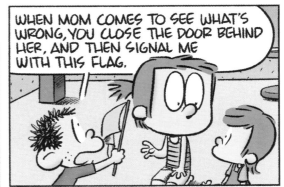

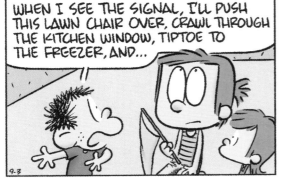

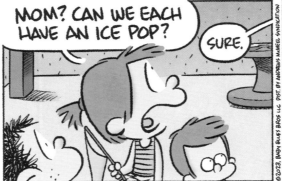

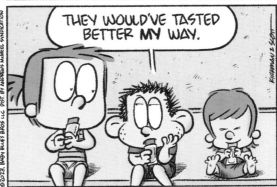

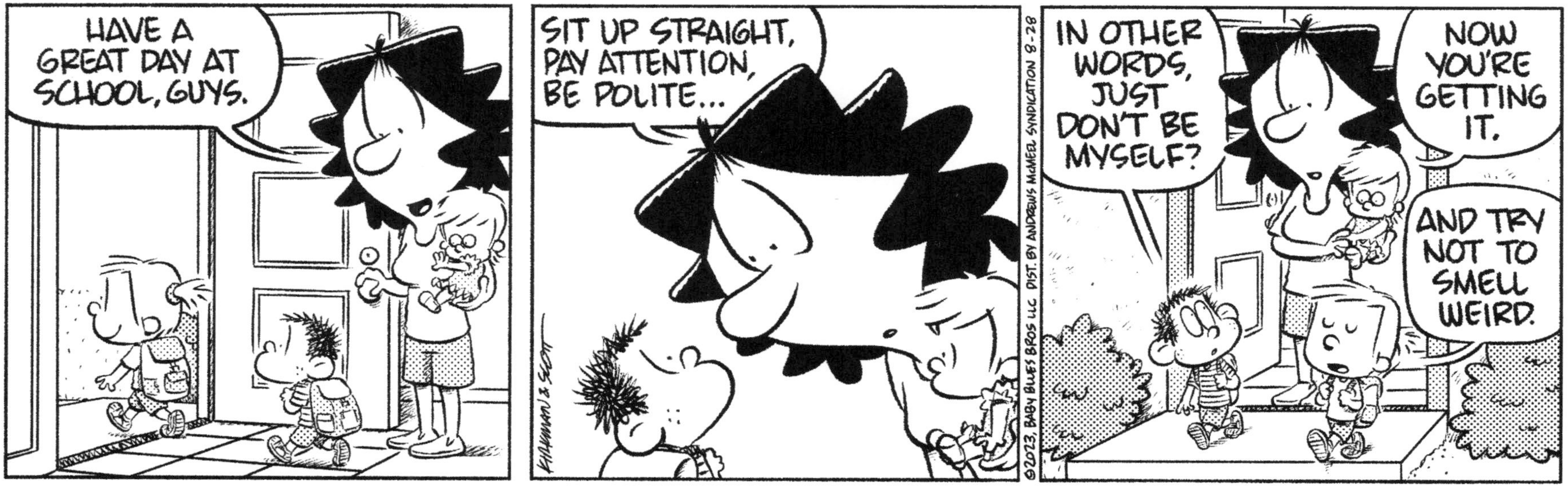
HAVE A GREAT DAY AT SCHOOL, GUYS.
SIT UP STRAIGHT, PAY ATTENTION, BE POLITE...
©2023, BABY BLUES BROS LLC DIST. BY ANDREWS McMEEL SYNDICATION 8-28
IN OTHER WORDS, JUST DON'T BE MYSELF?
NOW YOU'RE GETTING IT.
AND TRY NOT TO SMELL WEIRD.

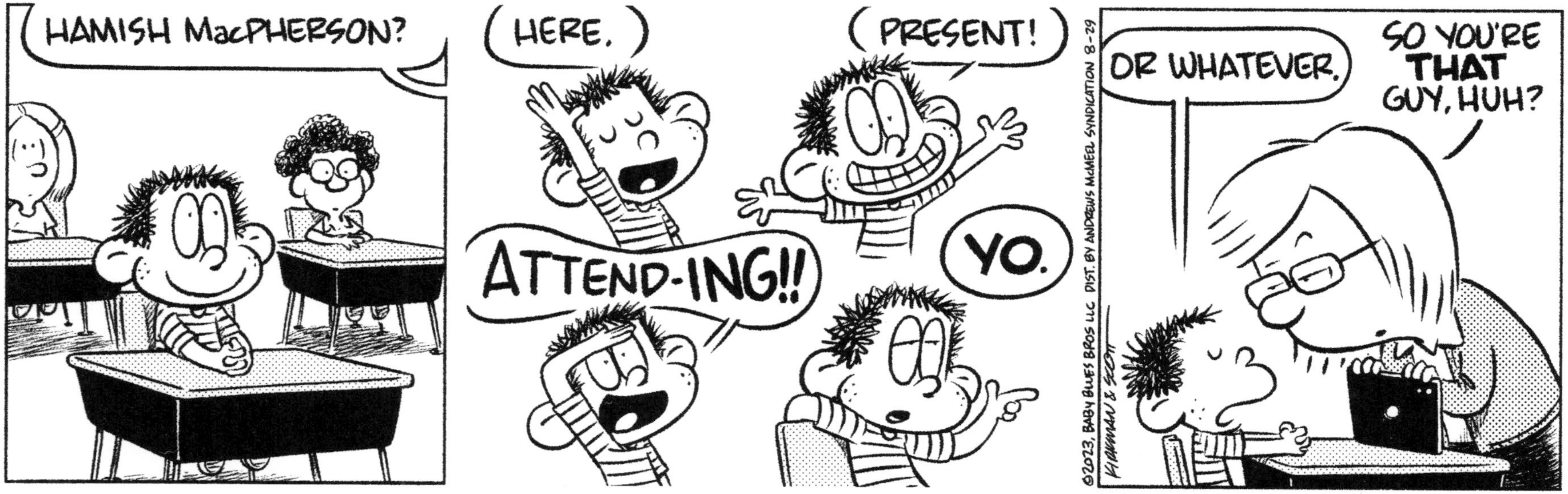
HAMISH MacPHERSON?
HERE.
PRESENT!
ATTEND-ING!!
YO.
©2023, BABY BLUES BROS LLC DIST. BY ANDREWS McMEEL SYNDICATION 8-29
OR WHATEVER.
SO YOU'RE **THAT** GUY, HUH?

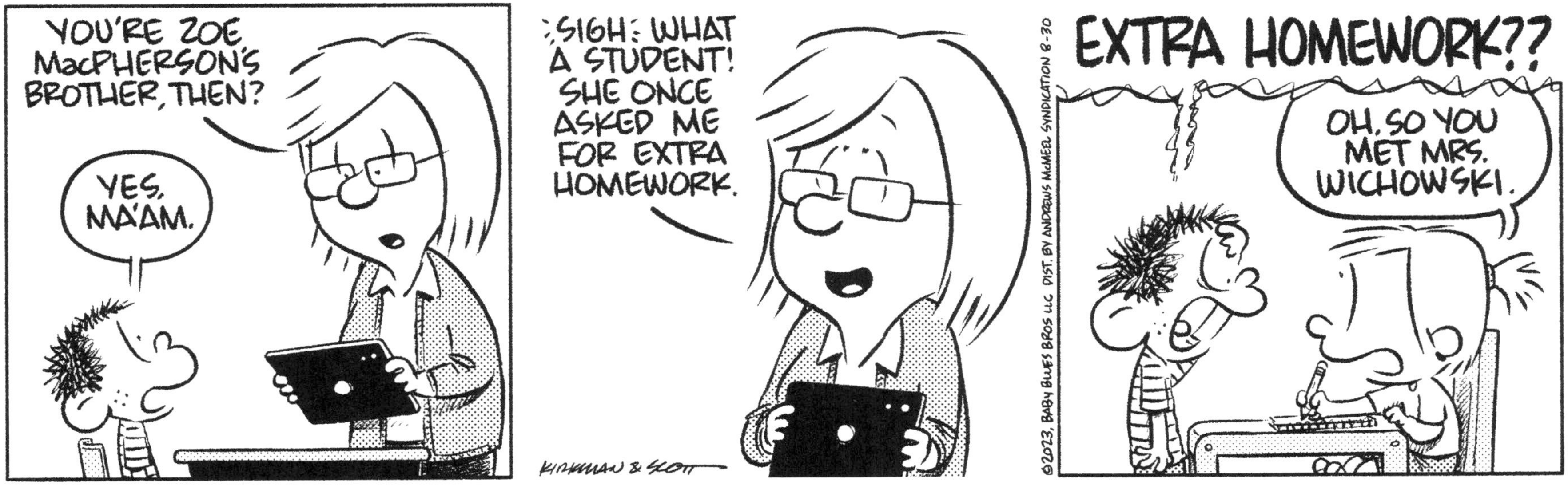
YOU'RE ZOE MacPHERSON'S BROTHER, THEN?
YES, MA'AM.
:SIGH: WHAT A STUDENT! SHE ONCE ASKED ME FOR EXTRA HOMEWORK.
KIRKMAN & SCOTT
©2023, BABY BLUES BROS LLC DIST. BY ANDREWS McMEEL SYNDICATION 8-30
EXTRA HOMEWORK??
OH, SO YOU MET MRS. WICHOWSKI.

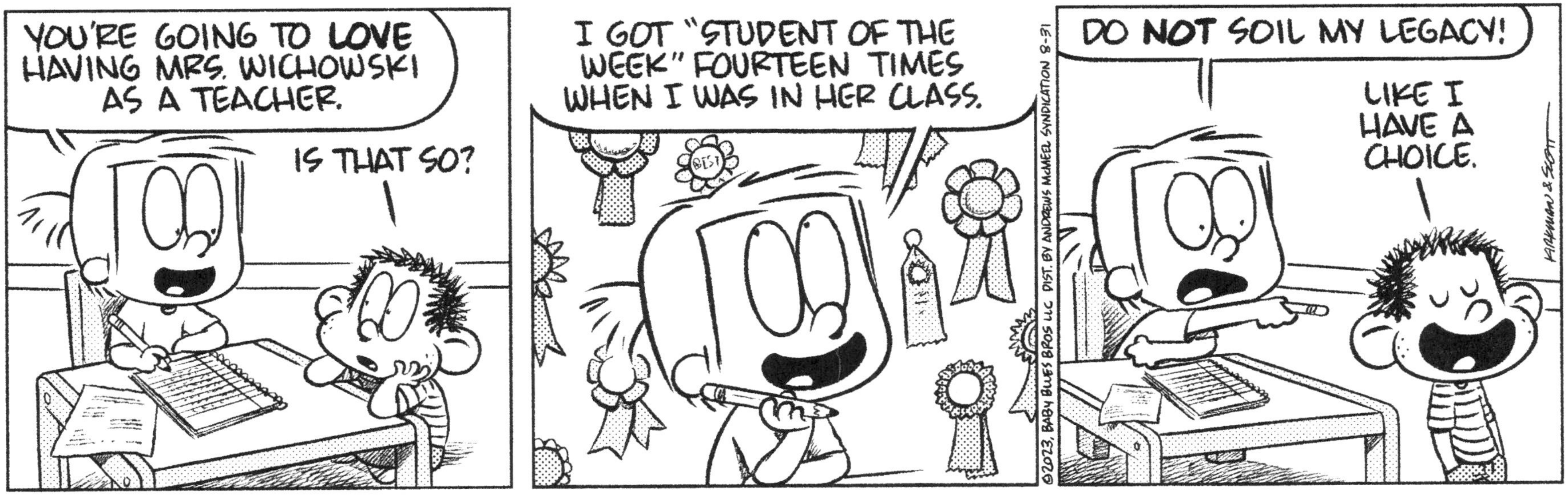
YOU'RE GOING TO **LOVE** HAVING MRS. WICHOWSKI AS A TEACHER.
IS THAT SO?
I GOT "STUDENT OF THE WEEK" FOURTEEN TIMES WHEN I WAS IN HER CLASS.
BEST
©2023, BABY BLUES BROS LLC DIST. BY ANDREWS McMEEL SYNDICATION 8-31
DO **NOT** SOIL MY LEGACY!
LIKE I HAVE A CHOICE.
KIRKMAN & SCOTT

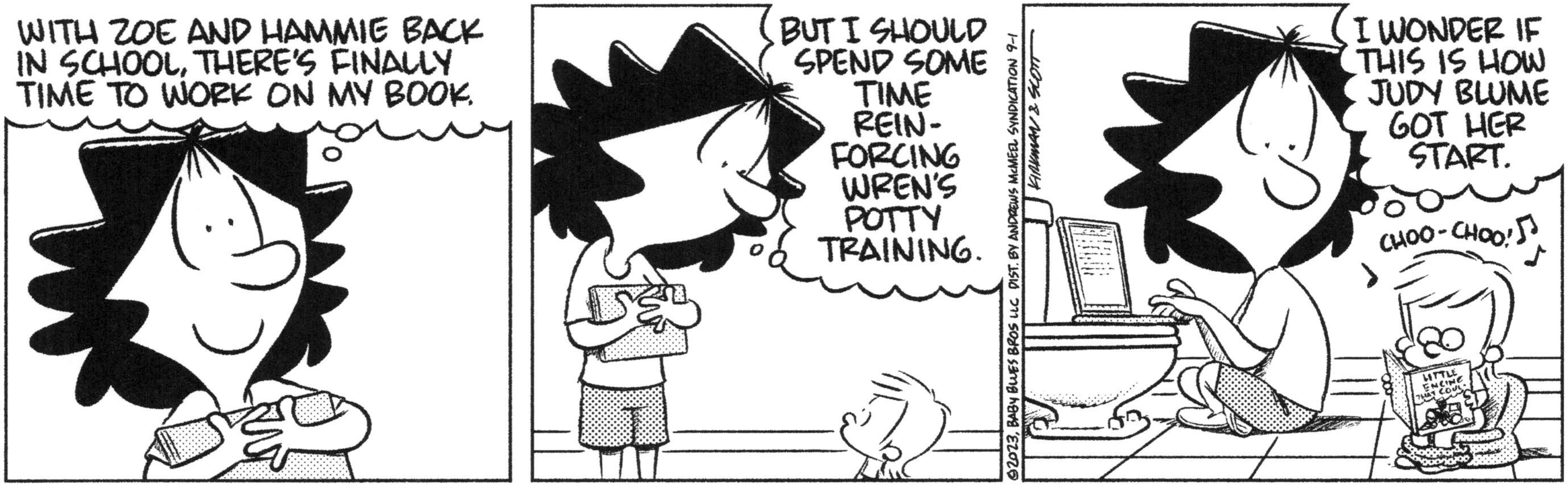
WITH ZOE AND HAMMIE BACK IN SCHOOL, THERE'S FINALLY TIME TO WORK ON MY BOOK.
BUT I SHOULD SPEND SOME TIME REIN-FORCING WREN'S POTTY TRAINING.
©2023, BABY BLUES BROS LLC DIST. BY ANDREWS MCMEEL SYNDICATION 9-1
KIRKMAN & SCOTT
I WONDER IF THIS IS HOW JUDY BLUME GOT HER START.
CHOO-CHOO!

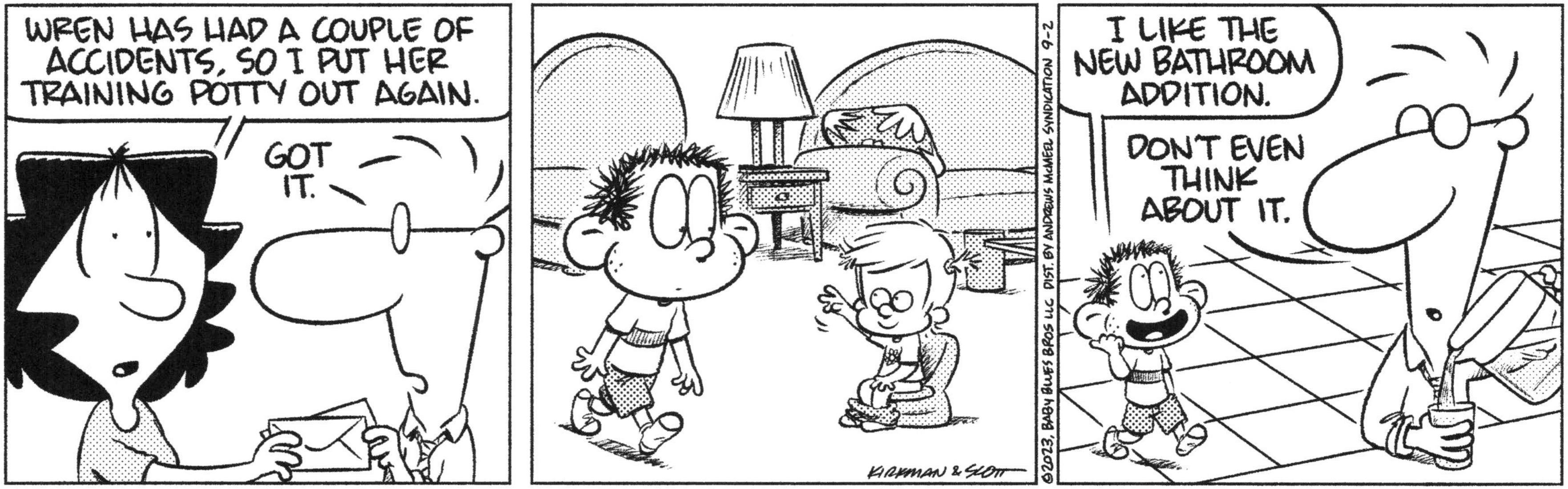
WREN HAS HAD A COUPLE OF ACCIDENTS, SO I PUT HER TRAINING POTTY OUT AGAIN.
GOT IT.
KIRKMAN & SCOTT
©2023, BABY BLUES BROS LLC DIST. BY ANDREWS MCMEEL SYNDICATION 9-2
I LIKE THE NEW BATHROOM ADDITION.
DON'T EVEN THINK ABOUT IT.

©2023, BABY BLUES BROS LLC DIST. BY ANDREWS MCMEEL SYNDICATION
LET'S TRY GENTLY ROLLING THE DICE FROM NOW ON, OKAY?
AW!
9-10

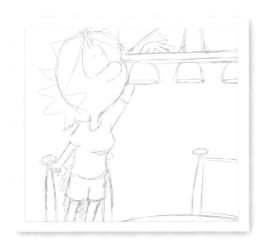

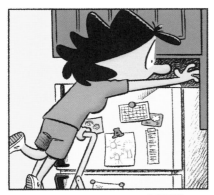

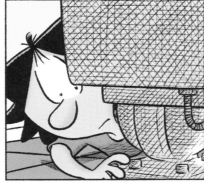

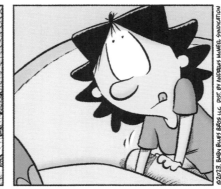

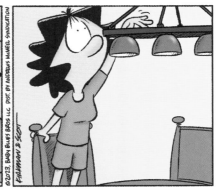

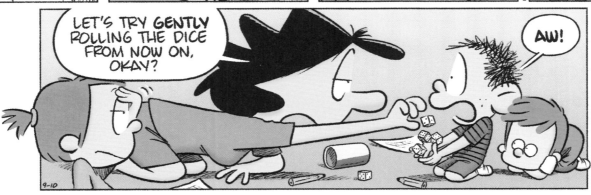

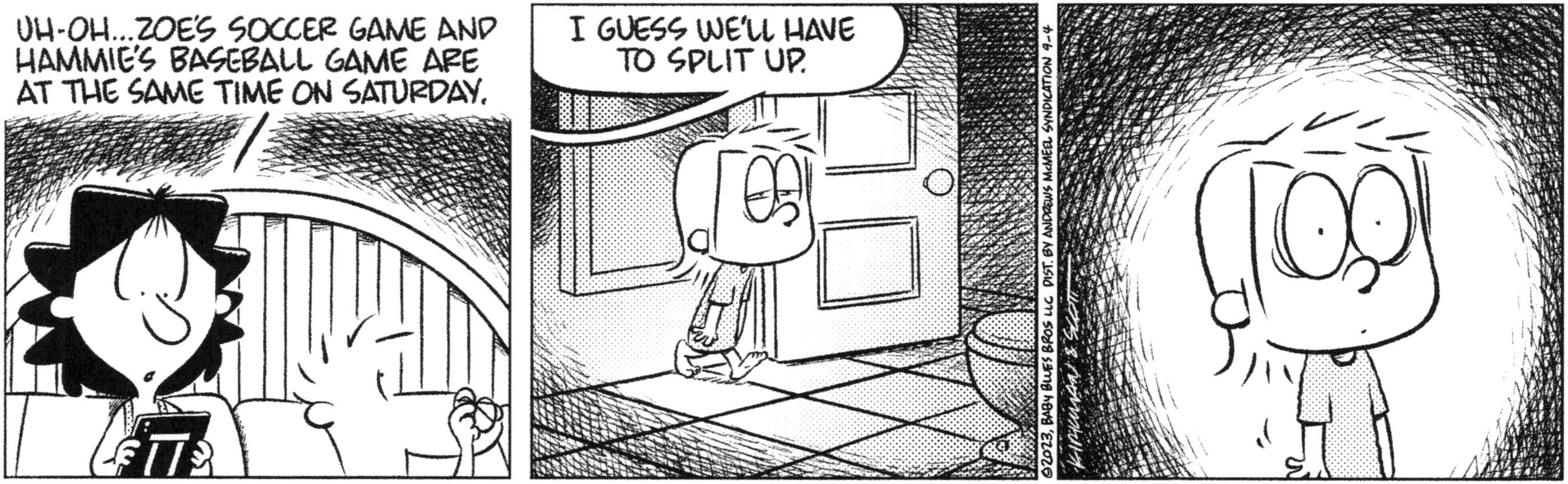
UH-OH...ZOE'S SOCCER GAME AND HAMMIE'S BASEBALL GAME ARE AT THE SAME TIME ON SATURDAY.
I GUESS WE'LL HAVE TO SPLIT UP.
©2023, BABY BLUES BROS LLC DIST. BY ANDREWS McMEEL SYNDICATION 9-4
KIRKMAN & SCOTT

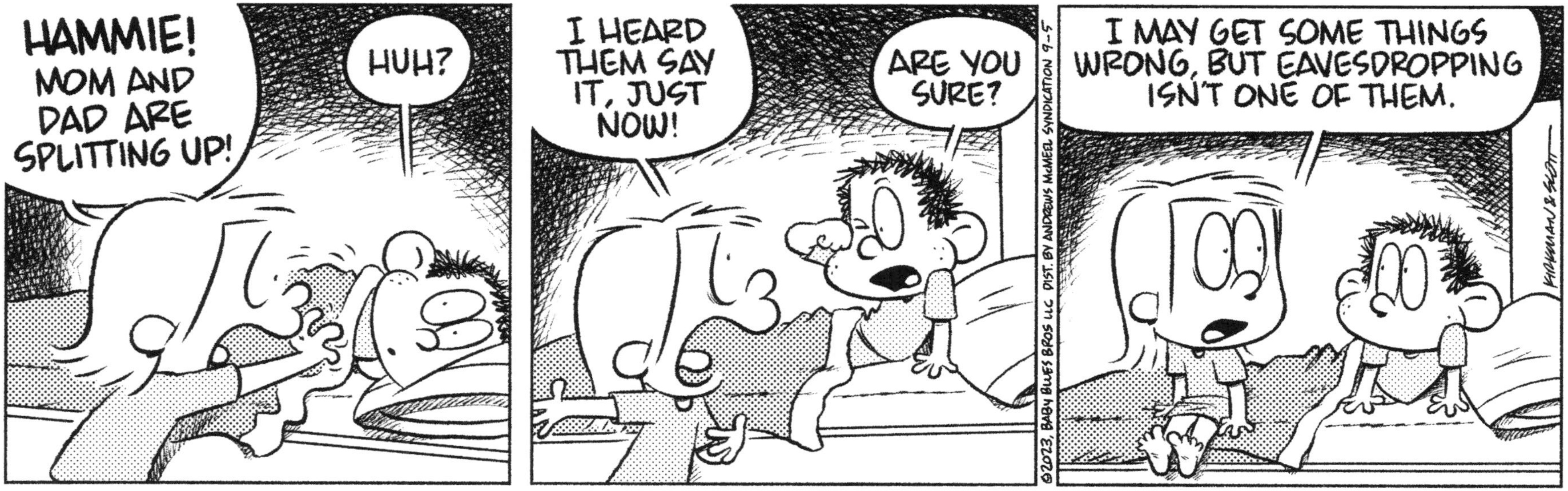
HAMMIE! MOM AND DAD ARE SPLITTING UP!
HUH?
I HEARD THEM SAY IT, JUST NOW!
ARE YOU SURE?
©2023, BABY BLUES BROS LLC DIST. BY ANDREWS McMEEL SYNDICATION 9-5
I MAY GET SOME THINGS WRONG, BUT EAVESDROPPING ISN'T ONE OF THEM.
KIRKMAN & SCOTT

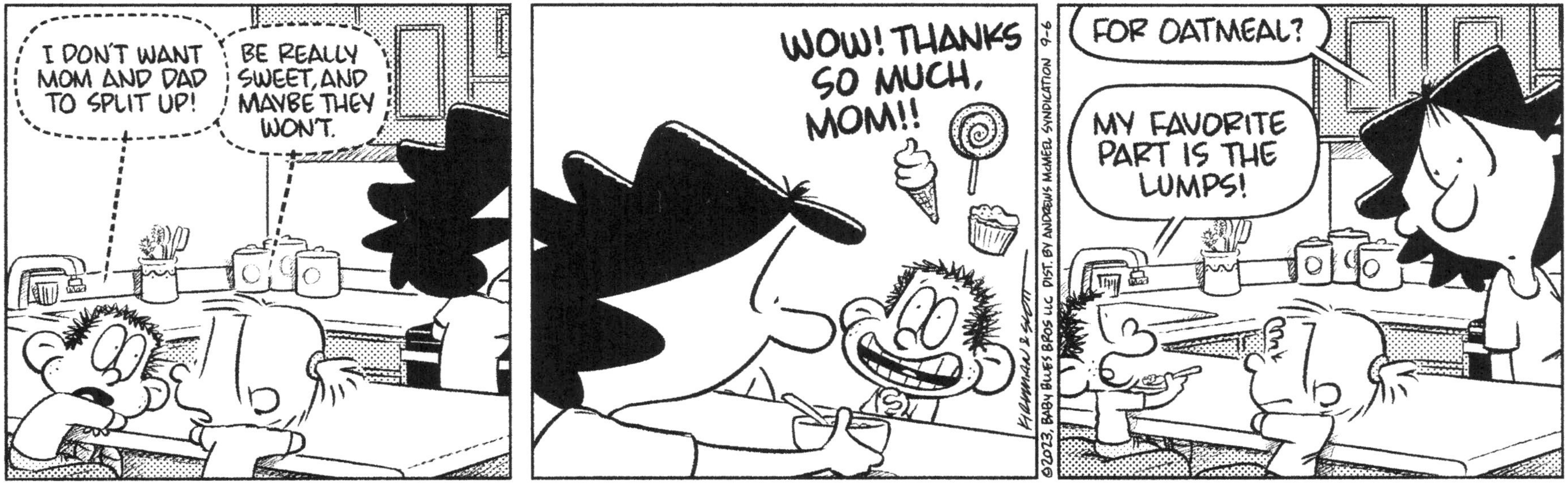
I DON'T WANT MOM AND DAD TO SPLIT UP!
BE REALLY SWEET, AND MAYBE THEY WON'T.
WOW! THANKS SO MUCH, MOM!!
KIRKMAN & SCOTT
©2023, BABY BLUES BROS LLC DIST. BY ANDREWS McMEEL SYNDICATION 9-6
FOR OATMEAL?
MY FAVORITE PART IS THE LUMPS!

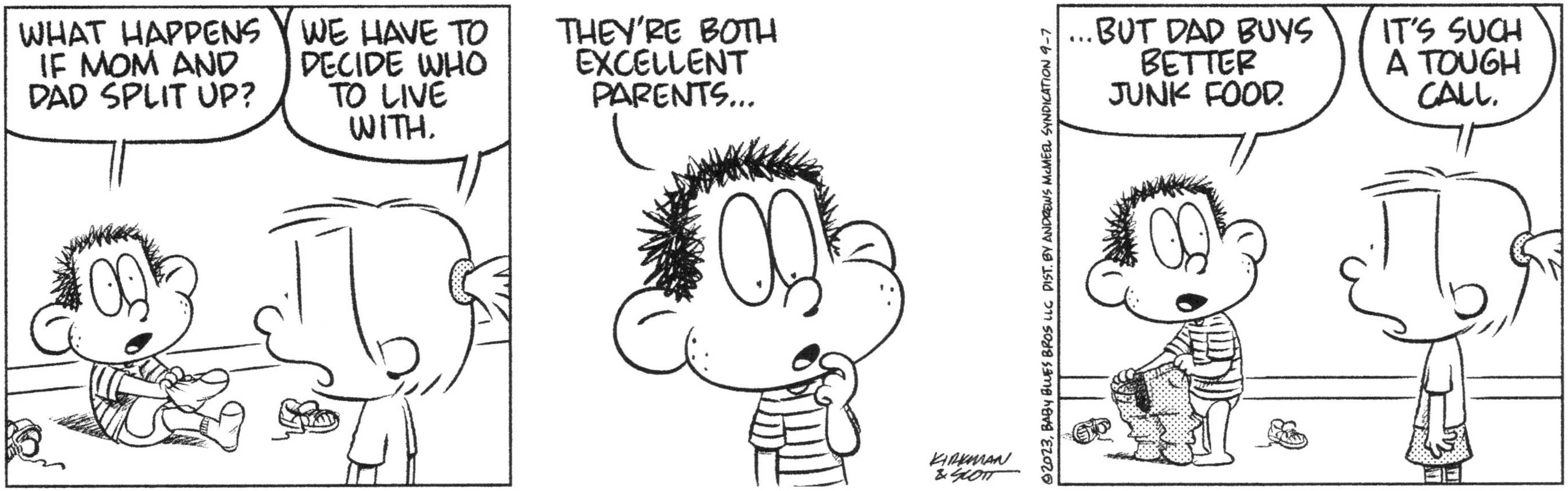
WHAT HAPPENS IF MOM AND DAD SPLIT UP?
WE HAVE TO DECIDE WHO TO LIVE WITH.
THEY'RE BOTH EXCELLENT PARENTS...
KIRKMAN & SCOTT
©2023, BABY BLUES BROS LLC DIST. BY ANDREWS McMEEL SYNDICATION 9-7
...BUT DAD BUYS BETTER JUNK FOOD.
IT'S SUCH A TOUGH CALL.

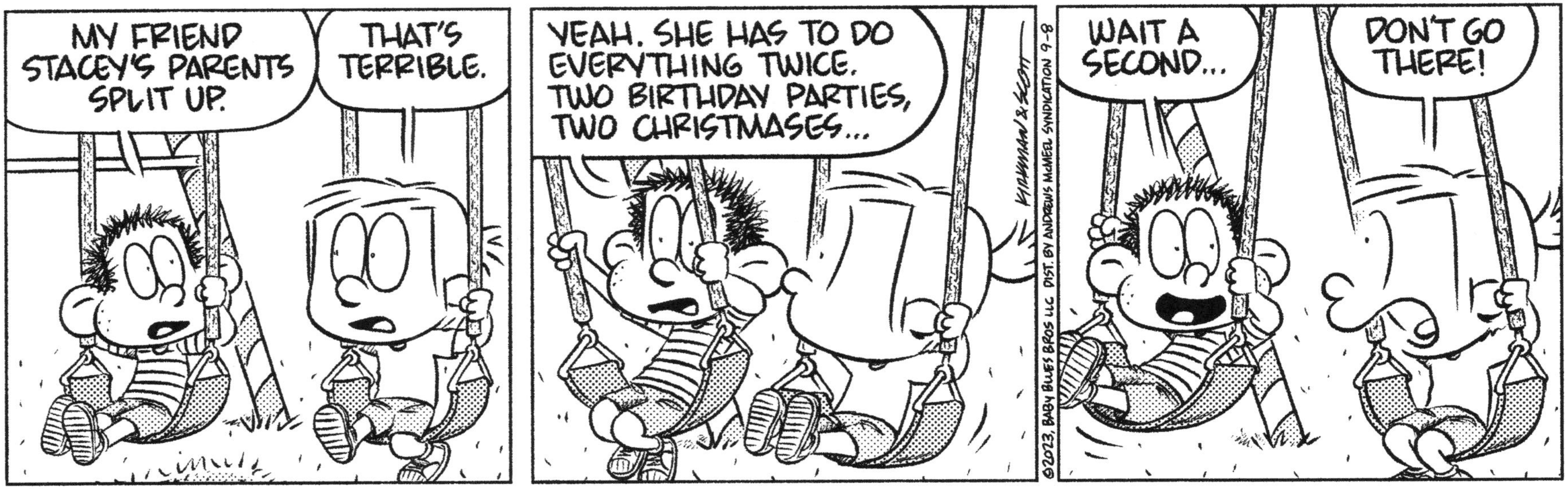
MY FRIEND STACEY'S PARENTS SPLIT UP.
THAT'S TERRIBLE.
YEAH. SHE HAS TO DO EVERYTHING TWICE. TWO BIRTHDAY PARTIES, TWO CHRISTMASES...
©2023, BABY BLUES BROS LLC DIST. BY ANDREWS MCMEEL SYNDICATION 9-8
KIRKMAN & SCOTT
WAIT A SECOND...
DON'T GO THERE!

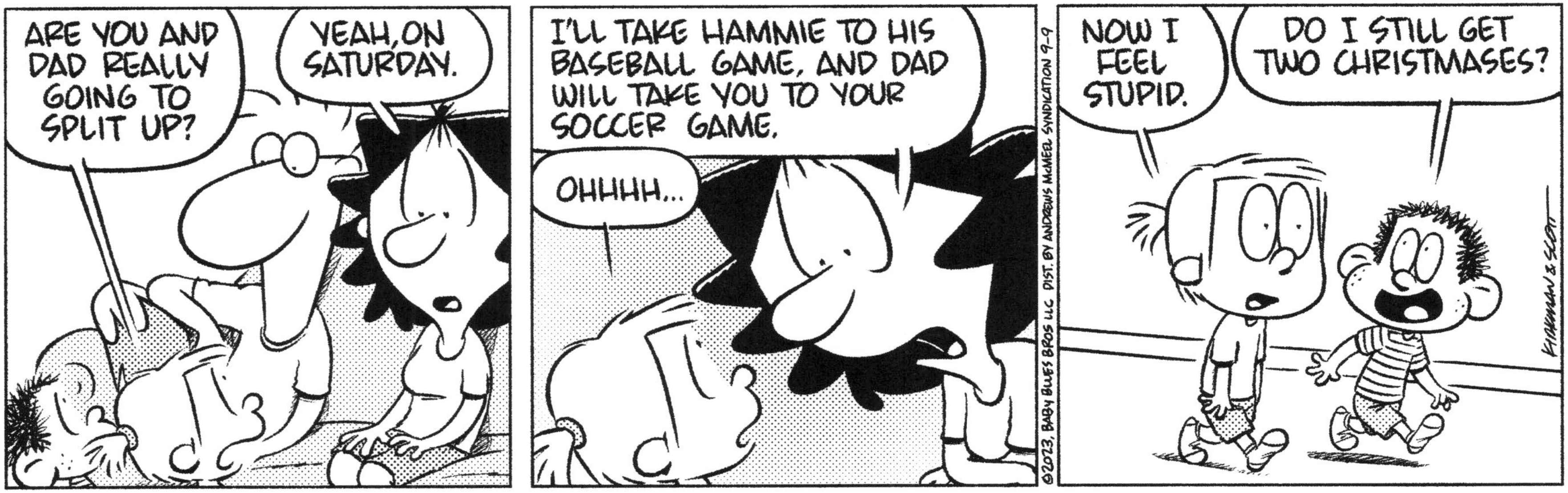
ARE YOU AND DAD REALLY GOING TO SPLIT UP?
YEAH, ON SATURDAY.
I'LL TAKE HAMMIE TO HIS BASEBALL GAME, AND DAD WILL TAKE YOU TO YOUR SOCCER GAME.
OHHHH...
©2023, BABY BLUES BROS LLC DIST. BY ANDREWS MCMEEL SYNDICATION 9-9
NOW I FEEL STUPID.
DO I STILL GET TWO CHRISTMASES?
KIRKMAN & SCOTT

PLOP!

YOU SURE LOOK COMFORTABLE.
OH, I AM.
WOULD YOU LIKE ME TO BRING YOU SOMETHING?
YOU'RE READING MY MIND, SWEETIE!
©2023, BABY BLUES BROS LLC DIST. BY ANDREWS MCMEEL SYNDICATION
ANYTHING IN PARTICULAR?
NO. WHATEVER LOOKS GOOD TO YOU IS FINE.
YOU SURE?
ABSOLUTELY.
PLOP!
KIRKMAN & SCOTT
9-17
NEXT TIME, I'M JUST GOING TO SAY, "POTATO CHIPS."

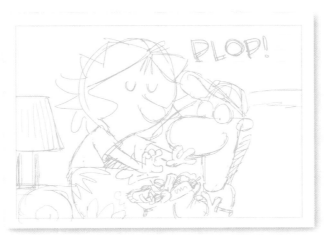

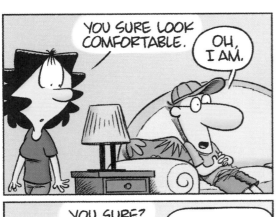

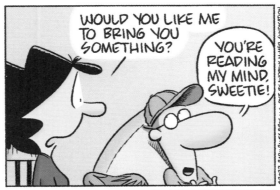

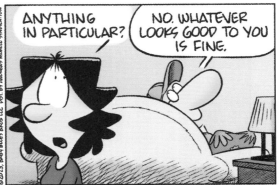

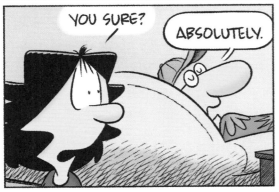

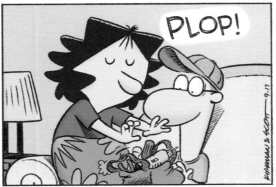

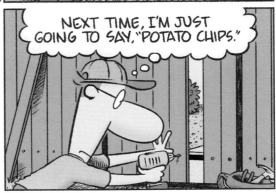

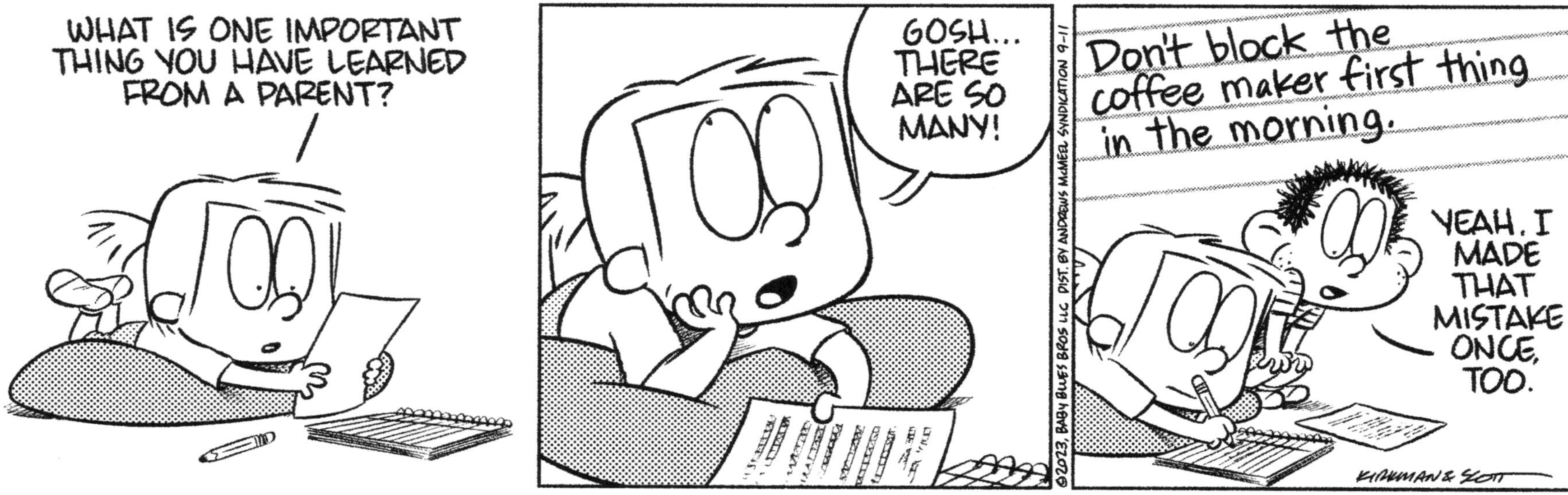
WHAT IS ONE IMPORTANT THING YOU HAVE LEARNED FROM A PARENT?
GOSH... THERE ARE SO MANY!
©2023, BABY BLUES BROS LLC DIST. BY ANDREWS McMEEL SYNDICATION 9-11
Don't block the coffee maker first thing in the morning.
YEAH. I MADE THAT MISTAKE ONCE, TOO.
KIRKMAN & SCOTT

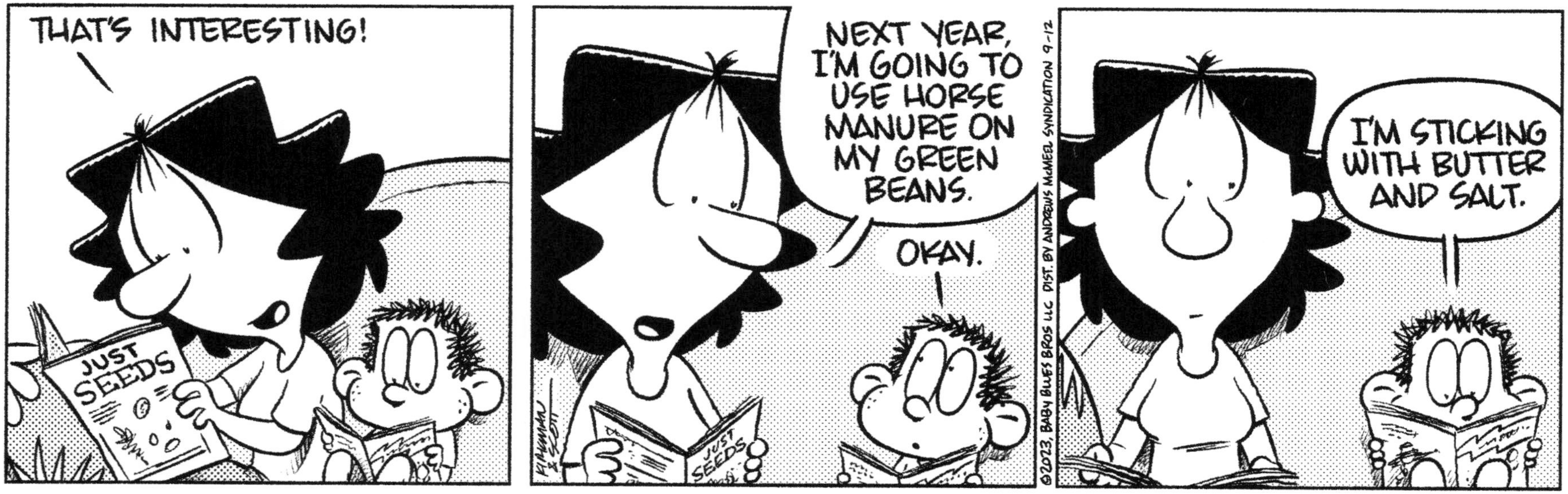
THAT'S INTERESTING!
JUST SEEDS
NEXT YEAR, I'M GOING TO USE HORSE MANURE ON MY GREEN BEANS.
OKAY.
©2023, BABY BLUES BROS LLC DIST. BY ANDREWS McMEEL SYNDICATION 9-12
I'M STICKING WITH BUTTER AND SALT.

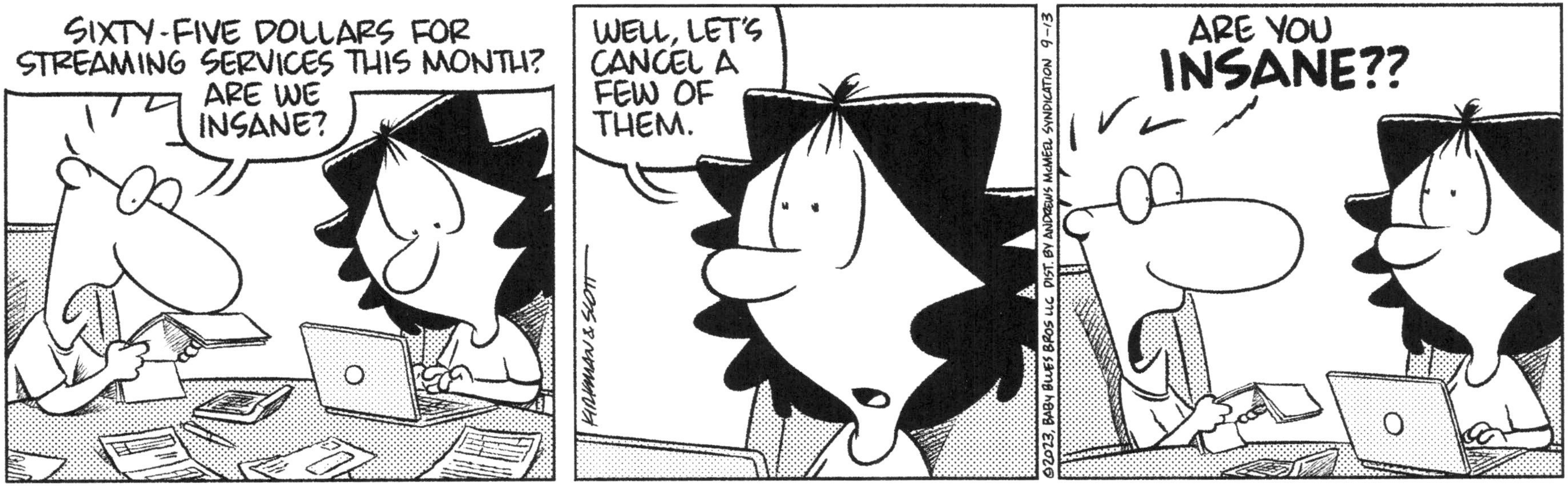
SIXTY-FIVE DOLLARS FOR STREAMING SERVICES THIS MONTH? ARE WE INSANE?
WELL, LET'S CANCEL A FEW OF THEM.
ARE YOU INSANE??
KIRKMAN & SCOTT
©2023, BABY BLUES BROS LLC DIST. BY ANDREWS MCMEEL SYNDICATION 9-13

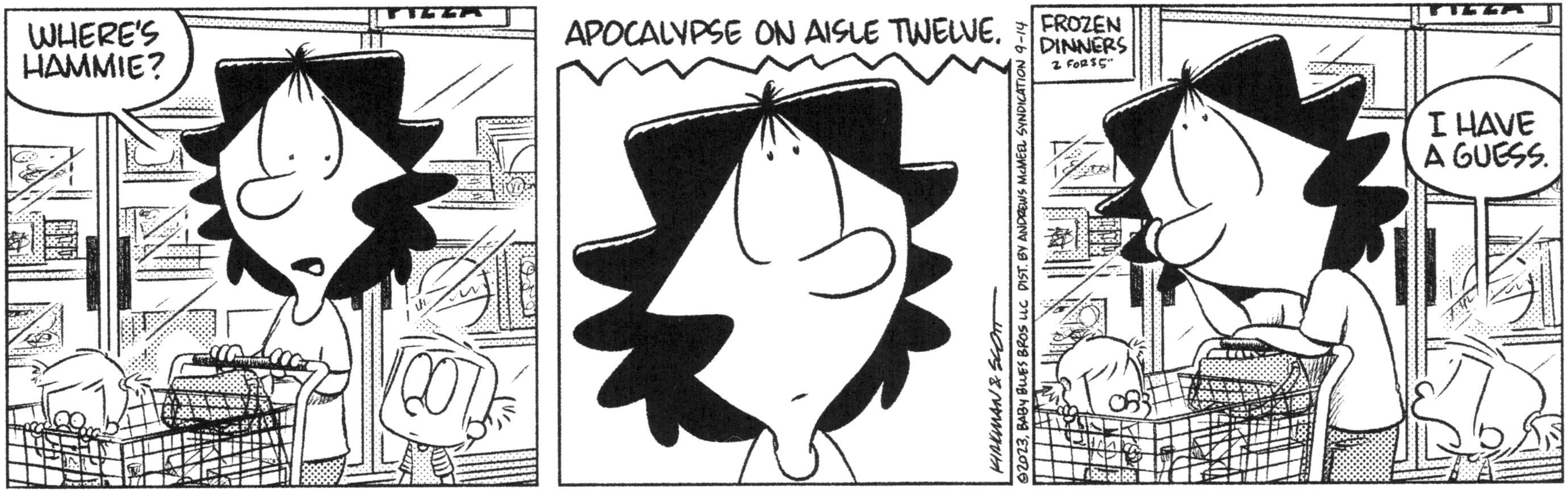
WHERE'S HAMMIE?
APOCALYPSE ON AISLE TWELVE.
FROZEN DINNERS 2 FOR $5
I HAVE A GUESS.
KIRKMAN & SCOTT
©2023, BABY BLUES BROS LLC DIST. BY ANDREWS MCMEEL SYNDICATION 9-14

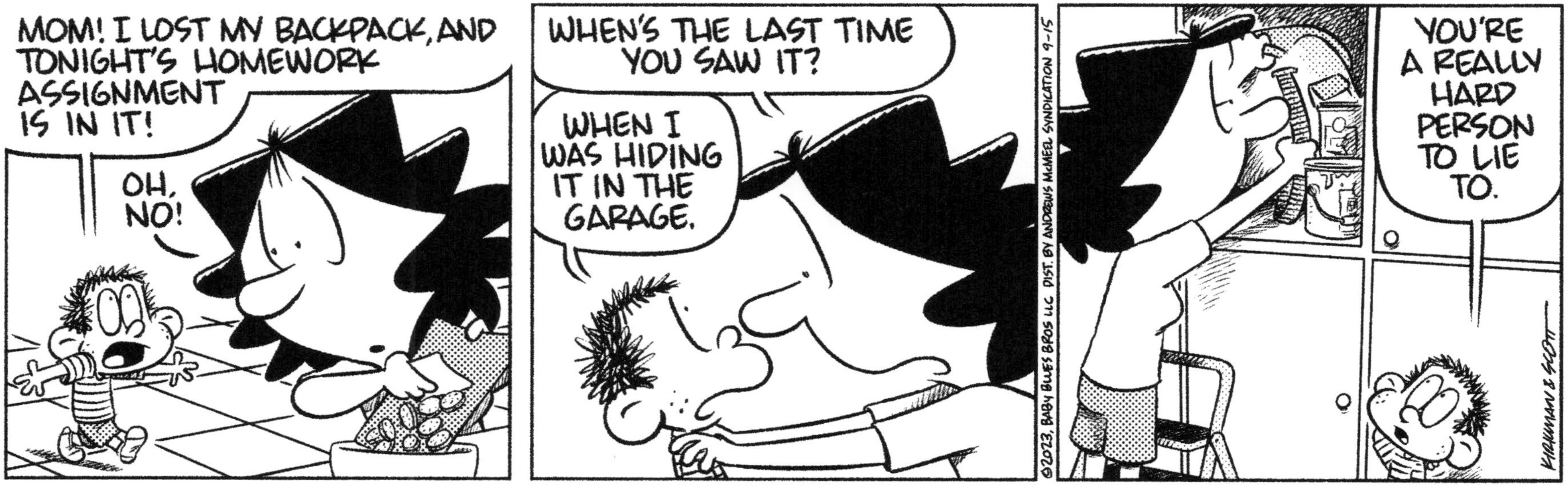
MOM! I LOST MY BACKPACK, AND TONIGHT'S HOMEWORK ASSIGNMENT IS IN IT!
OH, NO!
WHEN'S THE LAST TIME YOU SAW IT?
WHEN I WAS HIDING IT IN THE GARAGE.
YOU'RE A REALLY HARD PERSON TO LIE TO.
©2023, BABY BLUES BROS LLC DIST. BY ANDREWS MCMEEL SYNDICATION 9-15
KIRKMAN & SCOTT

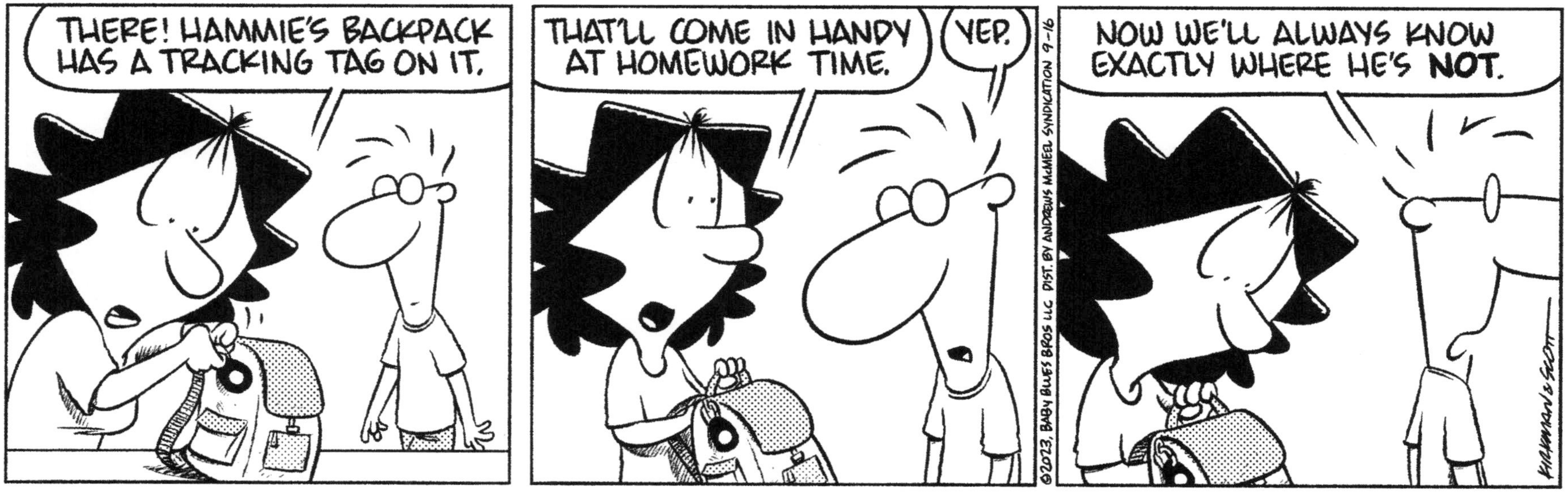
THERE! HAMMIE'S BACKPACK HAS A TRACKING TAG ON IT.
THAT'LL COME IN HANDY AT HOMEWORK TIME.
YEP.
NOW WE'LL ALWAYS KNOW EXACTLY WHERE HE'S **NOT**.
©2023, BABY BLUES BROS LLC DIST. BY ANDREWS MCMEEL SYNDICATION 9-16
KIRKMAN & SCOTT

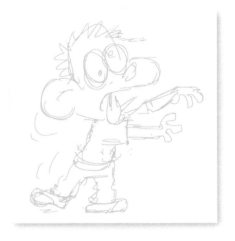

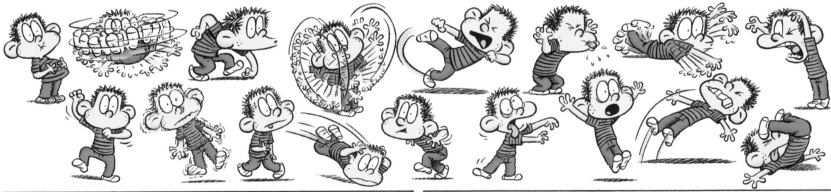

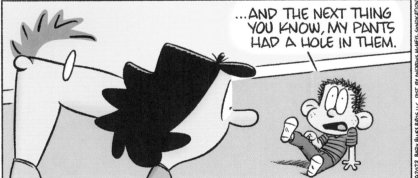

...AND THE NEXT THING YOU KNOW, MY PANTS HAD A HOLE IN THEM.
©2023, BABY BLUES BROS LLC DIST. BY ANDREWS McMEEL SYNDICATION
ELEMENTARY SCHOOL IS NOT FOR WIMPS.
IT SOUNDED MORE LIKE THE APOCALYPSE THAN RECESS.
KIRKMAN & SCOTT 9-24

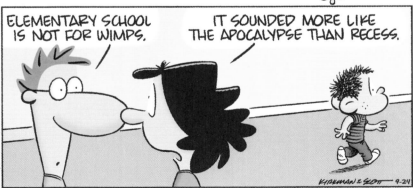

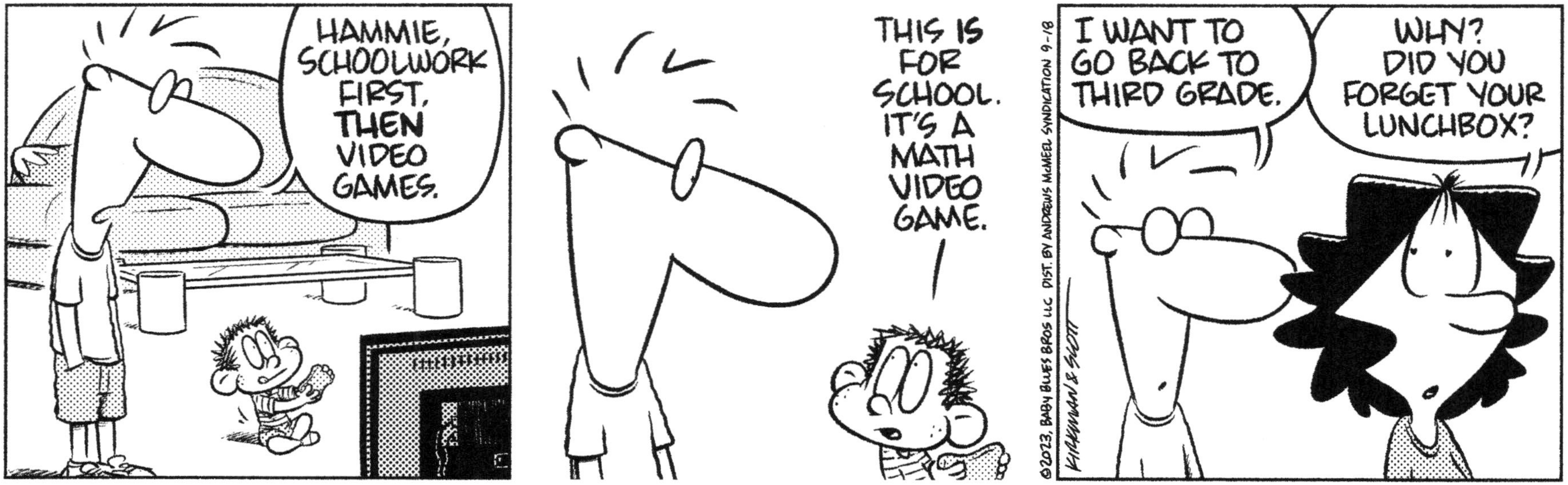
HAMMIE, SCHOOLWORK FIRST, THEN VIDEO GAMES.
THIS IS FOR SCHOOL. IT'S A MATH VIDEO GAME.
©2023, BABY BLUES BROS LLC DIST. BY ANDREWS McMEEL SYNDICATION 9-18
KIRKMAN & SCOTT
I WANT TO GO BACK TO THIRD GRADE.
WHY? DID YOU FORGET YOUR LUNCHBOX?

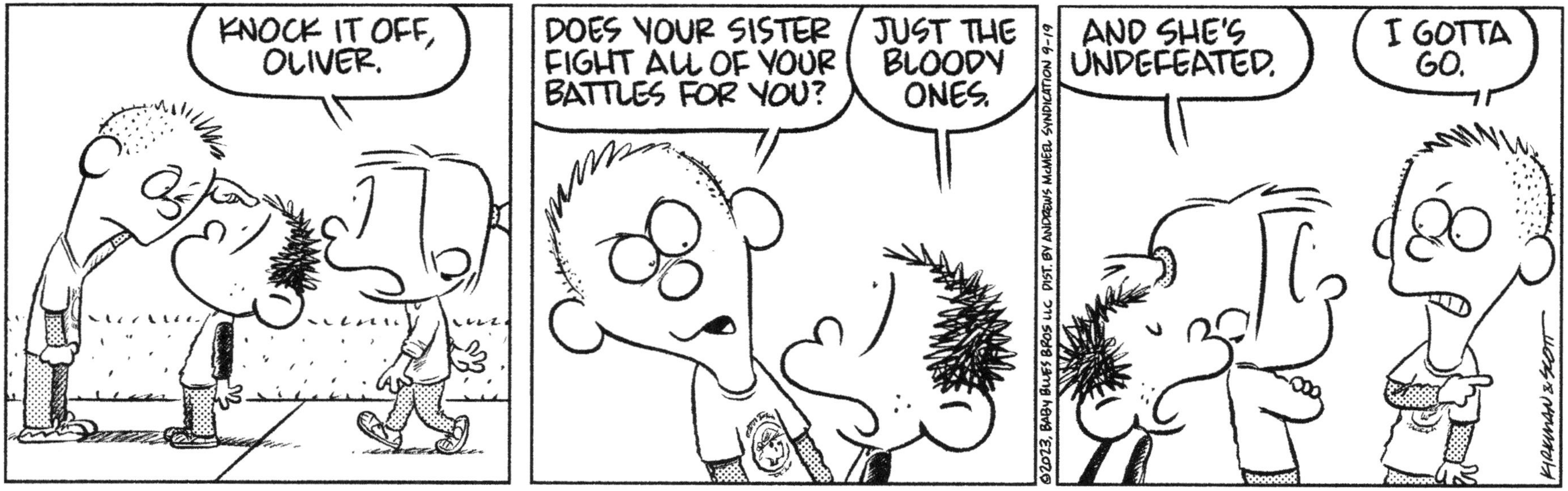
KNOCK IT OFF, OLIVER.
DOES YOUR SISTER FIGHT ALL OF YOUR BATTLES FOR YOU?
JUST THE BLOODY ONES.
©2023, BABY BLUES BROS LLC DIST. BY ANDREWS McMEEL SYNDICATION 9-19
AND SHE'S UNDEFEATED.
I GOTTA GO.
KIRKMAN & SCOTT

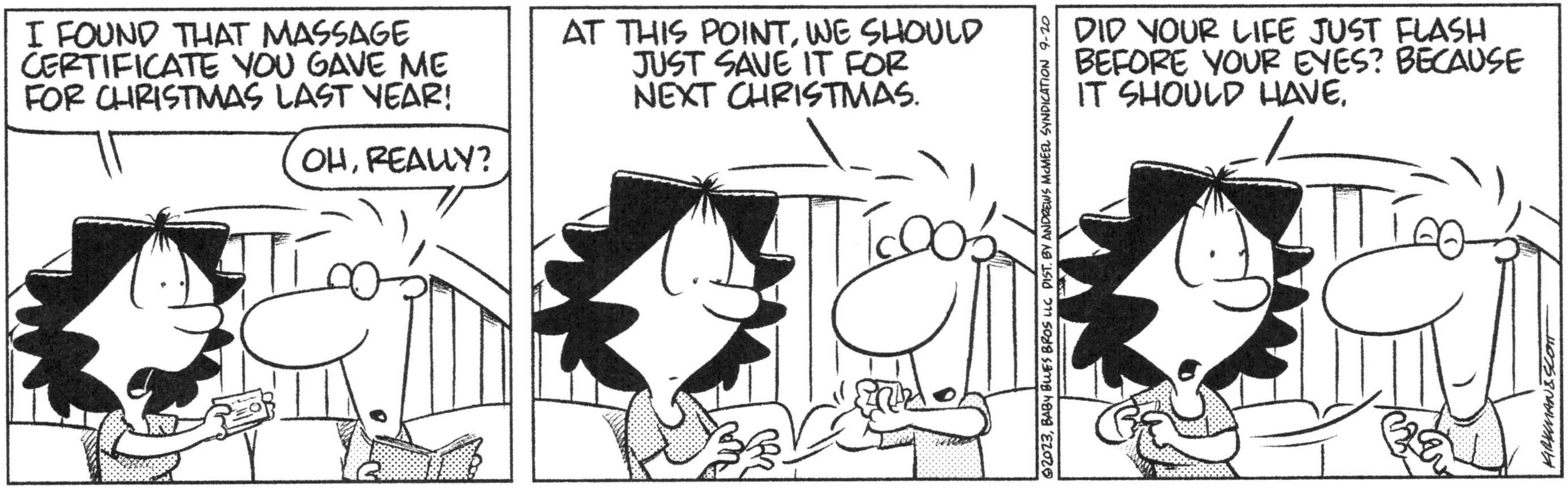
I FOUND THAT MASSAGE CERTIFICATE YOU GAVE ME FOR CHRISTMAS LAST YEAR!
OH, REALLY?
AT THIS POINT, WE SHOULD JUST SAVE IT FOR NEXT CHRISTMAS.
©2023, BABY BLUES BROS LLC DIST. BY ANDREWS McMEEL SYNDICATION 9-20
DID YOUR LIFE JUST FLASH BEFORE YOUR EYES? BECAUSE IT SHOULD HAVE.
KIRKMAN & SCOTT

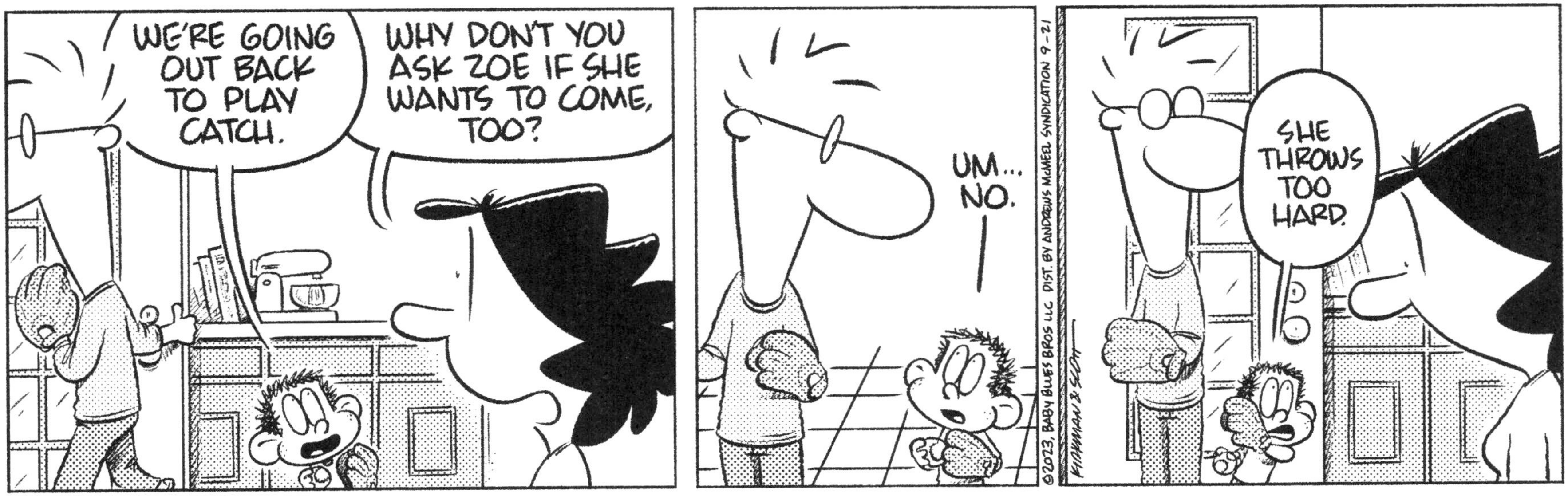
WE'RE GOING OUT BACK TO PLAY CATCH.
WHY DON'T YOU ASK ZOE IF SHE WANTS TO COME, TOO?
UM... NO.
©2023, BABY BLUES BROS LLC DIST. BY ANDREWS McMEEL SYNDICATION 9-21
KIRKMAN & SCOTT
SHE THROWS TOO HARD.

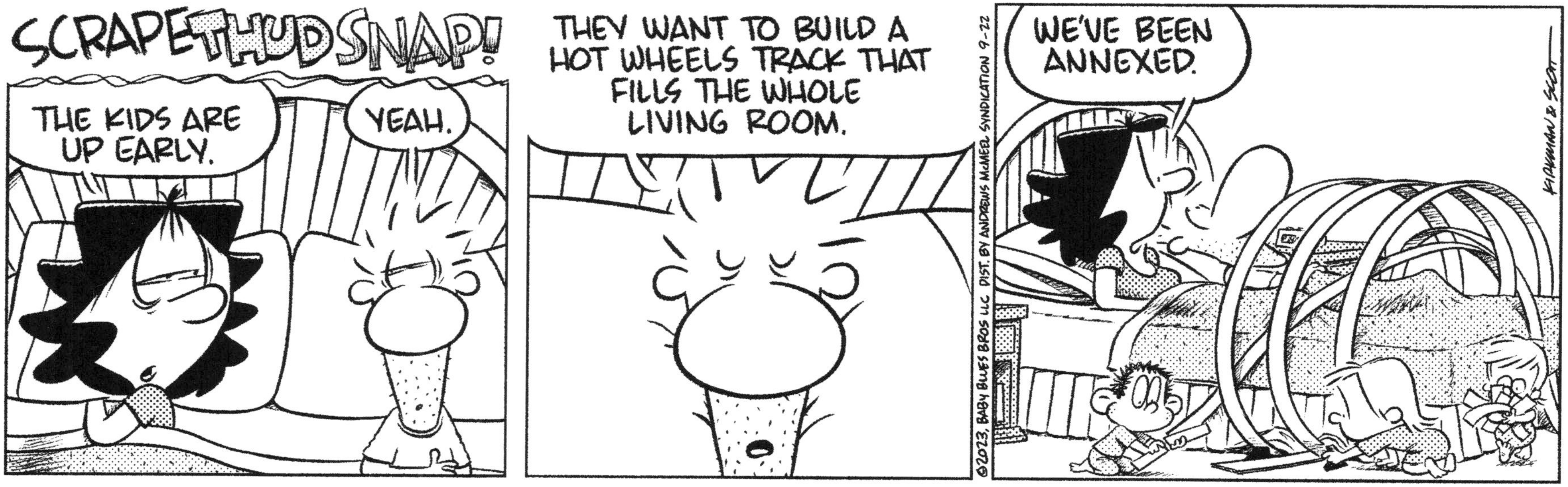
SCRAPE THUD SNAP!
THE KIDS ARE UP EARLY.
YEAH.
THEY WANT TO BUILD A HOT WHEELS TRACK THAT FILLS THE WHOLE LIVING ROOM.
©2023, BABY BLUES BROS LLC DIST. BY ANDREWS McMEEL SYNDICATION 9-22
WE'VE BEEN ANNEXED.
KIRKMAN & SCOTT

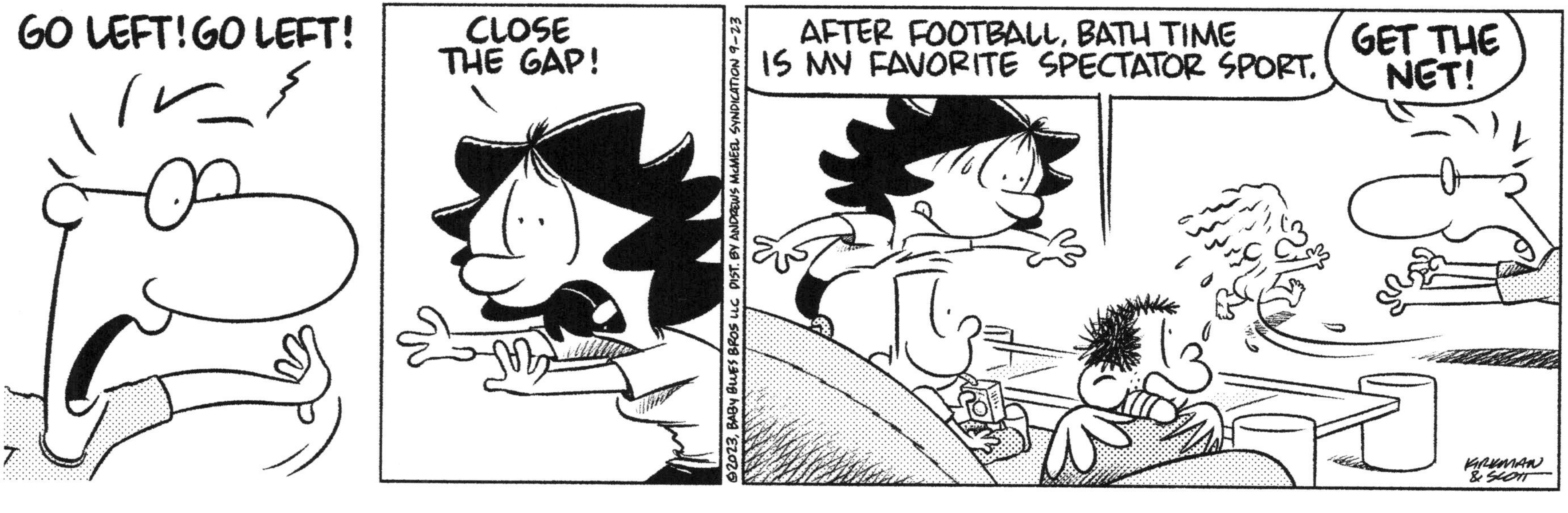
GO LEFT! GO LEFT!
CLOSE THE GAP!
©2023, BABY BLUES BROS LLC DIST. BY ANDREWS McMEEL SYNDICATION 9-23
AFTER FOOTBALL, BATH TIME IS MY FAVORITE SPECTATOR SPORT.
GET THE NET!
KIRKMAN & SCOTT

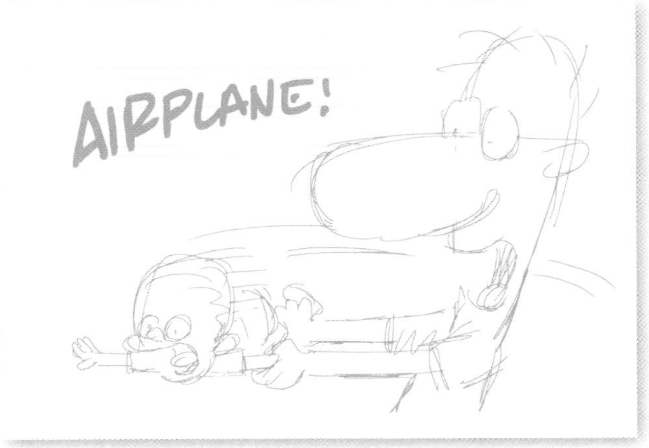
AIRPLANE!

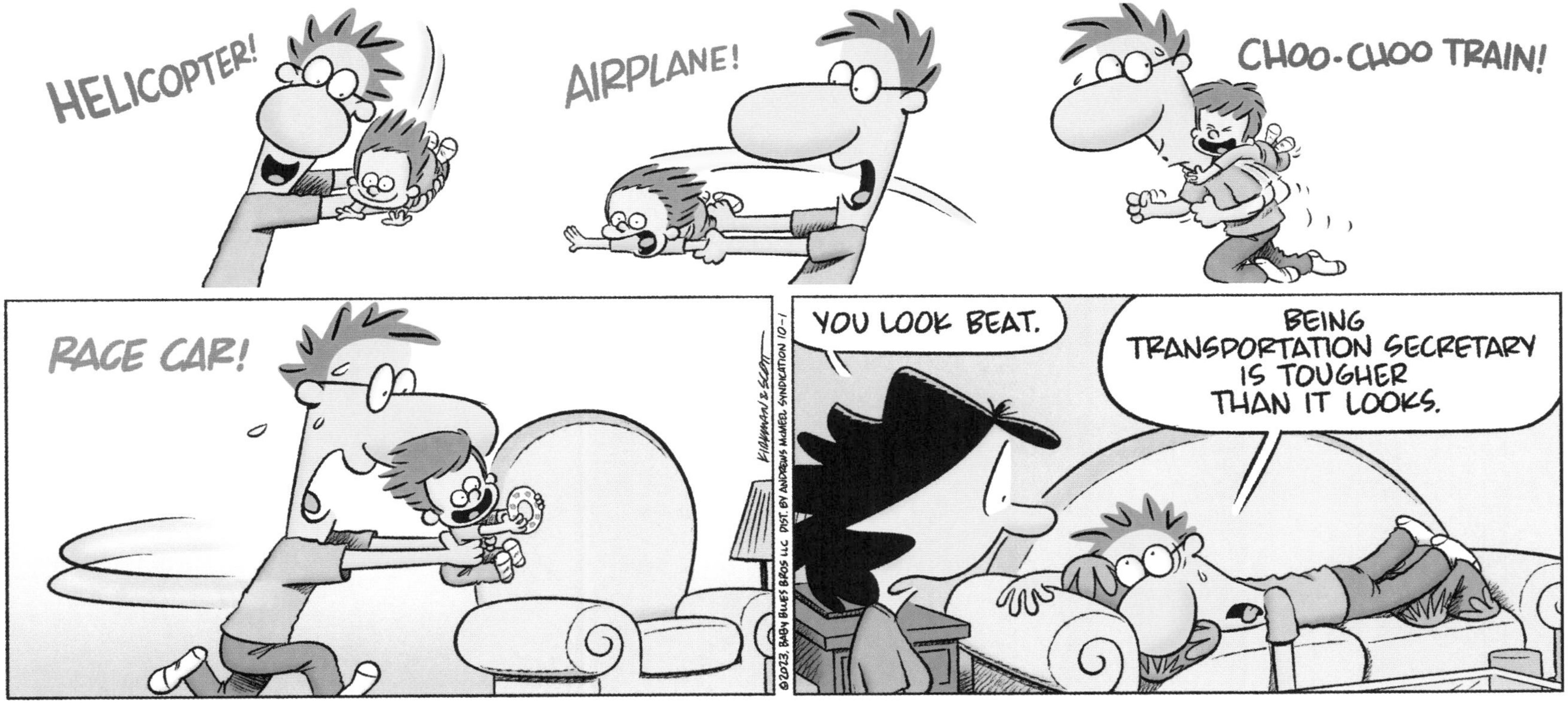
HELICOPTER!
AIRPLANE!
CHOO-CHOO TRAIN!
RACE CAR!
©2013, BABY BLUES BROS LLC DIST. BY ANDREWS MCMEEL SYNDICATION 10-1
YOU LOOK BEAT.
BEING TRANSPORTATION SECRETARY IS TOUGHER THAN IT LOOKS.

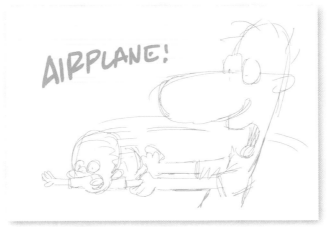

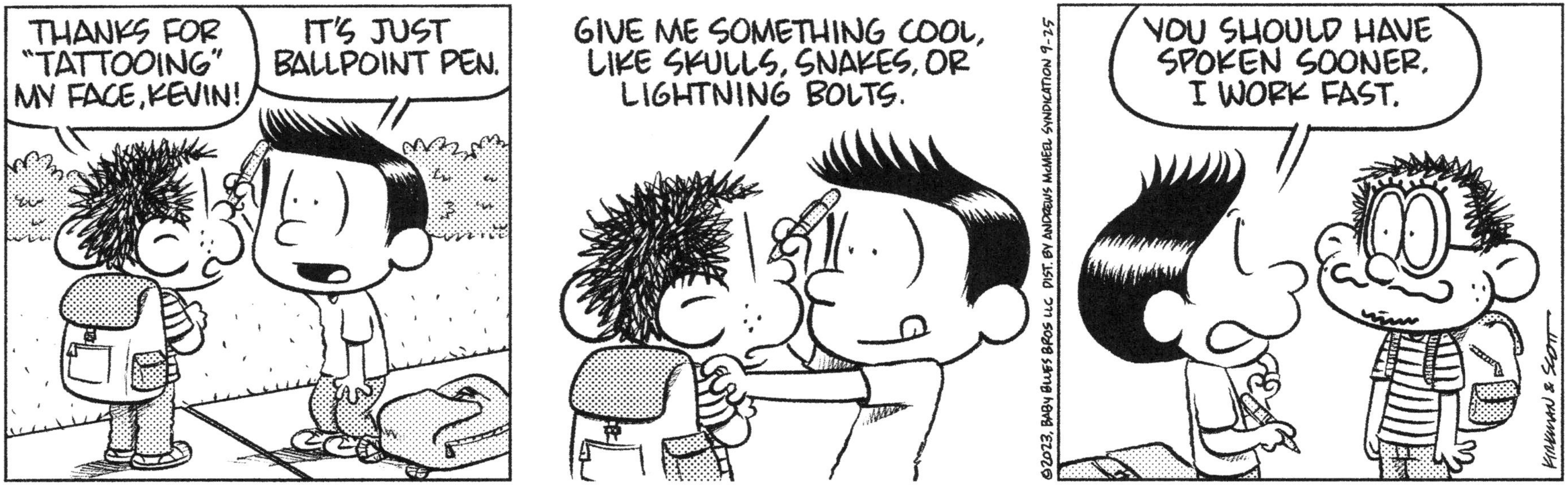
THANKS FOR "TATTOOING" MY FACE, KEVIN!
IT'S JUST BALLPOINT PEN.
GIVE ME SOMETHING COOL, LIKE SKULLS, SNAKES, OR LIGHTNING BOLTS.
©2023, BABY BLUES BROS LLC DIST. BY ANDREWS McMEEL SYNDICATION 9-25
YOU SHOULD HAVE SPOKEN SOONER. I WORK FAST.
KIRKMAN & SCOTT

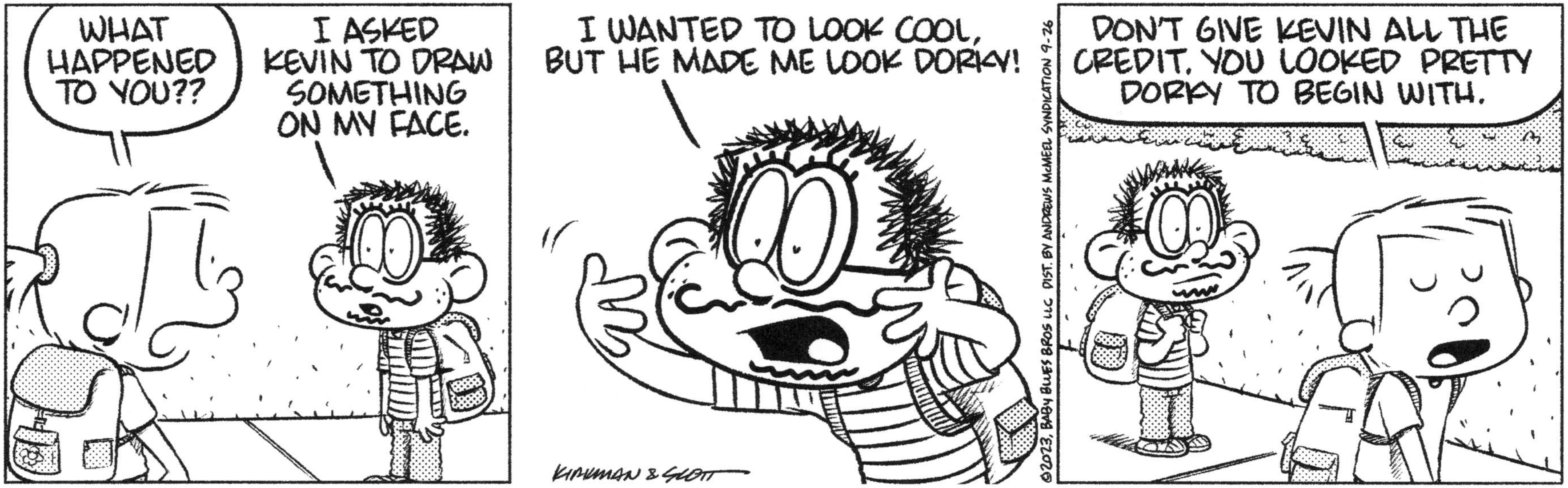
WHAT HAPPENED TO YOU??
I ASKED KEVIN TO DRAW SOMETHING ON MY FACE.
I WANTED TO LOOK COOL, BUT HE MADE ME LOOK DORKY!
KIRKMAN & SCOTT
©2023, BABY BLUES BROS LLC DIST. BY ANDREWS McMEEL SYNDICATION 9-26
DON'T GIVE KEVIN ALL THE CREDIT. YOU LOOKED PRETTY DORKY TO BEGIN WITH.

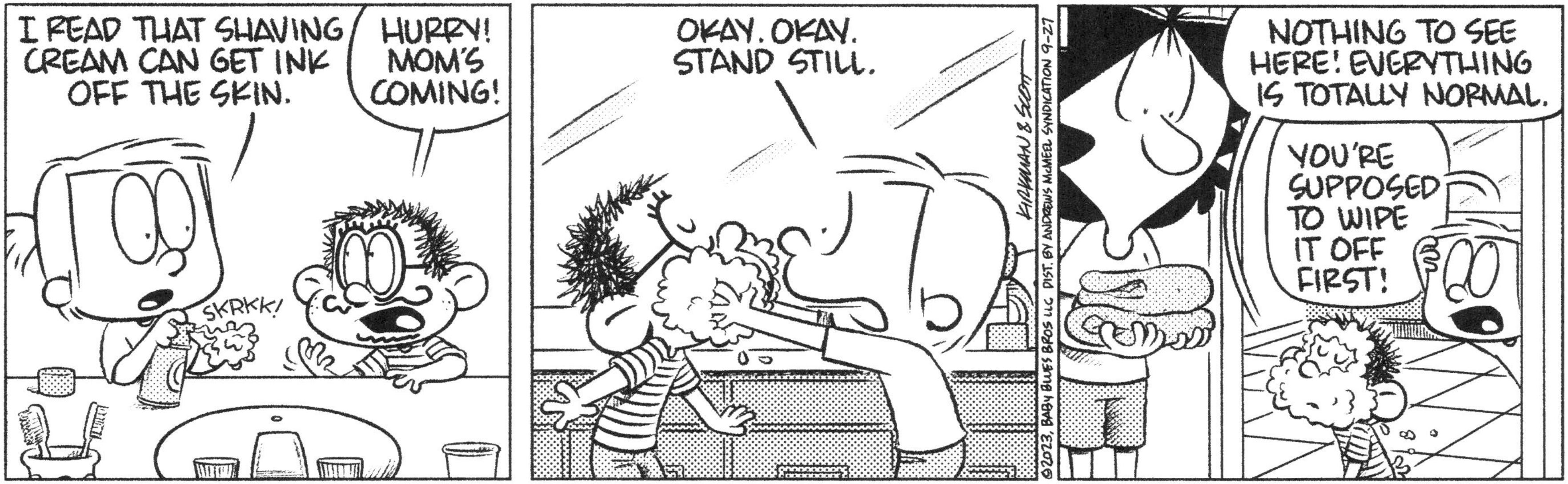
I READ THAT SHAVING CREAM CAN GET INK OFF THE SKIN.
HURRY! MOM'S COMING!
SKRKK!
OKAY. OKAY. STAND STILL.
KIRKMAN & SCOTT
©2023, BABY BLUES BROS LLC DIST. BY ANDREWS McMEEL SYNDICATION 9-27
NOTHING TO SEE HERE! EVERYTHING IS TOTALLY NORMAL.
YOU'RE SUPPOSED TO WIPE IT OFF FIRST!

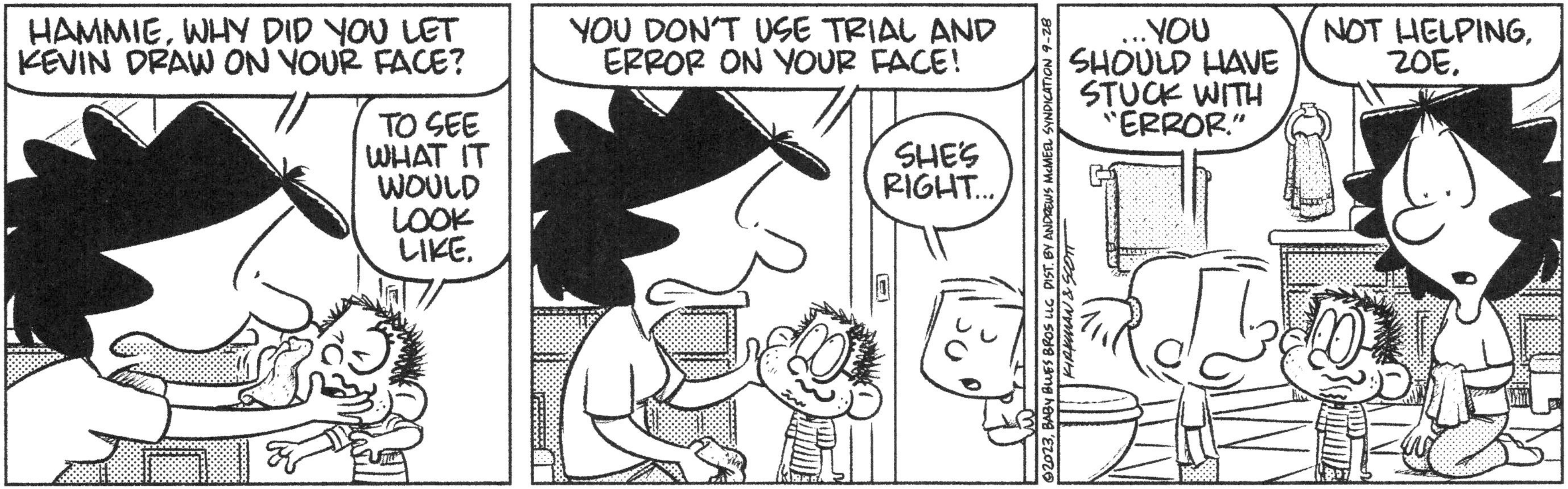
HAMMIE, WHY DID YOU LET KEVIN DRAW ON YOUR FACE?
TO SEE WHAT IT WOULD LOOK LIKE.
YOU DON'T USE TRIAL AND ERROR ON YOUR FACE!
SHE'S RIGHT...
©2023, BABY BLUES BROS LLC DIST. BY ANDREWS McMEEL SYNDICATION 9-28
KIRKMAN & SCOTT
...YOU SHOULD HAVE STUCK WITH "ERROR."
NOT HELPING, ZOE.

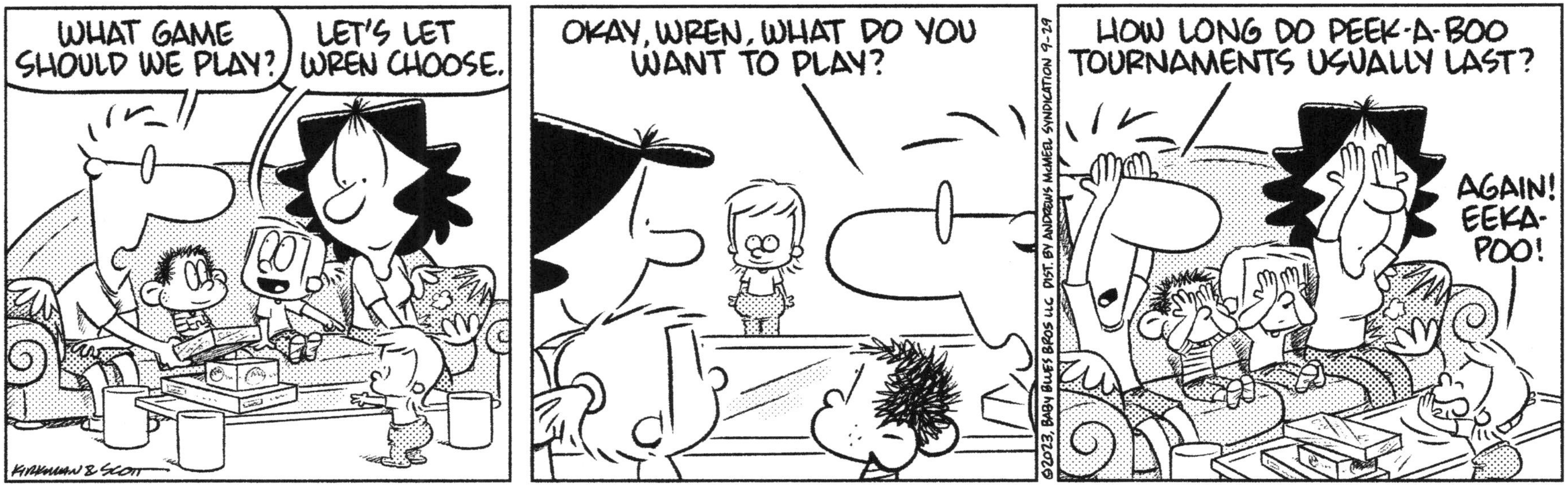
WHAT GAME SHOULD WE PLAY?
LET'S LET WREN CHOOSE.
KIRKMAN & SCOTT
OKAY, WREN, WHAT DO YOU WANT TO PLAY?
©2023, BABY BLUES BROS LLC DIST. BY ANDREWS McMEEL SYNDICATION 9-29
HOW LONG DO PEEK-A-BOO TOURNAMENTS USUALLY LAST?
AGAIN! EEKA-POO!

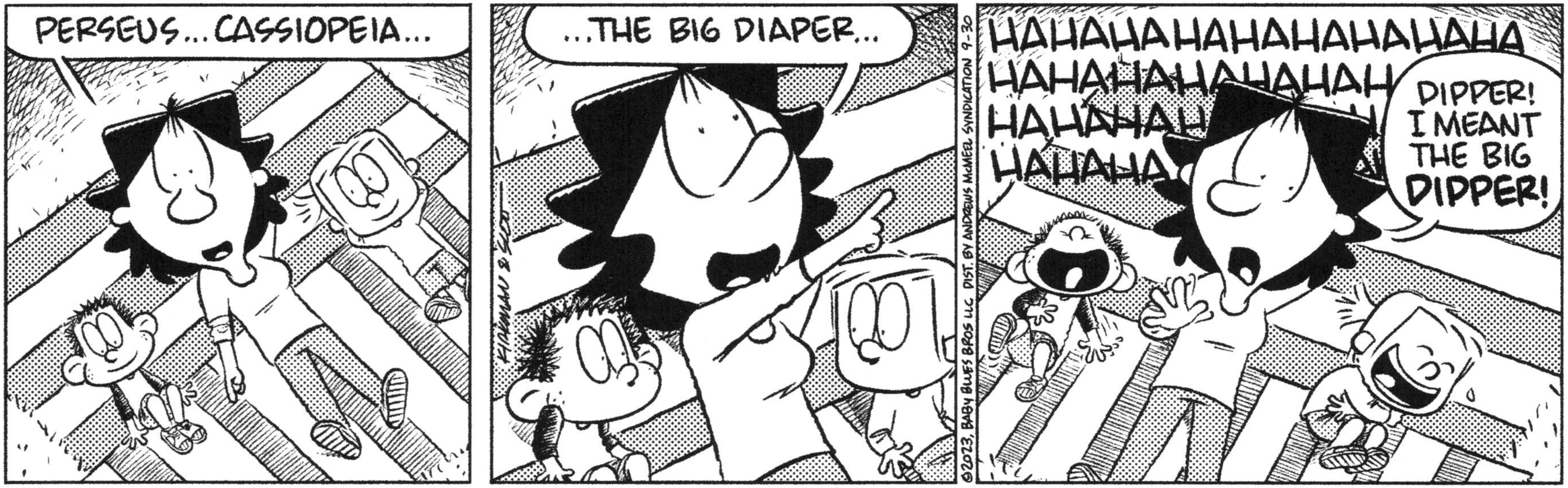
PERSEUS...CASSIOPEIA...
...THE BIG DIAPER...
KIRKMAN & SCOTT
©2023, BABY BLUES BROS LLC DIST. BY ANDREWS McMEEL SYNDICATION 9-30
HAHAHAHAHAHAHAHAHA
HAHAHAHAHAHAH
HAHAHAH
HAHAHA
DIPPER! I MEANT THE BIG DIPPER!

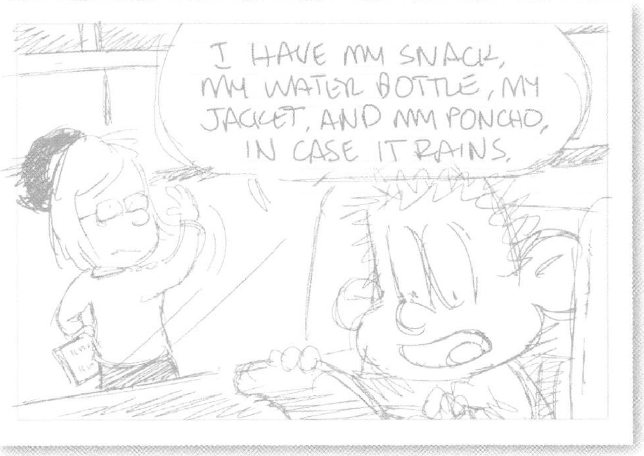
I HAVE MY SNACK, MY WATER BOTTLE, MY JACKET, AND MY PONCHO, IN CASE IT RAINS.

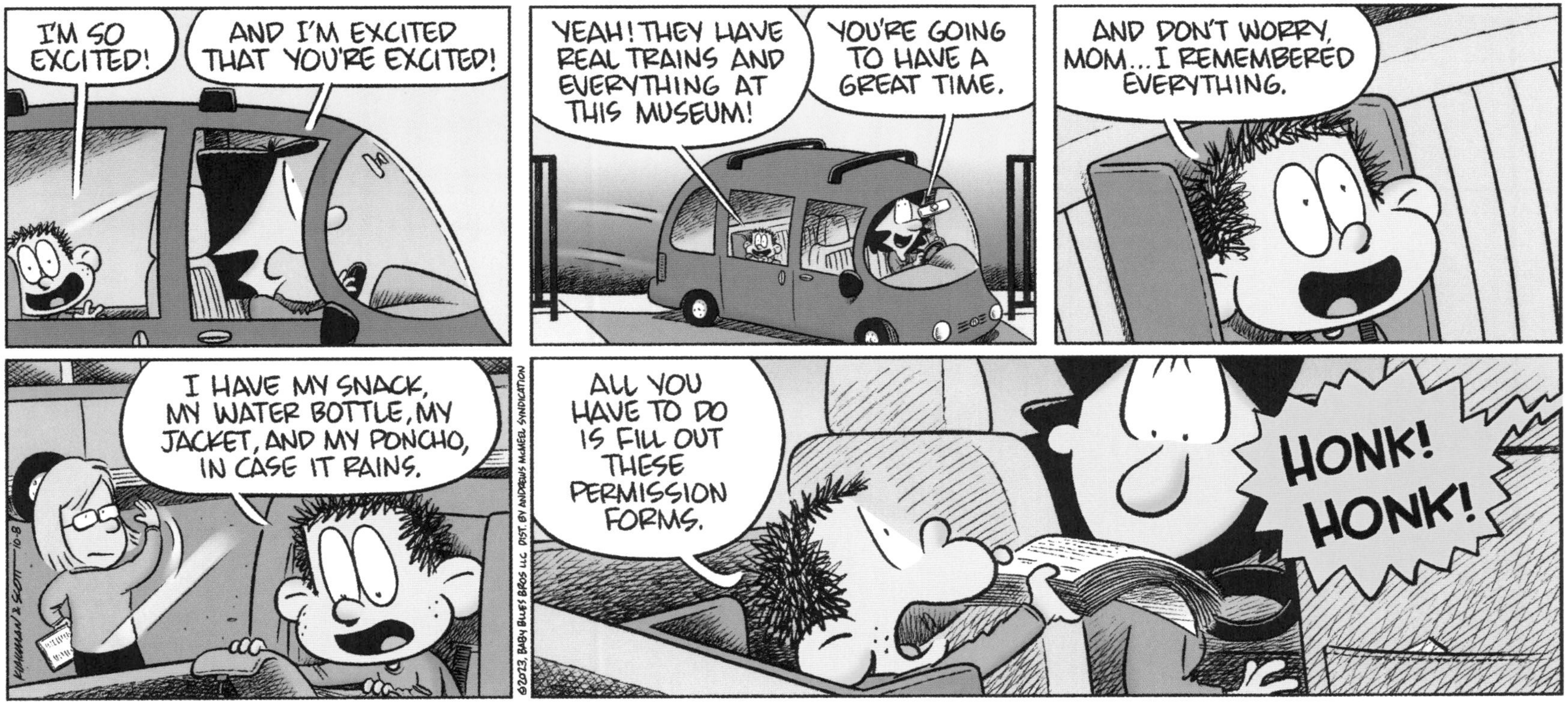
I'M SO EXCITED!
AND I'M EXCITED THAT YOU'RE EXCITED!
YEAH! THEY HAVE REAL TRAINS AND EVERYTHING AT THIS MUSEUM!
YOU'RE GOING TO HAVE A GREAT TIME.
AND DON'T WORRY, MOM... I REMEMBERED EVERYTHING.
I HAVE MY SNACK, MY WATER BOTTLE, MY JACKET, AND MY PONCHO, IN CASE IT RAINS.
ALL YOU HAVE TO DO IS FILL OUT THESE PERMISSION FORMS.
HONK! HONK!

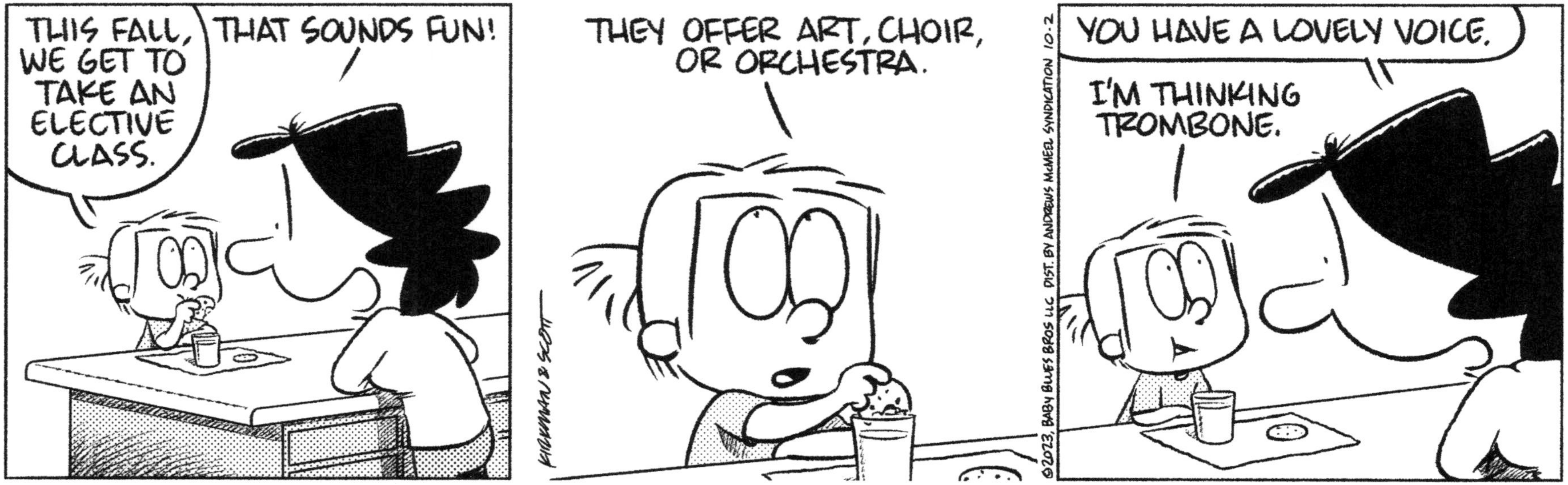
THIS FALL, WE GET TO TAKE AN ELECTIVE CLASS.
THAT SOUNDS FUN!
THEY OFFER ART, CHOIR, OR ORCHESTRA.
I'M THINKING TROMBONE.
YOU HAVE A LOVELY VOICE.
KIRKMAN & SCOTT
10-2
©2023, BABY BLUES BROS LLC DIST. BY ANDREWS MCMEEL SYNDICATION

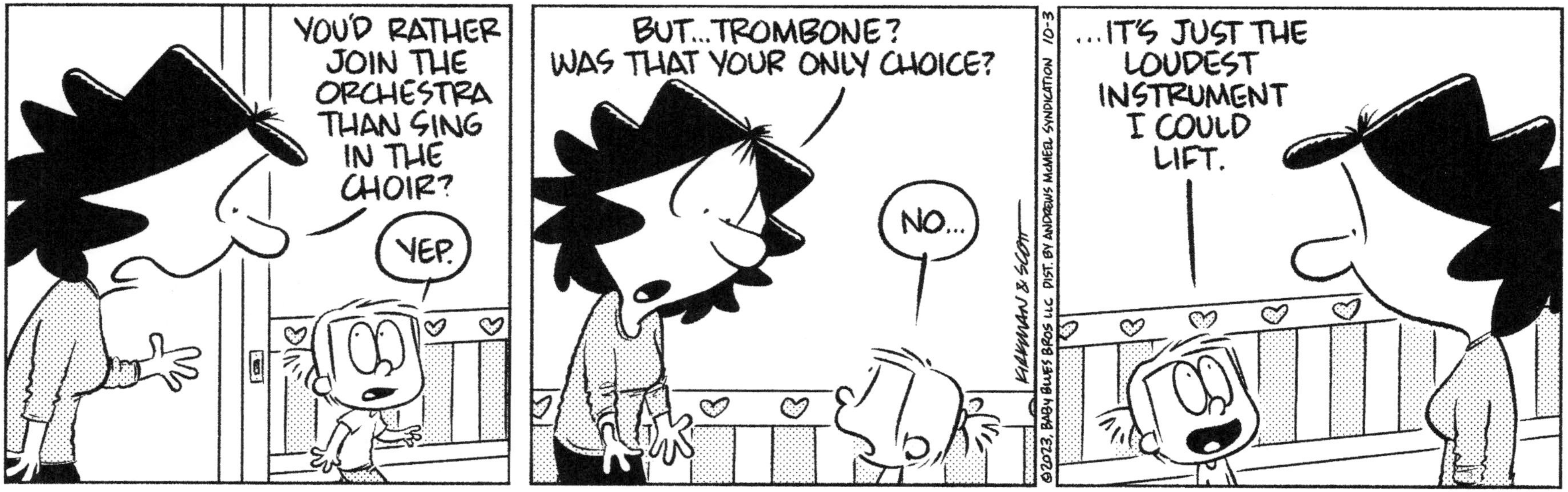
YOU'D RATHER JOIN THE ORCHESTRA THAN SING IN THE CHOIR?
YEP.
BUT...TROMBONE? WAS THAT YOUR ONLY CHOICE?
NO...
...IT'S JUST THE LOUDEST INSTRUMENT I COULD LIFT.
KIRKMAN & SCOTT
10-3
©2023, BABY BLUES BROS LLC DIST. BY ANDREWS MCMEEL SYNDICATION

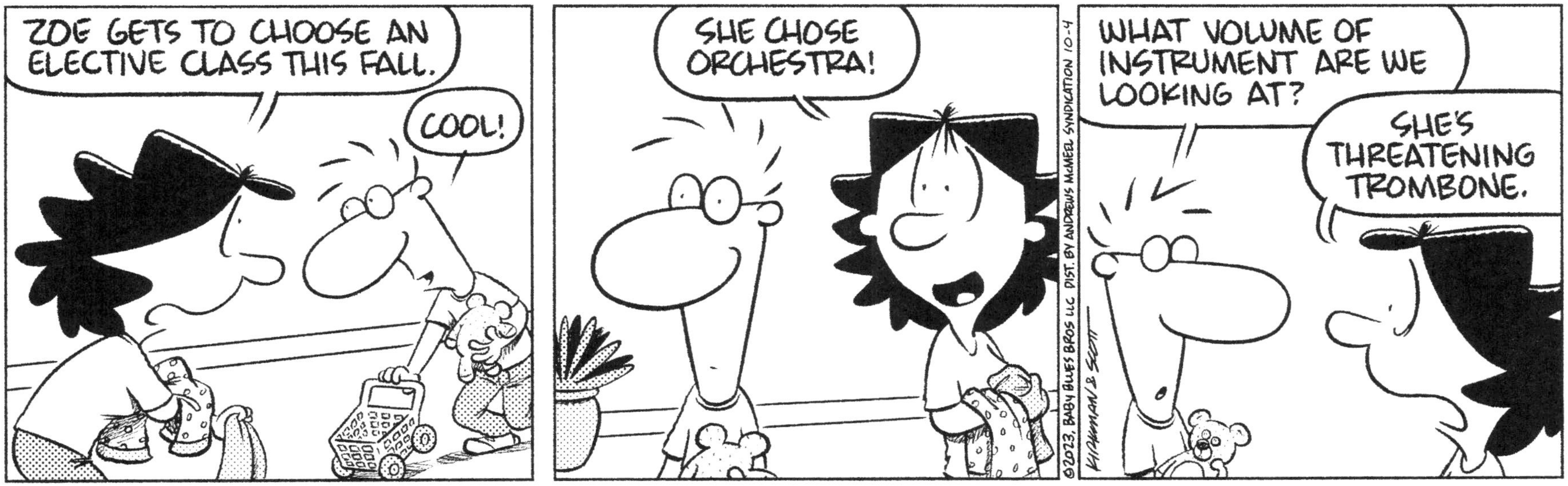
ZOE GETS TO CHOOSE AN ELECTIVE CLASS THIS FALL.
COOL!
SHE CHOSE ORCHESTRA!
©2023, BABY BLUES BROS LLC DIST. BY ANDREWS McMEEL SYNDICATION 10-4
KIRKMAN & SCOTT
WHAT VOLUME OF INSTRUMENT ARE WE LOOKING AT?
SHE'S THREATENING TROMBONE.

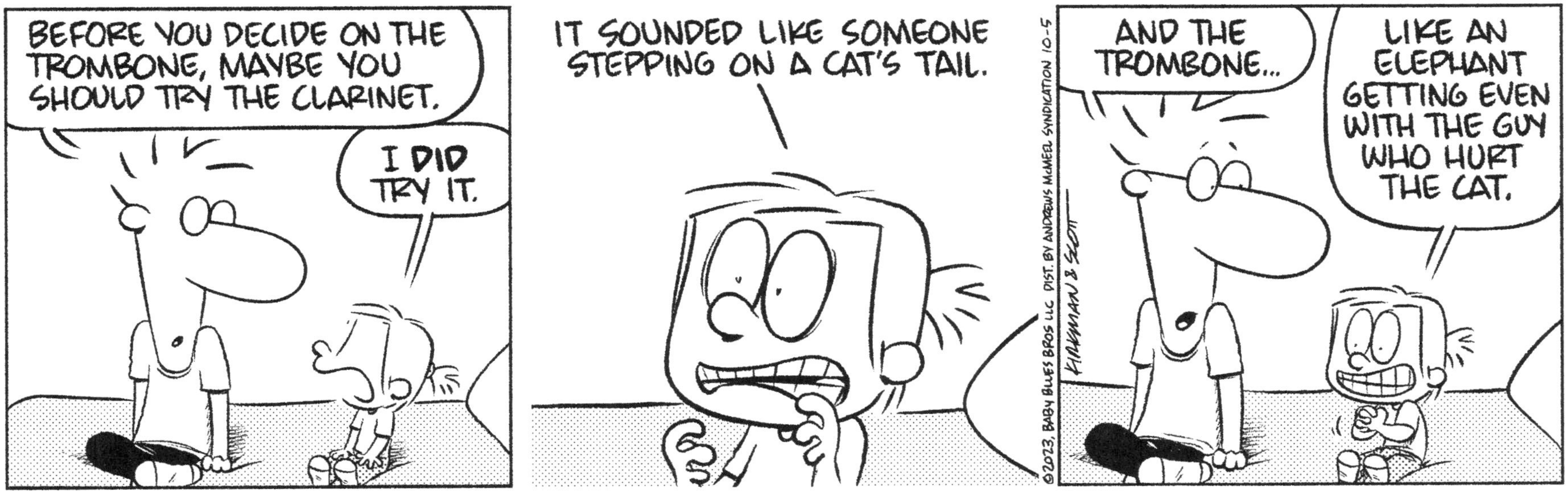
BEFORE YOU DECIDE ON THE TROMBONE, MAYBE YOU SHOULD TRY THE CLARINET.
I **DID** TRY IT.
IT SOUNDED LIKE SOMEONE STEPPING ON A CAT'S TAIL.
©2023, BABY BLUES BROS LLC DIST. BY ANDREWS McMEEL SYNDICATION 10-5
KIRKMAN & SCOTT
AND THE TROMBONE...
LIKE AN ELEPHANT GETTING EVEN WITH THE GUY WHO HURT THE CAT.

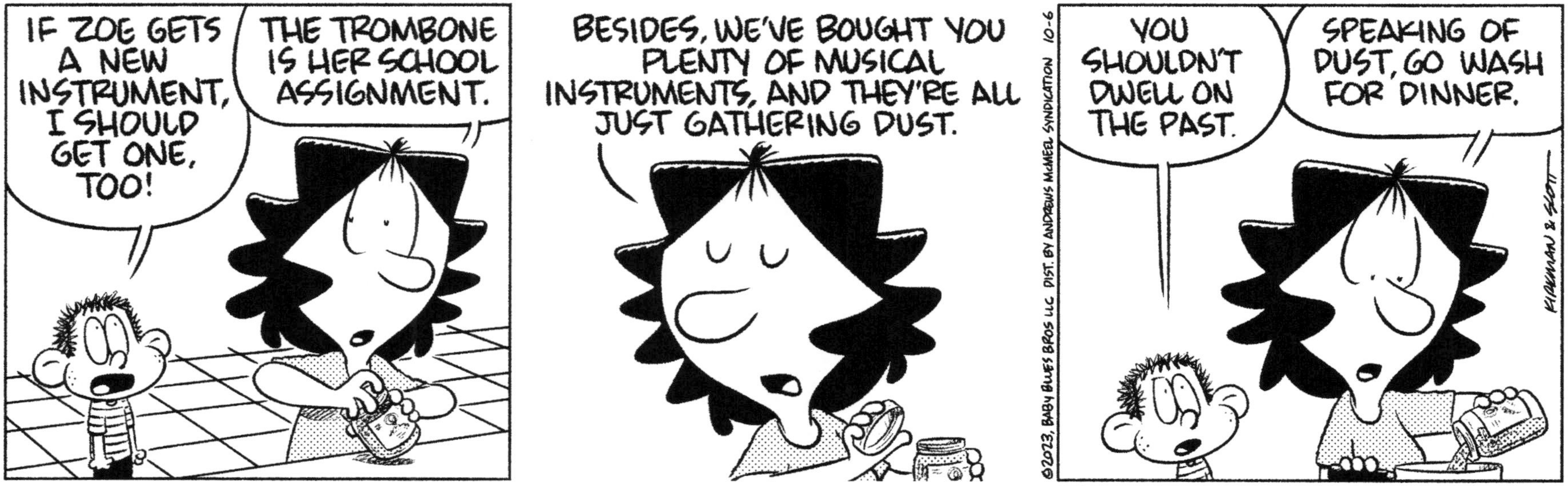
IF ZOE GETS A NEW INSTRUMENT, I SHOULD GET ONE, TOO!
THE TROMBONE IS HER SCHOOL ASSIGNMENT.
BESIDES, WE'VE BOUGHT YOU PLENTY OF MUSICAL INSTRUMENTS, AND THEY'RE ALL JUST GATHERING DUST.
10-6
©2023, BABY BLUES BROS LLC DIST. BY ANDREWS MCMEEL SYNDICATION
YOU SHOULDN'T DWELL ON THE PAST.
SPEAKING OF DUST, GO WASH FOR DINNER.
KIRKMAN & SCOTT

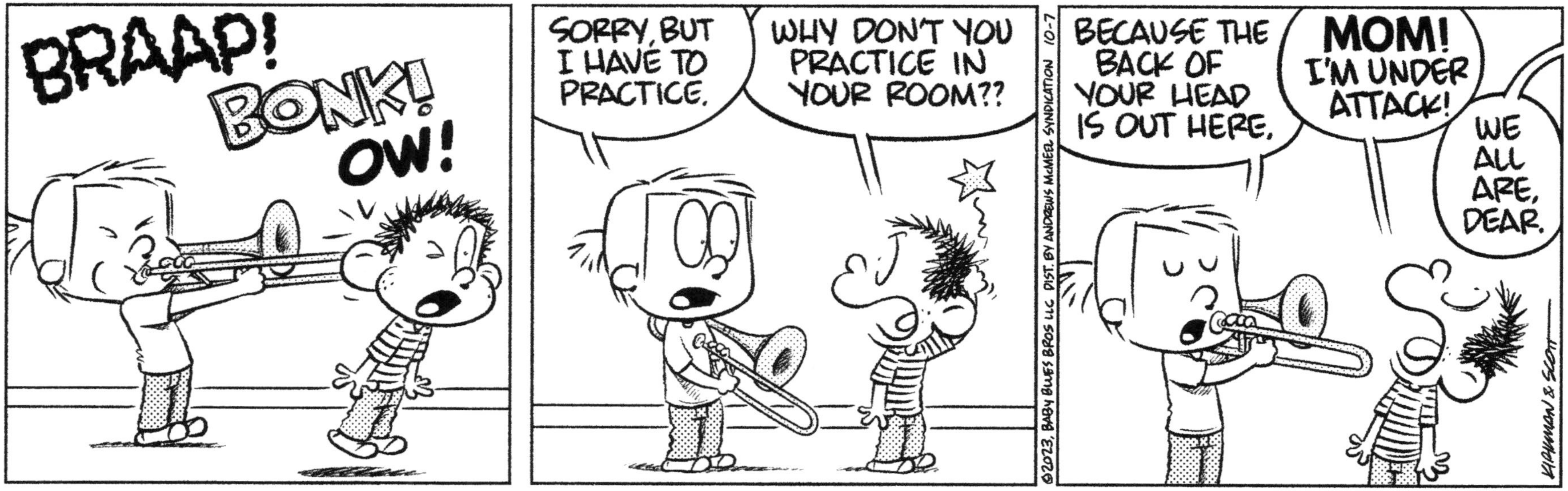
BRAAP!
BONK!
OW!
SORRY, BUT I HAVE TO PRACTICE.
WHY DON'T YOU PRACTICE IN YOUR ROOM??
10-7
©2023, BABY BLUES BROS LLC DIST. BY ANDREWS MCMEEL SYNDICATION
BECAUSE THE BACK OF YOUR HEAD IS OUT HERE.
MOM! I'M UNDER ATTACK!
WE ALL ARE, DEAR.
KIRKMAN & SCOTT

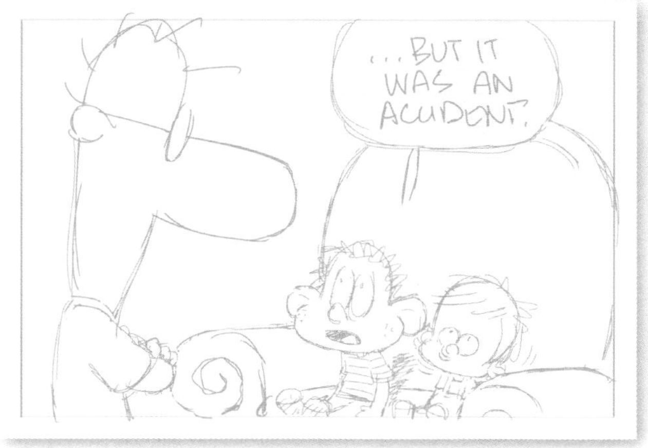
...BUT IT WAS AN ACCIDENT.

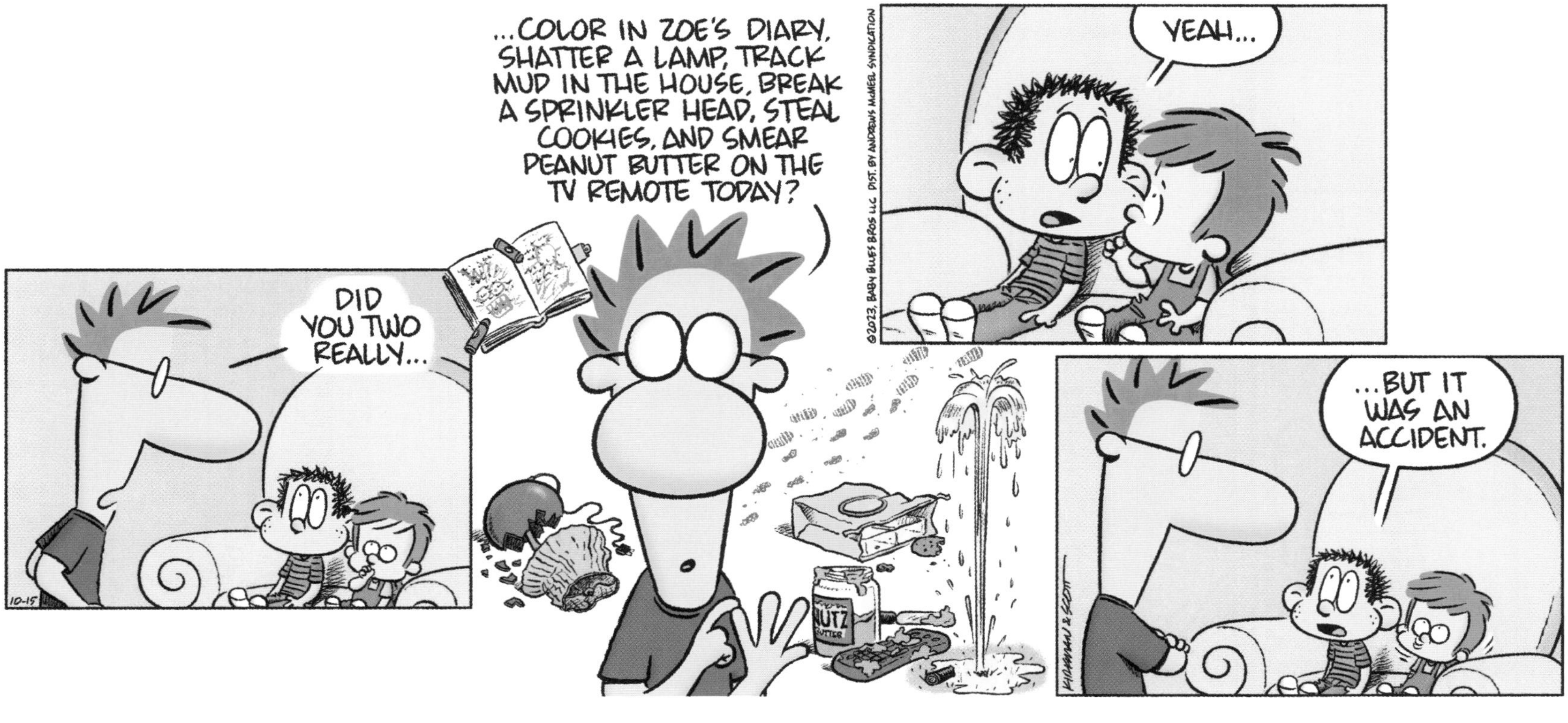
DID YOU TWO REALLY...
...COLOR IN ZOE'S DIARY, SHATTER A LAMP, TRACK MUD IN THE HOUSE, BREAK A SPRINKLER HEAD, STEAL COOKIES, AND SMEAR PEANUT BUTTER ON THE TV REMOTE TODAY?
NUTZ BUTTER
YEAH...
...BUT IT WAS AN ACCIDENT.
©2023, BABY BLUES BROS LLC DIST. BY ANDREWS MCMEEL SYNDICATION
KIRKMAN & SCOTT
10-15

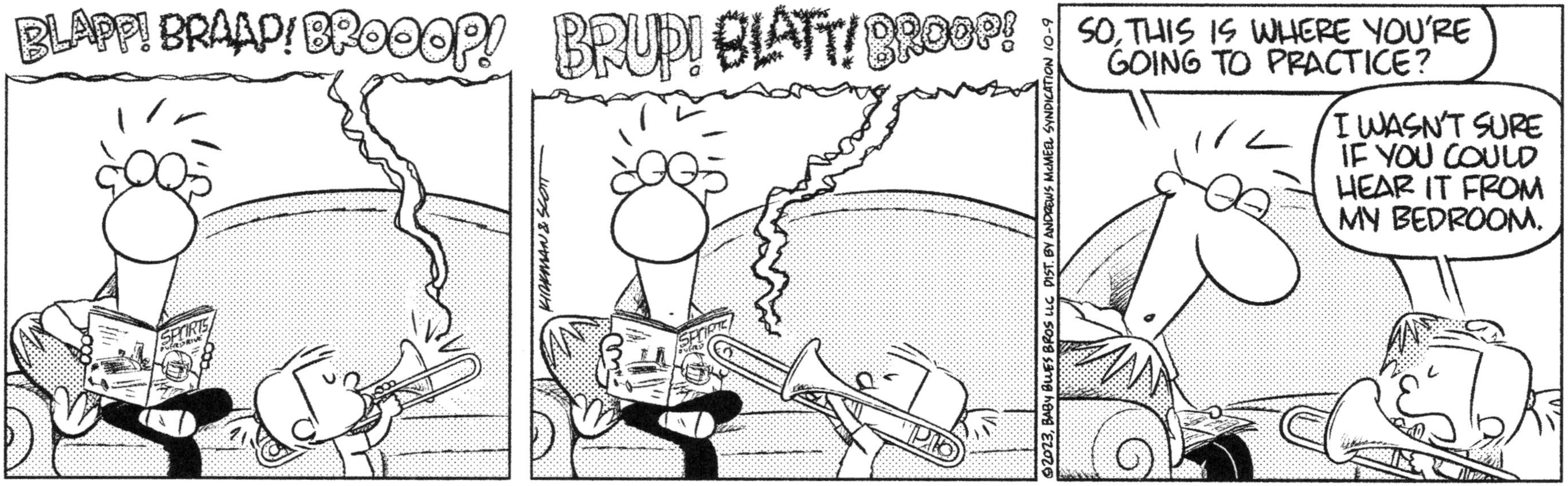
BLAPP! BRAAP! BROOOP!
BRUP! BLATT! BROOP!
KIRKMAN & SCOTT
©2023, BABY BLUES BROS LLC DIST. BY ANDREWS McMEEL SYNDICATION 10-9
SO, THIS IS WHERE YOU'RE GOING TO PRACTICE?
I WASN'T SURE IF YOU COULD HEAR IT FROM MY BEDROOM.

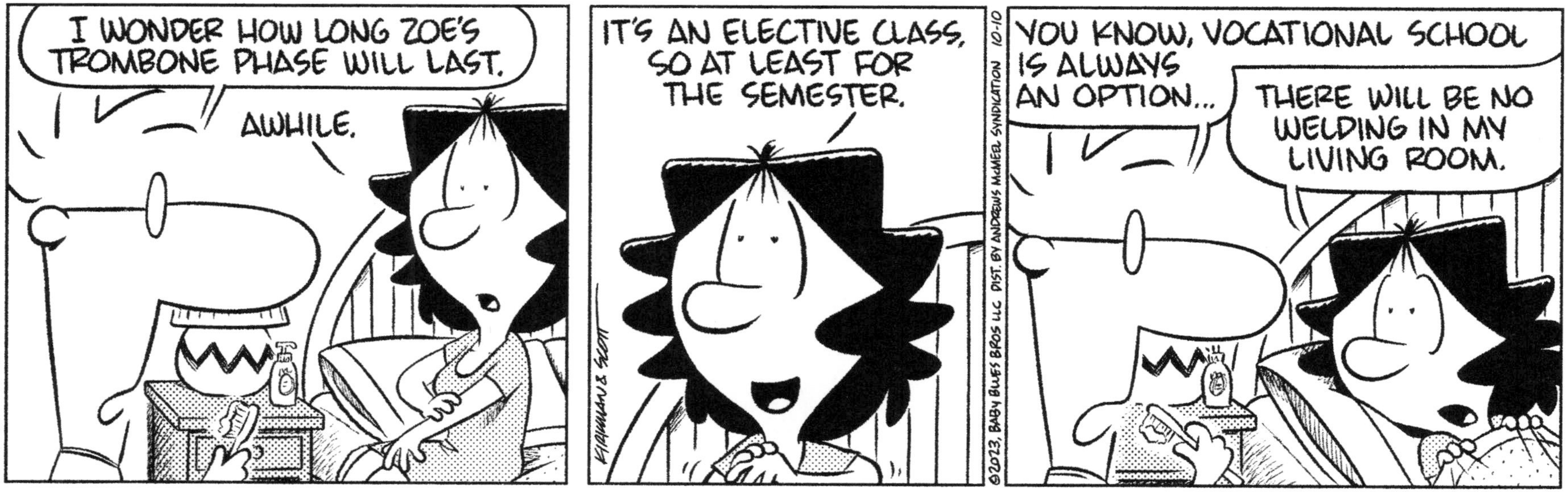
I WONDER HOW LONG ZOE'S TROMBONE PHASE WILL LAST.
AWHILE.
IT'S AN ELECTIVE CLASS, SO AT LEAST FOR THE SEMESTER.
KIRKMAN & SCOTT
©2023, BABY BLUES BROS LLC DIST. BY ANDREWS McMEEL SYNDICATION 10-10
YOU KNOW, VOCATIONAL SCHOOL IS ALWAYS AN OPTION...
THERE WILL BE NO WELDING IN MY LIVING ROOM.

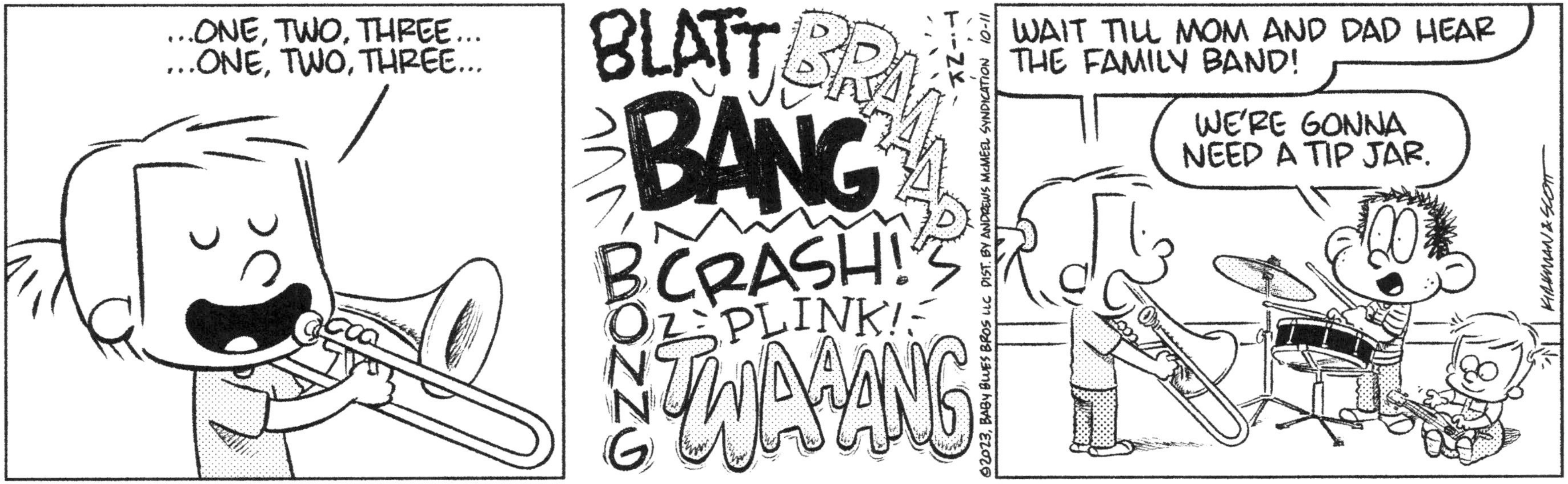

...ONE, TWO, THREE...
...ONE, TWO, THREE...
BLATT
BRAAAAP
BANG
BONG
CRASH!
PLINK!
TWAAANG
©2023, BABY BLUES BROS LLC DIST. BY ANDREWS McMEEL SYNDICATION 10-11
WAIT TILL MOM AND DAD HEAR THE FAMILY BAND!
WE'RE GONNA NEED A TIP JAR.
KIRKMAN & SCOTT

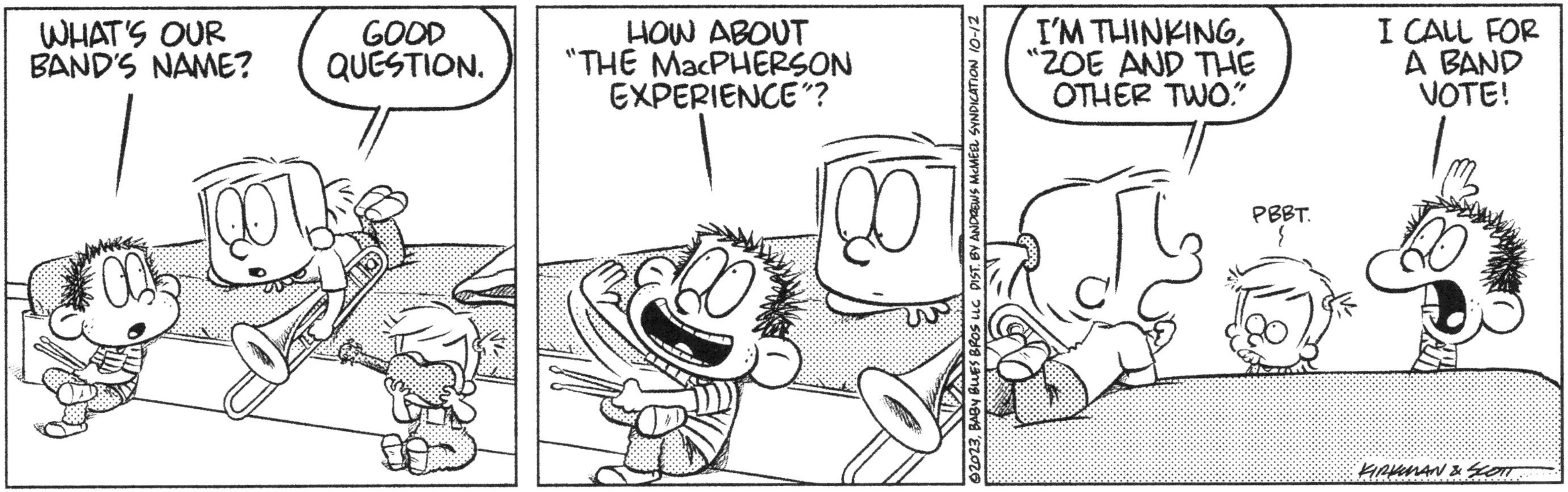

WHAT'S OUR BAND'S NAME?
GOOD QUESTION.
HOW ABOUT "THE MacPHERSON EXPERIENCE"?
©2023, BABY BLUES BROS LLC DIST. BY ANDREWS McMEEL SYNDICATION 10-12
I'M THINKING, "ZOE AND THE OTHER TWO."
PBBT.
I CALL FOR A BAND VOTE!
KIRKMAN & SCOTT

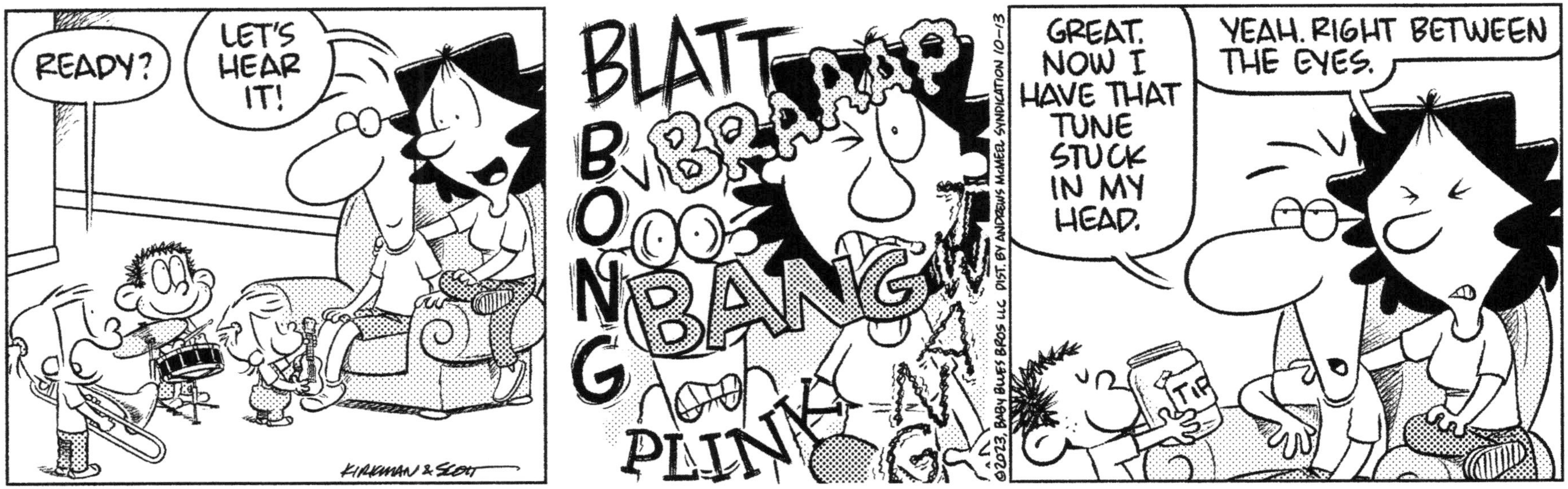
READY?
LET'S HEAR IT!
KIRKMAN & SCOTT
BLATT
BONG
BRAAAP
BANG
PLINK
©2023, BABY BLUES BROS LLC DIST. BY ANDREWS McMEEL SYNDICATION 10-13
GREAT. NOW I HAVE THAT TUNE STUCK IN MY HEAD.
YEAH. RIGHT BETWEEN THE EYES.
TIP

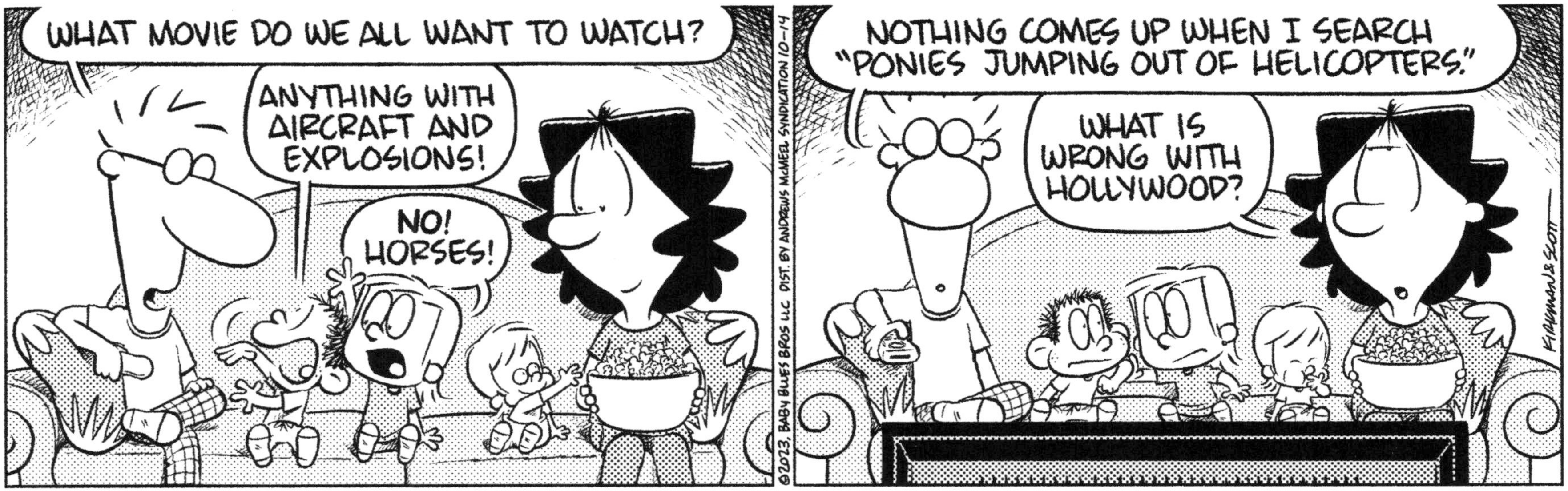
WHAT MOVIE DO WE ALL WANT TO WATCH?
ANYTHING WITH AIRCRAFT AND EXPLOSIONS!
NO! HORSES!
©2023, BABY BLUES BROS LLC DIST. BY ANDREWS McMEEL SYNDICATION 10-14
NOTHING COMES UP WHEN I SEARCH "PONIES JUMPING OUT OF HELICOPTERS."
WHAT IS WRONG WITH HOLLYWOOD?
KIRKMAN & SCOTT

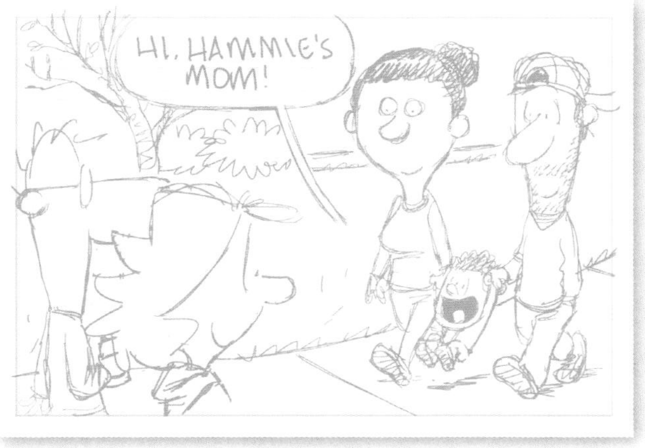
HI, HAMMIE'S MOM!

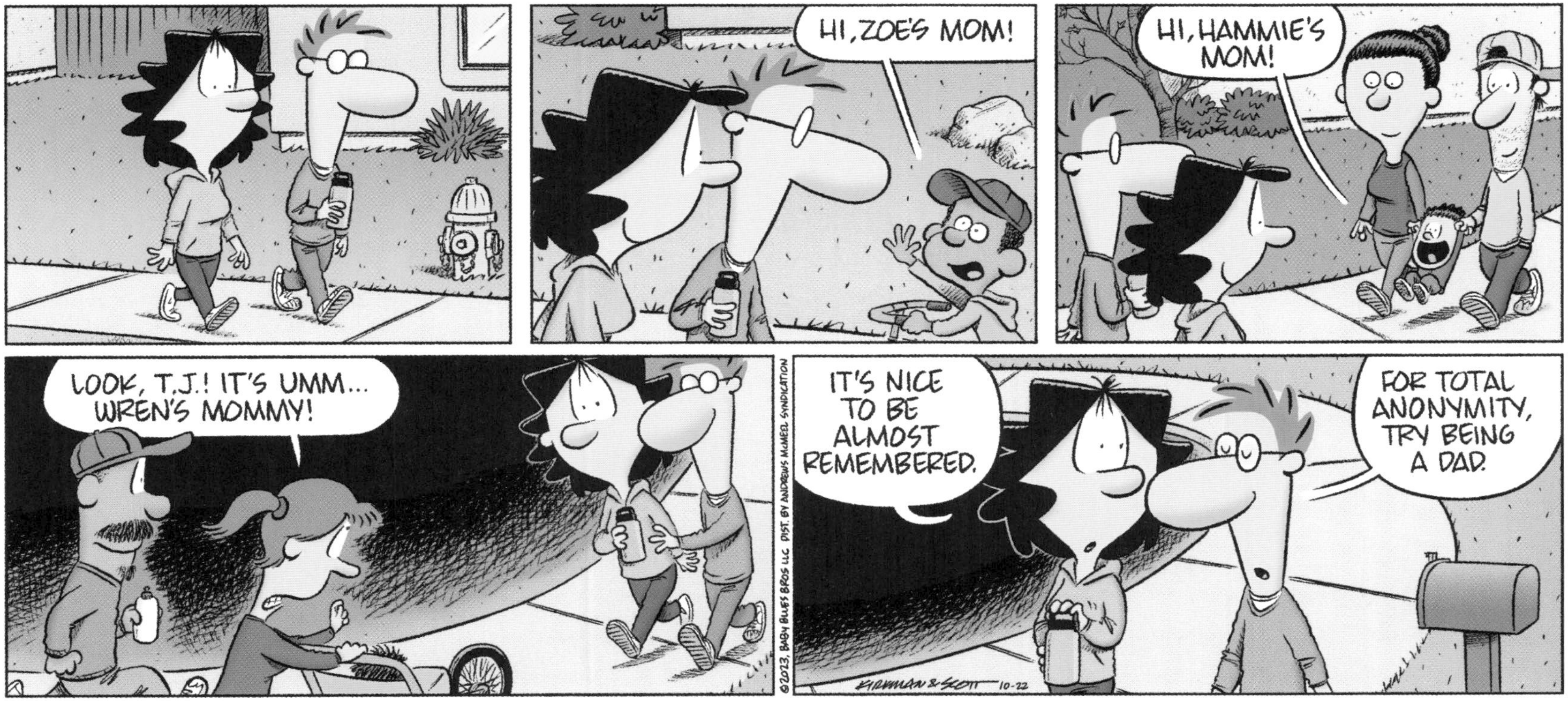
HI, ZOE'S MOM!
HI, HAMMIE'S MOM!
LOOK, T.J.! IT'S UMM... WREN'S MOMMY!
©2013, BABY BLUES BROS LLC DIST. BY ANDREWS MCMEEL SYNDICATION
IT'S NICE TO BE ALMOST REMEMBERED.
FOR TOTAL ANONYMITY, TRY BEING A DAD.
KIRKMAN & SCOTT 10-22

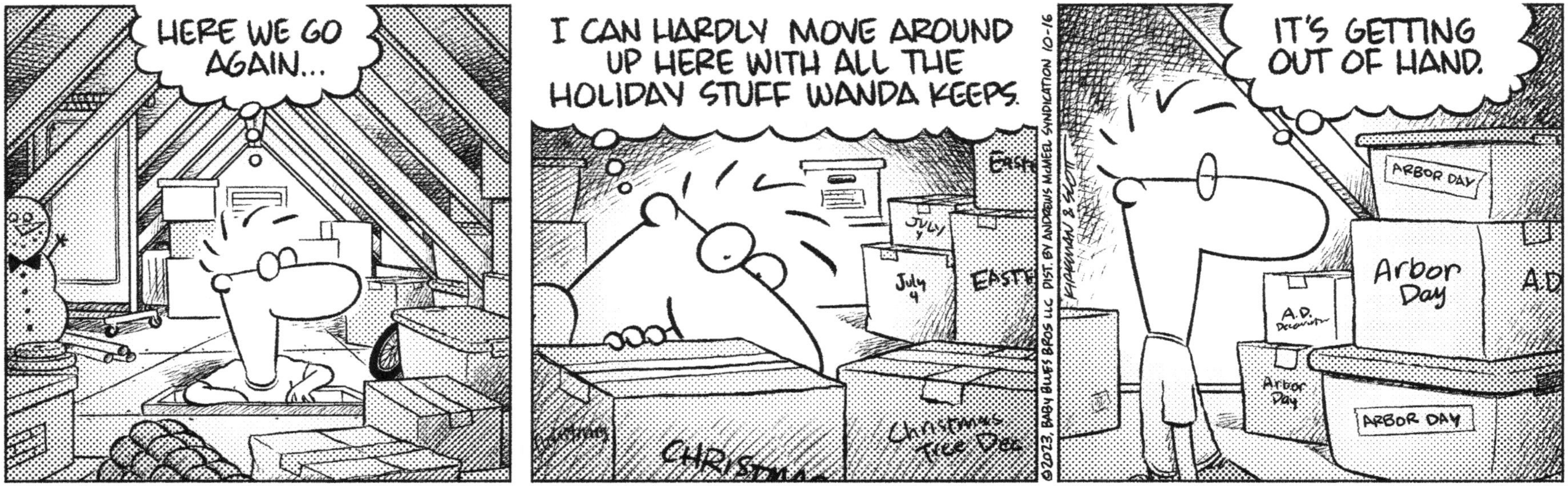
HERE WE GO AGAIN...
I CAN HARDLY MOVE AROUND UP HERE WITH ALL THE HOLIDAY STUFF WANDA KEEPS.
©2023, BABY BLUES BROS LLC DIST. BY ANDREWS McMEEL SYNDICATION 10-16
IT'S GETTING OUT OF HAND.
ARBOR DAY
Arbor Day
ARBOR DAY

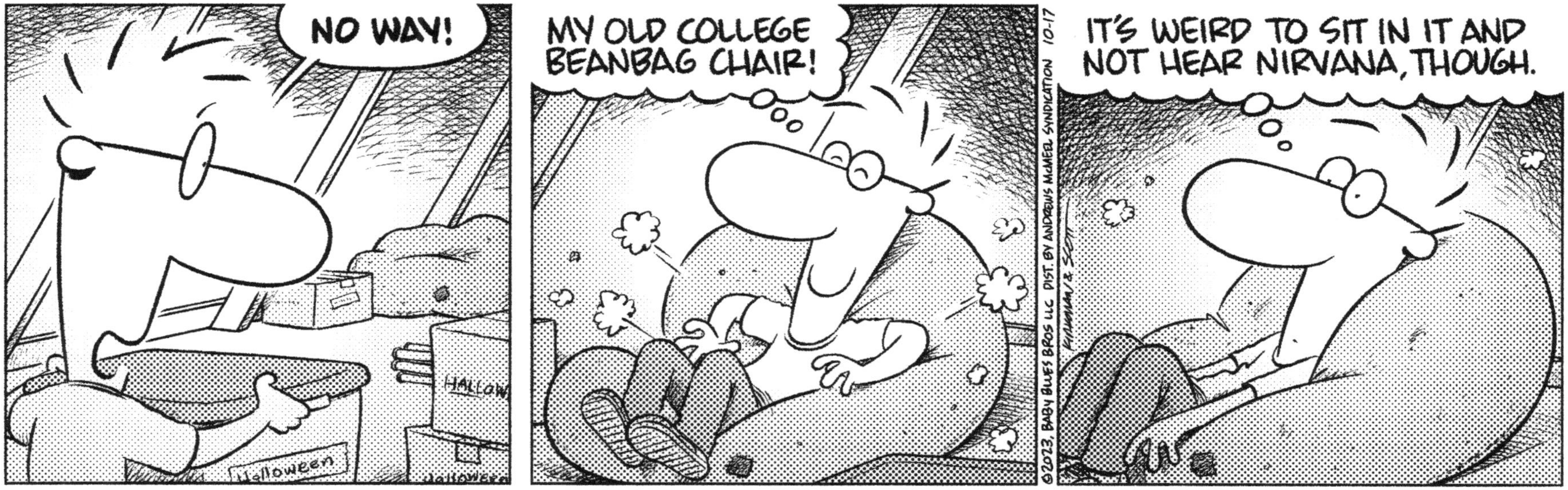
NO WAY!
Halloween
MY OLD COLLEGE BEANBAG CHAIR!
©2023, BABY BLUES BROS LLC DIST. BY ANDREWS McMEEL SYNDICATION 10-17
IT'S WEIRD TO SIT IN IT AND NOT HEAR NIRVANA, THOUGH.

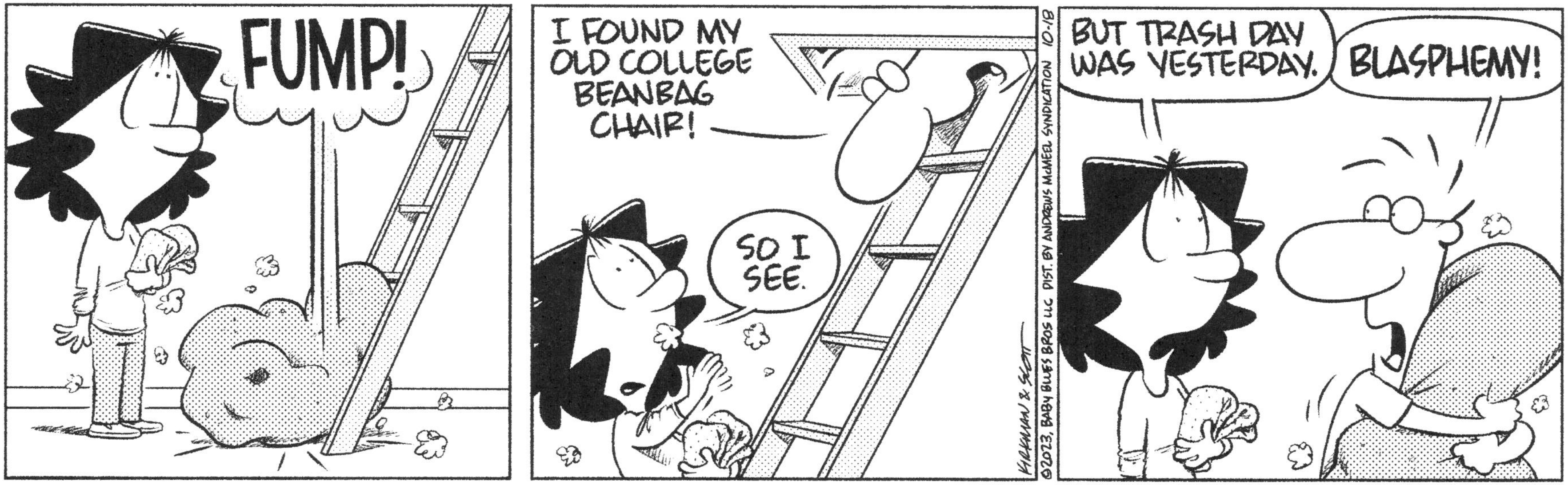
FUMP!
I FOUND MY OLD COLLEGE BEANBAG CHAIR!
SO I SEE.
10-18
©2023, BABY BLUES BROS LLC DIST. BY ANDREWS McMEEL SYNDICATION
KIRKMAN & SCOTT
BUT TRASH DAY WAS YESTERDAY.
BLASPHEMY!

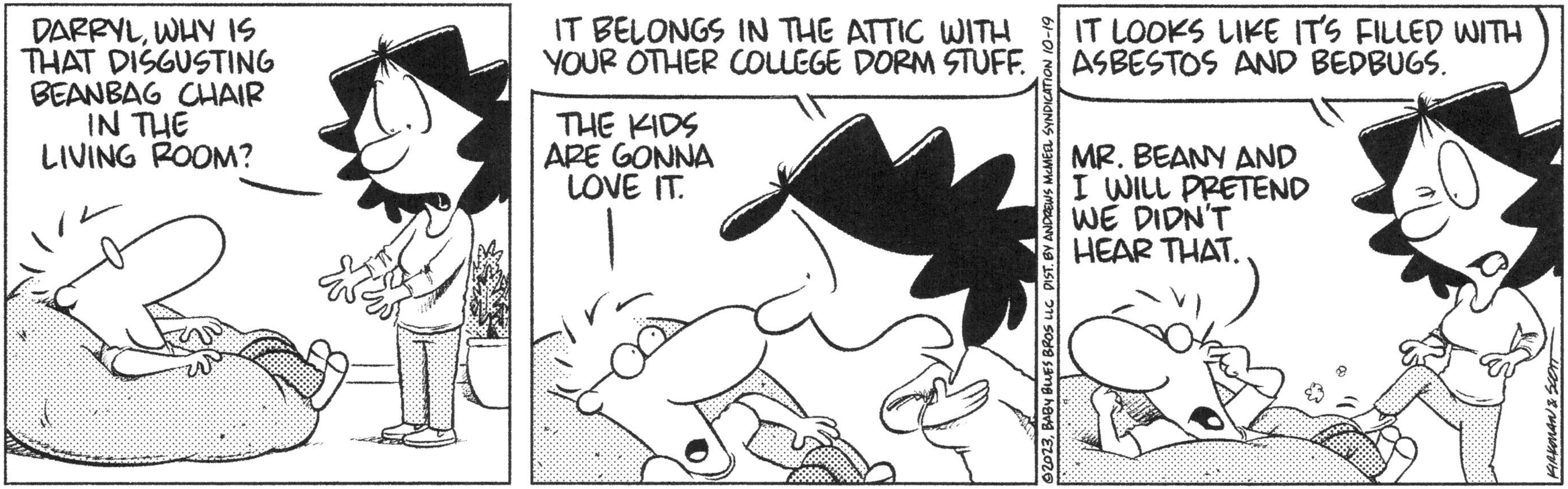
DARRYL, WHY IS THAT DISGUSTING BEANBAG CHAIR IN THE LIVING ROOM?
THE KIDS ARE GONNA LOVE IT.
IT BELONGS IN THE ATTIC WITH YOUR OTHER COLLEGE DORM STUFF.
10-19
©2023, BABY BLUES BROS LLC DIST. BY ANDREWS McMEEL SYNDICATION
IT LOOKS LIKE IT'S FILLED WITH ASBESTOS AND BEDBUGS.
MR. BEANY AND I WILL PRETEND WE DIDN'T HEAR THAT.
KIRKMAN & SCOTT

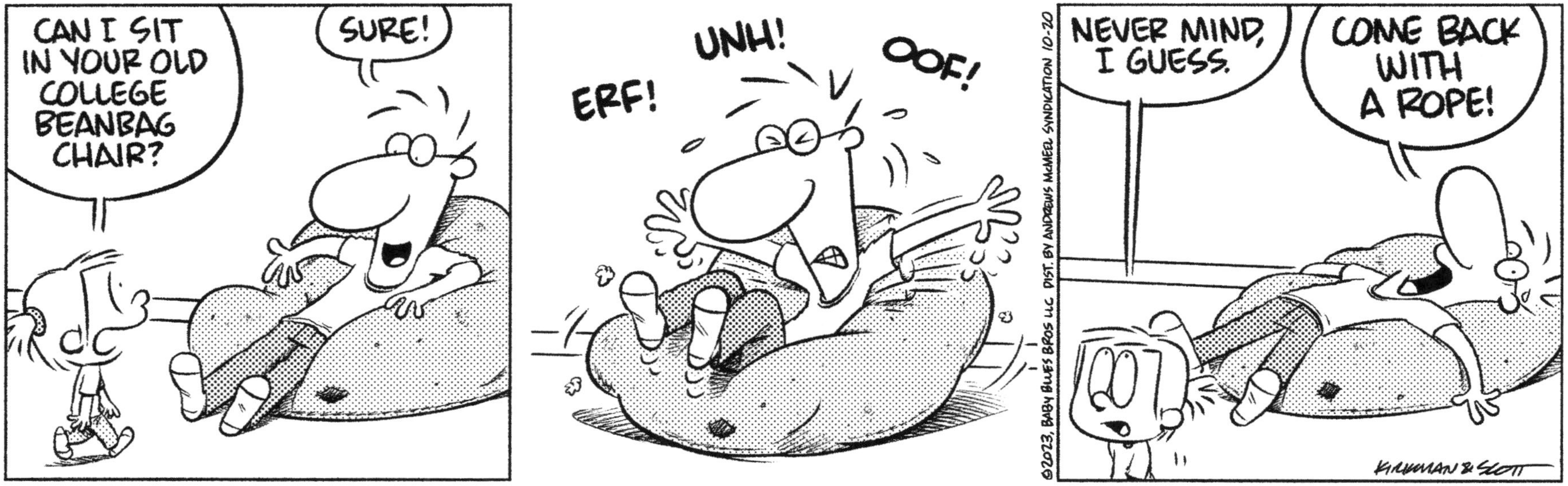
CAN I SIT IN YOUR OLD COLLEGE BEANBAG CHAIR?
SURE!
ERF!
UNH!
OOF!
NEVER MIND, I GUESS.
COME BACK WITH A ROPE!
©2023, BABY BLUES BROS LLC DIST. BY ANDREWS McMEEL SYNDICATION 10-20
KIRKMAN & SCOTT

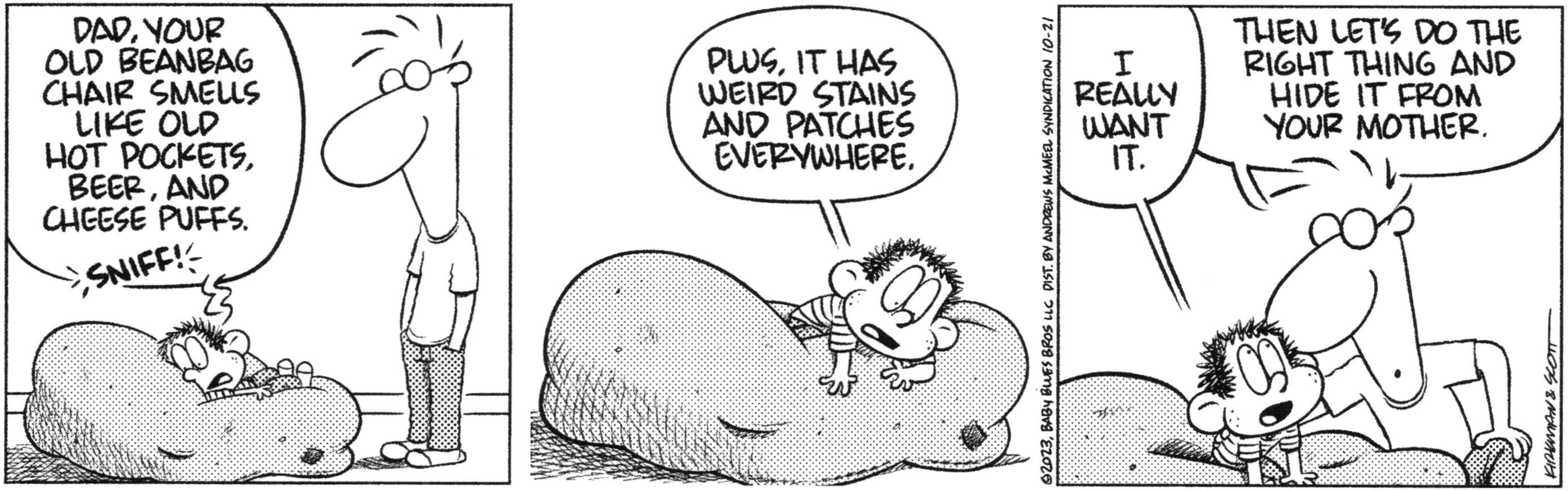
DAD, YOUR OLD BEANBAG CHAIR SMELLS LIKE OLD HOT POCKETS, BEER, AND CHEESE PUFFS.
SNIFF!
PLUS, IT HAS WEIRD STAINS AND PATCHES EVERYWHERE.
I REALLY WANT IT.
THEN LET'S DO THE RIGHT THING AND HIDE IT FROM YOUR MOTHER.
©2023, BABY BLUES BROS LLC DIST. BY ANDREWS McMEEL SYNDICATION 10-21
KIRKMAN & SCOTT

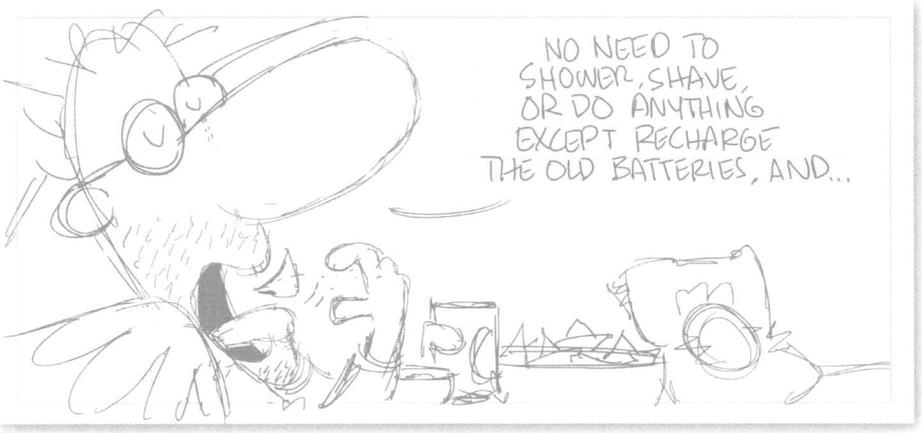
NO NEED TO SHOWER, SHAVE, OR DO ANYTHING EXCEPT RECHARGE THE OLD BATTERIES, AND...

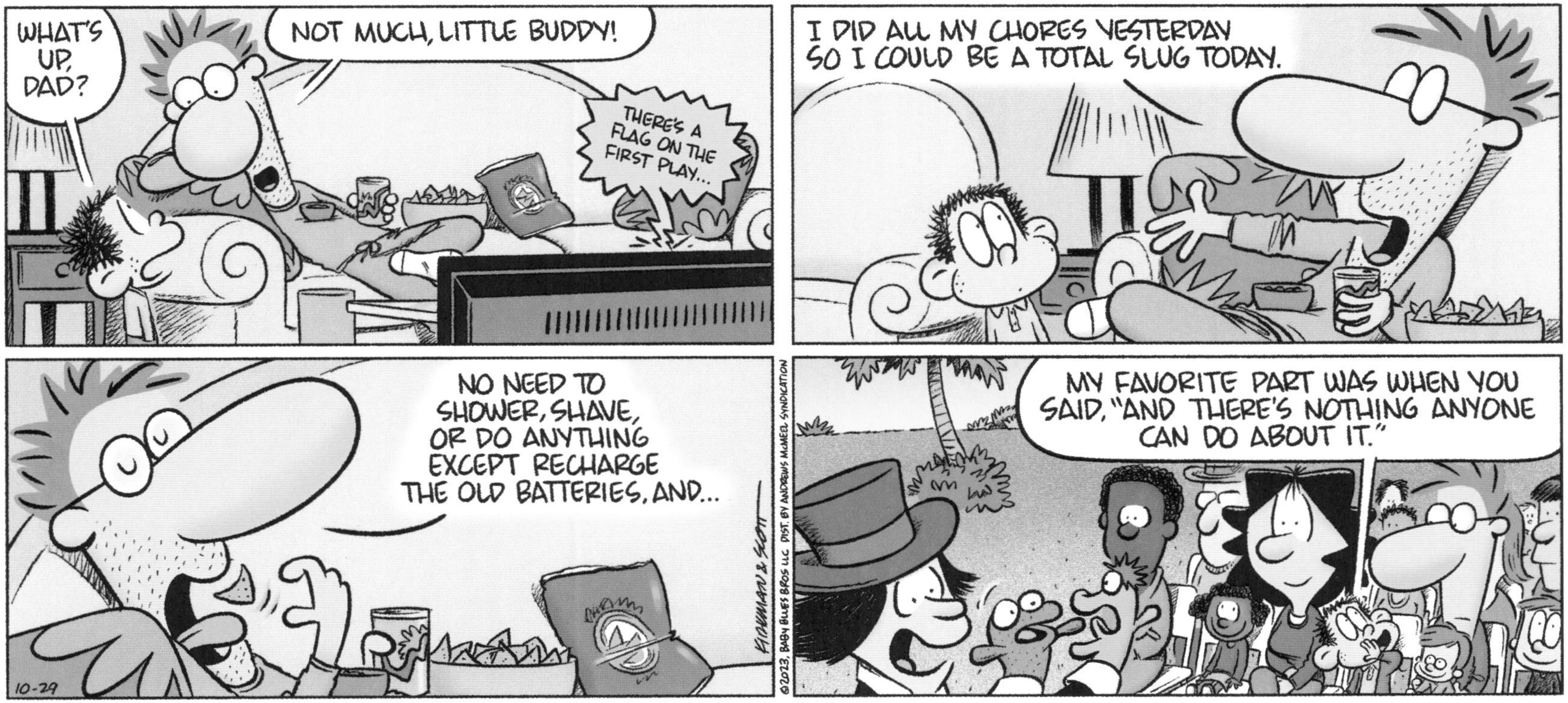
WHAT'S UP, DAD?
NOT MUCH, LITTLE BUDDY!
THERE'S A FLAG ON THE FIRST PLAY...
I DID ALL MY CHORES YESTERDAY SO I COULD BE A TOTAL SLUG TODAY.
NO NEED TO SHOWER, SHAVE, OR DO ANYTHING EXCEPT RECHARGE THE OLD BATTERIES, AND...
10-29
KIRKMAN & SCOTT
©2023, BABY BLUES BROS LLC DIST. BY ANDREWS MCMEEL SYNDICATION
MY FAVORITE PART WAS WHEN YOU SAID, "AND THERE'S NOTHING ANYONE CAN DO ABOUT IT."

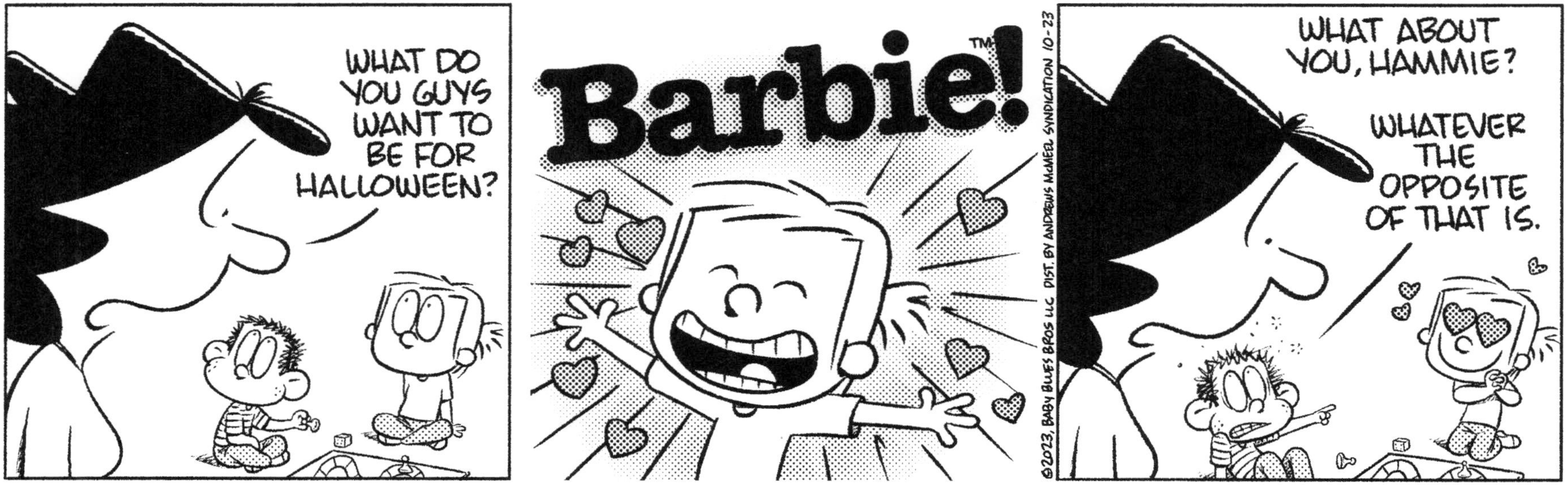
WHAT DO YOU GUYS WANT TO BE FOR HALLOWEEN?
Barbie!™
©2023, BABY BLUES BROS LLC DIST. BY ANDREWS McMEEL SYNDICATION 10-23
WHAT ABOUT YOU, HAMMIE?
WHATEVER THE OPPOSITE OF THAT IS.

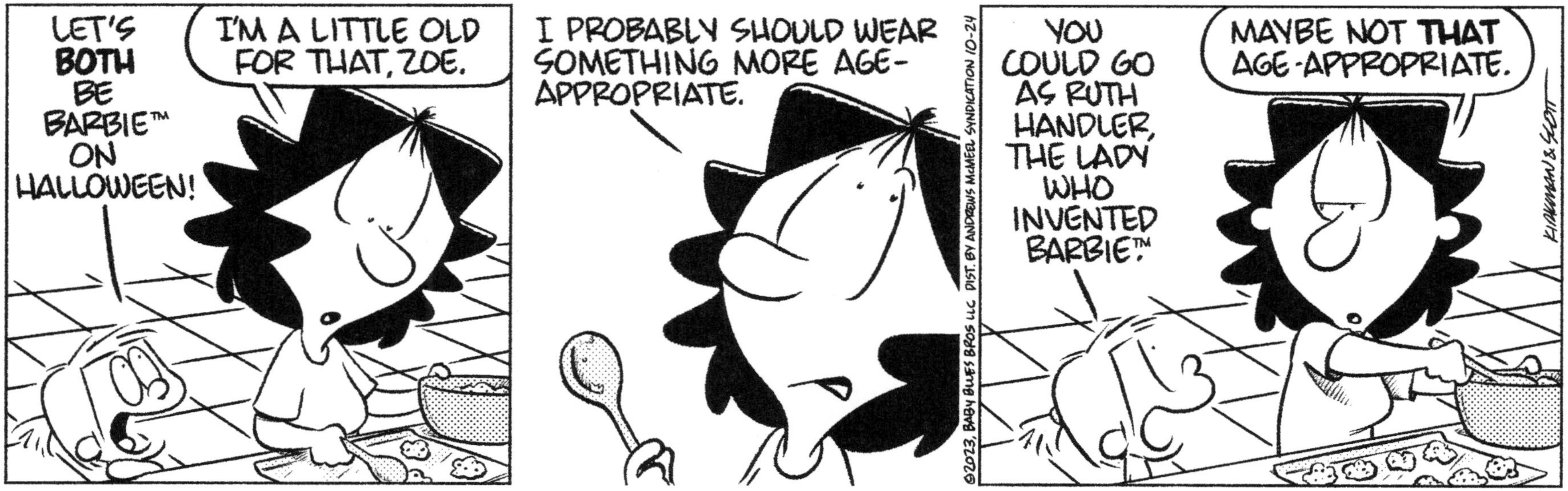
LET'S **BOTH** BE BARBIE™ ON HALLOWEEN!
I'M A LITTLE OLD FOR THAT, ZOE.
I PROBABLY SHOULD WEAR SOMETHING MORE AGE-APPROPRIATE.
©2023, BABY BLUES BROS LLC DIST. BY ANDREWS McMEEL SYNDICATION 10-24
YOU COULD GO AS RUTH HANDLER, THE LADY WHO INVENTED BARBIE™
MAYBE NOT **THAT** AGE-APPROPRIATE.
KIRKMAN & SCOTT

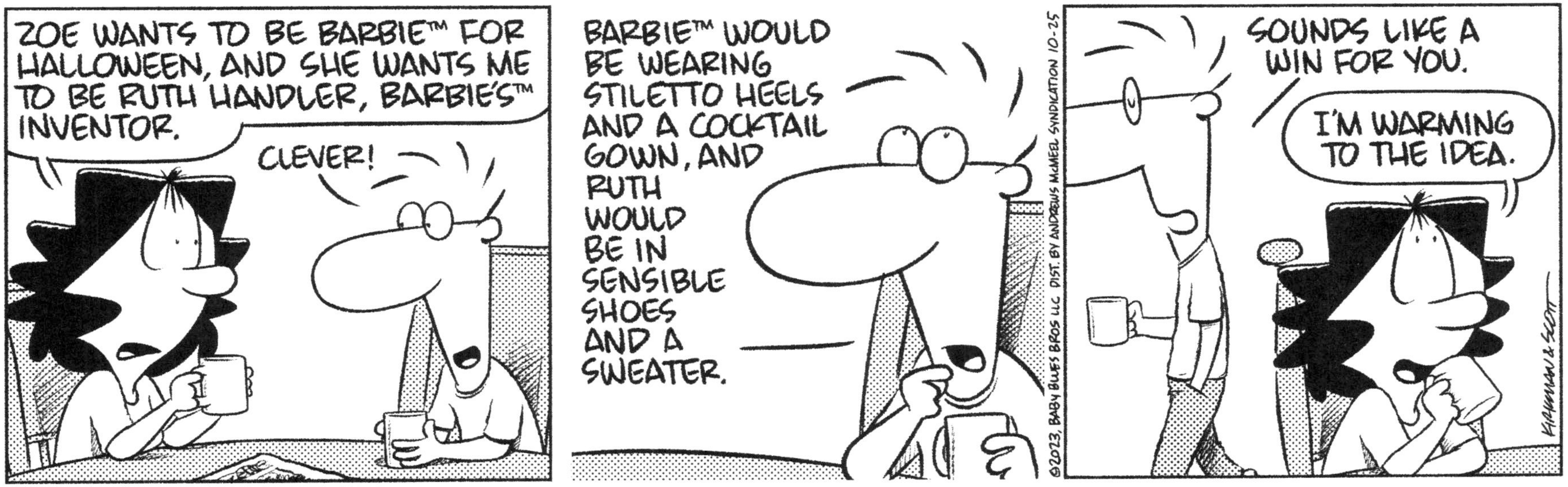
ZOE WANTS TO BE BARBIE™ FOR HALLOWEEN, AND SHE WANTS ME TO BE RUTH HANDLER, BARBIE'S™ INVENTOR.
CLEVER!
BARBIE™ WOULD BE WEARING STILETTO HEELS AND A COCKTAIL GOWN, AND RUTH WOULD BE IN SENSIBLE SHOES AND A SWEATER.
©2023, BABY BLUES BROS LLC DIST. BY ANDREWS MCMEEL SYNDICATION 10-25
SOUNDS LIKE A WIN FOR YOU.
I'M WARMING TO THE IDEA.
KIRKMAN & SCOTT

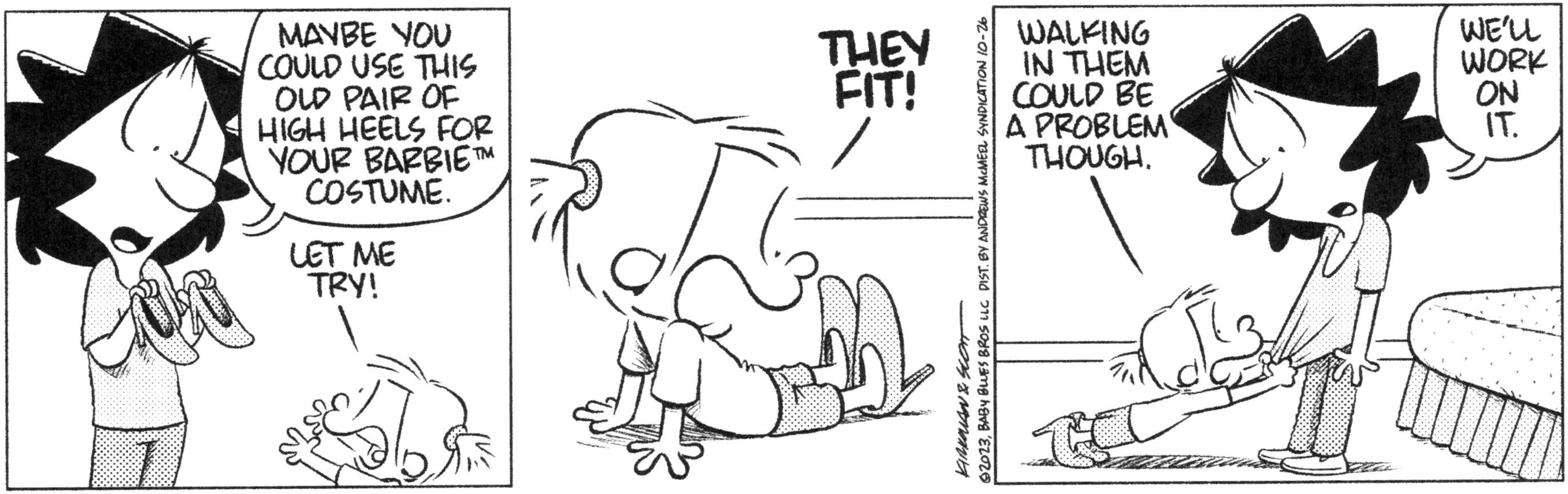
MAYBE YOU COULD USE THIS OLD PAIR OF HIGH HEELS FOR YOUR BARBIE™ COSTUME.
LET ME TRY!
THEY FIT!
KIRKMAN & SCOTT
©2023, BABY BLUES BROS LLC DIST. BY ANDREWS MCMEEL SYNDICATION 10-26
WALKING IN THEM COULD BE A PROBLEM THOUGH.
WE'LL WORK ON IT.

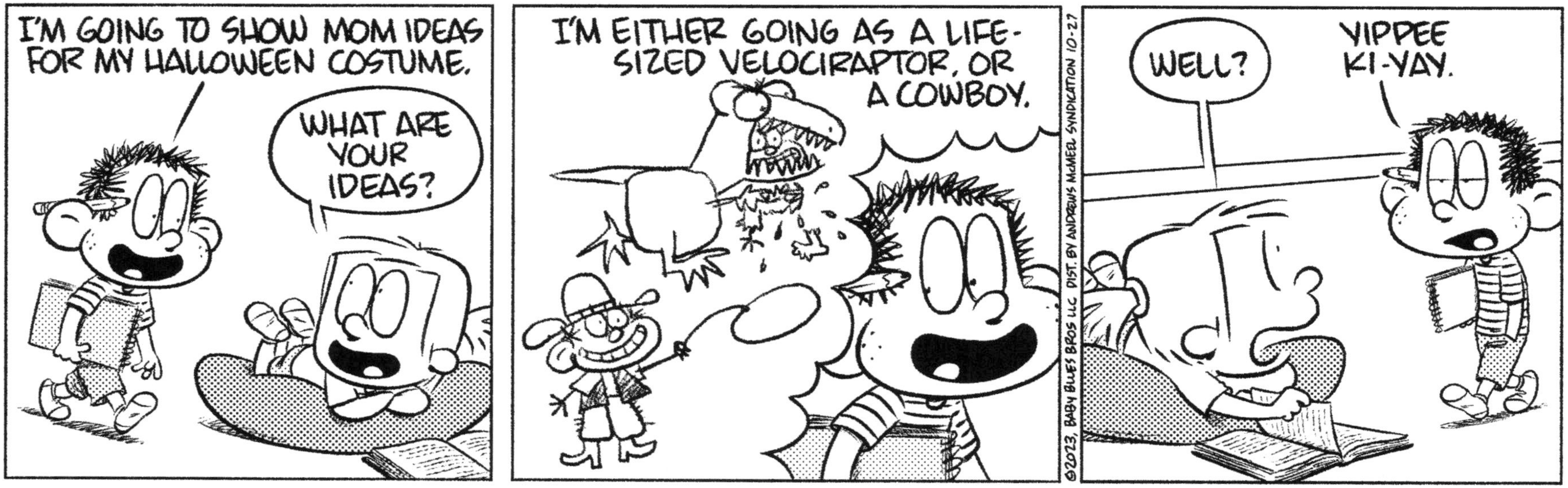
I'M GOING TO SHOW MOM IDEAS FOR MY HALLOWEEN COSTUME.
WHAT ARE YOUR IDEAS?
I'M EITHER GOING AS A LIFE-SIZED VELOCIRAPTOR, OR A COWBOY.
©2023, BABY BLUES BROS LLC DIST. BY ANDREWS MCMEEL SYNDICATION 10-27
WELL?
YIPPEE KI-YAY.

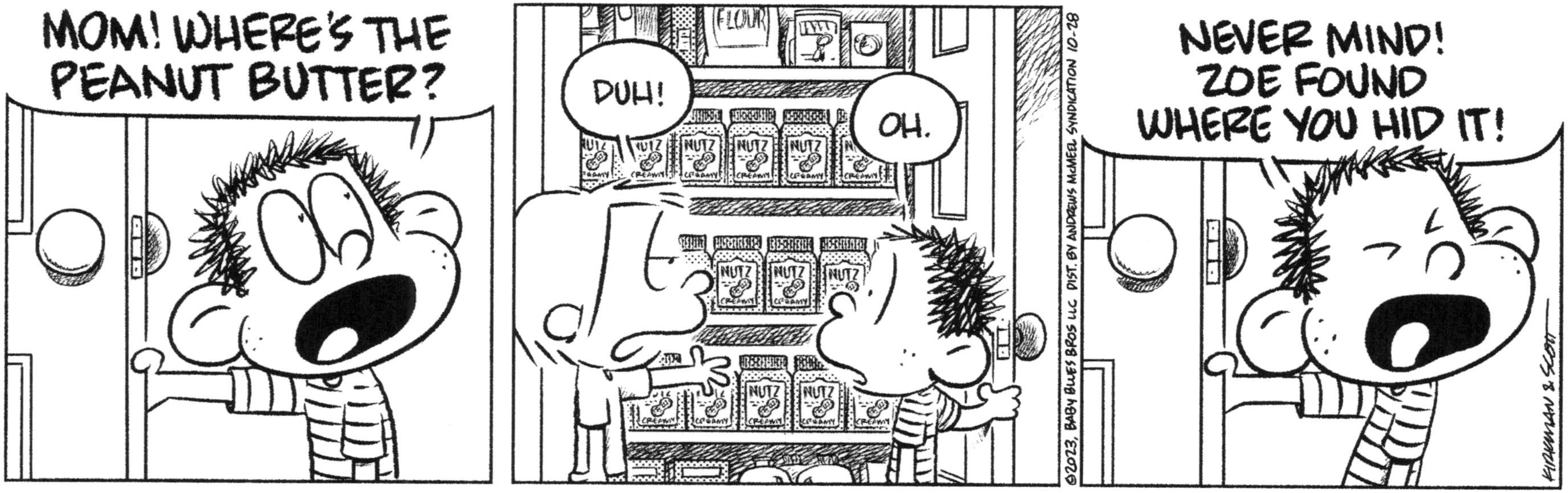
MOM! WHERE'S THE PEANUT BUTTER?
FLOUR
NUTZ CREAMY
DUH!
OH.
©2023, BABY BLUES BROS LLC DIST. BY ANDREWS MCMEEL SYNDICATION 10-28
NEVER MIND! ZOE FOUND WHERE YOU HID IT!
KIRKMAN & SCOTT

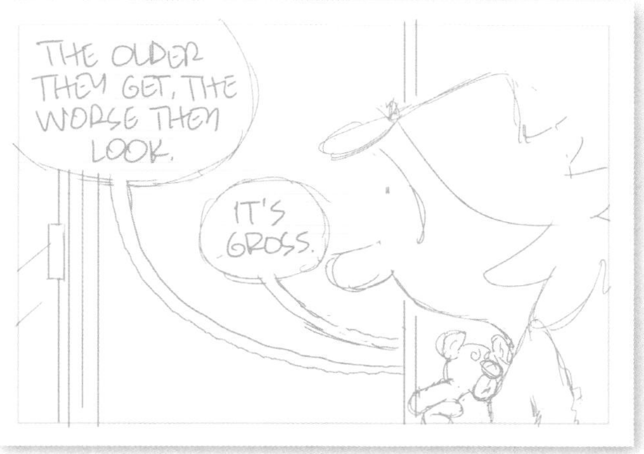
THE OLDER THEY GET, THE WORSE THEY LOOK.
IT'S GROSS.

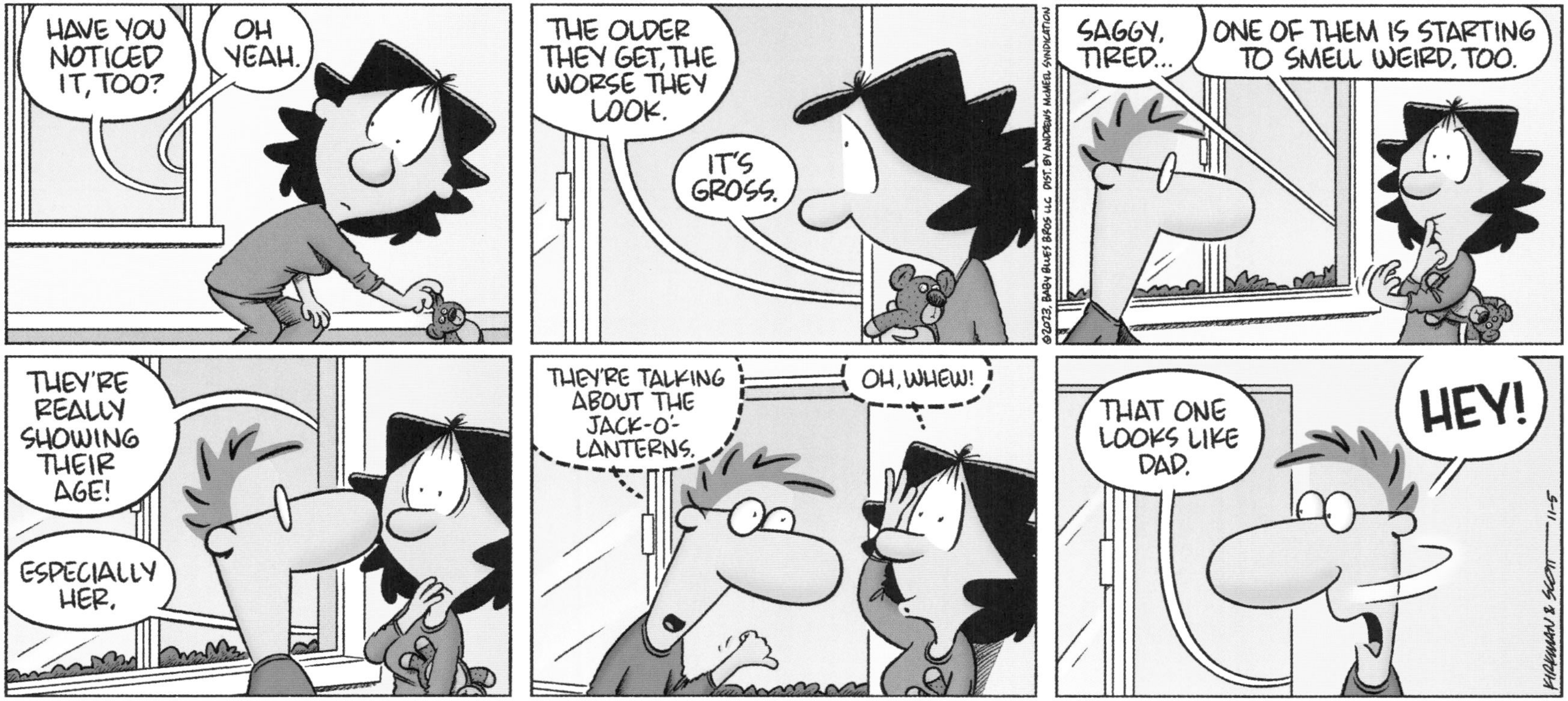
HAVE YOU NOTICED IT, TOO?
OH YEAH.
THE OLDER THEY GET, THE WORSE THEY LOOK.
IT'S GROSS.
©2023, BABY BLUES BROS LLC DIST. BY ANDREWS MCMEEL SYNDICATION
SAGGY, TIRED...
ONE OF THEM IS STARTING TO SMELL WEIRD, TOO.
THEY'RE REALLY SHOWING THEIR AGE!
ESPECIALLY HER.
THEY'RE TALKING ABOUT THE JACK-O'-LANTERNS.
OH, WHEW!
THAT ONE LOOKS LIKE DAD.
HEY!
KIRKMAN & SCOTT 11-5

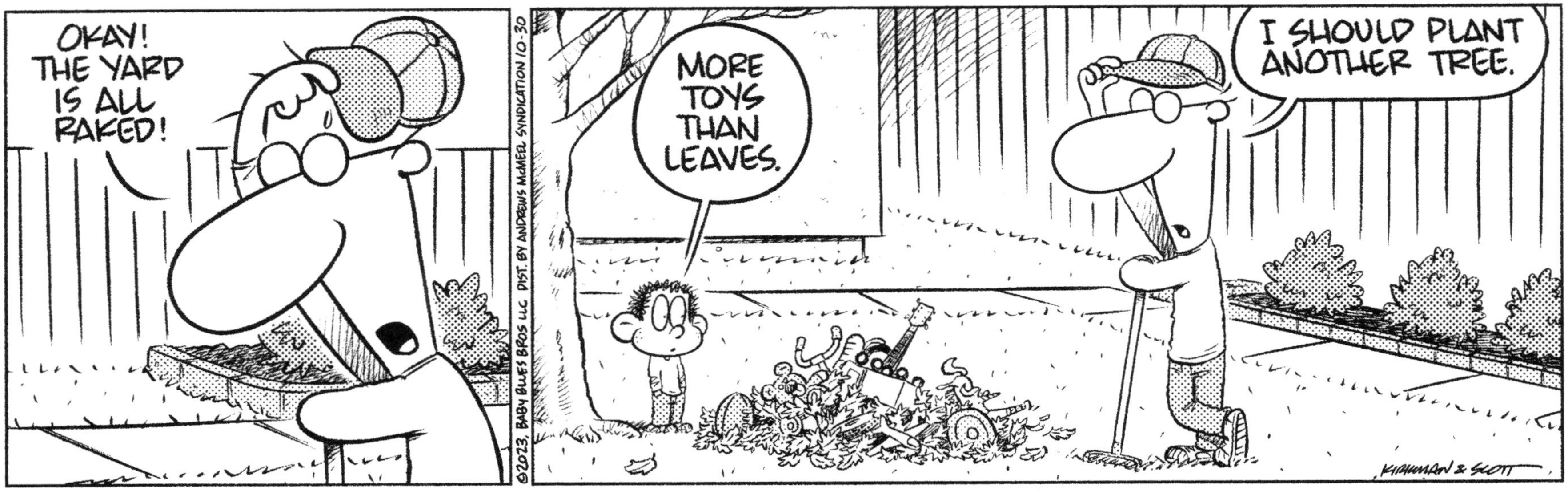
OKAY! THE YARD IS ALL RAKED!
MORE TOYS THAN LEAVES.
I SHOULD PLANT ANOTHER TREE.
©2023, BABY BLUES BROS LLC DIST. BY ANDREWS McMEEL SYNDICATION 10-30
KIRKMAN & SCOTT

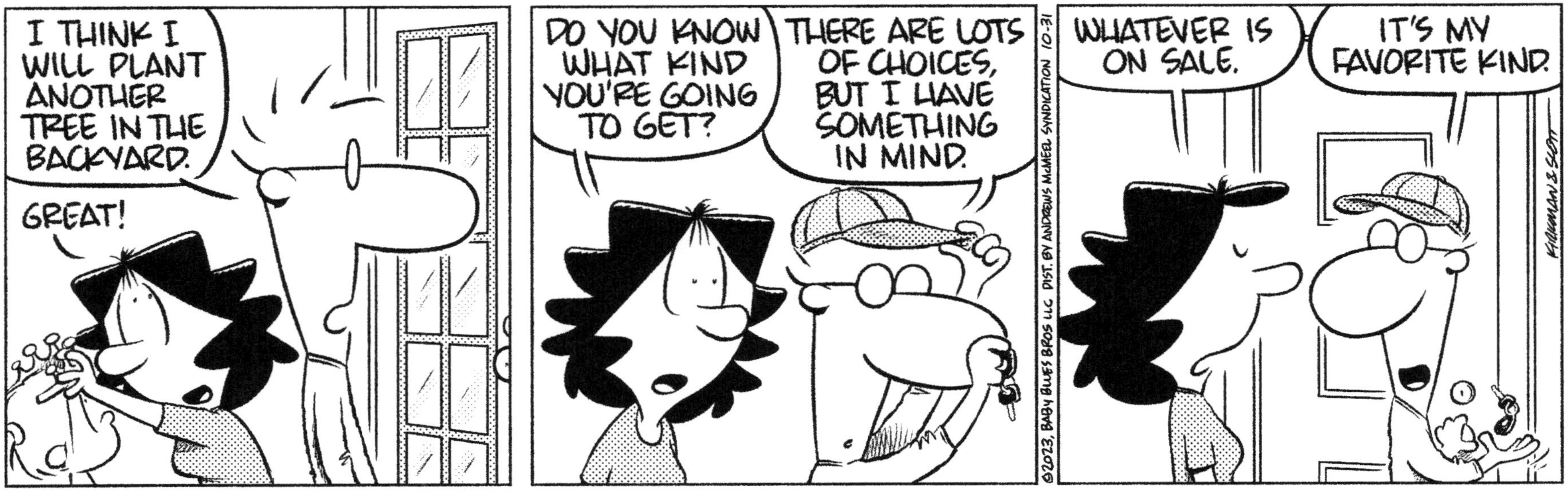
I THINK I WILL PLANT ANOTHER TREE IN THE BACKYARD.
GREAT!
DO YOU KNOW WHAT KIND YOU'RE GOING TO GET?
THERE ARE LOTS OF CHOICES, BUT I HAVE SOMETHING IN MIND.
WHATEVER IS ON SALE.
IT'S MY FAVORITE KIND.
©2023, BABY BLUES BROS LLC DIST. BY ANDREWS McMEEL SYNDICATION 10-31
KIRKMAN & SCOTT

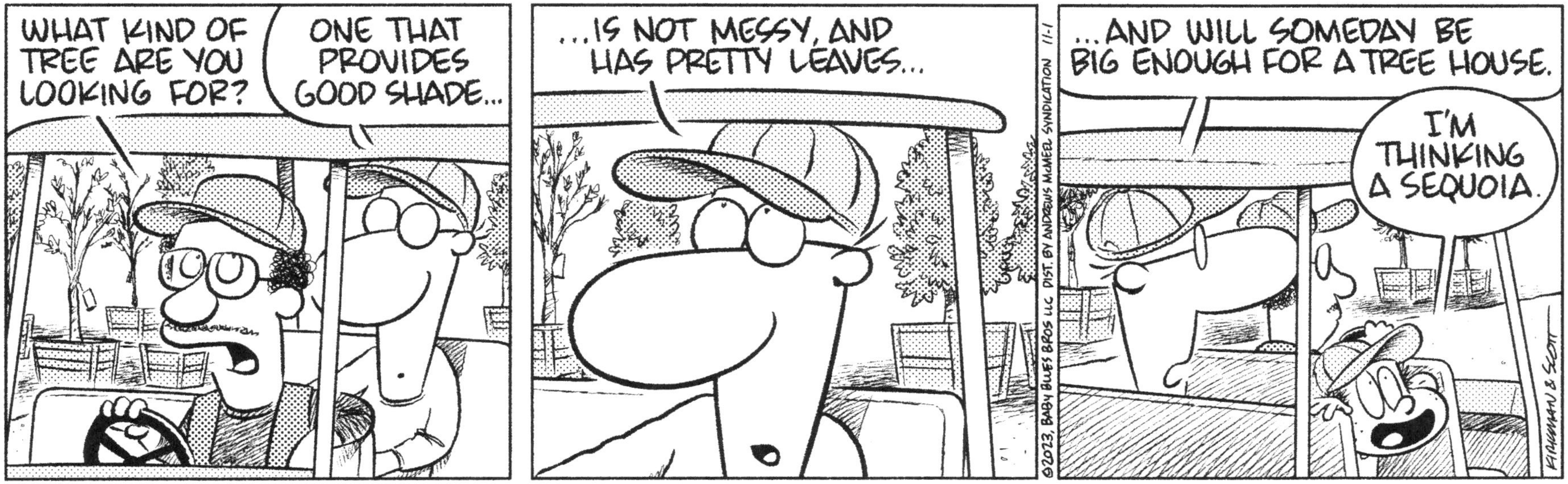
WHAT KIND OF TREE ARE YOU LOOKING FOR?
ONE THAT PROVIDES GOOD SHADE...
...IS NOT MESSY, AND HAS PRETTY LEAVES...
©2023, BABY BLUES BROS LLC DIST. BY ANDREWS McMEEL SYNDICATION 11-1
...AND WILL SOMEDAY BE BIG ENOUGH FOR A TREE HOUSE.
I'M THINKING A SEQUOIA.
KIRKMAN & SCOTT

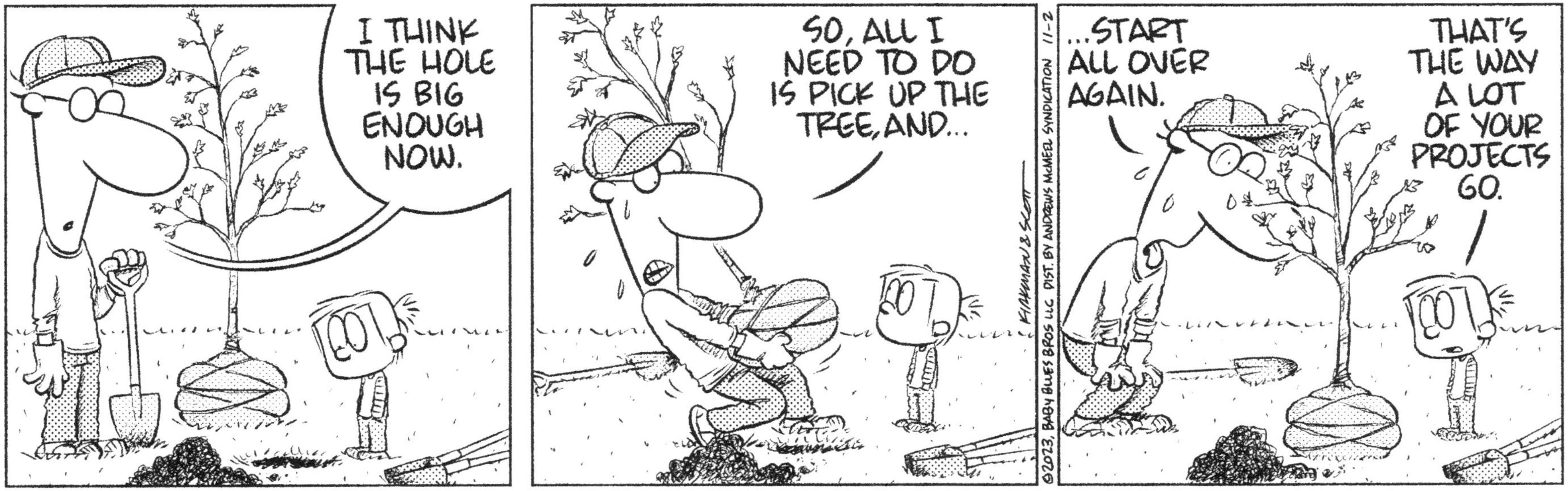
I THINK THE HOLE IS BIG ENOUGH NOW.
SO, ALL I NEED TO DO IS PICK UP THE TREE, AND...
KIRKMAN & SCOTT
©2023, BABY BLUES BROS LLC DIST. BY ANDREWS McMEEL SYNDICATION 11-2
...START ALL OVER AGAIN.
THAT'S THE WAY A LOT OF YOUR PROJECTS GO.

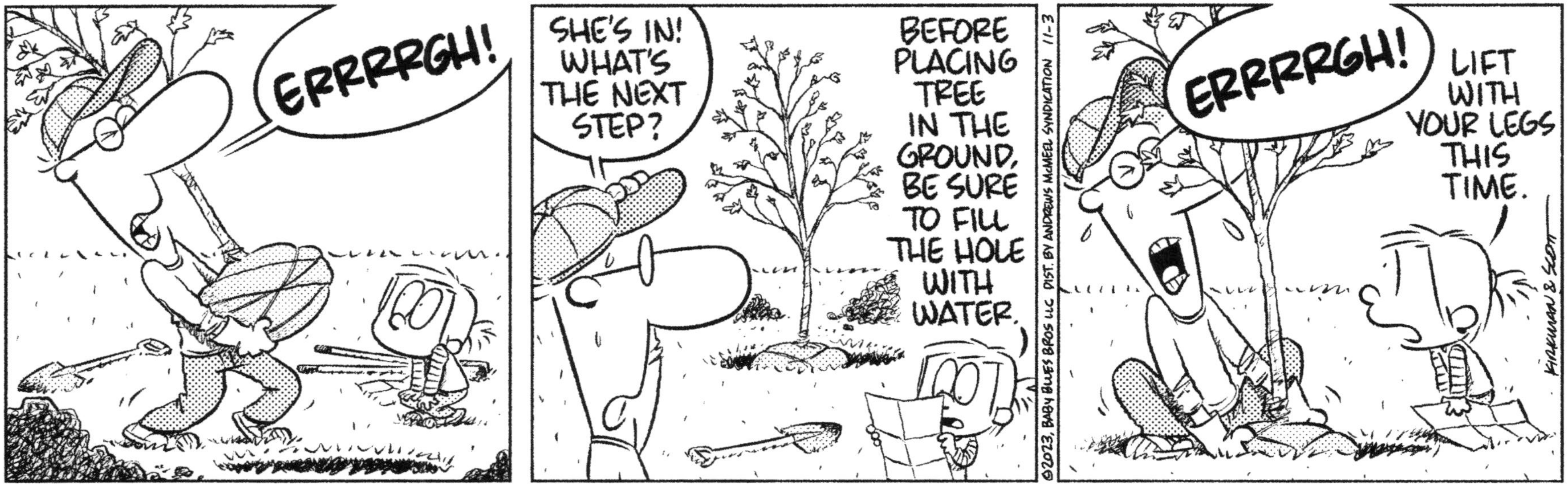
ERRRRGH!
SHE'S IN! WHAT'S THE NEXT STEP?
BEFORE PLACING TREE IN THE GROUND, BE SURE TO FILL THE HOLE WITH WATER.
©2023, BABY BLUES BROS LLC DIST. BY ANDREWS McMEEL SYNDICATION 11-3
ERRRRGH!
LIFT WITH YOUR LEGS THIS TIME.
KIRKMAN & SCOTT

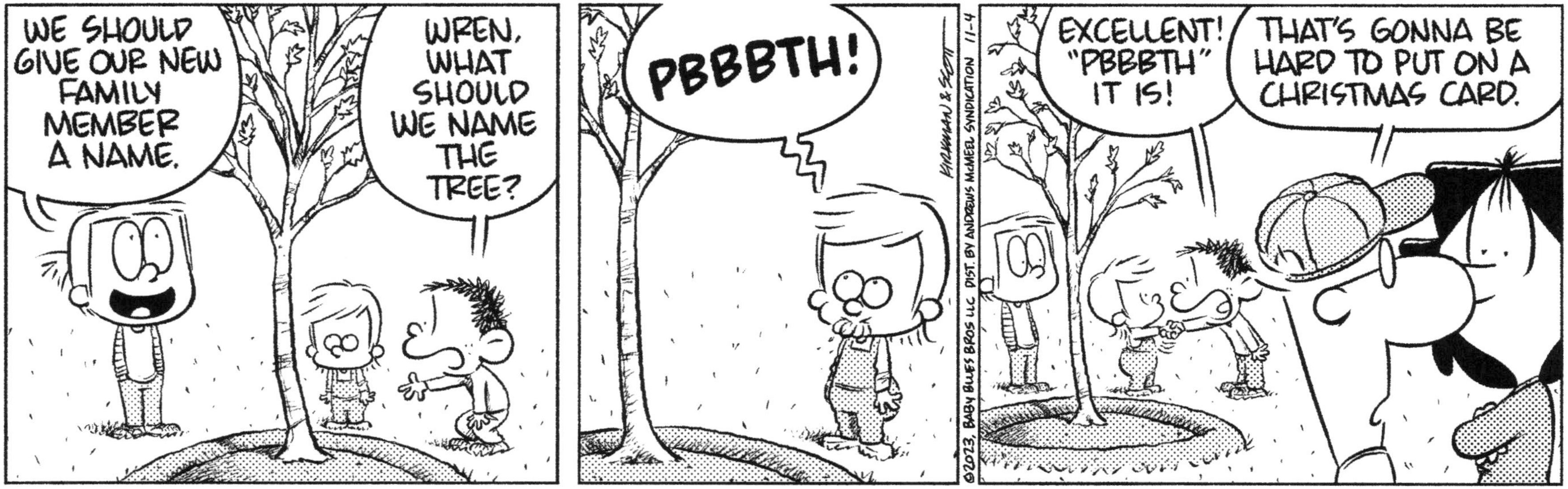
WE SHOULD GIVE OUR NEW FAMILY MEMBER A NAME.
WREN, WHAT SHOULD WE NAME THE TREE?
PBBBTH!
KIRKMAN & SCOTT
11-4
©2023, BABY BLUES BROS LLC DIST. BY ANDREWS McMEEL SYNDICATION
EXCELLENT! "PBBBTH" IT IS!
THAT'S GONNA BE HARD TO PUT ON A CHRISTMAS CARD.

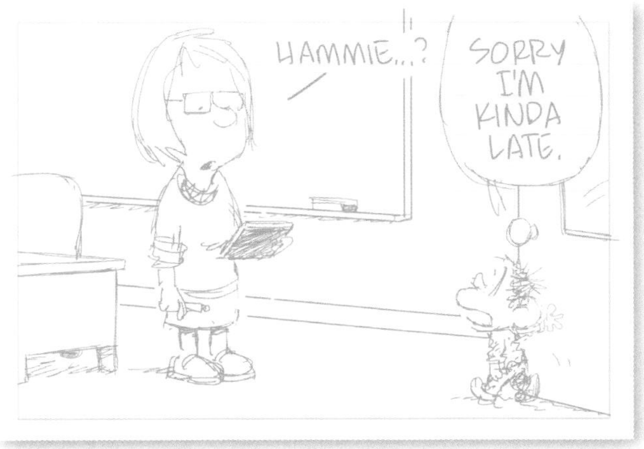
HAMMIE...?
SORRY I'M KINDA LATE.

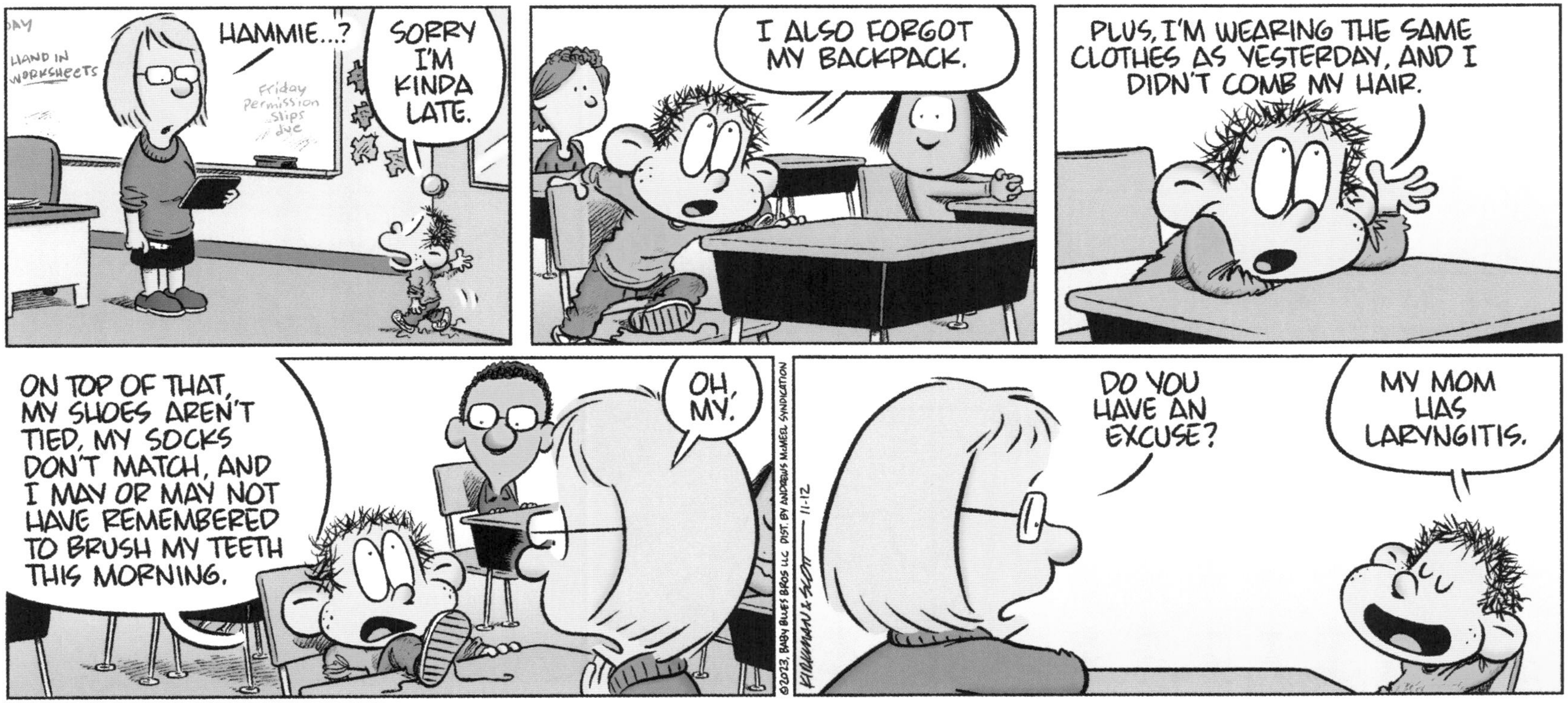
HAND IN WORKSHEETS
Friday Permission slips due
HAMMIE...?
SORRY I'M KINDA LATE.
I ALSO FORGOT MY BACKPACK.
PLUS, I'M WEARING THE SAME CLOTHES AS YESTERDAY, AND I DIDN'T COMB MY HAIR.
ON TOP OF THAT, MY SHOES AREN'T TIED, MY SOCKS DON'T MATCH, AND I MAY OR MAY NOT HAVE REMEMBERED TO BRUSH MY TEETH THIS MORNING.
OH, MY.
©2023, BABY BLUES BROS LLC. DIST. BY ANDREWS McMEEL SYNDICATION
KIRKMAN & SCOTT 11-12
DO YOU HAVE AN EXCUSE?
MY MOM HAS LARYNGITIS.

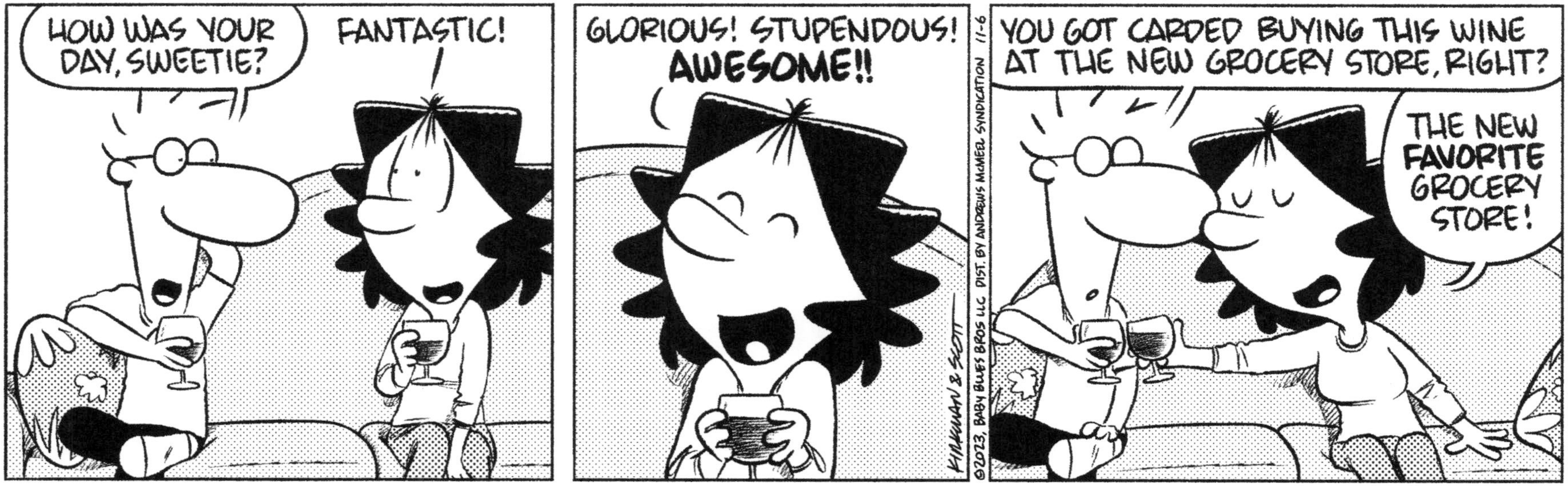
HOW WAS YOUR DAY, SWEETIE?
FANTASTIC!
GLORIOUS! STUPENDOUS! **AWESOME!!**
11-6
KIRKMAN & SCOTT
©2023, BABY BLUES BROS LLC DIST. BY ANDREWS MCMEEL SYNDICATION
YOU GOT CARDED BUYING THIS WINE AT THE NEW GROCERY STORE, RIGHT?
THE NEW **FAVORITE** GROCERY STORE!

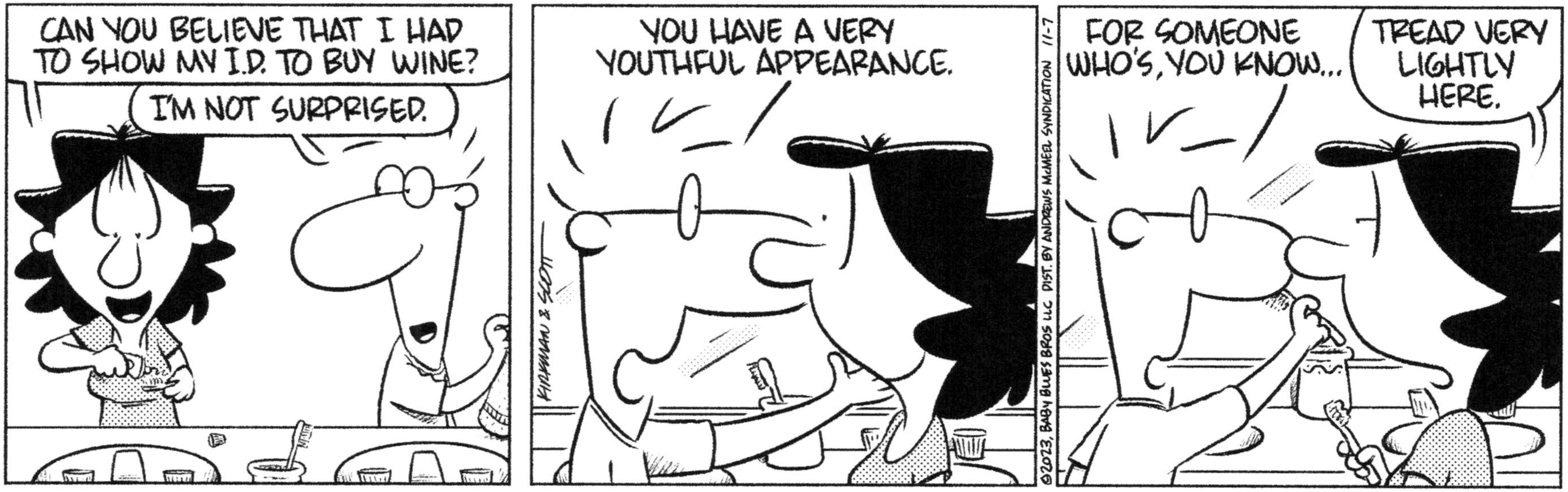
CAN YOU BELIEVE THAT I HAD TO SHOW MY I.D. TO BUY WINE?
I'M NOT SURPRISED.
KIRKMAN & SCOTT
YOU HAVE A VERY YOUTHFUL APPEARANCE.
11-7
©2023, BABY BLUES BROS LLC DIST. BY ANDREWS MCMEEL SYNDICATION
FOR SOMEONE WHO'S, YOU KNOW...
TREAD VERY LIGHTLY HERE.

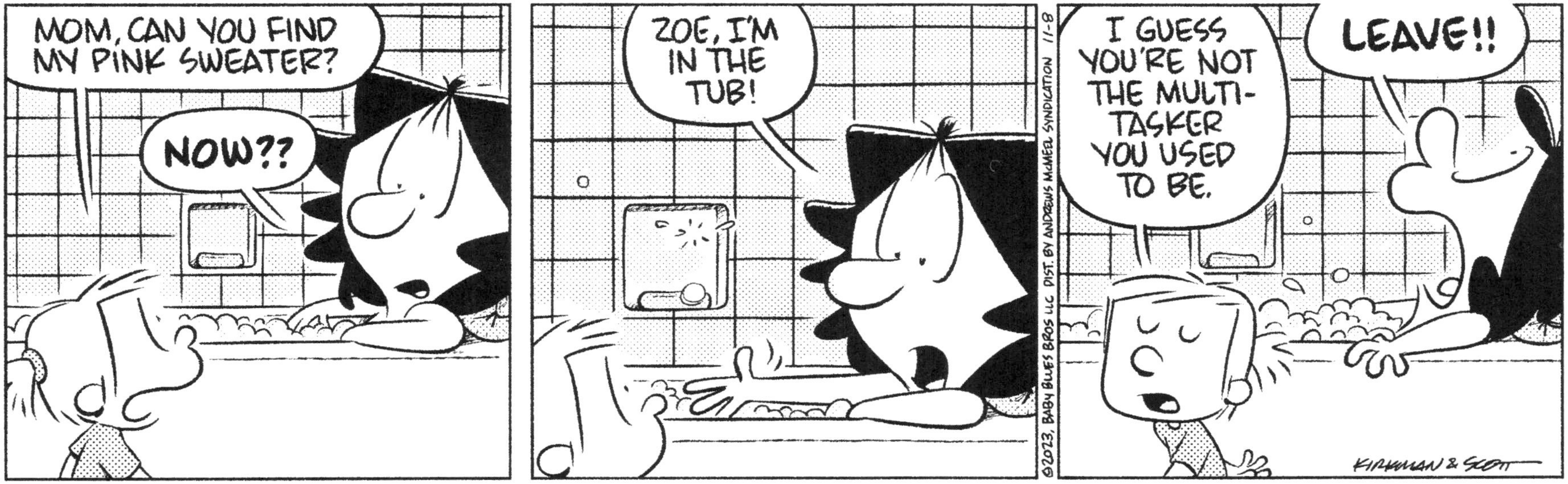
MOM, CAN YOU FIND MY PINK SWEATER?
NOW??
ZOE, I'M IN THE TUB!
I GUESS YOU'RE NOT THE MULTI-TASKER YOU USED TO BE.
LEAVE!!
©2023, BABY BLUES BROS LLC DIST. BY ANDREWS McMEEL SYNDICATION 11-8
KIRKMAN & SCOTT

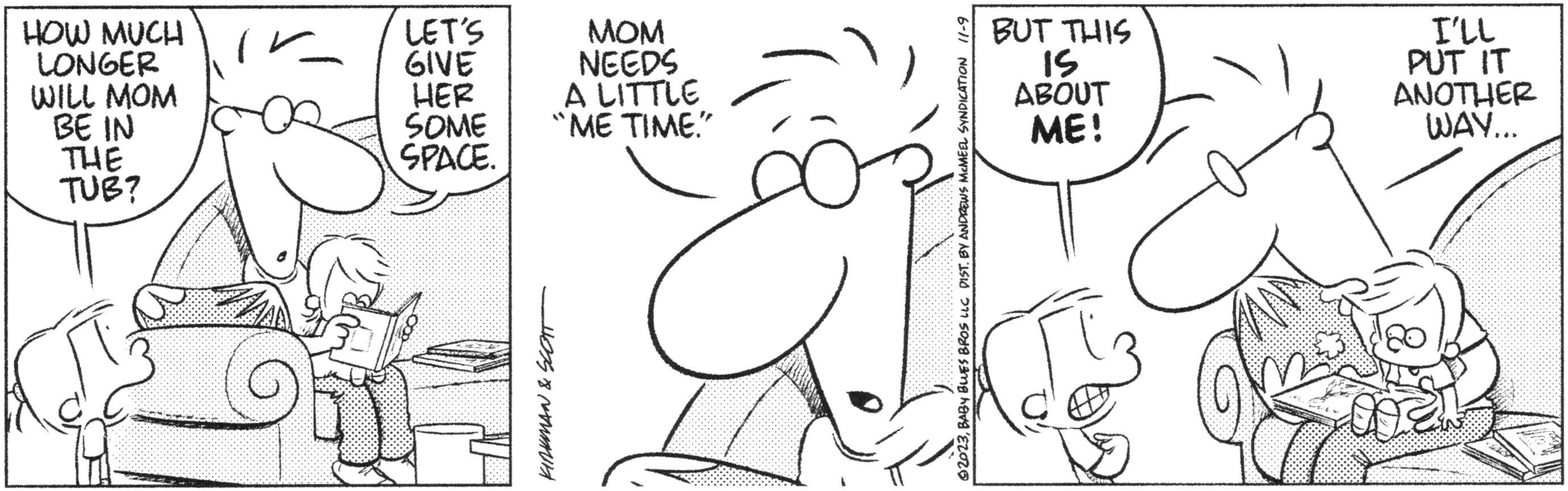
HOW MUCH LONGER WILL MOM BE IN THE TUB?
LET'S GIVE HER SOME SPACE.
KIRKMAN & SCOTT
MOM NEEDS A LITTLE "ME TIME."
BUT THIS IS ABOUT ME!
I'LL PUT IT ANOTHER WAY...
©2023, BABY BLUES BROS LLC DIST. BY ANDREWS McMEEL SYNDICATION 11-9

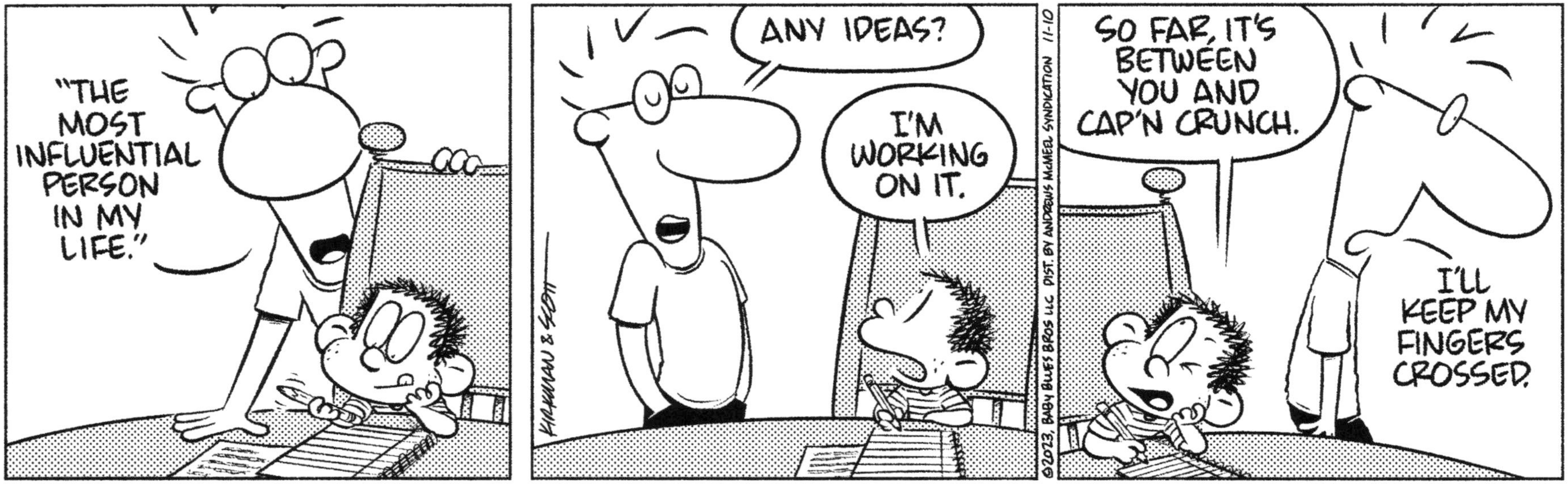
"THE MOST INFLUENTIAL PERSON IN MY LIFE."
ANY IDEAS?
I'M WORKING ON IT.
SO FAR, IT'S BETWEEN YOU AND CAP'N CRUNCH.
I'LL KEEP MY FINGERS CROSSED.
KIRKMAN & SCOTT
©2023, BABY BLUES BROS LLC DIST. BY ANDREWS McMEEL SYNDICATION 11-10

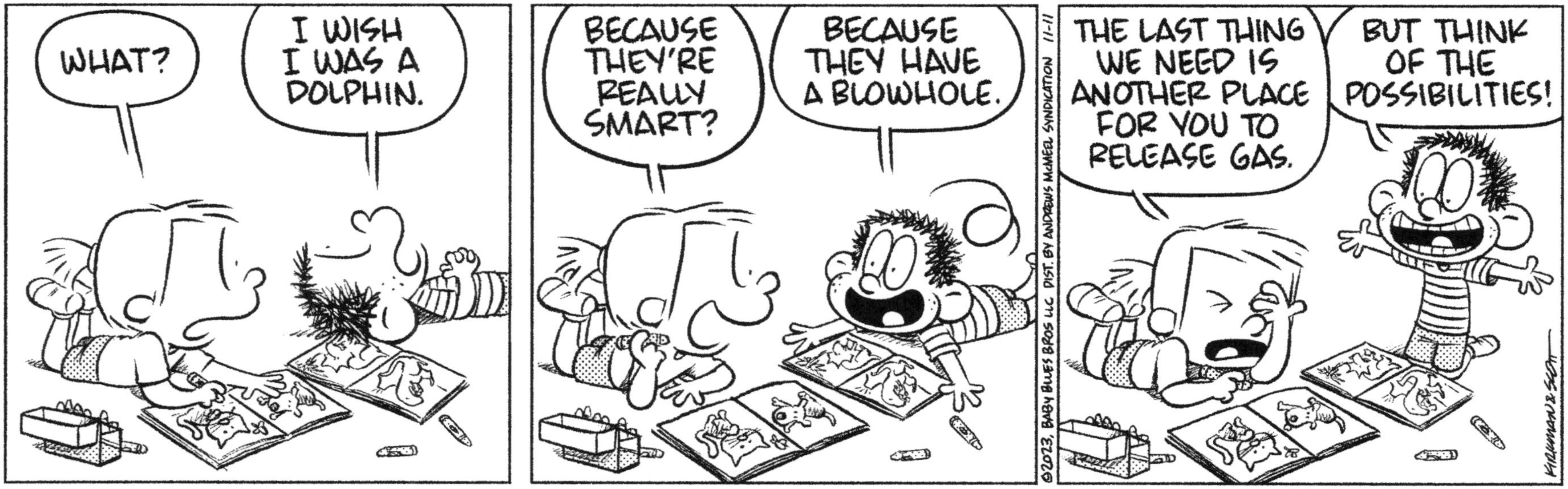
WHAT?
I WISH I WAS A DOLPHIN.
BECAUSE THEY'RE REALLY SMART?
BECAUSE THEY HAVE A BLOWHOLE.
THE LAST THING WE NEED IS ANOTHER PLACE FOR YOU TO RELEASE GAS.
BUT THINK OF THE POSSIBILITIES!
KIRKMAN & SCOTT
©2023, BABY BLUES BROS LLC DIST. BY ANDREWS McMEEL SYNDICATION 11-11

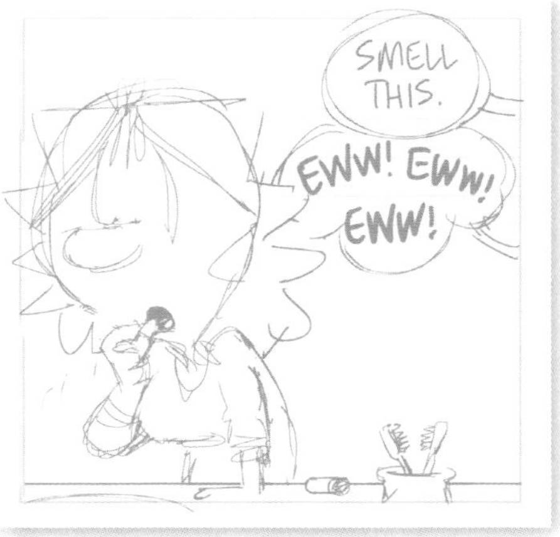
SMELL THIS.
EWW! EWW! EWW!

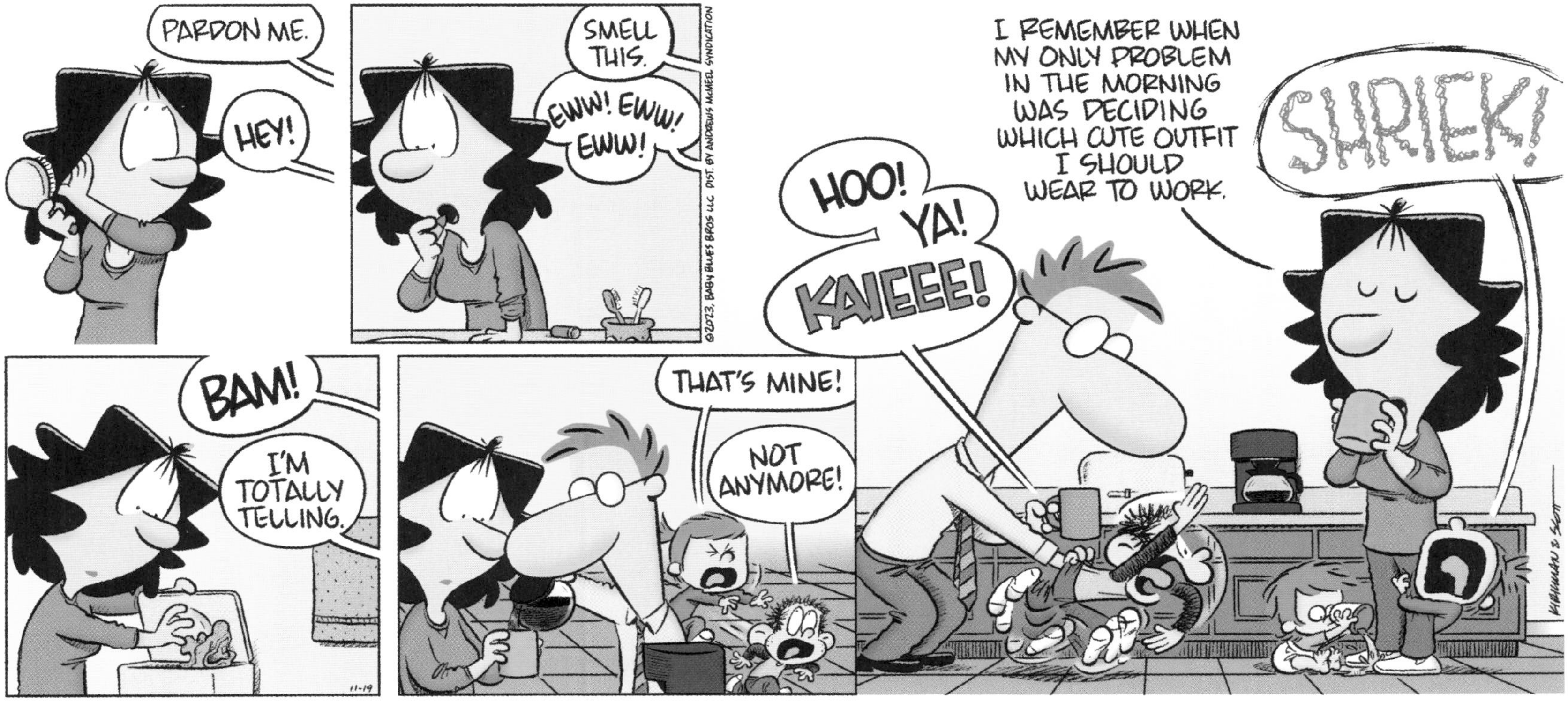
PARDON ME.
HEY!
SMELL THIS.
EWW! EWW! EWW!
©2023, BABY BLUES BROS LLC DIST. BY ANDREWS McMEEL SYNDICATION
BAM!
I'M TOTALLY TELLING.
11-19
THAT'S MINE!
NOT ANYMORE!
HOO! YA! KAIEEE!
I REMEMBER WHEN MY ONLY PROBLEM IN THE MORNING WAS DECIDING WHICH CUTE OUTFIT I SHOULD WEAR TO WORK.
SHRIEK!

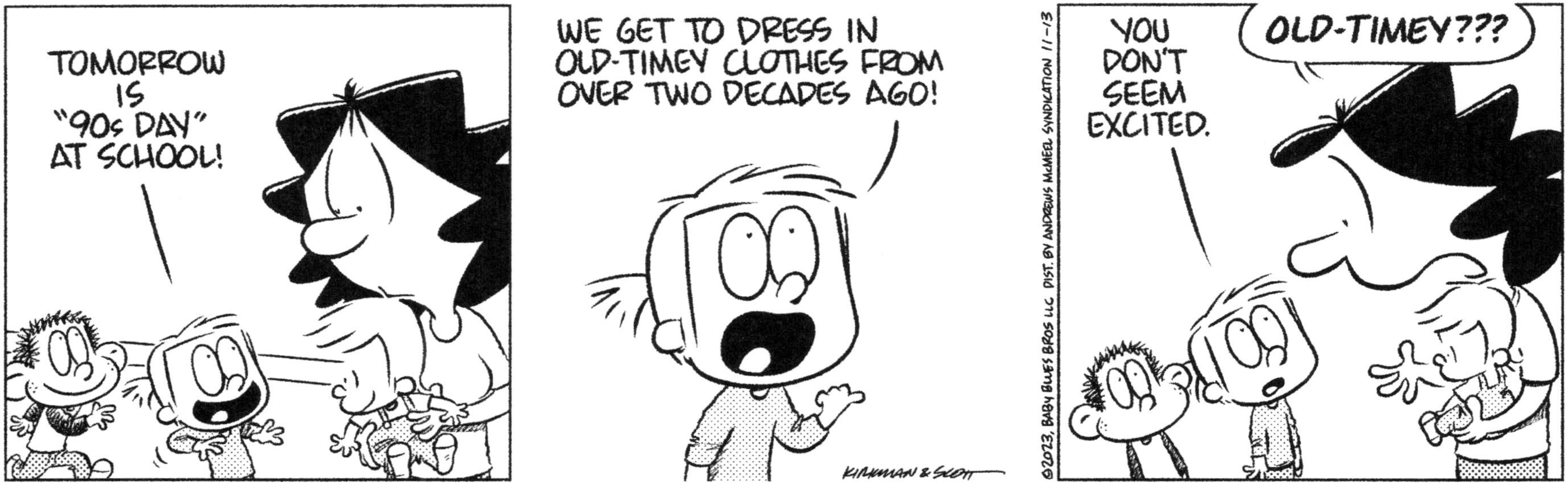
TOMORROW IS "90s DAY" AT SCHOOL!
WE GET TO DRESS IN OLD-TIMEY CLOTHES FROM OVER TWO DECADES AGO!
KIRKMAN & SCOTT
©2023, BABY BLUES BROS LLC DIST. BY ANDREWS MCMEEL SYNDICATION 11-13
YOU DON'T SEEM EXCITED.
OLD-TIMEY???

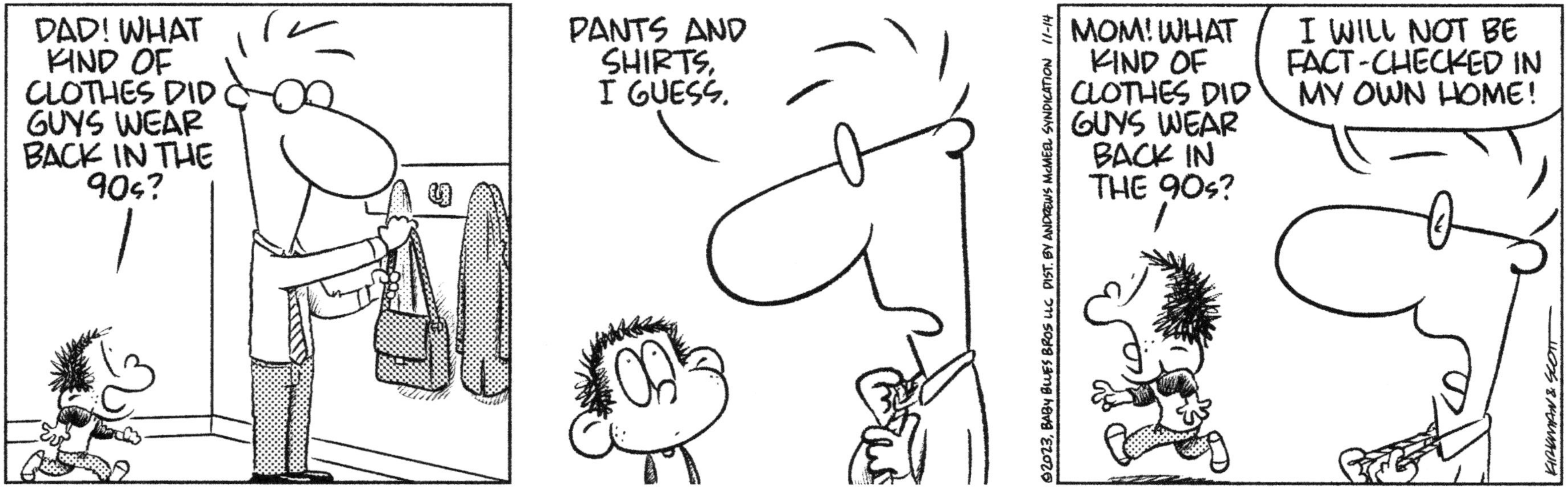
DAD! WHAT KIND OF CLOTHES DID GUYS WEAR BACK IN THE 90s?
PANTS AND SHIRTS, I GUESS.
©2023, BABY BLUES BROS LLC DIST. BY ANDREWS MCMEEL SYNDICATION 11-14
MOM! WHAT KIND OF CLOTHES DID GUYS WEAR BACK IN THE 90s?
I WILL NOT BE FACT-CHECKED IN MY OWN HOME!
KIRKMAN & SCOTT

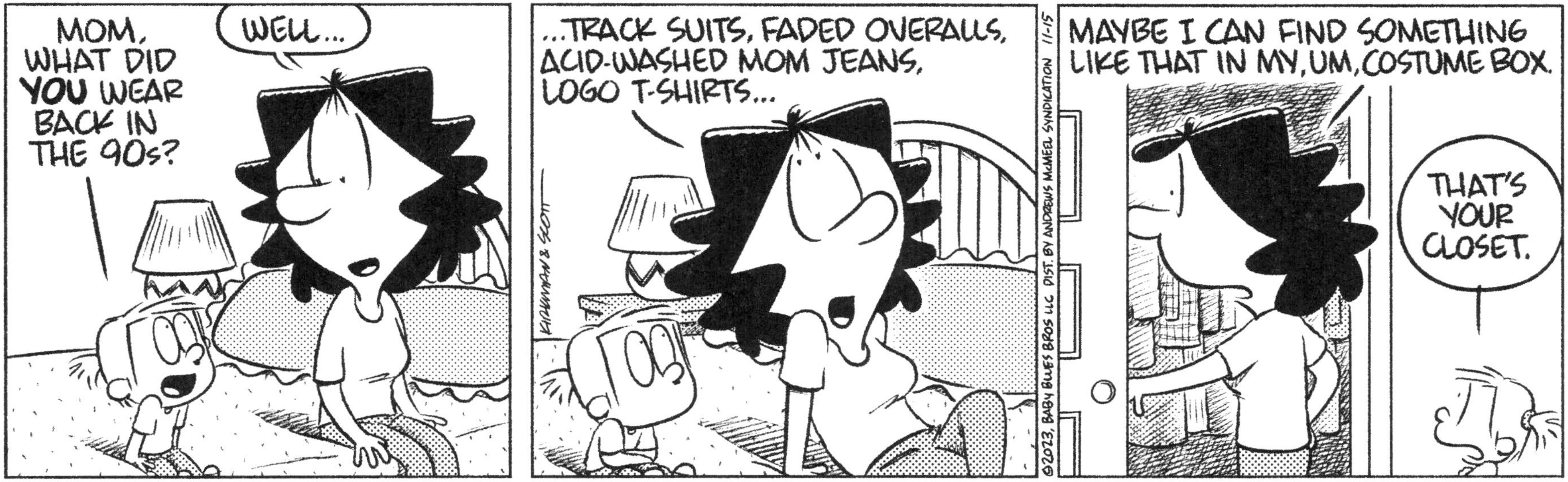
MOM, WHAT DID YOU WEAR BACK IN THE 90s?
WELL...
...TRACK SUITS, FADED OVERALLS, ACID-WASHED MOM JEANS, LOGO T-SHIRTS...
KIRKMAN & SCOTT
©2023, BABY BLUES BROS LLC DIST. BY ANDREWS MCMEEL SYNDICATION 11-15
MAYBE I CAN FIND SOMETHING LIKE THAT IN MY, UM, COSTUME BOX.
THAT'S YOUR CLOSET.

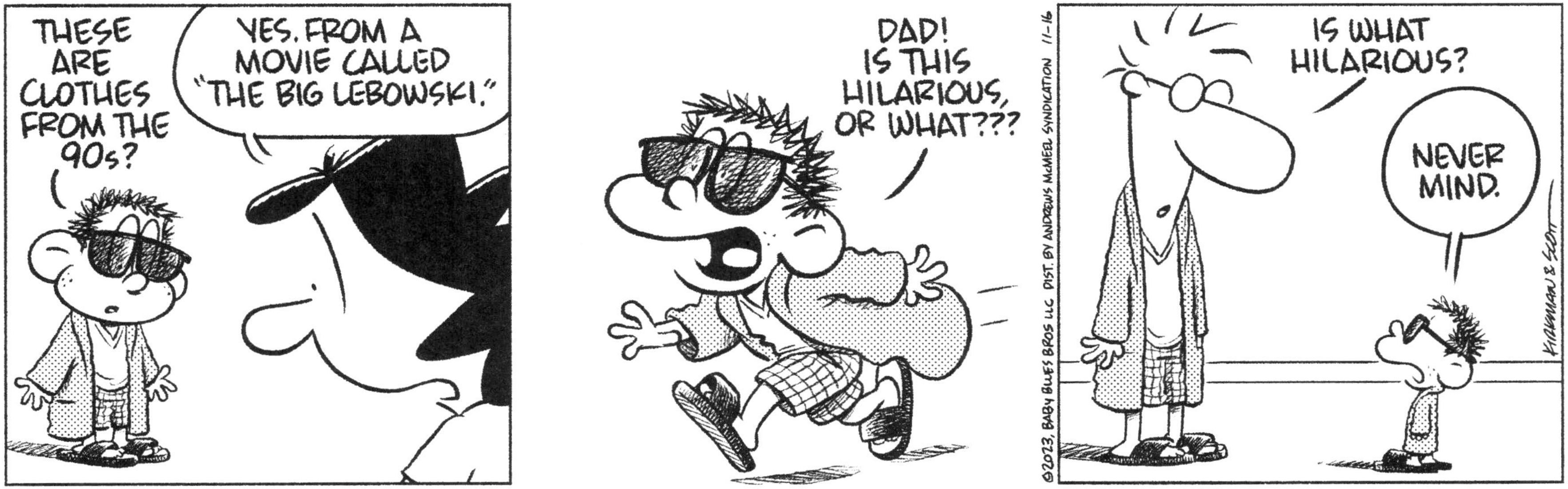
THESE ARE CLOTHES FROM THE 90s?
YES. FROM A MOVIE CALLED "THE BIG LEBOWSKI."
DAD! IS THIS HILARIOUS, OR WHAT???
©2023, BABY BLUES BROS LLC DIST. BY ANDREWS MCMEEL SYNDICATION 11-16
IS WHAT HILARIOUS?
NEVER MIND.
KIRKMAN & SCOTT

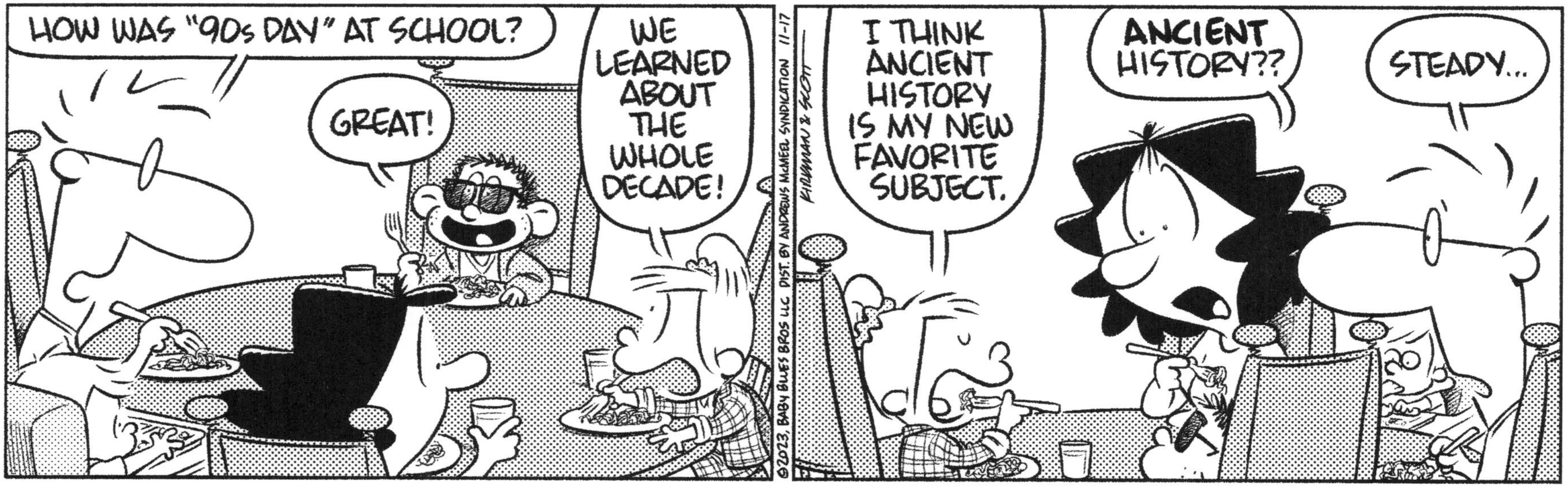
HOW WAS "90s DAY" AT SCHOOL?
GREAT!
WE LEARNED ABOUT THE WHOLE DECADE!
©2023, BABY BLUES BROS LLC DIST. BY ANDREWS McMEEL SYNDICATION 11-17
KIRKMAN & SCOTT
I THINK ANCIENT HISTORY IS MY NEW FAVORITE SUBJECT.
ANCIENT HISTORY??
STEADY...

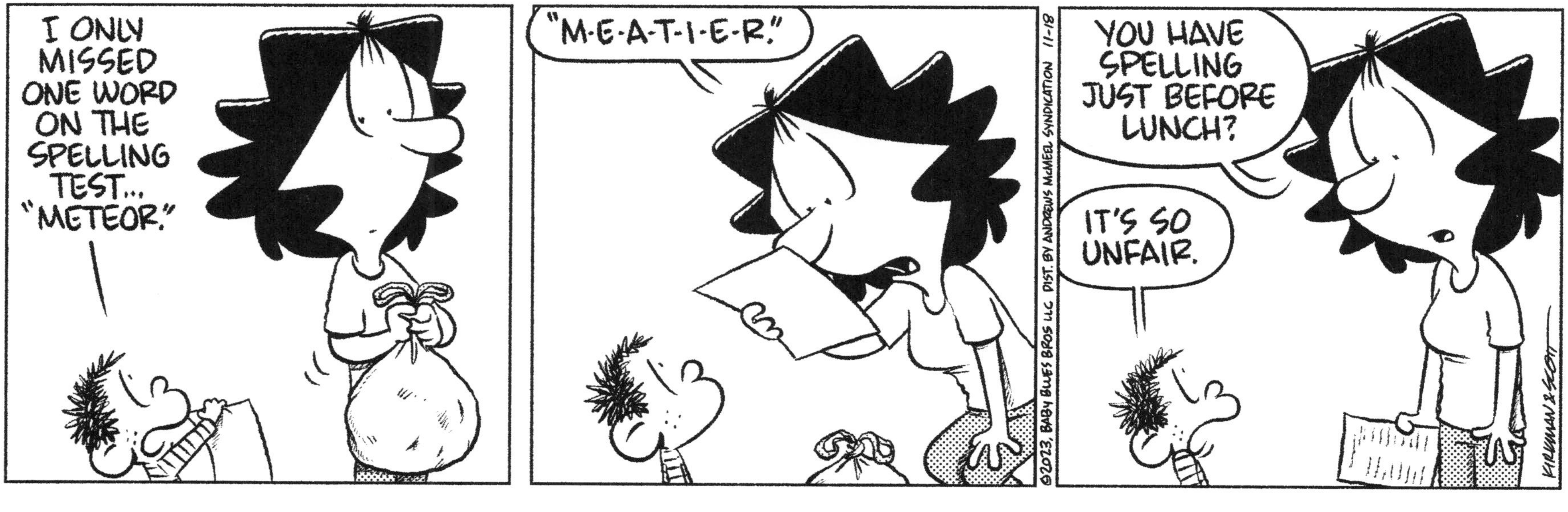
I ONLY MISSED ONE WORD ON THE SPELLING TEST... "METEOR."
"M-E-A-T-I-E-R."
©2023, BABY BLUES BROS LLC DIST. BY ANDREWS McMEEL SYNDICATION 11-18
YOU HAVE SPELLING JUST BEFORE LUNCH?
IT'S SO UNFAIR.
KIRKMAN & SCOTT

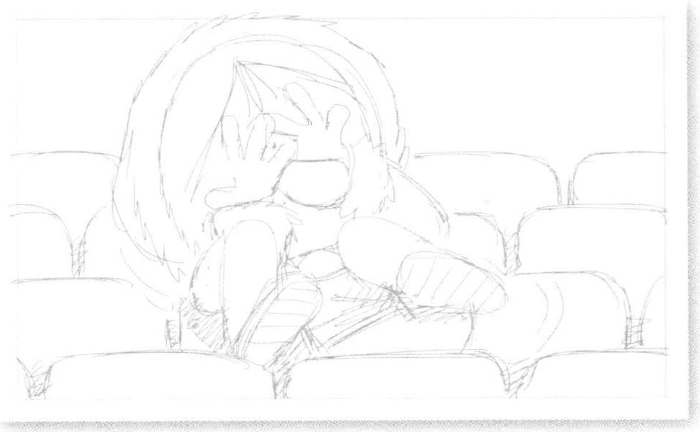

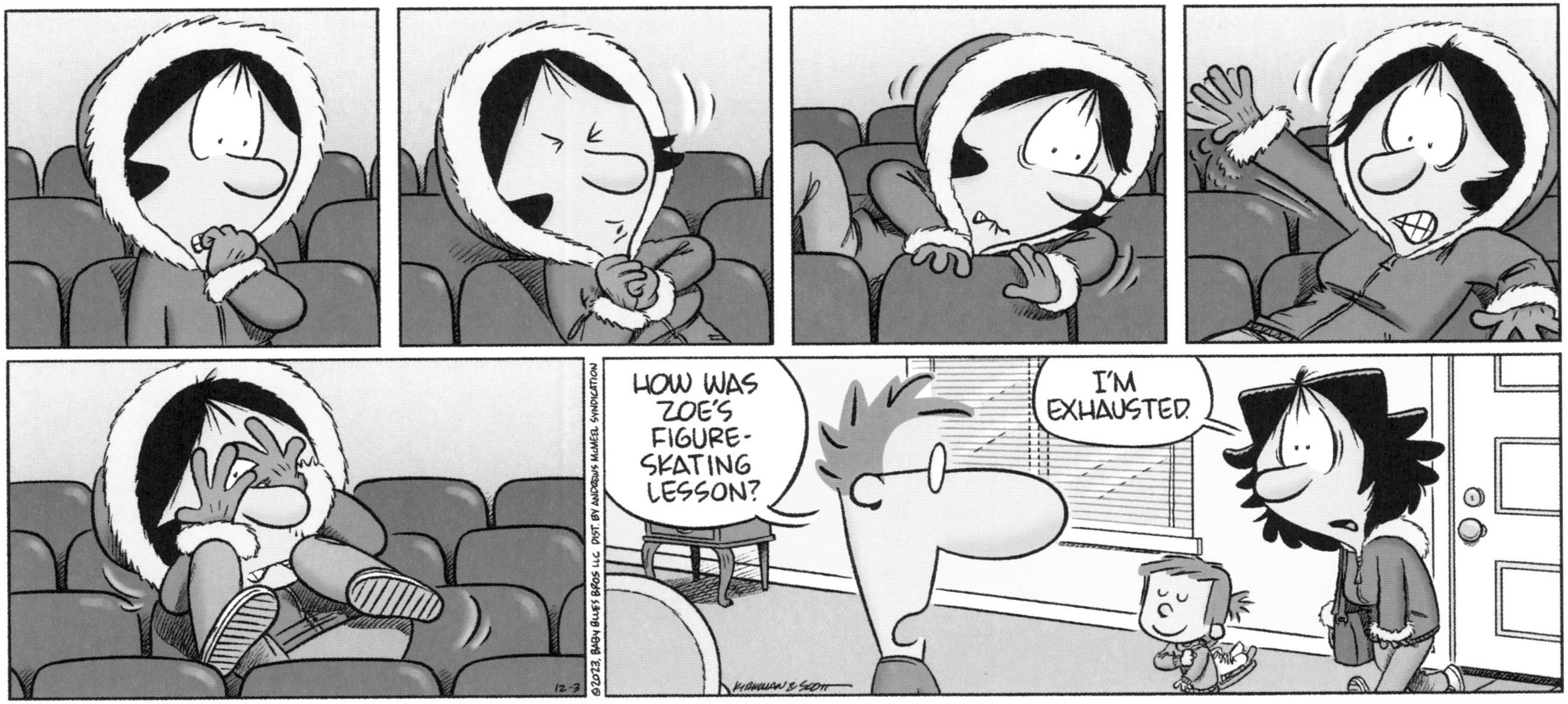
12-3
©2023, BABY BLUES BROS LLC DIST. BY ANDREWS McMEEL SYNDICATION
HOW WAS ZOE'S FIGURE-SKATING LESSON?
I'M EXHAUSTED.
KIRKMAN & SCOTT

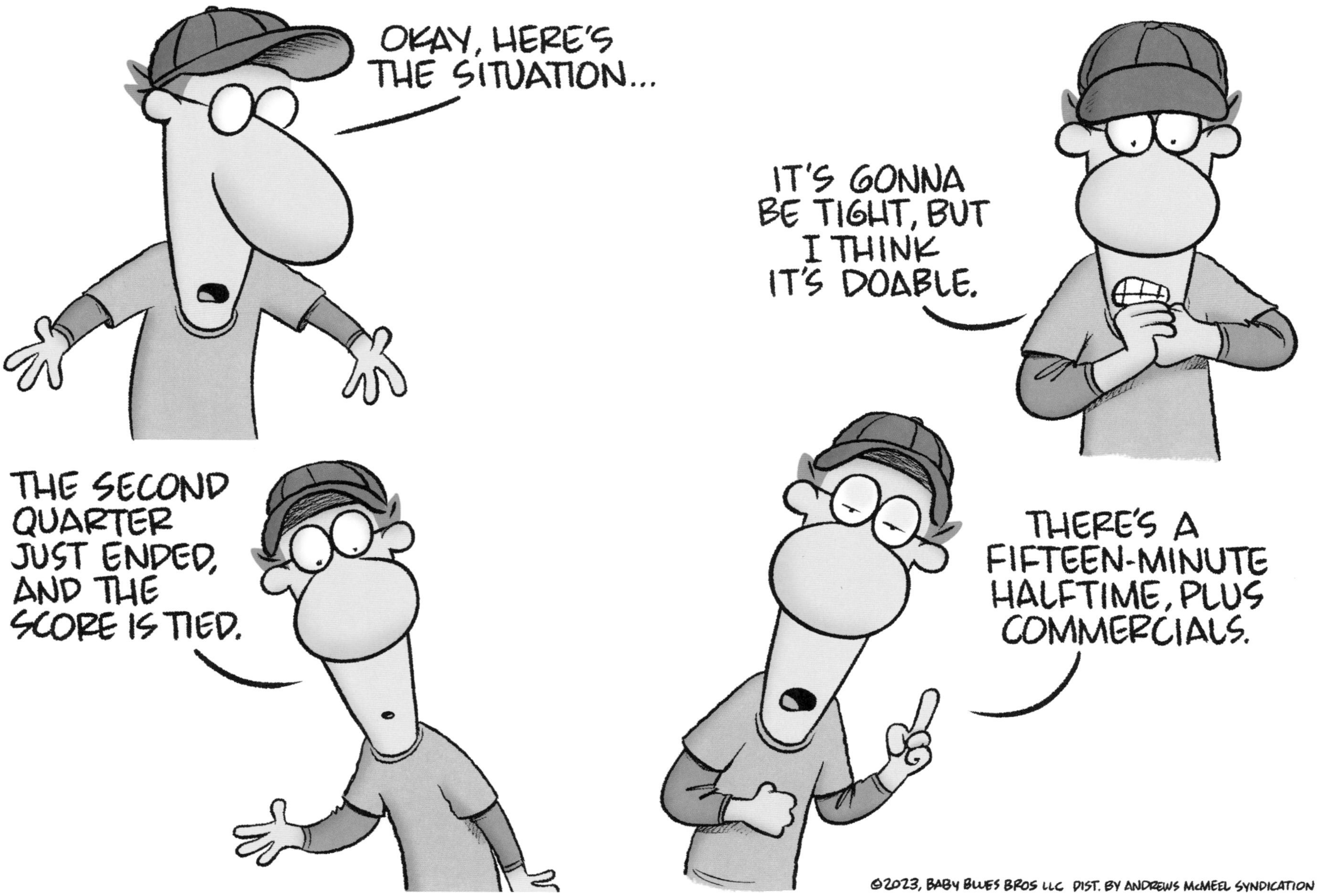
OKAY, HERE'S THE SITUATION...
THE SECOND QUARTER JUST ENDED, AND THE SCORE IS TIED.
THERE'S A FIFTEEN-MINUTE HALFTIME, PLUS COMMERCIALS.
IT'S GONNA BE TIGHT, BUT I THINK IT'S DOABLE.
©2023, BABY BLUES BROS LLC DIST. BY ANDREWS McMEEL SYNDICATION

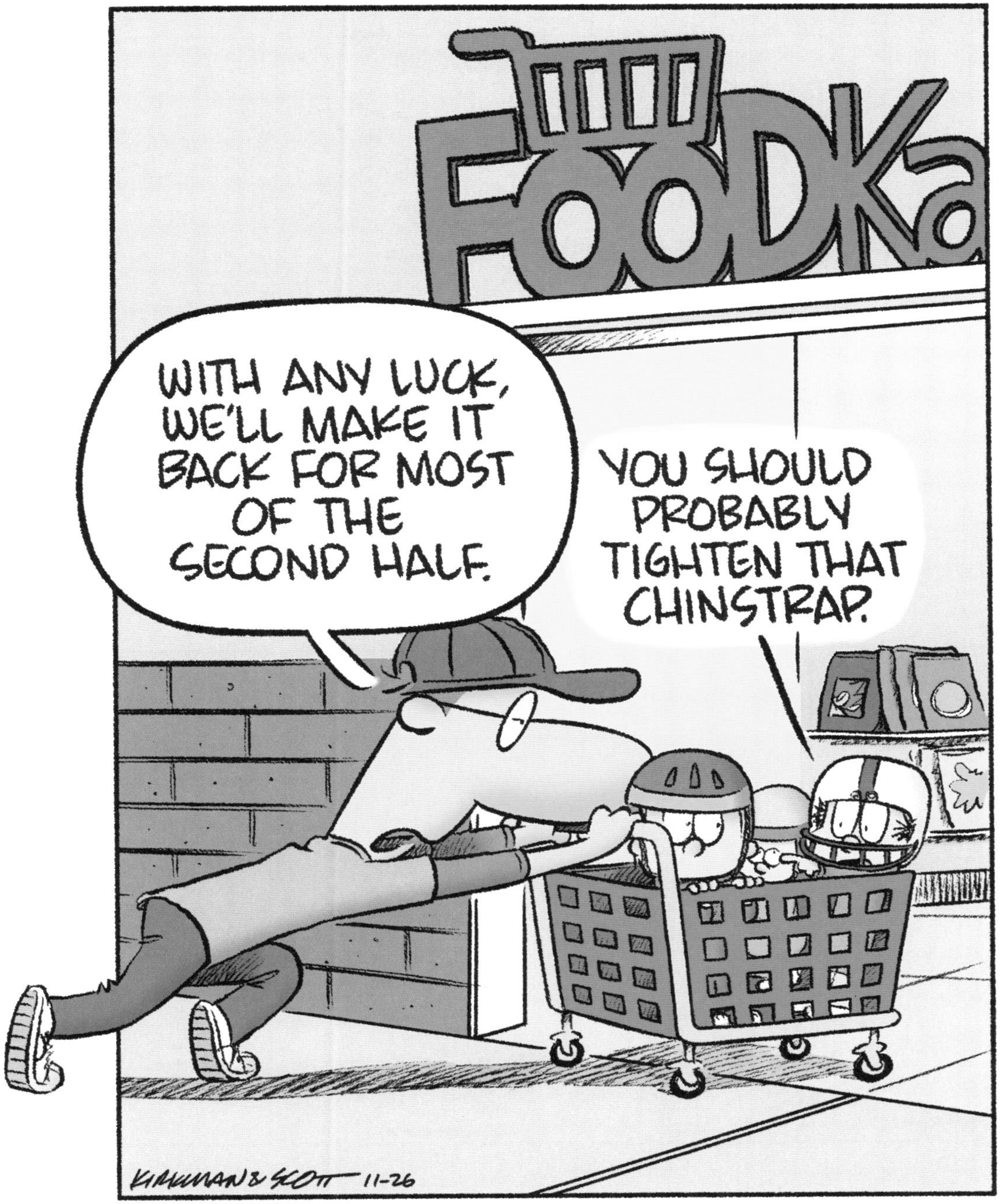
FooDKa
WITH ANY LUCK, WE'LL MAKE IT BACK FOR MOST OF THE SECOND HALF.
YOU SHOULD PROBABLY TIGHTEN THAT CHINSTRAP.
KIRKMAN & SCOTT 11-26

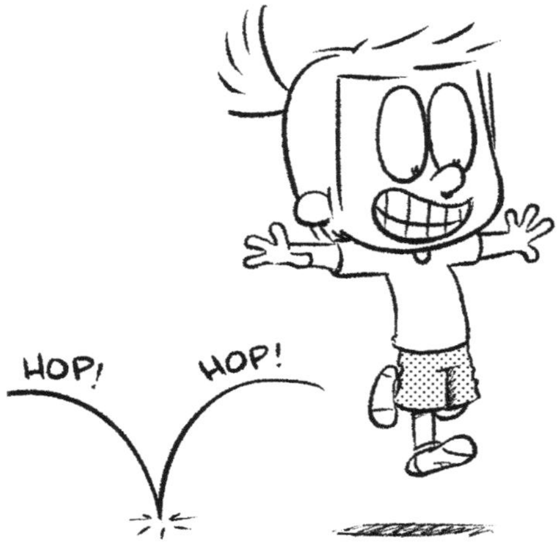
HOP!
HOP!

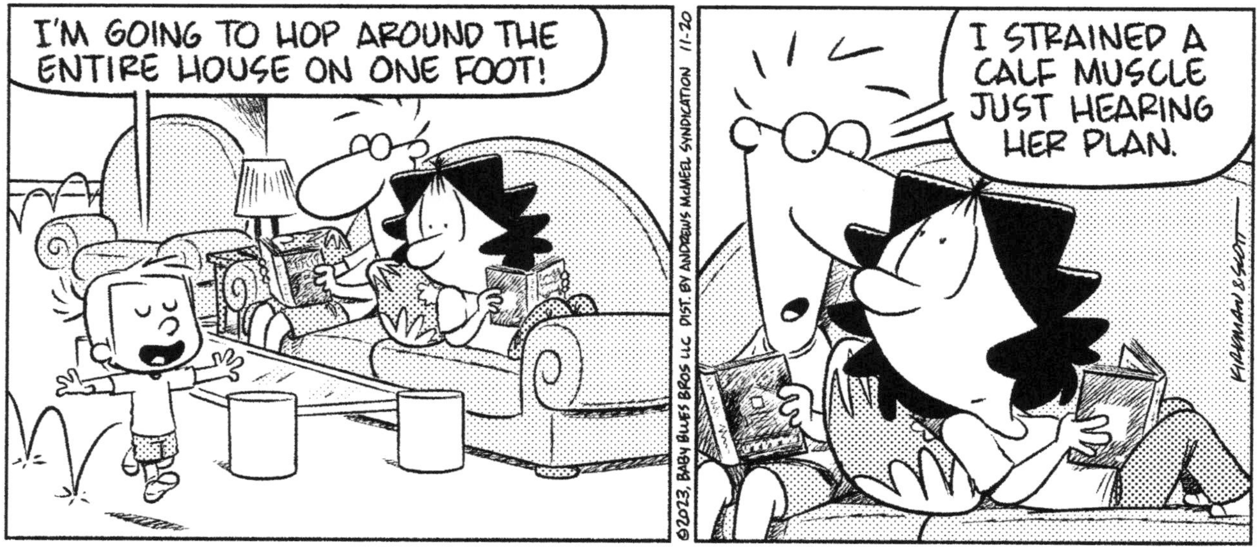
I'M GOING TO HOP AROUND THE ENTIRE HOUSE ON ONE FOOT!
11-20
©2023, BABY BLUES BROS LLC DIST. BY ANDREWS McMEEL SYNDICATION
I STRAINED A CALF MUSCLE JUST HEARING HER PLAN.
KIRKMAN & SCOTT

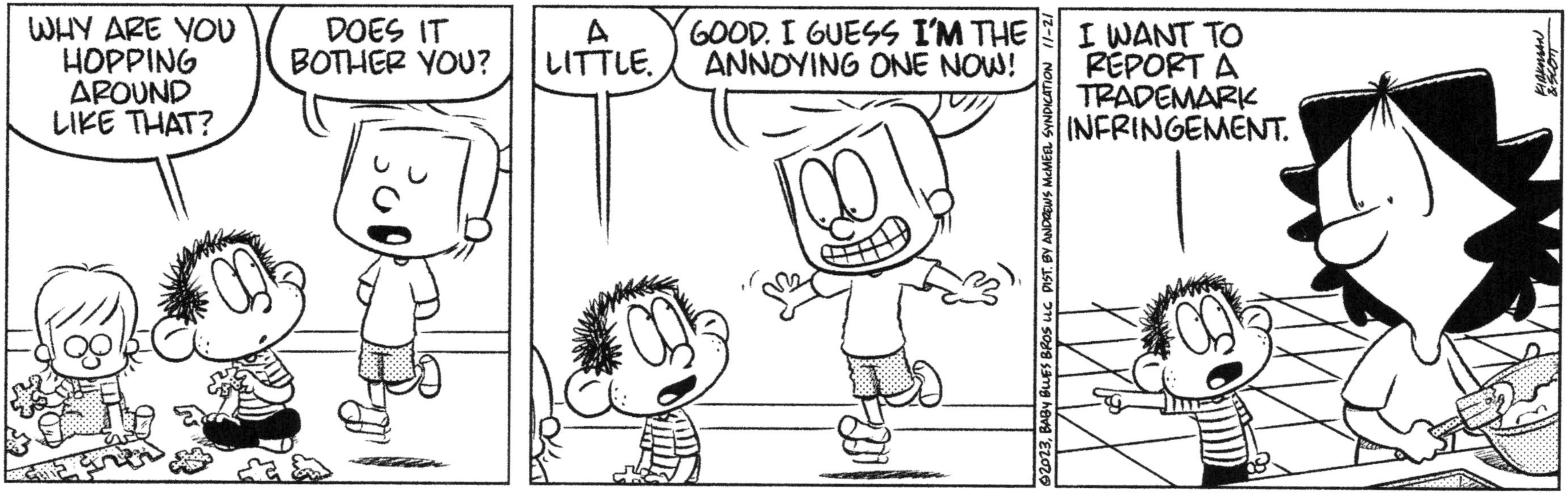
WHY ARE YOU HOPPING AROUND LIKE THAT?
DOES IT BOTHER YOU?
A LITTLE.
GOOD. I GUESS I'M THE ANNOYING ONE NOW!
11-21
©2023, BABY BLUES BROS LLC DIST. BY ANDREWS McMEEL SYNDICATION
I WANT TO REPORT A TRADEMARK INFRINGEMENT.
KIRKMAN & SCOTT

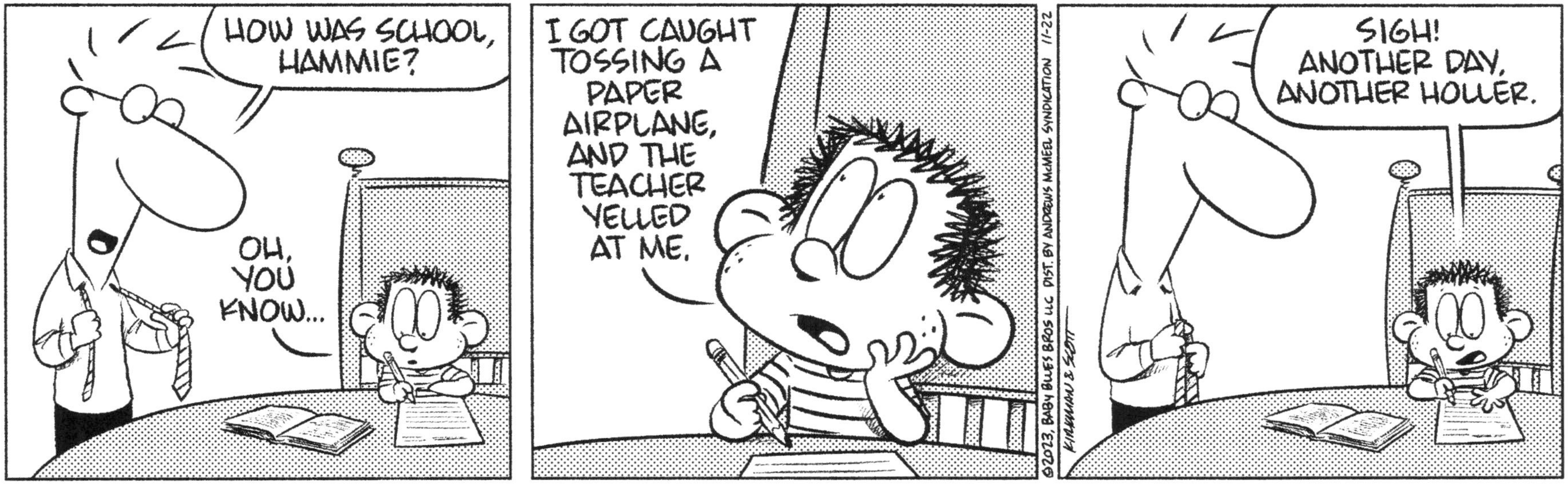
HOW WAS SCHOOL, HAMMIE?
OH, YOU KNOW...
I GOT CAUGHT TOSSING A PAPER AIRPLANE, AND THE TEACHER YELLED AT ME.
SIGH! ANOTHER DAY, ANOTHER HOLLER.
©2023, BABY BLUES BROS LLC DIST. BY ANDREWS McMEEL SYNDICATION 11-22
KIRKMAN & SCOTT

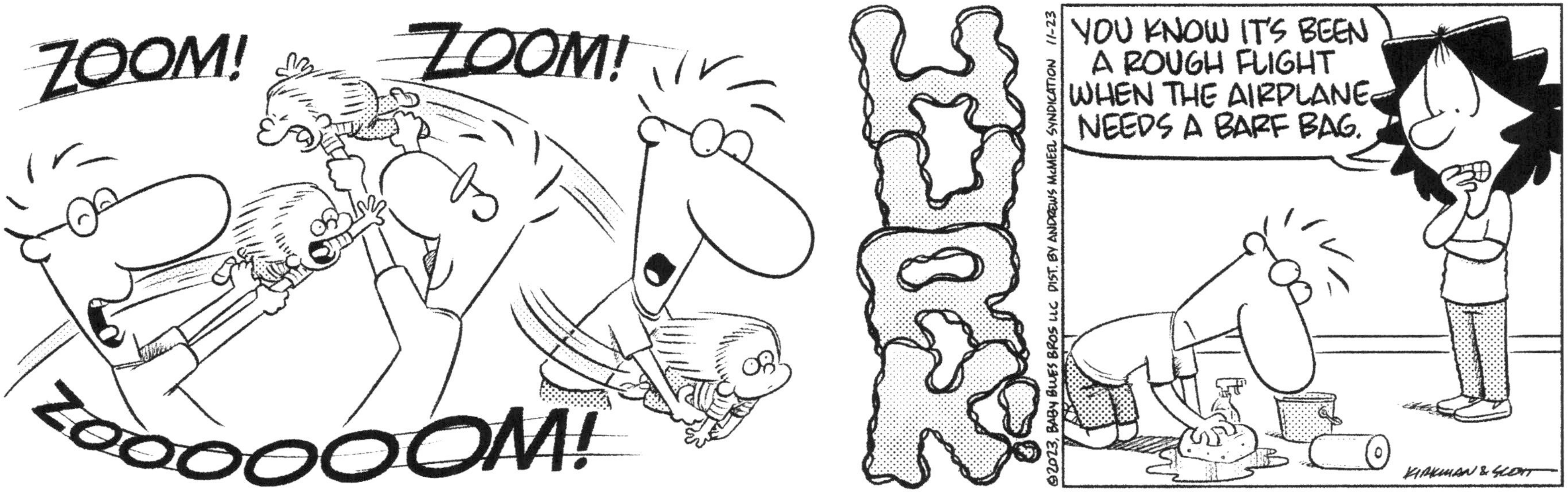
ZOOM!
ZOOM!
ZOOOOOOOOM!
HURK!
YOU KNOW IT'S BEEN A ROUGH FLIGHT WHEN THE AIRPLANE NEEDS A BARF BAG.
©2023, BABY BLUES BROS LLC DIST. BY ANDREWS McMEEL SYNDICATION 11-23
KIRKMAN & SCOTT

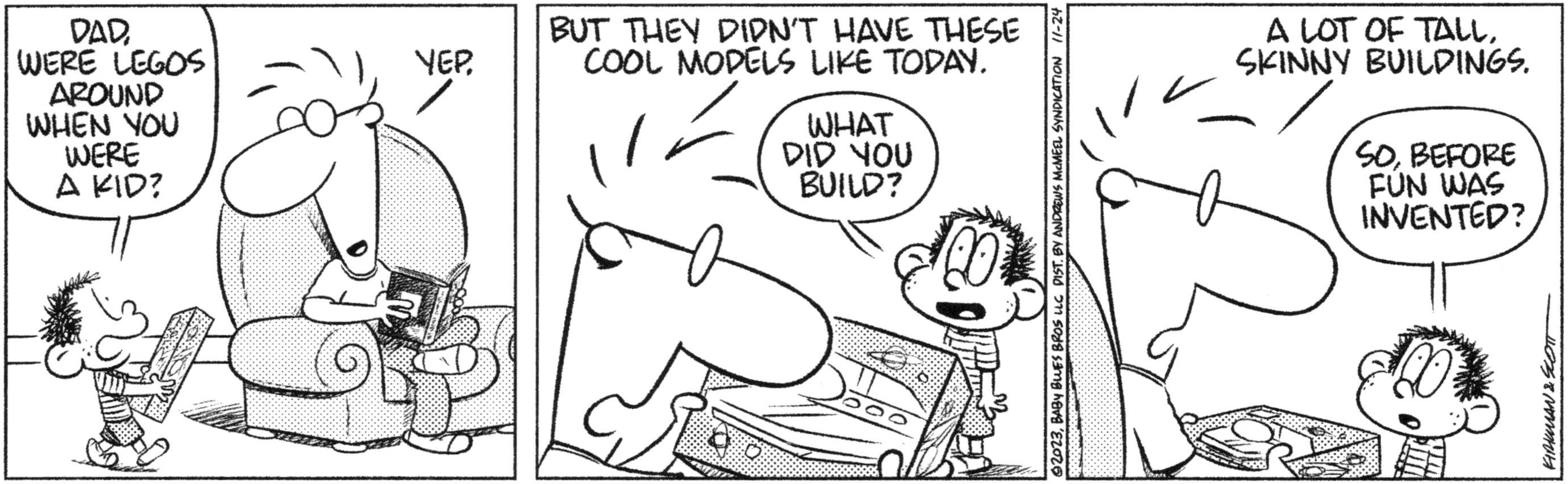
DAD, WERE LEGOS AROUND WHEN YOU WERE A KID?
YEP.
BUT THEY DIDN'T HAVE THESE COOL MODELS LIKE TODAY.
WHAT DID YOU BUILD?
©2023, BABY BLUES BROS LLC DIST. BY ANDREWS MCMEEL SYNDICATION 11-24
A LOT OF TALL, SKINNY BUILDINGS.
SO, BEFORE FUN WAS INVENTED?
KIRKMAN & SCOTT

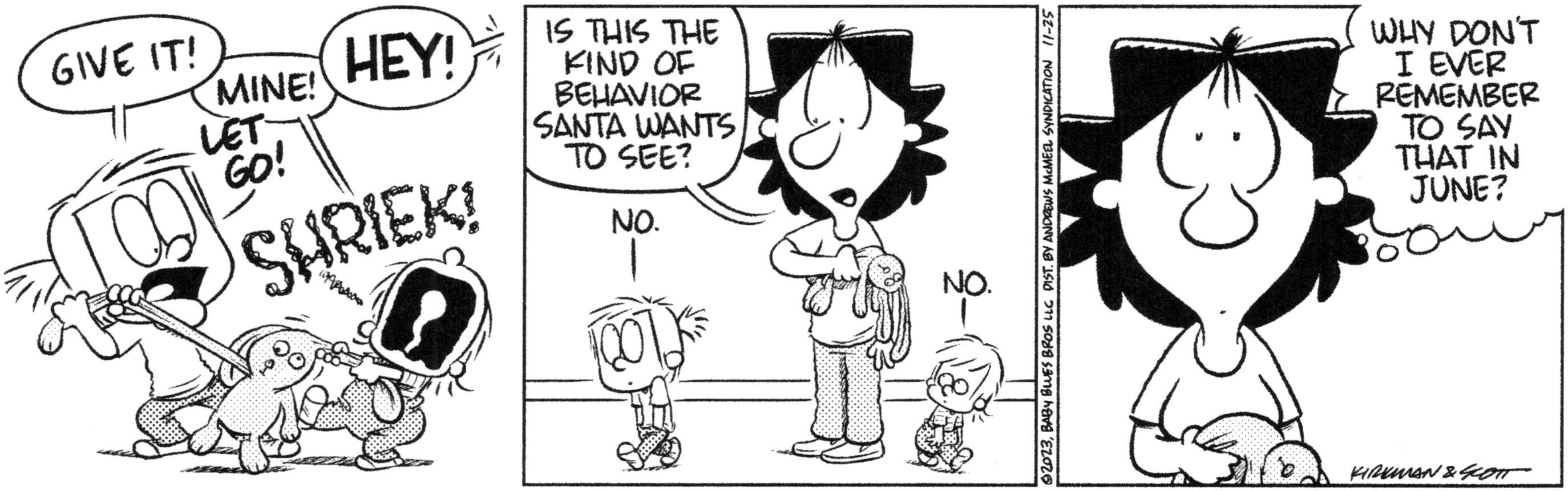
GIVE IT!
MINE!
HEY!
LET GO!
SHRIEK!
IS THIS THE KIND OF BEHAVIOR SANTA WANTS TO SEE?
NO.
NO.
©2023, BABY BLUES BROS LLC DIST. BY ANDREWS MCMEEL SYNDICATION 11-25
WHY DON'T I EVER REMEMBER TO SAY THAT IN JUNE?
KIRKMAN & SCOTT

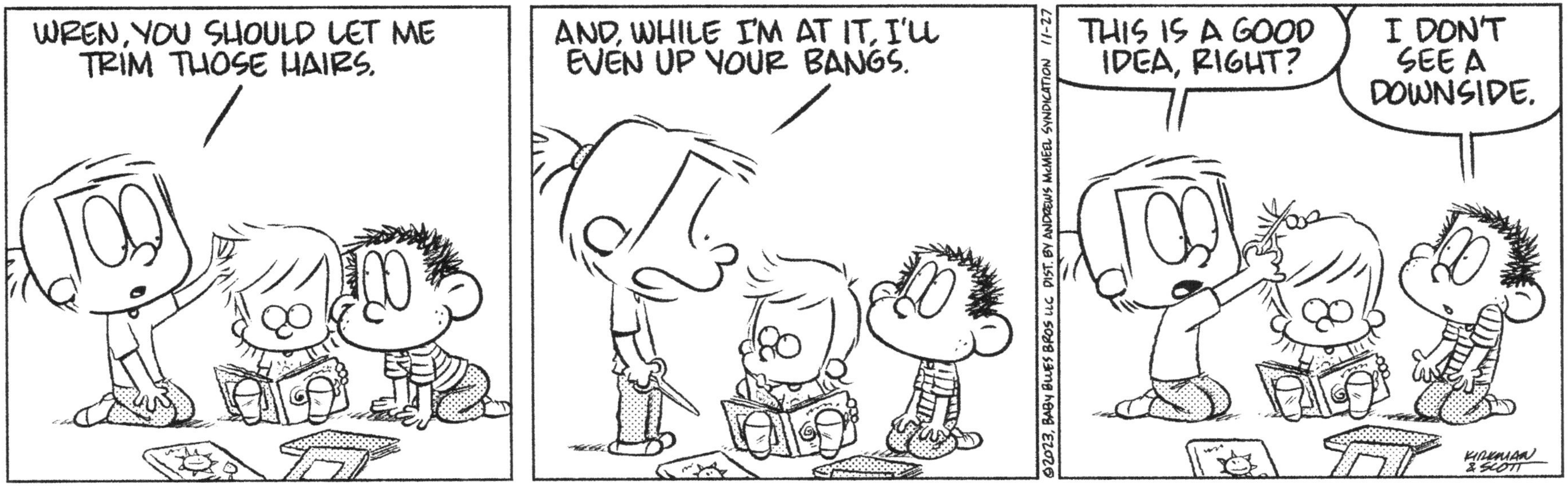
WREN, YOU SHOULD LET ME TRIM THOSE HAIRS.
AND, WHILE I'M AT IT, I'LL EVEN UP YOUR BANGS.
©2023, BABY BLUES BROS LLC DIST. BY ANDREWS McMEEL SYNDICATION 11-27
THIS IS A GOOD IDEA, RIGHT?
I DON'T SEE A DOWNSIDE.
KIRKMAN & SCOTT

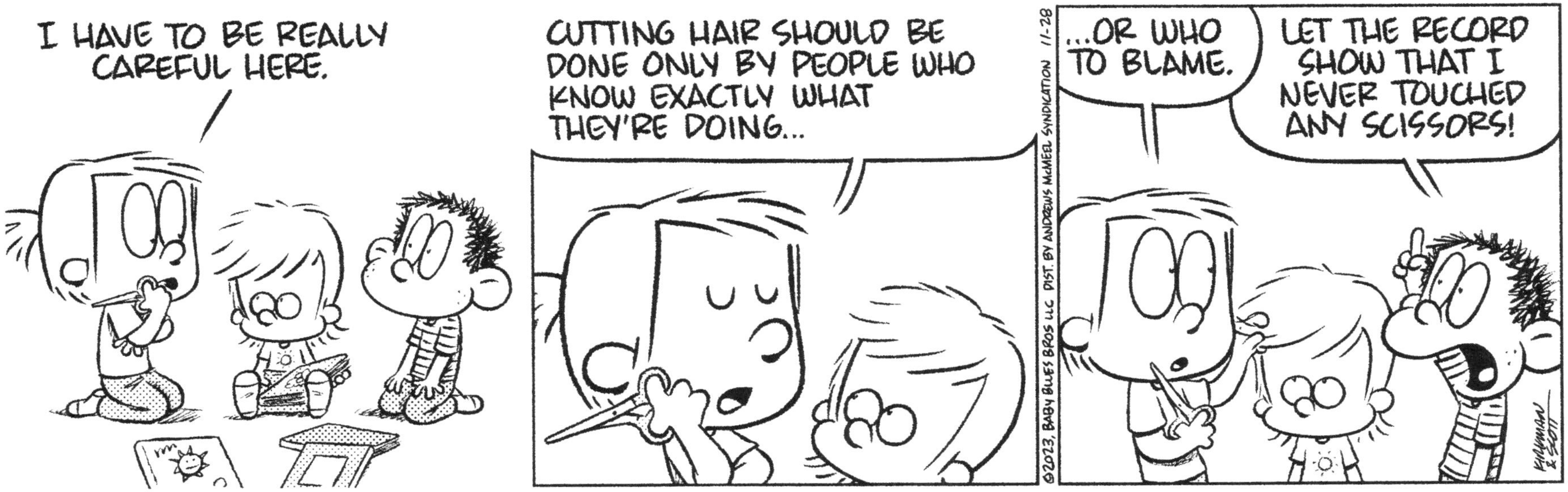
I HAVE TO BE REALLY CAREFUL HERE.
CUTTING HAIR SHOULD BE DONE ONLY BY PEOPLE WHO KNOW EXACTLY WHAT THEY'RE DOING...
©2023, BABY BLUES BROS LLC DIST. BY ANDREWS McMEEL SYNDICATION 11-28
...OR WHO TO BLAME.
LET THE RECORD SHOW THAT I NEVER TOUCHED ANY SCISSORS!
KIRKMAN & SCOTT

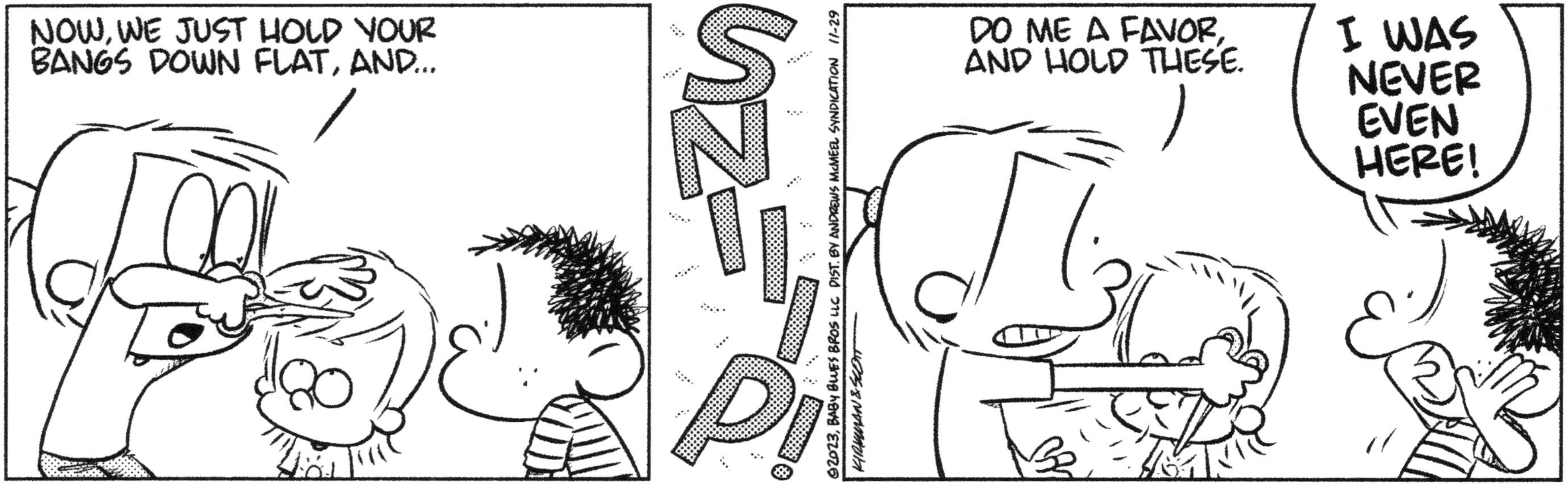
NOW, WE JUST HOLD YOUR BANGS DOWN FLAT, AND...
SNIIIP!
©2023, BABY BLUES BROS LLC DIST. BY ANDREWS McMEEL SYNDICATION 11-29
KIRKMAN & SCOTT
DO ME A FAVOR, AND HOLD THESE.
I WAS NEVER EVEN HERE!

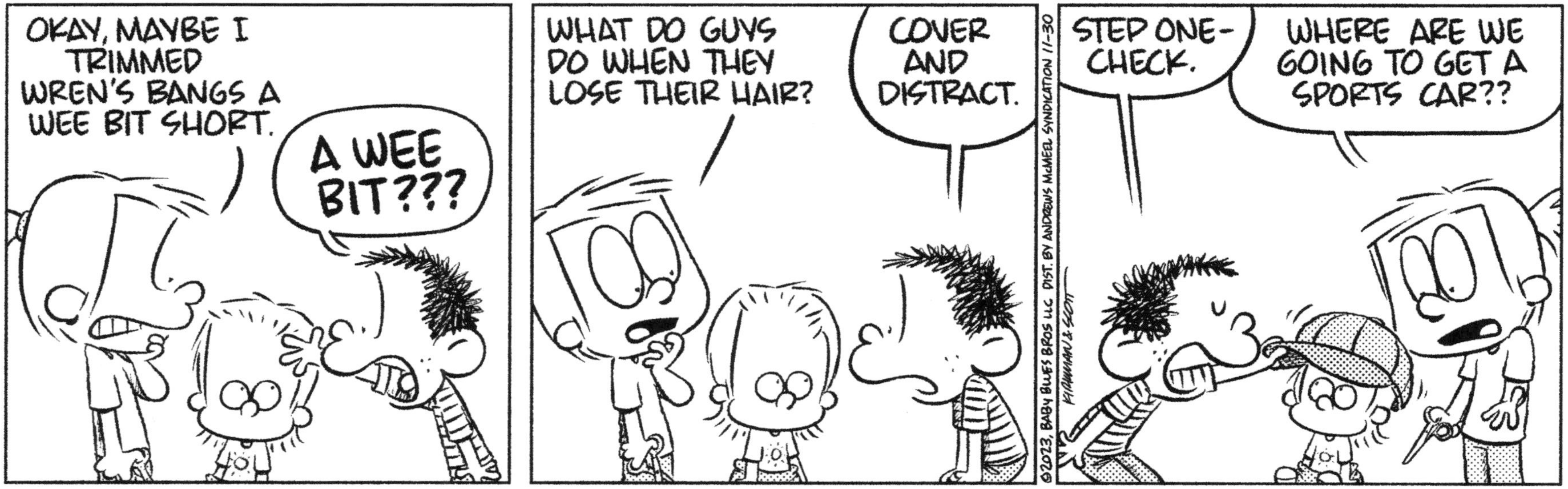
OKAY, MAYBE I TRIMMED WREN'S BANGS A WEE BIT SHORT.
A WEE BIT???
WHAT DO GUYS DO WHEN THEY LOSE THEIR HAIR?
COVER AND DISTRACT.
©2023, BABY BLUES BROS LLC DIST. BY ANDREWS McMEEL SYNDICATION 11-30
KIRKMAN & SCOTT
STEP ONE-CHECK.
WHERE ARE WE GOING TO GET A SPORTS CAR??

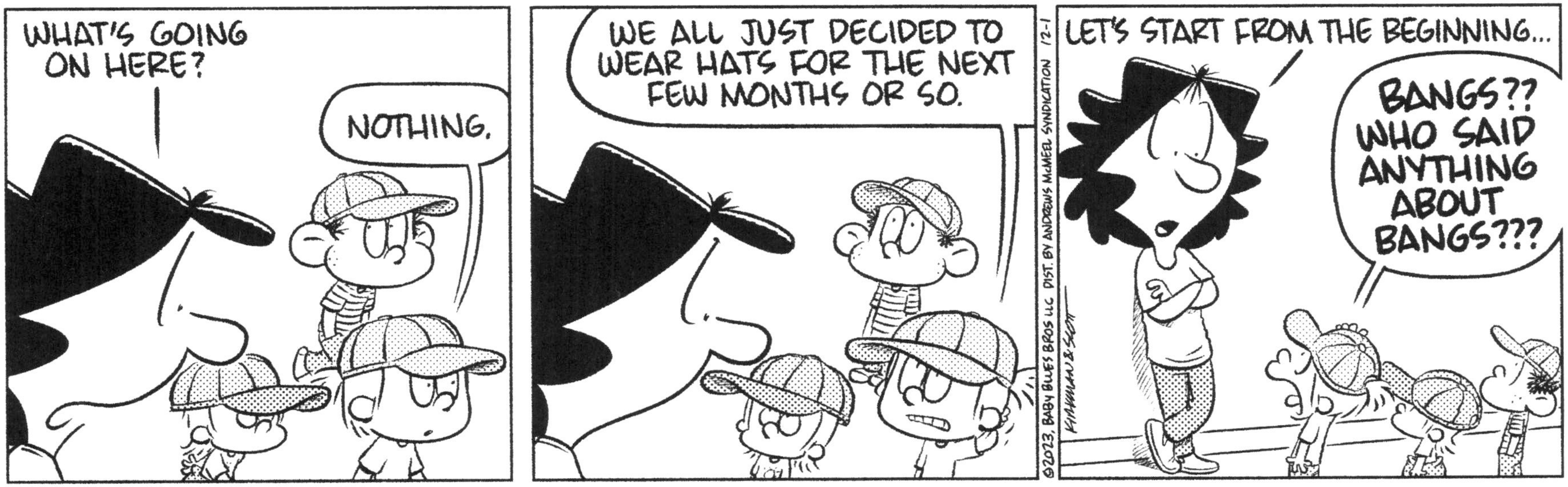
WHAT'S GOING ON HERE?
NOTHING.
WE ALL JUST DECIDED TO WEAR HATS FOR THE NEXT FEW MONTHS OR SO.
©2023, BABY BLUES BROS LLC DIST. BY ANDREWS McMEEL SYNDICATION 12-1
KIRKMAN & SCOTT
LET'S START FROM THE BEGINNING...
BANGS?? WHO SAID ANYTHING ABOUT BANGS???

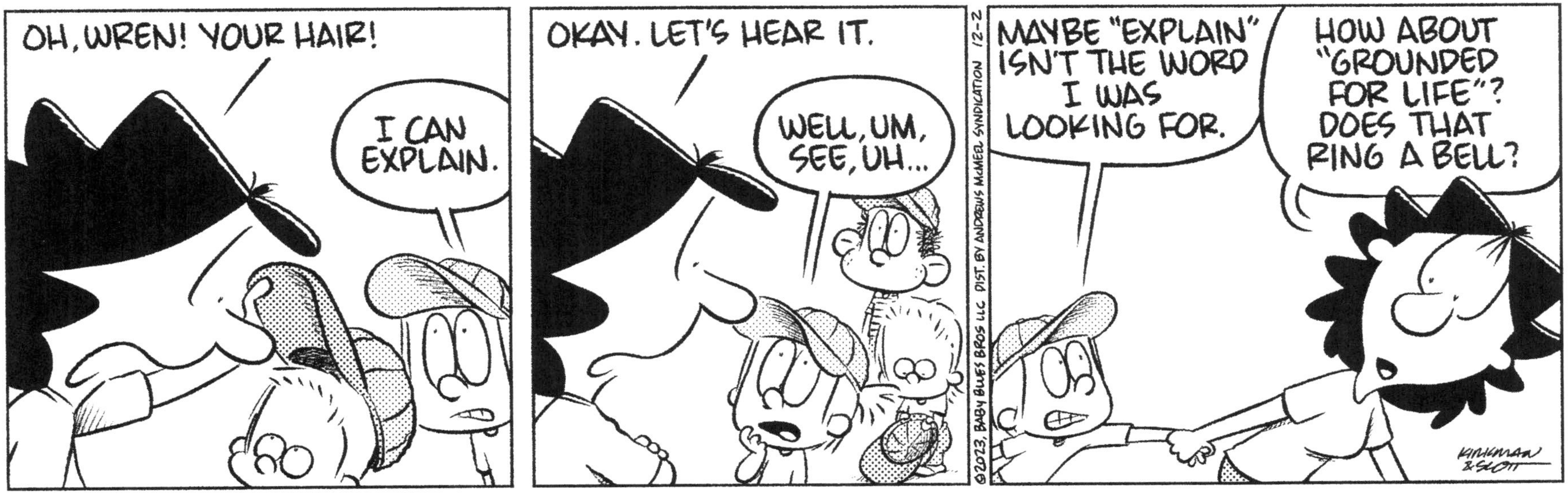
OH, WREN! YOUR HAIR!
I CAN EXPLAIN.
OKAY. LET'S HEAR IT.
WELL, UM, SEE, UH...
©2023, BABY BLUES BROS LLC DIST. BY ANDREWS McMEEL SYNDICATION 12-2
MAYBE "EXPLAIN" ISN'T THE WORD I WAS LOOKING FOR.
HOW ABOUT "GROUNDED FOR LIFE"? DOES THAT RING A BELL?
KIRKMAN & SCOTT

MO-O-MMM!
WHA-A-A-T??

MOM?
What?
MOM!
What?
MOM??
WHAT?
KIRKMAN & SCOTT
MO-O-MMM!
WHA-A-A-T??
12-10
MOMMY!
WHAT? WHAT? WHAT??
©2023, BABY BLUES BROS LLC DIST. BY ANDREWS McMEEL SYNDICATION
DO ANYTHING FUN TODAY?
I HOLLERED "WHAT" IN ABOUT FIVE DIFFERENT FONTS.

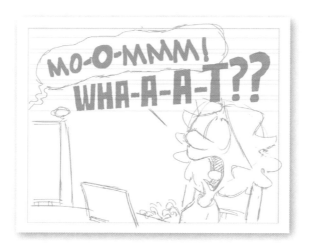

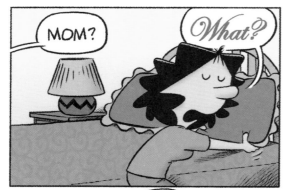

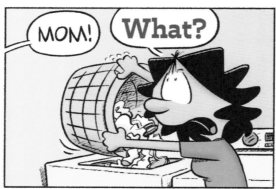

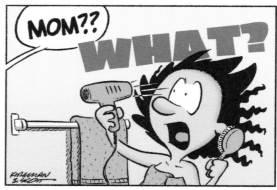

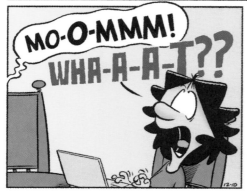

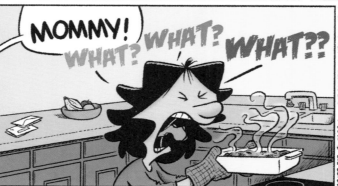

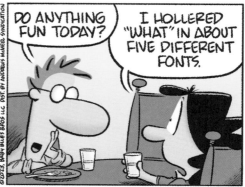

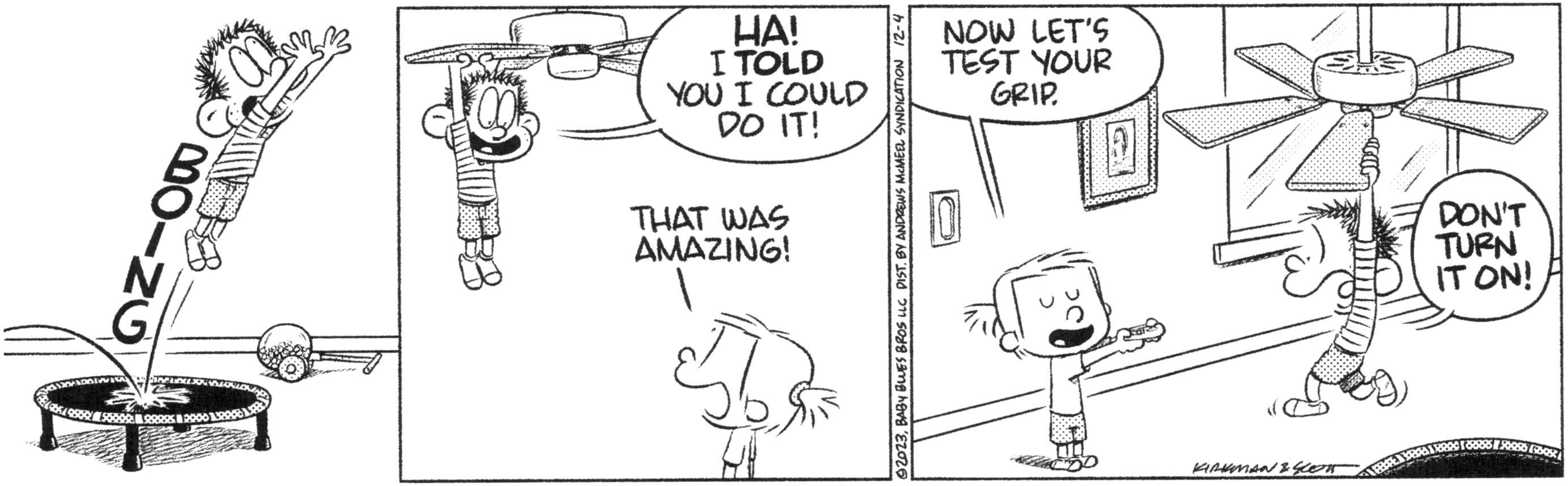
BOING
HA! I **TOLD** YOU I COULD DO IT!
THAT WAS AMAZING!
12-4
©2023, BABY BLUES BROS LLC DIST. BY ANDREWS McMEEL SYNDICATION
NOW LET'S TEST YOUR GRIP.
DON'T TURN IT ON!
KIRKMAN & SCOTT

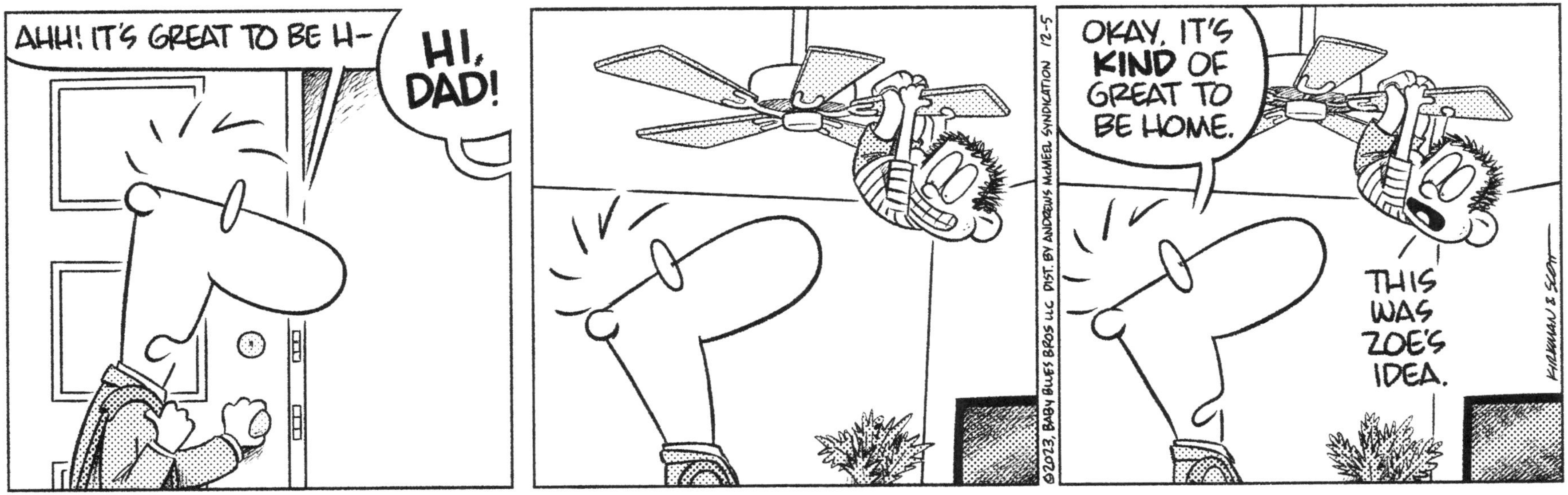
AHH! IT'S GREAT TO BE H–
HI, DAD!
12-5
©2023, BABY BLUES BROS LLC DIST. BY ANDREWS McMEEL SYNDICATION
OKAY, IT'S **KIND** OF GREAT TO BE HOME.
THIS WAS ZOE'S IDEA.
KIRKMAN & SCOTT

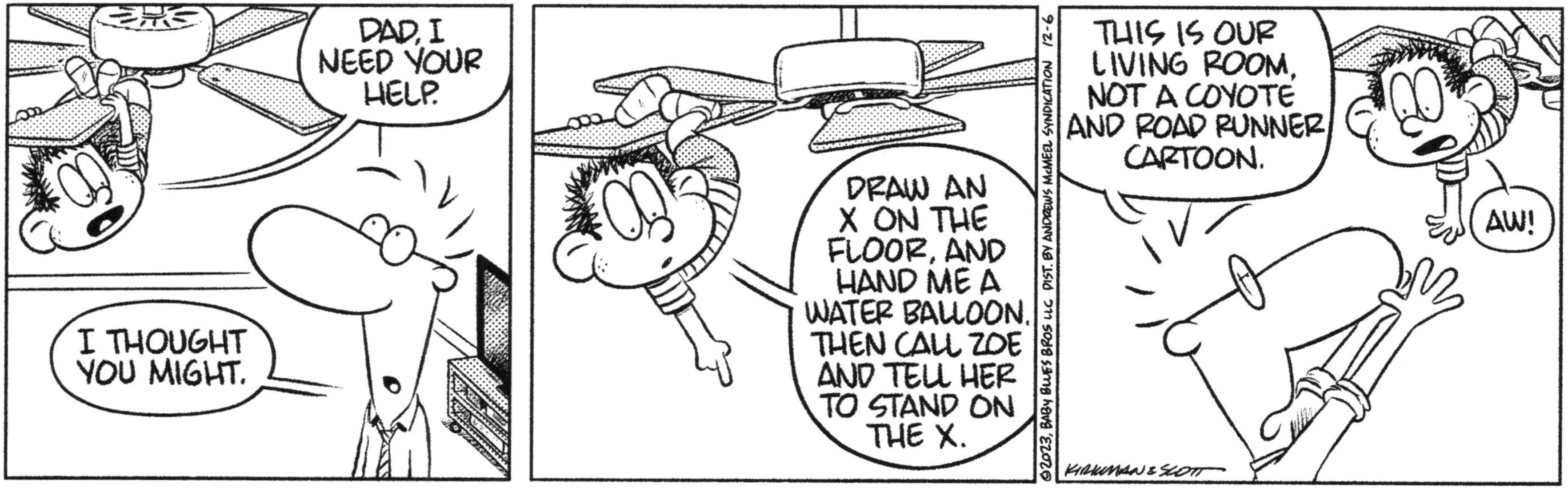
DAD, I NEED YOUR HELP.
I THOUGHT YOU MIGHT.
DRAW AN X ON THE FLOOR, AND HAND ME A WATER BALLOON. THEN CALL ZOE AND TELL HER TO STAND ON THE X.
©2023, BABY BLUES BROS LLC DIST. BY ANDREWS McMEEL SYNDICATION 12-6
THIS IS OUR LIVING ROOM, NOT A COYOTE AND ROAD RUNNER CARTOON.
AW!
KIRKMAN & SCOTT

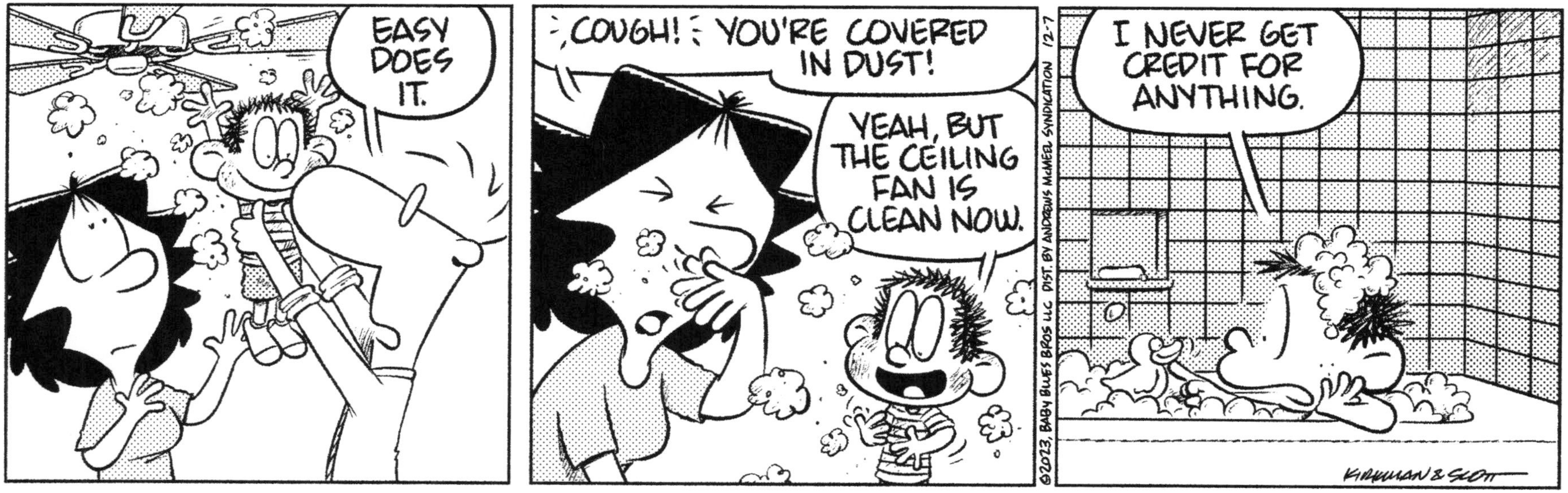
EASY DOES IT.
COUGH!
YOU'RE COVERED IN DUST!
YEAH, BUT THE CEILING FAN IS CLEAN NOW.
©2023, BABY BLUES BROS LLC DIST. BY ANDREWS McMEEL SYNDICATION 12-7
I NEVER GET CREDIT FOR ANYTHING.
KIRKMAN & SCOTT

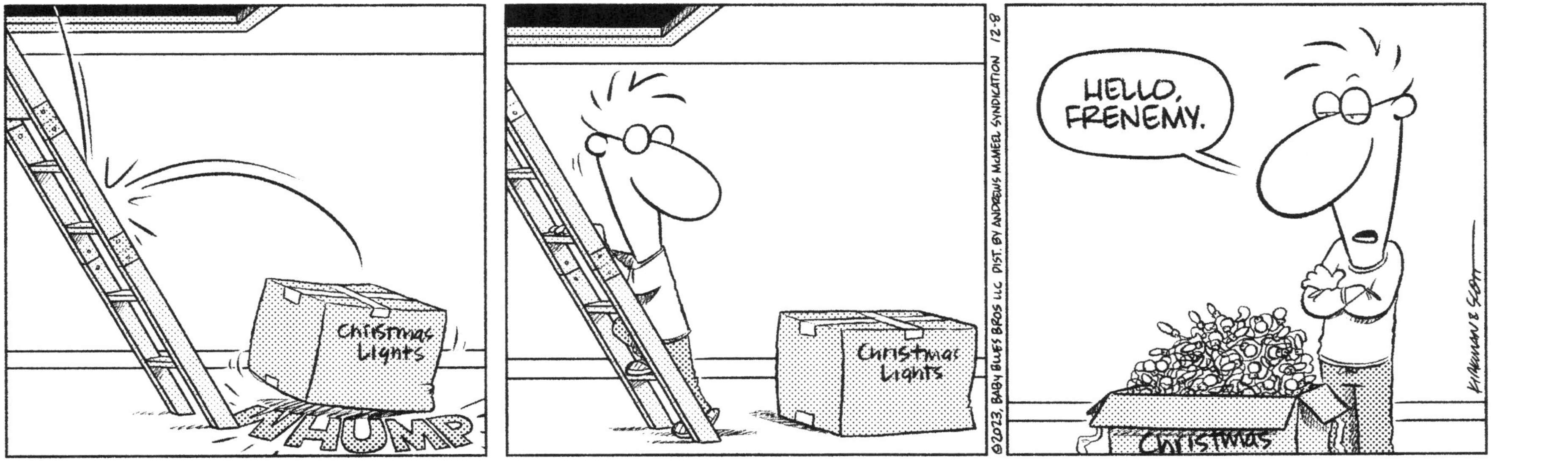
Christmas Lights
WHUMP
Christmas Lights
©2023, BABY BLUES BROS LLC DIST. BY ANDREWS McMEEL SYNDICATION 12-8
HELLO, FRENEMY.
Christmas
KIRKMAN & SCOTT

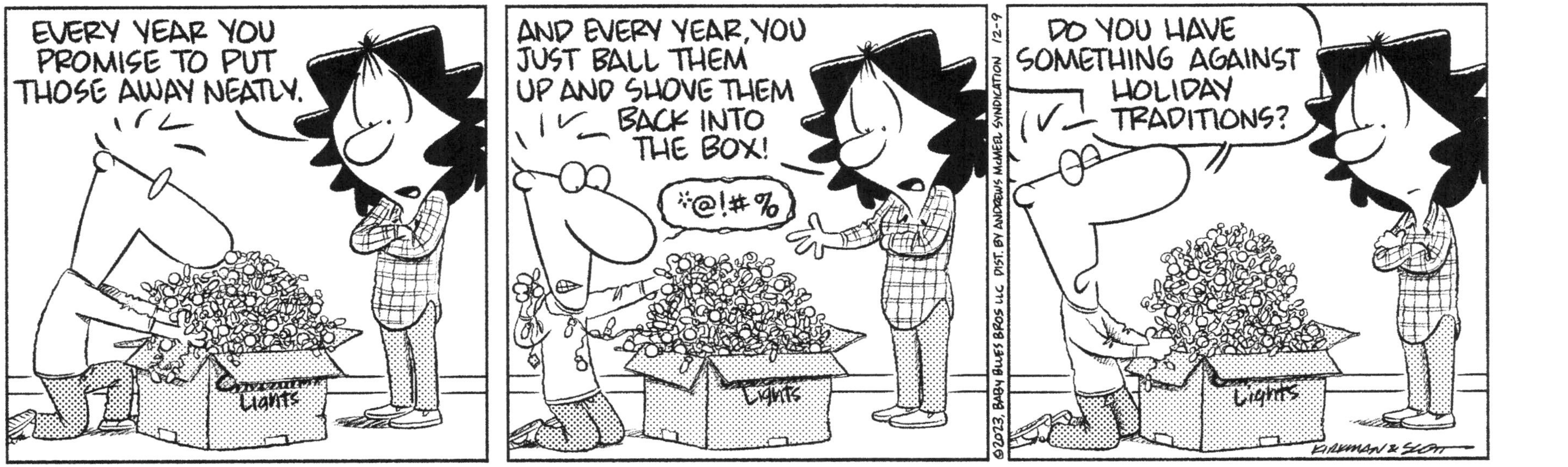
EVERY YEAR YOU PROMISE TO PUT THOSE AWAY NEATLY.
Lights
AND EVERY YEAR, YOU JUST BALL THEM UP AND SHOVE THEM BACK INTO THE BOX!
@!#%
Lights
©2023, BABY BLUES BROS LLC DIST. BY ANDREWS McMEEL SYNDICATION 12-9
DO YOU HAVE SOMETHING AGAINST HOLIDAY TRADITIONS?
Lights
KIRKMAN & SCOTT

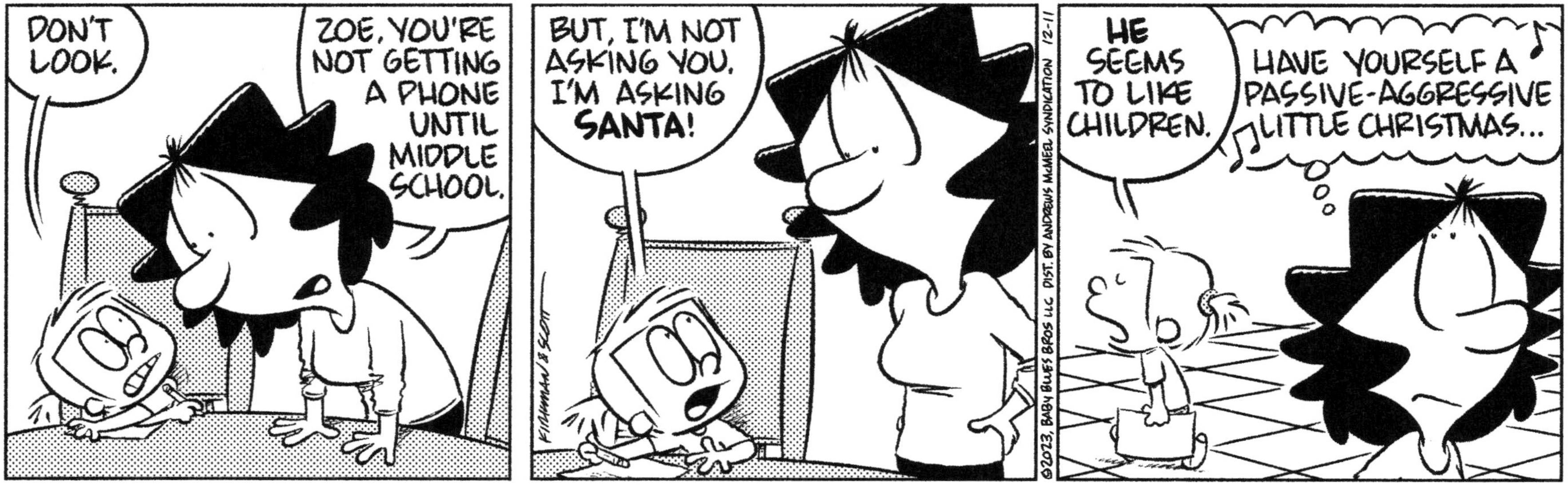
DON'T LOOK.
ZOE, YOU'RE NOT GETTING A PHONE UNTIL MIDDLE SCHOOL.
BUT, I'M NOT ASKING YOU. I'M ASKING **SANTA**!
HE SEEMS TO LIKE CHILDREN.
HAVE YOURSELF A PASSIVE-AGGRESSIVE LITTLE CHRISTMAS...
KIRKMAN/8 SCOTT
©2023, BABY BLUES BROS LLC DIST. BY ANDREWS McMEEL SYNDICATION 12-11

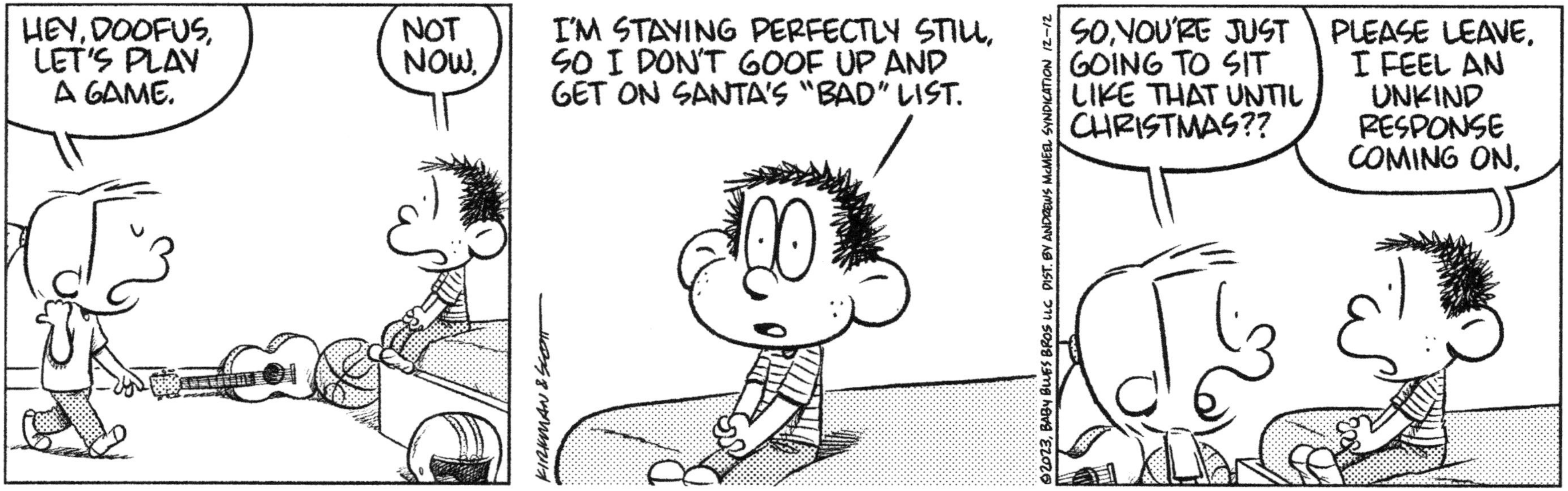
HEY, DOOFUS, LET'S PLAY A GAME.
NOT NOW.
I'M STAYING PERFECTLY STILL, SO I DON'T GOOF UP AND GET ON SANTA'S "BAD" LIST.
SO, YOU'RE JUST GOING TO SIT LIKE THAT UNTIL CHRISTMAS??
PLEASE LEAVE. I FEEL AN UNKIND RESPONSE COMING ON.
KIRKMAN & SCOTT
©2023, BABY BLUES BROS LLC DIST. BY ANDREWS McMEEL SYNDICATION 12-12

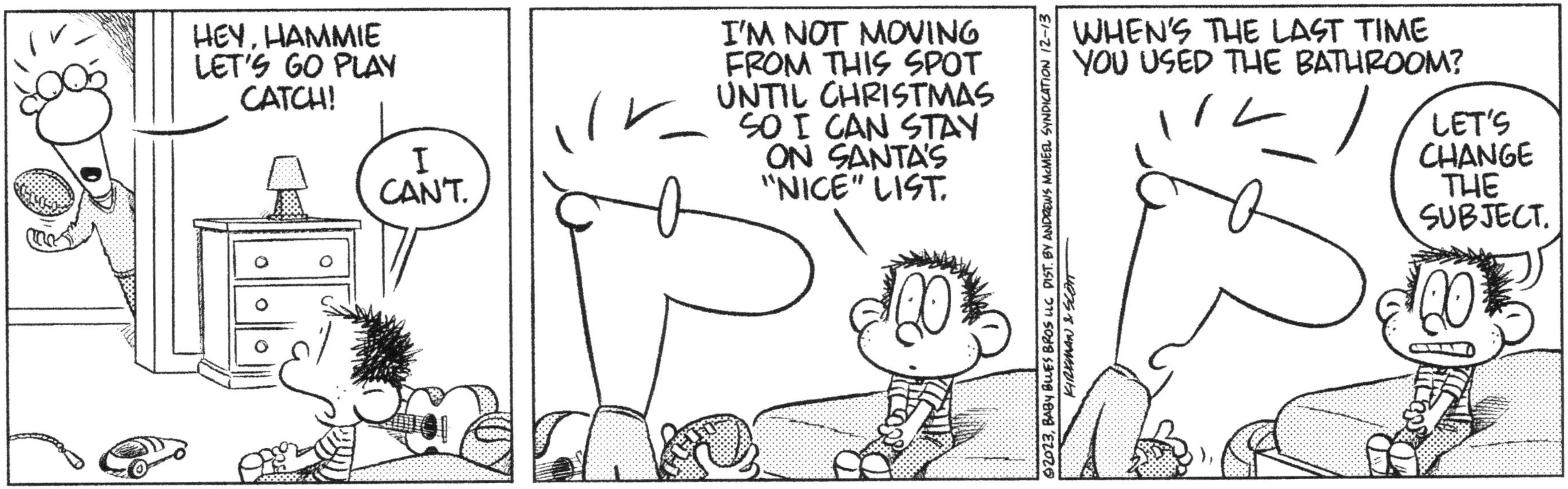
HEY, HAMMIE LET'S GO PLAY CATCH!
I CAN'T.
I'M NOT MOVING FROM THIS SPOT UNTIL CHRISTMAS SO I CAN STAY ON SANTA'S "NICE" LIST.
©2023, BABY BLUES BROS LLC DIST. BY ANDREWS McMEEL SYNDICATION 12-13
KIRKMAN & SCOTT
WHEN'S THE LAST TIME YOU USED THE BATHROOM?
LET'S CHANGE THE SUBJECT.

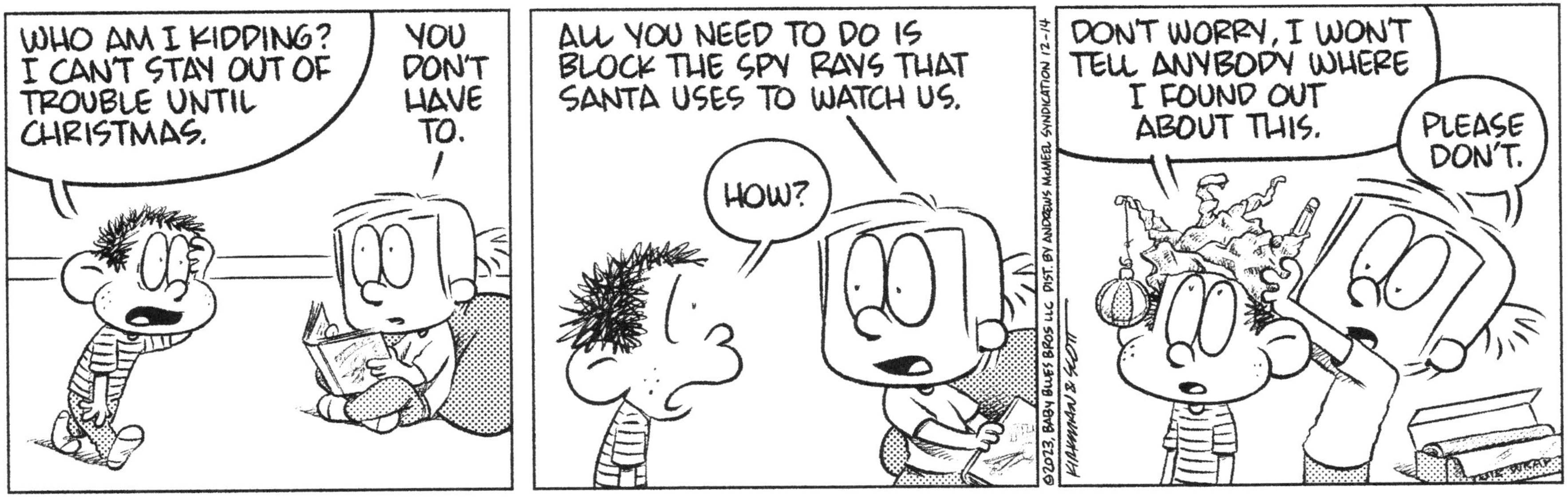
WHO AM I KIDDING? I CAN'T STAY OUT OF TROUBLE UNTIL CHRISTMAS.
YOU DON'T HAVE TO.
ALL YOU NEED TO DO IS BLOCK THE SPY RAYS THAT SANTA USES TO WATCH US.
HOW?
©2023, BABY BLUES BROS LLC DIST. BY ANDREWS McMEEL SYNDICATION 12-14
KIRKMAN & SCOTT
DON'T WORRY, I WON'T TELL ANYBODY WHERE I FOUND OUT ABOUT THIS.
PLEASE DON'T.

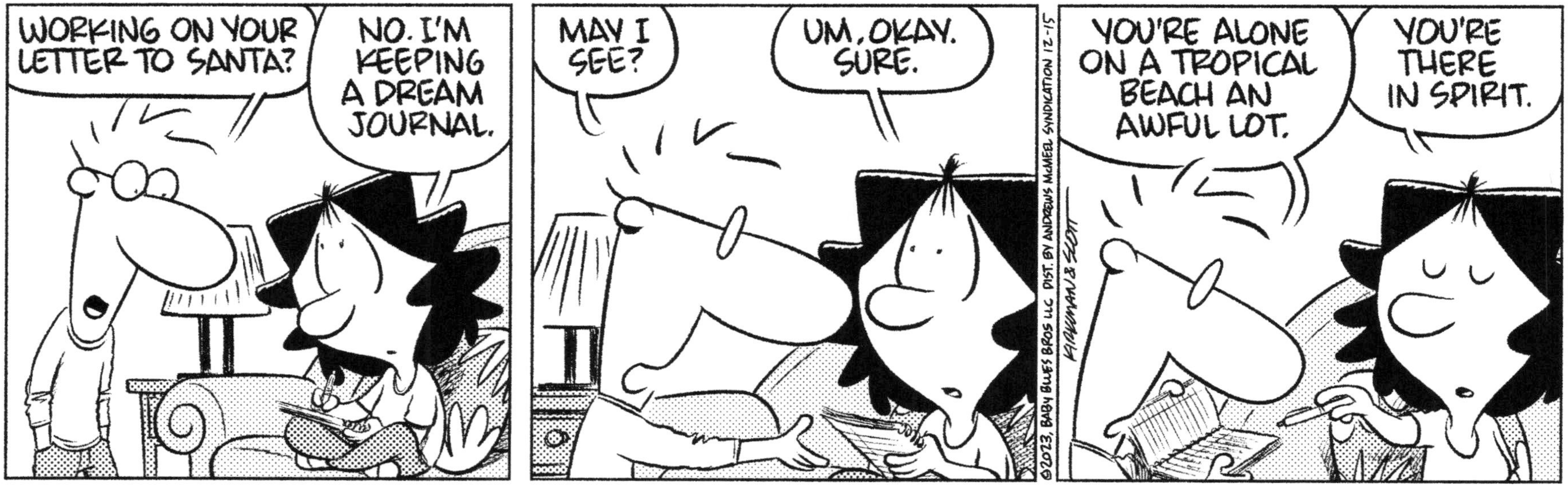
WORKING ON YOUR LETTER TO SANTA?
NO. I'M KEEPING A DREAM JOURNAL.
MAY I SEE?
UM, OKAY. SURE.
YOU'RE ALONE ON A TROPICAL BEACH AN AWFUL LOT.
YOU'RE THERE IN SPIRIT.
©2023, BABY BLUES BROS LLC DIST. BY ANDREWS McMEEL SYNDICATION 12-15
KIRKMAN & SCOTT

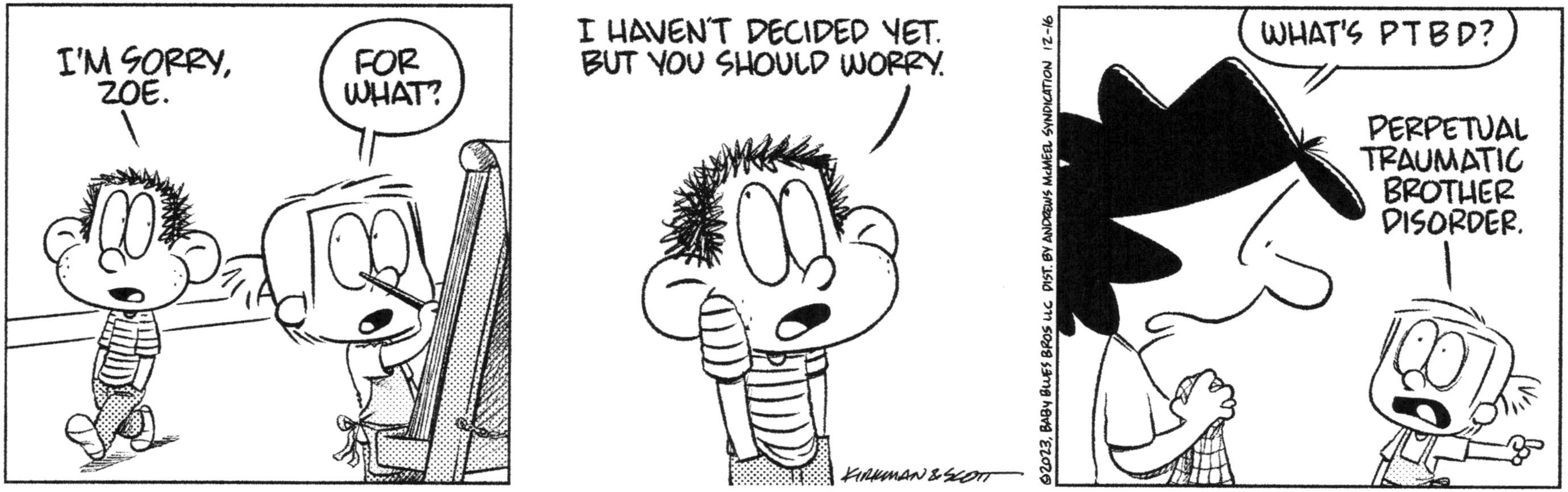
I'M SORRY, ZOE.
FOR WHAT?
I HAVEN'T DECIDED YET. BUT YOU SHOULD WORRY.
KIRKMAN & SCOTT
©2023, BABY BLUES BROS LLC DIST. BY ANDREWS McMEEL SYNDICATION 12-16
WHAT'S P T B D?
PERPETUAL TRAUMATIC BROTHER DISORDER.

THEY COUNT.
AUUUGH!

WREN! STOP!
YOU SHOULD NEVER TAKE DECORATIONS OFF A CHRISTMAS TREE.
EVEN THE CANDY CANES?
IF THE TREE ISN'T JUST RIGHT, SANTA CAN DEDUCT TOYS FROM OUR LISTS.
BUT CANDY CANES DON'T COUNT, RIGHT?
ANYTHING BUT A FULLY DECORATED TREE PUTS US ALL AT RISK FOR GETTING FEWER GIFTS.
EXCEPT FOR CANDY CANES! THEY CAN'T POSSIBLY COUNT!
12-17
THEY COUNT.
AUUUGH!
©2023, BABY BLUES BROS LLC DIST. BY ANDREWS MCMEEL SYNDICATION
I BELIEVE YOUR CANDY CANE PROBLEM HAS BEEN SOLVED.
WHY DO I FEEL LIKE I'M WORKING WITH THE MOB?
KIRKMAN & SCOTT

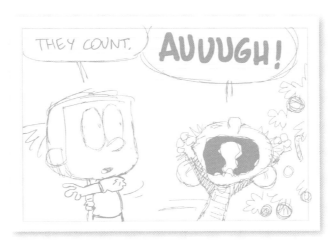

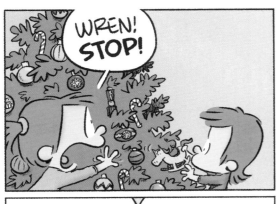

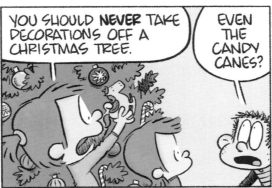

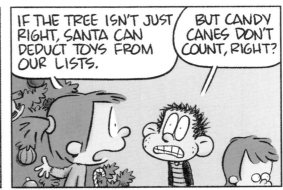

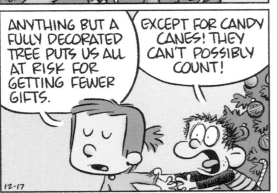

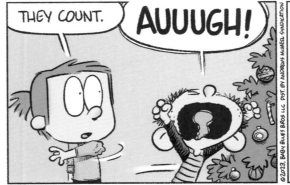

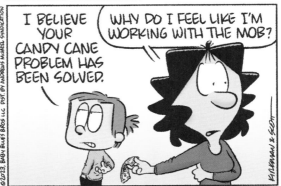

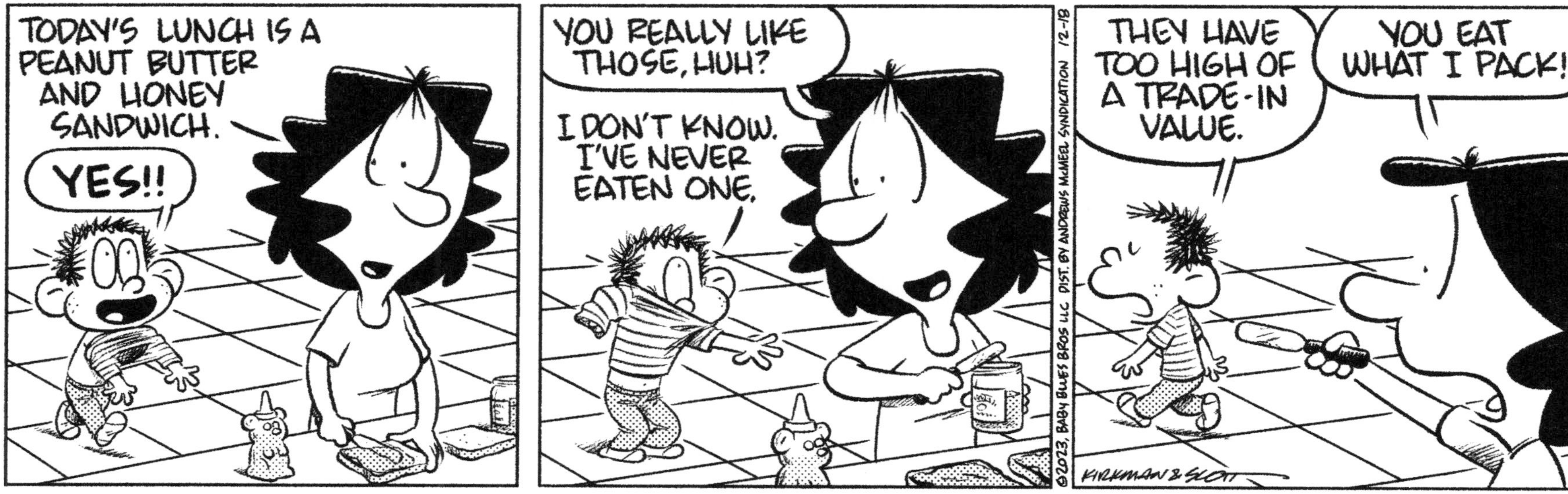
TODAY'S LUNCH IS A PEANUT BUTTER AND HONEY SANDWICH.
YES!!
YOU REALLY LIKE THOSE, HUH?
I DON'T KNOW. I'VE NEVER EATEN ONE.
©2023, BABY BLUES BROS LLC DIST. BY ANDREWS McMEEL SYNDICATION 12-18
THEY HAVE TOO HIGH OF A TRADE-IN VALUE.
YOU EAT WHAT I PACK!
KIRKMAN & SCOTT

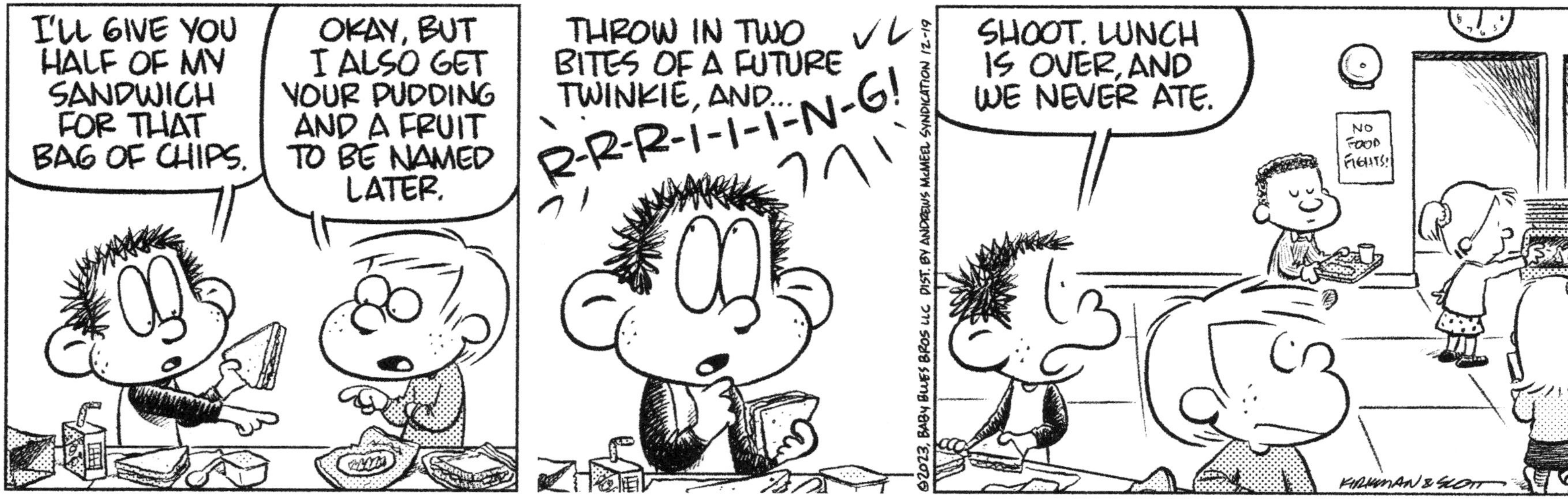
I'LL GIVE YOU HALF OF MY SANDWICH FOR THAT BAG OF CHIPS.
OKAY, BUT I ALSO GET YOUR PUDDING AND A FRUIT TO BE NAMED LATER.
THROW IN TWO BITES OF A FUTURE TWINKIE, AND...
R-R-R-I-I-I-N-G!
©2023, BABY BLUES BROS LLC DIST. BY ANDREWS McMEEL SYNDICATION 12-19
SHOOT. LUNCH IS OVER, AND WE NEVER ATE.
NO FOOD FIGHTS!
KIRKMAN & SCOTT

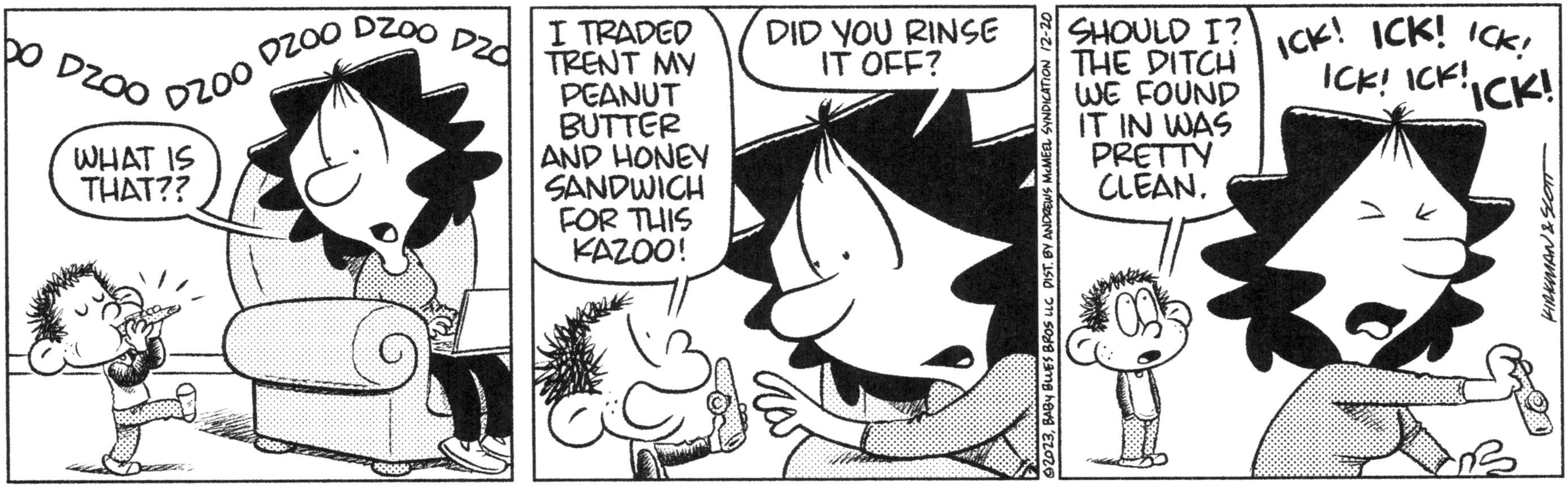
DZOO DZOO DZOO DZOO DZOO DZOO DZO
WHAT IS THAT??
I TRADED TRENT MY PEANUT BUTTER AND HONEY SANDWICH FOR THIS KAZOO!
DID YOU RINSE IT OFF?
SHOULD I? THE DITCH WE FOUND IT IN WAS PRETTY CLEAN.
ICK! ICK! ICK! ICK! ICK! ICK!
©2023, BABY BLUES BROS LLC DIST. BY ANDREWS McMEEL SYNDICATION 12-20
KIRKMAN & SCOTT

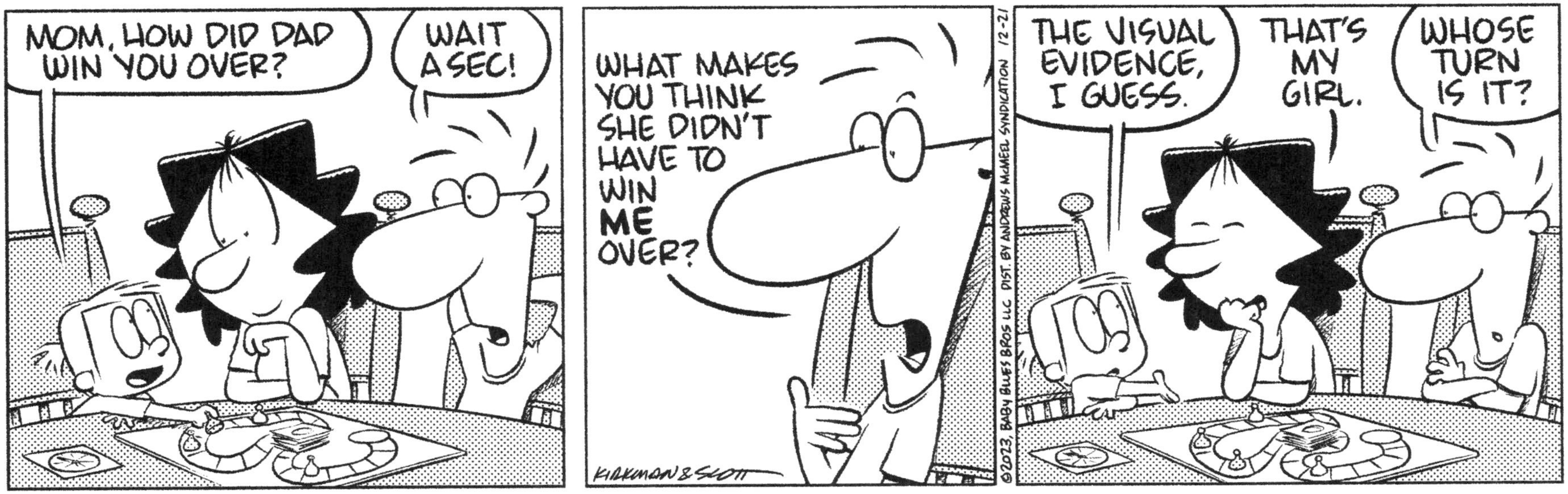
MOM, HOW DID DAD WIN YOU OVER?
WAIT A SEC!
WHAT MAKES YOU THINK SHE DIDN'T HAVE TO WIN **ME** OVER?
THE VISUAL EVIDENCE, I GUESS.
THAT'S MY GIRL.
WHOSE TURN IS IT?
©2023, BABY BLUES BROS LLC DIST. BY ANDREWS McMEEL SYNDICATION 12-21
KIRKMAN & SCOTT

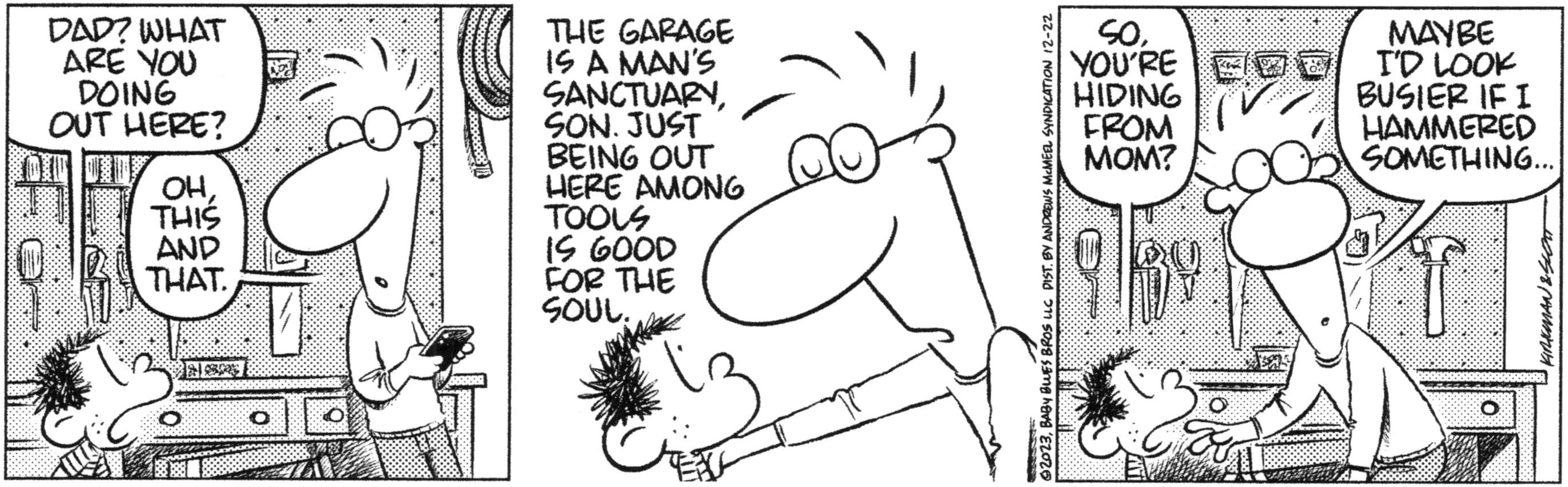
DAD? WHAT ARE YOU DOING OUT HERE?
OH, THIS AND THAT.
THE GARAGE IS A MAN'S SANCTUARY, SON. JUST BEING OUT HERE AMONG TOOLS IS GOOD FOR THE SOUL.
©2023, BABY BLUES BROS LLC DIST. BY ANDREWS McMEEL SYNDICATION 12-22
SO, YOU'RE HIDING FROM MOM?
MAYBE I'D LOOK BUSIER IF I HAMMERED SOMETHING...
KIRKMAN & SCOTT

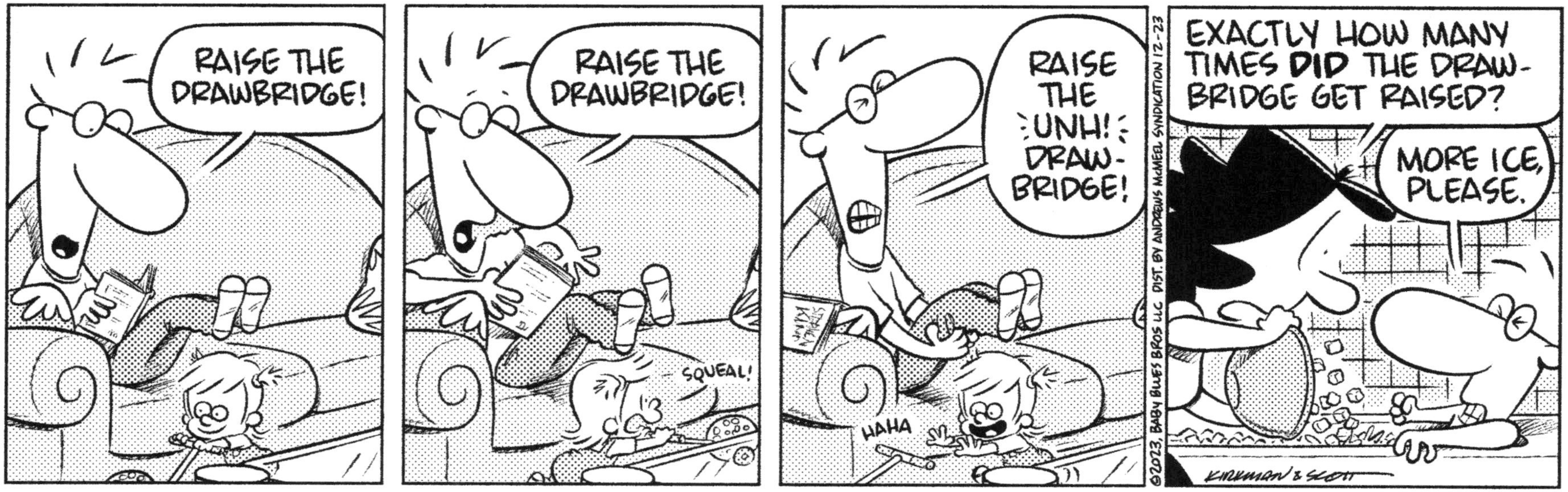
RAISE THE DRAWBRIDGE!
RAISE THE DRAWBRIDGE!
SQUEAL!
RAISE THE UNH! DRAW-BRIDGE!
HAHA
©2023, BABY BLUES BROS LLC DIST. BY ANDREWS McMEEL SYNDICATION 12-23
EXACTLY HOW MANY TIMES **DID** THE DRAW-BRIDGE GET RAISED?
MORE ICE, PLEASE.
KIRKMAN & SCOTT

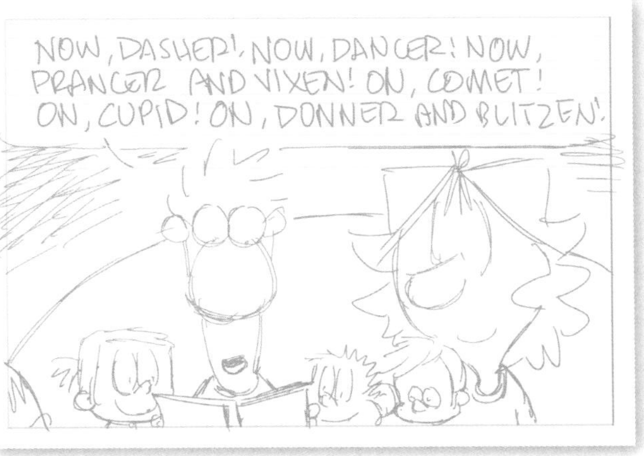
NOW, DASHER! NOW, DANCER! NOW, PRANCER AND VIXEN! ON, COMET! ON, CUPID! ON, DONNER AND BLITZEN!

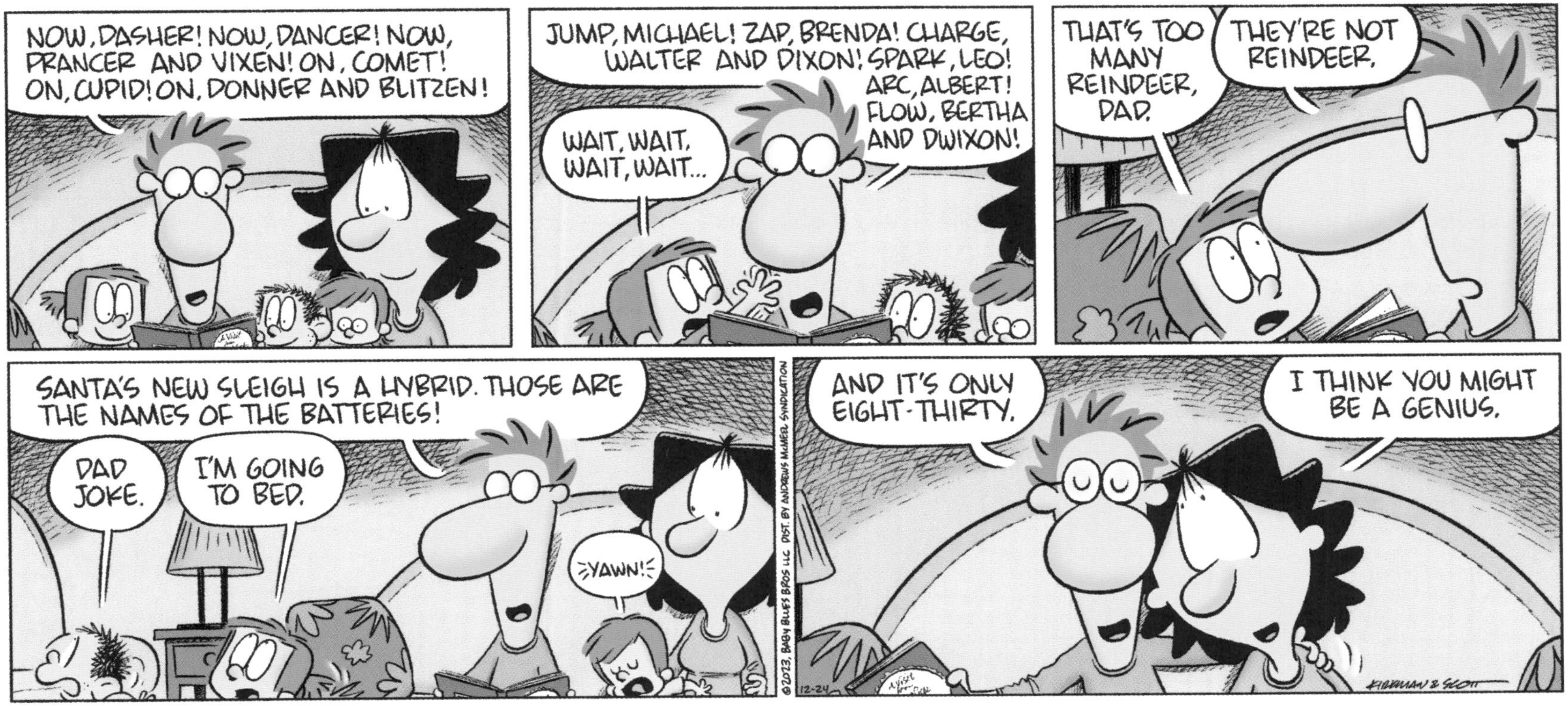
NOW, DASHER! NOW, DANCER! NOW, PRANCER AND VIXEN! ON, COMET! ON, CUPID! ON, DONNER AND BLITZEN!
JUMP, MICHAEL! ZAP, BRENDA! CHARGE, WALTER AND DIXON! SPARK, LEO! ARC, ALBERT! FLOW, BERTHA AND DWIXON!
WAIT, WAIT, WAIT, WAIT...
THAT'S TOO MANY REINDEER, DAD.
THEY'RE NOT REINDEER.
SANTA'S NEW SLEIGH IS A HYBRID. THOSE ARE THE NAMES OF THE BATTERIES!
DAD JOKE.
I'M GOING TO BED.
YAWN!
©2023, BABY BLUES BROS LLC DIST. BY ANDREWS McMEEL SYNDICATION
12-24
AND IT'S ONLY EIGHT-THIRTY.
I THINK YOU MIGHT BE A GENIUS.
KIRKMAN & SCOTT

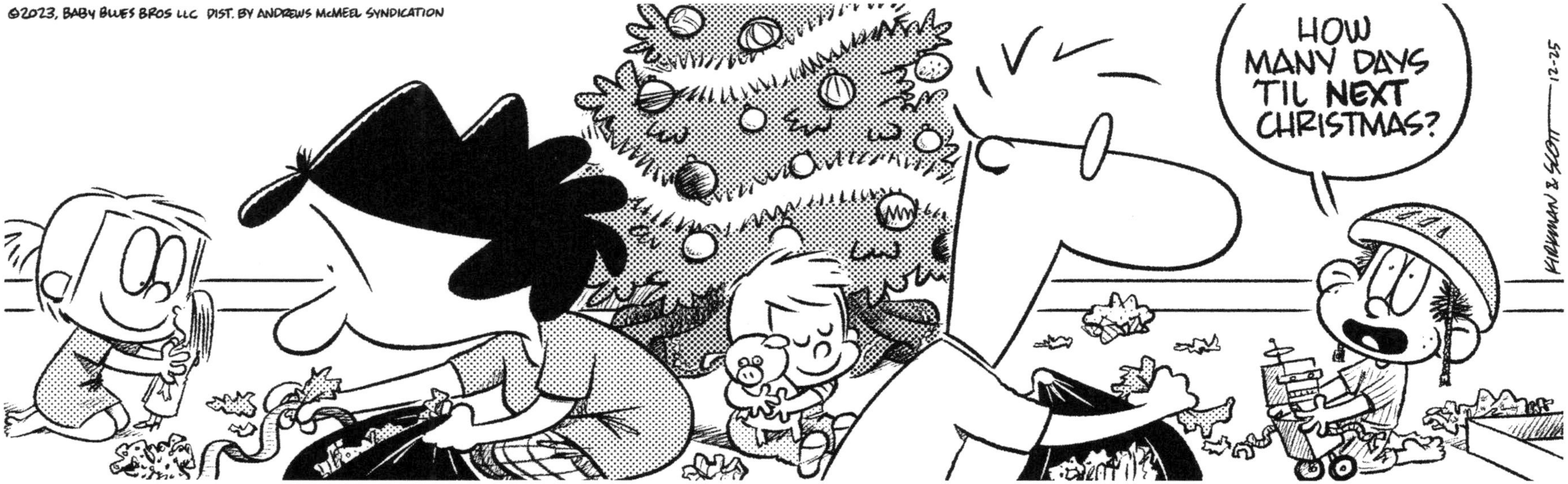
©2023, BABY BLUES BROS LLC DIST. BY ANDREWS McMEEL SYNDICATION
HOW MANY DAYS TIL **NEXT** CHRISTMAS?
12-25
KIRKMAN & SCOTT

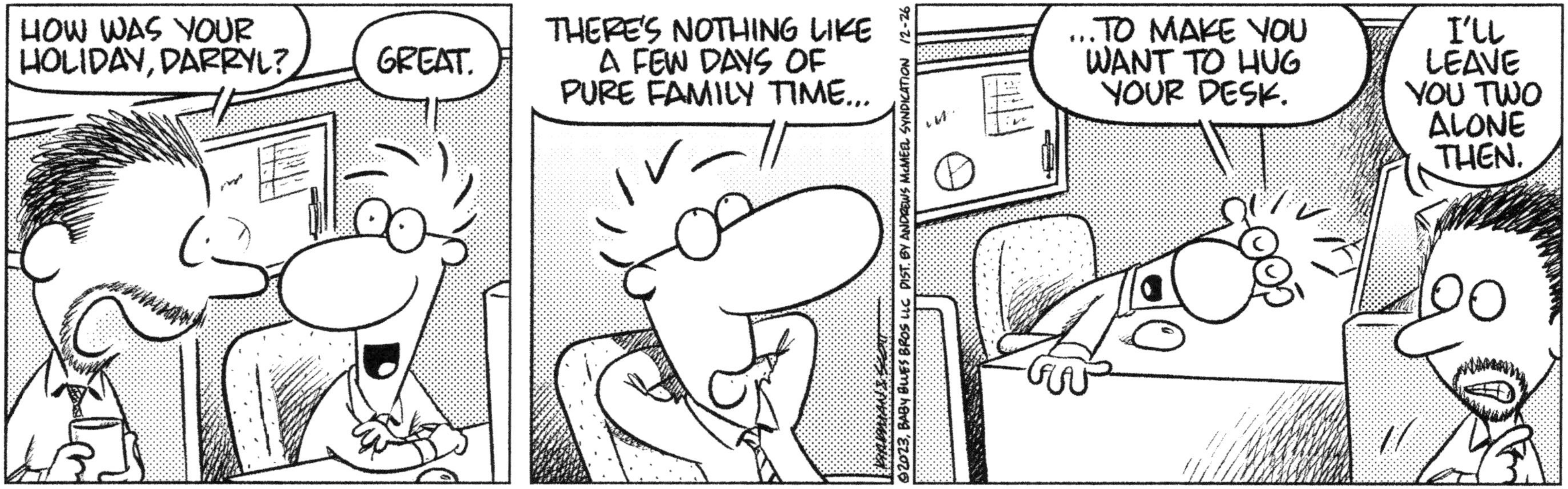
HOW WAS YOUR HOLIDAY, DARRYL?
GREAT.
THERE'S NOTHING LIKE A FEW DAYS OF PURE FAMILY TIME...
12-26
©2023, BABY BLUES BROS LLC DIST. BY ANDREWS McMEEL SYNDICATION
...TO MAKE YOU WANT TO HUG YOUR DESK.
I'LL LEAVE YOU TWO ALONE THEN.

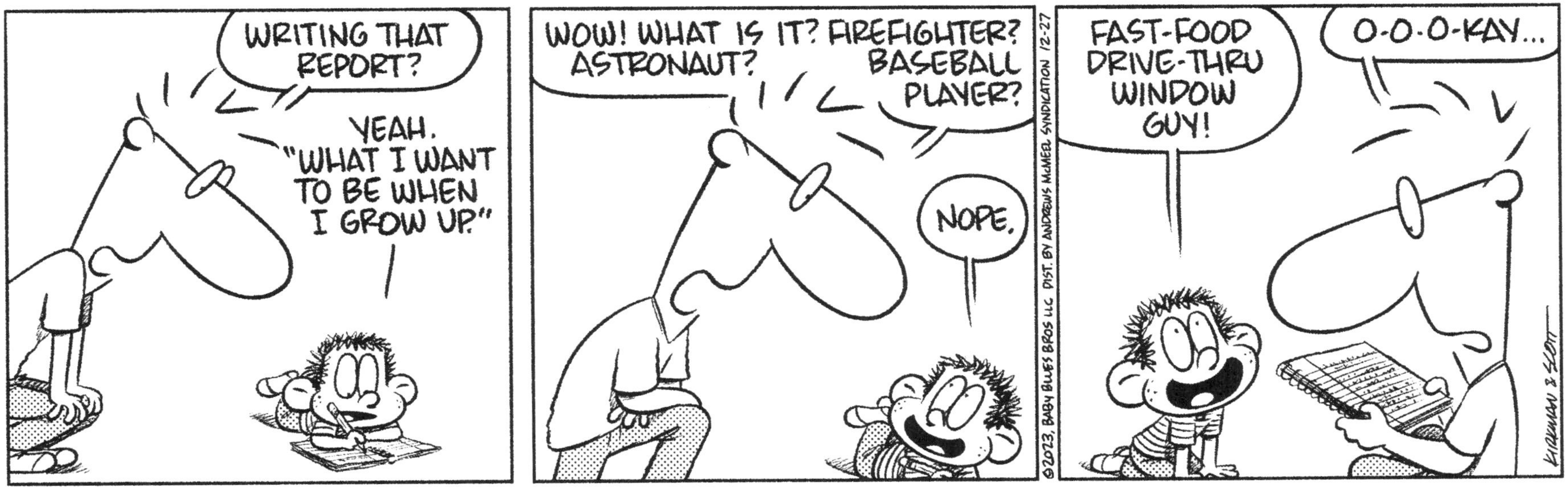
WRITING THAT REPORT?
YEAH. "WHAT I WANT TO BE WHEN I GROW UP."
WOW! WHAT IS IT? FIREFIGHTER? ASTRONAUT? BASEBALL PLAYER?
NOPE.
FAST-FOOD DRIVE-THRU WINDOW GUY!
O-O-O-KAY...
©2023, BABY BLUES BROS LLC DIST. BY ANDREWS McMEEL SYNDICATION 12-27
KIRKMAN & SCOTT

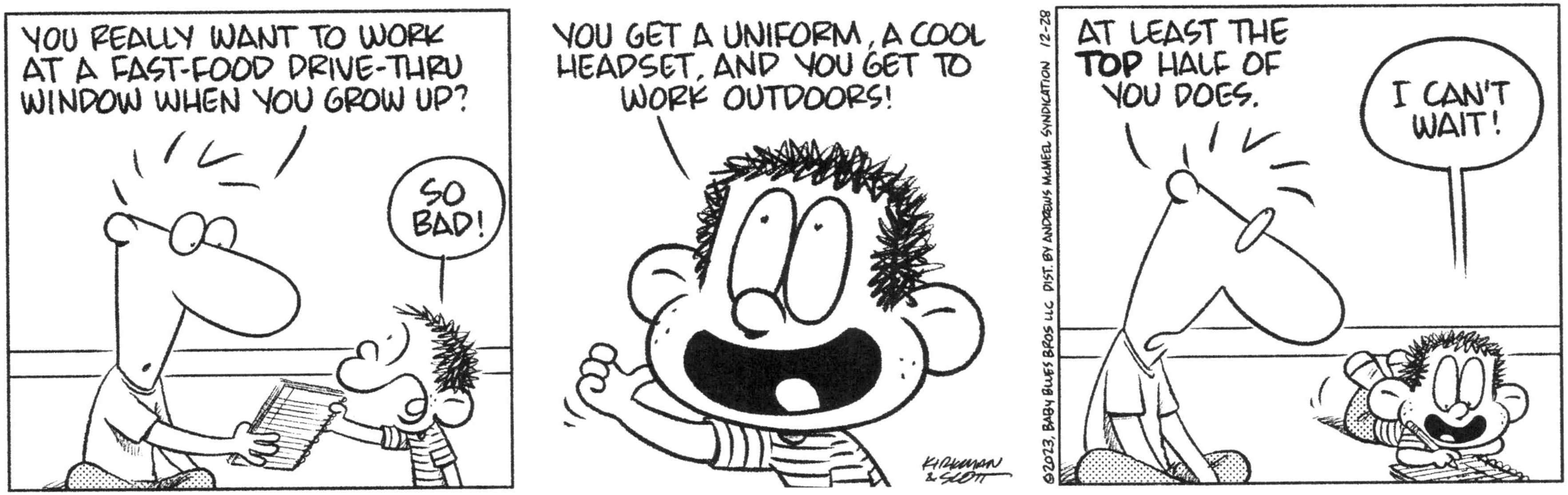
YOU REALLY WANT TO WORK AT A FAST-FOOD DRIVE-THRU WINDOW WHEN YOU GROW UP?
SO BAD!
YOU GET A UNIFORM, A COOL HEADSET, AND YOU GET TO WORK OUTDOORS!
AT LEAST THE **TOP** HALF OF YOU DOES.
I CAN'T WAIT!
©2023, BABY BLUES BROS LLC DIST. BY ANDREWS McMEEL SYNDICATION 12-28
KIRKMAN & SCOTT

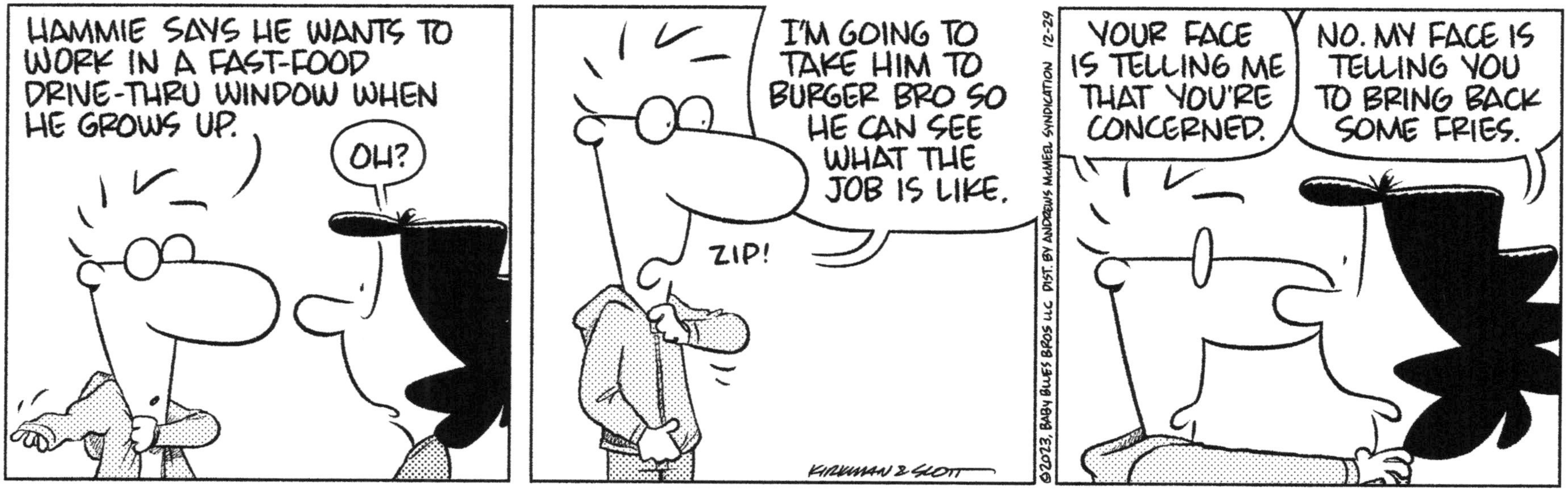
HAMMIE SAYS HE WANTS TO WORK IN A FAST-FOOD DRIVE-THRU WINDOW WHEN HE GROWS UP.
OH?
ZIP!
I'M GOING TO TAKE HIM TO BURGER BRO SO HE CAN SEE WHAT THE JOB IS LIKE.
KIRKMAN & SCOTT
©2023, BABY BLUES BROS LLC DIST. BY ANDREWS MCMEEL SYNDICATION 12-29
YOUR FACE IS TELLING ME THAT YOU'RE CONCERNED.
NO. MY FACE IS TELLING YOU TO BRING BACK SOME FRIES.

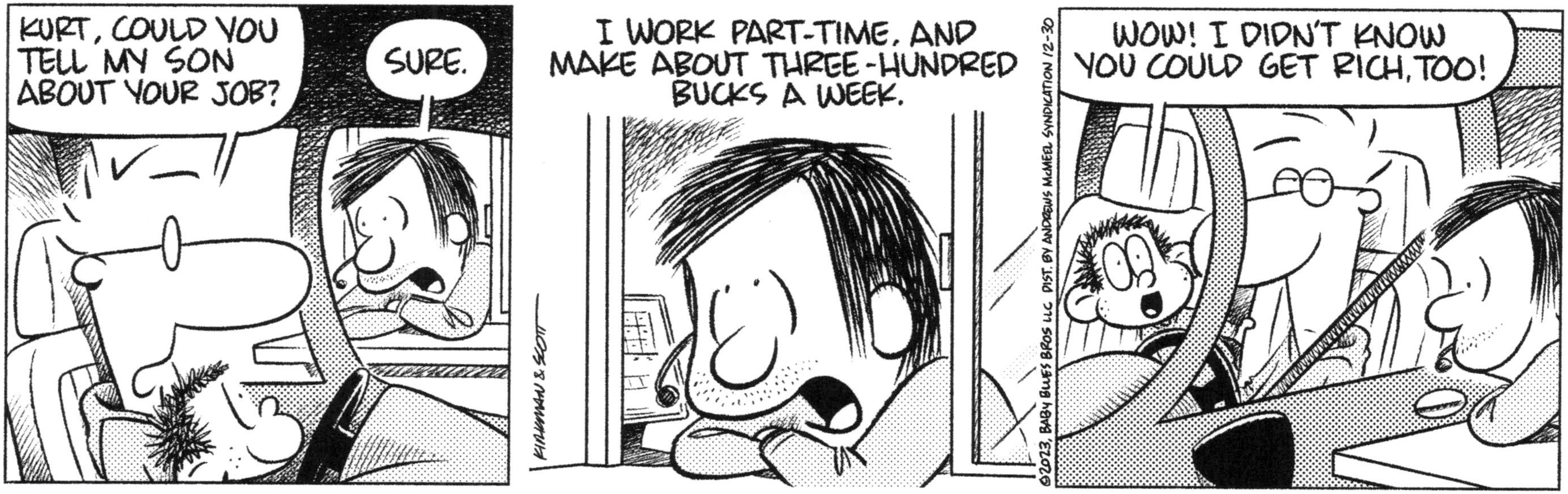
KURT, COULD YOU TELL MY SON ABOUT YOUR JOB?
SURE.
KIRKMAN & SCOTT
I WORK PART-TIME, AND MAKE ABOUT THREE-HUNDRED BUCKS A WEEK.
©2023, BABY BLUES BROS LLC DIST. BY ANDREWS MCMEEL SYNDICATION 12-30
WOW! I DIDN'T KNOW YOU COULD GET RICH, TOO!

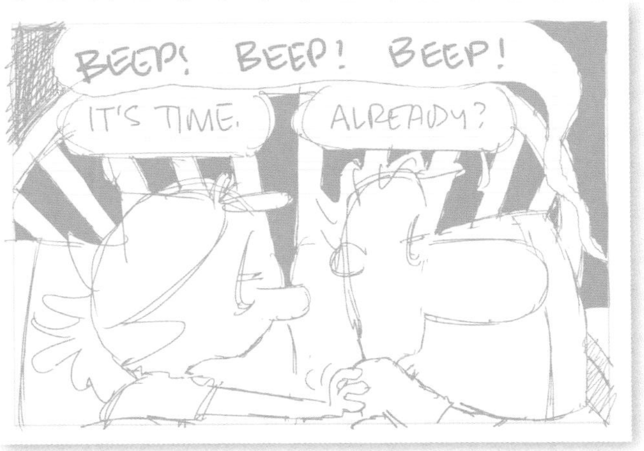
BEEP! BEEP! BEEP!
IT'S TIME.
ALREADY?

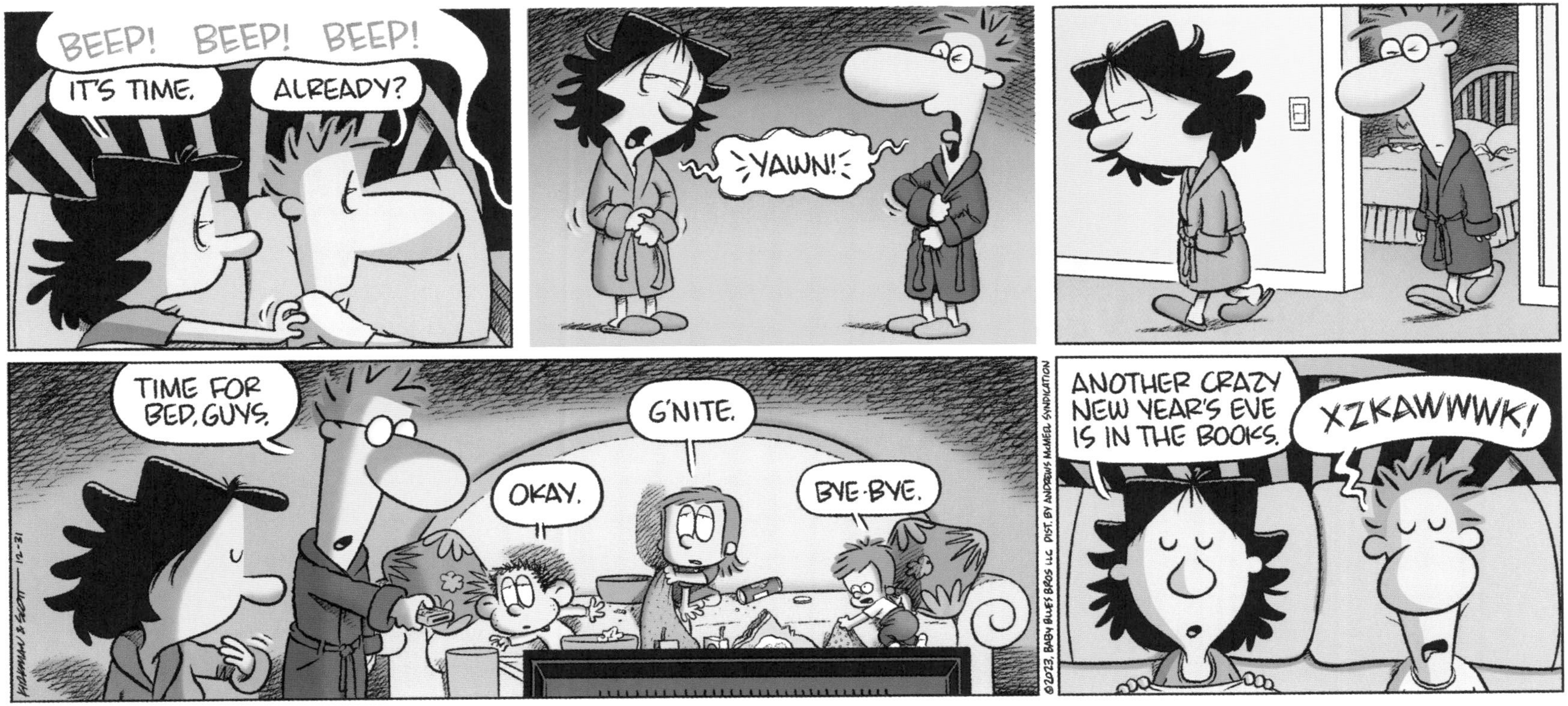
BEEP! BEEP! BEEP!
IT'S TIME.
ALREADY?
YAWN!
TIME FOR BED, GUYS.
G'NITE.
OKAY.
BYE-BYE.
KIRKMAN & SCOTT 12-31
©2023, BABY BLUES BROS LLC DIST. BY ANDREWS McMEEL SYNDICATION
ANOTHER CRAZY NEW YEAR'S EVE IS IN THE BOOKS.
XZKAWWWK!

Andrews McMeel Publishing
a division of Andrews McMeel Universal
1130 Walnut Street, Kansas City, Missouri 64106

www.andrewsmcmeel.com

24 25 26 27 28 SDB 10 9 8 7 6 5 4 3 2 1

ISBN: 978-1-5248-8779-7

Library of Congress Control Number: 2024933610
Editor: Lucas Wetzel
Designer/Art Director: Julie Barnes
Production Editor: Julie Railsback
Production Manager: Chuck Harper

Find *Baby Blues*® on the Web at www.babyblues.com.

ATTENTION: SCHOOLS AND BUSINESSES
Andrews McMeel books are available at quantity discounts with bulk purchase for educational, business, or sales promotional use. For information, please e-mail the Andrews McMeel Publishing Special Sales Department: sales@amuniversal.